THE FRENCH CANADIANS

1760-1967

MASON WADE

Revised edition, in two volumes

VOLUME ONE

1760-1911

Macmillan of Canada
A Division of Gage Publishing Limited
Toronto, Canada

This is a revised edition, in two volumes, of *The French Canadians 1760-1945*, which was first published in 1955.

First published in paperback 1968.

First published in the Laurentian Library 1975.

Reprinted 1983

ISBN 0-7715-9854-8

Revised paperback edition originally published in 1968 by The Macmillan Company
of Canada under ISBN 0-7705-1279-8.

Manufactured in Canada by Webcom Limited

FOR
JOHN BARTLET BREBNER

ABBREVIATIONS

AAQ: Archives of the Archdiocese of Quebec

APQ: Archives of the Province of Quebec

ASL: Archives seigneuriales de Lotbinière, Leclercville, Québec

ASTR: Archives du Séminaire des Trois-Rivières

Bib. St. Sulp.: Bibliothèque Saint-Sulpice, Montréal

Can. An. Rev.: The Canadian Annual Review

CAR: Canadian Archives Report

CHAR: Report of the Canadian Historical Association

CHR: The Canadian Historical Review

CJEPS: The Canadian Journal of Economics & Political Science

I.O.A.P.Q.: Inventaire des Œuvres Artistiques de la Province de Québec

LOC: The Library of Congress

NYPL: New York Public Library

PAC: The Public Archives of Canada

PIB: Press Information Bureau, Montreal

QLHS: Quebec Literary & Historical Society

QLHST: Transactions of the Quebec Literary & Historical Society

RAPQ: Report of the Archives of the Province of Quebec

RHAF: Revue de l'histoire de l'Amérique Française

TRSC: Transactions of the Royal Society of Canada

CONTENTS OF VOLUME ONE (*to* 1911)

CONTENTS OF VOLUME TWO (1911–1967)
(bound separately)

MAPS

ILLUSTRATIONS

PREFACE

THIS BOOK is essentially an attempt to explain why the French Canadians live, think, act, and react differently from English-speaking North Americans. It is also an account of what French Canadians call *le fait français en Amérique* — the French fact in North America — for only by tracing the intellectual and cultural history of French Canada from its beginnings can present-day Quebec be understood. French-Canadian culture is an intricate amalgam of the French heritage, the North American environment, and Roman, British, and American influences. The unifying thread in French-Canadian history is the spirit known as 'nationalism', which is actually an intense provincialism mingled with ethnic and religious factors. Therefore somewhat disproportionate attention will be devoted to the extremists of a generally placid and easy-going people, who possess a singular devotion to the golden mean as a rule of life; for this is an attempt to explain differences, not to stress resemblances.

This book is also the story of the ceaseless struggle of a minority group to maintain its cultural identity in the face of all manner of conscious and unconscious pressures to conform to the dominant civilization of other ethnic groups and another culture. The French Canadians are the *Sinn Feiners* of North America, for their strong group consciousness and cohesiveness arise from a basic loneliness and insecurity. It is the sense of 'ourselves alone' that motivates efforts at enhancement by stressing French Canada's peculiar ties with France and Rome. The attitudes of minority groups can often be explained only in psychological terms, and French Canada is no exception to this rule. Sir Wilfrid Laurier, one of the most eminent French Canadians, who had a profound understanding of both French and English Canadians,* once formulated this fact in the observation that 'Quebec does not have opinions, but only sentiments.' So this history will be in some measure a psychological study, whose findings may have some general validity for other minority groups.

Intellectual and cultural history is one of the broadest forms of non-specialized science. This book will be based on constitutional and political history, though by no means confined to it. It will use economic history and sociology, which do much to explain intellectual developments in this instance; it will employ literary and artistic history for illustrative pur-

---

* These terms are used for 'French-speaking' and 'English-speaking' throughout, and do not necessarily refer to ethnic origin.

poses. In so broad an attempt at synthesis in a field far from covered by
adequate special studies, comprehensiveness or finality is not to be expected, but it is hoped that this book may lead to a better understanding
of French Canada than previous histories largely concerned with political
events unrelated to economic and social developments. So far as possible,
this study is based upon primary sources, since many of the supposedly
standard works proved inaccurate and unreliable upon detailed investigation. But it has not proved feasible to carry this policy as far as the author
would have liked, largely because of the inadequacies of Canadian
archives and libraries and the wide dispersion of materials.* Considering
its scope and the immense amount of work that remains to be done in the
field, this book had to rely largely on the secondary sources which proved
trustworthy. Crucial episodes have generally been investigated in these
sources, and recourse has been had to the basic materials whenever the
secondary works were obviously unsatisfactory. This method has provided
a basic for critical judgement of earlier works, and the author has not
hesitated to differ with them. This book could not have been written without critical use of previous work, for scholarship is a cumulative process,
with an ungrateful tendency on the part of the laborer of the eleventh hour
to disparage earlier workers in the vineyards. But historical truth can only
emerge through continual sifting and winnowing of facts and theories in
the light of new knowledge and new perspectives.

This process has been particularly necessary, for until very recently it
has been the tradition in Canada to write history from a certain partisan
position: French or English, Catholic or Protestant, Liberal or Tory. This
tradition has had the unfortunate result of making the standard French
and English histories of Canada so dissimilar as to suggest that they are the
histories of two different countries. Such a situation, when members of the
two chief Canadian ethnic groups are largely educated in separate school
systems and different cultures, and are rarely thrown together until their
minds are formed, can have and has had tragic consequences. It is hoped
that this book will dispel some of the misunderstandings that are the basis
of much needless friction between Canadians of different cultural backgrounds. The author has sought to use and correlate all available French
and English sources, many of which are not available even throughout
Canada, and as a disinterested outsider to interpret them objectively in a
broader way than would be possible for a Canadian, subject to conscious
or unconscious bias and preoccupied with the national scene.

The author is committed to neither side in the ancient ethnic conflict in
Canada, and sympathetic to both, for his own ethnic and cultural heritage
is Scots and English, while he shares the faith of French Canada and is a
native of New England, a region whose history has many analogies with

* This situation has since vastly improved, thanks largely to the leadership of the
Dominion Archivist and National Librarian, Dr. W. Kaye Lamb.

that of Quebec and one which within the last century has become almost
as French as Quebec has become English. He claims freedom from ethnic
prejudice; and he believes that the Catholic historian's duty is best summarized by Leo XIII's dictum that the first law of history is not to lie, and
the second not to be afraid to tell the whole truth. In the course of this
book it has been necessary to state some hard truths; this has been done
without malice and without any other design than to do justice to the facts.
The ancient tradition of diplomatic relations between the French and
English in Canada has been outmoded by Canada's national development,
and frankness is now the best and most useful approach to their differences.

It doubtless seems presumptuous of the writer to take it upon himself to
write the history of a country of which he is not a native and whose mother
tongue is not his own. There are advantages, however, in such a course;
and perhaps particularly in this instance, where there has existed at times
an almost unbridgeable abyss between two peoples with a common history,
and where ancient quarrels have a fatal way of entering into the thinking
of each group about the other. The writer has devoted ten years to this
work; he lived in Quebec for two years, thanks to the Guggenheim
Foundation, and has made many extended visits there for research purposes, thanks to the Rockefeller Foundation and the Carnegie Corporation
of New York. The Corporation, through a grant to the Canada Foundation, has made publication possible. He has traveled through almost all
parts of the province, which is larger than France and Britain combined,
meeting and talking with all classes of its people, and learning some of the
things which are not to be found in books. He has taught in a French-
Canadian university and lectured on French Canada both in Quebec and
the other provinces, and through discussion learned much of both French
and English attitudes towards the matters with which this book is concerned. He is vastly indebted to many Canadians who undertook his
education in their history, and is grateful for the light they have shed upon
the problem with which he was concerned. He trusts that in these pages
they will find no cause to regret their courtesy and kindness to a stranger
in search of knowledge, who now seems to intervene in a family quarrel.

But the matters with which this book is concerned are not exclusively
Canadian in nature. While there are 5,500,000 French Canadians in
Canada, there are at least 2,000,000 Franco-Americans of Quebec and
Acadian stock in the United States. While their history, and consequently
their attitudes, like those of the French Canadians of the Maritime Provinces, Ontario, and the West, differ from those of the French Canadians of
Quebec, the old province on the St. Lawrence remains to various degrees
their cultural homeland, and they have deeply felt its influence. This book
is primarily concerned with Quebec, the heart of French Canada; but it
also deals with the history of the outlying groups when this has affected
Quebec, and the far-flung French-Canadian people have been re-united,

regardless of provincial or international frontiers. It has been impossible for the author, with the time and means at his disposal, to tell this broader story in detail, or even to sketch it fully. But the history of Quebec is essential to the understanding of these outlying minority groups, which in the past have shown varying tendencies to follow the Quebec tradition of standing apart and preserving their separateness from English-speaking North Americans; and there are common patterns, as well as significant differences, in the behavior of all minority groups. These are of concern to all North Americans, whether citizens of Canada or the United States, and indeed to all mankind, for only by the acceptance of diversity, through the understanding and reconciliation of cultural differences, can the great world problems of our time be solved.

It is unfortunately impracticable for reasons of space to acknowledge in detail all the obligations incurred by the writer in the course of ten years' work. Among many libraries the Dartmouth College Library offered extraordinary facilities for research throughout the undertaking. The staffs of the Public Archives of Canada and of the Quebec Provincial Archives were unfailingly helpful. The author is particularly indebted for criticism of the first draft to Professors J. B. Brebner of Columbia University, and Jean-Charles Falardeau and Jean-Charles Bonenfant of Laval University, who read the entire manuscript. Others who criticized one or more chapters include Professors E. R. Adair, J. I. Cooper, and F. R. Scott of McGill University, A. L. Burt of the University of Minnesota, G. F. G. Stanley of the Royal Military College of Canada, Miss Elizabeth Armstrong, M. G. Ballantyne, Dr. Pierre Dansereau, Dr. Eugene Forsey, the late J. K. Howard, and Major Gustave Lanctot. The late Paul Rainville, Gérard Morisset of the Quebec Provincial Museum, and A. J. H. Richardson of the Public Archives were of great assistance with the illustrations and maps. To these individuals and many others the writer wishes to express his gratitude, while absolving them of any responsibility for the views which he finally adopted after considering divergent points of view.

Mason Wade

Cornish, New Hampshire
   April 1954

PREFACE TO THE REVISED EDITION

IN PREPARING a revised edition of this book, concluded in 1950 and first published in 1955, I have added a new chapter, carrying the narrative down to 1966; I have sought to remedy factual errors in the older chapters; and I have added references to the major works published since that time. I have not attempted major revisions for two reasons: I do not find it necessary to change the basic interpretations or the main outlines, and while at the present time I might be inclined to write another and different book on the same theme, because of other commitments I could not attempt to write this one over again. Rereading my views of 1950, before beginning to write the new chapter, I was forcibly reminded of the warning of my historical father-in-God, J. Bartlet Brebner, about the dangers of writing contemporary history:

As we approach the present our inferences grow more and more subject to distortion. Circumstances which bear one kind of fruit in tranquility yield another kind in days of apprehension and still another in times of war. Secrecy and censorship veil huge areas of behavior so thoroughly that the same group of known events can be put together in half-a-dozen explanatory patterns, none of which will remain completely valid twenty-five years from now, and some of which will appear ridiculous. Any attempt to make the course of events intelligible, therefore, is like an exercise in algebra where the values of many of the components are unknown and where even time-tested formulas produce at best tentative results.*

Brebner was writing in time of war, but many of the same considerations have operated in the stormy post-war years of French Canada. Much of the evidence is simply not available to the historian, who in any case may have been too close to events to achieve a proper detachment. The best that one can do is to summarize developments in the light of one's personal knowledge and such documentary and other evidence as is available. There can be nothing definitive about contemporary history, since all the returns are not in, and a single new revelation may call for complete revision of one's judgements. But it still may be useful to attempt to find the pattern in the tangled skein of events, and, in order to aid the reader who wishes to make more detailed investigations in the period which I have attempted to summarize, a rather full bibliography of the wealth of materials available has been appended.

The publishers have supplied a new and much improved index, and

* J. Bartlet Brebner, *North Atlantic Triangle* (New Haven and Toronto, 1945), 304.

xvii

Major C. C. G. Bond has added greatly to the usefulness of the work with new maps. I am grateful to those individuals who were kind enough to make suggestions for revision of the older portion of the work and to those who offered criticism of the new chapter: F. R. Scott, Michael Oliver, Gérard Pelletier, G. V. Ferguson, M. Adelard Saudie, and Pierre Dansereau.

University of Western Ontario
London, Ontario

MASON WADE

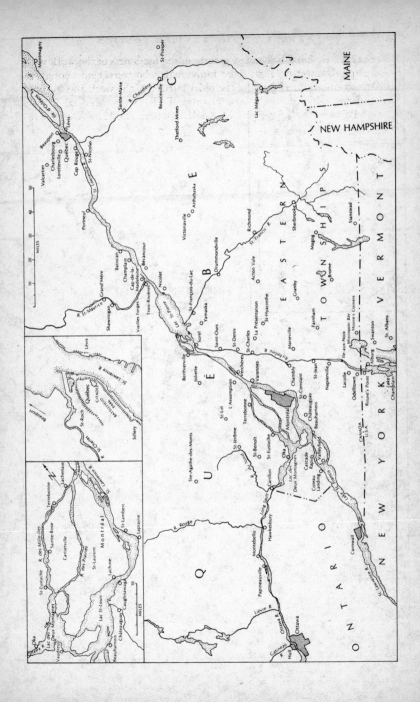

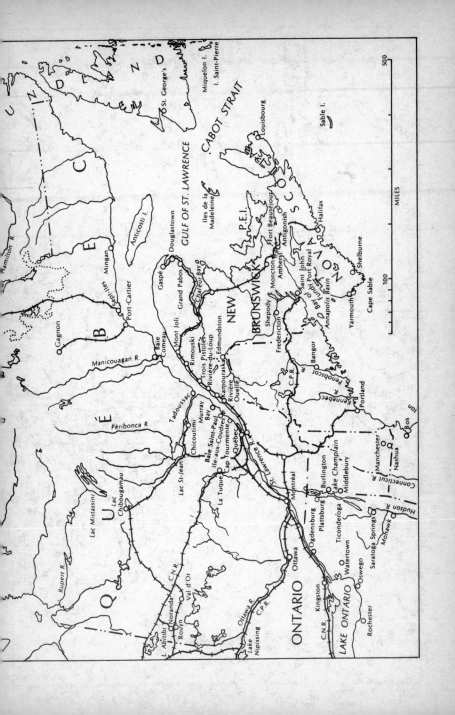

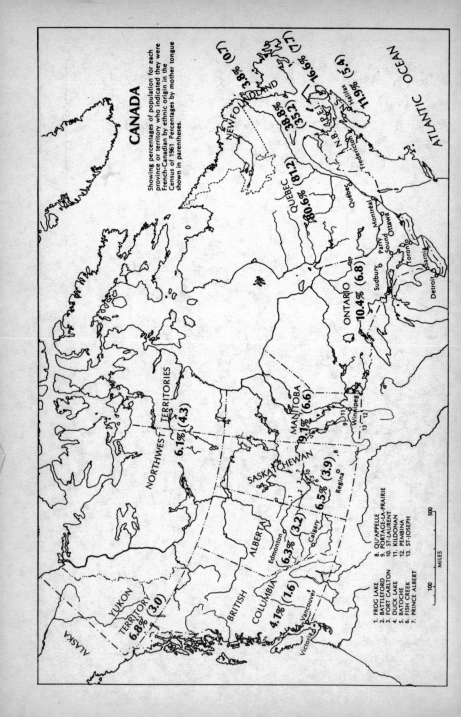

CANADA

Showing percentages of population for each province or territory who indicated they were French-Canadian by ethnic origin in the Census of 1961. Percentages by mother tongue shown in parentheses.

NEWFOUNDLAND 3.8% (0.7)

QUEBEC 81.2 (80.6% 38.8% (35.2) P.E.I. (6.6%

N.S. 11.9% (5.4) N.B. (7.7)

ONTARIO 10.4% (6.8)

MANITOBA 9.1% (6.6)

SASKATCHEWAN 6.5% (3.9)

ALBERTA 6.3% (3.2)

BRITISH COLUMBIA 4.1% (1.6)

NORTHWEST TERRITORIES 6.1% (4.3)

YUKON TERRITORY 6.8% (3.0)

ATLANTIC OCEAN

ALASKA

Detroit
Sarnia
Toronto
Ottawa
Montréal
Québec
Fredericton
Halifax
Parry Sound
Sudbury
Winnipeg
Regina
Calgary
Edmonton
Vancouver
Victoria

1. FROG LAKE
2. BATTLEFORD
3. FORT CARLTON
4. DUCK LAKE
5. EDMONTON
6. FISH CREEK
7. PRINCE ALBERT
8. QU'APPELLE
9. PORTAGE-LA-PRAIRIE
10. ST-LAURENT
11. PEMBINA
12. BATOCHE
13. ST-JOSEPH

MILES
100   500

THE FRENCH CANADIANS *1760-1967*

CHAPTER I

THE HERITAGE OF NEW FRANCE
(1534–1760)

NOWHERE in North America is the cult of the past stronger than in French Canada. Quebec's motto is '*Je me souviens*' ('I remember'), and this motto is no empty formula. French Canada has a sense of tradition unique in North America, and the French Canadians live in and on their past to a degree which it is difficult for English-speaking North Americans to appreciate. No real understanding of French Canada is possible without a realization of what its history—perhaps the most colorful, for its span of years, of any human record—means to the French Canadian, whose most popular historian has made familiar the phrase '*Notre maître, le passé*' ('Our master, the past') and established it as a principle for action in the present. [1]

What does '*Je me souviens*' mean to the French Canadian? Above all, it means that he remembers the days of New France, the heroic period of the French in America. The story of New France has been told too often and too well—most ably in English by Francis Parkman—to be retold once more at length, but its salient features must be recalled here because of their bearing on the subsequent periods with which this book is chiefly concerned. Some of the strongest forces in modern French Canada derive directly from the seventeenth century: the apostolic spirit of the Counter-Reformation or Catholic Revival, the cultural tradition of classicism, the political ideal of absolutism or benevolent despotism, and a semi-feudal hierarchical concept of society. To this golden age of French Canada its own historians have devoted disproportionate attention; every aspect of the French period (1534–1763) has been lovingly examined and re-examined, while many important phases of the English (1763–1867) and Canadian (1867 to the present) have been left untouched and unconsidered. The French Canadian consoles himself for an unhappy position in the present by dwelling upon the glories of his past. This very understandable psychological reaction also explains the tendency of the same historians to romanticize the history of New France, which is in itself so romantic as to need no added coloring. The staid Puritan Parkman is only one of many English-speaking writers to be moved by the same subject to excesses of romanticism. This general tendency has had the effect of be-clouding the facts in a golden haze of glorious legend.

I

The discovery of America came in an epoch of great and profound changes in the European world. With the invasion of Italy in 1494 by Charles VIII of France, the Renaissance spread more rapidly from Italy to northern Europe. The classical humanism of the great artists and writers of the Italian Renaissance enlarged the intellectual horizons of the European mind, while Columbus gave mankind a new world and Copernicus a new heaven. The old closed European world was shattered into fragments, as a new epoch of restless intel-lectual curiosity began. The great age of discoveries and explora-tions followed inevitably, and in the exploration of North America the French took the leading role from the Italians and Spaniards who had led in discovery. This was also the period of the Reforma-tion, when theological controversy and wars of religion racked the great nations of Europe. Bloody religious strife was carried across the sea from the Old World to New Spain, New France, and New England. Ribaut's French Protestants were massacred in Florida by Menendez' Spanish Catholics in the name of religion; while the French excluded Protestants from Canada, and the Puritans of New England barred Catholics from their colonies. In their in-fancy, the young colonies of New France and New England were opposed in religion; and the religious element was never absent from the long succession of wars which they waged against one another until the final downfall of New France. This fact has left its mark upon the mind of French Canada.

When New France was founded, France stood upon the thres-hold of its greatest age. Its population of some 14,000,000 was three times as large as that of England and Wales. Gibbon bears witness that Louis XIV was the master of a military establishment as great as that of the Roman Empire in its prime.[2] And then, as Macaulay puts it, 'France had, over the surrounding countries, at once the ascendency which Rome had over Greece, and the ascen-dency which Greece had over Rome,'[3] for French civilization was the model of all Europe. Latin at last yielded to French as the lan-guage of scholarship and diplomacy; the proud Spanish diplomat was forced to yield precedence to the Frenchman; French authority was supreme even in such minute matters as dress, cooking, and dancing. France was united as was no other European nation of the period; under the first three Bourbons—Henri IV, Louis XIII, and Louis XIV—the monarchy had become so absolute that Louis XIV could justly say—if he did—'I am the State,' and be supported in this position by Bossuet, the greatest French spokesman of the Church in his day.[4]

New France had an unequal share of the glories of France's greatest age. The absolutism and autocracy of the mother country affected every aspect of the life of the colony, but the needs of New France were often neglected by a monarch more concerned with Europe than America. A comparison of Quebec's Chateau Saint-Louis or Montreal's Chateau de Ramezay with the contemporary chateaux of the Loire reveals the pitiful inferiority of the colony to the mother country. The *seigneurs*, the much romanticized *petite noblesse* of New France, had little in common with the great nobles of France: in lineage, wealth, and power they were as nothing compared to the brilliant figures of the French court. The *haute noblesse* of France had little to do with Canada: some were fitfully interested in the fur trade and others lent the support of their names to the work of the missionaries, but few came to the colony themselves. Canada was commonly regarded in worldly France as the last resort of the ruined, the alternative to a prison cell, under both Louis XIII and Louis XIV, long before Voltaire dismissed it as 'several acres of snow.'[5] As with the great nobles, so with the kings: François I gave Jacques Cartier a ship and fifty crowns, and none of the Valois did more for New France. In the seventeenth century the Bourbons took a greater interest in Canada, but the colony still played only a minor part in their preoccupations.

The Bourbons, however, left a lasting mark on New France, and it was they and their ministers who shaped the development of the colony. Henri IV, the Protestant prince who became a Catholic king, gave France a degree of prosperity and national unity after the disruptive religious wars which permitted the founding of Port Royal and Quebec, the first settlements to be made after seventy-three years of regular voyages to the New World by French traders, explorers, and fishermen. Henri gave patents to develop New France to both Protestant and Catholic alike; if his example had been followed by later monarchs, the colony might have provided a refuge for the industrious Huguenots driven from France by the revocation of the Edict of Nantes and profited thereby; but Canada was destined by its founders to be a wholly Catholic land. Richelieu, through the Company of One Hundred Associates, tried to provide for the French traders of the northern seas the same support which the English and the Dutch had already given to their merchants of the Indies. Mazarin saved France from internal disruption and the loss of its European primacy, thus indirectly benefiting the colony, which was so dependent upon the mother country that in 1650 Marie de l'Incarnation, superior of the Quebec Ursulines, wrote home: 'Neither we nor all Canada can survive another two years without aid . . . if this aid is lacking, we must die or return to France, according to the opinion of the best thinkers.'[6] For seven years, from 1663 to 1670, Louis XIV gave the colony more support than it had yet received from the rulers of France; then European ambition replaced his zeal for colonization abroad. Colbert, the administrative genius behind the glory of the Sun King, left his mark on the colony, but with all his European concerns could never really give it the attention it deserved.

From the beginnings of the colony, the Church provided more support and encouragement than either crown or court. As the Puritans sought liberty of conscience in New England, so zealous priests, *réligieux*, and layfolk alike went forth from France to convert the savages and to build a new and more truly Catholic France in America. Missionary activity was not the primary purpose of the French in coming to America, and at first it was not their dominant concern, despite the claims of most French-Canadian writers; for New France was frequented by explorers and traders for nearly a century before the first missionaries came. The search for a Northwest Passage to the riches of the Indies; the lure of the flourishing fisheries of the Newfoundland and Nova Scotian banks; the hope that mines rivalling those of Spain might be discovered; the call of a continental treasure-house of furs—such were the motives which first brought the French to Canada. The fur trade remained the mainspring of the colony's life until long after the French period. Jacques Cartier paid lip service to the missionary motive, but his primary aims were exploration and the discovery of treasure. Champlain is the first writer on New France to stress a policy of Christianization; and he does not refer to it until his *Fourth Voyage* in 1613, and then as an afterthought: 'The desire that I have always had to make new discoveries in New France to the advantage, benefit, and glory of the French name, as well as to lead these poor peoples to the knowledge of God.'[7] But the missionary spirit was introduced into the life of New France early in the seventeenth century, and it has ever since remained a potent force in French Canada.

There is little truth, however, in the traditional opposition of a spiritual-minded New France to a materialistic New England. The French were first of all explorers and exploiters of the natural resources of the New World; and the great missionary effort of the seventeenth century was not unrelated to the necessity of winning the support of the Indians, whose goodwill was vital to the fur trade. Montreal was a fur-trading center long before Olier and Dauversière conceived the mission colony of Ville-Marie, and the Sulpicians placed the motto '*Hic evangelizabantur Indi*' ('Here the Indians were evangelized') above the entrance of their seminary in Montreal. Colonization, beyond the little necessary to assure the welfare of the fur trade, was discouraged by the great commercial monopolies who operated the trade. New France was ruled by transient Frenchmen for the benefit of France. On the other hand, the English colonists in the richer and milder region to the south had turned their backs upon their mother country, and they set about the creation of a New England upon a basis of permanent agricultural colonization. Only after that foundation had been firmly laid, by an effort which dwarfed that of New France, did they turn to trade by land with the Indians and by sea with the West Indies and with the French colonies themselves, neglected by a European-minded monarchy. These facts had an important bearing upon the conflict which soon developed between the rival empires of France and England in North America.

The destiny of New France was shaped by the fact that in the seventeenth century, the great age of the Catholic Revival in France, the renewed energy of the Church found in America an outlet from the restraint imposed at home by dominance of the state. The new religious spirit found heroic expression in the missionary activity of the Jesuits and Recollects* who saw to it that the Cross accompanied the *fleur-de-lis* from the Atlantic almost to the Rockies, from Hudson Bay to the Gulf of Mexico, as the French explorers bared the heart of the continent and traced out the principal waterways to which Jacques Cartier's '*grand fleuve de Hochelaga et chemin du Canada*,'[8] the 'river and road' of the St. Lawrence River system, led them. And while the missionaries made a continent familiar with their black and gray robes, devoted little bands of religious and pious layfolk cultivated the seeds of civilization on the banks of the St. Lawrence, where the fur traders had established only rude trading posts. Through these theocratic pioneers two great ecclesiastical disputes of the age of Louis XIV left their mark on the colony: the strife between Jesuit and Jansenist, and the struggle between Gallican and Ultramontane. The dominance of the Jesuits in New France gave short shrift to the doctrines of their enemies—the Jansenist *Anti-Coton* was burnt at Quebec in 1626—but nevertheless the ascetic and pietistic influence of Cornelius Jansen was felt through the close connections of the religious of Quebec and Montreal with their mother houses in France, which, like many of the pious lay supporters of the Canadian missions, felt the influence of the Port Royal movement. French-Canadian Catholicism has ever since had a strain of Jansenism in it, as American Protestantism has had a tinge of Puritanism.[9]

The strife between Louis XIV and Innocent XI over the relations of church and state was reflected in New France by bitter quarrels between bishop and governor and intendant, under the three-headed

---

* The Gray Friars, or Reformed Franciscans, a sixteenth-century foundation more devoted to asceticism and contemplation than the original order.

system of French colonial administration. But two of Bossuet's four fundamentals of gallicanism were reversed in the colony, where under the Jesuits and Bishop Laval the civil power came close to being considered subject to the spiritual one in temporal matters, and the Pope's authority was regarded as supreme and not subject to the usages of a national church. From the earliest days the leaders of the Church in New France had little use for Bossuet's reflection on the Papacy: 'Ocean itself, immense though it be, has its limits, and to break through at its own caprice would be to lay desolate the world.'[10] While gallicanism carried the day in Louis XIV's France, ultramontanism triumphed in New France under the championship of Bishop Laval, who vanquished the gallicanism of governor and intendant and established for himself a position which the Pope himself might have envied. Ever since, French Canada has remained a stronghold of clericalism, and very conscious of its spiritual dependence upon the Holy See.

2

It is appropriate that one of the three earliest written records of French Canada is Giovanni Battista Ramusio's *Navigationi e Viaggi* (1566), which contains Jacques Cartier's *Voyage au Canada en* 1534 and his *Bref récit . . . de la Navigation faite en MDXXXV et MDXXXVI*; for the rediscovery of America, after the Scandinavian explorations had been forgotten, was primarily the work of Italians: Columbus, the Cabots, Verrazano, and Amerigo Vespucci. Cartier is often credited by French-Canadian writers with the discovery of Canada, but John Cabot had touched at Cape Breton and planted the English flag on Newfoundland in 1497, while early in the sixteenth century Basques and Portuguese, as well as Frenchmen, were already swarming on the new fishing grounds discovered by searchers for a Northwest Passage to the Indies.* In an age of faith and abstinence, when the European consumption of fish was far greater than in modern times, the rich Newfoundland fisheries were a discovery well worth exploiting, and the French fishermen of Brittany, the Bay of Biscay, and the Channel ports at first outstripped their rivals. When Jacques Cartier set out in 1534 from Saint-Malo with a crew of fishermen and a commission from François I to consolidate Verrazano's claim of 1523 to the northeastern American coast as Nova Gallia, he was following a route already familiar to fishermen of France and many other countries, and not, like Columbus, blazing a path to the unknown. That year Cartier merely charted the Gulf of the St. Lawrence, where he met other French craft, and Chaleur Bay, without entering the great river which the Indians called the 'road of Canada.' He was looking for either a passage to

---

* The recent discovery of the ruins of a Viking settlement, occupied about 1000 A.D. at L'Anse-aux-Meadows at the northern tip of Newfoundland, confirms long-held theories that the Norsemen were the first Europeans to settle in North America.

the Pacific or a route into the interior of Asia, and François I hoped
he would forestall the Spaniards, who were already exploiting the
riches of the New World in the southwest. At Gaspé Cartier raised
a great cross which bore the *fleur-de-lis* and the words '*Vive le roi de
France*,'[11] a fitting symbol of the close relationship between church
and state in the New France thus claimed. Two Iroquoian Indians,
kidnapped while fishing in Chaleur Bay and taken back to France,
whetted François I's appetite for gold with their tales of the kingdoms
of Hochelaga, Stadacona, and the Saguenay, which might be new
Mexicos, Perus, or the outposts of Cathay itself. Cartier found rich
fisheries, fertile lands and a wealth of timber, but not the gold, silver,
jewels, and oriental staples which his pre-mercantilist monarch desired.

In the following year Cartier made his way up the St. Lawrence,
pausing at Tadoussac to marvel at the deep and mighty river which
the Indians told him led to the Kingdom of the Saguenay, rich in
copper, and touching at Ile-aux-Coudres before reaching the
Mohawk settlement of Stadacona (Quebec). Then, despite the
reluctance of the Indians to let him continue—the first instance of
the enduring Quebec-Montreal rivalry—he went on up the river to
the Huron or Onondaga center of Hochelaga (Montreal). There,
from the summit of Mount Royal, he looked out over the great plain
and saw the continental waterway stretching far beyond the Lachine
Rapids[12] which had stopped his progress. He heard of the Ottawa
River, leading to a land of silver and gold, from the Indians of
Hochelaga, to whom he read the Gospel of St. John and gave gifts,
after they had besought him to touch the sores of their sick, 'as if
God had come there to cure them.'[13] Finding no treasure among the
poverty-stricken northern Indians, whose bitter struggle for existence
made European tools and trinkets all the more valuable to them, the
French fell easily into the role of gods, which all the Indians assigned
to the white newcomers, and did not outrage their hosts as the
Spaniards did. In these few autumn months of 1535, Cartier traced
out the lifeline of New France, the waterway which was long to be
the limit of settlement. With a foreshadowing of that friendly
relationship with the Indians which was to be the great buckler of
New France in its struggle against the English, who long sought only
to exterminate the savages, Cartier observed: 'By what we have seen
and what little we have heard of this people, it seems that they would
be easy to tame.'[14] Returning to Stadacona, he spent the winter
there at the mouth of the Saint-Charles, losing twenty-five of his
men to scurvy as the ships lay frozen up for five months under four
feet and more of snow in a season whose severity appalled Frenchmen accustomed to a milder climate. In the spring he sailed back to
France with Donnacona, the 'King of Canada.' He did not return
until 1541, for François I was too involved in his struggle against

encirclement by the Holy Roman Empire of Charles V to concern himself with North America.

In that year the most ambitious French effort in the New World for nearly a century was begun, with colonization and conquest of the 'outer limit of Asia' as its aim, but in the end it came to nothing. The Sieur de Roberval was made lieutenant-general of the king in the New World, with Cartier as his subordinate. Ten ships were to be laden with sailors, soldiers, artisans, and colonists; full equipment and stores for two years, and even livestock, were to be carried; and the expedition was to establish a colony, as a base for further search for the Northwest Passage and for the discovery of the riches of the mythical Kingdom of the Saguenay, which had appeared to be a new Peru in the tall tales told by Donnacona. But Roberval was detained in Europe, and Cartier set off in the spring of 1541 with only five ships. After going up the St. Lawrence, as far as the Lachine Rapids, he wintered at Cap Rouge near Quebec, and then returned to France with a cargo of false gold and jewels—Thevet's 'diamants de Canada,'[15] meeting the belated Roberval with three more ships in June at St. John's, Newfoundland. Despite the latter's orders to accompany him back to Canada, Cartier continued on to France to get credit for his discoveries. Here he was joined by Roberval in the fall of 1543, after a winter exploration of the Saguenay and trouble with the Indians had frozen the colonizing spirit and revealed no treasure. Neither settlement nor new discovery resulted from this ill-starred expedition; and the discouraged court, preoccupied first with the Spanish conflict and then with religious and dynastic civil wars, lost interest in the New World. Montaigne summed up the prevailing French attitude to America when he remarked: 'I am afraid that our eyes are bigger than our bellies and that we have more curiosity than capacity, for we grasp at everything and catch nothing but air.'[16]

Meanwhile French fishermen frequented the waters which Cartier had carefully charted, and with the change from the green to the dry fishery, set up seasonal stations on the shores of Cape Breton, Nova Scotia, Gaspé, and the Gulf of St. Lawrence. The French were driven to the mainland, since the English had occupied the best portions of the Newfoundland coast for this purpose. Once contact had thus been established with the continent and its inhabitants, the fur trade became a profitable sideline of the fisheries. By the second half of the sixteenth century the trade came into its own; and Tadoussac, the Basque whaling post at the mouth of the Saguenay and at the head of the great waterway system used by the Algonkin tribes, became its center. The European demand for fur, a luxury which became a much desired staple after the discovery of the felting process, was as steady and as eager as the Indian demand for the iron weapons, tools, and utensils which were so superior to their

traditional implements of stone, wood, bone, and bark. But monopoly was as essential to the fur trade as individualism was to the
fisheries, and so the traders sought monopolies from the monarchy.
As early as 1588 two nephews of Jacques Cartier petitioned the king
to this effect, but not until ten years later did Henri IV grant the
Marquis de la Roche a monopoly in Acadia, and soon after assign
another in the Gulf and the Lower St. Lawrence to Pierre Chauvin,
a Huguenot merchant of Honfleur. The monarchy was ruined by
wars at home and abroad; the king had no money for colonization
efforts, but by obliging the monopolists to establish settlements he
hoped to gain his end at their expense. Colonization and the fur
trade were incompatible, however, and the collapse of de la Roche's
colony on Sable Island and the failure of Chauvin to establish a permanent post at Tadoussac supplied the first evidence of this fact.

In 1604 another monopoly was granted, with better results. The
Sieur de Monts headed the new company, which included some of
Chauvin's former associates, as well as the influential nobleman
Poutrincourt, the literary lawyer Marc Lescarbot, and the trading
associates Du Pont-Gravé and Samuel de Champlain, who had
explored the St. Lawrence during the previous year in behalf of the
colonization company of Aymar de Chastes. That spring an
expedition of some 125 people set out from France. After exploring
the Acadian coast, they settled on St. Croix Island, where Maine
now meets New Brunswick. In the following year the settlement
was moved across the Bay of Fundy to Port Royal on the
Annapolis Basin. Here a trading post was established, which
sheltered the banquets of the Order of the Good Time immorta-
lized by Lescarbot in his *Histoire de la Nouvelle France* (1609), and
where the same learned lawyer composed his *Muses de la Nouvelle
France*, the first literary production of the French in America. More
was accomplished than the writing of verses and the partaking of
good cheer, however, for vegetables and grain were cultivated and
some attempt at permanent settlement was made. But in 1607, at
the instigation of other jealous traders, de Monts' monopoly was
arbitrarily revoked by the minister Sully, and he abandoned the
whole venture in disgust. Poutrincourt and his son Biencourt continued fur trading in Acadia, but at the suggestion of Champlain,
who had already visited the St. Lawrence in 1603, de Monts was
induced in 1608 to try his luck once more in the latter region. This
move resulted in the lasting foundation of New France.

3

Samuel de Champlain was the true founder of French Canada.
He started life as a Huguenot soldier in the wars of the League, but in

1598, after becoming a Catholic, he turned mariner and sailed to Cadiz with a shipload of Spanish soldiers who had served in France. While there he was offered the command of a vessel bound to the West Indies and Mexico. This two-year voyage gave him a first-hand knowledge of the Spanish colonies and moved him to the thought of a Panama canal. It also furnished him with the material for his *Bref discours des choses les plus remarquables . . . aux Indes occidentales*. Brought to the notice of Henri IV by this work, which is illustrated by sixty-two curious drawings of the Indians and of tropical flora and fauna, Champlain was named a royal geographer. In 1603 he joined de Chastes' expedition to the St. Lawrence, which was under the command of Du Pont-Gravé of Saint-Malo, and was commissioned by the king to report on the expedition's discoveries. Thus he was formally launched upon his long career as an explorer and geographer. It is clear that his impelling motive was a love of discovery, for his explorations went far beyond the necessities of the fur trade in which he was nominally engaged, and his writings bear witness to the breadth of his curiosity. Champlain was a true man of the Renaissance, with a wide-ranging mind and a remarkable assortment of talents. He was at various times soldier, sailor, geographer, explorer, fur trader, historian, artist, architect, diplomat, governor, botanist, and gardener. But Lescarbot, the first historian of New France who was Champlain's companion at Port Royal, testifies that the latter's primary passion was discovery: 'Champlain promises never to cease his efforts until he has found either a western sea or a northern sea, opening the route to China which so many have sought in vain.'[17]

It was with this purpose that in the summer months of 1603 Champlain explored the Saguenay farther than any Frenchman had gone since Jacques Cartier discovered its mouth; that he followed the St. Lawrence up to the foot of the Lachine Rapids, and the Richelieu up to the rapids at Chambly. Thus convinced that there was no passage to the Indies by way of the great river, he inspected the Gaspé coast and Chaleur Bay in search of the elusive route which was the goal of all the great discoverers of the day. Laden with beaver skins and accompanied by some Indians, he sailed back to France, with his head full of the tales he had heard of great inland seas far up the St. Lawrence, beyond many rapids and a tremendous cataract. But his patron de Chastes had died during his absence, and de Monts, who succeeded to the monopoly, sought a milder climate than that which the traders had already experienced at Tadoussac and Quebec. So from 1604 to 1607 Champlain roamed along the seaboard from Nova Scotia to Martha's Vineyard, a coast which he was the first to map and name. So slowly and carefully did he do this work that he failed to reach the Connecticut and

Hudson Rivers, which led to richer and more naturally favored regions than that of the St. Lawrence.

In 1608 he came back to Quebec to stay. His reasons are revealed in his *Voyages* of 1613: 'So many voyages and discoveries vainly undertaken, with much labor and expense, have resolved we French these last years to try and make a permanent settlement in the land that we call New France, hoping more easily to accomplish this enterprise, since the voyage would begin in the land beyond the ocean, along which the search is made for the much sought passage.'[18] Thus, after almost seventy years, Cartier's work was resumed. Champlain left Du Pont-Gravé to barter with the Indians at Tadoussac, while he himself pushed on to the narrows of the St. Lawrence from which Quebec derives its name.[19] Here at the foot of the great rock he built the *habitation* of Quebec, the third settlement of the de Monts company and the one that was to endure. Of the twenty-eight white men who spent the winter there after Du Pont-Gravé sailed back to France, only eight survived. But the stout-hearted Champlain was not discouraged, unlike the earlier winterers at Quebec, and when summer came and Du Pont-Gravé brought support from France, he pushed on up the Richelieu to Lake Champlain, where not far from Ticonderoga he helped the Hurons and Algonkins of his party to defeat a band of Iroquois. He was forced thus to incur the lasting enmity of what proved to be the most powerful eastern savage confederation by the necessity of cultivating the friendship of the Indians who acted as his guides and furnished the French with furs. This motive comes out clearly in his account of the expedition against the Onondagas in 1615: 'It was very necessary to assist them both to put them the more under obligation to love us, and to facilitate my undertakings and discoveries which, as it seemed, could only be accomplished with their help, and also as this would lead to and prepare their conversion to Christianity.'[20] Here Champlain reveals the purposes of the founders of New France: first trade, then geographical curiosity, and finally missionary activity. This order is often reversed by French-Canadian historians, partly because history in French Canada has so largely been written by idealistic clerics.

Upon his arrival at Quebec in 1608, Champlain had found himself in the midst of a great Indian movement. The Algonkins and Montagnais, who were wandering hunters, were moving down from the north and replacing the sedentary, agricultural Iroquois and Hurons whom Cartier had earlier encountered at Stadacona and Hochelaga. The corn culture of the latter had not flourished in the St. Lawrence Valley, and as their enemies obtained superior iron tools and weapons from the French traders at Tadoussac, the Iroquois retired into northern New York, and the Hurons to the Georgian Bay region.

The balance between the two groups became more even when the Dutch came to New York in 1609 and began to supply the Iroquois with European arms in exchange for furs. This was the first known phase of a vast regional conflict based upon geography which has endured until the present day: a natural opposition of the St. Lawrence and Hudson-Mohawk river systems, the only eastern seaboard waterways which penetrated the mountain barriers and led to the heart of the continent. During the days of New France the two river systems were bitter rivals in the fur trade, for they provided the only channels of trade. Later, lumber and wheat were to replace fur as the staples of trade; canals to eliminate portages and carries; barges, steamers, and finally railroads to outmode canoes; but the opposition of the two systems remained, whether Indian, Frenchman, Dutchman, Englishman, or American controlled them.

Champlain, with his geographer's eye, was quick to appreciate the implications of the structure of the continent and to take action. In 1611 he cleared land for an establishment at Montreal, the meeting place of the two river systems and the predestined entrepôt of the St. Lawrence, because there ocean navigation ceased, interrupted by the Lachine Rapids, and all the traffic of the upper St. Lawrence, the Ottawa, and the Richelieu came together. In 1613 he went up the Ottawa in search of the mythical inland sea of which he had been told by a glib young Frenchman who had wintered with the Indians; and again in 1615 he followed the Ottawa to Lake Nipissing and Lake Huron, wintering with the Hurons of Georgian Bay, who served as middlemen for the French in the trade with the Western tribes. He went with them on an expedition against the Iroquois, who then fulfilled this same function for the Dutch, as they would later for the English. For commercial reasons the French had to incur the lasting enmity of the Five Nations, who already distrusted them as a result of Cartier's kidnapping exploits, and whose savage raids were almost to destroy New France in its infancy. The implications of geography and the relationship of the Indian tribes to the all-important trade overrode all other considerations, as the Recollect Frère Gabriel Sagard noted in his *Grand Voyage du Pays des Hurons* (1632): 'I had hoped to promote a peace between the Hurons and the Iroquois, so that Christianity could be spread among them, and to open the roads to trade with many nations which were not yet accessible, but some of the members of the Company advised me that it was not expedient, since if the Hurons were at peace with the Iroquois, the same Iroquois would lead the Hurons to trade with the Dutch and divert them from Quebec, which is more distant.'[21]

Champlain's activities were not confined to leadership in trade and war. In 1615 he brought the Recollects, or reformed Franciscans, to Quebec. Although the secular Abbé Jessé de Fléché had come to Port Royal in 1610 and the Jesuits Biard and Massé in 1611, these were the first priests in New France proper, and the only ones until the coming of the Jesuits ten years later. Of the first four Recollects, Pères Le Caron and Dolbeau went off immediately to missions among the Hurons of Georgian Bay and the Montagnais of the Saguenay-Lake St. John region—Le Caron was already established when Champlain reached Georgian Bay that fall—while the two others remained at Quebec in the convent which they built by the Saint-Charles River. With the coming of the Recollects, the mission of New France was born; with that of the Jesuits, the way was opened for the development of a theocracy such as France had never known. The energy and exaltation of the Catholic Revival in France found its fullest outlet in the colony, where the power of the king paled before the immediate power of the Church, whose heroic missionary effort and devoted social services at once gave it tremendous prestige and were essential to the life of New France.

The coming of the Recollects was the result of only one of the twenty voyages which Champlain made to and from France. He displayed no little statesmanship in maintaining the interest of king and court in the colony, despite contentions among the rival fur traders and the varying fortunes of the companies which held the monopoly of New France at different times. In 1617 he brought back from France the first true colonist, the Parisian apothecary Louis Hébert, and his family, which was the first to come to Quebec. Hébert had earlier shared the fortunes of Poutrincourt in Acadia and there, according to Lescarbot, had taken pleasure in working the soil. The Company was more interested, however, in his professional talents, and under the terms of his engagement Hébert had no chance to try his hand at agriculture for three years after his arrival. Then he was summoned to Tadoussac to act as de Caen's lieutenant, and in 1621 he was made royal procurator. But somehow in the midst of his official duties—no doubt with the aid of Champlain, who took an interest in gardens and knew their importance to the colony—Hébert managed to clear a bit of land atop the cliff at Quebec, high above the fort at its foot, and to grow peas and onions there. He had the farmer's love of land and obtained for himself the fiefs of Saut-au-Matelot and of the Saint-Charles River. But the actual pioneering of Hébert, the first Frenchman to attempt to settle in the New World, has been somewhat exaggerated in a Quebec which mistakenly considers itself to have been an agricultural region from the first. Only one and a half acres were cleared in the first twenty-two years of the colony, and no plow broke the soil of Quebec until 1628, the year after Hébert's death.[22] The successive companies which ruled the destinies of New France at this period made no effort to carry out the promises of colonization which they had given in exchange for a monopoly of the fur trade, since they would thus defeat their main purpose.

The first real colonization expedition to the St. Lawrence, sent out by Richelieu's powerful new Company of New France, was captured in the Gulf by two of the privateering Kirke brothers of Dieppe and London, while a third Kirke was demanding the surrender of Quebec from Champlain. The resolute governor concealed his pressing need for supplies and refused to yield, but after eking out another winter he was forced to capitulate on July 21, 1629. The Kirkes, who were half English and half Huguenot French, had the backing of both London and French Huguenot merchants and were supplied with letters of marque from Charles I of England. Their conquest thus marked the first round in that second Hundred Years' War between French and English which left a lasting mark on New France and finally brought about its downfall. It also marked the first assault of nationless capital upon French Canada. For three years the English flag waved over Quebec, until by the Treaty of Saint-Germain-en-Laye Charles exchanged New France and Acadia for the unpaid dowry of his wife, Henrietta Maria of France.

Then Champlain returned as governor and watched over the destinies of the colony until his death in 1635. But the great promise of the Company of New France had been blighted by the loss of almost its entire capital as a result of the Kirkes' activities. The company was forced to sublease its privileges and responsibilities, and so development of the colony continued in the old inadequate, hand-to-mouth fashion. By 1643 there were only 300 people in Quebec, instead of the 4,000 settlers that the company had promised to establish by that date. The most notable achievement in the field of colonization had been the granting of the fertile seigneury of Beauport to Robert Giffard in 1634, which established in a semi-feudal mold the pattern of settlement for the rest of the French regime. Aside from this beginning of real colonization, fur-trading posts were established at Trois-Rivières at the mouth of the Saint-Maurice in 1634 and at Fort Richelieu (Sorel) at the mouth of the Richelieu in 1642. Then, in the latter year, came the establishment of a colony at Montreal by a group of priests and pious folk, whose zeal for the conversion of the Indians was counted upon to secure this vital outpost of the trade.

It was the Church, rather than the monarchy or the trading companies, which gave the colony the support it needed during this difficult early period. The Jesuits, who came to New France in 1625 after the ill-starred Acadian mission of Biard and Massé in 1611–14, soon established a religious monopoly comparable to the commercial monopoly of the Company of New France. While their *Relations* served to arouse the mother country's interest in the colony and to bring a stream of missionaries and donations out from France, the Jesuits barred the Huguenots, who had thus far played a considerable part in New France, and soon crowded out their clerical rivals, the Recollects, who did not return until 1670, when the Jesuits had established a firm hold on the colony. The extent of that hold, and of the great missionary effort which is one of the most notable chapters in the history of the Society of Jesus, is revealed in the *Relations*, the annual reports of the mission of New France published in France from 1632 to 1673. The fact that the superior of the mission was responsible only to the general of the order in Rome set the ecclesiastical life of New France in an ultramontane pattern which differentiated it sharply from the mother country with its gallican-minded clergy dependent upon the monarchy.

The Jesuits sought to establish in Canada the closed theocracy which they later achieved in Paraguay. Their work among the Hurons of Georgian Bay was ended by the dispersion of that friendly nation by the Iroquois in 1649; but in the refugee Huron villages founded at Sillery near Quebec in 1637, and later on the Ile d'Orléans and at Lorette, they established the first of those theocratic Indian colonies where they sought successfully to christianize and gallicize the savages, while keeping them uncontaminated by the regrettably godless traders. After the downfall of the gentle Hurons, the Jesuits launched their mission to the Iroquois. Among this warlike people they had much less success in winning souls to Christianity—the little village of Caughnawaga, across the river from Montreal, easily held most of their converts—but they nevertheless served New France well by their influence on the bitterest enemies of the French. While the selfless heroism of the Jesuits has justly become legendary, their great work of learning and transcribing the Indian languages is less well known, though it played an important part in the development of the French empire in America.

Though the most notable work of the Jesuits was in the mission field, they were also the founders of the educational system of French Canada, for in 1635 they started a school at Quebec which eventually developed into a classical college with some of the attributes of a university. They were also instrumental in bringing out to New France Marie de l'Incarnation and her Ursuline nuns, whose school at Quebec for Indian girls was the humble beginning of a great tradition in the education of women in French Canada. The Jesuits also brought the Hospitalières, who came in the same ship with the Ursulines in 1639 to take charge of the Quebec hospital which had already been built by Père Le Jeune, who originated the project and obtained the necessary support from one of the pious ladies of the court. Similar backing permitted the realization of many another enterprise of the Jesuits in New France.

It was the Jesuit Père Vimont who accompanied the Society of Ville-Marie to their chosen mission field at Montreal in 1642, and it was the *Jesuit Relations* which inspired that foundation. The pious secret order known as the Company of the Holy Spirit also played an important part in the Montreal venture through its influence in high places at home. The leader in the New World of this group of dedicated priests and layfolk was the soldier Chomedey de Maisonneuve, who was driven by the fervor of a crusader in his determination to spread the Gospel among the Indians and to establish a bulwark against the Iroquois. With him was the devoted Jeanne Mance, who established a hospital at Montreal and ministered impartially to the sick, whether white or Indian, for the French had none of the English color prejudice. In 1657 Saint Marguérite Bourgeoys opened the first school at Montreal, and thus founded the great teaching order of the Congrégation de Notre-Dame, whose members were to play a major role in shaping the character of French-Canadian women throughout the colony. From such small beginnings much developed: by 1663 there were at Quebec some 150 members of religious communities out of a total population of about 500 souls. From the early days of settlement, education and the care of the sick and needy were included in the province of the Church, whose missionaries already performed governmental functions as diplomatic agents among the Indians and as financial agents in France. Thus the Church won a firm hold on the life of New France and soon achieved an ascendency in the colony.

During these first crucial years of the colony, the fur trade upon which its economic life depended developed slowly and uncertainly. After one sub-company had shown a profit of 300,000 *livres* for five years' activity, another promptly lost a greater sum in three years. Reorganization was inevitable under such circumstances; and the evils of absentee control were in some measure remedied by the formation in 1645 of the Habitants' Company, which took over the monopoly from the Company of New France. Two years later all citizens of the colony were permitted to trade with the Indians, provided they sold their furs to the company's stores at government-controlled prices. The governor, solely responsible in the days of Champlain and his successor Montmagny to the company, was assisted in 1647 by an appointed council of three Quebec merchants. In the following year the Council was revised to consist of the governor and ex-governor of the colony, the superior of the Jesuits, two inhabitants of Quebec, and three syndics. Later, additional elected members were added to the Council. These were nominated by the Council itself, but the syndics, or representatives of the people, of Quebec, Trois-Rivières, and Montreal had a voice in their election. Thus a certain measure of representative governmen

François de Montmorency-Laval, Vicar Apostolic of New France
(1659-74) and first Bishop of Quebec (1674-84)

Oil painting (c. 1671) by Claude François *dit* Frère Luc. This penetrating contemporary
portrait reveals both the autocrat and the ascetic in Bishop Laval, who has been hailed
both as a saint and as a tyrant. (Inventaire des Oeuvres Artistiques de la Province de
Québec.) (I.O.A.P.Q.)

France Bringing the Faith to the Indians of the New World

Oil painting by Frère Luc. The Recollect founder of the French-Canadian art here mixes the artistic traditions of the Old World and the scenes of the New. (I.O.A.P.Q.)

appeared for the first time in Canada. The colonists paid a high price for it, since no less than one quarter of the furs brought to the company's warehouses were taken as a tax to be applied to the support and defence of the colony. Meanwhile the supply of pelts was threatened by the attacks of the Iroquois upon both the French outposts and the villages of the Huron middlemen. The Iroquois set up a virtual fur blockade, which almost destroyed the French trading system by diverting the stream of pelts through their own hands into the Dutch warehouses of Orange (Albany) and New Amsterdam (New York). The Jesuits' mission to Onondaga, the very home of the Five Nations, and such exploits as Dollard's heroic stand in 1660 at the Long Sault on the Ottawa against the over-powering odds of an Iroquois war party, were defensive measures against this major threat to the survival of the colony.

4

At this crucial moment the rulers of France came to the rescue of the colony which they had so long neglected. Under Louis XIV and his great minister Colbert, the French colonial empire was given strong support by a paternalistic government under a mercantilist policy. In 1663 royal government was established at Quebec, and in the following year the great state corporation of the Company of the West Indies took over the monopoly of trade. In 1665 the Mar-quis de Tracy came with warships and soldiers, and in that same summer the new governor De Courcelles and the intendant Jean Talon arrived with shiploads of colonists and stores. Three forts were built to block the Iroquois warpath on the Richelieu; and in the following year de Tracy led the veterans of the Carignan-Salières Regiment, the *habitant* volunteers, and some Hurons and Algonkins deep into the Iroquois country. The expedition achieved little beyond the destruction of standing crops and grain stores—this was the first but not the last time that European soldiers found an Indian campaign in America like pursuing the will-o'-the-wisp—but the Iroquois, reduced in numbers by a generation's warfare, were impressed by the French show of force and sued for peace, which lasted for nearly twenty years.

This breathing spell was used to good advantage by the adminis-trators of the colony. The old order was swept away and New France was made over in the image of Louis XIV's France. The element of representative government in the old Sovereign Council was abolished in the new Superior Council, composed of governor, intendant, bishop, twelve councillors appointed by the king, the attorney-general, and a secretary. Through this body, at once administrative, legislative, and judicial, the governor and

B

intendant ruled the colony; while after 1726 they ruled virtually alone, as the Council lost most of its administrative power. These two officials, who represented in France the surviving authority of the great nobles of the district and the newer centralized power of the monarchy, often came into conflict; in New France a third head was added to the system, for François de Laval-Montmorency, the Jesuit-chosen bishop who arrived in 1659, had no sympathy with Colbert's gallican notions of the relations of church and state. Bishop Laval, who had risen under the regime of the ultramontane Queen Mother, was to cause the recall of no less than three governors and of the great intendant Talon himself under the gallican Louis XIV. The quarrels of the three leaders of the colony later imperiled its prospects, but for the moment the impetus of the new order carried all before it, and Talon's leadership was accepted.

Jean Talon was Colbert's chosen instrument for the remaking of New France. Colbert had decreed that 'the increase of the colony should be the rule and end of all the conduct of the intendant,'[23] and 2,000 settlers were sent out from France in the decade after 1663, many of them being soldiers who were induced to become colonists by liberal concessions. Practically all the provinces of France were represented in the emigration, although the greater number came from Normandy, Perche, Brittany, the Ile-de-France, and the western provinces. Colbert, through Talon, told the people of New France that 'their prosperity, their subsistance, and all that is dear to them depend upon a general resolution, never to be departed from, to marry youths at eighteen or nineteen years and girls at fourteen or fifteen.'[24] Early marriage and large families were rewarded by the state, while bachelorhood was penalized; and a paternalistic king sent over shiploads of his poor or orphaned wards, the *filles de roi*, to provide wives for veterans of the Carignan-Salières Regiment, and for the older colonists who had remained single in a land where white women were still rare. Thus was established the French-Canadian tradition of early marriage and large families, a tradition which has been one of the strongest forces in the tenacious survival and remarkable increase of this ethnic group. Large families were, of course, assets in the expanding agricultural economy of New France, though liabilities in the mother country.

Talon, too, was concerned about radically altering the way of life of New France, for Colbert had ordained that it was 'much more advantageous to the colony that the inhabitants devote themselves to cultivating and clearing the land, rather than to hunting, which can never be of any use to the colony.'[25] So Talon founded near Quebec the three model villages of Bourg Royal, Bourg la Reine, and Bourg Talon; but the nucleated village of ancient French tradition did not meet the needs of the colony, and the country parish was established as the basic unit of French-Canadian society. The necessity of close settlement for defence against the Indians, the use of waterways for transport and as a source of food, and the gregarious nature of the people combined to give the French-Canadian village its peculiar form. Land holdings were laid out in long narrow strips reaching back from the water, thus giving each settler access to the resources of river, fertile valley land, and forest; while the houses were set close together along first the river and then the single road which connected them with the church and *presbytère*. Early in the eighteenth century visitors to New France began to remark that the banks of the St. Lawrence resembled a continuous village.

Colbert believed in diversified economic activity and a measure of colonial self-sufficiency, so Talon encouraged shipbuilding, lumbering, tanning, flour milling, the salting of fish, and the extraction of oil from the porpoises and seals of the lower St. Lawrence. He investigated the iron deposits of Baie Saint-Paul and the Saint-Maurice, and the silver mines of Gaspé. He introduced the culture of hemp and flax, and encouraged home industry by importing wool for the domestic manufacture of cloth. Finding that the colonists were spending 100,000 *livres* a year for wine and brandy, and that the Church was up in arms against the ravages of strong drink among both the *habitants* and the Indians, Talon established a brewery, which checked both scandal and a considerable drain on the colony's slim resources.

Talon's vision was neither narrow nor dependent upon instructions from France. His mind was fascinated by the possibilities of the New World, and he dreamed great dreams, which sometimes alarmed the more cautious Colbert. Talon planned a road from Quebec to Acadia—now back in French hands in 1670, after an interlude of English rule for fifteen years and long negotiations which were part of Louis XIV's and Colbert's plan of empire. If his resources had been adequate to the task, the final fall of this first portion of New France to become English, half a century later, might have been prevented by its development along the same lines as the establishments on the St. Lawrence. He sent Saint-Simon and Père Albanel overland to Hudson Bay by way of the Saguenay, Lake St. John, and the Rupert in 1671-2, to offset the activities of the Company of Adventurers of England Trading into Hudson's Bay, which had just been formed in London by John Kirke, the youngest of the privateering brothers, on the strength of reports by the renegade *coureurs de bois* Groseilliers and Radisson. Then Saint-Lusson, backed by Jolliet, Perrot, and the Jesuit Allouez, was sent to Sault-Sainte-Marie to claim the whole West for Louis XIV, as the French moved on to the Great Lakes to meet the Western tribes whose furs they had once received through the agency of the vanished Hurons. The existence of English and Dutch settlements along the coast to the south was no bar to Talon's dreams of empire. He wrote home that 'nothing can prevent us from carrying the names and arms of His Majesty as far as Florida, New Sweden, New Holland, and New England.'[26] To realize this dream, Lake Ontario was to be fortified, while the Iroquois were warned by the governor in 1671 to refrain from trading north of the lake. First Jolliet and Père Marquette, then La Salle, traced out the Mississippi waterway, which enabled the French to cut off the English advance and to monopolize the trade of the heart of the continent. The French empire in America soon stretched in a great crescent from the mouth of the St. Lawrence to that of the Mississippi, hemming in the other European settlements on the Atlantic seaboard.

But Talon had not heeded Colbert's significant warning of 1666: 'It would be better to restrict yourselves to an extent of territory which the colony itself will be able to maintain than to embrace so much land that eventually a part may have to be abandoned, with some consequent discredit to His Majesty's Crown.'[27] Talon was called back to France for good in 1672—he had once been briefly recalled because of his quarrels with Bishop Laval—and his successors lacked his genius. Then, in the same year, Louis XIV became involved in the long series of European wars which meant the waning of royal interest and support for the colony across the ocean, whose pleas for more colonists were rejected by Colbert on the ground that France would be depopulated. Despite the efforts of Talon, there were only 7,000 Europeans in Quebec and 500 in Acadia by 1675; there were not then, and never were to be, enough men to implement the French claim to the vast expanses labeled New France on the maps of North America. Between the Atlantic seaboard and the Appalachians were confined the much more numerous and substantial English settlements; and when the great struggle for the continent opened in 1689, 200,000 Anglo-Americans faced 10,000 French Canadians. When the final episode of the Seven Years' War opened in 1756, 1,500,000 Anglo-Americans were opposed to 70,000 French Canadians. The simple facts of population, plus the major factor of Britain's new sea power, settled the fate of New France.

The period of French expansion continued until the close of the seventeenth century, however, with energy and daring compensating for lack of manpower. Frontenac, the new governor, carried on the Western policy which Talon had launched. This proud and vigorous old soldier knew instinctively how to deal with the Indians by alternating presents and threats with a high hand, and under no other governor was the prestige of the French higher with their enemies the Iroquois. Frontenac built the fort at Cataraqui (Kingston) which Talon had conceived, and gave the land about it to La Salle as a seigneury. This chosen lieutenant of the governor was no sedentary colonist, but a restless explorer and promoter who dreamed of putting the fur trade on a basis of large-scale operations. He built the first ships on the Great Lakes; established forts and trading posts on the Illinois; and explored the Mississippi to its mouth, near which he was to meet his death a few years later in an attempt to establish a base for the conquest of the Spanish mines of Mexico. While the intendant Duchesneau called for limitation of the numbers of the *coureurs de bois*—in 1679 their number was estimated at 500–600— and Bishop Laval demanded the end of the brandy traffic with the Indians, and both joined forces to oppose Frontenac's expansionism, the *coureurs de bois* were blazing new trails all over the West, and brandy went with them. Liquor had become an essential article in the fur trade; if the French had no brandy to offer, the English got the best furs with their rum. The frontier moved on: DuLuth explored the country beyond Lake Superior; Nicolas Perrot roamed about the Great Lakes; Père Hennepin explored the upper Mississippi; Tonty pioneered in the Illinois country; and Cadillac established the trading posts at Detroit and Michilimackinac, which were to the West what Montreal was to the East. And with the explorers and the traders went the Jesuits, who established missions at the posts set up along the arteries of trade and empire.

This wave of expansion did not fail to arouse opposition from the Iroquois, whose trading territory had been invaded, and from their English allies. Governor Dongan of New York wrote with bitterness: ''Tis a very hard thing that all Countryes a Frenchman walks over in America must belong to Canada.'[28] But Frontenac was recalled in disgrace, along with the intendant with whom he had quarreled, and his successors La Barre and Denonville lacked both his skill in dealing with the Indians and his fierce aggressiveness. After the collapse of La Barre's expedition against the Iroquois in 1684, the Five Nations and the English traders moved into the lower Great Lakes region. During the next two years furs from Michilimackinac reached New York. The supremacy of the St. Lawrence system was again threatened by its aggressive rival.

The only answer was war, and a new French movement towards the two other gateways to the heart of the continent: the Mississippi and Hudson Bay. La Salle attempted to found a colony on the Gulf of Mexico, and Iberville captured the English posts on James Bay. Along the upper St. Lawrence Denonville launched a fruitless expedition against the Senecas, which only brought reprisals from the Iroquois, who not only harried the trading routes but in 1689 even dared to fall upon Lachine and massacre its inhabitants, almost under the walls of the French stronghold of Montreal. War between France and England broke out in Europe as this disastrous stroke threatened the colony's lifeline, and in the emergency Frontenac was called back to save New France. With his usual aggressiveness he carried the war to the English: raiding parties composed of Indians led by Frenchmen suddenly issued from the winter woods and fell upon the frontier villages of New York, New Hampshire, and Maine. This was the sort of warfare the Indians understood and appreciated, and the French stock went up again and the trade routes to the West were reopened.

But the English had been goaded into action. The massacres, ruthless destruction, and subsequent mistreatment of captives in the raids to which the French had instigated their Indian allies woke the old European religious hatreds between the English and the French colonists. A great Protestant crusade against the 'papists' who had loosed the savages upon their frontier settlements was undertaken by New England and New York. Samuel Vetch, a Scot allied to the Albany fur traders and interested in Boston's commerce with Acadia, evolved the plan of a joint attack by sea up the St. Lawrence and by land over the Hudson-Champlain-Richelieu route—this was to be the standard English strategy in the American Hundred Years' War, and after several failures was eventually to win it—but the colonists did not succeed in coordinating their efforts, for the liberty-loving English colonies lacked the military unity of absolutist New France. The land expedition came to nothing; while Sir William Phips with the fleet succeeded in capturing Port Royal—on which the Boston merchants long had had an envious eye—though he failed to shake Frontenac's hold on Quebec after a week's futile siege. The old soldier governor, now almost eighty, became more aggressive than ever, once this great threat had been averted. In the West his lieutenants goaded their savage allies to take the war-path against the Iroquois, while the Acadians led bands of Micmacs against the New England settlements. Frontenac himself devastated the western New York stronghold of the Oneidas and Onondagas in 1696, while Iberville ranged from Hudson Bay to the Gulf of Mexico in a brilliant one-man war against the English by sea and by land. Though the conflict in Europe ended in 1697, the struggle in America continued until 1701, when the humbled Iroquois made peace with the French and their Indian allies. Under the Treaty of Ryswick, France regained Nova Scotia and retained all but one of the Hudson Bay forts.

The St. Lawrence and the Mississippi river systems were now guarded by a stronger chain of French forts; and Iberville had founded the French base at the mouth of the Mississippi which La Salle had failed to establish. If there had been time for the consolidation of these gains, the French empire in America might have endured, but its slender resources were again called upon by the War of the

Spanish Succession (Queen Anne's War). In America the action was confined to Acadia, New England, and Newfoundland, and for the French consisted of privateering, attacks on fishing establishments, and raids on border villages in Maine, New Hampshire, and Massachusetts. In 1709 and 1711 Colonel Nicholson waited in vain at the head of the Hudson for news of the British fleet, which was to proceed up the St. Lawrence against Quebec while he attacked Montreal by the Champlain-Richelieu route; but first the need for ships in Europe and then a savage storm in the Gulf which wrecked the fleet again spoiled the scheme of joint attack. Port Royal was won once more from the French, and part of the first French settlement in the New World then passed permanently to England, which was to conquer the whole of New France in the next half century as its sea power eclipsed that of France. The outcome of the great colonial struggle was already indicated, for though New France had been saved and enlarged by Frontenac and his chosen band of daring explorers, adventurers, and *coureurs de bois*, it had been drained of much of its bravest and most enterprising blood by the years of war.

5

This period of expansion was also marked by a great development of the intellectual life of New France. In 1664 Pierre Boucher, who had come to the colony at the age of twelve and grown up to be the governor of Trois-Rivières, published his *Histoire Véritable et Naturelle des Moeurs et Productions du Pays de la Nouvelle France*. This first history of Canada by a Canadian was dedicated to Colbert and written at the request of Louis XIV, to whom Boucher had been sent by the governor-general to report on the state of the colony, as 'being better acquainted with Canada than any other.'[29] Boucher was given the first Canadian patent of nobility, and on his return from France brought a number of colonists, as befitted his conviction that all that Canada lacked was inhabitants. His simple and straightforward book differs from the earlier accounts of Lescarbot and Sagard in that it is not a travel book, telling of wonders and marvels, but a sober emigrant's guide. The theocratic character of the colony, and the beginning of a distinction between transient Frenchmen and those who had thrown in their lot with that of the colony, are revealed by Boucher's forthright statement: 'In one word, good people may live here very contentedly; but not bad people, because they are too closely looked after here; therefore I do not advise any such to come, because they might be expelled from the country, or at the best compelled to leave it, as many have done already; and it is precisely those who loudly decry the country, not having found in it what they expected.'[30]

How different New France had become from the mother country is revealed by the astonished comments of the clever and cynical Baron de Lahontan, a French Jonathan Swift, in 1683:

One cannot have any pleasure, either at cards or in visiting the ladies, without the *curé* being told of it, and without his denouncing it from the pulpit. His indiscreet zeal goes so far as to name persons; and if he goes so far as to refuse Communion to noble ladies for wearing colored ribbons, for the rest you can judge for yourself. You can scarcely believe to what an extent the authority of these ecclesiastical seigneurs extends. I vow they are ridiculous in their actions: they excommunicate maskers, and even run to places where they are to be found, in order to unmask them and cover them with opprobrium; they watch over the conduct of the girls and women with more care than fathers and husbands. They persecute people who do not go to Communion monthly, and at Easter they oblige all sorts of people to carry tales to their confessors. They forbid and burn all books which are not concerned with devotion. I cannot think of this tyranny without protesting against the indiscreet zeal of the *curé* of this city. This cruel person, entering my host's house and finding some books on my table, threw himself bodily upon the romance of Petronius, which I regard more highly than my life because it is not expurgated. He tore nearly all the leaves out of it, with so little reason that if my host had not held me back when I saw the wretched remains, I should have hastened to the home of this turbulent pastor to pull out all the hairs of his beard in similar fashion. Not content with examining the actions of men, they wish even to search out their thoughts. Judge by this, Monsieur, what pleasure one has here.[31]

Lahontan burned to reform this theocratic society: 'One should commence by preventing clerics from making such frequent visits to the habitants, of whom they bluntly demand knowledge of their families' affairs down to the last detail, a practice which can often be contrary to the welfare of society, as you know.'[32] He noted the weariness of the colony under rule by excommunication, and the sad fate which befell governor or intendant who refused to accept clerical control. He paints a picture of every layman, from governor-general to simple officer, striving to keep on good terms with the clergy because of the power they wielded. Nevertheless, he admits that the people had great confidence in their priests, and that 'one is devout here in appearance.'[33] He summed up his impression of the French Canadians, whom he clearly considered a different people from his own, thus:

The Canadians or Creoles are well built, sturdy, tall, strong, vigorous, enterprising, brave, and indefatigable. They lack only the knowledge of literature. They are presumptuous and full of themselves, putting themselves ahead of all the nations of the earth; and unfortunately they do not have the respect that they might for their relatives (the French).

Quebec Seminary, *Procure* Wing

Constructed (1677–80) by Claude Baillif after the plans of Frère Luc, who was an architect as well as a painter. The top story was added after a fire in 1865. This is a fine example of the institutional building of the 17th century. The old elm in the centre of the court was treasured by all graduates of Laval until its recent loss. (I.O.A.P.Q.)

Montreal Seminary

Unsigned water color (c. 1826) attributed to John Drake, from Jacques Viger's *Album*. This is a view from the garden side of Francois Dollier de Casson's building of 1683, part of which still stands on Notre Dame Street. It was one of the many buildings designed and built by the great Sulpician. (I.O.A.P.Q.)

Villeneuve House, Charlesbourg

This late 17th century farmhouse is typical of the old dwellings in the Quebec district.
(I.O.A.P.Q.)

Beauchemin House, Varennes

This farmhouse built in 1770 is typical of the Montreal style. Though in the country, it has the high stone gables which were required in Montreal as a protection against fire leaping from roof to roof. Houses of this type may still be found, usually behind a tin curtain of advertising placards, in downtown Montreal. (I.O.A.P.Q.)

The blood of Canada is very good; the women are generally pretty; brunettes are rare, the wise are common, and the lazy are found in great enough number; they love luxury dearly, and it falls to the one who best traps a husband.[34]

Lahontan is not the most reliable of witnesses, but he is the most outspoken; and some of his observations are supported by unimpeachable testimony.

The truly religious spirit of the theocracy is revealed in the *Jesuit Relations*, which continued to be published annually in France until 1673, and in the stream of letters which Marie de l'Incarnation sent to her correspondents in France until her death a year earlier. These are absorbing documents, which throw a flood of light on the life of New France. Their literary quality is best indicated by the fact that Parkman made extensive use of them to enliven his vivid narratives. The crusader spirit of the founders of Montreal, which differed somewhat from the missionary zeal and mystic preoccupations of the Quebec writers, is mirrored in Dollier de Casson's *Histoire de Montréal* (1672-3), the first local history and a richly revealing picture of the times. After serving as a captain of cavalry under the great Turenne, Dollier entered the priesthood and came to Canada in 1666. At once missionary, explorer, architect, and engineer, Dollier became the superior of the Sulpicians and as such the seigneur of Montreal, over which he ruled like a military monk of the Middle Ages. Another old soldier, Frontenac, who was a friend of Molière, revived the drama in Canada with garrison theatricals staged at Quebec by officers of the Carignan-Salières Regiment. The great plays of Corneille, Racine, and Molière were thus performed in the colony soon after they were first given in France, but Bishop Saint-Vallier, Laval's successor, first frowned upon this frivolity and then condemned it, as he did dancing and immodest or overly gay dress.[35] The theater was not a vigorous form of artistic expression in Quebec until recent years, because of the Jansenist element in French-Canadian Catholicism, which also gave a puritanical tone to the colony's society in other respects.

Other schools came into being to supplement the establishments of the Jesuits and Ursulines at Quebec, and of Marguerite Bourgeoys at Montreal. Before the end of the seventeenth century there were no less than twenty-four, of which fifteen were in Quebec, Trois-Rivières, or Montreal, where the bulk of the population of some 15,000 was to be found. In 1668 Bishop Laval established the Petit Séminaire of Quebec, whose students received instruction from the Jesuits, to supplement the Grand Séminaire created in 1663 to prepare candidates for the priesthood; and the bishop and Talon joined forces to inaugurate the Saint-Joachim school for artists and artisans at nearby Cap Tourmente. The bishop needed trained hands to build and decorate churches; while the intendant was intent upon making the colony self-sufficient. They succeeded in establishing a popular artistic tradition, which persisted for nearly two centuries, of simple craftsmen working in the classic style of Louis XIV, first simplified and then embroidered to meet the expanding needs of the colony. The medieval tradition of craftsmanship, of long apprenticeship, and of preoccupation with making a beautiful thing as well as possible regardless of the cost in time and trouble, was thus introduced into the French-Canadian way of life. This tradition almost perished between 1840 and 1920, in a colonial culture's passion for imitation of foreign models, but it has been revived in recent years; and the provincial arts and trade schools now scattered through Quebec derive from the foundation of St. Joachim. Modern Laval University at Quebec also traces its tradition back to this same period; for from 1655 onward the Jesuit school offered the complete classical college course of seven years, and shortly thereafter advanced instruction in mathematics, navigation, surveying, engineering, and map-making was added. Aside from this training in applied science under Martin Boutet and Jean-Baptiste Franquelin, there was the pioneer research work of Michel Sarrazin, who was at once physician, surgeon, zoologist, and botanist.

Sarrazin deserves the title of father of French-Canadian science, and in this field he was a worthy contemporary of Frontenac, La Salle, and Iberville. He was not the first of his profession to come to New France: the surgeon Bonnerme had accompanied Champlain; another named Duchesnes had been the first to hold title to the Plains of Abraham; while Robert Giffard was the physician of the Hôtel-Dieu of Quebec as well as the seigneur of Beauport. But Sarrazin played a more important part in the life of the colony than any of his predecessors. A year after his arrival in 1685 he was named surgeon to the troops, and soon found himself serving the hospitals of both Quebec and Montreal. Perhaps influenced by his close friendship with the cartographer Franquelin, the most scientific mind in the colony, Sarrazin returned to France in 1694, where in less than four years he completed the seven-year course in scientific and clinical medicine given by the School of Paris.

Thus furnished with the best training then available, Sarrazin returned to New France, where he was soon named royal physician, with governors, intendants, and bishops among his patients. His studies had given him a passion for research, and amid his daily duties he found time to correspond with the Academy of Sciences in Paris, to which he furnished notable reports on the beaver, the muskrat, the porcupine, the seal, and ginseng—the root whose discovery by the Jesuits had involved the colony in trade with China, where it was highly valued as a drug. Sarrazin's major work, how-ever, was in botany. In five years he sent some 200 specimens of North American flora to Tournefort of the Jardin Royal, the great forerunner of Linnaeus. To accomplish this feat, Sarrazin enlisted the aid of officers at remote posts in the collection of speci-mens, which he then carefully studied and described. Tournefort gave the name of his zealous correspondent to the pitcher plant (*Sarracena purpurea*) to commemorate his painstaking work. With his studies of the sugar maple and the blueberry, Sarrazin paved the way for later exploitation of these Canadian natural resources, which were unknown in Europe. He even studied the mineral springs of Cap de la Madeleine, near Trois-Rivières, for which he over-optimistically foretold a future as great as those of the notable European spas. Concerned by the failure of French wheat to survive the Canadian winters, he imported the Swedish variety, which flourished and yielded richer crops than that on which the colonists had relied.

Correspondent of Réaumur, the Abbé Bignon, and Fontenelle, Sarrazin linked the colony with the great intellectual figures of the mother country. He became one of the notables of New France, and was named to the Superior Council and made keeper of the seals. The colony was not to see his like again until 1742, when Jean-François Gaulthier came out as royal physician, and under La Galissonnière, an associate of the Academy of Sciences of Paris and the founder of a Quebec Academy, revived the scientific tradition which Sarrazin had founded so brilliantly. After the English con-quest that tradition was forgotten for a century, and did not again become a force in Quebec life until recent years.

Another medieval cultural tradition was established in Canada by the Ursuline nuns, who taught the art of embroidery to both their white and Indian pupils. Marie de l'Incarnation and Madame de la Peltrie, like all convent-bred French ladies of the period, were great needle-workers; and this art, along with religion and languages, figured largely in the Ursuline curriculum. The needlework was chiefly upon altar decorations and clerical vestments. The most noted pupil of the Ursulines was Jeanne Le Ber, a daughter of the wealthiest merchant of Montreal who became the most famed recluse of New France, spending nineteen years in a chapel opening off the church of the Congrégation de Notre-Dame, where she divided her time between her devotions and needlework. Wool, silk, and thread of gold and silver, woven into the traditional flower, leaf, fruit, and geometric patterns, went into the making of the richly colored and ornamented vestments and altar linens which she created. Ex-amples of her art are still preserved in Montreal today, and modern French-Canadian work follows the same tradition. One curious result of the Ursulines' introduction of the art of embroidery was the development of a taste among the Indians for richly decorated costumes, which reached its peak in the nineteenth century. Such typical 'Indian' decorative motifs as the swastika and other geometric patterns have been derived by some authorities from the Ursulines' instruction of Huron girls in the seventeenth century.

During the latter part of the same century the architectural tradition of Quebec was also established. The first buildings were '*en colombage*' (squared timber frames filled with short logs or rubble), '*pièce sur pièce*' (squared timber laid horizontally), or '*en pile*' (upright logs planted in the ground as in a palisade). The log cabin was only introduced into Quebec in the nineteenth century from the United States. None of these early buildings have survived, but detailed descriptions of them may be found in the writings of Champlain and Marie de l'Incarnation.[36] Towards 1650 or 1675 more building in stone took place, as the colony became a permanent establishment, but unfamiliar varieties of stone and mortar and a very different climate played havoc with the work of French masons. Some of the first stone churches fell in ruins only twenty or thirty years after their construction. The differences of environment and of materials at hand played a part in the gradual modification of the imported style, which was a peasant and provincial version of that of Louis XIV.

Houses were of two main types: the Montreal stone mansion, narrow, deep, and massive, flanked by chimneys and protected against fires by endwalls raised well above the roof line; and the Quebec house of stone, or wooden frame filled with stone, long and shallow, with a central chimney and a steep roof pierced by dormer windows, above low and solid walls. The first type derived from a Breton model; the second from a Norman. Both were roofed with cedar shingles, unknown in France; and later with sheet iron as a protection against fire. Thatched roofs were found only in the districts of Trois-Rivières and Charlevoix, and then only on barns and outbuildings. The penetrating northeast wind of Quebec, which quickly broke up mortar, resulted in the practice of facing that quarter of the dwelling with wood to protect the stone-work. For further protection against the weather the other walls were often covered with whitewashed plaster. Thick walls, small windows, steeply pitched roofs, and the extension of the roof well beyond the walls to form the distinctive bell-shaped gable, were all adaptions to the rigorous climate of New France, with its nine months of bitter cold and heavy snowfall. A covered gallery in front or around the house met the needs of the three hot months.

Ecclesiastical architecture was conceived in the same simple spirit. Monasteries, convents, seminaries, and hospitals were built in the form of vast two- or three-story stone rectangles, with dormer windows on a steep roof dotted with chimneys. Later additions took the form of wings to the original structure. Forts were built after the same general pattern, but with thicker walls and stronger roofs. Stone windmills, which also served as strongholds in case of Indian raids, were common along the St. Lawrence between Quebec and Montreal. They took the form of round towers with very steep, conical roofs. The churches were of two main types: the traditional cruciform type of the French countryside, with two transepts and a semi-circular apse, and a very steep roof and a tower with one or two lanterns; and another with a single nave, closed by a false vault and a square apse. This later style, known by the name of the Recollects who introduced it after their return to Quebec in 1670, flourished for a time in the towns, but eventually yielded to the structurally stronger transepted type. The chief survival of the Recollect style is the tradition of luxurious interior decoration, which was introduced by artists of the school of Frère Luc, who worked in Quebec after 1670. Most buildings were planned by master stonemasons and carpenters; but the religious orders numbered some trained architects, such as Frère Luc of the Recollects and his disciples, and Dollier de Casson and Vachon de Belmont of the Sulpicians. The Jesuits, curiously enough, considering their dominance, never introduced into New France the artificial style known by their name; and they built only some simple mission chapels, which were not architecturally noteworthy. Some of the military engineers—Villeneuve, Gédéon de Catalogne, and the two Chaussegros de Léry—drew up unrealized plans for public buildings in the Jesuit style, but most of their work was in the manner of Louis XIV and Vauban. Quebec's architectural tradition was fixed in a popular style which could be carried on by master craftsmen and whose charm was based upon its honesty, simplicity, and good proportions.

6

From the Peace of Utrecht in 1713 until the beginning of the War of the Austrian Succession in 1744, New France enjoyed thirty years of peace, or at least of armed truce, welcome after thirty years of warfare that had tried its slender resources. The population stood at only 18,000, despite all the efforts made to swell it; the company entrusted with the fur monopoly had collapsed, bringing down in ruins the trade upon which the economic life of the colony depended; and Canada was flooded with card money, which was redeemed in 1714 at half its value—a loss to the colony of 800,000 *livres*. New France's military strength was sapped by the absence of recruits from the mother country to fill up the royal regiments, and by the failure of immigration to swell the ranks of the colonial militia; while the allegiance of the Indian allies was strained when a shortage of trade goods developed. The Iroquois had come under the official protection of the English, who used them as a constant threat to the vulnerable Lake Ontario link in the French lifeline of trade and empire. Hudson Bay, Newfoundland, and Acadia, the outposts of New France, were now all in English hands. The colony was on the defensive, and in 1716 Governor Vaudreuil thus described its policy: 'To profit from the peace by fortifying Canada.'[37]

France was a good deal less interested in the colony at the close of Louis XIV's reign than at the outset of it. Only four or five thousand immigrants came in the next forty years to meet the colony's major need of more manpower. They were not all the best of citizens: some of them were young men of good family who had fallen into disgrace, and were sent out under *lettres de cachet*. They were loath to work with their hands and so lived by their wits. Many of them acted as itinerant schoolmasters. They amused themselves gallantly with the *habitants'* wives and daughters, and introduced scandalous songs; and their loose behavior did nothing to increase the prestige of education with the right-thinking simple country folk. Nonetheless they enriched French-Canadian folklore with many a gay song whose origin goes back to the Middle Ages. Another immigrant group consisted of poachers, smugglers, and counterfeiters, whose enterprise made them more welcome additions to the population, while there was little censure or opportunity in the colony for the exercise of the peculiar talents which had brought about their deportation from the mother country. A lack of civic consciousness and a certain willingness to sail close to the wind of the law may be in part considered the contribution to the French-Canadian tradition of these newcomers, though these characteristics may also be traced back to the lawless *coureurs de bois* and the profound individualism of the French temperament. The bulk of the threefold increase of the population during these thirty years—the total amounted to 55,000 in 1754—must be assigned to the extraordinary vitality of this ethnic group, triumphing over poverty, plague, and war.

The military question was acute. The royal troops had dwindled to a mere 600, many of that number being old men or boys; and reinforcements from France were refused. The militia organized by Frontenac became the principal force of New France under a policy of universal service which exempted only a few officials. Each parish had its company under a *capitaine de côte*, the exact equivalent of the Anglo-American militia captain, who became the local representative of the central government in civil as well as military affairs and as such a threat to the old dominance of the *seigneur* and the *curé*. The companies were grouped under the governments of Quebec, Trois-Rivières, and Montreal, the whole force being under the orders of the governor-general. Fortifications were clearly necessary to supplement the shortage of men; and so the countryside was dotted with rude wooden palisades, with some stone forts at strategic points. The great fortress of Louisbourg, an American Gibraltar, was reared on Cape Breton Island to guard the mouth of the St. Lawrence, now threatened on either side by English Newfoundland and Acadia. But a naval base, no matter how powerful, is no stronger than the fleet which depends upon it; and in the absence of a powerful French fleet Louisbourg failed to fulfil its function and twice fell with astonishing ease when attacked by the English in 1745 and 1758.

In Acadia a passive resistance to English rule was maintained by the French farmers guided by their priests, while the Abenakis harried the expanding Maine settlements at the inspiration of their missionaries, who like their Acadian colleagues frequently confused religion and patriotism. In the West the French rebuilt Niagara to protect the line of communications between Canada, the Lake posts, and Louisiana; while at Crown Point on Lake Champlain they raised Fort Saint-Frédéric to block the traditional invasion path from the South. These fortifications were the work of the elder Chaussegros de Léry, an able disciple of Vauban. In the Illinois country the French fought a war of extermination—their first such Indian campaign—against the Foxes, who had been instigated to attack them by the English and the Iroquois. From 1731 to 1743 the La Vérendryes carried on the last great explorations of the French in America, reaching towards the Rockies in the last impulse of the old search for a passage to the Pacific and in the continuing effort to tap new fur territory.

During these years New France sought to evolve a sounder economy than it had yet known, with its sole reliance on the fur trade. Agriculture was encouraged by every device at the disposal of the governor and intendant, but it did not prosper and misery was often widespread. Commerce and industry fared as badly; the fur trade passed through its customary cycles of poverty and plenty; while inflation, shipwreck, and the profiteering of French merchants kept the prices of imports high, far beyond the means of most of the colonists. Local industry was alternately encouraged and then stamped out when it interfered with French manufacturing interests, under the mercantilist policy which prevailed at court; in 1702 it was still the king's view that 'The Colony of Canada is good only inasmuch as it can be useful to the Kingdom.'[38] Where noncompetitive industries could be established, they were encouraged with too lavish a hand, so that they never became self-sufficient. Corruption, the shortage of manpower and capital, the difficulties of communication and transportation, and absentee direction all combined to prevent New France from developing a strong and well-rounded economy.

Climate and the structure of society made the fur trade the major industry of New France: the long winters which hindered other enterprises favored this one; and soldier, gentleman, and unskilled laborer alike needed neither training nor capital to get rich quick in this wilderness trade. No less than 15,000 individuals left Montreal to engage in the trade during the seventeenth and eighteenth centuries; and they have left their mark in the French place names scattered over the continent, and in much mixed blood. But the free trader of the English colonies, with better and cheaper goods to offer in exchange for furs, and no rigid monopoly to hamstring his activities, soon drove the French trader farther and farther afield, or turned him into a dealer in contraband. As early as 1715, 50,000 pounds a year of beaver—a quarter or a sixth of the total yield— found its way deviously from Montreal to New York, while the French traders made increasing use of English trade goods, and more *coureurs de bois* deserted to the English. The transition had already begun from French monopoly to English control of the fur trade.

In the 1730's the first network of roads was built, and with this development colonization expanded and domestic commerce was liberated from six months of inaction while the waterways were frozen over. The colony supplied Louisbourg with part of its provisions, and this trade took on such proportions that when the fortress fell in 1745 the administrators of Canada sadly reported: 'The two colonies supported one another; today ours have no support.'[39] Louisbourg also served as entrepôt for a trade between Canada and the Antilles, which broke into but did not seriously threaten New England's long-established commerce in the Caribbean. These new developments brought about a great change in the colony's economic position. The land under cultivation increased from 63,000 *arpents* in 1719 to 163,000 fifteen years later; the wheat crop was tripled in thirteen years; and Intendant Dupuy proclaimed that wheat was destined to replace beaver as the chief Canadian export. The copper of Lake Superior and the iron of the Saint-Maurice were exploited on a small scale, while the lumber industry founded by Talon took on new life, with the nineteen sawmills of 1719 becoming fifty-two by 1734. Shipbuilding increased, though it never reached the proportions attained in the English colonies. In general, the colony exported raw materials and imported manufactured goods, and was slowly developing a favorable balance of trade when the return of war destroyed the carefully built economy. All this economic development had been the work of French officials, for the feckless tradition of the discoverers and the *coureurs de bois* still was dominant among the French Canadians. The minister at home noted regretfully in his dispatches to the governor-general that the Canadians wished always to go farther afield, without bothering about building up settlements in the interior, because they earned more and enjoyed greater independence when they were away from the settlements.

7

During the seventy-two years of Louis XIV's reign, New France developed the institutions which it was to preserve with singular tenacity, even after the English conquest of 1760. It was the King's lifelong ambition to concentrate all the power of the state in himself, believing as he did that division of power among the great resulted in corruption and disorder. But Louis XIV also thought of himself as the father of his people, and therefore his absolutism was tempered with paternalism. His great churchmen Bossuet and Jurieu likened him to God so fulsomely that Madame de Sévigné was moved to write: 'One is not content to compare him to God; the comparison is made in such a fashion that it can be clearly seen that God is only the copy of the King.'[40] His successor Louis XV acted on the same principles, but lacked Louis XIV's greatness. There was a major flaw in this benevolent despotism as far as the colony was concerned: the King could not occupy himself with all the details of the administration of New France, and the corruption and disorder that had been feared from division of power flourished when absolutism was applied at long range and through a series of subordinates.

The minister of the marine was given complete direction of the affairs of the colony. He exercised this power through the governor-general, charged with military and diplomatic functions, and the intendant, charged with judicial, police, financial, and economic authority. The governor-general was the personal representative of the King; his prestige was greater than that of the intendant, but the latter had more power. The governor was a noble and usually an old soldier; the intendant was a civil servant of bourgeois or *noblesse de la robe* background, and usually a much younger man; it was evident that the two officials, with conflicting powers and very different mentalities, would clash. Indeed it had been so planned at court, in order that no colonial dictatorship should develop to threaten the royal authority. Both governor and intendant were creatures of the King and could be recalled at will; each year they received the royal instructions and further dispatches from the minister to guide their actions. Any suggestions from the men on the spot had to wait a year for approval or disapproval at home, since the St. Lawrence was closed by ice to the frail vessels of the day at least six months in the year. Here again absolutism and paternalism put the colony at a grave disadvantage, though continuity in administration was supplied in some measure by the minister's long tenure of office.

Beneath the governor and intendant was the Superior Council, of which the former was honorary president and the latter the functioning head, while the bishop was a potent member. The Council became the battleground of the three heads of New France, and was soon shorn of all powers save the judicial, in order to quell their disruptive disputes. The Council has been called a parliament, but it is difficult to concede it that name in the English sense when its members were appointed by the executive, and the King had flatly ordained in 1726 that it should 'in no fashion, either direct or indirect, concern itself with governmental affairs.'[41] To the governor-general, who was also governor of Quebec, were subordinated the governors of Trois-Rivières and Montreal; while the regular troops were distributed among all three districts, with the majority at Montreal where the danger of Indian attack was most acute. The intendant had a chief assistant, the commissary of the marine, who was stationed at Montreal and charged with the support of the troops, while other assistants were scattered among the settlements and trading posts. Each district had its own courts, while the Superior Council served as the highest court in the colony. All told, the administration was carried on by 208 officials, paid by the King and usually sent out from France, in order that their interests might not be those of the colonists. When the extent of territory they governed is considered, their number surely was not excessive; and Parkman's charge that New France was 'all head'[42] loses some of its force. Unfortunately these officials were poorly paid, and the temptation to supplement their income by graft was irresistible in many cases. In the last days of New France the administrative system became riddled through and through with corruption on a gigantic scale; but long before the days of the infamous Intendant Bigot, official graft represented a serious drain on the colony's finances.

The people had practically no share in the government; their role was simply to take orders. In the early days the Council, then significantly known as 'Sovereign' rather than 'Superior,' served in some measure to represent the interests of the colonists as well as those of the mother country; but this representative function was soon extinguished. Later the syndics, at first representatives of the merchants and then of the towns, could be heard by the government, while any person was free to present requests or complaints. But these were matters of privilege and not of right; any subject could appeal to the King in his own name, but no one and no group had the right to speak in the name of all. The militia captain was a representative of the people, but he was also the agent of the government. This situation no doubt lies at the base of the French Canadian's lack of civic consciousness. Under French rule he had no real share in the government; under British rule he first had to struggle for the unfamiliar rights of representative government, and then found himself exploited by compatriots who acted in his name, but often for their own benefit rather than his. Another factor was the growing love of independence, which may be considered a North American trait grafted upon the French tradition of individualism. From the early days of the colony French administrators and travelers noted an independence of spirit to which they were not accustomed in the absolutist mother country. Lahontan observed that: 'None must say *habitant*, for the title of peasant is no better received here than in Spain, whether because they pay neither *sel ni taille* and have the liberty to hunt and fish, or because their easy life puts them on a level with the nobles.' In 1725 Vaudreuil remarked a 'spirit of mutiny and independence' among all the *habitants*; while in 1736 Hocquart noted that the Canadians were 'naturally indocile.'[43]

The truth of the matter is that the old social institutions of France developed along new lines in the colony, where the environment was so different. The annals of the colony are full of quarrels over precedence and privilege among all classes; the society of New France was not stable but constantly evolving, and the social ladder was open to whoever had the energy and the will to climb it. Poverty was too general and too widespread for wealth to be the basis of the social structure. There was noble blood to spare in the colony— and nobility was blithely assumed by those who lacked it, like the humble Gascon, Antoine Laumet, who came to call himself Antoine de Lamothe, Sieur de Cadillac. Some gentlemen of birth tilled the soil like peasants; and those who would not, from pride, entered the royal service, where they probably fared more wretchedly than the *habitant*, if more honorably by their lights.

The *seigneurs* were by no means all nobles; by the beginning of the eighteenth century *habitants* held a third of the seigneuries, and many others belonged to ecclesiastical bodies, officials, and merchants.[44] No *seigneur* could live in idleness on his small rents and feudal dues, and many of them labored beside their tenants. The seigneurial system was not established in Canada to create a privileged leisure class, but to encourage colonization. The *seigneur* might lose his fief if he did not succeed in establishing settlers upon it and in clearing the land. No less than one out of six seigneuries were thus withdrawn from their holders and reunited to the royal lands in 1741. The Jesuits, Sulpicians, and the Seminary of Quebec were the most successful *seigneurs*; for they carried on the work of settlement without interruption by warlike expeditions against the Indians or English, and they had the collective financial and intellectual resources to meet the problems of pioneering and cultivation under new and difficult conditions. The seigneurial system as a whole, however, cannot be said to have proved itself a successful method of colonization in New France, for it was too decentralized and uncoordinated in its workings. The long dependence upon the rivers as the sole highways confined settlement to the banks of the St. Lawrence until roads were finally built in the 1730's; then a second and sometimes a third line (*rang*) of concessions was opened up behind those fronting on the river, while settlement pushed up the St. Lawrence and the Ottawa from Montreal, and up the Richelieu and the Chaudière. Before the outbreak of the final struggle between France and England in America, plans were even launched to make substantial settlements about Lake Champlain, and to expand those in the Illinois country and at Detroit. But the fur trade and constant warfare offered too many temptations to the *seigneurs* for colonization to be their main concern.

There is little basis for the common claim that the French Canadians displayed from the first a peculiar genius for agricultural pioneering. Agriculture did not really come into its own in Quebec until the fur trade was taken over by the English after the Conquest and the call of the *pays-d'en-haut* (hinterland) waned. Many of the founders of New France were soldiers and adventurers; more were artisans, whose traditions have been carried down in the various handicrafts for which Quebec is still renowned; it took time to turn them into sedentary farmers. Another factor in the late development of agriculture was the gregarious nature of the people, who insisted on clustering together in the towns rather than isolating themselves in the country. By 1754 almost a quarter of the population was urban, and the colonial administrators were trying by ordinance after ordinance to restrain a still growing movement towards the towns. The tendency was engrained in the nature of the people, however, and today highly industrialized Greater Montreal includes half the population of a province which likes to think of itself as primarily rural and agricultural. By the beginning of the eighteenth century Montreal had already become the commercial center of the colony, while Quebec maintained its position as the administrative center and the terminus of ocean shipping. No real bourgeoisie arose; commerce was too firmly monopolized by the mother country for many Canadian merchants to grow prosperous, while most of the chief administrative posts were held by transient Frenchmen. Lawyers were excluded from the colony in order that justice might be more speedy, less expensive, and less sought after. Doctors came out from France, as did artists and architects. There were really only two classes in New France: the ruling élite of administrators, clergy, and noble *seigneurs*; and the mass of the people. The élite was either French or French by assimilation; the people called themselves

Canadians and were jealous of Frenchmen. This social division was to survive tenaciously in French Canada, and to set it apart from the rest of North America, whose greatest strength lies in a dominant middle class which plays no part in the traditional French-Canadian scheme of things.

8

Parkman has justly stressed the fundamental importance of the Catholic Church in New France: 'More even than the royal power she shaped the character and the destinies of the colony . . . The royal government was transient; the Church was permanent. The English conquest shattered the whole apparatus of civil administration at a blow, but it left her untouched.'[45] There can be little question that Bishop Laval had more influence on New France than Louis XIV during a long lifetime which appropriately paralleled Louis' reign. The development of the Church in New France may be said to be his work.

Laval came to the colony in 1659, having been named by Rome Vicar Apostolic of New France at the instigation of the Jesuits, who had maintained virtual ecclesiastical control of the colony since their arrival a quarter of a century before. The Abbé de Queylus, superior of the Montreal Sulpicians, had recently been appointed vicar of the Archbishop of Rouen, who claimed jurisdiction over New France. The Jesuits, who were barred from the bishopric by the rules of their order, nevertheless saw no reason why their rivals should have the office. The naming of de Queylus, who had likened the Jesuits to the Pharisees in a sermon preached in their stronghold of Quebec, was a definite threat to their dominance in the colony. With the aid of their powerful patron, Anne of Austria, Queen Mother and Regent of France, and of their influence at Rome, the Jesuits succeeded in having de Queylus supplanted by Laval, on the grounds that New France was a mission and that the naming of missionary bishops was a prerogative of the Papacy. Thus, at the moment of transition from mission to established church, the Church in New France was given an ultramontane rather than a gallican tendency. Under the regime of Laval, who had an inflexible will and an instinct for domination, ultramontanism was built into the very fabric of the Church in Quebec, which assumed a position very different from that which it held in gallican France.

From its foundation until about 1672, New France remained a mission in which the conversion of the savages was considered more important than the spiritual welfare of the colonists, except at Montreal, which was the parish as well as the seigneury of the Sulpicians. With the influx of immigrants under Colbert, the necessity of parish work became acute, for the new arrivals did not share the piety of the earlier settlers, and their behavior became a scandal to the Indian converts of the missionaries. The Carignan-Salières Regiment, fresh from long service in the Turkish war, introduced dissipations hitherto unknown in New France when they gave a ball at Quebec in 1667, the first in the colony, and staged theatricals. These innovations incurred the thunders of Bishops Laval and Saint-Vallier, who were singularly free with excommunications. The *coureur de bois*, descending upon the settlements after months in the wilderness, also upset the placid and pious colonists by his wild drinking, gambling, and wenching.

Laval had hardly disposed of the pretensions of his rival de Queylus when he tried to suppress the brandy traffic. Meeting opposition from the governors Argenson and Avaugour on this score, he returned to France and persuaded the government to recall the latter after he had disposed of the former. Laval came back with the new governor Mézy, who had been chosen on his recommendation, but with whom he soon quarreled and had recalled in turn over a question involving the bishop's position in the Council. This ascetic churchman who made a cult of personal humility belonged to one of the great families of France. By temperament and tradition he was inclined to stand upon the dignity of his office and the authority of the Church, which he considered to be lodged quite as absolutely in himself as Louis XIV considered the power of the state to lie in the monarchy. The bickering between bishop and governor went on until Laval went to France in 1672, returning clothed in the full dignity of Bishop of Quebec. There had been long negotiations between the Papacy and the French government on this score, and the latter had been forced to retire from its gallican position that the bishop should be named by the King. It was thus established that the Bishop of Quebec was to be in direct communication and dependence upon the Holy See; and this fact had important implications for the future.

Bishop Laval was no mere stickler for rank and rights; he was also a builder. Up to his time no Canadian had been ordained to the priesthood. Laval established the Séminaire de Québec in 1663 to prepare candidates for the priesthood. Meanwhile the Saint-Joachim School, also founded by Laval, trained craftsmen who helped to build the thirty churches reared between 1680 and 1730. Only 23 priests of Canadian origin came from the Quebec Seminary up to 1700, and 150 secular priests and 80 Jesuits from France supplemented them. Even after the growth of the colony had increased the number of candidates for the priesthood and provided for the support of a larger number of secular clergy—the Jesuit and Recollect missionaries were maintained by their orders—only 156 Canadian priests were ordained under the French regime, while 340 were brought from France to fill the gaps. Bishop Laval was an ultramontane centralizer, not a gallican or a believer in a national clergy. He was a churchman before he was a Canadian or a Frenchman; and under his guidance the Church in Quebec developed a tradition which it has preserved until today. Portraits of the Pope are found in French-Canadian homes more often than those of the Queen or of the prime ministers of Canada or Quebec, and the papal flag is displayed more frequently than at Rome.

Laval's centralizing tendencies found another outlet in his institution of *curés* who were re-assigned at the bishop's will, instead of being permanently fixed in one parish as in France. On this matter he had a long battle with the royal authorities who saw in this practice a dangerous extension of the episcopal power. Laval won this battle, as he won others with the state, and the secular clergy were controlled and supported by the seminary, which was headed by a superior chosen by the bishop. Laval's position in this matter was based upon local conditions, for few seigneuries were in a position to support a resident *curé*, as the king and Colbert wished. The first *curés* rivaled the Jesuit and Recollect missionaries in hardihood and devotion, as they made long journeys through the wilderness to visit their scattered flocks. The Seminary of Quebec was instituted as a branch of the Society of Foreign Missions of France, and the heroic labors of its first graduates validated this title. Bishop Laval retired to France in 1684 and resigned his charge, leaving his money, books, and furniture to the seminary; but he returned to Quebec in 1688, shortly after his successor Saint-Vallier had been installed in office. When the latter was captured at sea by the English, and was kept away from his diocese for thirteen years, the old bishop resumed office, which he held from 1700 to his death in 1708. In all, Laval guided the destinies of the Church in New France for thirty-four years, ruling in a more authoritarian and absolute fashion than any representative of the all-powerful Sun King. He left more of a mark upon the colony than any governor except the great Frontenac, with whom he had quarreled violently, as might have been expected when two autocrats were thrown together in a small settlement. There was no doubt to whom Frontenac was referring when he wrote to Colbert: 'Nearly all the disorders existing in New France have their origin in the ambition of the ecclesiastics, who wish to add to their spiritual authority an absolute power over temporal matters.'[46] The tradition of Bishop Laval has been a major force in the history of French Canada: his desire to subordinate state to Church, his authoritarianism, his Jansenism, his ultramontanism, have cropped up again and again in his spiritual heirs who have benefited from the prestige and ascendency which the first Bishop of Quebec won by his domineering will, his zeal, and his ceaseless effort.

After Laval's death the Church in Quebec was without a head for five years, before Bishop Saint-Vallier returned in 1713. He was then sixty, and though he maintained the prerogatives of the Church with a highly sensitive touchiness, he was unable to carry on where his predecessor had left off. After his death in 1727 the Church passed through evil days until the consecration of Bishop Pontbriand in 1741. Absentee bishops and a shortage of priests strengthened the hand of the seminary, which had already aroused the wrath of Bishop Saint-Vallier by 'the ideas it had formed of a new apostolic regime, where the seminary rather than the bishop led, and where all the ecclesiastics were to be subject to and dependent upon the seminary.'[47] The chapter of Quebec gave scandal by intrigues, idleness, and preoccupation with such worldly amusements as cards and good cheer, while it neglected its religious duties. The *curés* were seldom touched by such indictments; they continued their often arduous round of duties with zeal and devotion; they struggled to build churches; and as the only educated men in many districts, they gradually assumed a multitude of non-clerical functions, such as school-teaching and the drawing-up of notarial acts, which gave them an unequalled prestige and influence in their parishes. The theocratic tradition of early days was thus reinforced. Since the successors of Laval refused, despite constant pressure from the civil authorities, to establish fixed *curés*, the Bishop of Quebec had a stronger hold on the people than the governor, and the virtual local dictatorship of the *curé* was modified only by the fact that he was subject to recall at the bishop's will.

While the parochial and the hierarchical structure of the Church was built up and strengthened, missionary work was not neglected. In the Saguenay region the mission which had been abandoned in the seventeenth century while the colony was fighting for its life was resumed, and it was found that the Indians had handed down from generation to generation the tradition of the Mass and the hymns which the first Recollect missionaries had taught them. In Acadia the Jesuits continued their activity, which was both religious and political, for as Père Aubery frankly put it: 'Religion has been until the present the sole motive which has made the Abenaqui French, and when there will be no more missionaries there, they will become English and will alone be able to put the English in possession of the whole country at the first outbreak of war.'[48] Similarly the Abbé Le Loutre used his religious authority to keep French the Acadians of the peninsula, unwilling subjects of England since 1713, and lured them to the mainland and the French fortifications on the Isthmus of Chignecto. In the West the missionaries accom-

Shipwreck at Lévis

Oil painting (c. 1754) attributed to Paul Beaucourt, presented to the Shrine of Saint Anne de Beaupré as a token of thanks ("ex-voto") by the three survivors of a party whose boat was upset in the St. Lawrence while crossing from Lévis to Quebec. This charming primitive is notable for the detachment of the masculine survivors with regard to the drowning "*créatures*". (I.O.A.P.Q.)

Saint Peter's Church, Ile d'Orléans

Constructed in 1716 by artisans trained at the Saint-Joachim School. This is one of the finest examples of the typical transept church on the Norman model. The spire was added in 1830. (I.O.A.P.Q.)

panied the La Vérendryes; and no less than forty-five Jesuit priests and lay brothers maintained the missions of the hinterland. At Lorette, Saint-François, Bécancour, at Sault-Saint-Louis, Lac des Deux Montagnes, and La Présentation, villages of Christian Indians were established close to French centers, where in peacetime religion reigned in apostolic purity and in time of war useful auxiliaries for the slim French forces might be found.

9

Such was New France, as it developed its definitive form. It had become very different from the mother country, as the comments of French visitors reveal. Père Charlevoix, the Jesuit who twice visited Canada early in the eighteenth century and taught for a time at Quebec, has left us the best picture we possess of the old regime:

Everyone has the wherewithal of existence here; one pays little to the King; the *habitant* knows not the *taille*; he has cheap bread; meat and fish are not dear; but wine, cloth, and all things that must come from France cost a great deal. The gentlemen and officers, who have only their pay and who are charged with families, are the worst off. The women usually bring no other dowry to their husbands than much wit, love, their charms, and a great fertility; for God bestows upon the marriages in this country the benediction that he gave to those of the patriarchs; to provide subsistence for such numerous families requires that one also lead the life of the patriarchs, but the time for that has passed. There is more noble blood in New France than in all our other colonies together. The King still maintains twenty-eight companies of troops of the Marine, and three staffs. Several families have been ennobled, and several officers of the Carignan-Salières Regiment have remained there, so that the country is peopled with gentlemen, of whom the greater part are not at their ease. They would be still less well off, if trade were not permitted to them, and if hunting and fishing were not here open to all.

After all, it is somewhat their own fault if they suffer misery; the soil is good almost everywhere, and farming is not degrading. How many gentlemen in all the provinces of France would envy the lot of the simple *habitants* of Canada, if they knew it? And those who languish there in shameful poverty, can they be excused for not embracing a profession which only the corruption of morals and of the most sane maxims has degraded from its ancient nobility? We know no healthier climate in the world than there; there is no special sickness, the countryside and forest are full of marvelous remedies, and the trees distill balms of great virtue. These advantages should at least retain those whom Providence has caused to be born there, but frivolity, aversion to assiduous and regular labor, and the spirit of independence have always made a number of young men leave, and have prevented the colony from peopling itself.

These are, Madame, the faults with which most often and most justly the French Canadians are reproached. They are also those of the Savages.

It seems that the air which one breathes in this continent contributes to it, but the example and the habit of its natural inhabitants, who put all their happiness in liberty and independence, are more than sufficient to form this character.[49]

Père Charlevoix adds avarice, conceit, lack of scientific knowledge, ingratitude, overweening pride, inconstancy, impetuousness, and lack of respect for parents to his list of Canadian faults; but on the other hand he finds the colonists pious, religious, brave, and clever. Elsewhere, he remarks upon the provincialism of a society which had no news of its own and received that of Europe once a year, when the ships came in the spring, so that 'one talks ancient politics and conjectures on the future, with science and art having their turn in a conversation which never ceases.' He noticed no trace of accent, and thought the French spoken in the colony as pure as that anywhere. It is clear that he found the easy-going life of Canada pleasant, with its card-playing; its excursions in summer by *calèche* or canoe, in winter by sleigh or on skates; its fine hunting and fishing, which provided more than sport, since 'many gentlemen have only this resource to enable them to live at their ease.' He paints a sharp picture of Canadian society:

There are no rich people in this country; and that is unfortunate, for there is a great fondness for keeping up one's position there, and nearly no one amuses himself by thrift. Good cheer is supplied, if its provision leaves means enough to be well clothed; if not, one cuts down on the table in order to be well dressed. Our Creoles have benefited by the change. Everyone here is of good stature, and the best blood in the world is to be found in both sexes; lively wits, gentle and polite manners, are common to all; and boorishness of manner or language is unknown even in the backwoods.[50]

Père Charlevoix traveled widely in North America, and he makes an interesting comparison of the French Canadian with the English colonist:

The English colonist amasses means and makes no superfluous expense; the French enjoys what he has and often parades what he has not. The former works for his heirs; the latter leaves his in the need in which he is himself, to get along as best they can. The British Americans dislike war, because they have so much to lose; they do not humor the Savages, because they see no need to do so. The French youth, on the contrary, loathe peace and get along well with the natives, whose esteem they easily win in war and whose friendship they always earn.[51]

Later travelers made more casual but nonetheless interesting comments on New France. In 1736 Hocquart found that all the Canadians were devoted to religion, and he repeated this observation ten years later.[52] Peter Kalm, the Swedish traveler who visited

America in 1749, remarked that the French Canadians gave much more time to prayer and religious observances than the English or Dutch settlers to the south, and stated flatly: 'All those who have traveled in France admit that the French Canadian is a more fervent Catholic than his European cousin. Unfortunately, religion seems to consist here only of external observances.'[53] Kalm was impressed by the love of science displayed by his host La Galissonnière and by Lusignan, and compared this taste among the élite for natural history and for literature with the general scorn for the sciences in the English colonies, 'where the sole preoccupation of everyone seems to be to get rich quickly.'[54] He was astonished by the extent of La Galissonnière's knowledge, finding this 'other Linnaeus'[55] as much at home in politics, philosophy, and mathematics as in natural history. Kalm noted luxury among the merchants of Quebec and poverty among the *habitants*; politeness and a certain spirit of equality he found among all classes. Since he was fresh from the English colonies when he came to Quebec, he made many comparisons, finding the differences much the same as existed between the mother countries in Europe.

Young Bougainville, who came to Quebec as Montcalm's aide in 1756, has left a no less interesting account of New France than Peter Kalm's, though it is not as well known. The extent of the difference which had developed between Frenchman and Canadian is revealed in his comment: 'It seems that we are of a different nation, even an enemy one.'[56] He considered the Canadian 'vainglorious, mendacious, obliging, kindly, honest; tireless for hunting, racing, and journeys to the *pays-d'en-haut*; lazy at cultivation of the land.' He noted that 'a very great deal of brandy was drunk here'; and that 'there was little concern for the education of youth, since one early devoted oneself to hunting and warfare . . . It must be granted that despite this lack of education, the Canadians have natural wit, speak with ease, although they do not know how to write; their accent is as good as at Paris; their diction is full of vicious phrases borrowed from the Indian tongues or of nautical terms used in ordinary style.'[57] He found the orthodoxy of Quebec somewhat oppressive: 'No Jansenist is to be found here; there is even suspicion attached to people who know what one is.'[58] He judged that a prevailing spirit of gain destroyed the spirit of honor; that the commercial spirit was dimming the luster of military glory; and he reported the assurance of the Grand Vicar of Quebec that most penitents thought it only a mere peccadillo to steal from the king. On July 29, 1758 he wrote the epitaph of New France: 'Woe to this land! It will perish the victim of its prejudices, of its blind confidence, of the stupidity or crookedness of its chiefs. "This oracle is more certain than that of Calchas!"'[59]

Bougainville was right. New France fell like an over-ripe fruit before the last English assault in the American Hundred Years' War. In the final struggle Montcalm was hampered by the stupidity and jealousy of the Canadian-born governor Vaudreuil, and by the reluctance of France to supply the force he needed. The economic structure of the colony was rotted through by the gigantic swindles of Bigot and his gang of boodlers; division and dissension between Frenchman and French Canadian reigned until the moment of disaster came; and Wolfe won New France for Britain on the Plains of Abraham in September 1759. The Battle of the Plains might not have been conclusive if France had sent support for the army of Lévis, which defeated the English force, which it outnumbered three to one, at Sainte-Foy in the spring of 1760; but it was a British fleet which came up the St. Lawrence when the river opened, and thus the doom of New France was sealed. London had seen that the power of France might be broken on American battlefields as well as in Europe. Money and men had been poured across the ocean under the protection of British sea power; while France, fighting in Germany against Britain's allies, could spare few men and less money for the struggle in America. The old regime was dying and Voltaire celebrated the English victory at Quebec as the triumph of liberty over despotism, heralding the liberation of all America. The Reverend John Mayhew of Boston foretold that the Anglo-American colonies were destined to become 'in another century or two a mighty empire.'[60]

Parkman saw the great conflict which was concluded by the Treaty of Paris in 1763 as one between feudal, militant, and Catholic France and democratic, industrial, and Protestant England. Remove the religious terms from this equation, and it may better be restated as the conflict between the past and the future; for feudalism and military government in America were doomed by the mounting tide of democracy and industrialism, which soon made themselves felt in what had been the New France of Louis XIV and Bishop Laval.

Notes

[1] Canon Lionel Groulx, who has collected three volumes of historical studies under this title borrowed from the French writer André Beaunier (1869–1925), dramatic critic of *L'Echo de Paris* and literary critic of *La Revue de deux mondes*.

[2] Edward Gibbon, *The Decline and Fall of the Roman Empire*, Ch. I (Modern Library, New York, n.d.), I, 17.

[3] C. H. Firth (*ed.*), Macaulay's *History of England* (London, 1913), I, 387.

[4] C. W. Colby, *Canadian Types of the Old Regime* (New York, 1908), 21.

[5] Dom A. Jamet (*ed.*), Marie de l'Incarnation, *Ecrits spirituels et historiques* (Paris, 1929–39), III, 195 n.; Voltaire, *Candide*, Ch. 23; *Oeuvres complètes* (Paris, 1826), LIX, 317.

[6] Marie de l'Incarnation, *Ecrits*, IV, 295.

[7] H. P. Biggar et al. (eds.), The Works of Samuel de Champlain (Champlain Society, Toronto, 1925–36), II, 241.

[8] H. P. Biggar, The Voyages of Jacques Cartier (Ottawa, 1924), 106.

[9] Jansenism was a Catholicism strongly tinged with Calvinism. It was condemned as heresy in 1653 and again in 1713, but found support among French Catholics until the middle of the nineteenth century. Its adherents held that Christ died only for the elect; and this belief is symbolized by the Jansenist crucifix on which the arms of Christ are represented close together, not fully extended to embrace all mankind. Such a crucifix is among the earliest relics of the French in Acadia, and others have been found on the Ile d'Orléans near Quebec. Cf. J. C. Webster, Catalogue of Exhibits in the Ft. Beauséjour National Park Museum (Ottawa, 1937), no. 9, and Commission des monuments historiques de la Province de Québec, L'Ile d'Orléans (Québec, 1927), 47.

[10] Bossuet's comment on the Papacy is cited by Colby, Canadian Types, 39.

[11] Biggar, Cartier's Voyages, 64–5.

[12] These rapids, originally known as Sault-Saint-Louis, were nicknamed 'La Chine' by Dollier de Casson in mockery of La Salle's hope of finding a passage to the Orient in 1669. P.-G. Roy, Les Noms géographiques de la Province de Québec (Lévis, 1906), 232–3.

[13] Biggar, Cartier's Voyages, 165.

[14] Ibid., 186.

[15] Fr. André Thevet, Les Singularitez de la France Antarctique (Paris, 1878), Ch. 80.

[16] J. Florio (trans.), The Essays of Montaigne, Bk. I, Ch. 30, 'Of Cannibals' (Tudor Translations, London, 1892), I, 218.

[17] M. Lescarbot, Histoire de la Nouvelle France (Paris, 1866), Bk. III. This and other friendly references to Champlain were omitted in the 1617 edition, translated in the Champlain Society edition (Toronto, 1904–7).

[18] Biggar, Champlain's Works, I, 228–9.

[19] Roy, Noms géographiques, 328–31.

[20] Biggar, Champlain's Works, III, 31–2.

[21] F. Gabriel Sagard-Théodat, Histoire du Canada (Paris, 1865), Bk. IV, Ch. III, 811.

[22] Biggar, Champlain's Works, V, 298; VI, 486–7.

[23] P. Clément (ed.), Lettres, instructions et mémoires de Colbert (Paris, 1865), III–2, 402, Colbert-Bouteroue, Saint-Germain, 5 avril 1668.

[24] Talon's ordinance was based on Colbert-Bouteroue, Saint-Germain, 5 avril 1668; Clément, Lettres, III–2, 405.

[25] Clément, Lettres, III–2, 639, Colbert-Duchesneau; trans. in E. B. O'Callaghan (ed.), Documents Relating to the Colonial History of New York (Albany, 1855), IX, 792.

[26] RAPQ 1930–1, 32, Talon-Colbert, Québec, 4 octobre 1665; trans. in O'Callaghan, Colonial Documents, IX, 30.

[27] RAPQ 1930–1, 43, Colbert-Talon, Versailles, 5 avril 1666; trans. in O'Callaghan, Colonial Documents, IX, 41.

[28] O'Callaghan, Colonial Documents, III, 514, Dongan-Denonville, 25 October 1687.

[29] J. G. Shea (ed.), Charlevoix' History and General Description of New France (New York, 1900), III, 52.

[30] P. Boucher, Canada in the Seventeenth Century (Montreal, 1883), II.

[31] R. G. Thwaites (ed.), New Voyages to North America by the Baron de Lahontan (Chicago, 1905), I, 89–90.

[32] Ibid., I, 391.

[33] Ibid., 385.

[34] Ibid., 391.

[35] H. Têtu & C.-O. Gagnon, *Mandements, lettres pastorales et circulaires des évêques de Québec* (Québec, 1887), I, 170–2, 302–8, 413.

[36] R. Traquair, *The Old Architecture of Quebec* (Toronto, 1947), 5–17; C. W. Jeffreys & T. W. McLean, *The Picture Gallery of Canadian History* (Toronto, 1942), I, 116–17.

[37] APQ: Correspondence de Vaudreuil, 'Extrait du mémoire du M. Vaudreuil,' février 1716; cited G. Frégault, *La Civilisation de la Nouvelle-France, 1713-1744* (Montréal, 1944), 33 *n.* 23.

[38] PAC: B 23:85, 'Mémoire pour servir d'Instruction au Sr. de Beauharnois,' 6 mai 1702; cited Frégault, *Civilisation*, 72–3.

[39] PAC: C^{11} A, 83:14, Beauharnois & Hocquart-Maurepas, 12 septembre 1745; cited Frégault, *Civilisation*, 102.

[40] *Lettres choisies de Mme de Sévigné* (Paris, 1934), lettre du 13 juin 1685; cited Frégault, *Civilisation*, 129.

[41] PAC: B 49–2, 386, 'Mémoire du Roy à Beauharnois & Dupuis,' 14 mai 1726; cited G. Lanctot, *L'Administration de la Nouvelle-France* (Paris, 1929), 111.

[42] F. Parkman, *The Pioneers of France in the New World* (Frontenac ed., Boston, 1899), I, xcvi.

[43] Thwaites, *Lahontan's Voyages*, I, 34–5; Hocquart, 'Détail de toute la colonie, 1736,' in *Collections des mémoires et de relations sur l'histoire ancienne du Canada*, 2; APQ: Corr. de Vaudreuil, Vaudreuil-Maurepas, 18 mai 1725; cited Frégault, *Civilisation*, 165. *CHAR 1940*, 98-9, A. L. Burt, 'The Frontier in the History of New France.'

[44] Frégault, *Civilisation*, 184.

[45] F. Parkman, *The Old Regime in Canada* (Boston, 1899), II, 203.

[46] P. Margry (*ed.*), *Découvertes et Etablissements des Français* (Paris, 1876), I, 302, Frontenac-Colbert, 1677.

[47] *RAPQ 1941-2*, 180: I. Caron, 'Inventaire des documents,' Saint-Vallier-Conseil de Marine, 3 novembre 1717 (?); cited Frégault, *Civilisation*, 231.

[48] PAC: C^{11} A, 49: 597–8, 'Canada, sur les Abénakis'; cited Frégault, *Civilisation*, 245.

[49] L. P. Kellogg (*ed.*), *Charlevoix' Journal of a Voyage to North America* (Chicago, 1923), I, 245–7.

[50] Kellogg, *Charlevoix' Journal*, 116–17.

[51] *Ibid.*, 117–18.

[52] PAC: C^{11} A, 85: 55, Hocquart & Beauharnois-Maurepas, 7 octobre 1746; cited Frégault, *Civilisation*, 272–3.

[53] A. B. Benson (*ed.*), *Peter Kalm's Travels in North America* (New York, 1937), II, 396, 544.

[54] *Ibid.*, I, 375–6.

[55] *Ibid.*, II, 504.

[56] Bougainville; cited L. Groulx, *La Naissance d'une race* (Montréal, 1919), 239–40.

[57] *RAPQ 1923-4*, Bougainville, 'Mémoire sur l'état de la Nouvelle-France, 1757,' 57–61.

[58] R. de Kérallain, *La Jeunesse de Bougainville* (Paris, 1896), 63, 68, 99–100, 110.

[59] F. Parkman, *Montcalm and Wolfe* (Boston, 1899), III, 169–70.

[60] F. Parkman, *Pioneers of France in the New World* (Boston, 1899), I, xcv-xcviii.

CHAPTER II

THE LEGACY OF CONQUEST

(1760–91)

WHEN THE French Canadian says '*Je me souviens,*' he not only remembers the days of New France but also the fact that he belongs to a conquered people. This fact is deeply embedded in his consciousness, although he may protest that New France was not conquered by the English but rather abandoned by the French; and it is an important factor in his psychological makeup —and in that of the English Canadian.[1] From it stem the persecution and inferiority complexes which underlie much French-Canadian thinking. These attitudes are mirrored in the work of certain French-Canadian historians,[2] who paint the early days of British rule in dark colors contrasting sharply with their brightly tinted pictures of New France.

It is still possible today to start bitter controversy in Quebec by pointing out that the first British rulers of Canada did not try to crush the French Canadians under the yoke of military government, but on the contrary actually befriended them against the pretensions of the swarm of campfollowers and commercial adventurers who descended upon the newly conquered land like a cloud of locusts.[3] Such, however, is the picture which emerges from sober study of the contemporary documents. In this age of ruthless oppression of conquered peoples the peaceful transition of Quebec from French to British rule is remarkable and noteworthy. The English conquest might well have meant the end of French Canada as a cultural entity in North America, and of the French Canadians as an ethnic group; instead the survival of both was assured by legislation adopted a decade after the peace treaty had been signed. The French Canadians benefited by the confusion of British politics from 1760 to 1774, when colonial affairs were almost completely neglected in George III's bitter struggle with the Whig majority. But their survival was not dependent upon either British magnanimity or the force of circumstances; for French Canada possessed an indomitable will to live, witnessed in the first decade after the conquest by the attainment of the highest birthrate (65.3 per 1,000) ever recorded for any white people.[4] The whole history of Quebec since 1760 reveals how completely the French Canadians concentrated their resources and devoted them to the struggle for survival. This effort still continues, long after survival has been assured.

I

When the struggle began, the position of the French Canadians was indeed desperate, and few contemporary observers would have risked much on their survival. The New France which had been so utterly dependent upon the mother country throughout its existence was now separated and isolated from the France which had supplied its rulers, its educators, and its apostles. If the French Canadians were to remain French, they had to do so on the strength of their own resources, under the aegis of a foreign power whose religion, language, laws, and customs were very different from their own. This foreign power had been the traditional enemy of the conquered people ever since the first seeds of French settlement had been sown in the New World. France and England had fought a second Hundred Years' War in North America, and when that war ended some 70,000 French Canadians and Acadians faced more than 2,000,000 British North Americans. The French Canadians had lost much of their boldest and bravest blood in the wars which had occupied half their history, and they were exhausted by the long battle against overpowering odds. Their economic position was equally sorry: France had left them a legacy of 41,000,000 *livres* ($8,200,000) of inflated paper money, on which payment had been suspended and which was only partially redeemed years after the conquest.[5] Merchant and farmer alike were ruined; Quebec stood shattered after two months' bombardment, and the lower St. Lawrence countryside had been systematically devastated by the conquerors as they advanced up the river.[6]

Brigadier James Murray, who became military governor of Quebec soon after Wolfe's victory, thus depicted the 'miserable situation of His Majesty's Canadian subjects' to Amherst, the commander-in-chief in North America, on January 1, 1761:

... to describe it is really beyond my powers and to think of it is shocking to Humanity. It has afforded the King's British Subjects an opportunity of exerting that Benevolence and charity inseparable from the Sentiments which the freedom of our laws of church and state must ever inspire. The merchants and officers have made a collection of five hundred pounds Halifax currency and the Soldiers insist on giving one day's provision in a month for the support of the indigent, without these aids many must have perished and still I fear (in spite of all we can do) a famine unless a supply of corn is sent from Montreal or the British Provinces.[7]

Thus faced with common misery, British and French Canadians lived together, as Murray put it a few days later, 'in perfect harmony and good humour.'[8] Good relations had been established between the conquerors and the conquered soon after the Battle of the Plains in 1759. General Townshend lent Bougainville enough money to care for the French sick and wounded, though his own troops consequently went unpaid. All British officers, regardless of their sentiments about 'papistry,' were ordered to pay religious processions the 'compliment of the hat,' while the Ursulines knitted long woolen stockings for the kilted Highlanders during their first winter in Quebec.[9] The nuns of the Hôpital-Général and the Hôtel-Dieu, whose nursing had saved many British lives, were given special aid: the Hôpital-Général received £400 from Moncton, and all three communities were supplied with provisions and fuel during the first winter of British rule at Quebec.[10] The capitulations of Quebec and Montreal granted just and generous terms to the vanquished: the honor of the troops was preserved, while the people were assured the free exercise of their religion and of their civil and property rights.

Garneau and some later French-Canadian writers have been misled by the fact that Canada was governed by martial law from September 8, 1760 to August 10, 1764, and because of the traditional sternness of such government, have painted this period as one of tyrannical oppression. In fact, the military governments of Murray at Quebec, of Burton at Trois-Rivières, and of Gage at Montreal were all too tender to the French Canadians, at least in the minds of His Majesty's 'old subjects' who came flocking from Britain and the American colonies to exploit the conquest. No civil government could be set up until the peace treaty was signed in 1763, and after that, under the terms of the Peace of Paris, eighteen months were to elapse before British rule was officially established. Meanwhile the English military governors were supplemented by Swiss Protestant or Huguenot secretaries—Cramahé at Quebec, Bruyères at Trois-Rivières, and Maturin at Montreal, with Haldimand replacing Burton at Trois-Rivières in 1762—and so the strangeness of British rule was modified for the *habitant* by the fact that it was carried on in French.

There was little friction between the military and the French Canadians—the feudal structure of Quebec society appealed to the military mind—and Murray was justified in writing to his London agent early in 1764:

No Military government was ever conducted with more disinterestedness and more moderation than this has been. Hitherto it has not been easy to satisfy a Conquering army, a Conquered People, and a set of Merchants who have resorted to a Country where there is no money, who think themselves superior in rank and fortune to the Soldier and the Canadian, as they are pleased to deem the first Voluntary and the second born Slaves.[11]

He felt that he had won the 'affection and attachment of all the Canadian subjects,' and he protested his friendly sentiments towards the colony in a letter written in French to M. de Montesson, a prominent *seigneur*: 'I love it as much by inclination as by duty and my greatest pleasure will be to make its fortune, so far as that depends upon me.'[12] *Seigneurs* and British officers were soon upon the best of terms, and the intimacy of their personal relations is witnessed by the number of marriages contracted by British officers in the colony. Murray and Burton exchanged letters on the problems raised by the 'Matrimonial Distemper,' and the wife of the Quebec garrison chaplain remarked 'the extreme partiality for English officers' among the French-Canadian ladies.[13]

One of the best indices of good relations between English and French is the fact that '130 seigneurs, 100 gentlemen and bourgeois, 125 notable merchants, 25 legal authorities and lawyers (of whom several had belonged to the Superior Council), 25 to 30 doctors and surgeons, and nearly as many notaries'[14] remained in Quebec, instead of returning to France as they were permitted to do by the peace treaty. The French soldiers and officials, and some hundred of the colonial *noblesse*, deprived of their old opportunities for soldiering and fur-trading, were the only portion of the élite to emigrate. The clergy remained at their posts, and since their position alone among the élite was not affected by the conquest, their prestige as leaders of the people was strongly reinforced. The great mass of the population, the *habitants*, were little disturbed by the change of rule.[15]

To a singular degree the transition from French to British rule was unmarked by any radical changes. The new military governments continued the old administrative districts of Quebec, Trois-Rivières, and Montreal. The *curés* and the militia captains remained the agents of the central power, and through them the new oath of allegiance was administered in the rural parishes. The *habitants* objected more to giving up their arms than to taking the oath, and the regulations on this score were eased by the conquerors, who shared the *habitants*' passion for hunting. The militia captain became in some measure the magistrate of his parish, as well as its policeman. Murray revived the Superior Council of the old regime as the highest court of the colony, while British officers served as judges in cases appealed from the militia captain's jurisdiction. Some French Canadians were given office on the basis of their legal knowledge:

Jean-Claude Panet was made chief clerk of the Council, while J.-B. de la Fontaine was created attorney-general for the south shore and Joseph-Etienne Cugnet attorney-general for the north shore. The laws of the country were taken over and applied as they had existed under the French regime, and of necessity many Canadians found posts as clerks and assistants in the courts. In September 1761 an Englishman who was sued by a Canadian in the Quebec court had to get a copy of the charge against him translated into English. Furthermore, he was ordered to reply to it in French, for 'such was the language of the country.'[16] This was in a British court conducted by English officers under martial law. Notaries and land surveyors, like the militia captains, were recommissioned and continued in their functions. The military governors combined the roles of both governor and intendant under the old regime, and they did so in the same spirit of paternalism. Vicar-General Briand of Quebec paid tribute to them: 'Do not these noble conquerors succeed in forgetting that they have been our enemies, and concern themselves only with our needs and how to meet them?'[17]

The cherished laws, institutions, and customs of the French Canadians were thus early given toleration and a chance to survive. As regards their equally cherished religion, still more fundamental a part of French-Canadian culture, the situation was somewhat different. According to the capitulation of Quebec, 'the free exercise of the roman religion is granted, likewise safeguards to all religious persons, as well as to the Bishop, who shall be at liberty to come and exercise, freely and with decency, the functions of his office,' pending a treaty; and churches and convents were to be safeguarded.[18] According to the more comprehensive capitulation of Montreal, 'the free exercise of the Catholic, Apostolic, and Roman religion, shall subsist entire, in such manner that all the states and the people of the towns and countries, places and distant posts, shall continue to assemble in the churches, and to frequent the sacraments as before, without being molested in any manner, directly or indirectly' so far as the laws of England permitted, but the continuance of the tithe awaited 'the King's pleasure,' as did the privileges of the Jesuits, Sulpicians, and Recollects.[19] Vaudreuil had proposed, in good gallican fashion, that the French monarch should retain the right to name the Bishop of Quebec. This was refused by Amherst, and Quebec remained without a bishop, for Pontbriand had died four months before Montreal was surrendered, and no successor was named in the interval. The Church in Quebec was left without a head, and its future was imperiled. No new priests might be ordained without a bishop, and no recruits from France could supplement the numbers of the Canadian clergy, as in the past. Financial support from France was also withdrawn by the severance of relations with the mother country, while the tithe enjoyed no legal sanction.

The thorny question of the bishop was to drag on unsolved for six years, but for the rest the Church was treated with great tolerance by the conquerors, considering the Protestant prejudices of the time. It must not be forgotten that the frenzy of eighteenth-century hatred of 'papistry' reached its height during the French and Indian War. [20] But the American militiamen, who were most imbued with this fever, were sent home soon after the conquest, and the British regulars who remained were put under strict orders to show 'civility to the people who have chosen to live under our laws.' [21] To be sure, the Jesuits were turned out of their college in Quebec, which was the only undamaged building large enough to serve as barracks and government storehouse in the ruined Upper Town; and they, the Recollects, and the Sulpicians were forbidden to recruit their numbers; but at this same period even Catholic countries were expelling the Jesuits and prejudice against the religious orders ran high.

Though the conquerors were ordered by London to refrain from 'uncharitable reflections on the errors of that mistaken religion which they (the French Canadians) unhappily profess,' [22] and these orders were enforced, it is clear from Murray's correspondence that toleration was extended to Catholicism solely as a matter of policy and expediency. In June 1764 Murray, in writing to Lord Halifax about the renegade Jesuit Roubaud whom he had sent to London, revealed his private view that the French Canadians could be won from their religion:

He is a Man of extraordinary parts and great learning and is as Eloquent as Cicero. He is possessed of a thorough knowledge of the Views, Sentiments, & Faculties of the popish clergy of this province and perfectly sensible of the errors of their doctrine. He proposed Publickly renouncing the Roman Catholick Religion here, but such a measure would rather frustrate, than promote my schemes for the reform of the inhabitants of this colony. For that reason I send him to London where he may be useful and cooperate with me under the immediate direction of His Majesty's Servants in the great task I undertake of converting a great part of the Canadians.

I think I am not too sanguine in my hopes, I am at heart sure my attempt cannot be attended with any bad consequence, because nothing but mild and persuasive measures, the very reverse of persecution, shall be used, and therefore I rejoice to find Monsr. Charest has met with so favorable a reception at London, as I flatter myself that every indulgence that can be given will be granted these people. Great progress is already made; the National Antipathy is entirely got the better of on the side of the Canadians. I wish I could say as much of the British subjects, several from New England now established here are most inveterate fanaticks, a little address however may even make them of advantage, a proper contradiction of their insults will gain and strengthen the confidence of the Canadians to Govermt., which confidence being the Main Spring must be perpetually kept in order and cannot fail of perfecting the business I charge myself with, which is no less than the reformation of the greatest part of the inhabitants of this colony.[23]

Etienne Charest, *seigneur* of Lauzon and a leading Quebec merchant, had been sent to London in the fall of 1763 to present the petitions of the cathedral chapter of Quebec and of the Catholics of the whole colony for a bishop. The Abbé Montgolfier, superior of the Montreal Sulpicians, who had been named bishop by the chapter, left for Europe at the same time to have his nomination confirmed by the Holy See and to win the consent of the British government to his consecration. Murray opposed Montgolfier's nomination in a letter to Shelburne of September 14, 1763: 'If a priest as haughty and imperious, and so well connected in France, is placed at the head of this Church, he can later cause much trouble.'[24] So Charest was subjected to endless if polite delays in London, while Rome judged Montgolfier's election null, on the grounds that the canons had exceeded their powers in choosing a bishop. Under these circumstances Montgolfier withdrew and left the way clear for the nomination of Jean-Olivier Briand, Grand Vicar of Quebec and a friend of Murray, who praised his candor, moderation, and disinterestedness to Shelburne, concluding, 'I know no one of his cloth who more justly deserves the Royal favor.'[25]

Briand in turn departed for London, where he struggled for sixteen months against the ministry's reluctance to admit papal jurisdiction in a British possession—particularly when anti-Catholic feeling was running high at home. Finally he was informed unofficially that his consecration would be tolerated and that he could perform his episcopal functions in the colony, if he would content himself with the strange title of 'superintendant of the Romish church.' In June 1766 he returned to Quebec, where the Canadians congratulated one another happily and crowded the church to see their new bishop, 'Whom they regard as the support of their religion and as an earnest of the paternal kindness of the King towards them,'[26] according to the two-year-old bilingual Quebec *Gazette*, the first newspaper ever printed in Canada, where no press had been established under French rule.

Hardly had the foundation of French-Canadian survival been laid by Murray's military government when it was threatened by the institution of civil government according to the less liberal views of the Board of Trade, the forerunner of the Colonial Office of later days. These views were contained in the Royal Proclamation of October 7, 1763; Murray's commission as governor-general of

November 21, 1763; and his instructions of December 7. In accordance with the provisions of the peace treaty, Murray did not assume his new position until August 10, 1764, so the new order did not come into effect until that date. The proclamation gave the colony the name of the Province of Quebec, and it sharply reduced its old boundaries. The Labrador coast as far west as the St. John River was placed under the naval government of Newfoundland, since it was uncomfortably close to France's last foothold in the islands of St. Pierre and Miquelon. The new southern boundary ran from Restigouche Bay to the St. Lawrence, pretty much along the present Quebec provincial line, thus barring the Canadians from land which they had not yet settled and which might become more securely British if left to Nova Scotia and New England. The whole western hinterland was cut off from Quebec and turned into an Indian reserve, chiefly with the object of eliminating the causes of savage unrest, already evident in the conspiracy of Pontiac, the last great rising of the red man against encroachment by the white. The northern boundary ran from Lake Nipissing through Lake St. John to the head of the St. John River; but at that time and indeed until very recent times the far northeastern portion of the continent was of no great concern either to Canada or to England.

Much more important for the moment were the promises of a general assembly and of the laws of England which were made in the proclamation and implemented in Murray's commission and instructions. The tenor of the drastic new program of government has been admirably summed up thus: 'An old French colony was to be remade into an English colony.'[27] English laws and English courts were established; and provision was made for a large influx of British settlers, drawn either from old soldiers or from the crowded American colonies to the south. Assimilation was to be the order of the day; lands were set aside for the support of Protestant clergymen and schoolmasters, 'To the End that the Church of England may be established both in Principle and Practice, and that the said Inhabitants may by Degrees be induced to embrace the Protestant Religion, and their Children be brought up in the Principles of it.' The governor was even urged to report 'by what other Means the Protestant Religion may be promoted.'[28]

The outlook for the French Canadians would have been dark indeed if Murray had applied the ideas of the Board of Trade literally. He did not attempt to do so, however, because of their obvious impossibility, because of the sympathy he had formed for the French Canadians, and because of the quarrels in which he was already engaged with the English merchants and with General Burton, who was named commander of all the troops within the province and

made absolutely independent of the governor's control. Murray
poured out his woes to Elibank on September 16, 1764:

It is by the Military force we are to Govern the lately Conquer'd
Province in which there doeth not exist above fifty Protestant Subjects
Exclusive of the Troops and by my instructions of these fifty protestants
must be Composed the Magistracy: But what force, what weight can
such a Magistracy have unless the Supme. Magistrate has Authority
with the Troops? It is Evident the Brigadier must in fact be the Governor,
that the people must be Oppress'd by the Soldiery. That the Civil
Governor and his Magistrates must be Contemptable, and in place of
being the means of preserving order and promoting the happiness of the
Subjects, they must from the Natural Jealousie which such an establishment will produce become the Bane of Peace. And the Weak Effort they
will of Course make to Exert their Authority, will be productive of
Nothing but vexation and Confusion. The Reasons are so clear & simple
they should not have escaped the ministry.
   It will be too hard a task for me to Govern in the Civil Way a great
populated Country, of a different Religion, different language, different
Manners & Customs, without the Aid of the Troops or the Assistance of
the Law, for two [such] ignorant needy lawyers as are sent here from
England to distribute Justice to the people were never sent before from
any country.[29]

The 'two ignorant needy lawyers' were Chief Justice William
Gregory, fresh from an English debtor's prison, and Attorney-General
George Suckling, in search of new fields for his talents after a stormy
political and legal career in Nova Scotia. Suckling knew some law;
Gregory none; neither knew a word of French or much about human
nature. Such were the legal advisors of a governor who was a military man without legal training, and yet was supposed to legislate
for the colony, with the advice of his council, until an assembly
should be summoned.
   The Council was to be made up of the lieutenant-governors of
Trois-Rivières and Montreal—who promply refused to serve under
Murray, their former political equal and the military junior of
Gage—of the surveyor-general of the American customs, who was
seldom present; the chief justice; and eight members 'chosen from
amongst the most considerable' of the residents in the province.
The Council was at once a legislative, executive, and judicial body.
Since the anti-Catholic form of oath of office required barred any
French-Canadian Catholic from membership, its first members
were Colonel Paulus Aemelius Irving, later administrator of the
colony after Murray's departure; Captain Hector Theophilus Cramahé; Captain Samuel Holland, the engineer and surveyor-general;
Walter Murray, a relative of the governor; Dr. Adam Mabane,
an army surgeon; Benjamin Price and Thomas Dunn, English

merchants; and François Mounier, a Huguenot merchant who had settled in Canada shortly before the conquest. These men were chosen by Murray, and despite the fact that they were largely drawn from the army, they were sympathetic to the French Canadians and came to be known as the 'French party.' As the council remained, although governors came and went, these men and their successors practically governed Canada until 1787.[30]

Their power was not confined to the Council, for the chief justice presided over the King's Bench, while Mabane and Mounier were two of the three judges of the court of common pleas, whose prevailing language they at least understood, if they were ignorant of law. Under the governor's instructions from London, the magistrates and jurors had to be chosen from among the English merchants and retired officers, while the militia captains were excluded as Catholics. The only contact between government and people which had been developed since the conquest was thus cut, with the result that the political life of the colony became largely a struggle between the French have-nots and the English office-holders. The way was thus paved for the development of a new ethnic feeling to replace that 'National Antipathy' which Murray had congratulated himself on eliminating during the period of military government.

To these measures Murray was forced by orders from London, but he refused to call an assembly in which only the English merchants could have sat because of the anti-Catholic oaths required, and he sent Cramahé to London to urge the need of revising the government's policy in the interest of the French Canadians. On October 27, 1764 he himself wrote to Eglinton:

Mr. Cramahé has my Directions to lay everything before you, & I am sure You will do all in your power to assist him and a miserable People, who after having undergone the worst Calamities War can inflict, if not supported, must now either abandon their all or submit to the Persecution of the most cruel, Ignorant, rapacious Fanaticks who ever existed.

For my part, My Dear Lord, I will with Joy undertake anything to distress & reduce to reason my Royal Master's Enemies, but I cannot be the Instrument of destroying, perhaps, the best and bravest Race on this Globe, a Race that have already got the better of every National Antipathy to their Conquerors, and could they be indulged with a very few Privileges, which the laws of England do not allow to Catholics at home, must in a very short time become the most faithful & useful Set of Men in this American Empire.

If the Popular Clamour of England will not allow the humane Heart of the King to follow its own dictates & the [anti-] Popish Laws must be exerted with Rigour in Canada, for God's sake procure my Retreat, and reconcile it to Lord Bute, as I cannot be the Witness to the Misery of a people I love & admire.[31]

Such dispatches as this from the governor and the petitions from the people did much to help Cramahé bring about various modifications of the Board of Trade's policy. These changes led eventually to the Quebec Act and the utter overturn of the original policy. In 1765 the law officers of the Crown decided that the penal laws of England against Catholics did not apply in Quebec; and the Privy Council ordered that all discrimination against Canadians as jurors or lawyers should be abolished. In the following year a thorough revision of the judicial system was drafted, after the law officers of the Crown had condemned the administration of justice 'without the aid of the natives, not merely in new forms, but totally in an unknown tongue,' and the attempt to abolish 'all the usages and Customs of Canada with the rough hand of a Conqueror.'[32] Unfortunately this proposal was pigeon-holed at Whitehall when the elder Pitt replaced Rockingham as prime minister. The definitive solution of these vexing problems had to await the Quebec Act, while Murray tempered the English wind to the French-Canadian lamb as best he could.

Murray was having his own troubles, as the minority of English merchants—'the Licentious Fanaticks Trading here'[33]—grew more powerful and troublesome. Though only a small number of them had been born in the American colonies, most had spent some time there and had become infected with an unruly spirit of independence as well as anti-French sentiments. All claimed the right to be judged by English laws, and complained that their commercial operations were hindered by the unfamiliar French ordinances. These merchants were particularly numerous and influential in Montreal, the capital of the fur trade into which many of them forced their way soon after the conquest; and there was much friction between civilians who despised the military and an army which scorned shopkeepers. Murray observed in October 1764:

At Montreal the Civilians & the Military are Inveterate Enemies, I am ashamed to say, from the most trifling Circumstances: Every Art is used to improve the least Accident which may augment Popularity with the Troops: Discipline of Command must be neglected, the Canadian deemed an Alien and an irreconcilable Enemy to England, the few settled there held cheap, and everything in a Furoure. The Contagion may reach Quebec, but it cannot exist long, where the commander is not infected.[34]

As this last remark suggests, Murray was embroiled with his colleague Burton, as well as with the merchants of Montreal.

The latter had strong connections in London, and eventually they brought about Murray's downfall. The three-cornered quarrels which marked the closing years of his government are reminiscent of those between bishop, governor, and intendant under the French regime. No stick was too small to beat the governor with, and finally he was recalled to London for an investigation of the province's affairs. Murray learned the unwelcome news from his enemies the merchants, whose commercial correspondence was speedier than the official dispatches. He returned home undaunted by the charge of tyranny which had been raised against him: 'The Canadians who have lived under my government six years Shall be the best Judges of the truth of that Aspersion. They will to a man Vouch that all the Malice & Clamour which have been exhibited in England against me proceed from the protection that I have given them, and the inflexible aversion I have on all Occasions Shewn to Oppression & the National English Prejudice.'[35] It was even so, but in later years French Canadians were to echo the charges of Murray's English enemies, without realizing that they were attacking a great friend.

2

Guy Carleton, who in 1766 replaced Murray with the temporary rank of lieutenant-governor, and Burton as commander of the troops, was an Anglo-Irish soldier whose career was to be closely bound up with that of Quebec until the close of the century. He lacked the easy friendliness and frankness of Murray, who had done much to father the great Quebec legend that the Scots are sympathetic friends of the French Canadian, while the English are racial enemies.* But Carleton was a statesman rather than a placeman, and he could not abide graft and corruption. These traits, plus the natural sympathy of a soldier and a member of the landed gentry for a semi-feudal society, were to make him quite as much of a friend to the French Canadians as his predecessor. Carleton was accompanied by a new chief justice, William Hey, a young lawyer whose promise was soon realized, and by a new attorney-general, Francis Maseres, a brilliant scholar whose Huguenot ancestry gave him a perfect command of French and a bigoted obsession against Catholicism.[36] All three entered upon their duties with a prejudice against Murray and all his works which had been instilled in them by the London agent of the Quebec merchants. Consequently they were opposed to the 'French party' in the Council, who still hoped for their leader's triumphant return after he had been heard at home. When this hope was extinguished and Carleton was confirmed as governor-in-chief, he found himself

---

* This legend was furthered by the settlement of the disbanded Highland battalions along the Lower St. Lawrence, notably at Murray Bay and Rivière-du-Loup, where they intermarried with the French Canadians and were largely assimilated by them.

gradually drawn to the 'French party,' which again became the 'King's party.'

But in the opening months of his administration Carleton struck hard blows at the old dominant faction and favoured the mercantile minority. He banished Irving and Mabane from the Council; and in his dispatches home he pleaded the cause of the Montreal fur traders, who were hampered by restrictions on the commerce of the Lake posts, and that of the Quebec merchants who carried on the seal fishery in the lower St. Lawrence. He also tolerated the refusal of the merchants to pay the old French customs duties which Murray had kept in force during the military regime, and which had been applied again in 1766. The merchants displayed a wholly American repugnance for paying taxes, with or without representation. When suits were brought against them by Maseres, juries made up of merchants refused to heed his arguments or the chief justice's instructions. This summary procedure gave the merchants a momentary victory, but it eventually cost them the right of trial by jury in civil suits, under the Quebec Act.

One of Carleton's major reforms was in the matter of fees, by which most of the public officials were remunerated in lieu of salaries. The scale of fees was based in theory upon that prevailing in colonies where the standard of living was much higher than in Quebec, and in practice unscrupulous officeholders charged what the traffic would bear. This was a source of great discontent among both French and English; for under the French regime justice had been free, while the English merchants revolted against the outrageous exactions of the officials, which surpassed anything they had ever known. At the outset of his administration Carleton launched his lifelong crusade against the system by dismissing some of the grossest offenders and by publicly renouncing his own perquisites.

Another major step, taken with the support of his legal advisors, both of whom opposed representative government in Canada, was Carleton's refusal of the old subjects' demand for an assembly in which no French Canadian could have sat. Before leaving England, Maseres had already placed on record his views on this question:

As to the erecting an assembly in that province, it is a measure which probably will not for some years to come be found expedient. If an assembly were now to be constituted, and the directions in the governor's commission, above alluded to, were to be observed, by which none of the members elected there are to be permitted to sit and vote in the assembly till they have subscribed the declaration against Popery, it would amount to an exclusion of all the Canadians, that is, of the bulk of the settled population of the province—An assembly so constituted, might pretend to be a representative of the people there, but in truth it would be a representative of only the 600 new English settlers, and an instrument in their hands of dominating over the 90,000 French. Can such an assembly be thought just or expedient, or likely to produce harmony and friendship between the two nations? Surely it must have a contrary effect.

On the other hand, it might be dangerous in these early days of their submission to admit the Canadians themselves to so great a degree of power. Bigotted, as they are, to the Popish religion, unacquainted with, and hitherto prejudiced against the laws and customs of England, they would be very unlikely, for some years to come, to promote such measures, as should gradually introduce the Protestant religion, the use of the English language, of the spirit of the British laws. It is more probable they would check all such endeavours, and quarrel with the governor and council, or with the English members of the assembly, for promoting them. Add to this, that they are almost universally ignorant of the English language, so as to be absolutely incapable of debating in it, and consequently must, if such an assembly were erected, carry on the business of it in the French language, which would tend to perpetuate that language, and with it their prejudices and affections to their former masters, and postpone to a very distant time, perhaps for ever, that coalition of the two nations, or the melting down the French nation into the English in point of language, affections, religion, and laws, which is so much to be wished for, and which otherwise a generation or two may perhaps effect, if proper measures are taken for that purpose.[37]

Carleton himself felt that 'the British Form of Government, transplanted into this Continent, never will produce the same Fruits as at Home, chiefly because it is impossible for the Dignity of the Throne, or Peerage to be represented in the American Forests.' Monarchy and aristocracy could not be forces in America, 'where all Men appear nearly upon a Level.' Carleton, with one eye on the colonies to the south, was convinced that democracy would become dominant in an assembly, and this was clearly to be avoided 'in a province so lately conquered and circumstanced as this is.' He agreed with Maseres that the Canadians did not desire an assembly, which was totally foreign to their traditions, and that it was sought most eagerly by some of the 'English adventurers,' for whom neither official had overmuch regard.[38]

Carleton was familiar with France—his wife had been brought up at the Court of Versailles—and he saw New France through eyes blurred by impressions of the old mother country. Aristocratic and autocratic himself, he regarded the *seigneurs* and the clergy as the real leaders of the French Canadians, and tried to restore a feudalism which had never existed in Canada. He pleaded for a revival of the royal bounty which had supplemented the slim purses of the *seigneurs* in the French period, and he urged that their sons be given commissions in the army. This latter measure he regarded as an important safeguard against a French war. Charged with the defence as well as the administration of the colony, he was not happy at the thought that his garrison of 1,500 regulars might be opposed to 9,000 Canadians who had served in the French forces, or that France could muster 170 officers who either were Canadians or had seen service in Canada. He recommended the construction of citadels at Quebec and New York, to be linked by strong fortifications at Crown Point, Ticonderoga, and Fort George—a measure that at once would cut the American colonies in twain if their current unrest ended in rebellion, and would also guard both colonies against possible French aggression.

To his mind it was clear that the Canadians must be 'inspired with a cordial attachment and zeal for the king's government,' and that their grievances on the score of laws, courts, and fees must be promptly redressed. He urged that 'three or four of their principal gentlemen' be added to the Council, and that some military units be raised amongst them, for 'as long as the Canadians are deprived of all places of trust and profit, they never can forget they are no longer under the dominion of their natural sovereign; tho' this immediately concerns but few, yet it affects the minds of all, from a national spirit which ever interests itself at the general exclusion of their countrymen.'[39] This 'national spirit,' or group consciousness, which Carleton remarked so soon after the conquest, has remained a vital factor in French Canada down to the present day. Once its existence was pointed out, London displayed an ability to make use of it by such measures as Carleton had suggested. Today, whenever Ottawa neglects this tradition of government, it is urgently reminded that Canada is made up not of one people, but of two.

As far as the Church was concerned, Carleton was confronted with two problems. Bishop Briand was anxious to prevent the reoccurrence of any such episcopal interregnum as had left the Church in Quebec leaderless for six years after the conquest; and so was seeking a coadjutor with the right of succession in case of his death. Carleton got wind of this activity, and went to the bishop, maintaining that it was one which concerned the government. Carleton favored the principle of a coadjutor, for it avoided the necessity of 'sending to foreign dominions' for the consecration of a new bishop; but he disliked the leading candidate for the office, the Abbé de la Joncaire, who had the fault of having lived twenty-seven years in France, though he was Canadian-born. Briand agreed to obtain the governor's consent before he exercized the right which Rome had given him of naming a successor; and for the moment the question went into abeyance. Just before Carleton returned to

England in 1770, he approved, without consulting anti-Catholic London, Briand's nomination as coadjutor of L.-P.-M. d'Esgly, the first Canadian-born bishop. Carleton had seen an opportunity to attach the Canadians to Britain by using his influence to reverse the old preference shown to priests of French rather than of Canadian origin. He also discouraged the coming of new priests from France by requiring that they procure passports from the Secretary of State's office in London. Thus the possibility of the continuation of French ecclesiastical domination in Canada, after French political rule had ended, was removed. The Church was left short-handed, but self-sufficient. Carleton also took one rather arbitrary and un-justified step when he refused to allow vacancies in the Quebec cathedral chapter to be filled; for this body, less under his control than was the bishop on whose nomination he had passed, seemed to him an embarrassing source of independent ecclesiastical authority. The chapter became extinct with the death of the last canon in 1795.

Carleton thus did much in the interest of the *seigneurs* and of the clergy, the two groups to which he was drawn by his aristocratic and autocratic turn of mind. The masses of the people were neg-lected, however, until a new constitution for Canada was embodied in the Quebec Act of 1774, which was not his work, but that of many minds. Murray began the reform of the judicial and legal system of the Proclamation of 1763 soon after it went into force. The dispatches and petitions he sent home, interpreted by his agent Cramahé, led to the report of the law officers Norton and de Grey, to the effect that the penal laws of England did not apply to the Catholics of Canada. The Board of Trade drafted two further reports, which were added to by Charles Yorke at Cramahé's suggestion. The proposed scheme of reform, completed in June 1766, was pigeon-holed when the Rockingham ministry fell, and was not brought up again for a year. Then the opposition in the House of Commons carried a resolution that 'the Province of Quebec, for a considerable time past has wanted, and does now stand in need of, further regulations and provisions relating to its civil government and religious establishment.'[40]

For the next seven years a flood of reports, dispatches, petitions, and memorials ensued, upon which was based the legislation which gave Canada its first constitution. The petitions of old and new subjects; Carleton's reports and personal evidence; Maseres' in-numerable writings on all sides of the subject; the representations of Chief Justice Hey and the *seigneur*, Chartier de Lotbinière; and the reports of Solicitor-General Wedderburn, Attorney-General Thurlow, and Advocate-General Marriott all went into the making of the Quebec Act, which was railroaded through parliament at the end of the session, while revolt smouldered in the American colonies. The imminence of the American Revolution precipitated the Quebec Act, but it did not cause it, as the Americans immediately assumed when they learned that Labrador and the Ohio-Mississippi hinterland were restored to Quebec, thus hemming in the expanding population on the seaboard; that the French Canadians were granted the whole of their ancient civil law, almost to the exclusion of the English common law; and that the Catholic Church was virtually established in Quebec, while representative government was denied. All these measures in favor of their ancient enemies seemed to be as great blows to the economic, political, and religious liberties of the American colonists as the four penal laws directed against them, the 'intolerable acts,' which were jammed through parliament along with the Quebec Act. Great Britain strengthened her hold upon the portion of North America which was to remain British by allowing it to remain French and Catholic; but it revived the old sectional rivalry of the American Hundred Years' War. It was not wholly a coincidence that American unrest broke out into open rebellion at Lexington and Concord a few days before the Quebec Act came into effect on May 1, 1775.

Since the Quebec Act is virtually the Magna Carta of the French Canadians, its provisions must be examined in some detail. Its re-establishment in large measure of the ancient boundaries of New France restored the health of the northern economy, and once more made the St. Lawrence system a powerful rival of the Hudson-Mohawk route. The New York and Albany traders were indignant at the prospect of being excluded from the Niagara and Detroit trade, which they had shared with Montreal under the Proclamation of 1763; while the colony on the St. Lawrence, which had always felt the pull of the West, was once more given scope for expansion in that direction. As an aftermath of the Revolution, which delayed the immediate application of the Quebec Act, much of that westward expansion was English rather than French, however, for the majority of the American Tories or Loyalists who fled to Canada eventually settled not in present-day Quebec, but in the wilderness to the west which became Ontario.

Much more important at the moment to the French Canadians was the fact that the Act revoked the whole tentative system of civil, judicial, and ecclesiastical government which had been based upon the Proclamation of 1763, and which had aimed at the assimilation of the French Canadians into an English colony governed under English laws in an English spirit. Catholicism was no longer merely tolerated out of expediency; Catholics were assured the free exercise of their religion, which was no longer to be an obstacle to preferment to any office or position, since a new form of oath was provided which did not offend Catholic principles. The Catholic clergy were assured their rights and accustomed dues from Catholics, while the tithes of non-Catholics were to be applied to the support of a Protestant clergy. All future disputes as to property and civil rights were to be determined according to the 'Laws and Customs of Canada,'[41] the old French civil law, although the Crown retained the right to grant lands in free and common soccage rather than in fief, and wills might be made according to English law if so desired. On the other hand, the criminal law of England was to be retained as a whole, to the exclusion of the French criminal law. Since it was 'at present inexpedient to call an Assembly,' the power to legislate for the peace, welfare, and good government of the province was confided to a Council of not less than seventeen or more than twenty-three appointed members, acting with the consent of the governor. The Council was granted no power to tax except for public roads and buildings. Its ordinances were to be submitted to the Crown for approval or disallowance within six months, while no religious regulation at all and no punishment greater than fines or short imprisonment might be ordained without royal assent. A separate bill, the Quebec Revenue Act, established a schedule of duties and license fees which were to be applied to the support of the civil government and of the administration of justice.

The victory of the new subjects over the old was almost complete. The French Canadians, who outnumbered the English-speaking people in the colony by thirty to one, were granted their faith, laws, and customs, with the exception of the old criminal law. As a matter of fact, the original draft of the Quebec Act had provided for the revival of the French criminal law, except in cases of treason and other capital offenses. This provision had been supported by Maseres, Carleton, the *seigneurs*, and Thurlow; but Chief Justice Hey and Wedderburn had strongly attacked it, and their opinion had prevailed. Of the four cherished essentials of French-Canadian survival, only the question of language was left unsettled. It really had not yet arisen, save in the courts, for before the Quebec Act, as after it, 'all proclamations were published in both French and English, and ordinances were passed in the same manner.'[42] Since French was the only language understood by all the members of the new Council, debate was now carried on in French, although the minutes were kept in English. This fact, plus the increased power of the Council, added the last straw to the grievances of the merchants, who found themselves deprived of such traditional English rights as the *habeas corpus*, trial by jury, English mercantile law, and representative government.

For the withholding of an assembly, the unruly behavior of the American colonies was as much to blame as the lack of French-Canadian interest in representative government. Chief Justice Hey

Quebec from Lévis

Water color from George Heriot's sketch book for September, 1793. This Scot was the first of a long line of British watercolorists who were fascinated by Montreal and Quebec. (Public Archives of Canada.)

The Main Altar, Ursuline Chapel, Quebec

This is all that remains of the Recollect Chapel which was Frère Luc's masterpiece. The gilding, wealth of ornament, and hand-carved wooden statues are typical of the best 17th and 18th century church decorations. (National Gallery of Canada.)

had testified to the Commons as they considered the Act that the French Canadians 'look upon the house of assembly as a house of riot, calculated for nothing but to disturb the government and obstruct public servants.'[43] The merchants' petitions for representative government had a tone which smacked to London of the sedition rife in the American assemblies. Finally there was the awkward fact that the French Canadians could not fairly be excluded from an assembly, while London was not inclined to risk entrusting power to a newly conquered people when colonies which had been British from the beginning were seething with revolt. It was intended that many of the merchants' grievances should be answered by gradual modifications of the French laws through ordinances of the Council, and such provisions were embodied in the governor's instructions. These secret instructions, of course, did not receive the publicity of the Act itself; and it is certain that the Quebec Act strengthened the old subjects' 'strong Bias to Republican Principles'[44] which Carleton had much earlier remarked. Their loyalty was soon to be tested and found wanting during the American invasion of 1775-6; while the gratitude of the clergy and the *seigneurs*, whose position was reinforced by the Act, was strikingly displayed in the part they played in resisting that effort to make Quebec the fourteenth American colony.

3

Although the Quebec Act was wholly satisfactory to neither French nor English in Canada, it did much to ensure that one portion of North America should remain British, while it contributed largely to the loss of the rest. For it was a red rag to the American colonial bull, already goaded into exasperation by the repressive trade ordinances. In an 'Address to the People of Great Britain' on October 21, 1774, the first Congress of the American colonies protested violently against this 'worst of laws,' which established a 'religion that has deluged our island in blood, and dispersed impiety, bigotry, persecution, murder, and rebellion throughout every part of the world.'[45] The old anti-'popish' frenzy—the spirit that had lent to the French and Indian Wars the air of crusades, though they were really wars of trade and empire—was roused once more in America. Desperate men are seldom oppressed by a need for consistency, however, and five days later the same Congress adopted an 'Address to the Inhabitants of the Province of Quebec,' which sought to convince the French Canadians that their true interest lay in uniting with the American colonies in the struggle for liberty, representative government, and freedom from economic persecution. In this remarkable document, which attempted to split the French-Canadian masses from the

élite benefited by the Quebec Act, the following words were put
into the mouth of the 'immortal Montesquieu,' whose ideas played
a great part in the whole appeal:

Seize the opportunity presented to you by Providence itself. You have
been conquered into liberty, if you act as you ought. This work is not of
man. You are a small people compared to those who with open arms
invite you into fellowship. A moment's reflection should convince you
which will be most for your interest and happiness, to have all the rest
of North America your unalterable friends, or your inveterate enemies.
The injuries of Boston have roused and associated every colony, from
Nova Scotia to Georgia. Your province is the only link that is wanting
to complete the bright strong chain of union. Nature has joined your
country to theirs. Do you join your political interests. For their own
sakes they will never desert or betray you. Be assured that the happiness
of a people inevitably depends on their liberty, and their spirit to assert it. [46]

And lest the difference of religion should prejudice the French
Canadians against the Americans—though 'the transcendent nature
of freedom elevates those, who unite in the cause, above all such low-
minded infirmities'—the example of the Swiss confederacy, a peaceful union of Catholic and Protestant states which together defied
tyranny, was carefully cited.

The American appeal was a moving one, but it ill befitted the
men who had just evoked English religious prejudice in support of
their cause. The clergy and the *seigneurs*, who were probably the
only French Canadians on whom the exalted language of Congress
was not largely wasted, did not fail to bring this hypocritical inconsistency to the attention of the *habitants* who listened to the American
appeal, which was rapidly spread throughout the province by
merchants who were British by origin but American by conviction,
sentiment, or interest. The double-faced attitude of the Congress,
which denounced Catholicism in England and praised freedom of
conscience in Quebec, destroyed much of the effectiveness of its
appeal, but nonetheless the new gospel of the *Bostonnais* caught the
ear of the Quebec masses, who did not welcome a return to the old
system of feudal dues and obligations. The French Canadians, a
people just emerging from a feudal economy, got a startling lesson
in revolutionary politics and *laissez-faire* economics, for Adam
Smith's *Wealth of Nations* appeared almost simultaneously with the
Quebec Act and the American Revolution, and its ideas were already
widely spread. No French-Canadian delegates went to Philadelphia,
as requested by Congress, but during the winter of 1774-5 the
habitant was willing to listen to the words of such American agents as
John Brown of Montreal, and this gave his rulers considerable
concern.

The immediate importance of the Quebec Act, like that of Magna Carta, has been overestimated. The French Canadians could hardly have been assimilated, even if there had been no such concession of their rights, for the ways of New France were more firmly fixed than the English realized· then or later; and for more than half a century the French vastly outnumbered the English in Canada. Even without a Quebec Act, it is almost inconceivable that the French Canadians would have thrown in their lot wholeheartedly with the Americans, for the old tradition of ethnic enmity and sectional rivalry, nourished by bitter religious differences, was too powerful. In the last analysis, perhaps, it was the ever potent geographic factor of the Appalachian barrier, rather than the Quebec Act, which saved French Canada and prevented the British from making effective use of Quebec as a base for operations against the American colonies.[47]

The real importance of the Quebec Act was for the future, and its effect was not confined to Canada. A new principle of empire was laid down when it was conceded that the French Canadians could be British without becoming English. A precedent was thus established for the creation of multi-national empires. The British Commonwealth of Nations has been called an outgrowth of the Quebec Act; a realization of what Lord Acton considered to be a higher species of political organism, a greater achievement in civilized life, than the old national state. Then, in the virtual establishment of Catholicism in Canada, there was an anticipation of that ending of the old religious hatreds which did not come in England itself until the Reform Bill of 1829. Tolerance was a necessity of the new political order, as a modern student of the Quebec Act has pointed out: 'In the long run, the unity of the whole is all the deeper for the diversity of its parts, and . . . on fidelity to the old, deep loyalties of local or provincial or national life, and only indeed on that sure foundation, can be built, if men are wise and patient, a broader and more generous communion of human fellowship and service.'[48] The political lesson of the Quebec Act has not yet been thoroughly learned, as the warring nationalisms of our own times bear bloody witness.

The active agitation of John Brown, agent of the Boston Committee of Correspondence, and such Canadian-American merchants as Thomas Walker during the winter of 1774-5 won many *habitants* to the interest of the Congress. Others, however, remembered the anti-Catholic fanaticism of the *Bostonnais*, and this deep-rooted heritage from the French and Indian Wars had much to do with keeping the majority neutral. The center of American sympathy was in Montreal, where the merchants talked of sending delegates to Congress, and where on the morning of May 1, 1775 the bust of

George III on the Place d'Armes was found with blackened face and decorated with a rosary of potatoes and the inscription: '*Voilà le Pape du Canada, ou le sot Anglois.*'*[49] More important than rebellious words or insults to statues were the melodramatic capture of Ticonderoga by Ethan Allen on May 10, and Benedict Arnold's subsequent seizure of Crown Point and St. Johns. As Carillon, Fort Frédéric, and Saint-Jean, these bastions of the traditional invasion route were all too well known in Canada, and their fall did much to increase American sympathies among the realistic French Canadians.

There was much searching of hearts in Canada over the question thus raised. Carleton summoned the militia on June 9, after urging Bishop Briand to call his flock to arms, which that prelate did with all the more willingness since England had just granted 'the practice of our laws, the free exercise of our religion, and the privileges and advantages of British subjects'[50] to the French Canadians. Threatened on the one hand by his spiritual leaders with the refusal of the sacraments if he refused to meet the obligation of defending his country; and urged on the other to throw off the renewed burdens of the tithe and seigneurial tenure, 'the irons of slavery which have been polished with so much care'[51] in the fine words of Congress, and to join with the Americans in the defense of liberty against British oppression, the French Canadian was undecided as to where to cast his lot.

Noting that the majority of old subjects at Montreal refused to enroll in the militia, he likewise refused, claiming a right of neutrality in what must have seemed an 'Anglo-Saxon' family quarrel to a very newly British people. The Montreal merchants did not neglect to point out to the perplexed *habitant* that he would be breaking the oath taken after the conquest if he bore arms against the Americans, who were lumped with the English as *les Anglois* in the popular speech. The contagion of Americanism was also evidenced in the fact that one of the *habitants'* chief objections to mobilization was an unwillingness to serve under the *seigneurs* who had become identified with the English, while another was popular disapproval of the active part taken by the clergy in the British interest. It was remarked with bitterness by good Catholic *habitants* that Bishop Briand's proper role was making priests rather than militiamen, while the overzealousness in recruiting of such *seigneurs* as Saint-Luc de la Corne, Rigauville, de Lanaudière, and de Tonnancourt defeated their object and brought on local revolts against mobilization at Terrebonne, Verchères, and Berthier.[52]

Meanwhile James Livingston, an American merchant of Chambly, spread word among the militia captains that the Americans would abolish the tithe and the seigneurial dues; and Ethan Allen launched

* 'Behold the Pope of Canada, or the English idiot.'

a rhetorical bombardment in favor of French-Canadian neutrality. An American army under Philip Schuyler and Robert Livingston's* son-in-law Richard Montgomery, an Irishman who had served in Canada with Wolfe and Amherst, came down Lake Champlain and established itself at Ile-aux-Noix on the Richelieu in September 1775. With the exception of the forts at St. Johns and Chambly, besieged by the invaders, the whole district south of Montreal fell at once into American hands. Its *congrèssiste* sympathies were soon evidenced by the raising of one French-Canadian regiment under James Livingston, and later of a second under Moses Hazen, another American settler on the Richelieu. Sizeable groups in Montreal and Quebec were loyalist, while on the other hand the militia of the Trois-Rivières district refused to march against the Americans. The Ile d'Orléans and the region south of the river below Quebec were also disaffected.[53] The majority of the *habitants* tried to preserve a neutrality whose bias was influenced by the shifting fortunes of the contending parties. Bishop Briand bears witness that no more than 500 joined the American forces, though nearly all desired the capture of Quebec.[54] There were many factors involved in this situation: at the base of it was the fact that the French Canadians were a people worn out by a century of border warfare against heavy odds, and by the long effort to explore a continent and carry on a continental trade with a minimum of manpower. The greater number had become sedentary folk, deeply attached to their land, and wishing only to dwell on it undisturbed by war.

Even the bellicose character of the *congrèssistes* was subject to sudden change, as Ethan Allen found at Longue Pointe, at the cost of three years' imprisonment, when he brashly attacked Montreal on September 25 with thirty Americans and eighty French Canadians from Chambly. After a sharp skirmish with 30 British regulars, some 80-100 British volunteers (including Guy Johnson's Tory rangers from the Mohawk Valley), and 120 loyalist French Canadians, the hero of Ticonderoga, the 'Notorious New Hampshire Incendiary' as Governor Tryon of New York called him, was forced to surrender with the 31 men who had not run that they might fight another day.[55]

Allen had been assured that Montreal was ready to yield to the forces of liberty; and indeed Carleton was uncertain of the ardor of the professed loyalists there. Great friend of the French Canadian though he was, Carleton wrote: 'I think there is nothing to fear from them while we are in a state of prosperity, and nothing to hope for while in distress.'[56] Though 1,200 *habitants* rallied to his standard in Montreal after the defeat of Allen, most of them developed a great interest in returning home for the fall plowing when Carleton refused to attack the Americans on the south shore of the St. Lawrence.

---

* Judge of the King's Bench Court, and prominent Revolutionary leader.

Simon Sanguinet, a hot loyalist of Montreal, who considered that Carleton's conduct showed lack of spirit, indicates another reason for the weakness of loyalist sentiment among the French Canadians: they suspected the *seigneurs*, whom Carleton trusted, of dealing secretly with the enemy. In at least one instance they were right, for Saint-Luc de la Corne secretly insured the neutrality of the mission Indians, and later went over openly to the Americans.[57]

Abandoning hope of defending Montreal, Carleton fled to Quebec on November 12, disguised as a *habitant* and guided through the American outposts at Sorel by the militiaman Jean-Baptiste Bouchette, skipper of a river craft and the founder of a notable French-Canadian family. Montreal capitulated to Montgomery, who had succeeded Schuyler in command, on the following day. Montgomery announced that his army had come 'to protect this province' and 'to accord it liberty and security.'[58] The *congrèssiste* inhabitants, with the Frenchman Valentin Jautard, three years later one of the founders of the Voltairean *Gazette littéraire de Montréal*, as their spokesman, sent Montgomery an address in which they rejoiced that 'our chains are broken' and declared that 'our hearts have always desired union, that we have always regarded and received the troops of the Union as our own.' The Montrealers were willing to join with their 'brothers of the colonies' in a permanent fellowship on the basis of the same laws, same rights, and proportional contribution.[59] Montgomery was not overly impressed by this eloquence; he judged the French Canadians much as Carleton had done and thought that they 'will be our friends as long as we are able to maintain our ground.'[60] Up to the walls of Quebec in late November the invasion was a triumphal progress for Montgomery, save for the heroic forty-five days' resistance of the garrison at St. Johns. Benedict Arnold, who led the other column of the American pincer movement against Quebec, and lost nearly half his command in the rigors of a march up the Kennebec and down the Chaudière at that season, was warmly welcomed and provisioned by the inhabitants of the Beauce when his men emerged from their epic battle with the wilderness.[61] He was already encamped before Quebec when Montgomery moved down the St. Lawrence from Montreal. The prospect of the rapid addition of the fourteenth colony to the rest was then at its brightest.

The tide soon turned. The defeat of Montgomery and Arnold's joint December 31 assault on Quebec marked the first setback of the American fortunes in Canada. In it the leaders were lost— Montgomery was killed and Arnold severely wounded; and their successor's one triumph was a political one, when in February 1776 General David Wooster ordered elections in the parishes, in order that the holders of royal commissions might be replaced by those with authority from Congress. This measure introduced into Quebec the new idea of the people's right to choose its own chiefs, and the innovation was exceedingly well received throughout the province. The concept of popular government thus implanted in the French-Canadian mind was to bear fruit in later years. Wooster also distributed a letter from George Washington, addressed 'to the People of Canada' and calling for the co-operation of the French Canadians, since 'the cause of liberty and America is the cause of all virtuous American citizens, whatever their religion, whatever the blood from which they originate.'[62] But this appeal was not very effective in the face of growing friction between the invaders and the French Canadians. The seizure and sending southward as prisoners of loyalist French Canadians was resented bitterly, and so was the persecution which the clergy had largely brought upon themselves by their loyalist activities. Among many others, the Sulpician superior Montgolfier, who was vicar general of Montreal, and Grand Vicar Saint-Ours of Trois-Rivières were distinguished by their anti-American sentiments and activities, which did nothing, of course, to relieve the Americans of their traditional anti-Catholic prejudices.[63]

The tide of French-Canadian public opinion really turned against the invaders when cash ran out, and the Americans resorted to requisition or to payment in paper, which soon became inflated. Quebec remembered all too well the exactions of Bigot's regime and the still unredeemed French paper which was the mother country's legacy to her abandoned colony. It also was impressed by the prevalence of disease and desertion among the besiegers of Quebec, and it remembered that British sea power had been decisive in 1759 and 1760. Since the Americans had failed to take Quebec by storm when its defenders were isolated, the French Canadians argued that the invaders would surely be repulsed in the spring, when the opening of the St. Lawrence brought British ships and reinforcements to the hard-pressed garrison. Still, news of the success or the failure of the rebels in their own land was eagerly followed, while the mass of the French Canadians continued to traffic with either British or Americans as circumstances dictated.

Congress realized too late the seriousness of the Canadian situation. It addressed another letter to the Canadians, offering reassurance to the friends of liberty;[64] but not until the spring of 1776 did it send three commissioners—Benjamin Franklin, Charles Carroll, and Samuel Chase—to Montreal, after the *congrèssistes* Saint-Luc de la Corne, Thomas Walker, and James Price had gone to Philadelphia to urge the necessity of vigorous measures. The commissioners were accompanied by the French-educated Jesuit John Carroll, later the first American Catholic bishop, and by the printer of Congress's appeals to the *habitants*, Fleury Mesplet, a wandering Frenchman whom Franklin had picked up in London.

Mesplet had the distinction of establishing the first purely French press in Canada, since the bilingual *Quebec Gazette* established in 1764 was published by Britishers and was a government organ. But it is somewhat excessive to call Mesplet, as his biographer has done, 'the founder of the free press in Canada,'[65] for his first function was to propagate American ideas in French. Two years later, however, his press gave birth to the *Gazette littéraire de Montréal*, the French forerunner of French-Canadian journalism. In 1776 Mesplet was not ready for business in the basement of the Chateau de Ramezay until the American commissioners and the army of invasion had retired southward with marked precipitation. The father of French-Canadian journalism spent the latter part of June and the first days of July in jail—an omen of his future fate, and also of that of many French-Canadian editors for half a century to come.

The American commissioners themselves, hampered by the delays which occasionally make one despair of democratic procedure, had only reached Montreal on April 29, while British reinforcements arrived at Quebec on May 6. The francophile Franklin, who in this instance suffered one of his rare diplomatic failures, found that there was little to be done to save a bad situation, while Father Carroll was unable to win over the inflexibly royalist French-Canadian clergy, who greeted the raising of the siege with a *Te Deum* and later invoked harsh sanctions against *congrèssistes*.[66] The arrival of the British reinforcements at Quebec started an American retreat which soon degenerated into a panic-stricken rush for home and safety. The American army was made up of amateur soldiers who had a healthy respect for British regulars; it was rotten with smallpox and dysentery; it lacked munitions, provisions, and credit; and it had dwindled away with the desertion of men who had volunteered for a quick and easy conquest which had not eventuated after nine months' hard service under miserable conditions. The Americans fell back along the St. Lawrence and the Richelieu, evacuating Sorel on June 14, Montreal on the 15th, Chambly on the 17th, and St. Johns on the 18th. They retired to Crown Point and Ticonderoga with 150 *congrèssistes* of Livingston's and Hazen's regiments, who constituted the second great exodus of French Canadians to what became the United States—the Acadian deportees of 1755 being the first.

Carleton did not press the pursuit vigorously or attempt an immediate counter-invasion. He was well aware that he had had a close escape, and that Canada stood in great need of being put in order after the American occupation had sapped its loyalty and set brother against brother. The British army spent the summer at Chambly and St. Johns, building boats in order to follow the Americans down Lake Champlain. The boats were not ready until early October, and then Carleton contented himself with destroying the American vessels on the lake and forcing the American defenders of Crown Point to burn the place and to retire to Ticonderoga.

Two thousand French Canadians had volunteered by the end of September, the greatest number to back their loyalism by action, but Carleton only accepted half of them, while he requisitioned the services of 1,200 *habitants* of the Richelieu for unpaid *corvées** in connection with the building and provisioning of the fleet. The army returned to Montreal for the winter, leaving the *habitants* of the Richelieu disgruntled and soon causing unrest in the city upon which it was quartered. No distinction was made by Carleton between those French Canadians who had been loyal and those who had sympathized with the Americans; and his conduct revealed more concern for American prisoners than for Canadian subjects.[67] Carleton's lack of energy in pursuing the campaign against the Americans and his attention to the prisoners may be explained by his conviction that these erring brethren might be led to see the error of their ways, while his confidence in the French Canadians had been badly shaken by their behavior during the invasion.

In any case he began to rule with a harsher hand. On March 29, 1777, the new Legislative Council, which had held few meetings during the difficult period through which the colony had just come, passed a Militia Act which imposed military service on all *habitants* from sixteen to sixty, and fixed heavy penalties for failure to comply. This act was even more unpopular with the people than the forced labor of the previous autumn, for fifteen years of freedom from military service, which had been compulsory under the French regime, made it seem an intolerable burden. In the enforcement of this law upon an unwilling people may be found a basis of the lasting French-Canadian dislike for compulsory military service.[68] Carleton was only able to raise 300 French-Canadian militiamen for Burgoyne's invasion force; and he realized 'how unwilling they were to engage in the affair.'[69] But *corvées* again rained upon the disgruntled *habitants*, in order that Burgoyne's unwieldy force might be launched upon its campaign; and friction between the British soldiers and their unwilling hosts did nothing to strengthen the loyalism of the people.[70]

Burgoyne's surrender at Saratoga in October 1777 at once raised the specter of a new American invasion; and, significantly enough, the articles of capitulation permitted Canadian prisoners to return

* Compulsory labor required under the feudal system.

home simply on their promise not to serve again. Congress had not
yet despaired of the 'fourteenth colony,' for the Articles of Confederation of 1777 stipulated that Canada could be 'admitted into
and entitled to all the advantages of this union.'[71] Quebec was
once more on the defensive, and in February 1778 Carleton ordered
the militiamen to hold themselves in readiness and provided payment for the *corvées* of the two previous years, as well as pensions
for the volunteers who had seen service.[72] With the French alliance of
that same month the chief result of Burgoyne's bungled campaign,
Quebec was once more exposed to American intrigue and propaganda; and official kindness rather than sternness towards the
French Canadians was clearly indicated. In the fall Lafayette's
plan of a joint Franco-American expedition by land and by sea
against Quebec was considered by Congress, while Admiral d'Estaing
issued a resounding manifesto to his 'compatriots of North America'
on the keynote: 'You were born French; you cannot cease to be
so.'[73] Despite the effect of such appeals upon Canadian lovers of the
old regime and sympathizers with the Americans, Canada profited
by division among her enemies. First Washington opposed an
enterprise which might restore Canada to a France whose ally
Spain controlled Louisiana, and thus might revive the old encirclement of the American colonies; and then the French had no desire
to see the Americans become self-sufficient and all-powerful on the
North American continent. The scheme of 1778 was considered
again in 1780 and 1781, but never carried into execution. The
threat of invasion by the ancient masters of Canada remained
strong enough, however, to contribute to differences between the
old and new subjects in Quebec.

A modern French-Canadian historian has judged that 'perhaps
no event has exercised so much influence upon Quebec, directly
or indirectly, as the American Revolution.'[74] This verdict seems
to be justified. The Revolution settled the fate of French feudalism
and absolutism; it caused a split between the largely pro-British
élite and the largely pro-American masses which had important and
lasting results. It was a potent lesson in politics; and from this
period onward democracy and liberty were forces in the French-
Canadian mind. One of the immediate aftermaths of the Revolution
was the introduction into Quebec of some 6,000 American Tories
or United Empire Loyalists—professed Loyalists, at least, but undoubtedly the loyalty of many was merely to good farm land. Major
André's executioner was discovered taking out land and provisions
at Kingston as a Loyalist refugee.[75] The newcomers, however,
numbered nearly a tenth of the French Canadians; they did not
settle among the French, except at William Henry (Sorel), but along
the unpopulated upper St. Lawrence and the southern Gaspé

coast; and their resourceful energy made them even more of a force than their number indicates.[76] Their coming clinched Wolfe's victory; Canada was not to be French, but French and English. It also caused within some years the virtual repeal of the Quebec Act, the granting of the elements of representative government, and the division of British North America into Upper (English) and Lower (French) Canada. That terminology has long been dropped; but much bitterness and ill feeling in Quebec could have been avoided if the psychological attitudes of superiority and inferiority appropriate to it had also disappeared.

The day of Carleton, the friend of the French Canadians, had come to an end. He had been superseded in 1777 as military commander by Burgoyne; he had become embroiled with the new Chief Justice Peter Livius, a New Hampshire Tory, over his practice of arbitrary government through an inner circle in the legislative council, a body which was beginning to show signs of independence; and he had quarrelled with Germain, the Colonial Secretary. Finally the embittered Carleton, disappointed in his hopes both for himself and for Canada, resigned his post. He was replaced in June 1778 by Frederick Haldimand, the Swiss soldier of fortune who had served at Montreal under Gage from 1760 to 1762, and had then replaced Burton as governor of Trois-Rivières, where he had remained until his return to England in 1765. Haldimand was thus no stranger to Canada, but he judged its problems in a very different light than Murray or Carleton.

4

Haldimand was the ablest of the Swiss Protestants who played a vital but little-recognized role in Canada during the early years of British rule. Trained to his profession in the armies of Holland, Sardinia, and Frederick the Great, along with his friend Henry Bouquet, who saved the Alleghany frontier of the American colonies after Braddock's defeat, Haldimand raised a battalion of the Royal Americans from among the German and Swedish settlers of Pennsylvania and Maryland when he first came to America in 1754. In 1758 he was a member of Abercromby's ill-fated expedition against the French forts on Lake Champlain, and was wounded in the unsuccessful assault of Carillon (Ticonderoga). He commanded Fort Edward on the Hudson during that winter, and rebuilt Fort Oswego in the following summer. In the great campaign of 1760 he marched with Amherst against Montreal, and was charged with the occupation of the city and the negotiations with the Chevalier de Lévis, since he was far more at home with the French language than with English.

When called to Trois-Rivières as governor of the district, he displayed marked political and economic ability: regulating the fur trade, reopening the Saint-Maurice forges, building roads, and encouraging agriculture, to the general satisfaction of all concerned. When a French-Canadian contingent of 300 men was raised in 1764 to serve against Pontiac and the western Indians, Haldimand found it easy to enlist a company in his bailiwick. His secretary at Trois-Rivières, Conrad Gugy, another Swiss, took such a fancy to the region that he bought the nearby seigneury of Machiche and settled there, playing an active role as a loyalist during the American invasion. Haldimand himself acquired the seigneury of Grand Pabos in Gaspé and also land at Shepody in Nova Scotia, which gave him a firsthand knowledge of the problems of settlement, one of his chief concerns as governor-general. Haldimand also had had singular success in winning the people of Trois-Rivières to their new allegiance: only two women, two children, and a servant left his district for France under the terms of the Treaty of 1763. As for the rest, he wrote: 'I am persuaded that they would be in despair were they to see a French fleet and troops arrive in this country in any number whatsoever; they begin to taste too well the sweets of liberty to be the dupes of the French.'[77] The interval between his departure from Canada in 1765 and his return as governor had been filled with six years as governor in Florida, two at New York and Boston, and three at home, since London wisely prefered at first not to use foreigners to put down the rebellion in the American colonies. Haldimand was now given the difficult task of keeping Quebec British, while its ancient masters were striving to win it from its new allegiance by every sort of intrigue, and were threatening to invade the country.

Under such circumstances the neutrality of the French Canadians was clearly not to be counted upon, nor could the governor rely, as in 1775-6, on the loyalty of the *noblesse* and the clergy. Haldimand was conscious of the altered conditions:

However sensible I am of the good conduct of the clergy in general during the invasion of the Province of the year 1775, I am well aware that since France was known to take part in the contest, and since the address of Count D'Estaing and a letter of M. de la Fayette to the Canadians and the Indians have been circulated in the Province, many of the Priests have changed their opinions, and in case of another Invasion would, I am afraid, adopt another system of conduct.[78]

The French priests who remained in the colony after the conquest still enjoyed a dominance over their Canadian colleagues, who had an inferior education. Under the altered circumstances, their loyalty to the government weakened, and they drew many of the native-born clergy with them.[79] Haldimand was obliged to make an example by deporting in 1778 a Sulpician, the Abbé Huet de la Valinière, who had come under suspicion during the American invasion and now openly advocated the return of Canada to France.[80] Despite this action the French proclamations still turned up on church doors, and the *presbytères* served as centers of seditious rumors. To Haldimand's mind, the only solution to a delicate problem was to import French-speaking priests from Savoy, who would be friendly to Great Britain, but London was slow to act on his advice.

The contagion of sedition was widespread among the élite, many of whom had relatives in France, and by no means confined to the French clergy.[81] Haldimand was obliged to arrest three prominent French citizens whose loyalty to Britain was more than suspect. The most notable was Pierre de Sales Laterrière, who had studied medicine in Paris under General Rochambeau's uncle, and had come to Canada in 1766 in the same ship with Hector Cramahé, Richard Montgomery, and the Jesuit La Jonquière. According to his *Mémoires*, a valuable if unorthodox picture of the period, Laterrière found Canada so agreeable that he thought himself in paradise. Since he was a gay young blade, the frivolity of 'my little new American Paris' was very much to his taste:

Never have I known any nation so fond of dancing as the Canadians; they still practice the French square dances and the minuet, to which they add the English dances. During the winter, which lasts eight months, the nights are passed in feasts, suppers, dinners, and balls. The ladies are much given to cards before and after the dances. All games are played, but the favorite is an English game called *Wisk*. . . .

One must admit that the Canadian ladies are beautiful; and that in general they receive more education by means of the schools and the nuns than the men; and that by their natural disposition they greatly surpass the men in *finesse*, in gentleness, and in manners. Demanding little, they do not take advantage of their superiority; and thus they attach the men to them, so that even strangers are obliged to give them credit. In general, the Canadian ladies are very economical, loving, and faithful spouses. It is very difficult for one who spends some years here to avoid marriage. The English felt this pressure after the conquest; many of them have married here, and at present the number has grown vastly.[82]

Laterrière became first the Quebec agent of the Saint-Maurice forges, and then the associate at Trois-Rivières of the manager, Christophe Pélissier. The latter was so thoroughly involved with the Americans, to whom he furnished bombs and tools during the siege of Quebec, that he was forced to leave the country with them. Laterrière succeeded him both in the business and in the affections of Madame Pélissier, who remained in Trois-Rivières as his companion. This domestic situation, with its suggestion of the complete opposition of the two men, at first preserved Laterrière from arrest as an American sympathizer, but by February 1779 there was clear evidence that he was preparing the way for a new invasion and encouraging Canadians to join the Americans. He was clapped into a cell in the Quebec jail, and soon joined there by Valentin Jautard and Fleury Mesplet, the Voltairean founders of the *Gazette de Montréal*, who had indulged in too much freedom of the press for Haldimand's taste.

Traffic with the Americans was not confined to Frenchmen, however, for the journalists were joined in the fall of 1780 by the Scot Charles Hey, one of the British merchants of Quebec who had prudently taken up residence on the Ile d'Orléans during the American siege, and who was a brother and faithful correspondent of the American quartermaster-general at Albany. Most of the leading plotters, however, were Frenchmen like François Cazeau and Boyer Pillon of Montreal, and most notably Pierre Du Calvet, whose vigorous pen has done much to give Haldimand the name of a tyrant. None of these political prisoners received a trial; but Laterrière was released in the summer of 1780 on his promise to leave the colony, and the others were set at liberty in May 1783, when the threat of American invasion was ended. They were held in light confinement, and Du Calvet was even allowed to carry on his business and to pen his blasts against Haldimand in his prison cell. It is difficult to censure Haldimand for detaining these men, since there was considerable evidence against them in Canada and their names appeared in the list of traitors sent up from New York by General Clinton, to whom Benedict Arnold had revealed the Canadian plots after his treason.[83]

The mood of the people was uncertain. Soon after his arrival Haldimand deplored the 'sentiments which the French Alliance with the Rebels has undoubtedly raised up in numbers of them, who in regard of the Rebellion were unquestionably attached to Government.'[84] He hoped to awe them into loyal behavior by strengthening the fortifications of the Richelieu and by making a stronghold of Sorel, which commanded both that traditional invasion path and the St. Francis River, and also the approach to Quebec from indefensible Montreal. During the winters of 1781-3, when the threat of invasion was always imminent, he prepared to evacuate all provisions from the southern part of the province in order to hamper an American advance. Haldimand barred the loyalists from settlement along the American frontier, proposing to leave the

Eastern Townships as a forest barrier against invasion, and as a reserve for future expansion of the French Canadians. He thought it 'good policy that the frontiers should be settled by people professing a different language, and accustomed to other laws and government from those of our restless and enterprising neighbours of New England.'[85]

With vision unusual in a professional soldier, Haldimand saw that French and English might be drawn more closely together if their cultures were shared. With this object in mind, he established the first public library in Canada, half English and half French. When the difficulty of obtaining French books because of the war resulted in only English works being sent out from London, Haldimand refused to open the library until the other books arrived, 'to prevent any jealousy.' The library was established in the Bishop's Palace at Quebec, and its subscribers included French-Canadian priests and laymen as well as most of the English-speaking residents. In writing on March 1, 1779, to his Swiss friend General Budé in London, Haldimand gave an account of his enterprise:

The few resources here, and the reason I have every day for perceiving that the ignorance of the people is one of the greatest obstacles that must be conquered to make them acquainted with their duties and their own interest, have given me the idea of establishing a public Library. I have led the Bishop and the Superior of the Seminary to see the advantage which would result from it. They have entered into my ideas, and I have had a subscription opened, which they have signed with me, as have several priests, almost all the British merchants and several Canadians. . . .[86]

According to the catalogue of 1785, this library included 1,000 French and 800 English books, mostly eighteenth-century works. This was a notable addition to the intellectual resources of Canada, for it has been estimated that there were only some 60,000 books there in 1765.[87]

During the French regime the most considerable libraries were in ecclesiastical hands. The important Jesuit collection at Quebec was dispersed by the suppression of the order, but the Sulpician library, perhaps the best and richest in the colony, remained available at Montreal. Some of the *curés* had notable collections— in the early years of the eighteenth century the Abbé Philippe Boucher of Saint-Joseph-de-Lévis possessed 400 volumes. The concentration of books in clerical hands naturally effected a somewhat rigorous selection, and books which might be considered dangerous or frivolous were exceedingly scarce in New France in the early days. There was, however, a relative abundance of religious works, of the Greek and Latin classics, and of legal works.

As the relations of the colony with the mother country increased during the prosperous first half of the eighteenth century, more books, and less proper ones, were to be found. The catalogue of the library of the Sieur Joseph Fournerie de Vézon of Montreal in 1760 includes such items as *Gil Blas*, Voltaire, Montesquieu, Machiavelli, Mirabeau, Rousseau, Boccaccio, and the *Arabian Nights*. Vézon was a French officer who only came to Canada in 1757, but most of the books probably belonged to his wife's first husband, a Canadian.

The old legend that Quebec never felt the influence of Voltaire and the encyclopedists has been disproved by the discovery of their works in Canadian libraries of both before and after the English conquest. The *Quebec Gazette* frequently printed selections from Voltaire after 1764, and a Voltairean academy flourished in Montreal in 1778. Voltaire and Rousseau were widely read in both England and America at this period, and their vogue in Quebec cannot be considered solely an English-inspired attempt to win the French Canadians from their faith. These men dominated the era everywhere that books were read, and their works were not strictly banned in Quebec until the middle of the nineteenth century, when a new tide of Jansenism set in, and the social consequences of their doctrines became apparent to the highly conservative religious leaders of the French Canadians.

Haldimand's reference to Canadian ignorance in his letter to General Budé reveals that this Swiss Huguenot did not share the high opinion of the French Canadians held by his English-speaking predecessors. Furthermore, he judged that 'no people in the world are more bigoted in their laws and usages,' and he considered that the clergy possessed an 'attachment for France, concealed under their zeal for the Preservation of their Religion.'[88] It is not unlikely that a certain confusion of a mild racism and nationalism with religion, which was to increase with the years, had already set in among the French Canadians, preoccupied as they were in this period of transition with insuring the survival of their faith, laws, customs, and language under the rule of men of another culture. But the Protestant Haldimand was no fanatical enemy of the French Canadians, as his resolutions upon taking office bear witness:

To give protection and to have much regard for the orders and the religious houses; to be always polite and obliging but also to be always watchful; not to be adopted by either party; to ask time to consider things of any importance, but also to make it an inviolable rule to do whatever has been promised; not to become heated in conversation, rather to leave the room under any pretext, as was the case with a bishop, who prayed in order to give his blood time to cool; to return immediately, to listen with patience and take time for deliberation; to favour commerce and distinguish the merchants who deserve it; to have respect for the officers which is due them, to associate with them at table and in parties with the Canadians, and to require from them good conduct and the regulation of their expenses; to have good manners and show confidence in the chief justice and procuror general and to consult them as occasion arises; to treat in the same way the Catholic clergy and make known to them the danger that their rights will be in if the rebels, and especially the *Bostonnais*, gain the upper hand, for it is these last who are the most interested in the reduction of Canada in order to people it with their own kind, assure their independence, and make themselves masters of commerce; their intolerance should be made known, the curés should speak to it. [89]

As can be seen from this entry in his journal, Haldimand's intention was to hold the balance more evenly between the French Canadians and the English merchants than had his predecessors; and this object he accomplished, so far as the grave peril of the colony permitted.

Haldimand has been called a persecutor of Catholicism because he banished the Abbé de la Valinière and two French Sulpicians who came to Canada disguised as laymen in 1783. But Vicar-General Montgolfier had himself proposed deporting La Valinière half a dozen years earlier, [90] and when England was at war with France Haldimand could hardly allow French priests to influence the Canadians against their rulers, as these three Sulpicians undoubtedly had done. He has also been denounced—Laterrière called him the 'cruel, hard, wicked Swiss'[91]—for making political prisoners and holding them without trial, but in the whole six years of his government, when British rule in Canada was put to its severest test, such arrests numbered only nineteen. The outraged Du Calvet's picture of jails bursting with innocent victims of the tyrannous governor is more than a little overdrawn. Then, after favoring the merchants at the outset of his administration, Haldimand gradually turned toward the 'French party'; and in the end both French and English combined to oppose him, demanding the repeal of the Quebec Act, the creation of an assembly with tax powers, and in short the establishment of Quebec as a British colony with British institutions and British rights. The effect of Haldimand's absolutist government and of the influence of American ideas upon the French Canadians was thus made evident.

The wartime governor was not the man to rule the colony in the postwar period of constitutional development; and Haldimand's long-standing request for leave was suddenly granted in 1784 by a London deluged with both French and English petitions against him. Guy Carleton, now Lord Dorchester, was sent out to replace him in 1786, and to finish the work begun in his earlier administration of making Canada secure as a loyal part of the British Empire.

D

5

Dorchester was not the same man as Carleton, however; he had lost his confidence in the French Canadians and in his understanding of their society. He was also old and ill. Under these circumstances the dominant figure in the new administration was the Tory Chief Justice William Smith, who had held the same office in New York when Carleton was commander-in-chief there during the Revolution. Both went to England in 1783, and were consulted by the government in its plans for consolidating what remained of British North America after the peace treaty of that year. Smith reported on the Canadian petitions of the following year and drafted an act to regulate the government of Canada. He also sketched out the new powers which should be given to Dorchester, whom he proposed as governor-general of all British North America.[92] Smith favored retaining the Quebec Act and setting up an assembly, while in his opinion the governor and legislative council could be counted upon to make all necessary adjustments of the system without recourse to the British parliament.

Smith wanted Dorchester to be a viceroy, but the ministry would only make him governor of Quebec, Nova Scotia, and New Brunswick, and commander-in-chief in all these provinces. Dorchester was also commissioned to report to the ministry in detail on the measures necessary to remedy discord in Canada. This compromise, with its limited anticipation of a united British North America, broke down through the force of geography and of transportation difficulties. After his arrival at Quebec in October 1786, Dorchester only once stirred from his seat of government, and then it was to visit the new 'United Empire Loyalist' settlements of American Tories on the upper St. Lawrence, while the lieutenant-governors of the Maritime Provinces reported direct to London as before.

Dorchester relied on Chief Justice Smith in all things save Loyalist matters, in which he followed the advice of Smith's influential disciple, Sir John Johnson, late master of the Mohawk Valley and now Superintendent of Indian Affairs for British North America. Quite apart from the influence of these advisers, Dorchester no longer saw only the French side of any question, for the behavior of the French Canadians under stress and the coming of the Loyalists to Canada had radically revised his outlook. Then Smith, who had seen peoples 'addicted to foreign laws and usages and understanding none but a foreign language'[93] absorbed to an English way of life in New York, New Jersey, and Pennsylvania, was confident that the French Canadians could likewise be assimilated in an English

Canada. He set about realizing this aim at once by a judicial decision which held that English civil law was in force in the province for old subjects. The 'French party,' already alarmed by the coming of the Loyalists and by the threat of anglicization, promptly launched a battle against Smith in the legislative council. Thanks to a six-hour attack by James Monk on the administration of justice, which was instigated by the merchants, a compromise bill, acceptable to both the chief justice and the 'French party,' was passed, while the governor was requested to investigate the courts. This investigation had no other immediate results than to reveal the chaotic confusion of judicial affairs, to discredit the judges of the 'French party,' and to bring about Monk's dismissal as attorney-general. But in the end its findings did much to support London's feeling that a new Canadian constitution must be drafted.

This feeling was also reinforced by the petitions of the merchants and the dispatches of the governor relating to the altered conditions of trade. The advance of the Spaniards up the Mississippi, and of the Americans into the western territory ceded (but not yet handed over to them) under the peace treaty, called for a liberation of the fur trade from the old restrictions. Then, despite the tenets of the old colonial system, the Richelieu trade with Vermont, which was still a republic independent of the American Union and flirting with annexation to Canada, was too valuable to be ruled out. The same question of commercial intercourse with the Americans in the case of the new settlements on the upper St. Lawrence and on the Great Lakes was likewise raised by the proposed division of the province, already being discussed in London. The Canadian merchants, anxious to replace the Americans as the source of supplies for Newfoundland and the British West Indies, also sought revision of the customs duties and of the Navigation Laws. Some half-hearted measures were taken by London, but the most vital decisions were put off until the question of a new constitution should be settled.

An investigation into the hitherto neglected question of education was also launched by Dorchester in 1787, when Amherst resumed his attempt to get, as a reward for his services in the conquest, the Jesuit Estates which had been confiscated in 1763. Under the French regime the Jesuits had acquired considerable property, which they used for the support of their Indian missions and for educational purposes. Forbidden to recruit new members under the terms of the capitulation of Montreal, the Canadian Jesuits had struggled on with dwindling numbers until suppression of the order in France in 1764 and the papal dissolution of the order in 1773 culminated the great upsurge of anti-Jesuit feeling which began as national phenomenon and ended as an international one supported by the Papacy.

The college at Quebec was closed in 1768, but the primary school survived there until 1776. The Jesuit Colleges in Quebec and Montreal were taken over by the English after the conquest for use as barracks, jails, and storehouses, but despite royal instructions in 1774 to suppress the order and to take over its property for the Crown, the Jesuits retained control of the rest, including ten seigneuries which brought in an annual revenue of eleven or twelve hundred pounds. By 1787 there were only four surviving Canadian members of the order, who used their income for poor relief, while the ultimate disposition of the property was still unsettled. Amherst's claim, first made after the conquest, had been delayed for almost twenty years by legal complications; now his renewed insistence raised a question which was not to be finally settled until 1888,* though the Crown took over the Estates in 1800 at the death of the last Jesuit.

At the moment, an order from London for a description of the Jesuit Estates raised a tumult in the colony, because both French and English Canadians felt that the revenue of the property should be used for its original purpose, the support of education, rather than be handed over to Amherst. The sole secondary schools for boys were the seminaries of Quebec and Montreal, while girls were educated in the convents of Quebec, Trois-Rivières, and Montreal. There were six elementary Protestant schools in Quebec, two in Trois-Rivières, and four in Montreal, as well as one each at Lachine, L'Assomption, and Sorel. These were small, inadequately staffed, and expensive by comparison with the Catholic schools, which were attended by many English children. Outside the cities and chief towns there were only a few small schools run by *curés* or nuns of the Congrégation de Notre Dame. The government supported four Protestant teachers, two in Quebec, one in Montreal, and one in Gaspé; the Catholic schools had to get along on their own resources.

The general ignorance was appalling; Hugh Finlay, the postmaster-general, who was in a good position to know the facts throughout the province, wrote home in 1784 that 'not one man in five knows how to read.'[94] Shortly after the conquest, Mrs. Frances Brooke, wife of the Quebec garrison chaplain, found the *habitants* 'ignorant, lazy, dirty, and stupid beyond all belief,' while she reported that 'all knowledge of language is confined to the sex, very few, even of the *seigneurs*, being able to write their own names.'[95] French-Canadian ignorance was a favorite theme of the English merchants, and it was said that the clergy deliberately kept the people ignorant in order to dominate them. Bishop Hubert denounced such statements in 1789, claiming that twenty-four to thirty people in each parish could read and write, and that the backwardness of his people was due to climatic and pioneering

* See Chapter VIII, pp. 423-9.

conditions. But his higher figure would give only some 4,000 literates out of a total French-Canadian population of 140,000.[96] To be sure, literacy was far from general in France or England at this period, but Canada was behind the more justly comparable American standard of the day.

Chief Justice Smith headed the committee on education and prepared the report which it issued in December 1789. It called for free parochial primary schools, with a system of free county secondary schools, whose curriculum would include such practical matters as bookkeeping and surveying. A university was to complete the educational structure. Theology was to be excluded, in order that both French and English might attend the same institution, whose governors were to include the Catholic and Anglican bishops, an equal number of prominent laymen of each faith, and the judges. Haldimand's library was to be taken over for the new university, which was to be housed in the Jesuit College at Quebec. A portion of the revenue of the Jesuit Estates was to serve as an initial endowment, to be completed by private contributions. Smith anticipated that such a university would make Quebec the intellectual capital of British North America, and that it might even attract American students, through the 'opportunity of acquiring one of the most universal languages of Europe.'[97] In contrast to the past, when education had been a monopoly of the Church, the new system 'would follow a single principle under the watchful eye of the Crown,' as Dorchester wrote to Grenville.[98]

This project, which was unanimously supported by the council, including the French Canadians J.-G. Chaussegros de Léry, François Baby, Charles de Lanaudière, and J.-B. Lecompte-Dupré, was opposed by both the Catholic and the Protestant bishops. The Anglican Bishop Inglis, who considered Quebec 'a French colony with an English garrison,' found the plan too kindly to the French Canadians and too indifferent to the rightful pre-eminence of his 'national church.'[99] The Catholic Bishop Hubert objected to it because of the difficulty of reconciling the educational interests of Catholics and Protestants, of French and English; while he blandly pointed out that if a university was urgently desired, nothing was simpler than to return the revenues of the Jesuits to their original purpose and to restore the Jesuit College of Quebec to its original function. For their part, the four surviving Jesuits offered to make over their revenues, less provision for themselves, to the Catholic bishop as an educational fund for the benefit of the Canadians.[100] But as discussion of the question dragged on, the establishment of a non-sectarian state university was supported by a petition of October 31, 1790, which bore the signatures of sixty French Canadians, including the coadjutor Bishop Bailly de Messein, the provincial of the Franciscans, and a director of the Quebec Seminary. Meanwhile the Montreal lawyer Simon Sanguinet left property worth four or five hundred pounds a year for the endowment of such a university. The Sulpicians applied for a charter for an affiliated institution in Montreal, to be known as Dorchester or Clarence College, which would teach the humanities, mathematics, engineering, and civil law, and which would be under the supervision of the Crown. All these projects were referred by the governor to London, which decided that they, like much else in Canada, must await the new constitution.

It is clear that Dorchester failed to perform his main function, which was to find a remedy for Canada's constitutional ills. In June 1787, when sending home reports at the request of London, he wrote: 'I confess myself as yet at a loss for any plan likely to give satisfaction.'[101] Sydney, the colonial secretary, writing to Dorchester on September 3, 1788, likewise confessed his perplexity: 'The variety of applications, which have from time to time been transmitted from thence upon this business, of so opposite a tendency to each other, render it extremely difficult to fix upon any Arrangements calculated to satisfy all the Parties interested in, or connected with it.'[102] But faced with a session of parliament and an unruly opposition, he called upon Dorchester for fuller information, to be supplied at once by an 'Extraordinary Packet Boat.' Dorchester's reply, which contained little if anything new, was drafted by Chief Justice Smith. It pointed out that an assembly was demanded chiefly by the English merchants of Quebec and Montreal, while the *habitants* were neutral in the matter, and the *seigneurs* opposed—in short that only one-fifth of the total population desired a 'change of the laws and form of government.'[103] The proposed division of the province was considered to be 'by no means advisable at present, either for the interests of the new, or the ancient districts.' While London delayed, the merchants filled the columns of the *Quebec Gazette* and the new *Herald* (founded, along with the French *Courrier de Québec*, in 1788) with controversial correspondence on the needs of the colony, and their representative Adam Lymburner agitated at London in their interest.

In July 1789 the younger Pitt's cousin Grenville succeeded Sydney in the Colonial Office, and by the end of August he had drafted the basis of the Constitutional Act of 1791. He postulated an assembly on the grounds that the colony must stand on its own financial feet in the future, and that taxation without representation would lead Canada into the American Union. A single legislature was impossible for geographical and ethnic reasons; therefore an English province in the West must be cut out of the present province, 'rather than these two bodies of People should be blended together in the first formation of the new Constitution, and before sufficient time has been allowed for the removal of ancient prejudices, by the habit of obedience, to the same Government, and by the sense of a common interest.'[104] The legislative council was to be separated from the executive council, and to have the status of the House of Lords in the English system, with members holding their seats for life or during good behavior, and rewarded with baronetcies or some other mark of honor. The governor was to have both civil and military executive power and the right to dispose of the Crown lands. Grenville was inclined to believe that Canada would ultimately separate from the Empire, whatever constitution was given it; but he felt that the bestowal of a British constitution, in which the monarchic, aristocratic, and democratic principles were properly balanced, would delay that separation. In any case, a British constitution could no longer be denied to a large body of British subjects living in close proximity to the lost American colonies and at a great distance from England, while revolution was breaking out in France. The force of the geographical argument was evidenced by the fact that delays of navigation kept Grenville's proposal of 1789 from traveling out to Canada for comment and returning to London in time to be considered during the session of 1790. Dorchester's and Smith's contributions to the original draft were negligible, for Grenville acted on his own ideas, which were also those of the younger Pitt. The final bill, which was passed on June 10, 1791, was little affected by its passage through parliament, and the debate upon it was chiefly notable for the irrelevant clash of Burke and Fox on the French Revolution.

The Constitutional Act of 1791 did not repeal the Quebec Act, but only that portion of it which dealt with the form of government. The position of the Church and the status of the laws were left untouched. The actual division of the Province of Quebec into Upper and Lower Canada was embodied in a later order-in-council rather than in the Act itself, because Britain still held the Western posts ceded to the Americans in 1783. The project of a united British North America was abandoned, as Chief Justice Smith noted with sorrow: 'I miss in it, however, the expected Establishment, to put what remains to Great Britain of Her Antient Dominions in North America, under one general direction, for the united interest and safety of every Branch of the Empire.'[105] To his Tory satisfaction, however, Canada was not 'abandoned to Democracy' like the old colonies.

The Act really satisfied no single group in Canada except the Loyalists of Upper Canada, who were delivered from an uneasy dependence upon Quebec, their ancient enemy. The French-Canadian masses were indifferent to the change, as were the clergy.

The *seigneurs* found their position threatened by the prospect of a democratically elected assembly and of the granting of the Crown lands in freehold tenure. The merchants were the unhappiest of all: the combination of the division of the province and of the institution of representative government perpetuated their minority status under French-Canadian control. The long-sought English commercial laws were not to be theirs, unless the French Canadians decided to adopt them. Pitt, in his reply to Fox's objection to the division of the province on an ethnic basis, made the government's hopes on this score clear:

As the honorable gentleman has said, it would be extremely desireable that the inhabitants of Canada were united and universally led to prefer English laws and the English constitution. The division of the province is probably the best means to obtain that object. The French subjects will thus become convinced that the British government has no intention of imposing English laws upon them. Then they will consider with a freer spirit the operation and the effects of these laws, comparing them with the operation and effects of theirs. Thus, with time, they will perhaps adopt ours by conviction. That will happen more probably than if the government suddenly undertook to submit all the inhabitants of Canada to the constitution and laws of this country. It will be experience which will teach them that English laws are the best. But it must be admitted that they ought to be governed to their satisfaction.[106]

Macaulay mourned that Pitt had not died in 1792, when his name would have identified with these ideas of peace, freedom, philanthropy, temperate reform, and mild and constitutional government—the ideas of what a later historian has called the Second British Empire.[107] It is to the younger Pitt and to his cousin William Grenville that the French Canadians owe the forms of British self-government, which were so unfamiliar to them in 1791 that the grant was not appreciated, but which were shortly put to such good use that French-Canadian survival was assured for all time. A half century of constitutional conflict lay ahead, but thanks to London the French Canadians were armed to meet it.

Notes

[1] The marked preference by French Canadians for the term 'cession' rather than 'conquest,' when there would have been no cession without a conquest, is a psychological defence. The latent English-Canadian tendency to think of the French as a 'conquered people' is a similar defence mechanism on the part of a dominant minority concerned about maintaining its position against increasing odds.

[2] Notably Garneau and Groulx.

[3] Witness the reception of Abbé Arthur Maheux's *Ton Histoire est une épopée*, I, *Nos Débuts sous le régime anglais* (Québec, 1941). To be sure, there are indications in the Murray Papers (PAC) that Abbé Maheux, like Canon Groulx, approached the subject with a predetermined thesis, though with an opposite purpose. Both writers cite only such passages as suit their divergent ends.

[4] The birthrate from 1760–70 was 65.3 per 1,000. G. Langlois, *Histoire de la population canadienne-française* (Montréal, 1934), 262. On French-Canadian vitality in general, see J. Davidson, 'The Growth of the French Canadian Race in North America,' *Annals of the American Academy of Political and Social Science*, VIII (Sept. 1896), 213–35.

[5] T. Chapais, *Cours d'histoire du Canada* (Québec, 1919), I, 23–4n.

[6] 'A Journal of the Expedition Up the St. Lawrence,' by a British officer, *New York Mercury*, No. 385 (31 Dec. 1759); cited by J.-C. Bracq, *L'Evolution du Canada Français* (Paris, 1927), 50. A French translation of this journal was published as a pamphlet at Quebec in 1855. A. G. Doughty & G. W. Parmelee, *The Siege of Quebec and the Battle of the Plains of Abraham* (Quebec, 1901), VI, 173.

[7] PAC: Murray Papers, III, 'Letters to & from Murray, 1759–89,' 49–50, Murray-Amherst, 1 Jan. 1761.

[8] *Ibid.*, III, 53, Murray-Amherst, 11 Jan. 1761.

[9] *The Journal of Captain John Knox* (Champlain Society, Toronto, 1914), II, 260, 156n.; cited by A. L. Burt, *The Old Province of Quebec* (Minneapolis, 1933), 18.

[10] Burt, 19.

[11] PAC: Murray Papers, II, 'Letter Book, 1763–5,' 53–5, Murray-George Ross, 26 Jan. 1764.

[12] *Ibid.*, II, 47, Murray-de Montesson, 14 Jan. 1764.

[13] *Ibid.*, II, 104, Murray-Burton, 22 March 1764; F. Brooke, *The History of Emily Montague* (London, 1769), I, 38, Letter VI.

[14] Juge Baby, *L'Exode des classes dirigéantes à la cession du Canada* (Montréal, 1899). Cf. Abbé L. Groulx, *Lendemains de Conquête* (Montréal, 1919–20), 39–51.

[15] Abbé I. Caron, *La Colonisation de Québec* (Québec, 1927), I, 3–10.

[16] PAC: 'Registre d'Audience du conseil militaire de Québec, 1760–62,' II, 121; cited Burt, 35.

[17] H. Têtu & C.-O. Gagnon, *Mandements des évêques de Québec* (Québec, 1888), II, 169, Briand's mandement, 4 juin 1763.

[18] A. Shortt & A. G. Doughty, *Documents Relating to the Constitutional History of Canada 1759–1791*, *CAR 1905*, III (Ottawa, 1907), 6–7, Capitulation of Quebec, Arts. VI & IX.

[19] *Ibid.*, 25, Capitulation of Montreal, Art. XXVII.

[20] Sister Mary Augustina [Ray], *American Opinion of Roman Catholicism in the Eighteenth Century* (New York, 1936), 395.

[21] *Knox's Journal*, II, 260.

[22] PAC: B (Haldimand Papers), 37, 10, Egremont-Amherst, 12 Dec. 1761.

[23] PAC: Murray Papers, II, 'Letter Book, 1763–65,' 139–41, Murray-Halifax, 26 June 1764.

[24] PAC: CO 42, I,——,Murray-Shelburne, 14 Sept. 1763; cited Chapais, I, 45.

[25] PAC: Q I, 258, Murray-Shelburne, n.d.

[26] *Quebec Gazette*, 3 July 1766; cited Chapais, I, 53.

[27] Burt, 82.

[28] Shortt & Doughty, *Const. Docs.*, *1759–91*, 139–40, Murray's Instructions, 7 Dec. 1763.

[29] PAC: Murray Papers, II, 'Letter Book, 1763–5,' 154–7, Murray-Elibank, 16 Sept. 1764.

[30] Burt, 88.

[31] PAC: Murray Papers, II, 'Letter Book, 1763–5,' 170, Murray-Eglinton, 27 Oct. 1764.

[32] Shortt & Doughty, *Const. Docs., 1759–91*, Report of Attorney and Solicitor-General, 13 May 1766. See Caron, I, 18, for Chief Justice Mansfield's censure of the Proclamation.

[33] Shortt & Doughty, *Const. Docs., 1759–91*, 167, Murray-Lords of Trade, 29 Oct., 1764.

[34] PAC: Murray Papers, II, 'Letter Book, 1763–5,' 181, Montreal-Halifax, 30 Oct. 1764.

[35] *Ibid.*, 290, Murray-George Ross, 4 Dec. 1765.

[36] W. S. Wallace, *The Maseres Letters, 1766–1768* (Toronto, 1919), 9.

[37] Shortt & Doughty, *Const. Docs., 1759–91*, 185–6, Maseres, 'Considerations on the Expediency of Procuring an Act of Parliament for the Settlement of the Province of Quebec,' 1766.

[38] *Ibid.*, 206–7, Carleton-Shelburne, 20 Jan. 1768.

[39] *Ibid.*, 205–6.

[40] Cited Burt, 152.

[41] Shortt & Doughty, *Const. Docs., 1759–91*, 404, Quebec Act.

[42] Burt, 258.

[43] W. P. M. Kennedy, *Statutes, Treaties and Documents of the Canadian Constitution, 1713–1929* (Oxford, 1930), 128.

[44] Shortt & Doughty, *Const. Docs., 1759–91*, 207, Carleton-Shelburne, 20 Jan. 1767.

[45] *Journals of the Continental Congress*, I (1774), 88; cited G. Lanctot, *Les Canadiens-français et leurs voisins du sud* (Montréal, 1941), 98, 'Le Québec et les Colonies américaines.'

[46] Kennedy, *Docs.*, 146, 'Address of the General Congress to the Inhabitants of Quebec, 26 Oct. 1774.'

[47] *CHAR 1939*, 13, R. G. Trotter, 'The Appalachian Barrier.'

[48] R. Coupland, *The Quebec Act* (Oxford, 1925), 196.

[49] PAC: Q 11, 170–3; cited Burt, 209.

[50] Têtu & Gagnon, *Mandements de Québec*, II, 264–5, Briand's mandement, 22 mai 1775. This pastoral letter was sent only to the districts of Montreal and Trois-Rivières, those most open to American influence. L. Laurent, *Québec et l'église aux Etats-Unis* (Washington, 1945), 36n. Vicar-General Montgolfier of Montreal backed up Carleton's proclamation of June 9 with a circular to his *curés* on June 13. Têtu & Gagnon, II, 265–6. It is noteworthy that Bishop Briand stressed that the French Canadians were bound by their religion, as well as by their oath of allegiance, to defend their country and king, while discounting the possibility of foreign service. The traditional British loyalty of the French-Canadian hierarchy and the traditional aversion to foreign wars are here first exemplified.

[51] Archives seigneuriales de Lotbinière, MS. 'Lettre du Congrès Général aux Canadiens. Mai ou juin 1775.' Cf. *Journals of Congress*, II(1775), 68–70, 29 May 1775; cited Lanctot, *Voisins*, 104. Abbé François-Louis Chartier de Lotbinière, the former Recollect Père Eustache, became chaplain of James Livingston's French-Canadian regiment in 1776 after displaying American sympathies the previous year. Laurent, *Québec & l'église*, 54–6.

[52] Abbé Aug. Gosselin, *L'Eglise au Canada après la conquête* (Québec, 1917), II, 87; Abbé Verreau (*ed.*), *L'Invasion du Canada* (Montréal, 1873), 39, 54, 63.

[53] Verreau, 166; Caron, I, 101.

[54] Gosselin, II, 87.

[55] J. H. Smith, *Our Struggle for the Fourteenth Colony* (New York, 1907), I, 381–94; E. Allen's *Narrative of the Capture of Ticonderoga and of His Captivity and Treatment by the British* (Burlington, 1849), 12–13.

[56] PAC: Q 12, 188, Carleton-Germain, 28 Sept. 1776; cited by C. Martin, *Empire and Commonwealth* (Oxford, 1929), 140.

[57] Verreau, 55–6; *ibid.*, 51–3, 60, 101.

[58] *Ibid.*, 83.

[59] *Ibid.*, 85–6.

[60] Lanctot, 107.

[61] Smith, I, 598–607.

[62] J. C. Fitzgerald (*ed.*), *The Writings of George Washington* (Washington, 1931), III, 480.

[63] Verreau, 95.

[64] *Ibid.*, 99; quoted Caron, I, 103–4.

[65] TRSC, XII (1906), Sec. II, 197–309, R. W. McLachlin, 'Fleury Mesplet, the First Printer of Montreal.'

[66] Laurent, 45–9; Caron, I, 105; Têtu & Gagnon, II, 269–79, Briand's mande- ment, juin 1776. Cf. Briand's letter to his sister, 27 sept. 1776, in *Revue canadienne*, VIII (1871), 441.

[67] Verreau, 135.

[68] C. P. Stacey, *Canada and the British Army, 1846–71* (London, 1936), 9.

[69] PAC: Q 13, 222, Carleton-Burgoyne, 29 May 1777; cited by Lanctot, 117.

[70] Verreau, 145–6, 155.

[71] *Journals of Congress*, 1777, 924; cited by Lanctot, 117.

[72] Verreau, 151–3.

[73] PAC: Q 16–1, 297, D'Estaing's proclamation, Boston, 28 Oct. 1778; Smith, II, 539. Cf. Caron, I, 109–10.

[74] Lanctot, 121–2.

[75] PAC: Q 16–1, 265; A. L. Burt, *The United States, Great Britain, and British North America* (New Haven, 1940), 121–2.

[76] Caron, I, 120–8.

[77] J. N. McIlwraith, *Sir Frederick Haldimand* (Toronto, 1906), 53.

[78] *Ibid.*, 128.

[79] Caron, I, 113–14.

[80] Laurent, 51–4.

[81] P. Aubert de Gaspé, *Mémoires* (Ottawa, 1866), 85, 90, 186.

[82] *Mémoires de Pierre de Sales Laterrière et de ses traverses* (Québec, 1873), 61–2, 52–3.

[83] Burt, *Old Prov.*, 296.

[84] PAC: Q 15, 268, Haldimand-Germaine, Sorel, 15 Oct. 1778; cited McIl- wraith, 140.

[85] PAC: B 56, 204, Haldimand-North, 27 Oct. 1783; cited Caron, I, 123.

[86] QLHST 1887–9, 37.

[87] Benjamin Sulte's estimate, in A. Fauteux, *Les bibliothèques canadiennes* (Mont- réal, 1916), 13.

[88] McIlwraith, 13, 181.

[89] *Ibid.*, 179–80.

[90] AAQ: 'Vicaires Généraux,' V, 54, Montgolfier-Briand, 21 Oct. 1776; cited by Laurent, 53.

[91] McIlwraith, 277.

[92] NYPL: Smith Papers, 'An act for the regulation of the Province of Quebec— June 11, 1785,' 'An act to repeal part of an act entitled "An act for making more effectual provision for the government of the Province of Quebec in North America" and for the better regulating of the British colonies on that continent'; cited by Burt, 426.

[93] NYPL; Smith Papers, Smith-Dorchester, 7 Nov. 1788; transcript in PAC, Q 39, 117–21; cited by Burt, 432.

[94] Finlay-Nepean, 22 Oct. 1784; cited by Abbé L. Groulx, *L'Enseignement français au Canada* (Montréal, 1931), I, 48.

[95] Brooke, *Emily Montague*, I, 35, Letter VI.

[96] Groulx, *L'Enseignement*, I, 51.

[97] Burt, 465.

[98] Groulx, *L'Enseignement*, I, 67.

[99] PAC: Inglis Papers, I, 154, Inglis-Canterbury, Halifax, 27 Aug. 1789.

[100] Durham, *Report on the Affairs of British North America* (London, 1839), App. D, 100.

[101] Shortt & Doughty, *Const. Docs., 1759–91*, 646, Dorchester-Sydney, 13 June 1787.

[102] *Ibid.*, 653, Sydney-Dorchester, 3 Sept. 1788.

[103] *Ibid.*, 655, Dorchester-Sydney, 8 Nov. 1788.

[104] *Ibid.*, 664, Grenville-Dorchester, 20 Oct. 1789.

[105] *Ibid.*, 685–6, Smith-Dorchester, 5 Oct. 1780.

[106] *Parliamentary History*, XXIX, 113; cited by Chapais, II, 22.

[107] *Encyclopedia Britannica* (11th ed.), XXI, 673, Macaulay, 'William Pitt'; cited by Chapais, II, 12.

CHAPTER III

THE STRUGGLE FOR SURVIVAL

(1791–1834)

THE ERA of representative government in Canada opened under happy circumstances which contrast sharply with the gloomy picture of the period painted by some French-Canadian historians, who see 'secret thoughts' and 'unjust motives' behind Grenville's plan for Canada and consider it only a 'caricature of British parliamentary government.'[1] These writers fail to recognize the shattering effect of the outbreak of the Terror upon British official opinion, which had previously been somewhat sympathetic to the ideals of 1789, or at least had been confident that a revolutionary France was no longer to be feared. The tolerant attitude earlier shown to the French Canadians was replaced after 1793 by a fear of everything French, whether Continental or Canadian. As Britain struggled for its life against revolutionary, republican, and imperial France for the next twenty years, an ethnic tension hitherto unknown in Canada was created, which left its mark on the French-Canadian mind.

The fault lay largely with those Loyalists who had been rewarded for their losses in the United States by offices in Canada. Their fear of everything French, based upon their traditional hatred of French 'papists' and their bitter suspicion of French intrigues among the American republicans who had stripped them of their old homes and possessions, became almost hysterical. They furthered their new careers and feathered their nests by seeing 'French emissaries' everywhere, and finding 'French conspiracies' in the French Canadians' efforts to practice the self-government which Pitt and Grenville had granted. They were badly scared men, who had lived through one revolution in America and dreaded another in Canada as the old eighteenth-century order crumbled. Their nervousness led them to confuse a growing French-Canadian nationalism and North American republicanism with a loyalty to France which had died with the Terror. Like other revolutionary victims, their reaction was so violent as to further in the long run the very revolution they feared. Their efforts to deprive the French Canadians of the self-government embodied in the constitution of 1791 helped to bring on the Rebellions of 1837–8, for the 'unquestioned Democratik

Enthusiasm'[2] which they noted with alarm in the 1790's was not to be repressed.

But when the new constitution took effect on December 28, 1791, its advent was celebrated by public dinners in both the upper and lower towns of Quebec, where French and English alike sat down to feast and rose to drink such toasts as 'The French Revolution and true liberty throughout the universe,' 'The abolition of the feudal system,' 'May the distinction between old and new subjects be buried in forgetfulness, and may the title of Canadian subjects survive forever,' 'May liberty extend to Hudson Bay,' and 'May the event of the day be a mortal blow to the prejudices which are contrary to civil and religious liberty and to commerce.'[3] Representatives of the gathering in the lower town carried a letter to that in the upper town, proposing the toast: 'The Constitution, and may the unanimity among all classes of citizens cause all distinctions and prejudices to disappear, make the country flourish, and render it always happy.' This sentiment was drunk simultaneously at both gatherings amid general applause, and that night the capital was illuminated in honor of the new constitution. A Constitutional Club was formed by the 160 men who had dined together on this occasion, which was 'enlivened by the Prince's band of music,' while a *Club de Patriotes* at Montreal avidly discussed and cheered the news from France at this period.[4] The Prince in question was Edward, the soldier Duke of Kent and father of Queen Victoria, who was stationed with his regiment at Quebec from August 1791 to January 1794; he fostered good feeling by his social talents, and made many friends among the French Canadians.[5]

I

The differences between French and English Canadians were not to subside, however, with the coming of representative government, but rather to increase. At the very outset the new subjects were offended by the division of the province into twenty-one counties, most of which were given incongruously English names. Then there were disorders involving ethnic differences at the elections held in June 1792.[6] The new assembly, whose members included *seigneurs*, lawyers, notaries, merchants, and *habitants*, numbered sixteen English-speaking members out of a total of fifty, though the English population numbered only some 10,000 out of a total of 156,000.[7] The French Canadians were in a distinct minority in the non-elective branches of the government: in the legislative council they had seven out of sixteen members, and in the executive council four out of nine.

At the first meeting of the new legislature the two ethnic groups came into conflict over the election of the speaker of the assembly:

Jean-Antoine Panet was nominated by the French members, while a choice among William Grant, James McGill, and Jacob Jordan was proposed by the English. A warm debate over the bilingual qualifications of the rival candidates sprang up, which was marked by the startling declaration of Pierre-Louis Panet, a cousin of the French nominee: 'It is absolutely necessary for the Canadians to adopt the English language in time, for this is the sole means to banish the antipathy and the suspicion which the diversity of language will maintain between two peoples united by circumstances and forced to live together. But while awaiting this happy revolution, I believe that it is only decent that the speaker whom we choose should be able to express himself in the English language when he addresses the representative of our sovereign.'[8] The notary Joseph Papineau made an eloquent rejoinder to the speeches of English members supporting this view, and when the vote was taken, Jean-Antoine Panet was elected speaker, despite the fact that his cousin Pierre-Louis Panet and the French-born François Dambourgès had joined the English-speaking bloc in opposing him.

This early conflict between French and English members was but a forewarning of a clash that soon followed over the question of which should be the official language of the legislature. Up to this date French had enjoyed no legal status, although it was commonly used for most of the colony's business, both public and private. Its dominance is indicated by the fact that all the English candidates for the speakership were bilingual, while Panet's qualifications in this respect were by his own admission imperfect. To the committee on rules, composed of four members of each group, Pierre-Amable de Bonne proposed that the journals of the assembly should be kept in both languages. John Richardson, the leader of the Montreal merchants, promptly offered an amendment that the English version be considered the legal text. A notable three-day debate followed, with Richardson, Pierre Panet, Grant, McGill, Lee, and Young opposed to de Bonne, Papineau, Bédard, de Lotbinière, Taschereau, and Rocheblave.

The most notable speech was made by Chartier de Lotbinière, who had upheld the rights of the French language before the British parliament when the Quebec Act was under consideration.[9] His desire was not to exclude English, but simply to provide that both languages should enjoy the same status. He pointed out that the Quebec Act insured to the French Canadians their religion, their laws, and their rights as citizens. To him it was clear that the division of the province into Upper and Lower Canada had been made 'in order that the French Canadians should have the right to make their laws in their language, according to their usages, their notions, and the present situation of their country.' He declared that the French

Canadians were loyal to the king, and that they were English at heart before they could speak a word of that tongue. Referring to France, then torn by the Revolution, he concluded: 'It is not by uniformity of language that nations are made more faithful or more united.' And Pierre Bédard, who soon became a parliamentary leader and was later to found the first French-Canadian newspaper, observed: 'If the conquered should speak the language of the conqueror, why don't the English still speak Norman? Is it not ridiculous to wish to make language the test of a people's loyalty?'[10]

Richardson's amendment was defeated by 26–13, with only Pierre Panet and Dambourgès crossing the ethnic line; a revised version was likewise defeated by 27–9, with two English members, Grant and McNider, voting with the French majority. The measure finally adopted by the assembly provided that all bills should be put into both languages by the clerk before being read, while members retained the right to bring in bills in their own language. It also ordained that the English text should be considered legal in the case of bills touching on the criminal law, which was of English origin, and the French text legal in the case of bills bearing upon the civil law, which was of French origin.[11] Thus the two languages were put upon a basis of equality, and both were given an official character, though English remained the language of the law at the insistence of London. Bilingualism was recognized in fact in 1792, if it was not to attain full legal status until 1867.[12] Thus representative government was used at the outset by the French Canadians to secure the last of the conditions of their national survival: official sanction of their language. Their religion, laws, and customs had already been secured by acts of the British parliament.

The English party soon became discontented with the assembly for which they had so long striven. Richardson, the leader of the opposition, confided his gloom about the new form of government to Alexander Ellice, the London partner of his great Montreal trading firm, in a letter of February 16, 1793:

Unhappily the Session commenced with a determined spirit of Party amongst the French members, for they had a private meeting, at which it was decided that an Englishman should on no account be elected speaker.

We wished to conciliate and be moderate, and that the choice should fall on whoever might be best qualified to fill the Chair, from ability, habits of public business, and knowledge in both languages, without distinction of Country. For this purpose three, Grant, McGill and Jordan, were proposed, of which they might select one, the most consonant to the general wish, but all was to no purpose, right or wrong, a Canadian must be the man, no matter how ill qualified; and the election fell on a Mr. Panet, a Quebec lawyer, whose ideas and talents were never calculated for anything beyond the quibble routine and formality of a Court of Common Pleas, such as this Country has hitherto experienced.

The same principle which induced this first Out of Door Meeting has hitherto governed all their proceedings.

. . . . .

I fear there are Two Parties amongst the French—one obnoxious to the New Constitution, as they opposed our procuring it—the other more dangerous as being infested with the detestable principles now prevalent in France. These being my fears, my hopes of course are slender—still, as questions will arise on which they will split, it will give the English (who have no wish but the happiness of this country as a British Colony) a preponderance.

. . . . .

Nothing can be so irksome as the situation of the English members—without numbers to do any good—doomed to the necessity of combating the absurdities of the majority, without a hope of success—were I rid of it, no consideration would induce me again to accept of such a trust—but as I am in, I am determined to give my opinion boldly for such measures as in my conscience I shall think really calculated to do this province a service, under the relation it stands in as a part of the B.[ritish] Empire. I am persuaded—if this House is not dissolved—the English will in the end be the most popular—as facts will speak for themselves, and gradually remove prejudices, interestedly fomented.[13]

This letter reveals the outlook of one of the ablest British merchants in the colony, who resented French party spirit while he blandly assumed that only a member of his own group was qualified for the post of speaker, viewed his French colleagues with suspicion, and resented the dominance of the majority over the minority, although this was a basic principle of the British form of government which the merchants had so long desired.

To be sure, Lieutenant-Governor Sir Alured Clark, who represented the Crown in Dorchester's absence, also noted at the outset of the session a 'jealous spirit' and 'some animosity,'[14] which he blamed chiefly on the fear of the French Canadians that the English intended to control the assembly and to use it to change their ancient laws and customs. But by the end of the session he was pleased to find that distinctions of origin had disappeared almost entirely, and that all the members sat down together for a final dinner marked by 'the greatest harmony and the best mutual dispositions.'

2

Though it is extremely doubtful whether many members of the assembly were infected with the 'detestable principles now prevalent in France,' as Richardson thought, it is certain that French Canada did not wholly escape the influence of the French Revolution, despite the cherished Quebec legend to that effect. The turbulent Citoyen Genet, who represented the French Republic in the United States from April 1793 until early in the following year, was not uninterested in Canada, and his successors followed in his path in this respect. They used Vermont, then dominated by the 'Frenchified' Allen brothers—Ethan, who died in 1791, was the nominal author of a deist work, *Reason, the Only Oracle of Man* (Bennington, 1784), and Ira dealt with the Directory—as a base for intrigues against the colony. The busy channels of trade between the neighboring regions brought to the St. Lawrence the propaganda of the Enlightenment and the Age of Reason, as well as Vermont timber, pot and pearl ash, grain, and provisions. One of Genet's appeals, entitled 'The Free French to their Brothers of Canada,' which had been drawn up on the advice of a young Montreal revolutionary sympathizer, read thus:

Imitate the examples of the peoples of America and of France. Break with a government which degenerates from day to day and which has become the cruelest enemy of the liberty of peoples. Everywhere one finds traces of the despotism, greed, and cruelty of the King of England. It is time to overturn the throne on which hypocrisy and imposture have sat too long. Fear nothing from George III, or from his soldiers, whose numbers are too small to oppose your valor. The moment is favorable, and insurrection is the holiest of duties for you. Remember that being born French, you will always be suspected and persecuted by the English kings, and that this title will be today more than ever a basis for exclusion from all employment . . . Canadians, arm yourselves; call the Indians to your aid. Count on the support of your neighbors and on that of the French.[15]

The old rumors of a French fleet bound for the St. Lawrence and of a new American invasion along the Richelieu passed once more through the province. There was foundation in fact for the first, and a possibility of the latter as the expansionist Vermonters reacted against a tightened frontier. The agitation reached its greatest heights in 1793–4 and 1796–7, when unrest and disorder were widespread. In May 1794 Dorchester called out the militia to repel the threat of invasion from Vermont, and the attempt to carry out this measure evoked new unrest, notably at Charlesbourg, near Quebec, where 300 armed men resisted 'in the name of the people, which is above the law.'[16] At Montreal there was an attempt to force the prisons, and messengers were sent out to raise the countryside against the government. In 1796 there was widespread unrest over the new Road Act, stimulated by French agents. In December Ira Allen, who had previously hoodwinked Haldimand in long negotiations for the union of Vermont with Canada, was captured by His Majesty's Navy in the English Channel aboard a vessel, inappropriately named the *Olive Branch*, which was laden with 20,000 muskets destined for French-Canadian use in case the French Revolution came to Canada. The agitation was brought to a close by the public execution for treason of David McLane at Quebec in July of the following year.[17]

The unrest was confined to the people, and it was opposed by the French-Canadian leaders, both lay and clerical. In November 1793 Bishop Hubert issued a firm circular letter to his clergy in which he declared that 'the bonds which attached them to France had been entirely broken, and that all the loyalty and obedience which they formerly owed to the King of France, they now owed to His Britannic Majesty.' It was their duty 'to drive the French from this Province.'[18] In the following year the Bishop headed the list of eminent French Canadians of Quebec who signed a loyalist manifest condemning 'with the greatest horror the seditious attempts lately made by wicked and evil-intentioned persons in circulating false and inflammatory writings, in exciting by false rumors the fears and doubts of our compatriots against the laws and the power of the government.'[19] A similar declaration was drawn up at Montreal by a committee headed by the leading French-Canadian citizens. In 1796 Bishop Hubert issued another circular to the clergy, in which he warned them against the 'mute and pernicious proceedings which tended to nothing less than to trouble entirely the peace, tranquility, and the happiness in which the inhabitants of the country rejoice under the government and protection of His Britannic Majesty.' He pointed out:

It does not suffice that we be loyal and faithful subjects, if the *habitants* confided to our care allow themselves to be seduced by the enemies of peace and good order . . . we believe it to be more than ever our duty to impress upon the people, either in our public instructions or our private conversations, how closely they are obliged to maintain themselves in the loyalty which they have sworn to the King of Great Britain, in prompt obedience to the laws, and in the avoidance of any spirit which might inspire them with the ideas of rebellion and independence, which have caused such sad ravages in recent years, and from which it is so much to be desired that this part of the globe ever be preserved.[20]

The clergy, shocked by the revolutionary attacks upon the Church in France and fearful of American influence, was moved to a greater loyalty to Great Britain. In June 1794 the Abbé Joseph-Octave Plessis, then *curé* of Quebec and later bishop, pronounced at the funeral of Bishop Briand an oration which was permeated with a warm loyalism:

Our conquerors, regarded with a supicious and jealous eye, inspired only horror and a foreboding chill. We could not persuade ourselves that men strange to our land, to our language, to our laws, to our usages, and to our belief would ever be able to give to Canada that which she had just lost in changing masters. Generous nation, which has proved with so much evidence how false were these prejudices; industrious nation, which has brought to bud the riches which this land enclosed within its bosom . . . charitable nation, which has just rescued with such humanity the most faithful and most maltreated subjects of the kingdom to which we formerly belonged; kind nation, which gives each day new proofs to Canada of your liberality; no, no, you are not our enemies, nor those of our Holy Religion, which you respect. Pardon this early distrust in a people who still had not the happiness to know you; and if, after having learned of the overturn of the state and of the destruction of the true Faith in France, and after having tasted during thirty-five years the mildness of your rule, some amongst us are still found so blind or so evil-intentioned as to entertain the same suspicions and to inspire in the people criminal desires to return to their ancient masters, blame not on the whole what is only the vice of a small number.[21]

The Abbé Plessis even went so far as to impute to Bishop Briand the realization at the time of the conquest that 'the Faith itself might gain by this change of rule'—a statement still much contested by French-Canadian ultranationalists who use Catholicism to bolster their separatism.[22] In 1798, when Nelson defeated the French fleet at Aboukir, Bishop Denaut ordained public thanksgiving for the news which 'spread joy in all hearts,' and reminded his flock of 'the debt they owe to Heaven for having put them under the rule and protection of His Britannic Majesty.' His coadjutor, Bishop Plessis, in a sermon on this same occasion, exclaimed: 'Alas, where would we be, brethren, if this country, by an unfortunate reverse, should return to its ancient masters?'[23]

This new British loyalty was not confined to fine words; in 1799 the assembly offered to vote £20,000 to help England meet the expenses of the war with France, while in 1800 and 1801 a long list of French Canadians, headed by the clergy, subscribed to the patriotic fund raised to support British arms against France.[24] Thanks to the French Revolution, the break with France was almost complete; and the influence of the *emigré* French clergy, some fifty[25] of whom helped to relieve the shortage of priests in Quebec, did much to give the French Canadians an enduring distrust of modern France. On the other hand, the coming of the *emigrés* fortified the prestige of French culture, for they were highly educated men and some of them brought books and pictures which constituted a notable addition to the cultural resources of French Canada, largely cut off from its mother culture since the conquest. Their influence was greater than their number would indicate, since they took a leading role in the educational revival of the period, which saw seven new classical colleges established between 1802 and 1832, as well as many schools.[26]

More important, perhaps, than the influence of the French Revolution upon Quebec was the delayed effect of the American Revolution, though the two were intricately involved, thanks to the support given French agents by American republicans. The doctrine of liberty had been instilled into the French-Canadian mind during the invasion of 1775–6, and after the American Revolution British officials and French-Canadian élite alike were disturbed by its manifestations. Haldimand, Hamilton, and Holland all found the Canadians 'much tinged with Yankey Politics,' and François-Joseph Cugnet was scandalized that 'everyone here, even in the class of the third estate, considers himself entitled to make suggestions to the Councils.'[27] The people insisted upon maintaining the practice, established during the American invason of 1775–6, of electing the militia captains, who were now called upon to ascertain the opinion of the people; and for the first time petitions were circulated and signed by people of the lower classes rather than by members of the élite. This new popular spirit was nourished by some of the American sympathizers among the British merchants, 'secret enemies from within'[28] as Haldimand called them, and by many of the humbler newly arrived Loyalists, who sought 'a Government similar or Superior to that under which they were born, had lived, and were happy.'

The new spirit manifested itself in opposition to some of the measures adopted by the legislature, particularly the Militia Act of 1794 and the Road Act of 1796. The Loyalist Attorney-General James Monk blamed the disturbances of this period, which were directed against both government and clergy, on the ferment of French revolutionary propaganda among the populace, though Dorchester attributed the opposition to the Militia Act to the *habitants* having lost the habit of military service, rather than to disloyalty.[29] In 1796 the passing of a highway act which laid the burden of new *corvées* upon the people caused renewed unrest and resistance to the government. The Loyalist Attorney-General Jonathan Sewell considered that trouble-making French emissaries were responsible;[30] but some of the blame must doubtless be assigned to the unwillingness of the people to assume the burdens, as well as the privileges, of representative government, so different from any form of rule they had previously known.

3

The new legislature proceeded slowly about its work, passing an average of only eight bills a session during the first twelve years of its existence. Inexperience was one reason for this slowness in dealing with the important matters that pressed upon its attention; another

was the fact that a quorum of thirty-four had been set, and ma⸤
members found themselves financially unable to attend, since th⸤
services were unrewarded. One of the popular leaders, the nota⸤
Joseph Papineau, had to be brought to the bar of the assembly ⸤
the sergeant-at-arms, after failing to take his seat in 1802 and 180⸤
and then sought exemption from attendance, which was granted aft⸤
long debate. Professional men and *habitants* gradually replaced t⸤
seigneurs in the assembly, while the latter found refuge in t⸤
legislative or executive council, allying themselves with the Engli⸤
ruling class after losing the confidence of the masses.

Among the principal measures adopted by the legislature we⸤
the Judicature Act of 1794, which established a system of courts th⸤
lasted for half a century; and the Revenue Acts of 1795, which add⸤
new import duties and increased those already established, wh⸤
laying new taxes on peddlers and inn-keepers. In 1805 a measu⸤
providing for the construction and maintenance of public institutio⸤
brought about a sharp conflict between the merchants, who favor⸤
a tax on land, and the majority of the assembly, which favored furth⸤
increases of the tariff and a sales tax. The principle of indirect tax⸤
tion, supported by the popular representatives, triumphed and ⸤
mained the basis of taxation in Quebec until modern times. T⸤
merchants took their defeat badly, and the critical editors of th⸤
organs, the *Montreal Gazette* (which had become English) and t⸤
new anti-French *Quebec Mercury*, were summoned to the bar of t⸤
assembly in 1806 for libel and contempt of that body. The cry ⸤
'French domination,' already becoming well-worn, was raised on⸤
more in English circles.[31]

Surprisingly enough, considering the emphasis on cultural s⸤
vival, the vital question of education was long left unsolved. The⸤
was a deadlock on this question between the English, who want⸤
state-controlled schools, and the French, to whom education wa⸤
religious matter which was a prerogative of the Church. In 179⸤
measure providing for the establishment of parochial schools, to ⸤
supported by the revenues of the Jesuit Estates, was allowed to ⸤
after reaching a first reading, while Dundas postponed action ⸤
Dorchester's educational proposals until a Protestant bishop ⸤
Quebec was appointed.[32] In 1800, with the death of Père Casot, t⸤
last Jesuit in the province, the question of the disposition of t⸤
Jesuit Estates, and with it the question of establishing a new syst⸤
of education, arose once more. The new lieutenant-governor, S⸤
Robert Shore Milnes, who was to show more hostility to the Fren⸤
Canadians than any British administrator had yet revealed, promp⸤
informed the assembly that he had been ordered to take possession⸤
the Estates in the name of the Crown, and that this had already be⸤
done.

The education bill which the assembly was called upon to consider in 1801 was based upon the ideas of Jacob Mountain, first Anglican Bishop of Quebec. Appointed to that office in 1793 as a protégé of Pitt's tutor and secretary, he was appalled by the fact that the French-Canadian masses were 'deplorably ignorant,' and showed no progress 'in the attainment of the language of the country under whose government they have the happiness to live'; while he deplored the upper classes' practice of sending their sons to 'Foreign America' as one 'pregnant with alarming mischief.'[33] In 1795 he had proposed to Dorchester that English Protestant schoolmasters be placed in every parish to teach English free and writing and arithmetic at low fees. This measure would, he thought, break down the barrier between English and French, and induce the latter 'to embrace by degrees the Protestant Religion.' Nothing was done, however, along those lines, perhaps because Dorchester resented the appointment of Mountain rather than his own candidate for the see, but more probably because of Dorchester's lack of sympathy with anglicization and his reluctance to provoke further popular unrest in troubled times. In 1799 Bishop Mountain finally won approval by the executive council of a projected system of free primary schools, to be staffed by English teachers paid by the government.[34] If the government set aside funds for this purpose, as he had proposed to Dorchester in 1785, he foresaw that 'in a few years a new race of men, of subjects, and of Christians will be formed in this country; the surest and most peaceful means will have been found to make ignorance disappear, to stimulate industry, to confirm the loyalty of the people by the gradual introduction of English ideas, customs, and sentiments; the thick cloud of bigotry and prejudice which hovers over the country will be dissipated; and the wall which separates Canadians and English will be broken down.'[35] Bishop Mountain's project found favor with the anglifying governor and with the colonial secretary; and in 1801 the Speech from the Throne called upon the assembly to provide for its establishment by law.

The project involved the creation of a state system of education, to be known as the Royal Institution for the Advancement of Learning. Its controlling body was to consist of the governor, the lieutenant-governor, the Anglican bishop, the chief justice, and the speaker of the assembly. This body, naturally dominated by the governor, was to control all the resources of the Royal Institution, and was to be charged with the direction of the free primary and secondary schools to be set up under its supervision, as well as with control of the teachers and students. Its regulations were to be subject to the approval of the governor, who was given the power to establish primary schools in the parishes and townships, as well as two royal grammar schools in Quebec and Montreal, and to choose school commissioners to administer the school property. The teachers were to be named by the governor and commissioned by him. Herman Witsius Ryland, the governor's francophobe secretary, justly considered the measure 'an extremely powerful means to increase the executive power and to modify gradually the political and religious sentiments of the French Canadians'; while Denis-Benjamin Viger, a Montreal lawyer who was becoming a leading French-Canadian spokesman, thought it 'worse than the university system established in France by Bonaparte.'[36]

This highly autocratic scheme doubtless owed something to Governor Milnes' conviction that 'the Canadian Habitants are, I really believe, an industrious, peaceable and well disposed People; but they are, from their want of Education and extreme simplicity, liable to be misled by designing and artful Men, and were they only once made fully sensible of their own Independence, the worst Consequences might ensue.'[37] Milnes feared the opposition of the Catholic clergy, whose independence, he found, 'tends to lessen the Influence of Government in this Province.' But with the exception of a rival bill proposed by Joseph-François Perrault, the pioneer French-Canadian educational reformer, which failed on second reading, the government's measure passed through the assembly without incident or protest, except for the addition of amendments which secured the independence of all church schools or private institutions, and which made the creation of a Royal Institution school in any parish dependent upon the will of the majority of the inhabitants. The clergy, which had blocked the less objectionable scheme of Loyalist Chief Justice Smith, remained mute; Bishop Plessis later remarked to Sir James Craig: 'You say that our Church never sleeps, but you will allow, however, that we were asleep, and very profoundly too, when we suffered that bill to pass.'[38] But the anglicizers were also asleep, or too much concerned with land speculation, for the Act of 1801 long remained a dead letter, and the proposed land grants for the support of the Royal Institution were never made.[39]

The creation of the Royal Institution was the first step in a campaign of anglicization which endangered the basic elements of French-Canadian survival, and hence aroused vigorous French-Canadian resistance. This campaign was the work of the English or Loyalist placemen who filled the executive and appointive offices of the colony—the so-called 'Chateau Clique'—and it was supported by the British merchants. It even enlisted the backing of some of the *seigneurs* and other members of the French-Canadian élite* who had been attached to the official party by patronage, after they had

---

* Such men were called '*les chouayens*' or '*les vendus*' by the popular party. The latter term has ever since continued to be applied by French-Canadian nationalists to compatriots accepting office from '*les Anglais*,' whether English or Canadian.

been ousted from the French party by the rising class of lawyers and notaries. In constitutional terms it was a battle between the executive council and the assembly, as most of the reactionary-minded governors did their best to upset Pitt and Grenville's en-lightened effort to give Lower Canada self-government adapted to the customs and the ideas of the French Canadians. [40] In religious terms it was a battle between the Anglican and Catholic Churches for supremacy as the established church of Quebec, with the Anglican bishop and governors natural allies. The campaign opened with Bishop Mountain's protests to the governor and to London that 'To authorize the Establishment of two Bishops of the same Diocese, of different religious persuasions, would be a solecism in Ecclesiastical Polity, which I believe never took place in the Christian world; to attempt the *union of different Churches* with the State would be, I hardly conceive, an experiment in the science of Government not less dangerous than novel.' [41]

The question of the position of the Catholic bishop dragged on until the eve of the War of 1812; but the political crisis came to a head in 1805, over the means of raising funds for the support of public institutions. The French majority, who represented agricul-tural interests, favored customs duties, while the English merchants wanted real estate taxes. Open warfare between the executive and the assembly ensued. The attacks of the *Montreal Gazette* and the *Quebec Mercury* on the assembly were followed by the establishment at Quebec of a French-Canadian organ, *Le Canadien*, on November 22, 1806. The rumor of this project was sufficient to induce one 'Anglicanus' to announce flatly in the *Mercury* of October 27: 'This province is already much too French for a British colony. To un-frenchify it as much as possible, if I may use the expression, should be our primary purpose.' [42] The reactionary spirit of the bureaucratic party was even more evident in another communication to the *Mercury*, on the day following the first appearance of *Le Canadien*:

What remains to be done? Withdraw these privileges which are represented as too few, but which are in reality too many, and in which the conquered rejoice too freely; and order matters so that the adminis-tration of public affairs will be carried on in English, by Englishmen, or men of English principles. This will be the first step, and the most efficacious one, towards the anglicization of the province. [43]

Le Canadien, with its much-echoed motto '*Fiat justitia, ruat caelum*,' breathed the spirit of the times. It was founded by three lawyers, Pierre Bédard, Jean-Thomas Taschereau, and Joseph-Louis Borgia, and a doctor, François Blanchet, all members of the as-sembly. It based its stand on the principles of British constitution-alism, which some French Canadians with the aid of two or three

Englishmen or Scots had managed to master so well within fift‹
years that they were already adept at the tactics of legislative ‹
struction. To the *Mercury* one 'Canadensis' replied in *Le Cana‹*
on December 6:

> You say that, far from adopting the sentiments of those in whose f‹
> steps you follow in order to prevent the Canadians from obtaining
> same advantages as you from the constitution, the intention of
> Majesty in dividing the province, as expressed by his prime minis
> and that of his parliament, was to give the Canadians a large majo‹
> in Lower Canada, in order to relieve them from the tyranny which
> would exercise on them. You say that the Canadians use their privile
> too freely for a conquered people, and you threaten them with the
> of those privileges. How dare you reproach them for enjoying the pr‹
> leges which the British Parliament has granted them? Was it not eno‹
> to have done all you could, to have made use of lies and calumnies
> prevent them from obtaining these privileges? . . . Ought you not fin‹
> to submit to what our sovereign and his parliament have ordained? W‹
> difference did they leave between you and the Canadians; from w‹
> right dare you derive this odious distinction of conquerors and c‹
> quered, when they wished to efface it forever? You ask absurdly whet‹
> the Canadians have the right to exercise these privileges in their o‹
> language. In what other tongue could they exercise them? Did not
> parliament of Great Britain know what their language was?[44]

On January 31, 1807, *Le Canadien* deplored the alliance between
placemen and the English members of the assembly, which divi‹
the legislature according to origin, and gave the English facti‹
which regarded itself as a privileged class to which all offices sho‹
be reserved, the appearance of 'being more concerned with c‹
serving its advantageous position than with the interests of ‹
inhabitants of the country.'[45] Such pronouncements seemed ‹
be deplorably tainted with a Jacobin spirit to Attorney-Gene‹
Jonathan Sewell, who rejoiced in an annual stipend of $12,6‹
or to the governor's secretary Ryland, who drew $5,000 fr‹
four offices. They were no less objectionable to Bishop Mounta‹
Receiver-General Henry Caldwell, Judges Alcock and Monk, a‹
such pillars of the English party in the assembly as Richards‹
and Young.

This party of placemen and merchants—most of them up to th‹
ears in speculation in the public lands, which were granted w‹
amazing liberality to the Chateau Clique and its friends—w‹
cheered by the appointment of Sir James Craig as governor ‹
October 1807. Craig was a professional soldier whose ideas ‹
colonial government were thoroughly eighteenth century in char‹
ter, and who was singularly jealous of the royal prerogative, wh‹
he saw endangered by an independent-minded assembly. Shor‹

after his arrival, Craig reported to London that 'The disposition of mind seems to be excellent in all parts of the province.'[46] Such was not long to be his conviction.

In 1808 the assembly declared Ezekiel Hart, a Jewish merchant of Trois-Rivières, ineligible to sit or vote with it on religious grounds, while the English faction strongly dissented from this attack on one of their economic class. The assembly also raised the question of banning judges from its midst, in an attack on Judge DeBonne, who had gradually become a partisan of the placemen, and during the previous year had opposed with extreme vigor an attempt of the French party to introduce allowances for members of the assembly. He had also founded a middle-of-the road French paper, the second *Courrier de Québec*, whose moderation under the editorship of Jacques Labrie had brought down upon it the thunders of *Le Canadien*. The bill declaring judges ineligible was passed by the assembly, but was promply rejected by the legislative council. The elections of 1808 were marked by the violent attacks of *Le Canadien* on the placemen, on the abuse of the royal prerogative, and on DeBonne, the leader of the '*Chouayens.*' Craig was moved by his advisers to cancel the militia commissions of the proprietors, on the grounds that he could have no confidence in the publishers of 'a seditious and libellous publication, that is actively disseminated through the province with great industry, and which is expressly calculated to vilify His Majesty's government, and to create a spirit of dissatisfaction and discontent among his subjects, as well as of disunion and animosity between the two parts of which they are composed.'[47]

War was now openly declared between the executive and the assembly, with Craig using his power of dissolution to counter French-Canadian obstructive tactics. Craig promptly prorogued the legislature in May 1809, when it again insisted upon expelling Ezekiel Hart, who had been re-elected, and the judges. But the elections of that fall returned much the same men to the assembly, and when the session opened in January 1810, a bill declaring judges ineligible was again quickly passed. The assembly also proposed to pay all the civil expenses of the government, thus attempting to weaken the control of the executive, and introducing a question which was to provide decades of discord. When the legislative council adopted the judicial ineligibility bill with an amendment protecting Judge DeBonne for the duration of the parliament, the assembly voted a resolution barring him. This was beyond its powers, and Craig promptly dissolved parliament the following day.

On March 17, a few days later, he seized the press of *Le Canadien* and jailed its printer; he filled the streets of Quebec with armed patrols; and he suspended the mail service. On March 19 he arrested Bédard, Blanchet, and Taschereau and jailed them without trial; while he followed these arbitrary acts with a curious proclamation in which he violently denounced these 'sowers of sedition' and querulously protested his innocence of any oppressive intentions.[48]   The people were unmoved by protestations of good will accompanied by acts of tyranny; and in the elections which followed they re-elected the opponents of the placemen, including the prisoners Bédard and Blanchet. Upon this failure of his policy, Craig sent his secretary Ryland to London to discover how far the imperial government would back him in what promised to be an epic struggle with an unruly legislature. After his first arbitrary dissolution of the assembly, he had been warned by Castlereagh, the colonial secretary, to 'avoid any Expression which can be construed as touching in any degree upon their supposed Privileges and the general Freedom of Inquiry and Debate.'[49]

With Ryland to London went a long dispatch, in which Craig poured out all his woes to Liverpool, Castlereagh's successor, who encouraged him to get along without an assembly, drawing on the British Treasury for expenses. This document of May 1, 1810 affords a good picture of Canada at the outset of the agitation for responsible government, provided that Craig's prejudices are discounted. It was based upon a memorandum[50] prepared by the Loyalist Chief Justice Sewell, which postulated the eternal antipathy of French and English; the necessity of anglicizing the province if it were to remain British; a recourse to massive American immigration to swamp the French Canadians; the establishment of high property restrictions upon the franchise, to prevent French dominance in the assembly; the union of Upper and Lower Canada for more prompt and certain anglicization; and nomination of the *curés* by the Crown, in order to destroy the power of the Church. In short, Sewell called for a complete repudiation of the policy of 1791 and a return to that of 1763.

Craig began his dispatch[51] by insisting upon the fact that Canada was a conquered country, of whose total population of 250,000 only 20,000 were English or American. In his view the remainder were French: 'I use the term designedly, My Lord, because I mean to say that they are in Language, in Religion, in manner and in attachment completely French—bound to us by no one tie, but that of a Common Government, and on the contrary viewing us with sentiments of mistrust and jealousy, with envy, and I believe I should not go too far, were I to say with hatred.' Under the tensions of the Napoleonic Wars, Craig here expressed a view which has been echoed down to the present with less excuse by English-speaking people unable to differentiate between Frenchman and French Canadian, and which reflects the same xenophobia of which they accuse the French Canadian. Craig amplified his views on this basic point:

. . . the line of distinction between us is completely drawn. Friendship (and) Cordiality are not to be found—even common intercourse scarcely exists—the lower class of people, to strengthen a term of contempt, add *Anglois*—and the better sort, with whom there formerly did exist some interchange of the common civilities of Society, have of late entirely withdrawn themselves—the alleged reason is that their circumstances have gradually declined in proportion as ours have increased in affluence; this may have had some effect, but the observation has been made also, that this abstraction has taken place exactly in proportion as the power of the French in England (Europe?) has become more firmly established.

This division along ethnic lines into 'haves' and 'have-nots,' which lasted for nearly a century, arose largely from the fact that the commercial-minded English had the governmental influence and the access to British capital which enabled them to exploit the Canadian commercial revolution, which began with the Peace of 1783 and the coming of the Loyalists, and had reached its halfway mark by 1810. The products of farm and forest had become the major staples as the fur trade declined, and this new trade was largely in English hands. Napoleon's Continental Blockade of 1807, which cut Britain off from Baltic timber, was largely responsible for the revival of a commercial imperialism which flooded Canada with British capital. Canada suddenly was linked with the industrial civilization of Britain. The number of ships clearing from Quebec tripled between 1807 and 1810, with every branch of the timber and lumber trade showing a similar expansion. The French Canadians, long largely ousted from the management of the fur trade, had fallen back on the professions, petty trades, agriculture, and unskilled labor. The professional men and tradesmen were not commercial-minded. The *habitants* were deeply traditional; they practiced subsistance rather than commercial farming. Their insistence upon an outmoded feudalism and their economic self-sufficiency were matters of equal irritation to the commercial-minded Englishman. *Le Canadien* spoke for the French Canadians as a people, with a few rare exceptions, when in 1808 it deplored the new commercialism and characterized a mercantile aristocracy as 'equally prejudicial to the authority of the Crown, to the interests of landowners, and to the liberties of the people.'[52]

Craig, under the influence of Bishop Mountain like his predecessor Milnes, was distressed by the position of the Catholic Church and the influence of its clergy:

The Bishop, tho' unknown to our Constitution and confirmed, if not appointed by a Foreign Power, has been suffered to exercise every Jurisdiction incident to the episcopal functions; he nominates to all the benefices of the Province, and removes at his pleasure from one living to another . . . His Patronage is at least equal to that of the Government, & it is so perfectly at his pleasure, that Government has no other notice of it, than that he usually once a year delivers to the Governor a list of such changes as have taken place during the preceding twelve months. . . . In truth the Catholic Bishop tho' unacknowledged as such, exercises now a much greater degree of authority than he did in the time of the French Government, because he has arrogated to himself every power which was then possessed by the Crown . . .

With the Curés themselves, no direct communication from the Government exists in any shape; a numerous and powerful body, dispersed in every corner of the Country, and certainly possessing a very considerable weight and influence with the people, scarcely know, and are hardly known to the Government. . . .

Craig found, in the face of abundant evidence to the contrary, that the clergy's 'attachment to France is equally undoubted, and it is now even supposed to be not a little directed to the Person of Bonaparte, who since the concordat, is considered among them as the Restorer of the Roman Catholic Religion.' The source of this curious conviction may be surmised when Craig praises the legislative council in the next sentence as 'composed of everything that is respectable in the Province' and 'animated by the best intentions towards His Majesty's Service & the public good.' The respectable members of the legislative council were then engaged in loading themselves with a plurality of offices, in dividing the public lands among themselves, and in withholding from the British Treasury the royal revenue. But at least they were not French, and hence suspect of Bonapartist sentiments; and so they found favor in Craig's eyes.

Representative government was not at all to Craig's absolutist taste, especially when 'To a People circumstanced as I have described these to be, ignorant and credulous in the extreme, having no one common tie of affection or union, viewing us with Jealousy, mistrust and hatred, having separate & distinct Interests, it has been thought proper to give a share in the Government of the Country, by a House of Representatives in which they must ever have the Majority.' Craig railed against the absence of a property qualification for members, and he blamed their unruly behavior on ignorance rather than malevolence:

. . . at present they are completely in the hands of the party which leads the House, Debate is out of the question, they do not understand it, they openly avow that the matter has been explained to them the night before by such & such persons, and they invariably vote accordingly. It is in this manner, at their nightly meetings which are held for the purpose, that every question is previously decided, and it is impossible that these people can ever be set right, for those who judge right never meet them outside of the House; they do not associate with them.

In such a House, certainly 'the most independent Assembly that exists in any known Government in the world,' the governor could have no influence, even that arising from personal intercourse, for 'I can have none with Blacksmiths, Millers, & Shopkeepers; even the Avocats & Notaries, who compose so considerable a portion of the House, are generally speaking such as I can nowhere meet.'

It was clear to Craig's suspicious mind that this 'set of unprincipled Avocats and Notaries . . . having everything to gain and nothing to lose by any change that they can bring about,' had been encouraged by the revival of France under Napoleon, and were 'using every endeavour to pave the way for a change of Dominion and a Return under that Government.' Indeed, such was the general conviction 'of all ranks with whom it is possible to converse on the Subject.' In his own opinion, 'the great Mass of the people are completely infected,' and he reported that the leaders of the popular party 'publickly declare that no officer of the Crown is to be trusted, or to be Elected into the House. These, together with all English in general, and their own Seigneurs, are entirely proscribed.' *Le Canadien*, whose purpose was defined as 'to vilify and degrade the officers of Government under the title of *Gens en place*, and to bring into contempt His Majesty's Government itself,' linked leaders and people; and 'Every topick that is calculated to mislead & inflame the people has at times occupied the pages of this paper.' In view of the fact that 'no circumstance whatever has occurred to awaken their attachment to their Mother Country, nor have any pains ever been taken to produce such a change, their habits, language and religion have remained as distinct from ours as they were before the Conquest. Indeed it seems to be a favorite object with them to be considered as (a) separate Nation; *La Nation canadienne* is their constant expression, and with regard to their having been hitherto quiet & faithful subjects, it need only be observed that no opportunity has presented them an encouragement to shew themselves otherwise.'

Craig judged that the public welfare and general prosperity would never be promoted by the assembly: 'Religious prejudices, Jealousy, and extreme ignorance all forbid the expectation, and these, I am afraid, must prevail among the Canadian part of it for a long period to come.' As an example he cited the fact that the Canadians were 'loud in their Clamours' against the introduction of American settlers into the Eastern Townships, 'as having a tendency, which of all others they are most anxious to assert, to impede the complete Establishment of a Canadian Nation.'

Judging the situation thus, Craig proposed nothing less than the revocation of the Constitution of 1791, since 'that Spirit of independence, that total insubordination among them, that freedom of conversation by which they communicate their Ideas of Government as they imbibe them from their Leaders, all of which have increased wonderfully within these last five or Six years, owe their origin entirely to the House of Assembly, and to the intrigues incident to Elections.' As an alternative to this admittedly delicate and difficult measure, Craig suggested 'the Reunion of the Two Provinces, so as to Balance the Canadian Party in the House,' though he was 'more inclined to keep the Province of Upper Canada as a foreign and distinct population, which may be produced as a resource against that of this Country in case of necessity.' This latter policy of playing one ethnic group against the other has survived until the present as one of the basic principles of Canadian politics, both federal and provincial. As another alternative, Craig proposed a new division of the province, giving more representation to the Eastern Townships and thus offsetting the French Canadians.

But whatever measure should be favored by London, if the assembly were to be continued, the qualifications for membership must be raised, since 'it really, My Lord, appears to me an absurdity that the Interests of certainly not an unimportant Colony, involving in them those also of no inconsiderable portion of the Commercial concerns of the British Empire, should be in the hands of six petty shopkeepers, a Blacksmith, a Miller, and fifteen ignorant peasants who form part of our present House; a Doctor or Apothecary, twelve Canadian Avocats and Notaries, and four so far respectable people that at least they do not keep shops, together with ten English members, compleat the list; there is not one person coming under the description of a Canadian Gentleman among them.'

Having thus scornfully dismissed the fathers of Canadian self-government with typical Tory arrogance, Craig turned again to the question of the Catholic bishop. Since 'the Person who at present exercises the episcopal functions is not, I think, of a turbulent disposition, but he is a Man of great ambitions and some art,' Craig proposed that Bishop Plessis be bribed into submitting to nomination of the *curés* by the Crown, which would give the government 'not only the most extensive' but also 'the most powerful and useful influence.' He also proposed that the Crown should take over the Sulpician Estates, since 'the Majority of the present Members of the Institution are French emigrant Priests, and are not among the least dangerous persons in the Colony; the Person at the head of it is particularly of that description, a very able, but a very artful, designing Man, whose prediliction for France is not doubted.' He suggested that the Sulpicians should be left two-fifths of the revenue of their estates, and the Seminary of Quebec should be assured of its property; 'the two together form an ample provision for the Education of their Youth.'

These drastic proposals were backed by Herman Ryland's ardent advocacy in London, but the British government found it inex-

Morin College, Quebec

The old Prison of Quebec, built in 1808 after the plans of François Baillairgé, the greatest of the builders who combined the French and British traditions at this period. The building subsequently was converted for the use of Morin College, an English institution affiliated with McGill, and now houses the Quebec Literary and Historical Society. (I.O.A.P.Q.)

Masson House, Terrebonne

The Manor House of the Seigneurs of Terrebonne, built in 1848 in the English style by one of the few French-Canadian families which prospered under the new commercial system introduced after the conquest. (National Gallery.)

pedient to launch a discussion of Lower Canadian affairs in parliament at that time. The question of the revocation or alteration of the Constitution of 1791 was thus put aside entirely, and the ministers delayed their opinion on the matters of the nomination of the *curés*, the disposition of the Jesuit and Sulpician Estates, and the settlement of the Crown lands. The growing prospect of war with the United States discouraged the adoption of any measures which might arouse unrest in Canada; and once again the French Canadians won concessions affecting their survival from the British government, lest Canada should join the lost American colonies.

London not only put aside Craig's recommendations, but also rejected the pretensions of the Anglican Bishop of Quebec. Bishop Mountain saw realized his fears of 1803 that 'unless some immediate and effectual remedy be applied to the abuses which have been gradually introduced . . . the Roman Catholic Church will be to all intents and purposes the established Religion of the Country; rapidly declining, as it should seem, in other parts of the world it will not only find here a safe asylum, but be raised to the pre-eminence and laid upon the broadest and most substantial Bases.' The early maneuvers of Bishop Mountain had been frowned on by the Colonial Secretary in 1804, when the latter advised the governor to discourage all differences between the two bishops.[53] The petition of Bishop Denaut for civil recognition of his office—made in 1805 at Attorney-General Sewell's instigation—likewise remained without response from London. Bishop Mountain, Sewell, and Ryland then joined forces to put the Catholic Church under the power of the Crown. Ryland's views on the Catholic clergy are clearly expressed in a letter of December 23, 1804:

I call them 'Popish' to distinguish them from the Clergy of the Established Church, and to express my contempt and detestation of a religion which sinks and debases the human mind, and which is a curse to every country where it prevails. This being my opinion, I have long since laid it down as a principle, which, in my judgment, no Governor of this Province ought to lose sight of for a moment, that by every possible means which prudence can suggest gradually to undermine the authority and influence of the Roman Catholic Priests. This great, this highest object that a Governor can here have, might have been accomplished (I am confident) before now, and may by judicious management be accomplished before ten years more shall have passed over. . . . We have been mad enough to allow a company of French rascals to deprive us for the moment of the means to accomplish this [i.e., establishment of the royal supremacy, abolition of papal authority, and the Protestantizing of Canada].[54]

In 1807 Bishop Mountain went to London to press the Anglican case, and there Ryland wrote him, complaining of the promptness with which the administrator of the colony had received Bishop Plessis as the successor of Bishop Denaut, and had agreed to the nomination of Bishop Panet as coadjutor. The last had the misfortune to be the brother of the speaker of the assembly, who was in ill odor with Ryland and the Chateau Clique.

The appointment of Sir James Craig as governor strengthened the hand of Bishop Mountain, Sewell, and Ryland, for they found in him a man who shared their objections to the Catholic Church. Bishop Plessis suspected the danger which might arise when Ryland went to London in 1810 with Craig's report, for he wrote to Adam Lymburner, now retired to London:

I should not be at all surprised if this occasion were used to calumny the clergy in the minds of the ministers. The revenues which our *curés* enjoy, the authority of the Catholic Bishop over them and the people, are long since the objects of jealousy. But I put all my hope in the Providence of the God I serve, and try to have served by my people, by inspiring them with the sentiments with which they should be permeated as Christians and as subjects.[55]

Somewhat unwisely at this crucial period, Bishop Plessis issued on October 25, 1810 a proclamation calling for public prayers for the Pope, in which he signed himself 'Bishop of Quebec by grace of the Holy Apostolic See.'[56] Ryland waved a copy of this document under the ministers' eyes in London, and called for criminal prosecution of the bishop for acknowledging a foreign jurisdiction in a British colony.[57]

After long delays the law officers of the Crown, to whom the proposals respecting the Church had been referred, finally reported that the King had the right of nomination of the *curés* and that the Sulpicians had no valid title to their estates. But they added that these matters had been so long neglected that rights of possession, difficult to upset, had arisen; and they entirely ignored the question of Bishop Plessis' proclamation. In December 1811, when the colonial secretary was about to send instructions to Craig covering the nomination of the *curés* and the disposition of the Sulpician Estates in accordance with the governor's views, the Lord Chancellor intervened, and Ryland went home disgruntled and empty-handed. Lord Chancellor Eldon was supported by Sir Robert Peel and Lord Castlereagh, the last of whom had, as colonial secretary some years before, thus dismissed Bishop Mountain's pretensions:

The Canada Act assures to the Catholics of Canada the free exercise of their religion, and to their clergy the right to receive the tithes paid by those who belong to this faith, saving the supremacy of His Majesty as established by the Act of Supremacy. The Supremacy of the King, according to this act, is limited to preventing strangers from exercising any spiritual jurisdiction in the possessions of the Crown. But the bishop of Quebec is not a stranger; he is chief of a religion which can be freely practiced by grace of the imperial parliament; he can claim and receive from Catholics the tithes and ordinary dues, and exercise upon them the rights which he had always enjoyed. It would be a very delicate business to intervene in the affairs of the Catholic religion at Quebec, or to force the titular bishop to abandon his titles and to act not as bishop, but only as superintendant.[58]

Sir James Craig's last effort as governor, in the spring of 1811, was an attempt to force Bishop Plessis to submit to his notion of the royal prerogative. Bishop Plessis has left an interesting account of the three interviews in which the governor tried without success by every means from threats to bribes to win the bishop to his way of thinking.[59] Then, thanks to the outstanding loyalty of the clergy in the War of 1812, the British government sent orders to the new governor, Sir George Prevost, that 'the salary of the Catholic Bishop of Quebec shall henceforth be increased to the sum recommended by you of £1,000 per annum, as a testimony to the sense which His Royal Highness entertains of the loyalty and good conduct of the gentleman who now fills that station and of the other Catholic clergy of the Province.'[60] Ryland, as secretary of the executive council, had to write with his own pen the words 'Catholic Bishop of Quebec,' after he had vainly tried to substitute 'superintendent of the Roman Church' for the phrase which the colonial secretary had used in his dispatch. The affirmation of the royal supremacy in the matter of the bishopric became a dead letter, and Bishop Plessis was justified in saying that a great danger had been averted and that the religious liberty of the French Canadians had been newly assured for the future.

4

Craig's 'Reign of Terror,' as French-Canadian historians call it, has tended to obscure the very important economic developments of the epoch, which underlaid the constitutional conflict between the Chateau Clique and the representatives of the people. The surrender to the United States in 1796 of most of the western trading posts marked the beginning of the decline of the Montreal fur trade; and the cannier merchants had already begun to turn their attention to new fields. The fur trade had been based upon a nomadic civilization, and was the enemy of colonization; the new economy was agricultural and based upon land ownership. Soon after the Loyalists settled along the Upper St. Lawrence, the Montreal merchants began dealing in wheat and flour from that region, as well as from the Richelieu Valley, and acting as middlemen for their Upper Canadian brethren in the London trade. They also took a hand in the growing commerce in American products, which were brought down the Richelieu from Lake Champlain and exported to England under colonial preference. The British fur traders, like their French predecessors, were finally conquered by the land, and acquired property in the neighbourhood of Montreal from the declining *seigneurs*. In many cases they established small industries on these seigneuries, flour and saw mills, potteries, and organized domestic industries, such as the production at L'Assomption of *ceintures fléchées* or woven-worsted sashes for the North West Company and later the Hudson's Bay Company. After the Crown Lands Proclamation of 1792 [61] the British merchants began to indulge in land speculation on a considerable scale.

This land speculation centered in the vast empty expanses of the Eastern Townships, which first had been left unsettled as a barrier to American aggression, and then reserved by Haldimand for colonization by the French Canadians, whose difference in blood, language, and religion might be counted upon to act as a check to American expansion. But geography was not to be denied in this region, which is a natural extension of Vermont and New Hampshire; and immigrants from New England began to settle there, drawn by the richness of the land. At first this movement of squatters was frowned upon by the authorities; but when both French and English Canadians alike refused to take up land in the Townships, 'the most unlimited encouragement' [62] was given to Americans. The French were loath to leave their familiar world of the St. Lawrence for this remote region of vast virgin hardwood forests with a system of tenure new to them, and most of the English were more interested in trade or in office-holding than in the back-breaking work of pioneering.

As conflict between the English minority and the French majority in the new assembly developed, the coming of Americans to swell the numbers of the former was welcomed by the Chateau Clique, who were also interested in finding purchasers for the land grants which were one of their chief perquisites of office. Officially, grants were limited to 1,200 acres for a single individual, with 200 acres the normal amount; but these regulations were evaded by the speculators, who made use of many names to conceal their holdings. In 1795 one single partnership, composed of Sir John Johnson's son-in-law, Patrick Langan; the Postmaster-General Hugh Finlay; Captain David Alexander Grant, who had married the *seigneuresse* of Longueuil; and John Jacob Astor of New York, planned to take out grants on no less than 2,000,000 acres—twenty-four whole townships. [63] To obtain the number of names of 'intending settlers' required by law, advertisements offering 200 acres to anyone who could produce a certificate declaring himself to be 'an honest, industrious Person, and peaceable Inhabitant' were placed in the American newspapers.⁶⁴ The northward movement of New Englanders, some Loyalist in sympathies and more merely hungry for new land, began immediately after the Proclamation of 1792; in five years some 2,000 settlers came into the Townships; and by 1805 the population there numbered more than 5,000, mostly Americans. The fertile lands of the numerous well-watered valleys were soon cleared and put under cultivation by a people accustomed to pioneering in similar country; land values rose; roads were built; and the first coach route from Quebec to Boston was established in 1811, through what had been an almost impenetrable forest barrier between the province and New England only a few years before.

The newcomers demanded representation, and found the officials at Quebec well disposed to their plea. Craig was inclined to favor them as a counterweight to the French Canadians. Then, too, the governor was surrounded by Loyalist officials who had begun life in the American colonies and had a natural sympathy for the newcomers. It was the Massachusetts-born Chief Justice Sewell who produced the memorandum upon which Craig based his conclusions on the matter. The grounds for encouraging the American settlers and increasing their numbers with a view to swamping the French were thus stated by Sewell: the newcomers were 'of English stock, professing the same religion, speaking the same language, and would therefore be more easily assimilated and would become better subjects than those which we now possess.'⁶⁵ Quite naturally, this officially-encouraged immigration of foreigners into French Canada did nothing to check the growth of ethnic feeling among the old inhabitants of the province. *Le Canadien* thundered against the introduction of 'a half-savage people, whose forays are as much to be feared in Canada as those made formerly by the Goths and Vandals into Italy,' while D.-B. Viger asked whether it was good policy for Britain to make 'an American province' out of Canada.⁶⁶

But to the minds of the official class and of the merchants, panicky about French plots, irritated by their conflict with the French-Canadian majority in the assembly, and eager to profit by land speculation, an American Canada was better than a French one. The basic motive of the Chateau Clique in this instance was not hatred of the French but self-interest; the editor of the *Quebec Mercury* remarked: 'I have no particular personal friendship for the American; still less have I any enmity to the Canadian; but I must be permitted to have an anxious wish to see so large a portion of the British dominions in a superior state to wilderness.'⁶⁷ Another factor was also involved, as was indicated by an anonymous pamphleteer who railed against the failure of the French to exploit the resources of the country:

The population of this Province forms a small compact body inert in its nature, without one principle of percussion; and exhibiting its infant face, surcharged with all the indications of old age and decay. During a lapse of two centuries, little more than the borders of the St. Lawrence have been put under cultivation; in a few places only, have settlements slumbered forth, on the minor streams, with manifest reluctance and regret.[68]

To British merchants interested in booming trade, French-Canadian conservatism and adherence to an outmoded semi-feudal agricultural way of life were deplorable, in the face of the manifest opportunities of a new commercial and industrial era.

'Jeremy Cockloft, the Elder, M.A., P.C.,' whose *Cursory Observations* is one of the scarcest * and most amusing Canadian books, paints a vivid picture of 'this dreary Province of Canada'[69] as seen through English commercial eyes in 1811 at the high tide of the Canadian economic revolution. 'Cockloft' is thought to have been a young Englishman sent out to Quebec in behalf of the London timber merchants. When not complaining about the prevailing dirt, the 'livid squalidness' of countenance, and the 'uncouthness' of dress among the French Canadians, he made some important economic observations. He found a general interest in the price of timber in England, which is not surprising, since timber exports had tripled between 1807 and 1810 and had become the basis of Quebec's prosperity, remaining such until the depression of 1833.[70] In Quebec he met an enterprising Bermudian, 'whose project was to make Bermuda a depot for the produce of both the other colonies' (Canada and the British West Indies), but the flaw in this scheme to him was that the West Indies could often get their provisions more cheaply from the United States, as they did according to Joseph Bouchette.[71] He also talked with Canadian gentlemen, who 'regretted the inert disposition of the 'Habitants, whom they said neither adversity nor prosperity could arouse from the torpid habits of their forefathers; that in general they planted no more now, although every species of provision had risen greatly in price, than they did four years ago when the trade was very trifling.' The go-ahead Englishman was appalled by the easy-going French Canadians: 'Their aversion to labor springs from pure, genuine, unadulterated *indolence*. Give a 'Habitant milk, a few roots, tobacco, wood for his stove, and a bonnet *rouge*, he works no longer;— like the native Savage, who seldom hunts but when driven by hunger.'[72]

'Cockloft' noted that Quebec imported cottons, woolens, hardware, bolt and bar iron, sheet lead, copper, tin, coals, salt, cordage, anchors, cables, sailcloth, mathematical instruments, earthen and glass ware, drugs, etc. from Britain; but that two-thirds of these

* But has been reprinted by Oxford University Press, Toronto, 1960.

imports went on to the United States. Quebec also imported rum, sugar, pimento, and coffee from the British West Indies; and codfish and whale oil from Newfoundland. Exports consisted of furs, timber, wheat, flour, oats, pot and pearl ashes, salted beef, pork, butter, hams, soap, lard, candles, and ships for the Britain–West Indies trade, but he observed that Quebec could not supply the West Indies. He found that the Quebec ships were not as well built as European ones, and that they were expensive because of the high cost of labor (double that in Europe); high freights, commissions, and insurance on all ingredients except timber; and the cost of sending out crews from England. With a mercantilist's regret he noted that the Canadians' consumption of imports was 'but trifling in comparison to the extent of their country, the 'Habitants in general manufacturing their own clothes, and in winter substituting skins for woolens. The wants of these people are very few; being perfectly free from any desire of luxury or finery . . . the 'Habitants seldom exert themselves to provide more than their immediate wants require; and if they sometimes get rid of their natural indolence, an exorbitant price is necessary as a stimulus for a continuance of their exertions.'[73]

'Cockloft' exempted the 'higher classes' from his general indictment of the *habitant*, but commented: 'In whatever place a paucity of natural enjoyment prevails, the mind of man is apt to descend to vulgar and idle, not to say criminal pleasure. This unfortunately is the case in Quebec. The liberal arts either have been frozen in some severe winter, have deserted to a more congenial clime, or perhaps have never visited the place.' The theater was encouraged chiefly by transients, while the two weekly newspapers seemed 'very weakly productions.' Instead of 'Newspaper animadversions, private gossips furnish an ample fund of anecdote and scandal, which circulates like the miasma of pestilence; and characters are stabbed in the dark, unconscious where the blow is derived, or by whom directed.' He briskly summed up the amusements of Quebec as 'gaming, scandal, licentiousness and drinking.'[74]

The insular 'Cockloft' was shocked to find that 'all the boys in Quebec speak English like Frenchmen, and indeed seldom speak it at all, when the French language will answer their purpose.' He noted an 'inveterate prejudice of the 'Habitants against the British.' He regretted that the Canadians had received 'the freedom of the British Constitution; which they did not at the time and I fear never will appreciate or rightly understand.'[75] Though most Englishmen of the trading class were strong mercantilist imperialists at this time, 'Cockloft' took a view more typical of the English Reformers after 1829:

Upon the whole, I think it very questionable, whether the Provinces of Canada are worth the expense of retaining under the British flag, even politically considered. The 'Habitants have certainly a strong predilection for the French, of which the universality of that language throughout the country must be admitted as a very presumptive proof,—more especially as it supersedes the English tongue in their legislature and courts of law, as well as in their private dealings with one another. The American people appear to have a great desire to possess the Canadas; and I really think the cession of the territory to them (especially if well paid for, as was the case with Louisiana) would be of great benefit to Great Britain, and an endless source of miseries and calamities to the Fredonians. . . .[76]

It is clear that 'Cockloft' remained too much of a traditional British imperialist to appreciate the workings of the new American economic imperialism which had already begun to invade Canada, regardless of sovereignty.

A new stage of the ancient rivalry of the St. Lawrence and Hudson trading systems had opened, and the American economy was beginning to push its Canadian rival to the wall. The old Canadian monopoly of the fur trade was broken forever when John Jacob Astor forced John Richardson and William McGillivray of Montreal into partnership with him in January 1811, and left only the Canadian North-West open to British traders. A flood of American manufactures was flowing into Canada under Jay's Treaty, as well as the timber for which the Continental Blockade had created such a demand in Great Britain. The Montreal and Quebec merchants benefited by the passage of American timber down the Richelieu and the St. Lawrence, but they found their monopoly of imported manufactured goods badly threatened. The American Embargo Act of 1807 could not stop the development of a north–south trade; the subsequent contraband traffic across a border which had become largely a legal fiction amounted to more than the previous legal trade.[77]

Hampered at home by the French majority's reluctance to protect commerce, the merchants sought relief in London by forming in 1809 the Committee of British North American Merchants, which served as a lobby at the seat of government for the commercial classes of Montreal and Quebec. In 1812 this body won the grant of imperial protection against the importation of commodities not the growth or manufacture of the United States, while the American tariffs were to be adopted on American imports except in the case of natural products, from which the Canadian merchants benefited.[78] The War of 1812 gave the Canadian merchants some cheer, for it suggested the possibility of regaining the lost hinterland, and with it monopoly of the fur trade. Thus the traders and the Indians united to oppose the westward American movement and the settlement which followed in its wake, dooming the old economy.

5

Despite all the glorification by nationalist historians of the French-Canadian part in the War of 1812, it was really a maritime and western war in which Quebec played little part. Though Joseph Bouchette, son of Carleton's guide in 1775, makes much of the 'insatiable desire for gain'[79] of the Americans—some of whom, like Massachusetts-born Philemon Wright, the founder of the Ottawa lumber trade, were displaying a most un-Canadian activity and industry—and Yankee designs on Quebec figure in many other French-Canadian accounts of the conflict,[80] it was really the American South and West that forced the war, and their interest in attacking Canada was a blow at Britain, not annexation. The Anglo-American maritime difficulties and the long delay in turning over the western posts, with consequent conflict between British traders and the Indians they controlled, and the Americans, had irritated the swelling national pride of the United States, which was in a few more years to burst out in the eagle-screaming doctrine of Manifest Destiny. Federalist New England, however, was opposed to what it regarded as a republican war designed to aid Napoleon, and even threatened secession because of it. The nine thousand transplanted New Englanders of the Eastern Townships supplied six battalions to the British army in Canada, and Vermont and New York provided two-thirds of that army's supplies.[81]

The annexation of Quebec no longer figured in Yankee thinking: the economic relations between New England and its northern neighbour had become so close and so profitable that an American could write: 'we would regret much (between ourselves) that Quebec should not remain in possession of the English. They charge us no Duties upon Exports down the River, and our produce being shipped from Canada as the products of a British Colony, we obtain the Bounty or Discriminating Duties.'[82] Again, in 1808 the Governor of Vermont assured John Henry, the double renegade then serving as a secret agent of Craig, that in case of war his state would adopt a neutral attitude towards Canada. Although Henry's disclosure to President Madison of British designs, after he was repudiated by Craig, played some part in increasing war-mindedness in New England, this attitude of neutrality was the one followed in fact during the war by the states bordering upon Quebec.

As war came closer, French agents were active in trying to arouse French-Canadian unrest after Craig's 'Reign of Terror'; but their efforts were doomed to failure by the mild and conciliating conduct of his successor, Sir George Prevost, another Swiss professional soldier with the customary talent for handling French-Canadian sensibilities. The proposed alliance of Napoleonic France with the United States against Britain enlisted no sympathy in a Quebec which was now opposed to 'the enterprises of any power whatsoever in Canada.'[83] *Le Canadien* refered to Napoleon as the 'lawless leader of France'[84] and Quebec City had been illuminated in honor of Nelson's victory at Trafalgar; there was little left of the old bond between French Canada and France. The French Canadians had been irritated by American immigration into the Townships and injured in their pride by Jefferson's reference to the proposed invasion of Canada as a 'mere matter of marching.'[85]

When Vicar-General Deschenaux, in Bishop Plessis' absence, issued a circular letter calling the people to the defence of the country and of 'our good government' in the name of interest, gratitude, and religion,[86] the French Canadians embraced the British cause with singular unanimity. The assembly cheerfully voted $928,000 for military and civil purposes, and authorized the emission of paper currency for war purposes. It also passed a new militia law, under which 6,000 men were raised without difficulty. In April 1812, before the outbreak of the war, Lieutenant-Colonel Charles Michel de Salaberry, a Canadian who under the patronage of the Duke of Kent had seen long service in the British Army in many quarters of the world, recruited the first French-Canadian regiment of regulars, the *Voltigeurs Canadiens*. The ranks were filled in a few days.

Most of the War of 1812 was fought in Upper Canada, and with the exception of the part played by the French-Canadian *voyageurs* and *engagés* of the fur trade in the battles about the posts on the Great Lakes, Quebec had little opportunity to translate its loyalty and willingness to fight into action. As far as Quebec was concerned, there were only three campaigns. In 1812 Dearborn advanced on Montreal from Plattsburg. He halted at the border when warlike enthusiasm waned among his militiamen, and returned to his base with his homesick army after an utterly bloodless campaign of four days. On October 26 of the following year Hampton marched within fifteen miles of the St. Lawrence with a force of 4,000 men, but a night attack at Chateauguay by 800 Canadians, including De Salaberry's *Voltigeurs*, was enough to make him renounce the conquest of Canada. In 1814 Prevost's advance against Plattsburg, with 7,000 veterans of Wellington's campaigns, collapsed when his fleet was destroyed by Macdonough on Lake Champlain on September 11. One wonders where the ardent loyalist Bouchette found the 'depraved ferocity'[87] of which he accuses the Americans. But some verbal violence must be permitted to a fire-eater frustrated by the quite evident desire of the New England states to prevent war from interfering with business, and by Prevost's equal willingness to accept the situation. Despite recent disputes along the Vermont–New York frontier, so much in doubt that in 1818 it was found that the American fort at Rouses Point had been built well within Canadian territory, no British move was made east of Lake Champlain.

The bellicose merchants of Montreal, who were constantly exhorting the government to greater effort, and whose traders, *engagés*, and the Indians they influenced made useful allies to the redcoats, did much to account for British successes in the West. Much of the old fur-trading empire was regained during the war, but once more British diplomacy, despite the merchants' insistence upon a new western boundary and the creation of an Indian barrier state, sacrificed the wartime gains in the Treaty of Ghent (1814). Astor's growing dominance in the fur trade was reinforced, while the Montreal traders found their last resource in the North-West threatened by Lord Selkirk's settlements after 1812 in the Red River country and by the expansion of the Hudson's Bay Company, which absorbed the North-West Company in 1821.

The War of 1812 weakened the British loyalty of the English in Quebec, while the French Canadians demonstrated much greater loyalty than they had shown in 1775. A new Canadian loyalty was beginning to spring up among both groups, who had fought together to repel invasion and whose doubts about the other had been dispelled by common effort. This new Canadianism was to be demonstrated in the years to come by a collaboration of members of both ethnic groups in favor of Canadian self-government and against British misrule.

6

This new spirit did not end the quarrels between the assembly and the executive; it merely altered the alignment of forces. Despite the mild and conciliatory attitude of the new governor, the assembly showed no disposition to forget its past grievances or to alter its intransigent attitude. Sir George Prevost had taken office when Britain, hard pressed on the Continent, was quite willing to make concessions to assure Canadian loyalty in the face of an American war. After a first examination of the situation, he had been struck by the prestige of the clergy in Quebec, and by his predecessor's error in alienating its support. It was at Prevost's request that Bishop Plessis prepared a memorial on the position of the Catholic bishop which served as the basis of the British government's grant of official recognition and support.[88] Prevost also attempted to conciliate the popular party by restoring to Pierre Bédard and Joseph Borgia the militia commissions which Craig had withdrawn as a penalty for their share in the publication of *Le Canadien*. A few months later he elevated Bédard to the bench. The francophobe Ryland was dismissed from his post as secretary to the governor; the executive council was given seven new members, of whom four were French Canadians; and several French Canadians were added to the legislative council.

Despite these conciliatory overtures, the assembly could not forget its past grievances. Though it gave the governor's war measures the fullest support in 1812, nevertheless it had formed a committee, composed of Bédard, Viger, Lee, Joseph Papineau, and his son Louis-Joseph Papineau among others, to enquire into the state of the province, the events of Craig's administration, and their causes. Nothing came of this move, which nonetheless indicated the unwillingness of the assembly to let bygones be bygones. The popular party also clashed with the legislative council over two war-time security measures, which consequently failed; and in 1813 it refused to grant the extended powers of martial law which the governor had specifically requested.

The most notable action of the assembly was its attempt to impeach its ancient Loyalist enemies, Chief Justice Sewell and his colleague Judge Monk. The instigator of this measure was James Stuart, a Nova Scotian Loyalist, who had been deprived of the attorney-generalship in 1809, as a result of his difficulties with Craig. He had seen Sewell's brother named to replace him, and doubtless personal feeling entered into his attack on the chief justice for his activities as adviser to Craig during the 'Reign of Terror.' Stuart acted as head of the popular party in the assembly, and thus for the first time in Canadian history was seen the spectacle of a man of one ethnic group leading a party dominated by the other. The governor refused to suspend the judges until the assembly's 'Heads of Impeachment,'[89] on which the legislative council had not been consulted and in which they did not concur, had been considered at London. As a result Prevost was promptly accused of violating the constitutional rights of the assembly; and then, after the legislators had had four days to cool off, was given a vote of confidence. The colonial secretary, Bathurst, disapproved of the action of the assembly, which involved the new principle of ministerial responsibility in a colonial government, while in 1815 the Privy Council handed down a judgment favorable to Sewell, who had gone to London to plead his case. Meanwhile the assembly's attempt to send Stuart to England to support its charges had been blocked by the refusal of the legislative council to approve a vote of funds for this purpose. The council had also rejected the proposal of the assembly to send Judge Bédard to London to act as agent of the province. The old deadlock between the two houses of the legislature thus continued, despite Prevost's efforts to reconcile them.

This feud resulted in the refusal of the legislative council, despite Prevost's approval, to pass the assembly's bill for the establishment of parish schools under local control. The Royal Institution had remained virtually a dead letter, thanks to the unanimous opposition of the French Canadians, but its supporters in the council were opposed to this encroachment upon its domain. Ryland considered the assembly's bill nothing short of 'a most effectual means for insurrection and revolution.'[90] The council still included Sewell, Bishop Mountain, Monk, Ryland, and others of the old Chateau Clique, who showed little inclination to adapt themselves to the new regime of conciliation. In self-protection the council also rejected the attempts of the assembly to declare judges ineligible to sit in the upper house, and to place a heavy tax on the revenues of civil office and on pensions.

In proroguing the session of 1814, Prevost deplored such domestic strife while the country was at war, but in his dispatches to London he said of the assembly that he had 'no reason to distrust their loyalty or attachment to His Majesty's Person and Government.'[91] Prevost was a realist: he saw that the English party was too weak to serve as a support to the government, and that consequently the good-will of the Canadians must be gained by taking into account their interests and claims. He believed that one solution of the recent difficulties was to admit Canadians to the offices which had hitherto been reserved to Englishmen: the leaders of the assembly were 'principally lawyers, who as it appears to me are merely seeking an opportunity to distinguish themselves as the Champions of the Public for the purpose of gaining popularity, and who are endeavouring to make themselves of consequence in the eyes of Government, in the hope of obtaining employment from it—some of them held Offices confered upon them by myself and all of them I have reason to think, was it necessary to purchase their Services, would be willing to barter them.'[92]

Unfortunately this governor who knew how to rule with moderation and by a judicious distribution of favors was called home in 1815 to answer charges based upon his exceedingly cautious military conduct during the War of 1812. The Chateau Clique used these charges to undermine Prevost's position in Canada, and he finished his term of office under a cloud which was never wholly cleared, since he died before his case was heard. He was temporarily replaced by the fire-eater Sir Gordon Drummond, who announced the Privy Council's decision in favor of Sewell to the assembly when it met in 1816, and promptly dissolved that body when it protested against the judgment. But the well-worn remedy of dissolution worked no cure of the ills of the body politic; the party of Stuart and his ally Louis-Joseph Papineau was returned in greater force; and when the new governor, Sir John Sherbrooke, arrived in July 1816 to take over from Drummond, he found a full-fledged political crisis raging. The placemen, cheered by Sewell's victory and the recall of Prevost, had celebrated the chief justice's return in triumph with a twenty-gun salute, an incident which had strengthened the popular party's conviction that the government was its enemy.

Sherbrooke, like Prevost, saw that continual dissolutions were no solution of the difficulty, and he was not inclined to follow the course suggested by Bathurst of governing without an assembly, although this was feasible, since the executive was not financially dependent upon that body. He reported to London that Sewell was anathema to all classes of the population and should have been induced to resign. But since the government had decided to re-instate him, a measure which would alienate popular support and prevent any harmonious development of the province, Sherbrooke proposed that the colony be given an agent at London to voice its grievances, and that Stuart be detached from the French party by the gift of office. As time went on Sherbrooke took other conciliatory measures which did much to reduce popular opposition to the executive: he named Bishop Plessis to the legislative council, and proposed that Louis-Joseph Papineau be added to the executive council. It was clear to him that 'the great evil of this country and the one most fruitful of discussions has been the lack of confidence in the executive government, not so far as regards the character of the governor but rather as regards the council, which has come to be considered as his adviser, and whose actions are regarded with a jealous suspicion which tends to hamstring all acts of government.'[93] Sherbrooke's policy was to win the confidence of the French Canadians and to reconcile them to the government by giving them a share in its responsibilities.

But neither Sherbrooke nor any governor until after 1840 was willing to let the prerogative of the Crown yield to the growing power of the assembly. Thus, when goodwill was lacking on the part of the governor and moderation on that of the assembly, the inevitable conflict of the two competing powers became acute. The Constitution of 1791 had established representative government with an irresponsible executive. It had left undefined the respective spheres of the British and provincial parliaments, thus providing two sources of friction between the Crown and the assembly. Then, as the Crown lost its financial independence based upon the Quebec Revenue Act of 1774 and became dependent upon votes of supply, the lines of conflict between the two powers became sharply defined.

7

Such was in brief the basis of the constitutional battles which culminated in rebellion in 1837. After the failure of Receiver-General Henry Caldwell, who in 1819 was found to be £97,000 short in his accounts, the chief issue was whether or not the government should be completely dependent upon the assembly for financial support.

The popular party was led by Louis-Joseph Papineau, son of the Montreal notary who had fought for the use of French in the first assembly in 1792, and who had carried dispatches for Carleton through the American lines in 1775–6. The younger Papineau, born in 1786 and educated at the Seminary of Quebec, became a lawyer after studying in D.-B. Viger's office, but he entered the assembly in 1808 and soon devoted his energies to politics. He early took a leading role, succeeding Panet in 1815 as speaker, a post which he held for the greater part of the next twenty years. Even as a small boy at the seminary he had revealed an oratorical talent which eclipsed that of his father, who was regarded, along with Pierre Bédard, as one of the most eloquent French-Canadian spokesmen of the day. This talent was developed by Papineau's wide reading, as was the natural independence of mind which made him one of the small group of members of the assembly who secretly met in 1812 to consider whether it might not be best to remain neutral in the coming conflict, and to let the British defend themselves from an American invasion. This course having been opposed by Bédard, Papineau cheerfully served as a militia staff captain during the three years of war. After his election as speaker, Papineau took no great part in party politics until 1820, but engaged in a study of history and constitutional law which later stood him in good stead.

The ideas of Papineau at the real beginning of his political career in that year are reflected in his eulogy on the death of George III, in which he compared 'the happy situation in which we find ourselves today with that of our ancestors when George III became their lawful monarch':

George III, a sovereign respected for his moral qualities and his devotion to his duties, succeeded Louis XV, a prince justly despised for his debauches, for his lack of attention to the needs of the people, and for his senseless prodigality to his favorites and mistresses. Since that epoch the reign of law has succeeded to that of violence; since that day the treasure, the fleet, and the armies of Great Britain have been employed to provide us with an effective protection against all foreign danger; since that day her best laws have become ours, while our faith, our property, and the laws by which they were governed have been conserved; soon afterwards the privileges of her free constitution were granted us, infallible guarantees of our domestic prosperity if it is observed. Now religious tolerance; trial by jury, the wisest guarantee which has ever been established for the protection of innocence; security against arbitrary imprisonment, thanks to the privilege of the *habeas corpus*; equal protection guaranteed by law to the person, honor, and property of citizens; the right to obey only laws made by us and adopted by our representatives—all these advantages have become our birthright, and will be, I hope, the lasting heritage of our posterity. In order to conserve them, we should act like British subjects and free men.[94]

It was this same insistence upon the rights of British subjects and free men which sent Papineau into exile with a price on his head within twenty years' time. The long battle over the right of the assembly to control the province's finances, a right essential to any real form of self-government and of representative institutions, began a few months after this patriotic utterance, with the coming of the arbitrary Lord Dalhousie, a governor whose name was to become associated in the French-Canadian mind with the hateful memory of Sir James Craig, despite the former's efforts to unite the two ethnic groups by founding the Literary and Historical Society of Quebec in 1824 and by setting up a joint monument to Wolfe and Montcalm at Quebec in 1827.[95]

Meanwhile the insistence of both the Lower and Upper Canadian assemblies on holding the purse-strings, and the quarrel between the two provinces over the division of import duties, seemed to offer to some minds an opportunity to settle both difficulties by a single measure, the reunion of Upper and Lower Canada into a single province—a measure often later revived and finally adopted in 1840. Thus the obstinate French-Canadian majority could be turned into a minority, and the financial difficulties of the young upper province could be assumed by the prosperous older one. This measure was favoured by the British ministers, weary of endless complaints from Canada; by the governing class in the colony, which saw its privileged position threatened by the rising power of the assembly; and by the Montreal merchants, who hoped thus to restore the commercial unity of the St. Lawrence system. They had long advocated the union of the Canadas, but now their pleas took on new force as the threat of the Hudson River system to its ancient rival became more acute with the completion of the Champlain Canal in 1822, which reversed the profitable Richelieu trade, and with the steady progress of the Erie Canal, which threatened to tap the commerce of the Great Lakes at the expense of the St.

Corpus Christi Procession at Quebec, 1821

Oil painting by Louis-Hubert Triand, professor of painting at the Ursuline Convent.
This painting, still in the possession of the Quebec Ursulines, shows the Cathedral at
the left, the old Jesuit College on the right, and the ancient houses on Buade Street
(many of which are still standing) in the center. The spire of the Anglican Cathedral,
built after Wren's plans by the Royal Engineers, towers in the background.
(I.O.A.P.Q.)

Cathedral and Market Place, Quebec

Crono-lithograph (1832) by C. Hullmandel after a drawing by W. Walton from a
sketch of Robert Sproule. Another view of the same scene from the Jesuit College.
(I.O.A.P.Q.)

Nicolet Seminary

Built 1827-32 by Jean-Baptiste Hébert from the plans of the Abbé Jérôme Demers. This building, the handsomest example of institutional architecture in the Province, shows a perfect fusing of the French and British traditions. (I.O.A.P.Q.)

Lawrence system. While the growing commercial power of the United States thus threatened them at home, the merchants saw England begin to shift from mercantilism to free trade. The preferential timber duties were reduced in 1822, and the Reformer Huskisson was already well on his way to the presidency of the Board of Trade.

The merchants felt the necessity of immediate planning, revolutionary legislation, and vast public expenditures to enable the St. Lawrence system to survive this double threat; and yet they found themselves at the mercy of a legislature which was anti-commercial and utterly unmoved by their pleas for action. The governor alone was sympathetic to the merchants, for Dalhousie saw that Montreal was the logical center of the new commercial system: 'It is the heart of the country, and from it circulates the lifeblood of Canada.'[96] Yet Quebec remained the administrative center, and as always viewed its rival with suspicion and was jealous of its own power and prestige. The *Montreal Gazette* bitterly protested that 'Quebec affords an example of centralization of Military, Civil, Financial, Clerical, Commercial, and Marine power, worthy of the policy of the late Napoleon Bonaparte.'[97] Thus hampered at home, the merchants turned to London, where they had a friend at court in the person of Edward Ellice, son of one of the great Montreal merchants and son-in-law of Lord Grey, head of the Whig Party. Ellice was at once *seigneur* of Beauharnois near Môntreal and a member of the British parliament; his friends were the leaders of the Montreal merchants, Richardson, Grant, and Molson. He brought their views to the ear of the ministers, and all but achieved the union of the Canadas which they so ardently desired.

Ellice's advocacy was supported by Judge Monk and Attorney-General Marshall, who found themselves in London to give advice on the question of customs duties; but the Attorney-General of Upper Canada, John Beverley Robinson, opposed the project of union in a memorandum which checked the growing resolution of the ministers in favor of union. He gave London the first statement of a new Canadianism, which was not dependent upon the ethnic background of its adherents:

The French habitants of Lower Canada, I am firmly convinced, are as peaceably disposed, as submissive to authority, and as loyally attached to the British government as any portion of His Majesty's subjects; and whatever be the embarrassment that their representatives can cause in refusing to provide in a permanent manner for the civil list, or on the questions of revenues or other matters, whatever they may be, between them and the executive power, it must not be attributed to the preponderance of French influence on the English, but to the desire which all popular assemblies display to affirm and to exercise as much as possible the segment of power which they believe granted to them by the constitution, and even to extend it, a disposition from which more inconveniences can be expected according to the degree of democracy of such a body. And I believe that the descendants of Englishmen, Irishmen, and Scots will be more inclined to persevere in such a course than the descendants of Frenchmen. If then the idea that the united legislature will be more reasonable on this score than the present legislature of Lower Canada seems perforce to render a union desirable, I do not believe that the result would justify the attempt.[98]

Robinson saw very clearly into the future, anticipating the collaboration of William Lyon Mackenzie with Papineau and of Robert Baldwin with Lafontaine in the achievement of responsible government for Canada—the natural outgrowth of the grant of representative institutions in 1791. But London was not yet ready to accept this development, and after receiving Robinson's opinion, which also sharply separated commercial matters from the project of political union, the government merely wavered in its resolution to join the two in a single bill. It was won back to its original intention by Ellice, and a bill 'to make more effective provision for the government of the provinces of Lower and Upper Canada, to regulate the trade thereof and for other purposes'[99] was consequently brought into the House of Commons in June 1822.

But there was also an anti-unionist group in parliament, whose spokesman was Sir James Mackintosh, a noted lawyer and social thinker and the chief orator of the opposition. When the bill was brought in, he protested against the introduction, at so late a stage in the session, of a measure which affected the most sacred rights of the Canadians, and declared his opposition to the project of union until the will of the people of Canada had been consulted. He was supported by Henry Bright, who objected to the injustice of a bill which had 'for its object to destroy the influence of Lower Canada and to give a certain superiority to the Protestant population over the Catholic population.'[100] Bright raised a telling question which served to generalize the debate: ' If Canada is deprived of its legislature, what security will the other English colonies have?' In the face of this opposition, the government cut the bill in two; the commercial provisions were passed as the Canada Trade Act, while the project of union failed of reconsideration before the end of the session. The Union Bill provided for a single legislative council and assembly, to be composed of the present members in both provinces. The power of naming new members to the legislative council was reserved to the governor, while the representation of Upper Canada in the assembly was increased from twenty-five to forty—that of Lower Canada remaining fifty—and the governor was authorized to erect new electoral districts in the Eastern Townships. The total future representation of either province was limited to sixty, and could not be altered without a two-thirds vote of both council and assembly. A property qualification of £500 was required of members. Four members of the executive council were to have the right to all the privileges of the assembly except that of voting. All records were to be kept in English, and after fifteen years English was to be the sole language of debate. *Curés* were to be named only with the consent of the governor.

Quite naturally, when news of this bill reached Quebec in September 1822, a tempest arose. The *Quebec Gazette*, the *Spectateur Canadien*, and the *Gazette Canadien* alike warned the people against this threat to their institutions, laws, and language. Public meetings were held at Montreal, where Denis-Benjamin Viger denounced the bill and its injustices. A committee of eighteen notable citizens drawn from both the bureaucratic and popular parties was formed, including Louis Guy, Charles de Saint-Ours, P.-D. Debartzch, L.-R. Chaussegros de Léry, C.-M. de Salaberry, L.-J. Papineau, Viger, Joseph Bédard, Augustin Cuvillier, and Louis Bourdages. Similar protest meetings were held at Quebec, where the committee included L.-A. de Salaberry, J.-F. Perrault, L.-J. Duchesnay, I.-A. de Gaspé, F.-J.-P. Taschereau, Andrew Stuart, John Neilson, and F.-X. Blanchet. French Canadians and Britishers joined forces to oppose the union; the leaders of the protest movement included members of the legislative council and of the assembly, office-holders and leading spirits of the opposition, merchants and *seigneurs*, doctors and lawyers. The unionists also held a meeting in Montreal under the chairmanship of John Richardson, at which James Stuart, now won over to the cause of the oligarchy by the promise of office, maintained that any objections to the scheme were founded on prejudices which must be stamped out, or on local interests which should not enter into the question. To which the *Spectateur Canadien* replied: 'As if the language, laws, and institutions of a people could be considered mere prejudices; as if the particular interests of a country could be counted for naught in that very country!'[101] The two anti-unionist committees adopted a joint resolution of protest to London against any change in the established form of government. This was backed by a petition to the same effect signed by 60,000 individuals; and early in 1823 Papineau and John Neilson were sent to London by the committees to convey the petition to the ministers and Parliament. Thus began Papineau's partnership with Neilson, the first major collaboration of Canadians of different ethnic backgrounds in the common interest.

Neilson had come to Canada in 1790 from Scotland, imbued with radical Whig sympathies, and after seven years' apprenticeship on the newspaper founded by his uncle and inherited by his brother, became editor and proprietor of the *Quebec Gazette* in 1796, after weathering the witch-hunt of 1794 in New York. He combined the publication of this semi-official organ with bookselling, among his wares being the works of the French classical and romantic writers. He was elected to the assembly in 1818, where he sat until 1834. As a legislator he took a special interest in educational, agricultural, and land-grant questions, and soon espoused the cause of the popular party. In 1822 Dalhousie objected to the reflection of these views in the *Gazette*, and decided to found an official journal. Already faced with the competition of the *Mercury*, the organ of the English party, and of *Le Canadien*, that of the popular party, Neilson turned over the business management of the *Gazette* to his son Samuel, the King's Printer, and William Cowan; while the paper was edited by the Reverend John Charleton Fisher, who later composed the inscription for the Wolfe-Montcalm monument. But this compromise did not satisfy the governor, who set up a new *Gazette*, 'published by authority,' which was under the sole control of Fisher, and which lasted for several years.

This blow at Neilson's livelihood no doubt helped to throw him completely into the arms of the popular party, and he soon joined forces with Papineau, Bédard, and Viger. Neilson was a strong supporter of the Constitution of 1791; and in writing to Papineau on June 22, 1822 to warn him of the ministers' determination to revoke it, he remarked: 'This is a case of the only lamb of the poor man, which is seized by the rich man to add to the luxury of his feast. What fate have the inhabitants of this country to hope for from people who proceed in such fashion?'[102] He added his opinion that union would lead to annexation. The two men exchanged many letters before their departure for London in January 1823, and a still greater intimacy grew up between them during their mission. After their return Papineau paid his new friend this tribute: 'I know no one who has a greater right than you to the regard of my country, nor no one whom I esteem more than you.'[103]

When the two commissioners arrived in England, they sought out Wilmot Horton, under-secretary for the colonies, and Sir James Mackintosh, whom Papineau had mentioned to Neilson as a suitable London agent for Lower Canada as early as 1821. Mackintosh assured them that there was little likelihood of the government bringing in the union measure during the current session. At the request of the colonial secretary, Neilson, with Papineau's aid, drafted a memorandum which Garneau calls 'one of our best state papers.'[104] The commissioners pointed out at the outset of this document that only a small minority favored union, while the petition they bore carried the protests of seven-tenths of the adult population. The measure was open to objection on the grounds that it was impossible to set a common and convenient meeting place for two vast provinces whose joint extent was 1,500 miles and which even had different climates. The laws, customs, usages, religions, and dominant prejudices of the two regions were dissimilar, and each section was firmly attached to its own ways. The economic interests of the two provinces were actually opposed. There would be no saving brought by the measure, since the expenses of government would be increased by the difficulties of communication and transportation. In the matter of representation the bill unjustly favored Upper Canada, which would have more than twice Lower Canada's in proportion to population, while the latter province had five times as many inhabitants as Upper Canada.

On the language question the commissioners made this noteworthy observation:

The common usage of two languages is embarrassing, but in many cases it is inevitable. It was thus in England after the Norman conquest, and the ill-advised measure of that barbarous epoch which proscribed the Saxon tongue suffered a deserved fate. The language of the majority of a nation whose elements have close mutual relations always ends by prevailing. The English language will inevitably become the dominant language in North America, with or without measures of law. There are probably not ten members of the present House of Assembly of Lower Canada who do not understand English; several speak it easily; and no citizen of the province having means or some notable situation neglects to have his children taught English. It is thus that things change with time and yield to circumstances. But the language of a father or mother, of family or friends, of first impressions and first memories, is dear to all. And this unjustified proscription of the language of the Canadian people has been violently resented in a country where this tongue did much to save the colony for Great Britain at the time of the American Revolution.[105]

The commissioners also pointed out that the article relating to the nomination of *curés* was an assault on the liberties which had been guaranteed to Catholics ever since the conquest. Such a measure, with its violations of the rights of the clergy as recognized even in English law, 'could not fail to arouse public opinion in Canada, and if ever applied, would inevitably cause those unfortunate differences between Catholics and Protestants which have desolated other countries and from which Canada has been so happily free under the benevolent and enlightened rule of His Majesty.' The commissioners concluded by urging that if the government was nevertheless determined to push through the bill, it should first order a complete census of both provinces, and authorize the governor to recommend to the legislature the appointment of one or more agents of the province, who could plead at London the case for the maintenance of the present constitution.

After submitting this memorandum, Neilson returned home, while Papineau remained in London until the end of the session, to guard against the surprise attack which Ellice threatened. The two rival spokesmen maintained social relations, however, and it was at Ellice's house that Papineau succeeded in winning over to his views Sir Francis Burdett, a noted Whig who felt his party would be compromised if it overrode the will of the Canadian majority by supporting the bill.

While the question of union was thus being argued in London, there was a lull in the conflict in Canada. But in 1824 it broke out once more, when the government found itself with an empty treasury, thanks to Receiver-General Caldwell's failure to make up the deficit in his accounts, and thus became dependent upon the assembly for a vote of funds. Papineau, who supported the Canada Trade Act when that piece of imperial legislation was attacked in the assembly on the grounds that British subjects could not be taxed without their consent, refused to support the vote of funds which the government demanded; and when the measure was nevertheless carried, he demanded that the salaries of officials be reduced by 25 per cent. On this last point he parted company with Neilson, whose deliberate calm often arrived at different conclusions from Papineau's passionate ardor. Believing that Canada was 'menaced by new injustices . . . on the part of the authorities in England,'[106] Papineau became more insistent on the appointment of Sir James Mackintosh as London agent of the colony, and on the necessity of making an alliance with 'the honest folk of Upper Canada to get from them more extensive information than we have and to encourage them to persist in their righteous resolutions.'[107] For William Lyon Mackenzie and the Reformers of Upper Canada were waging the same sort of constitutional warfare against the Family Compact of York as the followers of Papineau were engaged in against the Chateau Clique in Lower Canada.

In Lower Canada the conflict between the executive and the assembly had now clearly defined the issues: the government demanded a vote of the civil list for the life of the sovereign and control of the Crown revenue, while the assembly was only willing to approve the civil list annually and claimed the right to control the whole revenue. During the absence of Dalhousie in 1825 a clash was averted on this matter, for the administrator, Sir Francis Burton, agreed to the views of the assembly on the budget; but Burton's action was censured by the colonial secretary and repudiated by Dalhousie upon his return. There was a head-on collision between the executive and the assembly on this score in 1826; and when the assembly persisted in its stand the following year, Dalhousie promptly prorogued the legislature with a sharp speech to the effect that 'nothing likely to promote the public interest can now be expected from your deliberations.'[108] Papineau and six followers censured this address in a manifesto marked by violent indignation—he had already described Dalhousie's administration to Neilson as that of 'birds of prey and passage, who call enriching themselves governing us'[109]—and the elections which followed were stormy. At the beginning of the new session Dalhousie refused to accept Papineau as speaker of the assembly; and when that body persisted in its choice, he dissolved it two days after it had met. Parliamentary government was virtually paralyzed, and popular indignation was so strong that there was no difficulty in getting 87,000 'signatures'—of which 78,000 were marks, which led the bureaucrats to refer scornfully to the popular party as 'Knights of the Cross'—on a new petition to London for the redress of Canadian grievances. In January 1828 Neilson, Viger, and Cuvillier took ship for England with this document,[110] while at the same time 10,000 inhabitants of the Townships forwarded another petition which complained of their particular wrongs.[111]

Before Neilson's departure Papineau wrote him a letter which reveals the strength of their friendship and his own bitter disillusionment with the form of government which he had eulogized six years before:

So many private losses, so many public difficulties render wretched the state of our society. You are worth much more than me, for you have the same sensitiveness as I have, and the strength that I have not. There is no one that I like to see as much as you; more than once you have stiffened my weakening courage. The loss of my friends makes me melancholy to the extent that I am nearly reduced to a complete and stupid inaction, which is my wretched dominating inclination. The injustice done to my country destroys me and agitates me to such a degree that I am not always capable of taking counsel only of an enlightened patriotism, but rather of anger and hatred against its oppressors. . . . The descendants of the French have no right to equal rights with their masters of British origin. Some political arrangement must be found by which the privileged minority may govern the majority without being disturbed by the latter's complaints. . . . The history of no other colony presents a similar spectacle of immorality.

It is odious that when the laws do not exclude the Canadians from office, that practice should exclude them. They furnish nine-tenths of the revenue and receive barely one-tenth. Influence with the country is a title to persecution both for Europeans and natives. You are a European and persecuted because you have the regard of the country.[112]

Here Papineau in his discouragement reveals the temperamental instability which explains much of his later career, and which finally brought about his break with Neilson, after twelve years of close collaboration. He also shows a North American outlook reminiscent of that of the American revolutionary leaders, reacting against English misgovernment.

A new ministry headed by the Duke of Wellington had just taken office in England, and the colonial secretary to whom the delegates carried their complaints was William Huskisson, the Tory Reformer who made himself notable by supporting free trade and Catholic emancipation. After hearing the delegates and consulting with his colleagues, he suggested the appointment of a committee of the House of Commons to enquire into the state of the government of Canada. In proposing this motion, Huskisson singled out the financial question, calling for the establishment of a system 'which would give the Assembly the power to determine the application of all funds for the internal improvement of the province, and at the same time withdraw from its authority that which might be called the civil list.'[113] He found that the system desired by the assembly was 'not compatible with the independence and dignity of the representative of the Crown or of the judges.' In a debate marked by speeches by Sir James Mackintosh, Henry Labouchere, Wilmot Horton, Lord Stanley, and Joseph Hume, the motion was adopted.

The committee was made up of Huskisson, Wilmot Horton, Mackintosh, Labouchere, and seventeen other members. It sat for two months and heard the testimony of Neilson, Viger, Cuvillier, Samuel Gale, Ellice, Simon McGillivray, Wilmot Horton, and James Stephen. Neilson attacked the legislative council and demonstrated that eighteen of its twenty-seven members had accumulated so many offices that they annually divided $88,000 of the public revenue amongst themselves. Viger dealt with the judiciary, pointing out that only three of eleven judges, in a province composed of 400,000 French Canadians and 80,000 English, were French-speaking. He also arraigned the English judges as tools of a political faction, who did its work in the legislative and executive councils, thus at once making laws, ordering their enforcement, and rendering decisions on their observance or non-observance. Cuvillier dealt with financial matters, exposing the irregularities of the past. On the other hand Samuel Gale, the representative of the Eastern Townships, urged that English courts be established in his district, that English tenure be permitted in practice as it was in law, that the Townships be given representation in the assembly, and that English immigration no longer be discouraged. Gale, like Ellice and the old Montreal fur trader McGillivray, favored a legislative union of Upper and Lower Canada. These representatives of the commercial class also reviewed once more all the arguments against the French system of tenure and of law in general, and against duties on the trade between the United States and Canada. They called for the annexation of Montreal, the commercial capital, to Upper Canada, if the two Canadas were not united; and demanded the ascendency of British views and 'security for British capital.'[114] Huskisson and Wilmot Horton were won over to some extent to the views of the popular party during the proceedings, and the committee's report was regarded by Neilson, Viger, and Cuvillier as 'decidedly favorable to the desires of the petitioners,'[115] as they wrote home in triumph on July 22, 1828, the day it was made.

The report[116] recommended that representation should be based on territory as well as population, so that the Townships should have an equitable share in provincial affairs. It also favored the establishment of land registry and transfer offices in that region. As a remedy to the practice of conceding lands to officials who did not improve their nominal holdings, it recommended a tax on lands neither improved nor settled. It gave handsome recognition to French-Canadian rights:

> The committee cannot too strongly express its opinion that the Canadians of French extraction should be as little troubled as possible in their peaceful enjoyment of their religion, laws and privileges, as guaranteed by acts of the British Parliament, and far from demanding of them that they hold their lands according to English tenure, it is of the opinion that when the seigneurial lands shall be filled up, if the descendants of the first settlers still prefer the tenure *en fief et seigneurie*, it sees no objection against other portions of uninhabited lands in the province being granted to them in this latter tenure, provided that these lands be separated from the Townships and not contained therein.[117]

Most notably, the committee recommended that the receipt and outlay of the public revenue be put under the control of the assembly. Nevertheless it urged that the salaries of the governor, executive councilors, and judges be permanently assured and not left dependent upon an annual vote of funds. But all judges except the chief justice should be barred from the councils, while the majority of the legislative council was not to be dependent upon the executive for other offices. It recommended precautions against such financial disasters as the Caldwell failure, and suggested that the revenues of the Jesuit Estates be applied to education. The document's appearance coincided with the recall of Dalhousie, who was replaced by Sir James Kempt. The new governor promptly accepted Papineau as speaker of the assembly. The long drawn-out crisis was ended for the time being, with a virtual victory for the popular party.

8

During the two years of his administration Sir James Kempt played the role of conciliator with such success that the period was one of political truce. Without renouncing its claim to financial control, the assembly passed revenue bills which were acceptable to the legislative council. The electoral districts were redivided, and the Townships were given eight representatives. Despite the wails of the merchants, representatives of the English-speaking population, which was only one-sixth of the total, made up one-quarter of the assembly. The promised land offices were established in the Townships. But contention was not wholly dead: the assembly expelled Robert Christie, a Gaspé merchant, for contempt. He was four times re-elected, and four times re-expelled, to the detriment of his sympathy with the popular party in the *History of the Late Province of Lower Canada* which he later compiled. Kempt appointed leading members of the popular party, including Viger, Louis Guy, and de Beaujeu, to the legislative council, and even proposed that Papineau and Neilson should be added to the executive council. He was conscious, as he put it, that he was sitting on a barrel of gunpowder,[118] and he proceeded warily.

In the fall of 1830 Kempt was replaced by Lord Aylmer, who had been instructed by Goderich, the new colonial secretary, to follow a policy of conciliating the popular leaders. Aylmer named Papineau and Neilson to the executive council, but they refused office on the grounds that the regulations of the assembly did not permit them to accept a Crown appointment. A year later Aylmer included eight French Canadians among his eleven nominees to the legislative council. Reform was clearly in the saddle at Quebec as well as at London. In 1831 Aylmer offered the British government's solution of the financial question: it would renounce control of the revenue to the assembly in exchange for a permanent civil list covering the salaries of the governor and judges and certain pensions. The assembly refused this proposal, maintaining that it did not conform to the recommendation of the Commons Report of 1828, thus displaying the 'petty and spiteful spirit,'[119] which, along with a failure to exploit its successes, was to lead to disaster rather than to the responsible government it sought. John Neilson then proposed a moderate set of resolutions on Canadian grievances, which was passed after sharp attacks from the extremists.

From this time onward the popular party was divided into two groups, one headed by Neilson and the other by Papineau. The divergence of opinion between the two men was of some years' standing; Papineau defined it in a letter to Neilson on November 14, 1830:

You are disposed to believe that the government can be pushed into the right path and will follow it passably well; I am disposed to believe that it goes from bad to worse. You complain loudly of the men who have led it; *ab hoc et ab hac* you are right: you have drawn on the public, which still keeps on when you wish to stop yourself. You believe that debased men are no longer dangerous; that they will govern well because they no longer dare to do evil. The majority does not see that. It sees flagrant abuses which have not all been corrected, while their unpunished authors preserve the same principles as before, that is to say, the absence of all principle, indifference to the public welfare, the same ardor for conserving in their odious coterie the accumulation of offices which they have monopolized, the same means of vengeance that they have so unscrupulously employed, the same certainty of impunity so long as their phalanx is not broken. I cannot desist. The country is still the prey of determined and dangerous enemies, and the English ministry is more disposed to sustain them than to guide itself by the rules of justice towards us.

. . . [I am convinced] that it is essential to the peace and good government of the province that its constitution be amended by suppressing the present Legislative Council and replacing it with an elective Council, in which each county will have a member.

That the courts of justice, badly constituted and not enjoying the least respect or public confidence, could not be reformed in the interest of the citizen while the judges controlled the Council and could not consent to increase their work and responsibility.

That the ungranted lands ought to be put under such regulations as the Legislature will adopt, and that the Jesuit Estates ought to be put at its disposition to aide the general education of the province. That we must not proceed to any other measure until these grievances have been satisfied, and request a prorogation of several months to await the response to the representations made to the King and to Parliament.[120]

Again, on May 11, 1831, Papineau playfully rallied his friend on his tendency to accept the conciliatory gestures of the government at their face value:

Cherrier tells me that you are to come in some weeks to see your Montreal friends. You have as much need as any other to see the wolves* in order not to forget how to howl. You are becoming too confiding, and too disposed to pardon the wrongs of the public and to forget the past. If it were from charity, nothing could be more edifying, but if it is weariness of fighting or confidence that the placemen here begin to wish to reform and to think of their salvation, it is a mistake. May God keep you in the holy resolution to come and see your Montreal friends.[121]

But the split between the two was not to be healed, despite Papineau's effort to remind his friend that he had always been 'tout bon canadien,'[122] for Neilson was a moderate by nature and Papineau an extremist, and each attracted the support of the likeminded among the popular party.

In July 1831 Aylmer communicated to the assembly a long dispatch[123] from Goderich which offered remedies for the minor grievances contained in Neilson's resolutions and proposed to renounce control of the revenue in exchange for a civil list covering

---

* The Montrealers were popularly known as 'wolves,' Quebeckers as 'lambs.'

the salaries of the governor, his secretary, the provincial secretary, the attorney-general, and the solicitor-general. The assembly, grown somewhat overbearing with success, refused this virtual surrender to its demands since 1818. It also resumed its old quarrel with the legislative council over a motion of Bourdages, which would have put the temporal possessions of the Church under the control of democratic parish councils—in effect, miniature local parliaments. This motion was carried in the assembly by Papineau's group over the opposition of Neilson's; but it was defeated, to the great joy of the clergy, in the legislative council at the instance of Sewell, who remarked: 'In destroying the discipline of the Church, one strikes at religion itself.'[124] Thus a militant anti-French Protestant gratified the Catholic clergy by opposing a bill supported by the French-Canadian majority. Such opposition explained in part why Papineau began to develop the anti-clerical attitude which later led to his complete break with the Church; in 1829, apropos of the question of the Seminary's estates, he had remarked to Neilson: 'If priests nevertheless sometimes tell the truth, I have long distrusted them.'[125] As Papineau became more radical in his ideas, he found himself in greater opposition to the clergy, who took their stand beside the other forces of conservatism.[126]

The era of political truce was broken on May 21, 1832 by the deaths of three French Canadians, shot by troops summoned by the magistrates to quell an election riot in Montreal. The commanding officers were arrested, but the indictment against them was quashed by the grand jury. Aylmer expressed to them his pleasure at the verdict, and his disapproval of the popular tumult directed against them. *Le Canadien* observed heatedly: 'Not content with having insulted a generous people, the representative of our sovereign must confirm the assassination of the subjects confided to him by his august master, and must compliment the murderers in a fashion most outrageous and contemptuous to the Canadian people.'[127] At the opening of the session a vote of censure was passed against the governor, and Dominique Mondelet, who had just been appointed by him to the executive council, was expelled from the assembly. The proposal to make the legislative council elective was taken up once more, and Papineau rallied a majority to its support, despite the opposition of his old allies Neilson, Quesnel, and Cuvillier.

The final stage of the struggle between the assembly and the executive now opened, over the issues of an elective council and of control of the revenue. The session adjourned without the adoption of a satisfactory revenue bill, and the government was forced to carry on by the old illegal expedients. For instance, £47,000 of the net revenues of £49,000 of the Jesuit Estates from 1801 to 1831—35 per cent of the receipts having been charged off to 'administrative costs' by the commissioners—were expended for general purposes, including the expenses and pensions of such notables of the Chateau Clique as Sewell and Ryland, while only £12,389 had been devoted to education—and confined, at that, to the anglicizing Royal Institution and to the Royal Grammar Schools of Quebec, Montreal, and Kingston. In 1831 the government finally offered to devote the Jesuit Estates and their revenues to the benefit of the educational budget, which then amounted to only some £3,000, but the offer involved the provision of new barracks in return for renunciation of the old Jesuit College at Quebec. Since this would have absorbed the revenue for several years to come, and in addition set the precedent of contribution to defence in peacetime, the assembly refused the bargain, while education struggled along without adequate support.

Another matter envenomed the relations between the ethnic groups. Immigration, encouraged by the merchants of Montreal in order to people the Upper Canadian wilderness, to provide manpower for the great canal-building projects, and to offset French-Canadian preponderance, had risen steadily since 1825, reaching the figure of 50,254 in 1831. It was encouraged by the ministry in London, as unemployment and distress increased in England, Scotland, and Ireland. The poverty-stricken migrants were packed into the unhealthy holds of the timber ships coming back to Canada, as ballast. After a voyage which was more often than not a battle for survival, they were put ashore at Quebec and Montreal, often penniless and disease-ridden. Many, unable to proceed westward, became public charges; and in 1832 the assembly passed a bill establishing a head tax, to be paid by the captains of the emigrant ships, to offset the financial burden thus imposed. The merchants of Quebec and Montreal bitterly opposed this measure, and they were supported by interested Upper Canadians. Both saw in it an attempt 'to obstruct that influx of Europeans which by increasing the number of English inhabitants, threatens soon to merge the preponderance of the French Canadians in Lower Canada.'[128] There was no doubt something in this view, for the French Canadians, then as now, did not welcome a flood of British immigration which threatened to inundate them and to fill up the lands which they wished to reserve for their own descendents.

The real crisis of the immigration situation came in 1832 with an outbreak of Asiatic cholera, brought by the newcomers, which spread like wildfire along the St. Lawrence and decimated both immigrants and natives. Immigration became, to certain wild French-Canadian eyes, an English conspiracy to wipe them off the face of the earth. Edouard Rodier, a fiery spokesman of the extremist group, proclaimed:

It was not enough to send among us avaricious egotists, without any other spirit of liberty than that which could be bestowed by a simple education at the counter, to enrich themselves at the expense of the Canadians, and then to enslave them;—they must also rid themselves of their beggars and cast them by thousands on our shores; they must send us miserable beings, who, after having partaken of the bread of our children, will subject them to the horrors following upon hunger and misery; they must do still more, they must send us in their train pestilence and death."[129]

Even Neilson editorialized bitterly in the *Quebec Gazette* against immigration, describing its effect as 'similar to the passage of an immense army . . . leaving the inhabitants to take care of and provide for the sick, wounded, and disabled, and bury the dead.'[130] Papineau was confirmed in his melancholy view of the state of affairs as he wrote to Neilson during the height of the epidemic in August:

As for me, I have not had a moment of indisposition. I have great confidence in the merit of my temperament, which makes me indifferent enough about living or dying as a result of the indignation I feel against the policy under which each of our administrations in turn insults and tyrannizes the country. The most wretched of all is that of today. Its fear of the merchants has let it permit the entrance of the plague into the country. Its fear of the military has let it permit the shooting of electors. Its fear of appearing to sympathize with them has assured impunity to their murderers. And all these crimes are the known fruits of the Governor's character, and of the position that he has taken from the outset of allowing himself to be guided by the counsels of the Solicitor. Nine-tenths of the Europeans have applauded the murders of the 21st. It is the most violent condemnation that can possibly be made of our detestable scheme of government. They well know that at their will armed force can be used against the Canadians, but not against them. What means is there to prevent a similar conviction being established in the minds of both populations? The sole means is to extend infinitely more than it has been the system of elections. Only by this arrangement may each consider itself equally protected by law.[131]

The organization in London in 1832 of the British American Land Company, which acquired over half a million acres in the Townships for British immigrants; the growing power of the chartered banks established in 1817 and 1818 by the English merchants; and the division of port revenues between the two provinces were other sources of irritation to the French-Canadian party, which like its counterpart in Upper Canada, grew more violent in its opposition to the oligarchy.

The mounting agitation and unrest came to a head in 1834. At the opening of the session the assembly was in a rebellious mood, and it did not receive in kindly fashion the censures of Stanley, the new colonial secretary, on its past proceedings. Papineau savagely attacked Aylmer, and was attacked in turn by Conrad Augustus Gugy, a great-nephew of Haldimand's aide. The temper of the times is best indicated by the Ninety-Two Resolutions, drafted by Papineau, Augustin-Norbert Morin, and Elzéar Bédard, and introduced in the assembly on February 17 by the latter. This was the manifesto of the popular party, which may well be compared with the declarations of principles which foreshadowed the American and French Revolutions. To the *Patriotes*, as they had begun to call themselves, it seemed that 'Liberty had both feet and one arm in bonds,'[132] and they called for reforms which went far beyond the goals of the English reformers of the day. The Resolutions also reflect a comparison of the British and American systems of government, and contain the first hint of annexationist sentiment in the popular party.

All of Papineau's ideas and all of his passion were evident in the Resolutions,[133] which were carelessly drawn up, repetitious, and of widely varying merit. The first eight were statements of loyalty and a recapitulation of the assembly's struggle for redress of its grievances. The ninth to the fortieth reviewed the arguments of the assembly against an appointive legislative council and in favor of an elective one. The forty-first to fiftieth singled out superior features of the American system of government, and concluded with a vague threat of seeking independence. The fifty-first to fifty-fifth summed up the rights and injustices of the French Canadians. The fifty-sixth to sixty-second dealt with the Canada Tenure Act and demanded its repeal. The sixty-third defended the assembly's expulsion of Christie and Mondelet. The sixty-fourth to seventy-fourth dealt with control of the revenue. The seventy-fifth complained that the French Canadians held only 47 out of 194 public offices, while they formed more than five-sixths of the population. The seventy-sixth to seventy-eighth dealt with judicial matters and grievances on this score. The seventy-ninth to eighty-third asserted the right of the assembly to all the powers, privileges, and immunities of the British Parliament. The eighty-fourth listed sixteen specific grievances not already mentioned. The eighty-fifth and -sixth called for the impeachment of Aylmer. The eighty-seventh and -eighth were declarations of gratitude and confidence to Daniel O'Connell and Joseph Hume for their support of the assembly's petitions in the British parliament. The eighty-ninth called for the formation of committees of correspondence at Montreal and Quebec to keep in touch with Viger, the province's agent at London since 1831, O'Connell and Hume, and likeminded persons in the other colonies, in the interest of concerted resistance to arbitrary oppression. The ninetieth begged Viger to remain at London in the public interest, and the ninety-first declared that the assembly would contract a debt of honor to the committees of correspondence for their expenses. The ninety-second called for the expunging from the record of the governor's message at the opening of the session, which contained Stanley's sharp comments on the assembly's petition in favor of the abolition or the making elective of the legislative council.

Papineau led the debate on the Resolutions, saying: 'We have to inquire if today we have not reached the period in which the first authority of the state should recover the respect it has lost, and in which honor, fortune, liberty, and existence should be assured, or whether we are to reconcile ourselves to see the latter fall to the last degree of abasement and the former rise to excesses.'[134] He attacked the 'vicious and imperfect' Quebec Act, and accused the clergy of being attached to the government because of it. To him it seemed that, neglecting the cause of the people, they had found that measure 'good because it was advantageous.' He traced the whole political history of the French Canadians: the early ignorance of constitutional rights and the struggle of the assembly since 1810 to attain them. He concluded with an indication of how far he had already gone in his own mind: 'It is certain that before long all America is to be republican. Meanwhile, ought a change in our constitution, if necessary, be guided by this consideration; and is it criminal to raise the question?' He summed up the Ninety-Two Resolutions, proclaiming them a bill of rights which must be adopted if French-Canadian liberties were not to perish.

Elzéar Bédard, Bourdages, Sabrevoix de Bleury, George Vanfelson, and young Louis-Hippolyte Lafontaine all made supporting speeches. Neilson led the opposition of the moderate constitutional reformers, who feared that adoption of the Resolutions would block reform. Andrew Stuart pointed out that the grievances were really only those of a small group of professional men, the lay élite, while the masses were unconcerned. During the debate Quesnel and other followers broke with Papineau, but in the end the Ninety-Two Resolutions were adopted by a vote of 56–23, and an address to the British Parliament based upon them was sent to London in care of Morin, who was instructed to aid Viger in urging them upon the British ministry. While dissolving the assembly, Aylmer condemned the Resolutions, but popular agitation in their favor continued. In the elections of 1834 Papineau's followers emerged triumphant, while the opponents of the Resolutions, including Neilson, were defeated.

The English merchants of Quebec and Montreal, already made uneasy by the American financial panic of 1833 and by English attacks on the timber preference, were goaded into complete exasperation by the Ninety-Two Resolutions, which one of them termed 'the most insolent, disloyal, insane, and ridiculous productions that were ever submitted to the consideration of a deliberative body.'[135] They formed constitutional associations in their strongholds of Montreal, Quebec, Sorel, and in the Townships; and they contested the elections in militant fashion, denouncing the disloyalty of the popular party. Papineau countered in kind, suggesting a boycott of British goods and urging a run upon the banks, which were controlled by the merchants: 'The most efficacious and most immediate means which the Canadians have to protect themselves against the fury of their enemies is to attack them in their dearest parts—their pockets—in their strongest entrenchments, the Banks.'[136] In November there were runs on the Quebec Bank and the Bank of Montreal, and an alarmed Tory paper likened Papineau to 'a well-drugged Malay running a-muck.'[137] On November 17, when it became evident that they had lost the election, the Tories met at Tattersall's in Montreal, and protested that they would no longer 'submit to the domination of a party averse to emigration, to commerce, to internal improvements, and to all those interests which may be regarded as British.'[138]

Papineau and his fellow members of the Montreal committee of correspondence, already aroused by the Tory use in the elections of strong-arm squads of Irish canal-diggers, believed that still more violent plans had been made at this meeting, and for the first time they considered the possibility of reform by force rather than by constitutional means. On November 20 the Montreal committee wrote to its Quebec equivalent, which had complained of the Tories' electoral methods:

For the rest, like these last [the English party of Quebec] our adversaries in Montreal have also struck against all which is Canada and part of the liberties of the country; like them they have proclaimed European *ascendancy* by means of exclusion on one hand and terror on the other; like yours, they are going to have dinners whose end is to inflame against the security, the rights, and the very life of the people of the country those of their adepts who attend these gatherings. Today in their assembly at Tattersall's, these projects of oppression and these incendiary doctrines have been laid bare. Among other warmed-over plans discussed was that of a mission to Upper Canada to form among the people of the neighboring province associations of a sort to provide forces for the Montreal party of assassins, both to support the union of the provinces and the dismemberment of this one.
. . . We are so poor, so little organized to repel by force of arms a domination which has become so burdensome to us. Are we ready; are the people ready; are you ready? Should we take so great a responsibility upon ourselves? Have we authority to do so? Do there remain no more means of protection in constitutional legality, giving it all the extension which befits British subjects claiming their rights and free men

living in America? Here are questions to which you, like us, must soon reply.[139]

But the committees of correspondence decided to confine themselves to implementing the Ninety-Two Resolutions, to protesting against the British American Land Company and the whole system of land granting and administration, to achieving an understanding with the popular leaders in Upper Canada and other neighboring colonies on common interests, and to adopting countermeasures against 'the system of industrial and commercial exclusion launched by our adversaries.'[140] Meanwhile the Tory constitutional associations in Montreal and Quebec adopted manifestoes protesting against persecution of other classes by the French Canadians, accusing them of republicanism, and making much of their own imperial loyalty.[141]

Both groups were conscious of the coming crisis, and the tension was not relieved by the sounding of appeals to ethnic solidarity. What had been a conflict of interests and of classes, brought to a head by the ruling class' attempt to repudiate the Constitution of 1791, was showing unmistakeable signs of becoming a war between English and French.

Notes

[1] Garneau, II, 431–2; L. Groulx, *Nos luttes constitutionnelles* (Montreal, 1915), II, 5. Garneau fails to recognize that there were two successive but very different attitudes on the part of British officialdom to the French Revolution. Whig sympathy with the ideals of 1789 and the belief of such men as Grenville that France was no longer to be feared were replaced after the execution of Louis XVI and the outbreak of the Terror by a panicky fear of everything French. The pamphlets published at Quebec by the closely supervised presses of Samuel Neilson and William Vondenvelden reflect this change of attitude, with Arthur Young giving way to the Bishop of Landaff. See M. Casey, *Catalogue of the Pamphlets in the Public Archives of Canada*, I, *1493–1877* (Ottawa, 1931), 109, 119. D. F. Mcquat has recently discovered that young John Neilson, who had high Whig sympathies, found it expedient to flee from Monk's witchhunt at Quebec in September 1794 and did not return from exile on Long Island until May 1795, when he declared that he had had the 'character of a Democrat and thought it prudent to avoid the charge.' PAC: Q 66, 5, Declarations of Aliens, J. Neilson, 30 May 1795; Q 66, 171, Dorchester-Dundas, 23 October 1793.

[2] PAC: Q 69–1, 4, Monk-Dorchester, 21 May 1794.

[3] Chapais, II, 42.

[4] *Ibid.*, 43; R. Christie, *A History of the Late Province of Lower Canada* (Quebec, 1848), I, 124–5; LOC: France, Archives des Affaires Etrangères, Correspondance Politique, Etats-Unis, Vol. 37, Pt. 6, 419–23 *verso*: Mezière-Genet, 12 juin 1793.

[5] Caron, II, 'Les Cantons de l'Est,' 14 n. 2; Christie, I, 116–8. P.-A. de Gaspé, *Mémoires* (Ottawa, 1866) 31, 62–4.

[6] Chapais, II, 43; Caron, II, 14–5. Such tongue-twisters as Buckinghamshire. Northumberland, and Effingham must have troubled the Canadians.

[7] Chapais, II, 45; Langlois, 267, gives the total as 161, 311.

[8] *Quebec Gazette* (20 December 1792); Chapais, II, 51–2.

[9] Shortt & Doughty, *Const. Docs, 1759–1791*, 399; Chartier de Lotbinière, 'Things which must be considered . . .' 1774.

[10] *Quebec Gazette*, 31 January, 14 February, 1793; Chapais, II, 69–70 & Caron, II, 17; N.-E. Dionne, *Pierre Bédard et ses fils* (Québec, 1909), 19–21.

[11] *Journal of the Assembly*, 1793, 167; Chapais, II, 76.

[12] PAC: Q 65, 324; Dundas-Dorchester, 2 October 1793; Chapais, II, 80–1 and *n*.

[13] W. P. M. Kennedy, *Statutes, Treaties and Documents of the Canadian Constitution, 1713–1929* (Oxford, 1930), 212–4; Richardson-Ellice, 16 February 1793.

[14] PAC: Q 63–2, 307; Alured Clark-Dundas, 3 July 1793; Chapais, II, 77–80.

[15] Excerpts in PAC: Q 69–2, 224–6; printed in W. Kingsford, *History of Canada* (Toronto, 1894), VII, 387–9 *n*. The full printed text, dated June 1793, in LOC: France, Archives des Affaires Etrangères, Correspondence Politique, Etats-Unis, XXXVII, 439–442 *verso*.

[16] PAC: Q 69–1, 4–25, Monk-Dundas, 29 May 1794; Chapais, II, 114.

[17] Chilton Williamson, *Vermont in Quandary* (Montpelier, 1949); *CHR XXXI* (Dec. 1950), 345–68: M. Wade, 'Quebec and the French Revolution of 1789: The Missions of Henri Mezière.'

[18] Têtu & Gagnon, *Mandements*, II, 471–2; Hubert's circular, 9 November 1793.

[19] PAC: S 44–5, 'Loyal Association Addresses, Lower Canada, 1794.'

[20] Têtu & Gagnon, *Mandements*, II, 501–2; Hubert's circular, 5 November 1796.

[21] AAQ: J.-O. Plessis, 'Oraison funèbre de Mgr Jean-Olivier Briand, 27 juin 1796'; Chapais, II, 124–6 *n*.

[22] L. Groulx, *Notre maître, le passé*, IIIe série (Montréal, 1944), 125–64, 'La Providence et la conquête anglaise de la Nouvelle France.'

[23] Têtu & Gagnon, *Mandements*, II, 515–7; Denaut's mandement, 22 December 1798; PAC: Q 82, 211: Plessis' *Discours*, 10 January 1799; printed copies at Laval and Quebec Legislative Library.

[24] Christie, VI, 23–4; G. Lanctot, *Les Canadiens français et leurs voisins du Sud* (Montréal, 1941), 129. PAC: Q 83, 152–5, Souscription volontaire; Q 84, 158–67, List of Voluntary Subscriptions.

[25] N.-E. Dionne, *Les ecclésiastiques et les royalistes français refugiés au Canada*, (Québec, 1905), IX.

[26] L. Groulx, *L'Enseignement français au Canada*, I, *Dans le Québec* (Montreal, 1931), 181.

[27] PAC: CO 42, 17, Holland-Roberts, 9 November 1785; Lanctot, 126–7.

[28] Shortt & Doughty, *Const. Docs.*, *1759–1794*, 489, Haldimand-Germain, 25 October 1780; Lanctot, 125.

[29] PAC: Q 69–2, 254: Monk-Dundas, 30 May 1794; Q 71–1, 2: Dorchester-Dundas, 24 May 1794.

[30] *Ibid.*, Q 79–1, 19: Sewell-Prescott, 12 May 1797; printed in *CAR 1891*, 73–6: Note D, French Republican Designs on Canada, No. 17.

[31] Christie, I, 238–43; D. G. Creighton, *Commercial Empire of the St. Lawrence* (Toronto, 1937), 155–6.

[32] PAC: CO 42, 22, 258–9: Dundas-Dorchester, July 1793.

[33] Christie, VI, 39: Mountain-Milnes, 19 October 1799; E. A. Cruikshank, *Simcoe Correspondence* (Toronto, 1925) III, 91–4, Mountain-Dundas, 15 September 1794; PAC: Q 74–2, 207–13, Mountain-Dundas, 15 July 1795; T. R. Millman, *Jacob Mountain, First Lord Bishop of Quebec* (Toronto, 1947), 170–1.

[34] PAC: Q 84, 183–90: Letter of the Bishop of Quebec on Education, 19 October 1799; Millman, *Mountain*, 171.

[35] PAC: Q 74, 207–13, Mountain-Dorchester, 15 July 1795; Groulx, *Enseignement*, I, 76.

36 Shortt & Doughty, *Const. Docs.*, 1791–1818, 349, Ryland's Observations, May, 1808; PAC: Q 220–3, 545–69, D. Viger, *Remarques sur l'Etat de l'Education en Canada en* 1831; Groulx, *Enseignement*, I, 78.

37 PAC: Q 85, 228 Milnes-Portland, 1 November 1800; printed in Kennedy, 219, 218.

38 Shortt & Doughty, *Const. Docs.*, 1791–1818, 393: Craig-Liverpool, 1 May 1810; Groulx, *Enseignement*, I, 80.

39 In 1816 two royal grammar schools were established in Quebec and Montreal, supported by the revenues of the Jesuit Estates and staffed by English teachers. Similar institutions had been established at Lévis in 1805 and at Saint-Nicolas in 1816. Fourteen teachers appeared on the public accounts in 1809; twenty-six in 1814, among them seven French Canadians serving in Catholic parishes. The efforts of the assembly to set up a rival educational system came to nothing in 1814, 1815, and 1817.

The Royal Institution finally came into official being in 1818, largely to take advantage of a bequest by James McGill of Montreal, who died in 1813, leaving his estate 'Burnside' to the Institution as the site of a college or university. If the will were not carried into effect within ten years, the property was to revert to McGill's heirs. The Montreal merchant also left £10,000 to be paid to the Royal Institution as soon as the college or university was established, to defray the expenses of launching and maintaining it. The bequest was prompted by the Reverend John Strachan, then missionary at York (Toronto), who married the widow of McGill's brother (*Montreal Gazette*, 3 September 1829: letter of P. Chartran; cited Millman, 173). Of the nine syndics who controlled the Royal Institution, only one was a French Canadian. The only other invited, Bishop Plessis, had refused. As Arthur Buller noted in his report on 'The State of Education in Lower Canada,' (Durham Report, App. D), the Royal Institution had an 'exclusively British and Protestant character,' and left the wants of the French Canadians 'virtually untouched.'

40 H. T. Manning, *British Colonial Government, 1782–1820* (New Haven, 1933), 300, 337.

41 PAC: Q 92, 253: Mountain-Milnes, 6 June 1805; printed in *CAR 1892*, 20: Note C, Ecclesiastical Affairs in Lower Canada, No. 2. However 'dangerous and novel' the experiment, such was the intention of London. Both Burke and Sewell considered that the Catholic Church had been established in Quebec by the Quebec Act. *A Letter from the Right Hon. Edmund Burke, M.P., to Sir Hercules Langrishe, Bart., M.P. on the subject of Roman Catholics in Ireland* (London, 1792), 83–4; QDA: Series C, 2, 29; cited Millman, 284 *n*. Burke spoke of his vote in 1791 as one "for the establishment of the Church of England *conjointly* with the establishment which was made some years before by Act of Parliament, of the Roman Catholics in the French conquered country of Canada."

42 *Quebec Mercury*, 28 October 1806; Chapais, II, 179.

43 *Ibid.*, 24 November 1806; Chapais, II, 180.

44 *Le Canadien*, 6 December 1806; Chapais, II, 181.

45 *Le Canadien*, 31 January 1807; Chapais, II, 185.

46 PAC: Q 106–1, 5: Craig-Castlereagh, 9 November 1807; Chapais, II, 187.

47 PAC: Q 107, 313–6, Ryland-Plante, Panet, Taschereau, Bédard, Borgia, Blanchet, 14 June 1808; printed in Christie, I, 276 *n*.

48 Christie, I, 317–20 *n.*: Craig's proclamation, 21 March 1810.

49 Doughty & McArthur, *Const Docs.*, 1791–1818 (Ottawa, 1914), 365, Castlereagh-Craig, 7 September 1809.

50 *Ibid*, 400–5, Observations of Chief Justice Sewell on the Union of the Provinces.

51 *Ibid.*, 387–400, Craig-Liverpool, 1 May 1810.

52 *Le Canadien*, 22 November 1806; Creighton, 158.

⁵³ PAC: Q 92, 253, Mountain-Milnes, 6 June 1803; printed in *CAR 1892*, 20: Note C, Ecclesiastical Affairs in Lower Canada, No. 2; Q 92, 275, Hobart-Milnes, 9 January 1804; printed in *CAR 1892*, 22: Note C, No. 3.

⁵⁴ Christie, VI, 72–3, Ryland, 23 December 1804.

⁵⁵ Abbé Ferland, 'Mgr Plessis,' in *Le Foyer Canadien*, I, 140; Chapais, II, 156.

⁵⁶ Têtu & Gagnon, *Mandemens*, III, 51, Plessis' Mandement, 25 October 1810.

⁵⁷ Christie, VI, 196–9, Ryland-Peel, 19 February 1811.

⁵⁸ Chapais, II, 161.

⁵⁹ Têtu & Gagnon, *Mandemens*, III, 59–72: Plessis-Craig, May-June 1811. Cf. Plessis' conversations with Sewell in April and May 1805, Christie, VI, 74–82.

⁶⁰ Christie, VI, 312–3; Bathurst-Prevost, 2 July 1813; Ryland-Brenton, 28 October 1813; Brenton-Ryland, 2 November 1813; Ryland-Brenton, 5 November 1813.

⁶¹ Doughty & McArthur, *Const. Docs., 1791–1818*, 60. Crown Lands Proclamation, 1792.

⁶² PAC: Q 80–2, 278–9, Prescott-Portland, 13 August 1798; Lanctot, 131.

⁶³ Creighton, 122–3.

⁶⁴ PAC: Q 80–2, 279, 280, 299: Prescott-Portland, 13 August 1798; Lanctot, 131.

⁶⁵ Doughty & McArthur, *Const. Docs., 1791–1818*, 402: Sewell's Observations.

⁶⁶ *Le Canadien*, 12 December 1807; cited Creighton, 158; Viger, cited Lanctot, 132.

⁶⁷ *Quebec Mercury*, 3 April 1809; Creighton, 159.

⁶⁸ *An Apology for Great Britain* (Quebec, 1809), 22–3; Creighton, 160.

⁶⁹ J. Cockloft, *Cursory Observations, Made in Quebec, Province of Lower Canada, in the Year 1811* (Bermuda, n.d.), 3. Copy in QLHS.

⁷⁰ *Ibid.*, 4–6; Creighton, 150; H. Innis & A. R. M. Lower, *Select Documents in Canadian Economic History*, II, *1783–1885* (Toronto, 1933), 236, 247.

⁷¹ Cockloft, 8–9; J. Bouchette, *A Topographical Description of the Province of Lower Canada* (London, 1815), 83–4.

⁷² Cockloft, 11.

⁷³ *Ibid.*, 21–5.

⁷⁴ *Ibid.*, 30–2, 35, 37.

⁷⁵ *Ibid.*, 37, 42.

⁷⁶ *Ibid.*, 26–7.

⁷⁷ Innis & Lower, *Select Econ. Docs.*, 228–9.

⁷⁸ *Ibid.*, 235.

⁷⁹ Bouchette, *Topographical Description*, 186.

⁸⁰ *Ibid.*, ix. 9, 15; PAC: Journal de Labadie, 1794–1817, Cahier IV, Labadie-P. Bédard, 5 August 1811: 'Aujourd 'huy les Américains jaloux de notre liberté veulant nous la ravir.'

⁸¹ PAC: Q 128–1, 185–6, Prevost-Bathurst, 27 August 1814; Lanctot, 138.

⁸² Lanctot, 133–4.

⁸³ *Ibid.*, 135.

⁸⁴ *Le Canadien*, 24 September 1808; Chapais, II, 215. Labadie, '*comme canadien et bon anglois*,' produced a patriotic jingle on Napoleon: '*Ce consul implacable! Qui veut régner partout, Ce vautour redoubtable, Est en horreur chez nous.*' PAC: Journal, Cahier II, 1 February 1804.

⁸⁵ A. Shortt & A.G. Doughty, *Canada and Its Provinces*, (Toronto, 1814), III, 201: Jefferson-Monroe, 1812.

⁸⁶ Têtu & Gagnon, *Mandemens*, III, 87: Deschenaux à MM. les curés, 29 juin 1812. Vicar-General J.-H.-A. Roux of Montreal issued a similar mandement on July 3 (Têtu & Gagnon, III, 88–91), while Deschenaux added two more circulars to the *curés* on July 20 and August 24 (*ibid.*, 91, 92) at the governor's suggestion.

Bishop Plessis expressed the governor's satisfaction and his own pleasure at the *curés'* assistance in a circular of October 6 (*ibid.*, 93), while on October 29 he issued a mandement encouraging the militia and ordaining a *Te Deum* for Wellington's victory over the French in Spain in July (*ibid.*, 94–8). The loyalist zeal of the clergy doubtless had a certain element of self-interest, with the question of the bishop's status still unresolved, but it expressed a sincere horror of Napoleonic France and of American sympathizers with it.

[87] Bouchette, 613.

[88] Têtu & Gagnon, III, 79–86; Plessis, *Mémoire*, 15 mai 1812.

[89] Doughty & McArthur, *Const. Docs., 1791–1818*, 445–50: 'Heads of Impeachment,' 1814.

[90] Christie, VI, 337: Ryland's 'A Brief Review of the Political State of the Province of Lower Canada during the last Seven Years,' May 1814.

[91] PAC: Q 127, 266: Prevost-Bathurst, 18 March 1814; Doughty & McArthur, *Const. Docs., 1791–1818*, 464.

[92] PAC: Q 128–1, 200, Prevost-Bathurst, 4 September 1814; Doughty & McArthur, 467.

[93] PAC: Q 143, 392; Sherbrooke-Bathurst, 21 April 1817; Chapais, III, 68–9.

[94] *Quebec Gazette*, July 1820; Chapais, III, 92–3.

[95] *The Centenary Volume of the Literary and Historical Society of Quebec* (Quebec, 1924).

[96] Creighton, 214.

[97] *Montreal Gazette*, 10 November 1828; Creighton, 213.

[98] PAC: Q 163–2, 553: Robinson-Bathurst, 23 April 1822; printed in *CAR 1897*, 39: Note A, 'Proposed Union between Upper and Lower Canada,' No. 20.

[99] Kennedy, 243: Union Bill, June 1822.

[100] Hansard, II Series, VII, 1708; Chapais, III, 117.

[101] M. Bibaud, *Histoire du Canada sous la domination anglaise* (Montréal, 1844), 235; Chapais, III, 117.

[102] Bib. St. Sulp.: Correspondence Papineau-Neilson (1819–23); Neilson-Papineau, 22 June, 1822; transcripts at PAC.

[103] *Ibid.*, Papineau Neilson, 29 November 1823.

[104] Garneau, II, 582 *n*. 23.

[105] PAC: Q 164–1, 113: Papineau & Neilson-Horton, 10 May 1823; Chapais, III, 134–5.

[106] APQ: Fonds Papineau, XI, 'Papineau à divers personnes, 1809–1844, 503: Papineau-Neilson, 13 September 1824.

[107] PAC: Neilson Collection, XIV, Papineau-Neilson, 13 September 1821; 30 April 1825.

[108] Kennedy, 251: Dalhousie's speech proroguing Assembly, 1827.

[109] Bib. St. Sulp.: Corr. Papineau-Neilson, Papineau-Neilson, 26 June 1826.

[110] *Imperial Blue Books, 1820–1829*, 'Report of Committee of House of Commons 1828,' Ap.: Petition of 87,000 Inhabitants of Lower Canada, 1828.

[111] *Ibid.*, Petition of 10,000 from the Townships of the Lower Province, 1828.

[112] APQ: Fonds Papineau, XI, 509-A, Papineau-Neilson, 9 January 1828.

[113] *Hansard, II Series*, XIX, 300; Chapais, III, 207–8.

[114] Creighton, 257.

[115] *Affaires du Pays depuis 1828* (Quebec, 1834), 1; Chapais III, 214.

[116] Doughty & Storey, *Const. Docs., 1819–1828* in *CAR 1935*, Ap., 466–77: Report of Committee of House of Commons, 1828. Published as *Report from the Select Committee on the Civil Government of Canada* (London, 1828); republished in French at Quebec by Neilson & Cowan, 1828. Extracts in Kennedy, 254.

[117] Translated from Chapais, III, 216.

[118] PAC: Q 193–3, 377: Kempt-Murray, 2 March 1830; Chapais III, 229.

[119] Manning, 335.

[120] APQ: Fonds Papineau, XI, 516–7, Papineau-Neilson, 14 November 1830.

[121] PAC: Neilson Collection, XIV, 40, Papineau-Neilson, 11 May 1831.

[122] Bib. St. Sulp.: Corr. Papineau-Neilson, Papineau-Neilson, 20 August 1831.

[123] Chapais, III, 242: Goderich-Aylmer, 7 July 1831.

[124] Le Canadien, 12 January 1832; Chapais, III, 259.

[125] Bib. St. Sulp.: Corr. Papineau-Neilson, Papineau-Neilson, 12 November 1829.

[126] Quebec Gazette, 10 December 1831, Letter signed 'La Raison' (Abbé C.-F. Painchaud): 'The Canadian clergy, having no longer anything to hope from the House of Assembly, would be wise to detach its hopes from it and attach them to the executive.'; Chapais, III, 257.

[127] Christie, III, 396–7, gives many of the documents; Le Canadien, Chapais, IV, 8.

[128] Montreal Gazette, 27 October 1832; Creighton, 275.

[129] Ibid., 11 September 1832; Creighton, 275–6.

[130] Quebec Gazette, August, 11 November 1832; Christie, III, 355.

[131] APQ: Fonds Papineau, XI, 521, Papineau-Neilson, 11 August 1832.

[132] N.-E. Dionne, Les Trois comédies de Status Quo (Québec, 1909), 13.

[133] Kennedy, 274–90: Ninety-Two Resolutions, 21 February 1834; Chapais, IV, 18–25.

[134] Précis des debats de la Chambre d'Assemblée (Québec, 1834), 4–7; Chapais, IV, 27–9.

[135] PAC: Q 219–2, 216–31, letter from Montreal, 27 February 1834; Creighton, 289.

[136] Montreal Gazette, 11 December 1834; Creighton, 293.

[137] Ibid., 6, 8 November 1834; Creighton, 293.

[138] PAC: Sec. of State's Papers, Lower Canada, Molson et al.–Craig, 22 November 1834; Creighton, 294.

[139] PAC: Neilson Collection, XIV, 48–9: Montreal Committee (Morin, Papineau, R. Nelson, O'Callaghan, Lafontaine, Perrault)—Quebec Committee (Vanfelson, Beserin, A. Berthelot, E.-R. Caron, Dubord, H.-S. Huot, J. Blanchet, A. Godbout, N. Boissonault, E. Bédard, et al.), 20 November 1834.

[140] Ibid., 50.

[141] The Patriot, 16 January 1835; Creighton, 294. The Quebec Association under Neilson's leadership was more moderate and truly constitutional, opposing Union or the annexation of Montreal to Upper Canada.

CHAPTER IV

CRISIS AND CONFLICT

(1834–9)

T HE REBELLION of 1837–8 in Lower Canda was neither a clear-
cut conflict between the ethnic groups, as many French- and
English-Canadian writers have considered it, nor a struggle
between liberty-loving North Americans and reactionary Europeans,
as Papineau saw it.[1] Many of Papineau's chief lieutenants were
English Canadians,[2] and the *Patriotes* maintained close relations
with Mackenzie's Reformers in Upper Canada.[3] In both sections
the popular agrarian majority was in bitter conflict with the oligar-
chic minority of officials, placemen, and merchants; and in both
sections rebellion resulted from the increasing frustration of the
majority, whose odds in numbers were outweighed by their enemies'
monopoly of power. Both Papineau and Mackenzie were publicly
supported in the imperial parliament and privately encouraged by
the English Philosophical Radicals;[4] and the agitation in the Canadas
had much in common with the Chartist movement in England, which
came to a head after the Canadian uprisings had been suppressed.[5]

Reform was the spirit of the age in both Canada and Britain; but
Canada's proximity to the United States, and the time-lag between
the Colonial Office and Parliament, brought matters to a head sooner
in the colony than in the mother country. The rise of Jacksonian
democracy in the United States reinforced the long-established
influence of the American Revolution upon Canadian political
thinking; the outmoded colonial system became more intolerable
to the popular leaders, while the oligarchy was frightened into violent reaction by the crumbling of its wonted world. The political
crisis was rendered more acute by the severe agricultural and commercial depression of 1833–8, which made both parties more intransigent and thus hastened the coming of open conflict.

I

In London, during April 1834, John Arthur Roebuck, a Radical
M.P. who had been educated in Canada, savagely attacked the
colonial administration of Lord Stanley and supported the Ninety-
Two Resolutions. A month later another English Radical, Joseph

Hume, wrote Mackenzie a letter in which he referred to 'that crisis which is fast approaching in the affairs of the Canadas, and which will terminate in independence and freedom from the baneful domination of the mother country.'[6] But the Whig government was by no means of the same school of thought as these Radical spokesmen. In reply to Roebuck's attack, Stanley proposed a revival of the Committee of 1828 on Canadian affairs, and this course was followed. The committee heard the testimony of Viger, Morin, Sir James Kempt, Frederick Elliott of the Colonial Office, Ellice, James Stuart, and others. Finally on July 3 it turned in a terse, sibyline report, which maintained that the government had tried to act on the suggestions of 1828 and had been guided by the best interests of the colony. But difficulties had arisen between the assembly and the legislative council, and between the assembly and the executive, which had prevented the full achievement of the program of reform. The committee concluded its report by asserting its conviction that 'practical measures for the future government of Lower Canada may best be left to the mature consideration of the government responsible for their adoption and execution.'[7] In short, Grey's outgoing moderate Whig ministry left the problem to Peel's reformist Tory administration.

Just before handing over the Colonial Office to Thomas Spring-Rice, Stanley announced his intention of abrogating the law of 1831 which had renounced the government's claim to the Crown revenues, in anticipation of the grant of a civil list which had not been forthcoming. In addition to this old quarrel, Spring-Rice found himself confronted with new grievances in the form of resolutions against the British American Land Company and against Aylmer's appointment of the bureaucrat Samuel Gale to the bench in 1834. Spring-Rice scolded Aylmer for his lack of wisdom and tact in the latter matter, but sustained the land company. Meanwhile in Canada the assembly had met and chosen Papineau as speaker by a vote of 70-6 which indicated his decided dominance over that body. The now customary deadlock between the two branches of the government soon arose, and Aylmer prorogued the assembly after it had passed one bill.

London, weary of continual crises in Canada and moved by the spirit of reform then active at Westminster, appointed a royal commission to visit Canada and seek an end of the difficulties. In order to give the commission a free hand, Aylmer was recalled and replaced by Lord Gosford, who was named high commissioner as well as governor, with the Tory Sir Charles Grey and the Liberal Sir George Gipps as his colleagues. The commissioners arrived at Quebec on August 23, 1835. Gosford at once displayed a conciliatory spirit, and took pains to consult such *Patriote* leaders as Papineau,

L.-M. Viger, and Debartzch. In his speech from the throne at the opening of the session, he called for an end to dissension and promised redress of many grievances.

Meanwhile the commission set about its work. Its secretary, Frederick Elliott of the Colonial Office, found three opposed groups in Lower Canada: the Bureaucrats, jealous of their authority and privileges; the English party, made up of discontented merchants, *seigneurs*, and placemen, which he considered more likely to cut the tie with Britain than the French party, and more sympathetic to republicanism; and the French party, the majority in the assembly, made up of lawyers, doctors, and *habitants* and completely controlled by Papineau. The latter Elliott found personally charming, 'by nature, as much as by the position to which he has raised himself, the first of the French Canadians,'[8] but given to violence, lack of complete frankness, and bitter prejudice against the English. Elliott appreciated the uneasy position of the French Canadians, 'surrounded on all sides by millions whose language and customs are those whose influence they have so much reason to fear,' and he considered that their dread of the future extinction of their language and culture was well founded. He concluded that 'to reconcile the French Canadians and to guide them in the art of government is the surest and most convenient policy for the present, and also that which will lead to lasting and solid advantages in the future.' After arguing with the militant *Patriote* Etienne Parent, 'a little dyspeptic man, the editor of *Le Canadien*,' Elliott was surprised 'to see on what a friendly basis generally rest the ideas of the French Canadians, and how their understanding of political science is superior to that of the men by whom they have been so arrogantly despised.'

Gosford endeavored to further this friendly feeling. The high commissioner's display of conciliatory spirit was not confined merely to such social gestures as dining Papineau and Viger and showing special attention to Madame Elzéar Bédard, whose husband had sponsored the Ninety-Two Resolutions. When the ultra-loyalists of Montreal formed a British Rifle Corps, 'to preserve inviolate the connection which exists between Great Britain and Lower Canada,' the governor promptly suppressed it as being more apt 'to endanger the public tranquility' than to promote it.[9]

Under such temperate rule the split among the *Patriotes* was accentuated, with the moderates led by Elzéar Bédard and John Neilson acquiring such former followers of Papineau as Vanfelson, Berthelot, Caron, and Morin. By February 1836 Papineau could only muster a majority of one vote in the assembly. Indeed Gosford's mission was about to be crowned with success when the untimely disclosure of the instructions of the royal commission, made by Sir Francis Bond Head, the impetuous governor of Upper Canada, threw doubt on London's professed goodwill toward the colony. It was the Upper Canadian Reformer Mackenzie who sent damaging extracts from these instructions to Papineau, who promptly communicated them to the assembly.[10] Thanks to this incident, Papineau was put back in the saddle, for Gosford's communication to the assembly of a complete copy of his instructions, in order to remedy the harm done by a partial disclosure of their contents, did not restore his original favorable position. The suspicions of the *Patriotes* were also reinforced by the appointment to the bench of Bédard. The popular party had lost too many of its leaders in this fashion not to distrust the maneuver. Vanfelson succeeded Bédard as leader of the moderates, and called for a vote of confidence in Gosford and a truce in the long battle of the assembly with the executive. Papineau and his young disciple Louis-Hippolyte Lafontaine opposed this course in speeches of considerable violence, and the measure was defeated by eleven votes. The policy of conciliation had been rejected by those to whom it was directed; now coercion was to take its place, as an open break finally occurred.

A special twelve-day session in the fall of 1836, called by Gosford at the instigation of London in a last attempt to secure the support of the assembly, ended with that body announcing on September 30 its intention 'to adjourn our deliberations until His Majesty's government shall by its acts, especially by rendering the second branch of the Legislature conformable to the wishes and wants of the people, have commenced the great work of justice and reform, and created a confidence which alone can crown it with success.'[11] The intransigent attitude of the assembly in thus going on strike for an elective council, despite the governor's policy of conciliation, was in large measure due to the violent newspaper warfare of the period, which saw the publication of Adam Thom's savage 'Anti-Gallic Letters' in the *Montreal Herald*.

This Scottish school-teacher and lawyer made himself the journalistic spokesman of the hardshell Tory merchants, and poured scathing abuse upon French Canadians and governor alike. Thom upbraided Gosford in such terms as these: 'Good heavens, my lord of Gosford, are you mad enough to glory in your shame, hardened enough to rejoice in a delegated opportunity of doing evil, degraded enough to be "cheerful" under the double lash of a Frenchified cabinet and a French faction?'[12] The merchants were maddened to desperation by Gosford's policy of conciliating the French Canadians; in December 1835 the *Montreal Gazette* justified an appeal to force,[13] while in the following year Thom warned Gosford that the talk of a civil war to give scope to British capital and commerce was to be taken seriously: 'Your lordship may have been led to believe that the avowed determination of the constitutionalists, to resist the

extension of French domination, was merely an empty threat; but
they have not forgotten, that the glorious fields of Cressy, Poictiers,
Agincourt and Minden were won by "miserable" minorities of
Englishmen over vast majorities of Frenchmen.'[14] Under such
provocation Papineau grew still more violent, despite counsels of
patience and moderation from the English friends of the *Patriotes*,
and he was supported by such disciples as Lafontaine, Augustin
Morin, and Sabrevoix de Bleury. Even the moderate *Le Canadien*
proclaimed: 'The Colonial Secretary has only words to offer an
Assembly to which a long reign of corrupt abuse has given an ardent
thirst for effective reforms. The immediate result of all this is not
hard to anticipate.'[15]

The royal commission, less Gosford, who remained as governor,
returned to England during the winter of 1836-7 and made its
report.[16] On the whole the document was unfavorable to the claims
of the assembly, which it thus summarized: a responsible executive'
council, an elective legislative council, complete and immediate
cession to the assembly of control of all the revenue, the revocation of
the Tenure Act and the British American Land Company Act, and
basic control by the assembly over the administration and settlement
of public lands. The commissioners considered that with two elective
houses the Lower Canadian legislature would resemble too closely
the American system of government and would be dominated by
one party. They believed that a responsible executive council—the
'ministry' for which the French Canadians had long contended—was
incompatible with the maintenance of the tie between the mother
country and the colony. The commissioners recommended the
retention by the Crown of a portion of the revenue, the grant of a
civil list for the life of the sovereign or for at least seven years, the
maintenance of the land company, a modification of the election
law, and the abandonment of the project of uniting the two Canadas.
They also singled out the abuses of naming the same individuals
to both the executive and legislative councils, and of excluding the
French Canadians from public office.

There was not much in the report to satisfy the assembly, which
had taken its stand on the Ninety-Two Resolutions and refused to be
conciliated by anything less than complete capitulation to its
demands. To be sure, the abuses of which the Lower Canadian
assembly complained were to be found in the other British North
American provinces, and in Upper Canada, at least, produced very
much the same reaction. But the situation was more dangerous in
Lower Canada because of the division between a French majority and
an English minority, although there were some English Canadians
in the French party and some French Canadians in the English
party. In the face of an ethnic conflict which embittered a political

conflict, London sought to maintain the old doctrines of colonial government, while the Canadians demanded British responsible government with certain American features.

London was willing to reform but not to revise existing institutions —the same institutions which had produced the American Revolution. Some of the leading Bureaucrats were deprived of their offices under the reign of Goderich at the Colonial Office. Gosford's nominations to the legislative council in the spring of 1836, following those made since 1828, were designed to give that body a French-Canadian majority; by the same date the executive council numbered five French Canadians and three English Canadians; while four of the five new judges named since 1828 were French Canadians. But such concessions, particularly when they were used to deprive it of its leaders, did not satisfy the assembly, which held out for full control of the revenue, responsible government, and an elective legislative council. On the first point Gosford expressed the government's willingness to yield at long last. But London was not inclined to grant responsible government, when that meant putting power into the hands of Papineau and his party, nor an elective council, when such a concession would have made Papineau the master of both houses of the legislature, and left the English Canadians without protection.

The decision of the British government as to its Canadian policy was announced just four days after the report of the royal commission was made to parliament on March 2, 1837. Lord John Russell, the emancipator of the English Catholics and the proposer of the Reform Bill in 1832, presented his Ten Resolutions, based on the commission's report, which declared the creation of an elective legislative council inopportune but proposed to make it more popular, rejected the proposal of a responsible executive council, maintained the British American Land Company, offered hope of the revocation of the Tenure Act, authorized the governor to take the funds which the assembly had refused to grant from revenues in the receiver general's hands, provided for the cession of the Crown revenues to the assembly if the latter granted a civil list, and urged the legislatures of Upper and Lower Canada to settle their common interests.[17] The Resolutions evoked a three-day debate, in which O'Connell, Roebuck, and Hume opposed the government's proposals, and Labouchere, Peel, and Gladstone supported them. Young Gladstone, who was later to become the advocate of Home Rule for Ireland, proclaimed in the best Tory style: 'The question is not a question of party; it is simply whether one ought to consent to a virtual separation of Canada from England. . . . The question in dispute is not between the Assembly and the administration, but between the Assembly and the mother country, which has sanctioned all that the mother country has done.'[18] Except for the Radicals, the Commons supported the government's proposals; and in the House of Lords only Lord Brougham raised his eloquent voice against the measure. The Ten Resolutions touched off the explosive Canadian situation.

The Irish-born and French-educated Edmund Bailey O'Callaghan, a supporter of Papineau in the assembly and the editor of the three-year-old Irish *Vindicator* of Montreal, summed up the reaction of the popular party to the events in England thus:

A combined and dishonorable junction of Whigs and Tories, in a House of Commons 'reformed' but in name, may pass Resolutions to annihilate the last remnant of Liberty left in the Colonial Legislatures. A House of Lords, the fundamental principle of whose Constitution is inimical to human freedom, may endorse the determination of the combined enemies of freedom in the Lower House, but neither the Resolutions, their authors, nor their supporters, can change the nature of things. *Robbery will be robbery still.* . . . Our rights must not be violated with impunity. A howl of indignation must be raised from one extremity of the Province to the other, against the robbers, and against all who partake of the plunder.

HENCEFORTH, THERE MUST BE NO PEACE IN THE PROVINCE —no quarter for the plunderers. Agitate! *Agitate!! AGITATE!!!* Destroy the Revenue; denounce the oppressors. Everything is lawful when the fundamental liberties are in danger. 'The guards die—they never surrender.'[19]

And so the French-Canadian struggle for self-government abandoned constitutional means and had recourse to revolt, at the instigation of an Irish doctor quoting one of Napoleon's marshals. That revolt was an incident in the great struggle between the new and old orders launched by the American and French Revolutions, which had made 'liberty' and 'freedom' words capable of unleashing the energies of peoples against their rulers. Napoleon had risen to supremacy in Europe by using the social forces thus set in motion; it was not inappropriate that the proud words of one of his followers should serve to rouse the people of French Canada.

2

The Rebellion of 1837–8 in Lower Canada was a rebellion in spite of the intentions of its original leaders; like its counterpart in Upper Canada, it was a largely unpremeditated resort to arms to break the long constitutional deadlock between the people and the oligarchy, after much provocation from the latter. Looking back on his course of action after he had been forced to take refuge in the United States, Papineau proudly proclaimed: 'I offered constitutional opposition;

I did not offer any other. We did not conspire to overturn the government by force; we wished to cure it by [altering] its diet and way of life.'[20]

Thus the first form of resistance to Russell's Ten Resolutions was an attempt to dry up the sources of the revenue by boycotting imported goods, and by using only homemade or smuggled articles on which no duty was paid. In April 1837 Ludger Duvernay, the hot-headed *Patriote* who had founded the Saint-Jean-Baptiste Society in 1834, laid down the *Patriote* program in *La Minerve*:

Friend Jonathan will supply us with the articles which we cannot make here. Therefore let us aid the smuggler; from now on he is a brave fellow whom each of us will encourage. Vigorous youths, determined and well organized, must be trained for this career. Smuggling must be done on a grand scale. No more circumspection or temporizing. Major remedies are needed for major evils. The sources of the revenue must be dried up. The vaults will empty; the thieves will find nothing more there. Then England will listen to reason. Never has a struggle been more just. We have withheld the subsidies; this weapon is now taken from us and we must seek others more efficacious.[21]

The *Patriote* leaders held public meetings to spread the gospel of economic revolt. They practiced what they preached: when the assembly was summoned in August, the appearance of the Montreal members aroused the humor of the government-controlled *Quebec Mercury*:

Mr. Rodier's dress excited the greatest attention, being *unique*, with the exception of a pair of Berlin gloves, viz.: frock coat of granite colored *étoffe du pays*; inexpressibles and vest of the same material, striped blue and white; straw hat and beef shoes, with a pair of home-made socks, completed the *outré* attire. Mr. Rodier, it was remarked, had no shirt on, having doubtless been unable to smuggle or manufacture one.

Dr. O'Callaghan's 'rig out' was second only to that of Mr. Rodier, being complete with the exception of hat, boots, gloves, and shirt [he *had* a shirt!] and spectacles.[22]

But as in the American Revolution, passive resistance to the arbitrary measures of the mother country soon led to more violent opposition. The general mood was highly explosive, since Canada was undergoing one of the worst depressions it had ever known—the wheat crop of the previous year had been a failure, and the farmers were hard-pressed during the spring and summer of 1837, while the business community was severely shaken by financial panic both in London and the United States. A resort to violence no longer seemed unthinkable, but rather the only solution of bitter frustration. The newspapers continued to fan the flames, and during the spring and summer great public meetings were held, particularly in the region of Montreal, that most sharply affected by the economic crisis. At these gatherings impassioned orators waxed more and more intemperate in their protests against British oppression and in their proposals of counter action. At Saint-Ours on the Richelieu on May 7 Wolfred Nelson, Cyrille Côté, and Siméon Marchessault—two doctors and a school-teacher—denounced the Ten Resolutions as a violation of the social contract and expressed regret that Canada had not made common cause with the Americans in 1775. This echo of Rousseau and the reference to the American Revolution are interesting in the light they shed upon the sources of *Patriote* ideas. Papineau was hailed as the Canadian Daniel O'Connell, a personification of the people.

This meeting of 1,200 persons adopted twelve resolutions prepared by the *Patriotes*' Permanent Central Committee, which corresponded to the first American Congress's declaration of rights and grievances in 1774 and to the French declaration of the rights of man in 1789. They read thus:

I. It is with feelings of the most lively indignation that we have seen the resolutions proposed for adoption by the House of Commons on March 6 last, resolutions of which the inevitable effect is to deprive us of any guarantee of liberty and good government in the future for this province.

II. The adoption of these resolutions will be a flagrant violation on the part of the Commons, and of the government which proposed them, of the Capitulation, treaties, and constitutional acts which have been granted to this country. These acts, and these treaties, carry reciprocal obligations, to wit, on our part, love and obedience; on England's part, protection and the assurance of liberty; and they would be virtually annulled by the violation of the promises of one of the contracting parties.

III. In these circumstances we can only regard the government which would have recourse to injustice, force, and a violation of the social contract as an oppressive power and a government of force, to which henceforth the extent of our submission should be measured only by our numerical strength, joined to the sympathies that we find elsewhere.

IV. The machiavelianism which has accompanied all the acts of the government since the cession, the bad faith which has characterized it until now, the feebleness revealed by every page of the commissioners' report and by speeches of the ministers, who did not blush to cite our division and our small numbers as reasons for refusing us justice; all this inspires us only with the most profound disgust and the most pronounced scorn for the men who rule one of the greatest and noblest peoples of the earth, or are attached to such a government.

V. The people of this country have long awaited justice from the colonial administration at first, and later from the metropolitan government, and always in vain; during thirty years fear has broken some of our chains, while an insatiable love of power has added heavier ones. The high opinion that we had of the justice and honor of the English people made us hope that the parliament which represented it would provide a remedy for our grievances. Disillusioned of this last hope, we have renounced forever the idea of seeking justice on the other side of the ocean, and we have recognized at last how much this country has been misled by the lying promises which made it fight against a people which offered it liberty and equal rights in behalf of a people who prepared to enslave it. Sad experience forces us to recognize that our true friends and natural allies were on the other side of the 45th parallel.

VI. We deny to the English parliament the right to legislate on the internal affairs of this colony without our consent, our participation, and our request, since the non-exercise of this right by England has been guaranteed to us by the Constitution, and recognized by the mother country when she feared that we would accept the offers of liberty and independence made to us by the neighboring republic. Consequently, we regard as null and void the Tenure Act, the Canada Trade Act, the act which incorporated the company known as the 'Land Company,' and finally the act which will doubtless be based upon the resolutions just adopted by the Commons.

VII. Regarding ourselves as no longer bound except by force to the English government, we shall submit to it as to a government of force, expecting from God, our valid rights, and from circumstances a better fate, the favors of liberty and a juster government. Meanwhile, as our public funds which the home government dares to dispose of without any control are going to become in its hands a new means of pressure against us, we regard it as our duty, arising from our honor, to resist by all means now in our possession to a tyrannical power, in order to diminish as much as we can these means of oppression, and we resolve:

VIII. That we shall abstain, insofar as it may be in our power, from consuming imported goods, particularly those on which the higher duties are paid, such as tea, tobacco, wine, rum, etc. By preference we shall consume products manufactured in our country; we shall regard as deserving well of the homeland whoever establishes the manufacture of silk, cloth, sugar, spirits, etc. Considering the Trade Act as null, we shall regard as wholly lawful the commerce known as contraband; we shall judge this traffic as very honorable; we shall try to favor it by every means in our power, regarding those who devote themselves to it as deserving well of the homeland, and as infamous whoever denounces them.

IX. In order to render these resolutions more efficacious, this assembly is of the opinion that an association should be established in this country, with headquarters in Quebec or Montreal, whose purpose will be to bind its members to consume only products manufactured in this country, or imported without the payment of duties. . . .

X. In order to effect more efficaciously the regeneration of this country, all should rally around a single man, following the example of Ireland.

God has marked this man, like O'Connell, to be the political chief and the regenerator of a people. He has given him for that purpose an unsurpassed force of thought and word, a hatred of oppression, a love of country which no promise or threat of the powers-that-be can break down. This man, already singled out by the country, is L.-J. Papineau. This assembly, taking into consideration the happy results obtained in Ireland from the assessment known as 'O'Connell's Tribute,' is of the opinion that a similar assessment, called 'Papineau's Tribute,' ought to exist in this country. The committees of the association against importation would be charged with raising it.

XI. This assembly could not break up without extending its sincerest thanks to the orators, not numerous but zealous and able, who proclaimed the justice of our cause in the House of Commons, as well as to the honest and virtuous men who voted with them. The London workers, who with a spirit of liberty and of justice worthy of a free people presented a petition to the House of Commons in favor of this unhappy country, have an equal right to our profound gratitude. Our friends of the Political Union of Toronto also have a right to our thanks for the sympathy they manifested towards us in the resolution they adopted on April 17 against the ministers' measures of coercion.

XII. This assembly holds the conviction that in the general election with which the country is threatened at the instigation of weak and perverse men, as ignorant of public opinion in the present crisis as they are deprived of influence, the electorate will exhibit its gratitude to its faithful representatives by re-electing them and by rejecting those who have not fulfilled their promises and their duties, and who have betrayed the country either by siding with our enemies or by cowardly absence when the country expected from them an honest expression of their sentiments. [23]

This Declaration of Saint-Ours, a notable landmark in the development of French-Canadian nationalism, was spread through the province by publication in *La Minerve* and in the *Vindicator*. With its warning that the people might renounce their allegiance to Britain, and with its use of the threat of annexation to the United States, then in the throes of expansionism to the tune of Manifest Destiny, it went much farther than the Ninety-Two Resolutions of 1834, which were a parliamentary rather than popular expression of the same state of mind. It frightened the supporters of the government, and made such moderates as Etienne Parent, who characterized it as 'strange, absurd, and unrealizable,'[24] recoil before the prospect of either civil war or hopeless despair under new repression.

The vagueness of the Declaration's fine language was clarified and strengthened at the meetings which were held at Saint-Laurent, Chambly, Yamaska, Lachenaye, Quebec, Verchères, Saint-Hyacinthe, Sainte-Scholastique, and elsewhere in May and June. At Saint-Laurent on May 15 Papineau lashed out at 'the old enemies of the country: the governor, the two councils, the judges, the majority of the public servants, their creatures and their supports, whom your representatives have long denounced as forming a corrupt faction, hostile to the rights of the people and moved by self-interest alone to support a vicious system of government.'[25] He attacked Gosford as three times as detestable as Dalhousie and Aylmer, and denounced the British parliament which wished 'to steal your money to pay your servants, whom your representatives have refused to pay because they have been lazy, faithless, and incompetent.' He hailed the example of the Americans, who had successfully resisted a similar attempt to oppress them in 1774; and proclaimed the sympathy of the American government and the British people with the Canadians in their struggle for justice.[26]

But in reality, despite expressions of sympathy in both quarters, financial panic and economic distress preoccupied both Britain and the United States at this moment. Papineau, who was an idealist thinking in purely political terms, did not realize this fact, nor did he see that such agitation as he was conducting, with constant appeals to systematic illegality, must end in violence. Yet he quoted Lord Brougham, who in the debate on the Ten Resolutions had warned the British ministry: 'Yes, if you attempt to consummate your iniquitous works, the Canadians have a moral duty to resist you. Yes, if the same blood ran in their veins as that which produced Washingtons, Franklins, and Jeffersons, they would chase you from their country as you were justly chased from the old colonies.'[27] Papineau claimed that he was not held back from rebellion by either fear or scruple, but by the conviction that constitutional resistance, which had won so many triumphs in the past for the French Canadians, would suffice once more, although he now envisaged for the first time the future necessity of stronger measures. The leaders of the agitation began to talk of free trade with the United States and a general convention. The cooler-headed and more farsighted Etienne Parent, now denounced as a coward and a hypocrite by the *Patriotes*, warned the people that declarations of hostility to England were invitations for the use of force to crush a feeble Canada, unable to win its independence by arms.[28]

Outside of Montreal, the headquarters of the Permanent Central Committee of the *Patriotes*, which gradually dominated the county committees, the popular feeling was strongest in the Richelieu Valley, hard-hit by wheat-crop failures, and about Lac des Deux Montagnes. The districts of Trois-Rivières and Quebec were much calmer than that of Montreal, although Augustin-Norbert Morin and Robert Shore Milnes Bouchette held large meetings in May and June at the capital, whose Irish population first decided to make common cause with the *Patriotes* and then yielded to the inducements offered by the oligarchy. In June and July Papineau, Morin, Lafontaine, and

Girouard made a tour through the district of Quebec, whose *Patriote* fervor lagged behind the ever-swelling agitation in that of Montreal. In July, the opposition decided to fight fire with fire, holding constitutional assemblies at Montreal, Napierville, Trois-Rivières, and Quebec. But even the presence of the garrison troops at these gatherings could not swell their numbers to equal those of the *Patriote* meetings; and the fact that they were presided over by English Canadians, and that their chief speakers were either English- or French-Canadian bureaucrats, indicates that they were officially inspired and not true popular assemblies.

Both state and church were alarmed by the growing unrest, and took steps to check it, without much success. On June 15 Gosford issued a proclamation denouncing the seditious assemblies and urging all public officials to oppose the measures proposed at them.[29] Several magistrates and militia officers who took part in the *Patriote* agitation were relieved of their commissions in August, when the meetings continued nonetheless. On July 25, at a dinner celebrating the consecration of Bishop Bourget as his coadjutor, Bishop Lartigue of Montreal informally advised his clergy that 'it is never permissible to revolt against legitimate authority or to violate the laws of the land; that absolution should not be given in the tribunal of penitence to anyone who teaches that it is permissible to revolt against the government under which we have the happiness to live, or that it is permissible to violate the laws of the land, particularly those which forbid smuggling.'[30] This résumé of the bishop's remarks—at a banquet attended by nearly all the clergy of the diocese —was published in *L'Ami du Peuple*, an anti-*Patriote* journal of Montreal, under the heading 'Catholicism against M. Papineau'; and was promptly disputed by the *Patriote* organ *La Minerve*, which denied that the bishop had condemned smuggling.[31] During the course of his pastoral visits in July, Bishop Signay of Quebec also recommended prudence to his clergy. But despite these restraining influences the agitation continued to mount, and scuffles and duels between the partisans of the popular and bureaucratic groups became more frequent in Montreal and the surrounding countryside.

The death of King William IV and the succession of Queen Victoria was used as a pretext by Lord John Russell, who was no doubt influenced by reports from Canada, to announce on June 23 the suspension of the program laid down in his Ten Resolutions, since the government was unwilling to blight the opening of a new reign by the application of coercive measures. On July 3 the British Commons voted a sum to meet the arrears of Canadian government costs. Gosford had already been ordered to call the assembly as soon as possible, in a final attempt to win its submission. Meanwhile London busied itself with taking action, after long delays, on the measures of conciliation which Gosford had earlier recommended. It was alarmed by a visit which the French minister to the United States, M. de Pontois, paid to Lower Canada, where he dined with Papineau and attended a *Patriote* assembly at Saint-Constant. With French Canadians greeting each other as *citoyen*, singing the *Marseillaise*, and displaying the Tricolor, Palmerston may be excused for his alarm.

But while a belated effort at conciliation was being made by the home government, the agitation in Canada continued to swell. Gosford's proclamation, with its attack on the *Patriote* leaders, had heightened rather than reduced the unrest; and in August congregations walked out on the traditional *Te Deum* which followed the proclamation from the pulpit of the new monarch.[32] Gosford himself still hoped to avoid serious trouble by liberalization of the two councils, and refused to call in troops from New Brunswick and Nova Scotia, as he had been authorized to do by London, despite growing disorder in the Two Mountains district northwest of Montreal. At the opening of the session on August 18, he announced the government's inclination to avoid recourse to the program of the Ten Resolutions, if the assembly consented to grant the needed funds. He also outlined the reforms which he had recommended and which had actually been decided upon in London as he spoke. If action had been taken upon them a month earlier, the course of history might have been changed.

But in its reply, which Papineau inspired and Morin—unaware that he had just been named commissioner of Crown lands—delivered, the unruly assembly announced:

It is our duty, therefore, to tell the Mother Country that if she carries the spirit of these resolutions into effect in the Government of British North America, and of this province in particular, her supremacy therein will no longer depend upon the feelings of affection, of duty and of mutual interest which would best secure it, but upon physical and material force, an element dangerous to the governing party, at the same time that it subjects the governed to a degree of uncertainty as to their future existence and their dearest interests, which is scarcely to be found under the most absolute government of civilized Europe.[33]

The assembly decided to rest upon its old intransigent position, since no reform of the council had taken place. Meanwhile dispatches were actually on the way out from London with news of the appointment of seven French Canadians out of ten new legislative councilors. The bureaucratic delays of the Colonial Office, heightened by the varying policies of eight ministers in eleven years, brought about the breakdown of representative government in Canada. A moderate motion by Taschereau, supported by Huot and the now wavering Bleury, to grant the desired funds if reforms took place, was defeated by 46–18; and the Papineau-Morin reply was adopted by a majority of fifteen votes. On August 26 it was presented to Gosford, who expressed his regret that the assembly persisted in its determination to deprive the country of a local legislature; and when the members returned to their chamber, the last assembly of Lower Canada found itself dissolved by a proclamation placed on the seat of Speaker Papineau.

Gosford at last abandoned hope of conciliation. On September 2 he wrote to the colonial secretary:

It is evident that Papineau's party will not be satisfied with any concession which will not put it in a more favorable position to realize its ultimate intentions, that is to say, the separation of this country from England and the establishment of a republican government. M. Papineau has gone so far that he must persevere, or submit to a defeat which would destroy all his influence; the plan that he follows shows that he has decided to risk everything to reach his goal. The violent and unjustifiable attacks which have been made by the ultra-Tories against the French Canadians in general have created an animosity of which M. Papineau has not failed to take advantage, and I attribute to this cause much of his influence on a great many members of the house. M. Papineau has emissaries in all directions, and although I do not know that there is reason to take alarm, there is need of much precaution and vigilance to prevent and check the disorders which might take place, as a result of the efforts made to excite discontent among the people by the most abominable representations. The government needs to be invested with the fullest power, and according to my present opinion, you may be under the necessity of suspending the constitution. It is with the most profound regret that I announce this opinion; but my duty forces me to do so.[34]

Gosford was right; the hot blood of the youngsters was carrying the *Patriote* movement out of the hands of staider elders. Late in August the New Brunswick-born and Vermont-bred Thomas Storrow Brown, André Ouimet, and Amédée Papineau, son of the *Patriote* leader, organized a *Fils de la Liberté* association in Montreal, in obvious imitation of the American Sons of Liberty of revolutionary days. The *Fils de la Liberté* met publicly for military training to the strains of George Etienne Cartier's '*Avant tout, je suis Canadien,*' though they lacked arms. On October 1 they published a hotheaded manifesto in which they proclaimed their intention 'to emancipate our country from all human authority save that of the bold democracy residing within its bosom.'[35] The Tories of the disbanded British Rifle Corps, egged on by the *Herald*, had formed a rival organization, the British Legion or Doric Club, which masqueraded as a 'fraternal association' after Gosford had again frowned on their renewed proposal to form a volunteer military unit.[36]

Meanwhile the *Patriote* mass meetings continued, with the majority of the speakers more violent than ever. The Two Mountains committee decided on October 1 to elect its own justices of the peace and military officers by majority vote, to replace those deprived of office by Gosford, and did so at a meeting of *habitants* on October 15. The anti-*Patriote Le Populaire* hailed the news with: '*La Révolution commence!*' On October 23 5,000 people assembled at Saint-Charles on the Richelieu in the name of the Confederation of the Six Counties [of the Richelieu] to hear Papineau, L.-M. Viger, Dr. Côté, Rodier, Brown, and Amury Girod. Papineau, at last alarmed by the storm he had roused, advised against a recourse to arms, urging constitutional resistance and arguing that 'the best way to fight England is to refuse to buy anything from her.'[37] It was significant that Dr. Wolfred Nelson, the chairman of the meeting, interrupted the 'tribune of the people' to insist that the time for action had already come, that the moment 'to melt our spoons into bullets' was at hand. This assembly of the six counties of the Richelieu adopted thirteen resolutions, including a statement, clearly modelled on the American Declaration of Independence, of the rights of man, among which figured the people's right to change the form of government at will. The assembly called upon the citizens of the Richelieu to meet in December to elect judges and militia officers to replace those dismissed by the governor for their *Patriote* leanings. Military training and systematic resistance to officials appointed by Gosford were urged, and British soldiers were encouraged to desert. On the 24th the delegates called for the meeting of a convention to replace the 'nullified' legislature. This attempt to create a state within a state was inevitably the prelude to open rebellion.

The influence of the American and French Revolutions was more evident than ever: the organization of the *Fils de la Liberté* in Montreal was hailed as an example which each parish should follow, and a ceremony, modelled upon that of 1789 on the Champs de Mars in Paris, was held about a liberty pole, crowned with a Phrygian bonnet and bearing the inscription, 'To Papineau, his grateful compatriots, 1837.'[38] Young men took an oath, hand upon the pole, to be faithful to the fatherland and to conquer or die. The Saint-Charles meeting gave clear evidence that the movement was passing into more extreme hands than those of its original leaders: Papineau, the scheduled hero of the affair, was more moderate than at Saint-Laurent in the spring, but he was overruled by Dr. Nelson, as was his follower F.-X. Mailhot by the still more extreme Dr. Côté, who was echoed by Brown and Girod. Côté, the turbulent member for Lacadie and the circulator of Lamennais' *Les Paroles d'un croyant*, a revolutionary work condemned by Rome, concluded his fiery address with these words: 'The time for speeches has passed; we must now direct lead against our enemies.'[39]

On the day after this assembly at Saint-Charles, and a rival constitutionalist gathering at Montreal with Peter McGill as chairman, Bishop Lartigue issued a pastoral letter which *La Minerve* hailed, under the heading of 'More Politics in the Pulpit,' as a 'second edition of Gosford's proclamation.'[40] It was an attempt to avert the imminent danger of civil strife:

For a long time, brethren, we have heard only of agitation, even of revolt, in a country always renowned up to now for its loyalty, its peaceful spirit, and its love for the religion of its fathers. Everywhere brothers are seen arrayed against brothers, friends against friends, and citizens against their fellow citizens; and from one end of this diocese to the other discord seems to have broken 'the bonds of charity which existed between the members of one body, the children of one Church, of Catholicism which is a religion of unity.

We speak here on our own initiative, without any external pressure, solely from motives of conscience. We shall not give you our opinion, as a citizen, on the purely political question as to which is right or wrong among the diverse branches of the sovereign power (these are matters which God has left to the disputes of men: *munduns tradidit disputationi corum*); but the moral question, i.e., what are the duties of a Catholic toward the civil power established and constituted in each state, this moral question, I say, is within our domain and competence . . .

Do not let yourselves be seduced if some one wishes to engage you in rebellion against the established government, under the pretext that you form part of the 'Sovereign People'; the all-too famous National Convention of France, although forced to admit the sovereignty of the people since its existence was due to it, took good care itself to condemn popular insurrections, by inserting in the Declaration of Rights at the beginning of the Constitution of 1795 the statement that sovereignty resides not in a part nor even in a majority of the people, but in the whole body of the citizens: adding, 'that no individual, that no partial union of citizens, can pretend to the "Sovereignty".' But who would dare say that in this country the whole body of citizens desire the destruction of their government.

Have you ever considered seriously the horrors of civil strife? Have you pictured brooks of blood flooding your streets and your countryside, and the innocent engulfed with the guilty in the same sequence of misfortunes? Have you reflected on the fact that, nearly without exception, every popular revolution is a bloody business, as experience proves; and that the philosopher of Geneva, the author of the *Social Contract*, the demagogue of the sovereignty of the people, says somewhere that a revolution would be bought too dearly, if it cost a single drop of blood?[41]

Bishop Lartigue based his exposition of the duties of the citizen particularly on Gregory XVI's encyclical of August 15, 1832, and the papal brief of July of the same year to the Polish bishops, in which the Polish patriots were reproved and the Czar was declared their lawful sovereign. These papal utterances, permeated with the reactionary royalist sentiment of the period, had caused Lamennais' break with the Church and the publication of his *Les Paroles d'un croyant*, whose fervent denunciation of kings and priests found favor with the *Patriote* extremists.

Bishop Lartigue's intervention was greeted with anger, popular demonstrations, and anti-clerical counterblasts by the *Patriote* press. At Montreal, where 1,200 *Patriotes* paraded opposite St. James Cathedral at vespers, it was said that the pastoral letter would hasten the 'revolution,' while at Chambly three men left the church while it was being read and gathered a group who greeted Bishop Bourget and the clergy after Mass with cries of '*A bas le mandement!*' and '*Vive Papineau!*' Elsewhere *curés* were treated to the singing of the *Marseillaise* and the *Libera*. The popular feeling ran so high that Bishop Lartigue offered his resignation to Rome and planned to take refuge at the Seminary of Quebec against anti-royalist plots in what he called a 'civil war.' In November he published anonymously at Quebec a '*Défense du Mandement*,' refuting *Patriote* criticisms of his action in *La Minerve* and the *Vindicator*.[42]

On December 11 Bishop Signay, fearing the spread of the Montreal troubles, condemned recourse to revolt for the remedying of abuses as 'not only inefficacious, imprudent, and fatal to those who make use of it, but moreover criminal in the eyes of God and of our holy religion' and ordained prayers for peace.[43] Although the episcopal utterance was generally received with respect in the districts of Quebec and Trois-Rivières, there was opposition to it in the capital. Abbé Baillargeon, then *curé* and later bishop of Quebec, had already aroused a bitter storm of protest there when he counseled loyalty, prudence, and submission to lawful authority. The new *Patriote* organ of the capital, the bilingual *Liberal* edited by Robert Shore Milnes Bouchette, grandson of Carleton's guide in 1775 and son of the surveyor-general, and Charles Hunter, had then observed that 'It would be much better for the *curés* to receive quietly their tithes and the thousand other taxes raised on the ignorance of the people, as long as they can in return preach the moral doctrines of Christianity to their flocks, rather than for them to descend into the arena of political disputes, moved as they always are in these questions by their private interests.' Of the pastoral letters Bouchette remarked: 'The day is not far off when the bishops will regret having meddled in matters which did not concern them.'[44]

Etienne Parent's defense of the *curé* of Quebec caused *La Minerve* to censure both, and the Permanent Central Committee to denounce *Le Canadien* and Parent himself as one 'who has betrayed, and continues to betray, the interests of the country.'[45] In October Parent counseled the abandonment of illegal opposition by the *Minerve* group, and promised that all the French Canadians would rise as one man to demand or seek justice, if their opponents then indulged in excesses. But by that time the situation was already out of hand: disorders, directed chiefly against the English merchants, the *seigneurs*, and the '*Chouayens*' (as those French Canadians who would not join the *Patriote* movement were known), had already broken out in the Richelieu and Two Mountains regions near Montreal. Magistrates and militia officers favorable to the government were forced to resign their commissions, and even *curés* were troubled by assaults on their property. Apart from the spokesmen of the Church, Etienne Parent was now almost alone among French Canadians in raising his voice against the course the *Patriotes* were following. On November 22, the very eve of recourse to open rebellion, he delivered himself of a prophetic utterance in *Le Canadien:*

If we emerge from our present plight without being crushed, let it be an eternal lesson to those who have not been able to learn from history, where it is written on every page, of the folly of agitating a people, of questioning the fundamental principles of the established social order, unless the oppression is directly felt by the governed and there remain no alternatives other than hard and dishonorable slavery or armed resistance. The agitation which has been aroused in this country has resulted in placing part of the population in open opposition to the government. But who would now say that the present government, with all its faults, is not preferable by far to the state of affairs which exists today in the district of Montreal? Would not the worst government be better than the anarchy which now grips the upper part of the province, even if anarchy were to be succeeded by a state of liberty; but no, it will be followed here as elsewhere by military despotism. That is not all. After the sword of the soldier has cut off the thousand heads of anarchy, then will come the law, which will arm the government with repressive measures that will necessarily retard the progress of the liberal cause . . . Thus we shall perhaps soon see the government vested with extraordinary powers which its creatures will certainly abuse. What will have caused that? The fatal agitation which has been imprudently aroused in this country, and which the leaders are no longer able to control. Once again, let this be at least a lesson for the future, if Providence reserves for us a future, which we must still hope.[46]

Parent had an observant as well as a prophetic soul: the *Patriote* movement had indeed run away from its original idealistic leaders and fallen into more violent hands.

The inevitable clash soon followed. Ethnic feeling was aroused by the boisterous parades of the rival *Fils de la Liberté* and Doric Club in Montreal, and on November 6 a street fight developed after the loyalists had been urged to 'crush rebellion in its bud,' which ended with the *Patriotes* breaking the windows of a magistrate's house and the Doric Club sacking the premises of O'Callaghan's *Vindicator* and assaulting Papineau's home. The troops were called out by the magistrates, a body which, along with the rest of Montreal's judicial organization, had just been purged by Gosford of all *Patriote* sympathizers. Armed guards, who tended to wink at the proceedings of the Doric Club, now patrolled the streets. [47] On the very day of the brawl in Montreal Gosford wrote home requesting power to suspend the *Habeas Corpus* Act and to proclaim martial law, while he also informed the colonial secretary that he had at last requested reinforcements from the Maritimes and Upper Canada. [48] Volunteer regiments, largely composed of Bureaucrats and gallophobes, were raised at Montreal, Quebec, and in the Townships. [49] Sir John Colborne, the commander-in-chief, who had long urged repressive rather than conciliatory measures, now obtained the governor's support. Public meetings and processions were prohibited on November 12, and warrants were issued on November 16 for the arrest for treason of twenty-six principal *Patriote* leaders. Papineau, O'Callaghan, Rodolphe Desrivières, T. S. Brown, and Ovide Perrault escaped arrest by fleeing from Montreal to the Richelieu, while André Ouimet, president of the *Fils de la Liberté*, and other minor *Patriote* figures of Montreal were clapped into jail. Morin, Bouchette, and a few others were arrested at Quebec, but later released on bail.

On the night of November 16 a troop of Montreal Volunteer Cavalry, sent to St. Johns with a constable to arrest Dr. Davignon and the notary P.-P. Demaray, was ambushed between Chambly and Longueuil by a force of *Patriotes* commanded by Bonaventure Viger* and Dr. Timothée Kimber, local chiefs of the movement. [50] Shots were fired and blood was shed; the volunteers fled, leaving their prisoners behind; and civil war had at last broken out, after a long prelude which contrasts sharply with the briefness of actual strife. But never has so little bloodshed been so well remembered, for ethnic division added to the bitterness of civil war.

3

The news of the successful skirmish at Longueuil heartened the *Patriotes*, driven to open rebellion by Tory provocation and by the government's adoption of repressive measures. They began to gather with such poor arms as they possessed at Saint-Denis and Saint-Charles on the Richelieu, where they were soon joined by the fugitives from Montreal. Those at Saint-Denis were commanded by Dr. Wolfred Nelson, an English-born local member of the assembly,

---

* A distant cousin of D.-B. Viger.

while the force at Montreal was commanded by Thomas Storrow
Brown, a New Brunswick merchant of Montreal, who still bore
scars from the fray between the Doric Club and the *Fils de la Liberté*,
whose 'general' he had been.

Colborne had established, with the aid of the Montreal merchants
and the *Chouayens*, an efficient intelligence service, and was well
informed about *Patriote* doings. He promptly planned a joint expedition against the two centers of the disaffected Richelieu region,
in order to nip the rebellion in the bud. One force under Lieutenant-
Colonel Wetherall, consisting of a regiment of regular infantry, a
troop of the Montreal Volunteer Cavalry, and two field guns, had
already been sent to secure the lightly garrisoned fort at Chambly.
This body was to advance down the Richelieu, and then to join
forces at Saint-Denis with a detachment under Colonel Gore of
five companies of regulars, a troop of mounted volunteers, and
a field gun, which was to come up the river from the post at Sorel.
It was thus hoped to round up the fugitive *Patriote* leaders and to
disperse their followers. The plan was neatly conceived, but it
made no allowances for the condition of rural roads in November,
or for the military's unfamiliarity with the countryside and its
language.

On the night of November 22, lashed by rain and sleet, Gore's
force turned away from the main route along the river in order to
avoid Saint-Ours, which was held by the *Patriotes*, and fell into difficulties on a muddy back road. His proposed surprise attack by night
on Saint-Denis became a daylight attack by exhausted and half-
frozen soldiers on a fully alert and strongly defended village, whose
pealing bells alarmed the countryside and brought new defenders
swarming to the scene. After five hours of inconclusive fighting,
which resulted in the soldiers losing six killed and eighteen wounded,
Gore retreated first to Saint-Ours and then to Sorel. One hundred
and seventeen of his men failed to answer the roll call the evening
after the battle. The *Patriotes*, who included some veterans of the
War of 1812, lost eleven dead and seven wounded.[51] Among the dead
was Ovide Perrault, a promising young lawyer and member of the
assembly who was a devoted follower of Papineau. Young George
Etienne Cartier distinguished himself by bringing reinforcements
across the river to the *Patriotes* under fire.

The great tribune himself, with Dr. O'Callaghan, had left early
in the skirmish for Saint-Hyacinthe, another *Patriote* center, whence
they later fled to the United States. Papineau declared that he
adopted this course on the advice of Wolfred Nelson, who had said
to him: 'Do not expose yourself uselessly; you will be of more service
to us after the fight than here'; but Nelson later denied, after he
had broken with his former chief, that he had ever made any such

statement.[52] It may have been that Papineau, the undisputed chief of the movement, felt obliged to preserve himself from capture—it is said to have been agreed among the *Patriote* high command that Papineau should keep apart from all fighting, in order to be free to negotiate later with the government—or he may have been unwilling to participate in the open insurrection which he had always opposed. In any case his action at Saint-Denis, imitated later by most of the chiefs of the *Patriotes*, created a breach between the leaders and their followers which played no small part in the rapid collapse of the movement.

But a more important incident at Saint-Denis than Papineau's flight was the murder by the *Patriotes* of Lieutenant Weir, a dispatch carrier in civilian clothes who had missed Gore on the road from Sorel, thanks to the latter's detour, and who had been taken prisoner when he arrived at Saint-Denis before the troops. When the attack began, he was ordered off for safe-keeping to Saint-Charles, having given his word not to attempt escape. But, seeing the troops approach as he was being taken off, tightly bound, in a wagon, he leapt out and was promptly dispatched by the swords and guns of his guards and of the excited bystanders, whose traditional hatred of the English had been aroused. Weir's body was found lying in the Richelieu, weighted down by stones, when the British forces returned to Saint-Denis a week later; and the sight of the mutilated corpse so infuriated the soldiers that they sacked and burnt the greater part of the village. The slogan of the government forces during the rebellion became 'Remember Jack Weir,' and many later excesses on their part can be blamed on this incident.[53]

The savageness of *Patriote* feeling was not wholly ethnic in character, however, for on November 28 some *Patriotes* of St. Johns captured a French Canadian named Chartrand, who had enlisted in a loyalist volunteer corps and was reputed to be a government informer. After a drumhead court-martial, Chartrand was tied to a tree and shot.[54] Civil strife is rarely conducted according to the established rules of warfare, and the conduct of the unorganized *habitants* was not such as to either win the respect of the British professional soldiers or to calm the prejudices of the English-Canadian volunteers, excited by the Tory press and by wild rumors of *Patriote* outrages upon members of the English minority isolated in the countryside.

The initial victory at Saint-Denis was the sole battle which the insurgents won. The *Patriote* enthusiasm which it aroused was soon dampened by news from Saint-Charles. Colonel Wetherall left Chambly on November 22 about the same hour as Gore left Sorel. But according to Major Conrad Augustus Gugy, a Swiss-Canadian leader of the English party in the assembly who acted as a police inspector and intelligence officer during the rising and who accompanied Wetherall as guide and interpreter, 'not one of the Force knew anything of the roads or the people, nor do I believe that more than one spoke French.'[55] Through the same November rain and sleet, followed by frost, which beset Gore's force, Wetherall's detachment struggled on till he was persuaded to halt by Gugy's alarm at what might befall exhausted men 'in an enemy's country, surrounded by thousands of armed men.'[56] The column was still seven miles from Saint-Charles when Wetherall got word of Gore's reverse at Saint-Denis, and on Gugy's advice he sent back to Chambly for reinforcements. Awaiting their arrival took another day.

Meanwhile the *Patriotes* at Saint-Charles had fortified the manor house of the newly loyalist *seigneur* Debartzch, who had fled to Montreal. According to 'General' T. S. Brown, who had bruised some local feelings by assuming command, the *Patriotes* were less numerous there than the government supposed, a bare 200 men equipped with only 109 guns. The impossibility of any long-meditated recourse to rebellion is best witnessed by Brown's account of the *Patriote* armament:

Of ammunition we had some half dozen kegs of gun-powder and a little lead, which was cast into bullets; but as the fire-arms were of every calibre, the cartridges made were too large for many, which were consequently useless. We had two small rusty field pieces, but with neither carriages nor appointments they were as useless as two logs.

There was one old musket, but not a bayonet. The fire arms were common *fusils* [flintlocks], in all conditions of dilapidation, some tied together with strings, and very many with lock-springs so worn out, that they could not be discharged.[57]

The most active resistance encountered by the troops was waged by a force under Bonaventure Viger, which harried the advance of the column by destroying bridges and picking off skirmishers. Brown had placed pickets at the outskirts of the village, and these fell back from house to house as the troops slowly advanced, burning houses and barns as they came to rout out sharpshooters. Before launching an attack against the *Patriote* stronghold, Wetherall sent a message that the rebels would not be molested if they dispersed quietly. Brown dispatched a grandiloquent reply, offering free passage to the troops to Sorel, if they would lay down their arms. The engagement which ensued between Wetherall's fresh veterans and the *Patriotes*, whose enthusiasm and numbers had dwindled as they awaited the approach of the military, lasted less than an hour. The field pieces breached the rude log redoubt which had been raised about the manor house, and a bayonet charge soon cleared out the *Patriote* stronghold. Viger and some others escaped by swimming across the river; Brown tried vainly to rally fugitives at the village, whither he had gone in search of reinforcements, and then fled to Saint-Denis, a general without an army. The *Patriotes*, who were outnumbered by two to one, lost forty killed, thirty wounded, and thirty taken prisoner, while the soldiers reported three killed and eighteen wounded.[58]

This decisive defeat, which scattered the leaders and dispersed their followers, crushed the rebellion in the Richelieu region. The *Patriote* chiefs either went into hiding or fled across the frontier, hounded by search parties of French constables and English volunteers; their men disbanded, complaining of their leaders' conduct and of the lack of arms and ammunition. Wetherall, no doubt once more influenced by the alarmed Gugy, did not press on from Saint-Charles to Saint-Denis, but returned to Chambly and Montreal, as in fact an undelivered dispatch from Colborne had ordered him to do. He made a triumphal entry into Montreal, with thirty-two prisoners and the liberty pole from Saint-Charles.[59] Reinforced from Montreal, Gore revisited the scene of his defeat on December 1 and found all quiet. His men, goaded by the discovery of Weir's mutilated body, desecrated the church, looted and set fire to the village, whose people had taken good care, under Nelson's direction, of the British wounded left behind on November 23.[60] This action left a legacy of bitter anti-English feeling in the countryside, soon to be increased by other incidents.

Meanwhile the *Patriote* leaders who had fled across the Vermont and New York borders were hospitably received by the Americans, whose memories of their own struggle for liberty had been kept alive by impassioned Fourth of July orators, and who were affected by the same economic depression which had moved the *habitants* to rise in revolt. But benevolent neutrality rather than active aid was the part played in general by the people whom Papineau had so confidently hailed at Saint-Ours as 'our friends and our natural allies.'[61] In their schemes of a liberating invasion the French-Canadian exiles received little American assistance more substantial than that offered by the good ladies of Swanton, Vermont, who made the flags carried by the 200 armed men with whom E.-E. Malhiot and Robert Bouchette crossed the frontier on December 6, hoping to rouse the dispersed *Patriotes* once more. But just across the line, at Moore's Corners, the returning exiles, burdened with arms and ammunition for the force they hoped to rally, were met by a party of the Missisquoi Volunteers under Captain O. J. Kemp, who had been warned of their coming. In an evening ambush whose effectiveness was somewhat spoiled by the overeagerness of the loyalists whom Kemp had summoned from all quarters to supplement his force, the *Patriotes* were put to flight after a few minutes' fire. They retired hastily over the border, leaving one dead and three wounded behind them.[62] One of the wounded was Bouchette, who found himself once more arrested, as he had been earlier at Quebec. He was soon jailed at Montreal, along with Wolfred Nelson and Bonaventure Viger, who had been captured in the man-hunt now carried on in the disaffected region.

Most of the *Patriote* leaders found sanctuary beyond the frontier, however, and during the winter, spring, and summer of 1838 they foregathered in one border town or another in New York and Vermont. Their meetings were troubled by dissension between the peace party headed by Papineau, and the militant group led by Dr. Robert Nelson, the brother of the imprisoned leader at Saint-Denis, and including Dr. Côté, Rodier, Malhiot, Gagnon, and Duvernay. The confusion which followed the outbreak of open rebellion ended all coherence in the *Patriote* movement. So fervent a disciple of Papineau as Lafontaine had tried to calm the over-zealous at the last moment; and then upon hearing of the incident at Longueuil on November 18, had hurried to Quebec to beg Gosford to summon a sobered assembly. He turned against Papineau, and early in December journeyed again to Quebec with Leslie and other members of parliament to renew his request of the governor; but meeting refusal once more, he went to the States and thence to England, hoping to intercede with the authorities at London. Learning that a warrant had been issued against him for treason, he retired to Paris, where he kept in touch with the *Patriotes'* English friends.[63]

After Gosford had issued a proclamation on November 29 calling upon the population to return to its loyalty, martial law was declared on December 5 for the third time since 1760. On November 29 and December 1 Gosford put prices on the heads of the chief *Patriote* leaders.[64] The *habitants* were ordered to give up their arms, and the magistrates to re-establish peace; while pressure was brought to bear through Gugy upon the Richelieu *curés* to use the Church as a tranquilizing force. Many of the *curés* did not need prompting from government sources; their sentiments were those of Bishop Signay who condemned the insurrection in his pastoral letter of December 11. Indeed, one of them was reprimanded for his zeal in making himself 'a crier or herald for the state' by the *Patriote*-minded Bishop Bourget, whose superior Bishop Lartigue nonetheless formally ordered the clergy of the diocese of Montreal on January 8, 1838, to refuse the sacraments and Christian burial to unrepentant rebels, as he and his coadjutor had already done since the outbreak of the rising in several instances. The *curés* of the Montreal district were more sympathetic to the *Patriote* cause. Bishop

View in Montreal, Canada

Oil painting (c. 1835) by W. H. B. Bartlett, showing the Great Blondin walking the tight-rope across Notre Dame Street between the Old Seminary Church and unfinished Notre Dame Church. (Victor Spark Gallery, New York.) (National Gallery.)

Saint-Ferréol Falls

Oil painting (c. 1840) by Joseph Legaré, one of the most interesting native painters
of Quebec. (I.O.A.P.Q.)

Lartigue placed Abbé Etienne Chartier, who took an active revolutionary role, under interdict, but he protected two others, the Abbés Augustin-Magloire Blanchet* and F.-M. Turcot, who were 'arbitrarily imprisoned.'[66] Bishop Bourget urged the *curés* to follow the example of the clergy of France and Spain, but showed great sympathy with Chartier, Blanchet, and other *Patriote* prisoners.

Meanwhile the most serious encounter of the whole rebellion took place at Saint-Eustache on December 14. At the news of the victory at Saint-Denis the long turbulent county of Two Mountains, northwest of Montreal, boiled over in revolt. It was the constituency of William Henry Scott, one of Papineau's English followers, but the actual leader of the revolt there was a Swiss agronomist and adventurer, Amury Girod, whose plausible tongue had won him credentials from Papineau. His violence and audacity had enabled him to dominate the local *Patriote* leaders, Joseph Girouard and Dr. Jean Chénier. Girod had no high opinion of his colleagues, for in the secret journal which he kept in German and Italian he remarked: 'It is easier to prove to a Goose that it should not Cackle, than to make a Canadian hold his tongue.'[67] On the night of November 29 some two hundred *Patriotes* under the command of Girod and Chénier broke into the Hudson's Bay Company stores at the Indian mission of Oka, where they seized a few guns and ammunition. They also took an old three-pounder, the cherished possession of the superior, Abbé Dufresne. Girod failed to persuade the Indian chief to lend his people's arms to the insurgents. Upon their return to Saint-Eustache, the insurgents occupied a newly completed but empty convent in defiance of the loyalist Curé Jacques Paquin's orders, and made their headquarters there. Apart from guarding the Abord-à-Plouffe bridge, which connected this region with the Island of Montreal, Sir John Colborne ignored the northern insurrection until the Richelieu rising had been suppressed.

News of the defeat at Saint-Charles and the influence of Curé Paquin of Saint-Eustache dampened the ardor of some of the *Patriotes*, but not that of Chénier, who did not hesitate to put both the *curé* and his vicar under virtual arrest. In any case the inflammatory speeches of Abbé Etienne Chartier, *curé* of nearby Saint-Benoît and one of the few priests wholeheartedly to adopt the *Patriote* cause, offset the activities of the loyalist clerics. Girod succeeded in gathering together nearly 1,000 men, including Irish as well as French Canadians, though many of them lacked weapons and to his disgust the whole body passed its time in drinking, dancing, and quarreling, instead of drilling and making ready for the inevitable clash. He noted in his journal that 'Chénier is a lazy and foolish fellow—his Brother is a drunkard, and both cause a

---

* Later Bishop of Walla-Walla and Nesqually, Washington.

G

deal of confusion through their bad example.'[68] Girod had already
quarreled with the moderate Scott and Girouard; and among the
local leaders only the despised Chénier and the Abbé Chartier
stood by him when he made himself unpopular by imposing discipline upon the disorderly assembly, which included much riffraff
and many peaceably disposed persons who had been impressed
into service by bellicose *Patriotes*. The numbers in the camp fluctuated
widely, and on the eve of the conflict Girod was forced to set a
guard about the village to prevent desertions.

On December 13 Colborne moved against this self-elected general
and his disorderly following with three regiments of regulars and
two of volunteer cavalry, as well as artillery—a force of more than
2,000 well-equipped men. On the following day this small army
crossed the Rivière-des-Mille-Iles on the ice and reached Saint-
Eustache, finding some 250 insurgents barricaded in the church, the
rectory, the convent, and the house of Scott—the most substantial
buildings of the place. The church was the chief *Patriote* stronghold,
and against it the artillery was directed. While cannon balls scarred
the façade, men of the Royals set fire first to the rectory and then to
the rear of the church. Forced out by the flames, the *Patriotes* were shot
down by the soldiers as they jumped from the windows. Chénier and
seventy others were thus killed, while many charred bodies were later
found in the ruins of the church. Over a hundred prisoners were
taken, while the soldiers reported only one killed and nine wounded.
Eye-witnesses, however, estimated the military losses as high as
150.[69] Among the wounded was the ubiquitous Major Gugy,
who had led the way across the ice and distinguished himself in the
attack on the church. Girod, who had fled to Saint-Benoît after
disposing his men for the attack under the resolute Chénier, shot
himself four days later, when threatened with capture near Montreal.
Placed under interdict by Bishop Lartigue, the Abbé Chartier
escaped to the United States, where after a voyage to France he
later had parishes in New York, Indiana, and Louisiana before
returning to Canada in 1845. Girouard and other *Patriote* chiefs
of the region were soon rounded up and jailed.

Most of Saint-Eustache was devoured by flames, after it had been
pillaged by the soldiers, some of whom paraded drunkenly through
the streets in vestments taken from the church. On December 15
the troops set out for nearby Saint-Benoît, which on the advice of
Girouard and the Abbé Defresne surrendered at their approach
and that of a large body of volunteers from the Ottawa Valley, but
the village was nevertheless sacked and burnt to the ground, while
the church was abominably desecrated. According to one of the
British officers, this inexcusable action was the work of the volunteers, who were 'not to be controlled, and who were in every case,

I believe, the instrument of infliction.'[70] Many of the volunteers were local men who had been ill-treated while the *Patriotes* were dominant. But Colborne, with 1,800 regulars at his command, can hardly be freed from blame for the devastation of a village whose inhabitants had surrendered to him and had offered no resistance whatsoever. The following day Colborne dismissed the unruly volunteers and returned quietly to Montreal with the regulars, while the volunteers looted and burnt their way home.

So ended the rebellion of 1837; for the rest of the province heeded the voice of the bishops and remained quiet, save for the village of Montmagny below Quebec, where Dr. Etienne-Pascal Taché was the mainspring of a minor disturbance. Thanks to the impromptu character of the revolt and to the irresolution of all the leaders save Chénier, who alone fought to the last, the resort to arms was a fiasco, like its counterpart in Upper Canada. But the authorities had had a bad scare, and Lower Canada soon became an armed camp. During December three regiments of regulars made an epic march overland to Quebec and Montreal from the Maritimes, and the cities and the military posts were soon strongly garrisoned, while parties of volunteers combed the countryside for the fugitive *Patriote* leaders. The conduct of the volunteers was such as to add to the bitter memories of Saint-Denis, Saint-Eustache, and Saint-Benoît, as was also the behaviour of the triumphant loyalist mob in Montreal when *Patriote* prisoners were brought to jail there. Gallophobia and anglophobia raged with new vigor in the uneasy province, though nominal peace had been imposed by force of arms.

On February 7, 1838, Bishop Signay issued a pastoral letter calling for thanksgiving at the return of peace and urging 'that Christian charity which ought to unite to one another the citizens of the same city, the dwellers in the same parish, and the subjects of the same province.' Bishop Lartigue followed suit, while both prelates encouraged their clergy to sign a petition to the Queen and British Parliament, protesting their loyalty, condemning the rising, and pleading against a union of Lower with Upper Canada and the loss of the French Canadians' rights and privileges. But this intervention of the clergy merely increased their unpopularity with the people, while the *Patriotes* remained convinced that union of the Canadas would lead inevitably to independence or annexation to the United States. Two days after thanksgiving had been duly made on February 26 for the return of peace, the *Patriotes* rose again.[71]

4

The rebellions in the Canadas had a profound effect in England, and at last brought the action which had so long been demanded.

Parliament met early in 1838 and on February 10 suspended the constitution of Lower Canada until November 1, 1840 and provided for the nomination by the governor of a council with legislative powers. Lord Durham was appointed governor-general and high commissioner to investigate Canadian grievances and to report on a remedy. On May 29 he took over from Sir John Colborne, who had become administrator of the colony when the ill and disheartened Gosford returned to England in February.

Colborne had appointed a special council of eleven English and eleven French Canadians—all Tories, Bureaucrats, or *Chouayens* [72]— that was given extraordinary powers under the proclamation of March 29 which suspended the constitution. The chief action of the council was to suspend the Habeas Corpus Act for three months, in order that the prisoners taken under martial law might still be held when the emergency measure was repealed in April. Colborne, who became the dominant force in Lower Canada after the rebellion broke out, governed with a hard hand, but not with brutality. Of the some 500 prisoners who had been taken during and after the rebellion, 200 were released by the end of January, and another hundred-odd by the first of May. Seventy-two of the remaining 161 were considered by him to be important offenders, and he left their fate to be determined by Durham, who had been instructed to temper justice with mercy.

The new governor-general's first act was to dismiss Colborne's packed special council, so 'that his administrative conduct should be free from all suspicions of political influence or party feeling; that it should rest on his own undivided responsibility.' [73] In its place he appointed a new executive council of five members, three of whom were drawn from his own staff, while the other two, the provincial secretary and commissary-general, were non-political functionaries. On June 25 he appointed a new special council, made up of the senior military and naval officers and three members of his own staff. Charles Buller and Colonel George Couper served on both councils.

These acts were typical of the man, who combined a regal arrogance and strong dictatorial tendencies with Liberal and indeed Radical opinions. He was the son of a wealthy colliery owner, who had been a member of parliament for the city of Durham. Educated at Eton, young Lambton had served for a year or two in the dragoons, and then succeeded to his father's seat in parliament, where he soon became a leader among the Whig Reformers and a bitter opponent of Liverpool, Castlereagh, and Peel. His second marriage to the daughter of Lord Grey, the leader of the Whigs, strengthened his political position; and he entered his father-in-law's cabinet as Lord Privy Seal in 1830, after having been elevated to the peerage in 1828. He was one of the committee of four which drafted the Reform Bill of 1832. Forced from the cabinet by ill health in the following year, he was given an earldom and sent on a special mission to Russia, where he pleaded the cause of the Polish rebels who were then being treated with great severity. Upon his return he took a leading role in the liberal wing of the Whig party, and in 1835 he was made ambassador to Russia, chiefly to get him out of the more moderate government's way. The same motive played a part in his appointment to Canada, for he was the hero of both advanced Whigs and moderate Radicals, and was much spoken of as a future prime minister. His reports on Russia and Belgium, where he had played a part in the establishment of Leopold I as king, had given him a great reputation as a political analyst. His brilliant abilities were offset by temperamental instability and lack of tact; while his arrogance and love of pomp and circumstance contrasted strangely with his professed Liberal sentiments.

Quebec was dazzled by the splendor of Durham's regal retinue, numbering no less than eight aides-de-camp and so large that it took over the Legislative Buildings as well as the Chateau Saint-Louis. Popular confidence was in great measure won for Durham by the proclamation which he issued upon landing, expressing his desire to hasten the return of constitutional government and to be considered a friend and arbitrator, ready at all times to hear the people's will and griefs, and determined to act with the strictest impartiality.[74] His immediate dismissal of Colborne's council gave evidence that these were more than mere fine words. Etienne Parent at once displayed great friendliness to Durham, and on June 8 *Le Canadien* carried an ode to the new governor from the pen of the future historian Garneau, which closed with the assurance, later to become wearisomely familiar in patriotic orations, that 'Canada would be the last defender of old England on this great continent.'[75] Durham at once turned the bright young men of his entourage loose on an investigation of the state of the province, while he himself held a splendid court in the Chateau Saint-Louis, to which both French and English flocked to enjoy themselves and to win the governor to their respective ways of thinking.

The new governor's first great problem was the disposal of the imprisoned *Patriotes*. It would be difficult to obtain their conviction from a French-Canadian jury, and little less than judicial murder if they were tried by an English-Canadian jury. In any case their trial would reawaken the agitation which had happily subsided. In the columns of the *Montreal Herald* Adam Thom still demanded that the rebels be brought to the gallows, but there seemed to be no way to send them there except without trial. Faced with this situation, Durham determined upon an ingenious if arbitrary course of action. He obtained a signed confession of guilt from eight of the principal prisoners, including Wolfred Nelson, Bouchette, and Bonaventure Viger, who at his suggestion threw themselves upon his mercy and prayed that the public peace should not be troubled by their trial.[76] By an ordinance of June 28—Victoria's Coronation Day—Durham exiled these eight prisoners to Bermuda, under pain of capital punishment if they returned without authorization. Sixteen other leaders of the rebellion, who had fled abroad and were under indictment for high treason, were forbidden to return to Canada under pain of death. Those named were Papineau, Côté, O'Callaghan, Robert Nelson, Rodier, Brown, Duvernay, Chartier, Gagnon, Cartier, the two John Ryans, Perrault, Demaray, Davignon, and Gauthier.[77] Another proclamation of the same date extended a complete amnesty to all other prisoners and refugees, except those involved in the murders of Weir and Chartrand, on condition of future good conduct.[78] These merciful and wise—if illegal—measures received general acclaim in Canada, except in the pages of the *Montreal Herald*, and established Durham's position as a peacemaker.

Unfortunately, they also aroused a storm of protest in England, which was unaware of local conditions and somewhat obsessed with legality. Deportation without trial and the arbitrary decreeing of the death penalty had an ugly sound to liberty-loving English ears. Lord Brougham, a bitter political enemy of Durham, was not slow to launch a savage attack in the House of Lords upon these measures. Melbourne and Glenelg, who had already congratulated Durham unofficially upon his solution of a difficult problem, were forced to bow to the storm which Brougham raised and to disavow the governor's action. While this political battle went on in England, Durham was making a royal progress through Lower and Upper Canada, and sketching out his plans for administrative reorganization.

One of his first concerns had been to avert the threat of official or unofficial American intervention into the Canadian troubles. Both Upper and Lower Canadian exiles were then trying to achieve just such a step, and had won considerable sympathy in New York official circles. But President Van Buren protested to Durham's brother-in-law and unofficial envoy, Colonel Charles Grey, when his government was accused of favoring the rebels for its own purposes, that he judged annexation 'directly contrary to the interests of the United States.'[79] Colonel Grey met with similar assurances from the American Secretaries of State and War, and steps were taken by the authorities on both sides of the border to prevent the re-occurrence of the hit-and-run warfare previously carried on by both rebels and loyalists over the frontier. Durham himself publicly drank the President's health while visiting Niagara Falls, and extended special courtesy to all Americans he encountered. These acts, capping his clemency to the rebellion prisoners, did much to calm American public opinion, which had been aroused in favor of the insurgents by the refugees.

Apart from such diplomatic activity, Durham appointed sub-commissions to study the vital problems of public lands, education, and municipal institutions. Adam Thom was named to the municipal commission along with Dr. Taché, who refused to serve with him; and this appointment of their most notorious enemy made the French Canadians uneasy. Their confidence in Durham might have been further shaken if they had known that Thom also acted as liaison officer between the governor and the Tory merchants. Before he left England Durham had been approached by the merchants' representatives, for Edward Ellice happened to be his close friend. He did not hesitate to lay his plan for federating British North America before a committee of seven merchants chosen by Peter McGill of the Bank of Montreal, a month before the lieutenant-governors of the Maritime provinces were summoned to Quebec in August to consult officially with him on the project, which was further discussed by delegations from the Maritimes at Quebec in September.

Meanwhile members of Durham's suite sought information and opinion in all quarters. The chief figure among them was Charles Buller, a brilliant young Radical M.P., who was aided as chief secretary of the high commission by Thomas Turton, an able young Calcutta lawyer who had drafted the Reform Bill of 1832, but whose reputation was clouded by a sensational divorce case in which he had figured. William Kennedy, an expert on municipal reform, headed the commission on municipal organization. Another aide was Edward Gibbon Wakefield, a budding expert on colonial affairs who, after drafting the *Report's* section on public lands and emigration became a member of the Canadian parliament and ended his career as adviser of the Governor of New Zealand. Wakefield's appointment had also revived a scandal, that of his runaway marriage with a schoolgirl heiress, for which he had been imprisoned. Buller's brother, Arthur, the younger Edward Ellice, and a number of other bright young men also aided in the investigation of Canadian affairs. Durham's insistence upon the appointment of Turton and Wakefield had aroused criticism in England, as had the regal scale upon which he established his mission. The ground was thus well prepared for future attacks at home upon the high commissioner.

5

Durham's *Report on the Affairs of British North America*, which is generally considered one of the greatest studies of colonial government and the most epoch-making state paper in Canadian history, owes much to these aides of the governor. Charles Buller's informal account of the mission[80] has come to have an importance only second to that of the *Report* itself, but other documents which went into the making of the state paper are less well known.

Among the most interesting are the letters of Stewart Derbishire, a London lawyer and journalist who was employed as a confidential investigator by Durham and began his work in Canada before the latter's arrival at Quebec. On his way to Canada Derbishire interviewed W. L. Mackenzie, John Rolph, and Dr. O'Callaghan in New York, where Upper and Lower Canadian popular leaders had at last succeeded in achieving the close co-operation which had been lacking in 1837. In Montreal he cultivated the one-time London agent of Lower Canada, Denis-Benjamin Viger, whom he thought must be 'reckoned among the most intelligent of the Confederates (I fear I must so call him) of Papineau.'[81] After encountering considerable difficulty in getting French Canadians to speak freely with a stranger about the rebellion, Derbishire arrived at this conclusion:

I am compelled to say that my impression at the present moment is, that the *habitants* up to the period of their revolt laboured under no practical grievances; and that their condition, social and political, was an enviable one, as compared with that of all other people upon the face of the globe. They knew not the sight of a tax-gatherer. Their imposts in the shape of rent were exceedingly light; and every man could obtain land in small or large quantities, or in addition to that which he possessed, according to his ambition or means of cultivation. . . . In his religion the french Catholic of Canada has enjoyed perfect freedom, the Catholic and Protestant contributing funds towards the creation of each other's ecclesiastical edifices, & the state of opinion and the laws so perfectly harmonizing as to religious toleration that there never has, so far as I can learn, been a ruffle to disturb the peace of society upon the score of a difference in creed. The freedom of person, of political opinion, and of the Press have been secured to the *habitant* by equal laws impartially administered.[82]

This glowing picture of conditions in Canada doubtless owes some of its rosy hues to the fact that Derbishire had been a special newspaper correspondent in the late Carlist Revolution and was contrasting the lot of the Canadian *habitant* with that of the unhappy Spanish peasant.

Derbishire judged, however, that the events of 1837 had altered matters considerably. He recounted the outrages of the loyalist volunteers, for whom he himself showed little sympathy and of whom Viger remarked that they 'had left wounds in the minds of the Canadians that could never be healed.'[83] Derbishire quoted a French-Canadian estimate that damage amounting to £85,000 had been caused in the six parishes visited by the military. They had burnt 297 buildings, including two churches, two rectories, and a convent—thus outraging the religious feelings of the people— twelve granaries, which were scarcely military objectives, and no less than eighty-nine houses at Saint-Benoît, where no resistance at all had been offered. Derbishire reported Papineau's advice that an amnesty for all political prisoners would do much to mend matters —Durham thus seems to have acted on a suggestion of the *Patriote* leader, which had also been made to him by Lafontaine before he left England[84]—and also Viger's comment that the rising had been 'no rebellion,' but an attempt to win justice. He also gave Viger's explanation of the ethnic animosity displayed by the *Patriotes*: 'The Scotch were disliked on account of their haughty, over-bearing manners, & the Irish for their irregularities, violence, and bad faith.'[85] He cited as 'strictly true' Papineau's remark to an English gentleman—probably Roebuck, whom Derbishire had met before leaving England—about the French Canadians: '"Our people," he said, "don't want english capital nor English people here,—they have no ambition beyond their present possessions, & never want to go beyond the sound of their own Church Bells."'[86]

Thus supplied with a useful hint by the tribune of the people, Derbishire made a penetrating explanation of the popular unrest which had culminated in revolt:

... with a people thus wedded to their own ways, & thus limited in their views, it may be readily understood that they would look with jealousy upon a race of more active and enterprising *habitants* who came to settle among them. The resistance offered to the English in this Country may be regarded as emanating from a kind of social or political *vis inertiae*. When to these feelings of aversion towards the intruder is added the alarm, oft sounded, of an intention on the part of the 'for-eigners' to abolish the laws & language of the 'conquered nation,' to 'anglicize' the Province and destroy every vestige of a distinctive race in the original settlers,—notions diligently inculcated by the revolutionary leaders and ably seconded by the newspaper organs of the English party in the current of contemptuous abuse they have never ceased to pour down upon the *habitants*, & in their frequent demands to keep them down; and when the Papineau & his Confederates' appeals to the nationality of this vain people, to their gallantry, to their numbers, to the local and general advantages of emancipating themselves from foreign thraldom & becoming masters of the soil are taken into consideration; and, above all, when due weight is allowed to the erroneous impression spread through the Country as to the conscious weakness of the Government by the tone of personal insult & scorn permitted Mr. Papineau towards the highest Functionary in the Province, the Representative of Majesty, the conduct of the people last Autumn will no longer appear extraordinary.[87]

He also reported the noteworthy observation of the Abbé Ducharme, *curé* of Sainte-Thérèse: 'It was the educated men, the doctors, notaries, and lawyers, who were at the head of the rebellion & were the great seducers of the people, and he seemed to derive from it an argument against educating the lower orders.'[88] The professional class has always been the most liberal one in French-Canadian society and one which has produced many dissidents with the clergy's conservatism and their rivals for leadership of the people.

Derbishire attached considerable importance to the views of a *calèche* driver, recommended by Viger, who drove him about the countryside. These views, which he considered representative of the average French Canadian of the day, might well be those of a similar individual in one of the back-country districts of modern Quebec:

. . . the french were the older inhabitants of the Country & the most numerous, & ought not to be subjected to the minority who cared nothing for them or the Country—but as they could make money out of it to carry away to spend elsewhere, and who for that purpose would '*fouler aux pieds les lois et les coutûmes des habitants* (trample under foot the laws and customs of the inhabitants)'.[89]

Derbishire also summed up the psychology of the **French Canadians** with some acuteness and considerable sharpness:

The *habitants* are a sluggish race, fond of indolent pleasures, lighthearted and gay. They resemble the french in many of their qualities, & have all the national conceit of that people. They consider themselves superior to all the other peoples, and too good to mix with any other race. I believe that from the highest to the lowest they live in a perpetual atmosphere of self-adulation. They are, I believe, an innocent and virtuous race, have retained a character of primitive simplicity, & even in the lowest orders have that naturally good manner, mid-way between servility and familiarity, which distinguishes the same class among the natives of the old Country. The ambition of bettering their condition seems never to have visited their minds: Locomotive faculties they seem to have none. . . . There seems to be no decorative taste in the people, no active spirit of improvement, no ambition beyond the mere supply of the wants of nature.[90]

Though the investigator thus echoed some of the critical observations of the English party, he thought that 'the violence with which the British talk of the French here almost surpasses credence.' As one measure of improving relations between the two groups, he proposed the establishment of 'a Paper of moderate tone and liberal principles,'[91] since he found the English press entirely Tory.

Thanks to the wide range and informal nature of his contact with the French Canadians, this almost forgotten investigator achieved a more profound insight into French Canada in a few weeks than his exalted employer was to achieve in five months. It is also evident, from a letter Derbishire wrote to Charles Buller in August, after interviewing the exiled Dr. Côté at Rouses Point, and in which he observed, 'To become *Masters* of the Country has, I fear, become a national sentiment with them,'[92] that Derbishire formed a more accurate view of the future than Durham, who thought that the French Canadians could be assimilated into a wholly English Canada. It is clear that Derbishire's initial report, written upon Durham's arrival in Canada in May had considerable influence at the outset in the high commissioner's course of action, though it was later supplanted by less impartial opinions. In its seventy-seven pages are outlined the chief elements of modern French-Canadian ultra-nationalism, which traces its origin to the Rebellion of 1837 and to the reaction to Durham's *Report*.

While his staff was still busy gathering material, Durham himself learned in September from an American newspaper that his ordinance on the rebellion prisoners had been disallowed, and that his 'despotic' action had been generally condemned in England. Humiliated and hurt, the sensitive Durham at once sent his resignation to the colonial secretary and, without waiting for its acceptance, made plans to leave Canada at once. Since extraordinary powers had been deliberately vested in him by the government, he wrote: 'I shall not blush to hear that I have exercised a despotism; I shall feel anxious only to know how well and wisely I have used, or rather exhibited an intention of using, my great powers.'[93] When news of his impending departure got about, Durham was deluged with sympathetic addresses from all camps, while the press echoed the popular regret that this well-disposed governor should leave and that his clement policy should be repudiated. In a remarkable farewell proclamation Durham explained the reasons for his resignation, and virtually appealed from the decision of the British government to Canadian public opinion.[94] This action resulted in *The Times* christening him the 'Lord High Seditioner.' Charles Buller, who remained behind in Canada to wind up the work of the commission, found, however, that the proclamation dispelled the unrest caused by Durham's departure: 'No disorder, no increase of disaffection ensued; on the contrary, all parties in the Province expressed a revival of confidence.'[95] After only five months in Canada, Durham left Quebec on a bleak November day, passing through streets lined by respectful crowds whose 'deep silence marked the general grief.'[96] The ship which bore him homeward was appropriately named the *Inconstant*.

6

Durham had hardly left the soil of Canada before the troubles which he had tried to remedy broke out once more, as they had before his arrival. Ever since the rising had been crushed in December 1837, the refugees, led by Robert Nelson and Dr. Côté, had been intriguing along the Vermont and New York border and in Canada itself, and their emissaries had ripened rebellion in the frontier counties of Lacadie, Laprairie, and Beauharnois. Robert Nelson, embittered by having been arbitrarily imprisoned for his brother Wolfred's acts in 1837, had joined forces with the turbulent Dr. Côté in organizing the frontier 'troublutions' of which Papineau disapproved, after breaking with the *Patriote* chief and Dr. O'Callaghan at an assembly of the exiles at Middlebury, Vermont, in January 1838.

The leaders had vainly sought aid and support from the officials of New York and Vermont, whose governors issued proclamations against aiding the rebels.[97] Papineau and O'Callaghan had even sounded out President Van Buren, who warned them that the United States, racked by financial crisis, had no intention of risking a war with Britain by maintaining anything but the strictest neutrality as far as the Canadian troubles were concerned. Van Buren issued a proclamation of neutrality on January 5, 1838, which was later implemented by the Neutrality Act of 1838. Papineau and O'Callaghan knew that without American support there was no hope for a Lower Canadian independence movement, and the old leader warned the undaunted Nelson that he would draw down new misfortunes upon their compatriots if he persisted. Nevertheless Nelson went ahead with his plans of provoking a new rising in Lower Canada by invading the province, timing his foray to coincide with those of the Upper Canadian rebels from Watertown, Ogdensburg, Buffalo, and Detroit.

Aided by some American sympathizers, and with 1,000 muskets from the arsenal at Elizabethtown, N.Y., Nelson crossed the border at Alburg on February 28, 1838; and under the self-assumed title of President of the Provisional Government of Lower Canada, he issued a declaration of independence announcing that the province had been relieved of its British allegiance and had become a republic.[98] This document decreed the separation of church and state, with the consequent suppression of the tithe; the abolition of seigneurial tenure, of the death penalty, except for murder, and of imprisonment for debt; and proclaimed freedom of the press, universal manhood suffrage (including the Indians, who were to be admitted to all rights of citizenship), and the secret ballot. The Crown lands and those of the British American Land Company were to be nationalized. A committee of delegates named by the people was to be charged with the drafting of a constitution subject to popular ratification. Both the French and English languages were to be used for all public affairs. A second proclamation appealed to the 'people of Canada' to rise against tyranny.[99] Though Nelson retreated across the frontier on the following day, when it became evident to him that the British and American authorities were co-operating to avoid border incidents,[100] this proclamation was spread abroad among the *habitants*, who in their discontent at the punitive measures adopted by the government after the 1837 rising, and at the repressive role played by the clergy, found much therein which appealed to them, particularly the prospect of liberation from seigneurial tenure and the tithe.

After a brief stay with Côté in an American jail for violating the frontier regulations, Nelson and his associates organized a secret society, the Hunters' Lodges or *Frères Chasseurs*, whose aim was the invasion of Canada and the achievement of independence. This semi-military organization, in which both Upper and Lower Canadian exiles made common cause and which enlisted some American adventurers, established itself during the summer of 1838 in the frontier states from Maine to Michigan and in both Upper and Lower Canada. Each district was commanded by a 'Great Eagle'—E.-E. Malhiot for the Richelieu—who had authority over the 'Eagles,' or company commanders, whose lieutenants, known as 'Castors,' directed the 'Raquettes,' who each commanded nine 'Chasseurs.' Each company had fifty men, commanded by five 'Raquettes' under a 'Castor.' There were horrendous secret oaths and ceremonies, and an elaborate system of signs and passwords by which the brethren recognized one another. The influence of Freemasonry was evident in the organization, whose French-Canadian centers were at Plattsburg, Montreal, and Quebec.

The leaders planned an invasion of Lower Canada five days after Upper Canada had been attacked, and the troops thus drawn off to the upper province. St. Johns, Montreal, and Quebec were to be assailed simultaneously under the command of three 'French generals,' recruited from among the European revolutionary exiles of 1830 in New York. Nelson was to exact £80,000 from John Molson, the Montreal merchant and banker, in reparation of the latter's wrongs against the province, while the banks, the Lachine Canal, and the customs station at St. Johns were to be confiscated to supply revenue for the new republic. All Jews were to be strangled and their goods confiscated. The minor centers of this conspiracy were at Chateauguay, Beauharnois, Napierville, and Laprairie, with a few in the Townships. As in 1837, the agitation centered in the region south of Montreal, but the *Chasseurs* were unable to evoke much enthusiasm in the stricken region north of the city which was still recovering from the devastation of the previous year. But Colborne, once more administrator of the province, after Durham's departure, estimated that the association had 200,000 members in Canada and the United States, with 3,000 in Montreal alone. This estimate is undoubtedly too high,[101] but the strength of the movement is evidenced by the fact that the *Chasseur* Félix Poutré, who later turned informer, was able to raise 3,000 men around St. Johns, though the majority were more eager to talk over their grievances than to bear arms.[102]

The conspiracy gained many new supporters when Durham's farewell proclamation of October 9, gave notice of his aim to 'elevate the Province of Lower Canada to a thoroughly British character,' 'to raise the defective institutions of Lower Canada to the level of British civilization and freedom, to remove all impediments to the course of British enterprise in this Province,' and to 'touch ancient laws and habits, as well as deep-rooted abuses.'[103] These remarks sounded all too much like the proposals of Adam Thom and the Montreal merchants, rephrased with elegance; at the prospect of national extinction many of the French-Canadian moderates joined with the extremists, and this time the clergy made no effort to check the agitation. Bishop Lartigue, who in June had objected to Durham's flooding the country with proclamations by the channel of the bishops, took refuge in Quebec against a Canadian Sicilian Vespers which was to involve 'a general massacre of Royalists.'[103a] In December he offered his resignation to Rome, since he had aroused the hatred of much of his diocese. The *Patriote* press had declared him guilty of high treason to the Canadian nation, for all his opposition to Durham.

The 1838 revolt began as planned on November 3, after the harvest was gathered, but little else went as the *Patriotes* had foreseen. The competent leadership and the supply of arms needed for so vast an uprising were lacking. Instead of the projected simultaneous risings at such key points as Quebec, Sorel, Chambly, Montreal, and Lac des Deux Montagnes, only the region southwest of Montreal revolted. Some 400 men seized the manor house of Edward Ellice at Beauharnois, while another 150 took possession there of the steamer *Henry Brougham*, which linked Lachine and the Cascade Rapids. By the morning of November 4, 600 men had gathered at Beauharnois, and the Bureaucrats of the region had been disarmed or taken prisoner. The *Patriotes* of Chateauguay succeeded in disarming the Scottish loyalists of the place, but came to grief when they tried to seize the arms of the Indians at Caughnawagha, and were themselves taken prisoners by the indignant savages. At Laprairie, where the local *Patriotes*, joined by a force from the United States, were to seize the barracks and the ferry linking the St. Johns railroad with Montreal, the revolt collapsed when no aid appeared, though some of the railroad was torn up. At Terrebonne the police and the *Patriotes* made a 'treaty,' after a few brushes. In the Richelieu parishes, less enthusiastic for revolt after the harsh repressive measures of the previous year, the *Patriotes* disbanded after they had vainly waited two days for the leaders and the arms which had been promised them.

Meanwhile Nelson had crossed the border and established himself on November 4 at Napierville, where 2,000-3,000 *Patriotes* had gathered under Dr. Côté. Nelson issued his declaration of independence of the previous February, and was proclaimed president of the new republic. But Nelson had only brought a handful of supporters with him, including two French soldiers of revolutionary views, Charles Hindenlang and one Touvrey, instead of the 'army' of which the *Chasseur* organizers had talked so confidently. Hindenlang found himself charged with the task of organizing into an army the mob which had gathered. Only 200-300 had any sort of guns, the rest being equipped only with pikes, pitchforks, or mere sharpened sticks. Thanks to the neutrality measures taken by the American government, Nelson had been able to secure in the States only 250 muskets and a single cannon, while the American membership of the *Chasseurs* had melted away. Several hundred more muskets and a cannon awaited the insurgents at Rouses Point on the boundary, but the force under Côté which was sent to fetch them on November 6 was driven across the border the following day by loyalist volunteers, after a skirmish at Lacolle. Nelson was thus cut off from his American base and deprived of badly needed arms, which fell into loyalist hands.

On November 8 he learned that Colborne was advancing against him from Laprairie with a force of 5,000-6,000 men, including volunteers and Indians. Retreating to Odelltown, just north of the border, with about 1,000 men, Nelson was checked there the following day by the loyalist garrison of 200, strongly established in the village and making good use of the captured cannon. Some of his followers had already mutinied and attempted to turn him over to the volunteers. Nelson fled across the frontier on November 9, while his men retired to Napierville, having lost fifty dead and as many wounded. On the following day Colborne entered Napierville, and the panic-stricken *Patriotes* dispersed in small bands which were pursued by the troops.

Meanwhile another column of regulars and the Glengarry Volunteers scattered the insurgents at Beauharnois and set fire to the village. Throughout the disaffected region, but particularly in the county of Laprairie, the houses of known rebels were burnt down. As in 1837, the volunteers entered with such zest into this work that even Adam Thom's *Montreal Herald* was moved to a curious display of humanity mixed with intolerance:

> Sunday night all the country back of Laprairie presented the frightful spectacle of a vast expanse of livid flames, and it is reported that not a single rebel house has been left standing . . . God knows what will become of the Canadians who have not perished, of their wives and families, during the winter which approaches, since they have in prospect only the horrors of hunger and cold. It is sad to reflect on the terrible consequences of the revolt, of the irreparable ruin of so great a number of human beings, whether innocent or guilty. Nevertheless the supremacy of the laws must be maintained inviolate, the integrity of the Empire respected, and peace and prosperity assured to the English, even at the expense of the whole Canadian people.[104]

For his part in permitting these excesses Colborne won the name of 'Old Firebrand,' though once again the devastation seems to have been largely the work of the volunteers, aroused to new heights of fury by the second rebellion.

Colborne, who warned his troops of the expected attack 'by a horde of rapacious brigands' on November 1, proclaimed martial law on November 4, while the *habeas corpus* was once again suspended by the special council on November 8.[105] Girouard, D.-B. Viger, Lafontaine, and Edouard Fabre were among those arrested on suspicion in Montreal. Colborne showed no inclination to trifle with the large number of prisoners who were taken during the single week of insurrection. By December 19, the prisoners numbered 753. One hundred and eight were promptly brought to trial before courts-martial, while three French-Canadian judges, Panet, Bédard, and Vallières de Saint-Réal, who regarded suspension of the *habeas corpus* as unconstitutional and attempted to force the government to give the prisoners civil trial by jury, were suspended by Colborne.[106] Ninety-nine of the accused were condemned to death, but only twelve of these were executed, while fifty-eight were deported to the Australian penal colonies, two banished, and twenty-seven freed under bond for good behaviour.[107]

The Tories protested at such mildness, while the French Canadians muttered against Colborne's 'bloodthirsty tyranny.' As Lady Colborne wrote on December 10, 1838, her husband was unable to please either group: 'As you will see by the *Herald* nothing can satisfy the ultra-British party, and with one party he must be content to be stigmatized as a tyrant, with the other as shamefully lenient.'[108] While Adam Thom and his colleagues of the Doric Club howled for more *Patriote* blood, the *Morning Chronicle*, a moderate Bureaucratic organ, reproved the *Herald* for losing sight of the purpose of punishment, 'which is to assure the safety of the community and not to arouse sympathy in behalf the sufferers and hatred against the government which permits such an effusion of blood.'[109] Since rebels were not allowed to defend rebels, French-Canadian lawyers were barred from the courts-martial. Lewis Thomas Drummond, a young Irish lawyer, and Charles Hart, the son of the much expelled Ezekiel, defended the Rebellion prisoners in the early trials, while Charles Mondelet, who was himself arrested on suspicion in 1838, a year later won from a French-Canadian jury the acquittal of those charged with the murder of Lieutenant Weir. Of the twelve executed men, two were the murderers of the loyalist Chartrand, four had killed an English settler in the Beauharnois troubles, and two more had benefited from Durham's amnesty for their actions in 1837, only to take up arms once more. None was a real leader of the insurrection. The most notable was the French 'General' Hindenlang, who refused to save his neck by turning state's evidence. A case can be made for the other four as innocent victims of enthusiasm aroused by impassioned politicians who left their followers in the lurch at the critical moment.

One of the curious features of the Rebellions of 1837-8 is that only the rank and file suffered penalties, while the leaders went almost scot-free and later rose to eminently respectable positions in Canadian or American life. After his futile negotiations with New York politicians for intervention in Canada, Papineau sailed for France in February 1839, hoping to interest the French press in Canada, as he had been urged to do by M. de Pontois some months earlier. In Paris, during the following May, he began a *Histoire de l'Insurrection du Canada*, of which the first portion was published in the *Revue du progrès* there, and reprinted some months later by Ludger Duvernay's refugee *Le Patriote Canadien* press at Burlington, Vermont. This work was a hotly-worded assault on Durham's *Report*, and its errors of fact and interpretation were promptly refuted by Papineau's former follower Sabrevoix de Bleury. The latter's nomination to the legislative council in August 1837 had involved him in a duel with Duvernay, who accused him of abandoning the *Patriote* cause for the sake of office.

After reporting a remarkable—if true—conversation with Lord Bathurst in 1823, in which the colonial secretary anticipated the American Civil War and the European struggle between reform and reaction, Papineau professed his complete lack of faith in Durham's remedies, since they involved the union of the Canadas which he had always opposed, the absorption of the French Canadians, and the maintenance of monarchical institutions. Papineau was convinced that Britain might maintain for a time its 'military occupation' of Canada, but it could no longer govern the country by civil means. He saw the independence of Canada as the only solution of the problem, with separation from Britain being accomplished either by voluntary consent of the imperial government, or by the French intervention which he sought on the basis of the violation of the Treaty of 1763, or by the war between Britain and the United States which then seemed imminent to his American friends. Papineau still dreamed of American aid for the Canadian reformers and underestimated the restraint which Van Buren had placed upon the anglophobe warhawks at Durham's earnest behest. Charles Buller was justified in writing to John Stuart Mill on October 13, 1838, that one of his chief's greatest achievements was that he 'had re-established goodwill with the United States, and rooted out from that people all sympathy with Canadian rebellion.' [110]

In Paris, however, Papineau found more congenial company than that of his inconstant American sympathizers in the persons of Louis Blanc and the *Républicains rouges* who shortly were to launch the French Revolution of 1848. It was their ideas, and those of Lamennais and Béranger, that he brought back to Canada when he was permitted to return in 1845. Papineau also busied himself in Paris with researches into the French colonial history of Canada, and met his English Radical friends Hume and Leader, although Lord Brougham, now reconciled to Durham and his policy, refused to see him. After his return Papineau sat in the Canadian parliament from 1847 to 1854, but the lifelong leader of the opposition was lost in a new era in which a younger generation had taken the helm. His influence was no longer paramount in politics, but remained important in the intellectual world.

His young disciples of Rebellion days fared better than the old tribune in the new Canada. Lafontaine, Morin, Cartier, and Taché all became prime ministers. Wolfred Nelson was re-elected to parliament in 1844; Thomas Storrow Brown returned to his business and the writing of reminiscences in Montreal; and Robert Bouchette became collector of customs at Ottawa. A few exiles remained in the States: Robert Nelson practiced medicine in New York City and Dr. O'Callaghan became the state historian of New York, editing valuable works on the colonial history of the continent.

The chief aftermath of the rebellions, as far as the mass of the French Canadians was concerned, was on one hand a marked development of emigration across the frontier, from motives of discontent and unrest, and on the other a vague conviction that the *Patriote* cause was not dead and that a leader in Papineau's tradition would appear when the occasion demanded him. Like Napoleon, Papineau had captured the imagination of a people, and his memory has lingered long in Quebec. One group, echoing the refrain of a *Chouayen* ballad of the period—'*C'est la faute à Papineau!*' ('Papineau is to blame!')—lays all later French-Canadian difficulties to his account, while another cherishes his memory as that of the first great French-Canadian nationalist. Today it is clear to French and English alike that he was a great Canadian, who played an important role in the evolution of Canada as a nation by blending the political ideas of Britain, France, and the United States.

7

Before the echoes of the second rising had died down, Lord Durham presented his solution of the Canadian problem to the British government. The *Report* was published in February 1839 in both English and French, and was immediately greeted in London as a notable state paper, before the party lines were drawn for its consideration in parliament. The London *Times* published a first instalment of the document before it was officially presented, and other English newspapers followed suit, giving the *Report* a wide circulation. In Canada Etienne Parent published the *Report* in French in *Le Canadien*, while Francis Hincks issued a pamphlet edition, dedicated to Robert Baldwin, at Toronto, and Joseph Howe reprinted it in the *Nova Scotian* at Halifax.

In both Lower and Upper Canada Durham's exceedingly plain speech grated on tender susceptibilities. Each of the *Report's* two main recommendations—union of the two provinces and responsible government—gratified one group and maddened the other. The Tories of both provinces were given the legislative union which they had long demanded, but they loathed the prospect of democratic responsible government which it recommended, and they were injured by Durham's castigation of the Chateau Clique and the Family Compact. The *Patriotes* and the Reformers received the long-sought prize of responsible government, but it was responsible government within the framework of imperial administration rather than an autonomy leading to the independent nationhood which both French and English radicals had lately come to favor. Upper Canadians in general were pained by the superficial, hasty, and ill-informed consideration given to their province, while the terms in which the recommendations of union and responsible government were made produced a sense of injustice and injury in French Canada which has survived in some measure to the present day.

Lord Durham's *Report* has a vastly lower reputation in French Canada than in English-speaking circles. For not only did it recommend the union of the Canadas, so long favored by the French Canadians' most bitter opponents, but it called for the absorption of the French Canadians into a wholly British North America. Far from showing sympathy with the *Patriote* doctrine of a '*nation canadienne*' whose needs were unique and peculiar and demanded independence, the opening paragraphs of the *Report* echoed Durham's predetermined conviction that confederation was the solution of British North American difficulties. Firsthand observation only reinforced his original view, for Durham remarked at the outset of the *Report* 'how inseparably connected I found the interests of Your Majesty's Provinces in North America, to what degree I met with common disorders, requiring common remedies.'[111] Federation of the British North American provinces had already been proposed by Roebuck in the Commons and advocated by him in a memorandum of which Durham made great use; it was approved by Durham's friends Edward Ellice and Lord Howick, the future third Earl Grey; it might be termed a Liberal if not a Radical idea.[112]

But another preconceived notion mirrored in the opening sentences of the *Report* was not at all Radical or Liberal: the idea that the solution of the Canadian difficulties should be based upon the mother country's interest. It was thus eloquently phrased by Durham:

The country which has founded and maintained these Colonies at a vast expense of blood and treasure, may justly expect its compensation in turning their unappropriated resources to the account of its own redundant population; they are the rightful patrimony of the English people, the ample appanage which God and Nature have set aside in the New World for those whose lot has assigned them but insufficient portions in the Old. Under wise and free institutions, these great advantages may yet be secured to Your Majesty's subjects; and a connexion secured by the link of kindred origin and mutual benefits may continue to bind to the British Empire the ample territories of its North American provinces, and the large and flourishing population by which they will assuredly be filled.[113]

Such full-blooded imperialism, nourished by a sense of the divine right of the English, was worthy of a Tory rather than a Liberal leader, and offered short shrift to colonial notions of independent nationhood. Durham was no believer in the tenets of the Little Englandism which found so many disciples among his political friends and was becoming more and more dominant in the mother country at this period. The fundamental dichotomy of Durham's mind is reflected in the first pages of the *Report*, which reveal the mentality of a radical aristocrat and a benevolent despot.

Then Durham goes on to show a racist outlook which grated on a minority proud of its cultural differences from the Anglo-Americans, and which has ever vitiated the merits of the *Report* in the French-Canadian mind. He remarked that he had come to Canada expecting to find a dispute between the people and the executive, but instead 'found two nations warring in the bosom of a single state: I found a struggle, not of principles, but of races.' Durham stoutly maintained that: 'Our happy immunity from any feelings of national hostility, renders it difficult for us to comprehend the intensity of hatred which the difference of language, of laws, and of manners creates between those who inhabit the same village, and are citizens of the same state';[114] and assigned to personal experience in Canada his conclusion that the struggle was primarily a racial one. But his secretary Charles Buller bears witness that, on the voyage out to Canada, 'I used indeed then to think that Lord Durham had too strong a feeling against the French Canadians on account of their recent insurrection'; and that 'he had made up his mind that no quarter should be shown to the absurd pretensions of race, and that he must throw himself upon the support of British feelings, and aim at making Canada thoroughly British.'[115] This attitude hardly suggests that 'happy immunity' from racist feelings which Durham claimed as the heritage of Englishmen, and it reveals the influence that Ellice and the Montreal merchants had established over the governor-general even before he left England. Naturally this initial tendency was reinforced by Durham's association with Adam Thom and the group the latter represented in Canada.

In any case Durham observed: 'The national feud forces itself on the very senses, irresistibly and palpably, as the origin or essence of every dispute which divides the community; we discover that dissensions, which appear to have another origin, are but forms of this constant and all-pervading quarrel; and that every contest is one of French and English in the outset, or becomes so ere it has run its course.'[116] To his mind, the 'vicious system of government' had long concealed the racial quarrel, since the races were divided among both government and popular parties, and individuals could be found in the opposite camp from the majority of their national group. The national hostility had long been confined to Quebec and Montreal, while isolated groups of either race in the countryside were free from it. But year by year it had been increasing, and the insurrection had completed the division: 'Since the resort to arms the two races have been distinctly and completely arrayed against one another. . . . A few exceptions mark the existence, rather than militate against the truth, of the general rule of national hostility.'[117]

Durham reconciled his racism and his liberalism by remarking, with a measure of justice, that both French and English parties had been fighting under false colors: 'the French appear to have used their democratic arms for conservative purposes, rather than those of liberal and enlightened movement; and the sympathies of the friends of reform are naturally enlisted on the side of sound amelioration which the English minority in vain attempted to introduce into the antiquated laws of the Province.' He found it difficult to believe that 'the hostility of the races was the effect, and not the cause, of the pertinacity with which the desired reforms were pressed or resisted.' Hewing to his racist line, he maintained that 'the contest, which had been represented as a contest of classes, was, in fact, a contest of the races.' And in his opinion French and English were incompatible: 'It is scarcely possible to conceive descendants of any of the great European nations more unlike each other in character and temperament, more totally separated from each other by language, laws, and modes of life, or placed in circumstances more calculated to produce mutual misunderstanding, jealousy and hatred.'[118] Such sentiments were of course natural in a member of the English ruling class, a few years after the conclusion of the Second Hundred Years' War between Britain and France.

This last consideration also helped to shape Durham's view of the French Canadians. He saw them as the children of a 'central, ill-organized, unimproving and repressive despotism . . . calculated to repress the intelligence and freedom of the great mass of the people.' He pictured them thus:

. . . a race of men habituated to the incessant labour of a rude and unskilled agriculture, and habitually fond of social enjoyments, congregated together in rural communities, occupying portions of the wholly unappropriated soil, sufficient to provide each family with material comforts, far beyond their ancient means, or almost their conceptions; that they made little advance beyond the first progress in comfort which the bounty of the soil absolutely forced upon them; that under the same institutions they remained the same uninstructed, inactive, unprogressive people . . . The mass of the community exhibited in the New World the characteristics of the peasantry of Europe . . . They clung to ancient prejudices, ancient customs and ancient laws, not from any strong sense of their beneficial effects, but with the unreasoning tenacity of an uneducated and unprogressive people. . . . The Conquest has changed them but little. The higher classes, and the inhabitants of the towns, have adopted some English customs and feelings; but the continued negligence of the British government left the mass of the people without any of the institutions which would have elevated them in freedom and civilization. It has left them without the education and without the institutions of local self-government, that would have assimilated their character and habits, in the easiest and best way, to those of the Empire of which they became a part. They remain an old and stationary society, in a new and progressive world. In all essentials they are still French; but French in every respect dissimilar to those of France in the present day. They resemble rather the French of the provinces under the old regime.

Durham noted the 'remarkable equality of properties and conditions,' and the prevailing want of education among the *habitants*. He had kind words, however, for the secondary education of the province: 'I know of no people among whom a larger provision exists for the higher kinds of elementary education, or among whom such education is really extended to a larger proportion of the population.' This Old Etonian judged that the education provided by the classical colleges 'greatly resembles the kind given in the English public schools, though it is rather more varied.' But the existence of a highly educated class in a closed society created a great problem, since careers in the army, navy, and civil service were largely barred to French Canadians, and all must become priests, lawyers, notaries, or doctors, though these 'professions are greatly overstocked.' Since the educated man sprang from the people and was 'separated by no barrier of manners, or pride, or distinct interests, from the singularly ignorant peasantry . . . he combines, therefore, the influences of superior education and social equality, and wields a power over the mass, which I do not believe that the educated class of any other portion of the world possesses.'[119] To this state of affairs Durham attributed the extraordinary influence of the French-Canadian popular leaders, whom he called 'demagogues'—a term frequently applied to himself by his English political opponents.

Despite his racist prejudices, Durham was not overly kind to the English Canadians. He had some of the traditional English scorn for colonials, and his Liberal principles were outraged by the outdated Canadian oligarchy. He convicted the officials and army officers of forming 'a kind of privileged class, occupying the first place in the community, and excluding the higher class of the natives from society, as well as from the government of their own country.' He detected in them an 'exclusiveness of demeanour, which was more revolting to a sensitive and polite people than the monopoly of power and profit.' But he noted that 'the active and regular habits of the English capitalist drove out of all the more profitable kinds of industry their inert and careless competitors of the French race,' so that 'all felt yet more acutely the gradual increase of a class of strangers in whose hands the wealth of the country appeared to centre, and whose expenditure and influence eclipsed those of the class which had previously occupied the first place in the country.' He gave the English full credit for developing new fields of industry, as well as improving old ones:

The ascendency which an unjust favouritism had contributed to give to the English race in the government and the legal profession, their own superior energy, skill and capital secured to them in every branch of industry. They have developed the resources of the country; they have constructed or improved its means of communication; they have created its internal and foreign commerce. The entire wholesale, and a large proportion of the retail trade of the Province, with the most profitable and flourishing farms, are now in the hands of this numerical minority of the population.[120]

Consequently most of the French-Canadian workers found themselves in the employ of English capitalists; and the coming of British immigrants, who adopted the prejudices of their compatriots without the reservations imposed by education and prudence, divided along racial lines a working class whose interests were really common.

In discussing the basis of the conflict between the races, Durham spoke with frankness and penetration. He judged that the difference of language was the first factor in an inevitable collision. Then, contradicting his earlier assertion of English immunity from racism, he remarked: 'It is not anywhere a virtue of the English race to look with complacency on any manners, customs or laws which appear strange to them; accustomed to form a high estimate of their own superiority, they take no pains to conceal from others their contempt and intolerance of their usages.' The newcomers to Canada, conscious of being a chosen people, 'found the French Canadians filled with an equal amount of national pride.' As time went on, 'The French could not but feel the superiority of English enterprize; they could not shut their eyes to their success in every undertaking in which they came into contact, and to the constant superiority which they were acquiring. They looked upon their rivals with alarm, with jealousy, and finally with hatred. The English repaid them with a scorn, which soon assumed the same form of hatred.' Charges of arrogance and injustice on one side were countered by charges of meanness and disloyalty on the other, with evil results: 'The entire mistrust which the two races have thus learned to conceive of each other's intentions, induces them to put the worst construction on the most innocent conduct; to judge every word, every act, and every intention unfairly; to attribute the most odious designs, and reject every overture of kindness or fairness, as covering secret designs of treachery and malignity.' Separated by language, the two races also lacked the bonds of a common religion or a common education. The result was the development of two distinct mentalities: 'the arguments which convince the one, are calculated to appear utterly unintelligible to the other,' while the events of the day were seen in utterly different lights by each.

Intercourse between the two races was almost non-existent in either business or society, while racial animosities were played upon when French commercial energy belatedly awoke and founded the *Banque du Peuple* in 1835, to compete with John Molson's and Peter McGill's Bank of Montreal, established in 1817, and a rival steamship line to Molson's St. Lawrence service, begun in 1809. Citing the facts that he had 'heard of but one house in Quebec in which both races meet on pretty equal and amicable terms,' and that intermarriages, frequent in post-conquest days, had become rare, Durham multiplied his illustrations of the curious abyss between the French and English worlds in Canada, which remains one of the first and most striking impressions of the visitor even today.[121]

After giving his classic account of the fundamental cleft in Canada, Durham observed that political strife arising of such a situation was inevitable:

The French regarded with jealousy the influence in politics of a daily increasing body of strangers, whom they so much disliked and dreaded; the wealthy English were offended at finding that their property gave them no influence over their French dependents, who were acting under the guidance of leaders of their own race; and the farmers and traders of the same race were not long before they began to bear with impatience their utter political nullity in the midst of a population, whose ignorance they condemned and whose political views and conduct seemed utterly at variance with their own notions of the principles and practice of self government.

It was clear to Durham that 'the superior political and practical intelligence of the English cannot be, for a moment, disputed,' while 'the greater amount of refinement, of speculative thought, and of the knowledge that books can give, is, with some brilliant exceptions, to be found among the French.' But he pointed out: 'That a race which felt itself thus superior in political activity and intelligence should submit with patience to a rule of a majority which it could not respect, was impossible.' And 'appeals to the national pride and the animosities of the French, became more direct and general on the occasion of the abortive attempt to re-unite Upper and Lower Canada in 1822, which the leaders of the assembly viewed or represented as a blow aimed at the institutions of their province,' while 'the anger of the English was excited by the denunciation of themselves, which, subsequently to this period, they were in the habit of hearing.'[122] The abuses of the executive power long postponed racial strife by aligning the have-nots, regardless of origin, against the haves; but the assembly was finally opposed by the whole English population because of its lack of interest in public works and in an alteration of the laws.

That body dominated by the French Canadians 'looked with considerable jealousy and dislike on the increase and prosperity of what they regarded as a foreign and hostile race; they looked on the Province as the patrimony of their own race; they viewed it not as a country to be settled, but as one already settled; and instead of legislating in the American spirit, and first providing for the future population of the Province, their primary care was, in the spirit of legislation which prevails in the old world, to guard the interests and feelings of the present race of inhabitants, to whom they consider the newcomers as subordinate.' Meanwhile the English 'regarded the policy of the assembly as a plan for preventing any further emigration to the Province, of stopping the growth of English wealth, and of rendering precarious the English property already invested or acquired in Lower Canada.' Thus grew up the 'singular alliance between the English population and the Colonial officials, who combined from perfectly different motives, and with perfectly different objects, against a common enemy.' The racial division thus begun was completed by the French-Canadian resort to arms in 1837–8: 'It is not difficult to conceive how greatly the evils, which I have described as previously existing, have been aggravated by the war; how terror and revenge nourished in each portion of the population, a bitter and irreconcilable hatred to each other, and to the institutions of the country.'[123]

Using to the full his powers of eloquence and psychological penetration, Durham painted a vivid picture of the respective outlooks of the two races on the morrow of the Rebellion—outlooks which still survive deep in the two folk memories today:

[The French] brood in sullen silence over the memory of their fallen countrymen, of their burnt villages, of their ruined property, of their extinguished ascendency, and of their humbled nationality. To the Government and the English they ascribe these wrongs, and nourish against both an indiscriminating and eternal animosity. Nor have the English inhabitants forgotten in their triumph the terror with which they suddenly saw themselves surrounded by an insurgent majority, and the incidents which alone appeared to save them from the unchecked domination of their antagonists. They find themselves still a minority in the midst of a hostile and organized people; apprehensions of secret conspiracies and sanguinary designs haunt them unceasingly, and their only hope of safety is supposed to rest on systematically terrifying and disabling the French, and in preventing a majority of that race from ever again being predominant in any portion of the legislature of the Province.

Representative government, the militia system, the course of justice and of trade, all found themselves obstructed by this situation, for which Durham foresaw no solution within his lifetime. The French

Canadians wished to revenge themselves upon the English by forming a republic; or even by annexation to the United States, at the expense of preserving their nationality; while the English extremists stated that 'Lower Canada must be *English*, at the expense, if necessary, of not being *British*.'[124] Exasperated to the point of desperation with the government, the self-styled loyalist English were willing to conceive of annexation, which would involve both their immediate commercial advantage and the extinction of French-Canadian national pretensions. Here Durham singled out the first instance of a practice oft to be repeated in Canadian history, of annexation talk being used as a threat by either English or French Canadians against the other ethnic group, whenever relations between them reached a crisis, or the economic position of either group became too uncomfortable.

In summing up his survey of the problem, Durham observed: 'A jealousy between two races, so long habituated to regard each other with hereditary enmity, and so differing in habits, in language and in laws, would have been inevitable under any form of government'; but nevertheless he roundly condemned the old imperial policy of divide and rule. To his mind French Canada should either have been left to the French, or rapidly and completely been assimilated by the English. A start had been made in 1764 on the second 'and wiser' of the two policies, but it had been abandoned with the coming of the American Revolution. Then Canada had been divided into two provinces, one French and one British, but with grave inconsistency Lower Canada had not been left wholly to the French or under French institutions. 'The error, therefore, to which the present contest must be attributed, is the vain endeavour to preserve a French-Canadian nationality in the midst of Anglo-American colonies and States'; for: 'It will be acknowledged by everyone who has observed the progress of Anglo-Saxon colonization in America, that sooner or later the English race was sure to predominate even numerically in Lower Canada, as they predominate already, by their superior knowledge, energy, enterprize and wealth.' Durham also flayed the continued errors of the government: 'A policy founded upon imperfect information, and conducted by continually changing hands, has exhibited to the Colony a system of vacillation which was in effect no system at all. The alternate concessions to the contending races have only irritated both, impaired the authority of Government, and, by keeping alive the hopes of a French-Canadian nationality, counteracted the influences which might, ere this, have brought the quarrel to its natural and necessary termination.' Durham concluded his survey of the problem by stating: 'The struggle between the Government and the Assembly, has aggravated the animosities of race; and the animosities of race have rendered the political difference irreconcilable. No remedy can be efficient that does not operate upon both evils.'[125]

8

The remedy which Lord Durham proposed for the ills of Canada did indeed 'operate upon both evils.' His solution for the political difficulty owed much to the Upper Canadian Reformer Robert Baldwin of York (Toronto), who in August 1838 had won from Durham the hearing for his arguments in favor of responsible government which the Colonial Office had refused to grant him in 1836. At their meeting Baldwin gave Durham the memorandum which he and his father had drafted in 1828, and which now played a notable part in fixing Durham's ideas.[126]

Durham contended that representative government had long been established in Canada, and could not be revoked. Therefore, 'the Crown must submit to the necessary consequences of representative institutions; and if it has to carry on the Government in unison with a representative body, it must consent to carry it on by means of those in whom that representative body has confidence.' This was daring doctrine in application to colonial affairs at the time, but Durham pointed out that responsible government had long been considered an 'indisputable and essential part' of the British constitution; that its absence had been the cause of the collisions between the executive and representative bodies not only in the two Canadas, but in all the British North American colonies. In traditional Whig style Durham caustically criticized those 'who imagined that in any colony of England a body invested with the name and character of a representative Assembly, could be deprived of any of those powers which, in the opinion of Englishmen, are inherent in a popular legislature . . . To suppose that such a system would work well there, implies a belief that the French Canadians have enjoyed representative institutions for half a century, without acquiring any of the characteristics of a free people; that Englishmen renounce every political opinion and feeling when they enter a colony, or that the spirit of Anglo-Saxon freedom is utterly changed and weakened among those who are transplanted across the Atlantic.' To his mind, 'the Legislative Council was practically hardly anything but a veto in the hands of the public functionaries on all the acts of that popular branch of the legislature in which they were always in a minority.'[127]

Faced with this situation, the assembly fell into 'a constant warfare with the executive, for the purpose of obtaining the powers inherent in a representative body by the very nature of representative government.' Thus it was led to pervert the constitution by such practices as adopting temporary legislation, tacking measures it desired onto essential supply bills, and abusing the quorum. In the absence of local institutions of government and in the face of executive monopoly of patronage, it had developed a vast new field of patronage by grants for local improvements and for education, to make up for its long exclusion from places and privileges. Here Durham revealed his understanding of the vital role of patronage in parliamentary government.[128]

Misgovernment was thus general. Durham censured the absence of any real representative of the Crown in the colony, thanks to the subordination of the governor to a Colonial Office which was both constitutionally irresponsible and prone to dangerous delays. He condemned the executive council as irresponsible and 'composed of persons placed in it long ago,' so that a new governor was obliged to take the advice of persons in whom he had no confidence. There was no administrative system outside the three chief cities, and the French-Canadian population lacked both municipal institutions and the capacity for self-government developed through them. 'Accustomed to rely entirely on the Government, it has no power of doing anything for itself, much less of aiding the central authority.' The laws and judicial system of Lower Canada presented a chaotic picture, with no party feeling 'the slightest confidence in the administration of criminal justice' or 'in the honest administration of the laws.'[129]

In his observations and recommendations on education, Durham closely followed Arthur Buller's report on 'The State of Education in Lower Canada,' which was printed as an appendix to the *Report*.[130] In the absence of proper provision for education by the government, ignorance was general: 'The English are hardly better off than the French for the means of education for their children, and indeed possess scarcely any, except in the cities.' Though Durham had little hope of immediately establishing a sound general system of education, he found that 'there existed among the French population a very general and deep sense of their own deficiencies in this respect, and a great desire to provide means for giving their children those advantages which had been denied to themselves. Among the English the same desire was equally felt; and I believe that the population of either origin would be willing to submit to local assessments for this purpose.' But the clergy of most of the churches opposed non-sectarian education, while any other system 'would be particularly mischievous in this Province, inasmuch as its inevitable effect would be to aggravate and perpetuate the existing distinctions of origin.' Given the opposition of the laity of every denomination to 'these narrow views' of the clergy, Durham was confident that strong popular government would lead to the establishment of 'a liberal and general system of public education.'[131] He did not hesitate to censure the British government for not having done, or even attempted to do, anything for education; and for its misappropriation of the revenues of the Jesuit Estates.

Although Durham was opposed to clerical control of education, he was, as might be expected of an advocate of Catholic emancipation in England, by no means anti-Catholic. He noted that there was in Lower Canada: 'a degree of practical toleration, known in very few communities,' and added that 'the Catholic priesthood of this Province have, to a very remarkable degree, conciliated the good-will of persons of all creeds; and I know of no parochial clergy in the world whose practice of all the Christian virtues, and zealous discharge of their clerical duties, is more universally admitted, and has been productive of more beneficial consequences. . . . Intimately acquainted with the wants and characters of their neighbours, they have been the promoters and dispensers of charity, and the effectual guardians of the morals of the people; and in the general absence of any permanent institutions of civil government, the Catholic Church has presented almost the only semblance of stability and organization, and furnished the only effectual support for civilization and order.' To the Catholic clergy he also paid tribute for 'their eminent services in resisting the arts of the disaffected' during the Rebellion.

Durham blamed the failure of the French Canadians to expand beyond the limits of the crowded seigneuries on the absence of parochial institutions in the new settlements, and urged such provision by the government 'in order to encourage them to spread their population, and to seek for comfort and prosperity in new settlements.' For, as he shrewdly observed, 'the religious observances of the French Canadians are so intermingled with all their business, and all their amusements, that the priests and the church are with them, more than with any other people, the centres of their little communities.' Finally he was convinced that 'the feelings and interests of the Catholic clergy and population should invariably meet with due consideration from the Government.'[132]

Durham's Liberalism was also revealed in his refusal to accept the official doctrine that 'the principles which are productive of harmony and good government in the mother country, are by no means applicable to a colonial dependency.' He proposed putting the management of internal affairs into Canadian hands, leaving to the mother country only control over the form of government, the regulation of foreign relations and trade, and the management of public lands and immigration; since 'A perfect subordination, on the part of the Colony, on these points, is secured by the advantages which it finds in the continuance of its connexion with the Empire.' He observed: 'The colonists may not always know what laws are best for them, or which of their countrymen are the fittest for conducting their affairs; but, at least, they have a greater interest in coming to a right judgment on these points, and will take greater pains to do so, than those whose welfare is very remotely and slightly affected by the good or bad legislation of these portions of the Empire.' Rejecting an old tenet of colonial government, he remarked: 'it surely cannot be the duty or interest of Great Britain to keep a most expensive military possession of these Colonies, in order that a Governor or Secretary of State may be able to confer colonial appointments on one rather than another set of persons in the Colonies.' He concluded that: 'The British people of the North American Colonies are a people on whom we may safely rely, and to whom we must not grudge power.'

But he did not believe that London could be restrained from 'injudicious interference' with the internal affairs of the colonies; 'while they remain the petty and divided communities which they now are.' Such interference or neglect would be avoided 'if these important and extensive Colonies should speak with one voice, if it were felt that every error of our colonial policy must cause a common suffering and a common discontent throughout the whole wide extent of British America.'[133] Here is vaguely reflected that initial conception of a united British North America with which Durham had begun his labors. It was first definitely formulated by Chief Justice William Smith in 1790, and had been urged upon Durham before his departure from England by Roebuck.

Its realization was to grow out of Durham's work, though the *Report* reluctantly abandoned the idea, on the grounds that the French Canadians could not be trusted with control of Lower Canada. Durham made only a few reservations in his recommendation of responsible government: the constitution of the form of government, the regulation of foreign relations and trade, and the disposal of public lands. He proposed that money votes should be subject to the consent of the Crown, as at Westminster, and that a system of municipal institutions should be established, since a 'general legislature, which manages the private business of every parish, in addition to the common business of the country, wields a power which no single body, however popular its constitution, ought to have; a power which is destructive of any constitutional balance.'[134] An appendix to the *Report* dealt with a proposed imperial system of land management, which remained a dead letter.[135]

But for the French Canadian the most notable recommendation of the *Report*—the proposal which vitiated the long-sought grant of responsible government and deprived the document of all merit in his eyes—was that Lower Canada should be made English by legislative union with Upper Canada. This was Durham's great error. The French Canadian can hardly be blamed for calling the *Report* a 'blueprint of assimilation' when Durham stated flatly:

I entertain no doubt of the national character which must be given to Lower Canada; it must be that of the British Empire; that of the majority of British America; that of the great race which must, in the lapse of no long period of time, be predominant over the whole North American Continent. Without effecting the change so rapidly or roughly as to shock the feelings and trample on the welfare of the existing generation, it must henceforth be the first and steady purpose of the British Government to establish an English population, with English laws and language, in this Province, and to trust its government to none but a decidedly English Legislature.

Durham, who had defended the Belgians against the Dutch and the Poles against the Russians, anticipated the objections to such a course: 'that this is a hard measure to a conquered people; that the French were originally the whole, and still are the bulk of the population of Lower Canada; that the English are newcomers, who have no right to demand the extinction of the nationality of the people, among whom commercial enterprize has drawn them.' He granted that: 'It may be said, that, if the French are not so civilized, so energetic, or so money-making a race as that by which they are surrounded, they are an amiable, a virtuous, and a contented people, possessing all the essentials of material comfort, and not to be despised, or ill-used, because they seek to enjoy what they have, without emulating the spirit of accumulation, which influences their neighbours.' He pointed out that: 'Their nationality is, after all, an inheritance; and they must not be too severely punished, because they have dreamed of maintaining on the distant banks of the St. Lawrence, and transmitting to their posterity, the language, the manners, and the institutions of that great nation that for two centuries gave the tone of thought to the European Continent.' And with a recognition of the great English principle of majority rule, Durham admitted that: 'it may be urged that justice demands that the minority should be compelled to acquiesce in the supremacy of the ancient and most numerous occupants of the Province, and not pretend to force their own institutions and customs on the majority.'[136]

But Durham had an eye both to the economic situation and to the future—two factors which the French Canadians, with their idealistic and traditionalist cast of mind, have always disregarded or underestimated—and so he replied thus to the objections he himself had raised:

But before deciding which of the two races is now to be placed in the ascendant, it is but prudent to inquire which of them must ultimately prevail; for it is not wise to establish today that which must, after a hard

struggle, be reversed tomorrow. The pretensions of the French Canadians
to the exclusive possession of Lower Canada would debar the yet larger
English population of Upper Canada and the Townships from access to
the great natural channel of that trade which they alone have created,
and now carry on. The possession of the mouth of the St. Lawrence
concerns not only those who happen to have made their settlements along
the narrow line which borders it, but all who now dwell, or will hereafter
dwell, in the great basin of that river. For we must not look to the present
alone. The question is, by what race is it likely that the wilderness which
now covers the rich and ample regions surrounding the comparatively
small and contracted districts in which the French Canadians are located,
is eventually to be converted into a settled and flourishing country? If
this is to be done in the British dominions, as in the rest of North America,
by some speedier process than the ordinary growth of population, it must
be by immigration from the English Isles, or from the United States—
the countries which supply the only settlers that have entered, or will
enter, the Canadas in any large numbers. This immigration can neither
be debarred from a passage through Lower Canada, nor even be prevented from settling in that Province. The whole interior of the British
dominions must, ere long, be filled with an English population, every year
rapidly increasing its numerical superiority over the French. Is it just that
the prosperity of this great majority, and of this vast tract of country,
should be for ever, or even for a while, impeded by the artificial bar which
the backward laws and civilization of a part, and a part only, of Lower
Canada, would place between them and the ocean? Is it to be supposed
that such an English population will ever submit to such a sacrifice of
its interests?

I must not, however, assume it to be possible that the English Government shall adopt the course of placing or allowing any check to the influx
of English immigration into Lower Canada, or any impediment to the
profitable employment of that English capital which is already vested
therein. The English have already in their hands the majority of the
larger masses of property in the country; they have the decided superiority
of intelligence on their side; they have the certainty that colonization
must swell their numbers to a majority; and they belong to the race
which wields the Imperial Government, and predominates on the
American Continent. If we now leave them in a minority, they will never
abandon the assurance of being a majority hereafter, and never cease to
continue the present contest with all the fierceness with which it now
rages. In such a contest they will rely on the sympathy of their countrymen at home, and if that is denied them, they feel very confident of being
able to awaken the sympathy of their neighbours of kindred origin. They
feel that if the British Government intends to maintain its hold of the
Canadas, it can rely on the English population alone; that if it abandons
its colonial possessions, they must speedily become a portion of t' at great
Union which will speedily send forth its swarms of settlers, and, by force
of numbers and activity, quickly master every other race. The French
Canadians, on the other hand, are but the remnants of an ancient colonization, and are and ever must be isolated in the midst of an Anglo-Saxon

H

world. Whatever may happen, whatever government should be established over them, British or American, they can see no hope for their nationality. They can only sever themselves from the British Empire by waiting until some general cause of dissatisfaction alienates them, together with the surrounding colonies, and leaves them part of an English confederacy; or, if they are able, by effecting a separation singly, and so either merging in the American Union, or keeping up for a few years a wretched semblance of feeble independence, which would expose them more than ever to the intrusion of the surrounding population. I am far from wishing to encourage indiscriminately these pretensions to superiority on the part of any particular race; but while the greater part of every portion of the American Continent is still uncleared and unoccupied, and while the English exhibit such a constant and marked activity in colonization, so long will it be idle to imagine that there is any portion of that Continent into which that race will not penetrate, or in which, when it has penetrated, it will not predominate. It is but a question of time and mode; it is but to determine whether the small number of French who now inhabit Lower Canada shall be made English, under a Government which can protect them, or whether the process shall be delayed until a much larger number shall have to undergo, at the rude hands of its uncontrolled rivals, the extinction of a nationality strengthened and embittered by continuance.[137]

Durham thus admirably summed up the hard logic of geographic and economic facts over which French-Canadian ultra-nationalists have never ceased to stumble, in a rude awakening from their dreams of separatism and an independent French state.

But Durham, perhaps blinded by the very racism which he disowned, badly underestimated the French Canadians and their national will to live. The remedy which he proposed was brutal but merciful in his eyes, because of what he called their 'hopeless inferiority':

I know of no national distinction marking and continuing a more hopeless inferiority. The language, the laws, the character of the North American Continent are English; and every race but the English (I apply this to all who speak the English language) appears there in a condition of inferiority. It is to elevate them from that inferiority that I desire to give the Canadians our English character. I desire it for the sake of the educated classes, whom the distinction of language and manners keeps apart from the great Empire to which they belong. At the best, the fate of the educated and aspiring colonist is, at present, one of little hope, and little activity; but the French Canadian is cast still further into the shade, by a language and habits foreign to those of the Imperial Government. A spirit of exclusion has closed the highest professions on the educated classes of the French Canadians, more, perhaps, than was absolutely necessary; but it is impossible for the utmost liberality on the part of the British Government to give an equal position in the general competition of its vast population to those who speak a foreign language. I desire the amalgamation still more for the sake of the humbler classes. Their present state of rude and equal plenty is fast deteriorating under the pressure of population in the narrow limits to which they are confined. If they attempt to better their condition, by extending themselves over the neighbouring country, they will necessarily get more and more mingled with an English population: if they prefer remaining stationary, the greater part of them must be labourers in the employ of English capitalists. In either case it would appear, that the great mass of the French Canadians are doomed, in some measure, to occupy an inferior position, and be dependent upon the English for employment. The evils of poverty and dependence would merely be aggravated in a ten-fold degree, by a spirit of jealous and resentful nationality, which would separate the working classes of the community from the possessors of wealth and employers of labour.[138]

Durham thus foresaw a good measure of the future development of French Canada under the impact of the industrial revolution and capitalism, though he badly misjudged the strength of the national spirit. He saw, too, that the old closed agricultural system was doomed; and cited Andrew Stuart's report of 1826 which pointed out that since 1784 the population of the seigneuries had quadrupled, while the number of cattle had only doubled, and the amount of land under cultivation had only increased one-third. He predicted future developments with remarkable accuracy: 'If they wish to maintain the same kind of rude but well-provided agricultural existence, it must be by removing into those parts of the country in which the English are settled; or if they cling to their present residence, they can only obtain a livelihood by deserting their present employment, and working for wages on farms, or in commercial occupations under English capitalists.' In contrasting the depopulation and impoverishment of Canada with the rapid increase of population and wealth in the United States, Durham had already noted 'a large annual emigration of young men to the northern states . . . from which they generally return to their homes in a few months or years . . . a great many now take up their permanent residence in the United States.' Relying on the 'stationary habits and local attachments of the French Canadians,' Durham underestimated the future development of this trend, which was one result of the agricultural situation he described, and which he thought would put the French Canadians in a position 'similar to that of the poorest of the Irish peasantry.'[139]

Then, to justify his recommendation of national extinction, Durham wrote the words for which he has never been forgiven by the French Canadians, and which were taken as a challenge that became the impulse for a great intellectual awakening of French Canada and for a crystalization of its sense of nationality:

There can hardly be conceived a nationality more destitute of all that can invigorate and elevate a people, than that which is exhibited by the descendants of the French in Lower Canada, owing to their retaining their peculiar language and manners. They are a people with no history and no literature. The literature of England is written in a language which is not theirs; and the only literature which their language renders familiar to them, is that of a nation from which they have been separated by eighty years of a foreign rule, and still more by those changes which the Revolution and its consequences have wrought in the whole political, moral and social state of France. Yet it is on a people whom recent history, manners and modes of thought, so entirely separate from them, that the French Canadians are wholly dependent for almost all the instruction and amusement derived from books: it is on this essentially foreign literature, which is conversant about events, opinions, and habits of life, perfectly strange and unintelligible to them, that they are compelled to be dependent. Their newspapers are written mostly by natives of France, who have either come to try their fortunes in the Province, or have been brought to it by the party leaders, in order to supply the dearth of literary talent available for the political press. In the same way their nationality operates to deprive them of the enjoyments and civilizing influence of the arts. Though descended from the people in the world that most generally love, and have most successfully cultivated the drama —though living on a continent, in which almost every town, great or small, has an English theatre, the French population of Lower Canada, cut off from every people that speaks its own language, can support no national stage.

In these circumstances, I should indeed be surprised if the more reflecting part of the French Canadians entertain at present any hope of continuing to preserve their nationality. Much as they struggle against it, it is obvious that the process of assimilation to English habits is already commencing. The English language is gaining ground, as the language of the rich and of the employers of labour naturally will.[140]

This cultural indictment was largely true, though it was unjust in crediting the exceedingly lively press, the cradle of later French-Canadian literature, to the pens of Frenchmen from France, for that stage of cultural colonialism had been past for thirty years. It also neglected to note that the Jansenism of French-Canadian Catholicism frowned on the drama, which was thus reduced to an arid literary form. If Durham had cared to make similar observations about the English Canadians, he would have been forced to observe that such culture as they had developed was wholly colonial, with the British-born John Neilson and Adam Thom their leading journalists, and an English stage maintained by English touring companies. The Americans, whom Durham tended to lump with the English Canadians, were as yet not much farther on the way to cultural independence. But Durham's words spurred a young French-Canadian notary, François-Xavier Garneau, to write the epic of his people, and thus to lay the foundations of a nationalist literature obsessed with the history and the way of life of the French Canadians. The national pride was injured by Durham's frank indictment, and one of the unforeseen consequences of the *Report* was a strengthening of the instinct of national survival and the creation of more vigorous opposition to assimilative influences.

To his credit, Durham flatly rejected various plans for absolutist government of Lower Canada, 'constituted on an entirely despotic footing, or on one that would vest it entirely in the hands of the British minority.' Such a scheme would have the worst consequences, in his view, upon both the French and the English, and upon the United States, whose sympathy he thought it a matter of the greatest importance to preserve. Therefore he pronounced: 'The only power that can be effectual at once in coercing the present dissatisfaction, and hereafter obliterating the nationality of the French Canadians, is that of a numerical majority of a loyal and English population; and the only stable government will be one more popular than has hitherto existed in the North American Colonies.' He cited Louisiana as an example of the peaceful amalgamation of a minority group to the majority which could be achieved by such means; and then proposed a legislative union of Upper and Lower Canada to attain this object in the case of the French Canadians. Durham was unwilling 'to subject the French Canadians to the rule of the identical English minority with which they have so long been contending; but from a majority, emanating from so much more extended a source, I do not think that they would have any oppression or injustice to fear; and in this case, the far greater part of the majority never having been brought into previous collision, would regard them with no animosity that could warp their natural sense of equity.' Union would 'secure to Upper Canada the present great objects of its desire,' while 'the French, when once placed, by the legitimate course of events and the working of natural causes, in a minority, would abandon their vain hopes of nationality.'[141] But Durham fatally neglected the close connection between the political and cultural rights of minority groups.

Durham regretted that 'great practical difficulties' had forced him to abandon his initial idea of a federal union of all the British North American colonies:

Such a union would at once decisively settle the question of races; it would enable all the Provinces to co-operate for all common purposes; and, above all, it would form a great and powerful people, possessing the means of securing good and responsible government for itself, and which, under the protection of the British Empire, might in some measure counterbalance the preponderant and increasing influence of the United States on the American continent. . . . If we wish to prevent the extension of this influence, it can only be done by raising up for the North American colonist some nationality of his own; by elevating these small and unimportant communities into a society having some objects of national importance; and by thus giving their inhabitants a country which they will be unwilling to see absorbed even into one more powerful.

With another of his remarkable insights into the future, Durham observed that 'it would be the tendency of a federation sanctioned and consolidated by a monarchical Government gradually to become a complete legislative union; and that thus, while conciliating the French of Lower Canada, by leaving them the government of their own Province and their own internal legislation, I might provide for the protection of British interests by the general government, and for the gradual transition of the Provinces into an united and homogeneous community.'[142] But the morrow of armed rebellion was no moment for gradualism, and so the birth of modern Canada had to wait another quarter of a century.

The concluding pages of Durham's *Report* indicate how clearly he envisaged such a development. At the end of this eloquent and farsighted state paper, which stands as a great landmark in the development of colonial government, Durham protested his 'earnest desire to perpetuate and strengthen the connexion between this Empire and the North American Colonies, which would then form one of the brightest ornaments in Your Majesty's Imperial Crown.'[143] Though the purpose of the Union was defeated by its operation, and the French Canadians were not assimilated but came rather to hold the balance of power under responsible government, it cannot be gainsaid that the great Reformer, who was dying of tuberculosis as he wrote the *Report*, did much to attain his goal.

Notes

[1] Ever since Durham announced his conclusion that it was 'a struggle not of principles but of races,' English writers have tended to follow his lead. Kingsford (Vols. IX and X) is the leader of the racist authorities. D. G. Creighton (*Commercial Empire*, 310–20) upset the traditional racist interpretation by stressing the common economic factors behind both the Lower and Upper Canadian risings, despite his lack of sympathy with the French Canadians and with Reform principles. Garneau and Christie, writing while the ethnic cleavage brought about by the rebellions still persisted, are strongly affected by it. Groulx paints a battle of races, while the most detailed French-Canadian account, G. Filteau's *Histoire des Patriotes* (Montréal, 1938–42), is violently racist. A. Fauteaux's *Patriotes de 1837–38* (Montréal, 1950), a biographical dictionary with a prefatory historical summary by Félix Leclerc, is the most scholarly and objective French work.

[2] Notably Edmund Bailey O'Callaghan, Wolfred and Robert Nelson, Thomas Storrow Brown. Amury Girod was a Swiss.

[3] *Mackenzie's Own Narrative* (Toronto, 1838), 6-7; Christie, V, 110-11. W. S. Wallace, *The Family Compact* (Chronicles of Canada, Toronto, 1915), 117-18, 123, 125.

[4] Roebuck, Hume, O'Connell, and Brougham were the leading English spokesmen for the Canadian Patriots.

[5] See the reply of the Permanent Central Committee of the County of Montreal to the address of the Workingmen's Association of London, Christie, V, 57-63. This was sent previous to the risings in 1837, though only published in 1838. G.-E. Cartier and Chevalier de Lorimier were joint secretaries of the committee, which originated in 1834. Papineau was its leader and its headquarters were Edouard Fabre's bookstore. Filteau, II, 80-1.

[6] *Colonial Advocate*, 22 May 1834: Hume-Mackenzie.

[7] Christie, IV, 3-4.

[8] *CAR 1883*: Elliott's Letters, 160-7 and Notes A1 and A2; Chapais, IV, 63-9, 72. See also G. M. Fairchild, jr., *Lower Canada Affairs in 1836* (Quebec, 1910).

[9] Christie, IV, 142-50. The exasperated Tories belatedly dissolved the Rifle Corps after a proclamation had stamped it as 'unconstitutional and illegal,' but regretted that 'the day has arrived when, in a Colony conquered by British arms, a body of loyal subjects has been treated as traitors, by a British governor, for no other crime than that of rousing themselves to protect their persons and property, and to assist in maintaining the rights and privileges granted to them by the Constitution.' *Ibid.*, 145.

[10] Christie, IV, 155-7; Kennedy, *Documents*, 307-18, Gosford's instructions, 17 July 1835.

[11] Christie, IV, 341.

[12] 'Camillus' [A. Thom], *Anti-Gallic Letters* (Montreal, 1836), 129; cited Chapais, IV, 94.

[13] Creighton, *Commercial Empire*, 297.

[14] *Ibid.*

[15] Chapais, IV, 99.

[16] PAC: Q 232-5, Report of Royal Commission, 1837.

[17] Kennedy, *Documents*, 342-3, Russell's Ten Resolutions, 6 March 1837.

[18] *Hansard, IIIrd Series*, xxxiv, 95-6; Chapais, IV, 127.

[19] *The Vindicator*; Christie, IV, 351-2 n.

[20] APQ: Fonds Papineau, 530, Papineau-J.-G. Nancrède, 14 mai 1838.

[21] *La Minerve*, 27 avril 1837; Chapais, IV, 135.

[22] Christie, IV, 373-4 n.

[23] *La Minerve*, 11 mai 1837; Filteau, *Patriotes*, II, 83-7; Christie, IV, 352-6.

[24] *Le Canadien*, 15 mai 1837; Filteau, II, 103.

[25] *The Vindicator*, *La Minerve*, 16 mai 1837; Filteau, II, 106.

[26] Filteau, 108-11.

[27] *Ibid.*, 109-10.

[28] *Le Canadien*, 15 mai 1837; Chapais, IV, 137-40.

[29] *CAR 1922-3*, 270-1.

[30] *L'Ami du Peuple*, 26 juillet 1837; quoted Groulx, *Notre Maître*, II, 92-3.

[31] *La Minerve*, 27 juillet 1837; Filteau, II, 132-3; paraphrased in *CAR 1922-3*, 243. Cf. Groulx, II, 90-6, and L.-A. Desrosiers, 'Correspondence de Mgr Jean-Jacques Lartigue de 1836 à 1838,' in *RAPQ 1944-5*, 247: Lartigue-Mgr Signay, 29 juillet 1837; 255, Lartigue-Mgr Mai, 15 octobre 1837.

[32] Filteau, II, 134-6; Christie, IV, 391-2.

[33] Christie, IV, 384.

[34] PAC: Q 238-1, 71, Gosford-Glenelg, 2 September 1837; Chapais, IV, 166-7.

[35] Christie, IV, 395; Filteau, II, 172-6.

36 Filteau, II, 171–2; Christie, IV, 398.

37 Fauteux, 29; Filteau, II, 182.

38 *The Vindicator*, 24 October 1837; Christie, IV, 400–10 *n.*; Fauteux, 29–30.

39 Filteau, II, 182.

40 *La Minerve*, 2 novembre 1837.

41 *Mandements des évêques de Montréal* (Montréal, 1867), I, 14: Lartigue, 24 October 1837. Translation in Christie, IV, 415–9.

42 *RAPQ 1944–5*: L.-A. Desrosiers, 'Correspondence de Mgr Jean-Jacques Lartigue de 1836 à 1838,' 257, Lartigue-Demers, 30 October 1837; 260, Lartigue-Superieur de Saint-Sulpice (Paris), 25 November 1837. *RAPQ 1945–6*: L.-A. Desrosiers, 'Correspondence de Mgr Lartique et de son coadjuteur Mgr Bourget de 1837 à 1840,' 142–3, Bourget-Sidyme (Turgeon), 26 October 1837; 143, Bourget-P. M.-Mignault, 6 November 1837; 144, Bourget-Sidyme, 13 November 1837. Cf. Groulx, 104–17.

43 *Mandements de Québec*, III, 371: Signay, 11 December 1837.

44 *The Liberal*, 3 November 1837; Chapais, IV, 173; Filteau, II, 195.

45 *La Minerve*, cited without date by Chapais, IV, 175.

46 *Le Canadien*, 22 November 1837; Chapais, IV, 183–4. For other extracts from Parent's writings at this period, see Chapais, 175–83.

47 PAC: Q 239–1, 4; Chapais, IV, 195.

48 Christie, IV, 426–37, gives the conflicting accounts of the *Montreal Herald*, *Montreal Gazette*, *L'Ami du Peuple*, *La Minerve*, and *Morning Courier* of the affair on November 6. Cf. Filteau, II, 217–24, which assigns the riot to a loyalist conspiracy.

49 Christie, V, 2–3 *n.*

50 PAC: Q 239–1, 98, Gosford-Glenelg, 22 November 1837; *RAPQ 1925–6*, 151–3, I. Caron, 'Les Evénements de 1837 et 1838,' Docs. 50–70; L.-O. David, *Les Patriotes de 1837–38* (Montréal, 1936), 25; Christie, IV, 448–50.

51 Christie, IV, 461, quotes the official figures of six killed and eleven wounded among the troops. Filteau, III, 28–9, puts the military losses at 116. Christie puts the *Patriote* dead at thirteen, Filteau at ten dead and seven wounded.

52 Christie, IV, 466–70 and *n.*, 507–40, gives many of the documents in the Papineau-Nelson dispute.

53 *RAPQ 1925–6*, 166–7, Docs. 358–80; Christie, IV, 471–4, 511–16; Filteau, III, 14–15, 22–3.

54 *RAPQ 1925–6*, 167, 168–70; Docs. 377–80, 381–440; Christie, IV, 474–5; Filteau, III, 50–1.

55 Christie, V, 23, Gugy-Christie, 8 April 1853.

56 *Ibid.*, 24.

57 Christie, IV, 520, Brown-Nelson, 25 November 1851.

58 Christie, IV, 465, gives the official return for the troops and quotes an estimate of more than 150 killed and more than 300 wounded for the *Patriotes*. Filteau, III, 44–5, estimates the *Patriote* losses as 40 dead, 30 wounded, and 30 prisoners, and states that the troops lost at least 30 men.

59 Christie, IV, 466.

60 *Ibid.*, 476–8, 513; Filteau, III, 58, 61–3.

61 Lanctot, *Voisins*, 194; Papineau at Saint-Ours.

62 Christie, IV, 481–3, Kempt-Colborne, 7 December 1837; 483–4 *n.*, Knowlton-Colborne, 7 December 1837; Filteau, III, 64–7.

63 *CAR 1922–3*, 373, 'Giroud's Journal,' 22 November 1837; 167–8, Lafontaine-J. Parkes, 10 March 1838; Lafontaine-E. Ellice, 15 March 1838; 170, Lafontaine-Ellice, 17 April 1838; *CAR 1901*, Q 239–2, 291, 295, Gosford-Glenelg, 28 December 1837 and Lafontaine warrant. PAC: Q 239–2, Gosford-Glenelg, 6 December 1837.

64 *CAR 1901*, 1011.

65 Christie, IV, 486-9, Proclamation of November 29; 490-1 *n.*, reward of $4,000 for Papineau, 1 December 1837; 491-2, rewards of $2,000 for W. Nelson, T. S. Brown, E. B. O'Callaghan, C.-H.-O. Côté, J.-T. Drolet, J.-J. Girouard, W. H. Scott, E.-E. Rodier, A. Girod, J.-O. Chénier, and $400 for P.-P. Demaray, J.-F. Davignon, J. [L.] Gagnon, P. Amiot, L. Perrault, L. Gauthier, and R. Des Rivières, 29 November 1837; 492-3 *n.*, proclamation of martial law, 5 December 1837. Most of the proclamations offering rewards are reproduced in their English and French versions in *RAPQ 1925-6*, 160, 176, 208, 216, 224.

66 *RAPQ 1945-6*, 151, Bourget-La Motte, 11 December 1837; *Mandements de Montréal*, I, 24, Lartigue's mandement, 8 January 1838; *RAPQ 1945-6*, 145, Bourget-Lefebvre, 4 November 1937; Bourget-Bellenger, 5 December 1937; 47, Lartigue-Blanchet, 27 January 1838; 145, Bourget-Quiblier, 20 November 1837; 151-2, Bourget-Chartier, 12 December 1837; 156, Bourget-Mousseau.

67 *CAR 1922-3*, 375, Girod's *Journal*.

68 *Ibid.*, 379.

69 Christie, V, 6 *n.*; Filteau, III, 92.

70 *RAPQ 1945-6*, 158, Bourget-Sidyme, 26 January 1838; A. Descelles, *The Patriotes of 1837* (Chronicles of Canada, Toronto, 1916), 101.

71 *Mandements de Québec*, III, 374-7, Signay's mandement, 6 February 1838; 377-8, circular on petition, 7 February 1837; 378-81, text of petition. This petition was the idea of Abbé J.-C. Prince of the Seminary of Saint Hyacinthe, and Bishop Bourget had advocated it to Bishop Turgeon as early as November 20 as a means 'to satisfy the moderate *Patriotes* and protect the interests of the clergy without being the tool of M. Papineau.' He thought that it would restore the confidence of the people in the clergy (*RAPQ 1945-6*, 146, Bourget-Sidyme, 20 November 1837). A draft of the petition was drawn up by Bishop Lartigue in November before the fighting at Saint-Denis and Saint-Charles, which caused the project to be postponed (*RAPQ 1944-5*, 260). But Bourget's hopes were not realized, for after the petition was sent he noted that the people had turned against the clergy (*RAPQ 1945-6*, 167, Bourget-Belcourt, 24 April 1838).

72 Christie, V, 51, lists the members, who included Neilson, James Stuart, and Peter McGill.

73 Christie, V, 151 *n.*, Buller-executive councilors, 31 May 1838.

74 Christie, V, 145-8, Durham's proclamation, 29 May 1838.

75 Chapais, IV, 224-5, gives excerpts.

76 Christie, V, 160 *n.* and 223-9, prisoners' letters of 18 and 26 June and Nelson and Bouchette's explanation of 19 October 1838.

77 *Ibid.*, 161-6, ordinance of 28 June 1838.

78 *Ibid.*, 174-7, proclamation of amnesty, 28 June 1838.

79 *CAR 1923*, 315, Colonel Grey's Report, 22 June 1838.

80 *Ibid.*, 341-69, Buller's 'Sketch of Lord Durham's Mission to Canada in 1838,' 1840.

81 *CHR 1937*, 51, N. Storey (*ed.*), 'Stewart Derbishire's Report to Lord Durham on Lower Canada, 1838.'

82 *Ibid.*

83 *Ibid.*, 53.

84 *Ibid.*, 52-3; P.-J.-O. Chauveau, *F.-X. Garneau et son oeuvre* (Montréal, 1883), ccxiii-iv.

85 *CHR 1937*, 54, 55.

86 *Ibid.*, 57.

87 *Ibid.*, 57-8.

88 *Ibid.*, 60.

89 *Ibid.*, 57.

90 *Ibid.*, 57.

91 *Ibid.*, 62.

⁹² *Ibid.*, 64.

⁹³ PAC: Durham Papers, II, 126, Durham-Glenelg, 28 September 1838.

⁹⁴ Christie, V, 211–21, Durham's farewell proclamation, 9 October 1838.

⁹⁵ *CAR 1923*, 361, Buller's *Sketch*.

⁹⁶ *Ibid.*, 363.

⁹⁷ Christie, V, 15–8, proclamation of Governor Jenison of Vermont, 13 December 1837; 83–4, proclamation of Governor Marcy of New York, 19 December 1837.

⁹⁸ Christie, V, 42–5, Nelson's proclamation, 28 February 1838.

⁹⁹ *Ibid.*, 45–6.

¹⁰⁰ Colborne continued martial law in the district of Montreal by proclamation on February 27, the day he took over the government from Gosford. On February 22 he had ordered the inhabitants of the counties of Laprairie, Chambly, and L'Acadie to give up their arms (Christie, V, 38–9). The official communiqué on the Caldwell's Manor episode clearly indicates that Nelson's invasion was anticipated (*ibid.*, 40–2). According to the *Burlington Sentinel*, Colonel John E. Wool, the U.S. commanding officer at Plattsburg, kept Colborne informed of the *Patriote* plans, and he was conveniently at hand to accept Nelson's surrender. Fauteux, *Patriotes*, 54; A. B. Corey, *The Crisis of 1830–1842 in Canadian-American Relations* (Toronto, 1941), 41–2.

¹⁰¹ TRSC 1926, III, 20, I, 17–34, I. Caron, 'Une Société Secrète dans le Bas Canada en 1838.' Corey, 75, estimates the membership at 40–50,000 members, with 107 lodges in Vermont, 283 in New York, 74 in New Hampshire, and 99 in Maine.

¹⁰² Félix Poutré, *Echappé de la Potence: Souvenirs d'un Prisonnier d'Etat en 1838* (Montréal, 1869).

¹⁰³ Christie, V, 213, 217, 218, Durham's farewell proclamation, 9 October, 1838.

¹⁰³ᵃ *RAPQ 1945–6*, 64, Lartigue-Turgeon, 6 June 1838; 80, Lartigue-Signay, 29 September 1838; 95, Lartigue-Provender, 21 August 1839.

¹⁰⁴ *Montreal Herald*, 14 November 1838; Chapais, IV, 218–19 *n.*

¹⁰⁵ Christie, V, 239–40, 263.

¹⁰⁶ *Ibid.*, 263–73, gives extracts from the loyalist and *Patriote* press.

¹⁰⁷ Fauteux, 75–9, identifies the prisoners and their fates.

¹⁰⁸ Chapais, IV, 224 *n.*

¹⁰⁹ Quoted in *L'Aurore*, 18 January 1839; Filteau, III, 208.

¹¹⁰ *CAR 1923*, Buller-J. S. Mill, 13 October 1838.

¹¹¹ C. P. Lucas, *Lord Durham's Report* (Oxford, 1912), II, 9.

¹¹² *CHR 1939*, 128, C. New, 'The British Background of the Durham Report.'

¹¹³ Lucas, II, 13.

¹¹⁴ *Ibid.*, 16–17.

¹¹⁵ *Ibid.*, III, 340.

¹¹⁶ *Ibid.*, II, 17.

¹¹⁷ *Ibid.*, 19–20.

¹¹⁸ *Ibid.*, 22, 23, 27.

¹¹⁹ *Ibid.*, 27, 28–31, 32, 33.

¹²⁰ *Ibid.*, 34, 35, 36–7.

¹²¹ *Ibid.*, 38, 40, 43.

¹²² *Ibid.*, 45–6, 47.

¹²³ *Ibid.*, 48–9, 51, 52.

¹²⁴ *Ibid.*, 52–3.

¹²⁵ *Ibid.*, 63, 70, 71, 72.

¹²⁶ *CAR 1923*, 326–8, R. Baldwin-Durham, 23 August 1838; 329–37, R. Baldwin-Glenelg, 13 July 1836; *CHR 1939*, 188, C. Martin, 'Lord Durham's Report and its Consequences.'

[127] Lucas, II, 278, 76, 82.

[128] *CHR 1938*, 22-30, J. B. Brebner, 'Patronage and Parliamentary Government.'

[129] Lucas, II, 110, 113, 128, 130.

[130] *Report on the Affairs of British North America from the Earl of Durham, Her Majesty's High Commissioner, &c. &c. &c.* (London, 1839), Appendix D.

[131] Lucas, II, 134, 135, 136.

[132] *Ibid.*, 137, 138, 139, 140.

[133] *Ibid.*, 280, 282, 282-3, 283, 285.

[134] *Ibid.*, 287.

[135] Report (London, 1839), Appendix B; Lucas, III, 34-130.

[136] Lucas, II, 288-9.

[137] *Ibid.*, 289-92.

[138] *Ibid.*, 292-3.

[139] *Ibid.*, 294. Emigration of French Canadians to U.S., 243, 262.

[140] *Ibid.*, 294-6.

[141] *Ibid.*, 296, 299, 307.

[142] *Ibid.*, 305.

[143] *Ibid.*, 333.

CHAPTER V

THE EMERGENCE OF A NATION—I

(1840-9)

THE FRENCH CANADIANS had lost their struggle for survival by resort to arms; they were to win it by resort to the arts of peace. Spurred by the direct attack on their culture which Durham had made, and by the threat of the assimilation which he recommended, they soon overturned the political system which was designed to effect it, and gave vigorous evidence of their cultural strength. The period between 1840 and 1867 is one of the most notable chapters in the French-Canadian past.

Faced with the prospect of national extinction, the French Canadians closed their ranks and won the peaceful victory which insured their national survival. They were favored by the curious fatality which befell the first governors-general of United Canada—three of whom served a total of only seven years, and were overtaken by death, while two were repudiated at home and two in Canada. They were fortunate in their own political leaders, Louis-Hippolyte Lafontaine and George Etienne Cartier, who displayed qualities of statesmanship as yet unrevealed by French Canadians: and they benefited by alliance with Robert Baldwin's Upper Canadian Reformers. They also profited by disunion among the English-Canadian Tories, accentuated by economic disorders that were of less concern to a people as yet largely unconcerned with trade and commerce. Then French Canada produced a national historian, François-Xavier Garneau, and a national poet, Octave Crémazie, at the very moment when a sense of nationality was necessary for survival. A spirit of liberalism and progress infused new life into a traditional culture at the very period when it became essential that that culture should change or perish. This notable era began with French Canada deprived of representative government and condemned to extinction in a wholly British North America; it closed with the dualism of Canada recognized by a new constitution and with a French-Canadian cultural tradition firmly established.

I

Such results were unthinkable at the outset of the period. The union of the two Canadas had been decided upon by the British government as a result of Durham's *Report*, but the grant of responsible government was withheld. The first Union Bill proposed by the British government in 1839 was withdrawn because of the protests it aroused in Upper Canada. The Reformers in both provinces were given new hope by Durham's backing of the principle of responsible government, while both groups of Tories united to denounce this dangerous suggestion. All parties were in some measure aggrieved by Durham's frankness. A committee of the legislative council of Upper Canada declared that the adoption of Durham's plan 'must lead to the overthrow of the great colonial empire of England.'[1] With a singular anticipation of the Tory annexationist sentiment of a decade later, this body proclaimed:

If England withdraw her influence, and leave her governors to be the shuttle between colonial parties, no loyalty now existing among any of these parties will prevent their seeking another influence in the neighbouring republic, to replace the one needlessly withdrawn; and as the French of Lower Canada sought the alliance of their ancient enemies, the Anglo-American population of the neighbouring States, to give them the means of overwhelming the British population—for the time left without the countenance or support of the British government—so will the losing party, in either colony, seek some external influence to aid their cause. England refuses the umpirage, and there can be no doubt but that it will be readily offered, before many years, to the United States.[2]

In the face of such provocative statements, the British government, which was not yet ready to consider parting with its colonies, sent out Charles Poulett Thomson, a disciple of Durham, as governor-general, with instructions to gather further information on Canadian affairs to serve in drawing up a new Canada bill. To him Lord John Russell, the colonial secretary and his close friend, expressed the government's anxiety 'to consult and, so far as may be possible, to defer to public opinion in the Canadas on the subject of constitutional changes,' and at the same time its great reluctance to depart from the principles of 'a legislative Union of the two provinces—a just regard to the claims of either province in adjusting the terms of that Union—the maintenance of the three estates of the provincial legislature, the settlement of a permanent civil list for securing the independence of the judges, and to the executive government that freedom of action which is essential for the public good—and the establishment of a system of local government by representative bodies, freely elected in the various cities and rural districts.'[3]

In the face of continued Canadian agitation for responsible government, Russell further advised Thomson that he was to give no encouragement to the 'movement for what is absurdly called responsible government.' He granted the existence of that system in England, but he did not favor its extension to the colonies:

But if we seek to apply such a practice to a colony, we shall at once find ourselves at fault. The power for which a minister is responsible in England, is not his own power, but the power of the Crown, of which he is for the time the organ. It is obvious that the executive councillor of a colony is in a situation totally different. The Governor under whom he serves receives his orders from the Crown of England. But can the colonial council be the advisers to the Crown of England? Evidently not, for the Crown has other advisers, for the same functions, and with superior authority.

It may happen, therefore, that the Governor receives at one and the same time instructions from the Queen, and advice from his executive council, totally at variance with each other. If he is to obey his instructions from England, the parallel of constitutional responsibility entirely fails; if, on the other hand, he is to follow the advice of his council, he is no longer a subordinate officer, but an independent sovereign. [4]

While objecting to the fundamental principle, Russell found none to 'the practical views of colonial government recommended by Lord Durham.' In short, he proposed that the fruits of Durham's plan be attained while the root was withheld. In his view this miracle was to be achieved by the exercise of forbearance on the part of both the executive and the assembly: 'The Governor must only oppose the wishes of the Assembly where the honour of the Crown, or the interests of the empire are deeply concerned; and the Assembly must be ready to modify some of its measures for the sake of harmony, and from a reverent attachment to the authority of Great Britain.' [5] Such an interest in harmony and such 'reverent attachment' were hardly to be expected from those who had recently been at one another's throats; only genius could make the policy briefly workable, and it was foredoomed to the failure which befell it within a few years.

2

Poulett Thomson, who was shortly raised to the peerage as Baron Sydenham of Sydenham and Toronto—an appropriate title, since he was to govern in the interests of England and Upper Canada— was singularly well equipped for the difficult task thus set him of working out a practical implementation of Durham's policy. He was neither a Tory soldier, like most of the governors who had preceded him, nor a benevolent Liberal like Durham; but a businessman who had been trained as a merchant and who had represented Manchester, the capital of the new industrialism, in Parliament for ten years. He was at home with facts, figures, statistics and financial problems; he had served for five years as president of the Board of Trade and was considered a likely choice for chancellor of the exchequer.

It had been demonstrated that Upper and Lower Canada could not exist economically separate; it seemed unlikely that they could live politically united. But if any man could bring about a successful working of the Union, it was Thomson, who was both an able parliamentarian and an able businessman, though a businessman of a very different stamp from the Canadian merchants, since he was a Whig, a free-trader, and a former Baltic timber dealer, and thus triply anathema to them.

He was as much opposed to responsible government as they were, however, and as set upon the Union as a device by which bankrupt Upper Canada, with its debt of £1,200,000 (the interest on which the revenue did not suffice to pay), could be saved by amalgamation with the prosperous lower province, whose debt amounted only to £95,000. Though no mention was made of the matter in his official instructions, he had been secretly authorized by the Cabinet to grant at his discretion a British guarantee for a loan of a million and a half sterling to Upper Canada, to diminish the interest burden and to continue the canal and road program which was largely responsible for the upper province's debt.[6] It was no problem for the iron-willed and self-confident Thomson to win support for the Union project from the new special council of Lower Canada, made up of creatures of the government selected by Colborne; while the terms he offered of a permanent civil list, equal representation for each province, and the charging of the Upper Canadian debt upon the general revenue, won over the Upper Canadian legislature after some resistance.

The governor overcame by personal intervention opposition from members of the Tory Family Compact, who proposed that Lower Canada should have only fifty voices to Upper Canada's sixty-two in the new assembly, that the capital should be in the latter province, that English should be the sole language of legislation, and that a property qualification should be established for members. The city fathers of Toronto went one step farther by demanding in their address of welcome that the same rights and privileges given to the 'loyal British population of these provinces' should not be extended to 'that portion of the population which by education, habits, and prejudices is alien to our nation.'[7] Despite these excessively vigorous protestations of loyalty which a largely immigrant stock directed against the natives of their common country, Thomson confided to a friend that the reconciliation of Upper Canada to the Union was 'a more difficult matter' than that of Lower Canada, where 'The *Canadien* and the *Montreal Herald* lie down together upon this point. In short, the unanimity is wonderful.'[8] Thomson himself thought 'a despotism would be by far the best thing for Lower Canada for the next ten years,' but he recognized 'that cannot be.'[9] As for Upper Canadian loyalism, he commented dryly that 'The people have got into the habit of talking so much *separation*, that they begin to believe in it. The Constitutional party is as bad or worse than the other, in spite of all their professions of loyalty.'[10] Thomson was no gentler in describing the state of Lower Canada a few months later: 'They have only one feeling—the French hate the English and would cut all their throats if they could—the English hate the French and only desire to ride rough shod over them.'[11]

With Canadian consent obtained either by force or pressure exercised by the governor-general, the imperial parliament passed the Union Act[12] on July 23, 1840. The bill, introduced by Lord John Russell on March 23, established the Province of Canada, with a legislative council named for life and an elected assembly composed of forty-two members from Lower Canada and forty-two from Upper Canada. Any change in the number of representatives demanded a two-thirds vote of both houses. A property qualification of £500 was established. English was to be the only language of original record for the legislature,[13] but the existing laws of the two provinces were preserved. The revenues of the Crown were renounced to the new province in exchange for a civil list of £45,000, covering the salaries of the governor and judges, and of £30,000, covering the salaries of the principal civil servants. Thomson had urgently advised Russell: 'You must take a *large* civil list. Govt. in this country depends on your not being obliged to go to the Assembly for what you want.'[14] The governor was given the right to erect new counties or townships, and to name personal deputies. Bills relative to the rights of the clergy and of the Crown were to be submitted to the imperial parliament, which also retained power over the regulation of trade and navigation between Canada and other countries. The governor preserved the right of veto and the right to reserve legislation for the royal sanction, while the Queen could disavow any bill within a period of two years.

By giving the same representation to the 650,000 people of Lower Canada as to the 450,000 of Upper Canada, the bill violated one of Durham's major recommendations, that in favor of representation by population. By merging the revenues of the two provinces and their public debts, Lower Canada was saddled with the enormous debt of the upper province, largely contracted, to be sure, for the St. Lawrence canals which would be of mutual value in the future, though at present of benefit mainly to Upper Canada. The article establishing English as the sole official language was deeply resented by the French Canadians. It was the first official measure directed against an essential element of their survival, and the first step in Durham's proposed program of anglicization.

The bill was supported in the House by both parties, with Russell, Charles Buller, Gladstone, Peel, and Ellice backing it, while the only notable opposition was raised by Daniel O'Connell. He protested against the inequality of representation and the fact that the people of Lower Canada had not been consulted, seeing only disaffection and a weakening of the bonds between the two countries as the results of such a measure. But even Hume, long the champion of the Canadians, refused to vote against the bill, and it was carried with only six opposing voices in the House. In the Lords the opposition to the bill, led by Wellington, Gosford, Ellenborough, Brougham, and Hardwick, was more vigorous. Gosford protested that 'I do not believe that in any of our Colonies Her Majesty has more loyal subjects than the French Canadians of Lower Canada.'[15] Denouncing the inequality of representation and the merging of the debts, he exclaimed: 'There could be nothing more arbitrary and unjust.' But despite these objections of the former governor, and the petitions of 10,000 inhabitants of Quebec and of the bishops and clergy of Montreal and Quebec, the measure was carried.

One powerful force behind the Union Act was that of the banking firm of Baring Brothers, which had underwritten almost all the Upper Canadian securities whose value was now in question. One of the principals of this firm, Francis T. Baring, was chancellor of the exchequer in the Melbourne cabinet, and the Baring interests may have had something to do with the determination of the cabinet to shift the burden of Upper Canadian bankruptcy onto the shoulders of the prosperous lower province. Young Pierre Chauveau was moved to bitter verse by this banker's constitution:

> C'est le jour des banquiers, demain sera notre heure.
> Aujourd'hui l'oppression, demain la liberté;
> Aujourd'hui l'on fustige un peuple entier qui pleure,
> Demain l'on voit debout tout un peuple ameuté;
> Aujourd'hui le forfait, et demain la vengéance,
> Aujourd'hui c'est de l'or, et demain c'est du fer . . .
> C'est le jour des banquiers, vous dis-je! c'est leur gloire
> Que les placards royaux affichent sur nos murs;
> L'Union que l'on proclame est leur chant de victoire,
> Et tout devait céder à des motifs si purs! . . .
> Ces vieux lords décrépits, ces ministres peureux . . .
> Cependant, si Baring leur dit: moi, je le veux,
> Enlacés comme ils sont aux filets de sa banque,
> Ils n'ont rien à repondre et jamais il ne fait
> D'inutile calcul, ni de projet qui manque.
> Il voudrait l'univers, il leur demanderait
> Le sang des nations pour verser dans sa caisse,
> Que l'illustre Russell d'une tremblante main,
> Jaloux de prévenir et d'écarter la baisse
> Signerait aussitôt l'absurde parchemin. . . .*[16]

> *It is the banker's day, tomorrow will be ours,
> Today oppression, tomorrow liberty,

While the young poet thus inveighed in prosy verse against British economic conspiracy—which French Canadians were to suspect with more and more frequency in the years to come—the businessman governor-general lapsed into lyricism in proclaiming the establishment of the Union on February 10, 1841:

Inhabitants of the Province of Canada: Henceforth may you be united in sentiment as you are from this day in name! Who can visit, as it has been my good fortune to do, the extensive regions which are now united in one common denomination, and fail to acknowledge the vast resources they present, for all that can conduce to the comforts and happiness of man? A part of the Mighty Empire of England—protected by Her arms—assisted by Her Treasury, admitted to all the benefits of Trade as Her citizens—your freedom guaranteed by Her Laws, and your rights supported by the sympathy of your Fellow-Subjects there—Canada enjoys a position unsurpassed by any Country in the world. It is for you, its Inhabitants, to cultivate these advantages—to avail yourselves of the new Era which now opens upon you.[17]

3

Though Sydenham was 'not a bit afraid of the responsible government cry,'[18] he was deeply disturbed by the home government's failure to establish under the Union Act a system of local government, which Durham had recommended and which he himself strongly favored. He wrote home:

No man in his senses would think for a moment of the Union without its being accompanied by some sort of Local Government, in which the people may control their own officers, and the executive at the same time obtain some influence in the country districts. Without a breakwater of this kind between the Central Government and the people, Government with an Assembly is impossible in Lower Canada, and most

> Today a weeping people is beaten,
> Tomorrow a people will be up in arms,
> Today the forfeit, tomorrow the vengeance,
> Today is gold's, tomorrow steel's . . .
> It is the banker's day, I say, it is their glory
> Of which the royal placards give notice on our walls.
> The Union thus proclaimed is their song of victory,
> And all ought to yield to motives so pure! . . .
> These decrepit old lords, these fearful ministers
> If Baring says to them: 'I wish it';
> Entrapped as they are in the meshes of his bank,
> They have nothing to say, and never does he make
> A useless calculation or a project doomed to fail.
> If he wished the universe, he would ask of them
> The blood of nations, to pour it in his safe;
> Let the noted Russell, with a trembling hand,
> Anxious to prevent and avoid a crash,
> Sign at once the absurd parchment . . .

difficult in Upper Canada; and it is absurd to expect that any good system will be established by the Provincial Legislature, even if time admitted of its being proposed to them . . . not only has all chance of the Union Bill working well been destroyed, but also a change of system throughout all the Provinces . . . The establishment of Municipal Government by Act of Parliament is as much a part of the intended, scheme of Government for the Canadas as the union of the two Legislatures, and the more important of the two.[19]

There was some injured pride of authorship behind this indignation, for Sydenham himself had drafted the scheme which was omitted from the bill, at the insistence of Peel and Stanley, because of 'the want of Canadian authority.'[20]

It was easy to remedy the omission in the case of Lower Canada, for all Sydenham had to do was to have an ordinance establishing his scheme passed by the special council. He thought it particularly important to do so, for:

The Priest and the Lawyer return the member *now* and *that* without any control, or upon any ground except hatred to English Govt. and the English name. Establish a field in which the Inhabitants can discuss their own interests, and parties will soon be split in the different parishes and districts, and set there someone in the confidence of the Govt. who will expose the misrepresentations which are made, and you will either get different members or have a good check on them.[21]

But to get the measure through the first parliament of the Union required all his skill as a parliamentarian. An interesting light on the man and on his concept of his role in the new government is furnished by the account he gave of this episode to his brother:

My last feat has been to carry the Municipal District Bill for Upper Canada, word for word after my own ordinance for the Lower Province; thereby not only giving the complement to the Union (for you know I always declared that without such institutions the Union could not work), but setting up my own particular legislation by the sanction of the United Parliament. The bill has passed both houses, and I proceed to-day in state to give it the royal assent, in order to make perfectly sure of its being law, even if I were to quit this world the day after. But the trouble I have had to do this has completely justified all my anticipations of the next to impossibility of our getting such a measure through a Provincial Assembly, and the utter hopelessness of the effort, but for the course I followed of dictating it, while I was dictator, for one part of the province first. One party hated the measure because it was to give power to the people; another because it placed that power under wholesome control by the Crown; a third because it deprived the members of the Assembly of all their past power of jobbing. But I beat them all three, to the utter astonishment of the spectators; and at last carried my work, the Bill, the whole Bill, and nothing but the Bill, by a majority of forty-two to twenty-nine, or more than one third. I have now accomplished all I set much value on; for whether the rest be done now or some sessions hence, matters little. The five great works I aimed at have been got through—the establishment of a board of works with ample powers; the admission of aliens; a new system of county courts; the regulation of the public lands ceded by the Crown under the Union Act; and lastly, this District Council Bill. [22]

This letter reveals Sydenham's policy of being his own prime minister, and the success which crowned his energetic pursuit of the program of reconstruction on which he had decided.

But parliamentary government was at a different stage of growth in Canada than at Westminster or Washington. Lord John Russell knew what responsible government meant in England in 1839, but both he and the Canadian governors were puzzled by a concept of patronage which owed more to American than British precedents. For Papineau, Lafontaine, and Baldwin, under the influence of Jacksonianism, the spoils system was a cornerstone of their constitutional concepts. Their demands for the extension of the elective principle to the councils* and other public offices ran counter to the traditional eighteenth-century concept of patronage held by the governors, who sought to emulate George III. Metcalfe saw the conflict in Canada not as one about a principle of government but as to 'whether the patronage of the Crown should be surrendered to the Council for the purchase of Parliamentary support.' [23] But responsible government and patronage were inextricably linked in Canadian constitutional development, as the course of party politics from 1841 to 1847 gave evidence. Both Baldwin and Lafontaine made control of patronage the criterion of their taking office. The demand for a share of patronage was particularly strong among the now politically conscious French Canadians, after their long exclusion from office by French and British placemen under the old imperial systems. Political office had special attractions for them, since other fields were largely dominated by English Canadians. Sydenham, and his successors until Elgin, ignored these facts, and their blindness cost them dear.

Sydenham named an executive council composed of four Tories and three Reformers, with not a single French-Canadian member. In explaining his action privately to Russell, the governor-general observed: 'The worst of it is, that there is really not a French Canadian to whom it is possible to give an office.' [24] To be sure, he had tried to induce Lafontaine to become solicitor-general of Lower Canada, promising in the future to call only Reformers to office from that section, but the latter had refused, not wishing to give his

* Baldwin, unlike his Lower Canadian friends, opposed an elective legislative council.

support to either the Union or to a government hostile to the French Canadians.

Since April 1839, when Francis Hincks had written him offering the co-operation of the Upper Canadian Reformers in achieving 'liberal institutions and economical government,'[25] Lafontaine had been in close touch with the leaders of that party. In 1840 he visited Robert Baldwin, and their acquaintance ripened into a lasting friendship and political alliance. Baldwin and Hincks preferred to join with men of their own political convictions rather than to accept the ethnic alliance offered by the British party in Lower Canada, for Baldwin held that 'There is, and must be, no question of races—It were madness on one side, and guilt, deep guilt on both to make such a question.'[26] Hincks kept urging Lafontaine to accept the Union and to act with the governor, assuring him that 'your brother Reformers in Upper Canada will meet you and your compatriots as Canadians, that no national animosities will be entertained, that we desire your friendship, esteem, and co-operation if we can obtain them consistent with our principles.'[27] When Baldwin accepted office as solicitor-general of Upper Canada, Hincks defended his course, and later urged Lafontaine to follow it, arguing that Reform influence in the government would thus be strengthened.[28]

Sydenham merely gathered in one cabinet representatives of the various factions whose support he needed to enact his policy; he did not choose a responsible ministry. He favored a dictatorship for Lower Canada, and he set about achieving the position of a dictator within the framework of the Union Act. The legislative council was in his power, since he named its members; the assembly offered more difficulties, since its members must be elected. But the governor took an active part in the elections held in the spring of 1841, talking freely of 'my candidates' and gerrymandering constituencies in order to achieve their election, notably at Montreal and Quebec:

I shall reduce the limits of Montreal & Quebec to the Cities and cut off the suburbs, which will cause a great clatter with the French and their Allies, but you might just as well have given no representation at all to either city as far as the Trade and the British Mercantile Interest is concerned, as not to do so. *With* the suburbs, these towns are as much French Counties as the Counties of the same names.[29]

Where such tactics were not sufficient, he established the polling places in strongholds of the government, and winked at the intimidation of voters. By such means nineteen unionists were elected out of Lower Canada's forty-two representatives. Sydenham reported to Russell:

. . . considering that two years ago the people were cutting each other's throats and in arms against each other while the French Canadian press and leaders have been doing everything in their power to excite the passion of the People, I am quite surprised that they [the elections] went off so well.[30]

Lafontaine was defeated in Terrebonne, where several hundred strongarm men had been brought in from Montreal and Glengarry to support Sydenham's candidate. Faced with the prospect of involving his supporters in a murderous and hopeless battle at the polls, Lafontaine withdrew from the contest. At the outset of the election he had issued a manifesto which served as a new political program for the French Canadians. In it he pointed out that Canada was not only their ancestral home, but also the adopted home of the English who had established themselves there, and that the happiness and welfare of both groups were dependent upon social equality and political liberty. He defined the latter as:

The sanction by the popular will of the adoption of laws; it is its consent to vote taxes and to control disbursements; again, it is its effective participation in the action of its government; it is its legitimate influence in making the wheels of the administration turn and its effective and constitutional control on the individuals most immediately placed to make the administration function; it is, in a word, the great question of the day: responsible government, such as was avowed and promised to the Assembly of Upper Canada, in order to obtain its consent to the principal of Union, and not such perhaps as is now explained in certain quarters.[31]

Lafontaine had no confidence in Sydenham's promises of responsible government, and stated his belief that the governor would be guided in his actions by the character of the new assembly. He expressed his own faith in the principle of responsible government:

I see in its working the sole guarantees that we can have of good and effective government. The colonials should have the management of their own affairs. They should direct all their efforts to this end; and to succeed, the colonial administration must be formed and directed by and with the majority of the representatives of the people.

He condemned the Union of the two provinces:

An act of injustice and despotism, in that it is imposed upon us without our consent; in that it deprives Lower Canada of the legitimate number of its representatives; in that it deprives us of the use of our language in the proceedings of the legislature, against the spirit of the treaties and the word of the governor-general; in that it makes us pay, without our consent, a debt that we have not contracted; in that it permits the executive power to seize illegally under the name of a civil list, and without the vote of the representatives of the people, an enormous part of the revenues of the country.

Lafontaine flatly rejected the policies of French-Canadian abstention from public life or of a strong demand for the revocation of the Union Act; the representatives of Lower Canada 'should pause before adopting a decision whose immediate result might be to throw us back again under the liberty-killing rule of a Special Council and to leave us without any representation.'

His answer to the problem was an alliance with the Reformers of Upper Canada:

Our cause is common. It is to the interest of the Reformers of the two provinces to meet on the legislative ground in a spirit of peace, union, friendship, and fraternity. Unity of action is more necessary than ever. I have no doubt that, like us, the Reformers of Upper Canada feel the need of it, and that in the first legislative session they will give us non-equivocal proofs of it, which I hope will be the gage of a reciprocal and lasting confidence.

This statesmanlike policy was followed during the next eight years; it laid the foundation of that collaboration between French and English which ended in the achievement of responsible government. Lafontaine's manifesto was hailed by the Upper Canadian Reformers and published in full in Francis Hincks's *Toronto Examiner*, one of their chief organs. Etienne Parent and Augustin Morin of Quebec gave it their support, while embittered John Neilson opposed the Union Act without holding out any hope for the success of a joint alliance against it.

In the absence of Lafontaine, who published another letter to his electors in which he said he had been defeated by Sydenham himself and that 'there were defeats more honorable than victory,'[32] Morin was the leading French-Canadian representative in the new assembly. He was immediately questioned by Hincks on the disposition of the Lower Canadian majority. Morin expressed his hope that the Reformers of the two provinces would act together, 'even though there are among you those who approve of the Union because of the advantages that it gives to Upper Canada, while we are opposed to it because none of its provisions are either just or advantageous for us. But natural justice on one side, and common ideas and interests on the other, should lead to an entente even on this very delicate point.'[33] He rejected an alliance with the Tories of Upper Canada, who were opposed to the Union, but also opposed to the idea of responsible government; and concluded:

You, the Reformers, are our only natural friends. We have been too sincere in our aspirations after liberty and reform—however unknown and ill rewarded they have been—to join now with men of another political faith. Such, at least, is the idea that I conceive of the attitude that my fellow citizens will take; an attitude independent of the executive, but which is not hostile to it and which would even leave us ready to aid and support it, if it wished to hear our sincere opinions and to offer us the guarantee of men possessing the public confidence in its councils.

The ground was thus paved for a working alliance between the Reformers of the two provinces.

When the first assembly of United Canada met at Kingston on June 14, 1841, Sydenham had 'his' majority. Only eight of the twenty-four legislative councilors, named five days before the session began, were French Canadians, and only four or five were independent of the government. Sydenham wrote Russell: 'I wish there were more and better French names amongst them, but few are loyal, and of these some do not like the expense or trouble.'[34] Among the Upper Canadians in the assembly there were twenty-six Reformers favorable to the Union, six members favorable to the government, and only ten Tory anti-unionists. Etienne Parent, now member for Saguenay, was pessimistic about the prospects of the Lower Canadian representatives in his dispatches to *Le Canadien*: 'In the circumstances, all they can do is to protest vigorously against the injustices committed against their country, to submit their cause to the whole world and to appeal from the present to the future. God in His mercy has left hope to the oppressed, and it is all that remains to us.'[35]

Some immediate encouragement was found, however, in the election of Augustin Cuvillier, the former colleague of Papineau and D.-B. Viger, as speaker, and in the defeat of the Tory candidate for that post, Sir Allan MacNab. Then Robert Baldwin, the leader of the Upper Canadian Reformers who had set his face firmly against racial discrimination, resigned from the executive council on the opening day of the session, when Sydenham failed to meet his request to dismiss the Tory members of the council and to include some Lower Canadians in that body. The governor, who had considered Baldwin's appointment in 1840 'the greatest possible *coup*,' now dismissed him as 'the most crotchety impractical enthusiast I ever had to deal with.'[36] The way was thus cleared for a closer alliance between the English and French Reformers, since they had no representatives in the government and were left free to oppose it.

In the debate on the speech from the throne, the Reformers also wrung from the government spokesman an admission that the ministers would resign if unsupported by a majority, and John Neilson was able to win twenty-five votes, including those of Baldwin and Hincks, for his amendment protesting against the Union Act. Only five of the Upper Canadian Reformers joined their fellows from the lower province in this protest, for Sydenham had secured their support by his promise of an imperial guarantee for a loan of £1,500,000, two-thirds of which would be spent in Upper Canada on the vast program of public works which he proposed. The early part of the session justified Sydenham's letter to Lord John Russell of June 27, in which he declared his system of government: 'What I have seen and what I have had to do during the last three weeks, fortifies my opinion as to the absolute necessity of sending as my successor someone having parliamentary and ministerial experience, someone who will not be afraid of work and who will govern himself, as I do.'[37]

The most noteworthy event of the first session of the legislature under the Union was the adoption of the resolutions of September 3, 1841. These were proposed by Baldwin and contained the basic principles of the responsible government which he had long supported. Faced with the prospect of their support by the united Reformers, Sydenham avoided the appearance of defeat by having similar resolutions proposed by his spokesman and adopted. The principal resolution read thus:

That in order to preserve that harmony between the different branches of the Provincial Parliament which is essential to the happy conduct of public affairs the principal of such subordinate officers, advisors of the representative of the Sovereign and constituting as such the provincial administration under him as the head of the Provincial Government, ought always to be men possessed of the public confidence whose opinions and policy harmonizing with those of the representatives of the people, would afford a guarantee that the well-understood wishes and interests of the people, which our gracious Sovereign has declared shall be the rule of the Provincial Government, will at all times be faithfully represented to the head of that government and through him to the Sovereign and Imperial Parliament.[38]

The passage of this resolution was one victory of the Reformers over Sydenham's maneuvers. This bill was rejected, of course, by the government-controlled legislative council. Sydenham's project of establishing a Canadian bank of issue was also turned down by the assembly, and one article of his cherished Municipal District Bill was carried by only one voice. The assembly had begun to feel its power, and the personal government system of Sydenham was already becoming untenable.

The only man who could make it function, by his willingness to 'breathe, eat, drink, and sleep on nothing but government and politics,'[39] died two days after parliament had been prorogued.

He had broken his leg in a fall from his horse two weeks before; the gout with which he was much troubled caused complications; and lockjaw ensued. Sydenham had created an efficient and economical administration for the new United Canada; he had launched a program of reconstruction and recovery which restored the credit of Canada and opened up its resources. He was not unworthy of the moderate Conservative Egerton Ryerson's epitaph: 'Lord Sydenham has done more in two years to strengthen and consolidate British power in Canada by his matchless industry and truly liberal conservative policy, than had been done during the past ten years by the increase of a standing army and the erection of military fortification.'[40] But if Sydenham saved 'millions to England,' as Ryerson said, he scarcely 'secured the affections of Canada.' Sydenham had not been the friend of the French Canadians —he informed Russell that 'any one district of it (Upper Canada) contains more real wealth and intelligence than all Lower Canada (exclusive of the Townships)' and that 'as for the French nothing but time will do anything with them. They hate British rule— British connexion—British improvement of all kinds whether in their Laws or their roads. So they sulk, and will try, that is, their Leaders, to do all the mischief they can.'[41] But Sydenham had made new allies for the French Canadians by his despotic policy of personal government.

4

It was ironic that Lafontaine was named a representative of York (Toronto) on the day before Sydenham was buried at Kingston. The man whom the late governor had kept out of the assembly now entered it through the courtesy of Robert Baldwin, who had been elected in both Hastings and York, and had asked his friends in the latter constituency to choose Lafontaine in his place. The incident was a proclamation of the alliance between the Reformers of the two provinces, and of that collaboration between French and English which was to create a different Canada than Durham had envisaged. A former lieutenant of Papineau, a man against whom a warrant for high treason had been issued four years before, a Catholic French Canadian, was elected from the stronghold of Protestant English Canada. The times had indeed changed. Etienne Parent hailed the electors of York in *Le Canadien*: 'It is on the principle of true equal justice that they intend to live with their brethren of Lower Canada, as the step they have officially taken indicates. They elect Mr. Lafontaine to show, they say, their sympathy for the Lower Canadians and their detestation of the ill treatment and the injustices to which we have been exposed.'[42]

A similar political revolution had also taken place in England, where the Whigs, who had held power for nearly eleven years, with but one brief interruption, fell before the Conservatives in the elections of June 1841. The new cabinet formed under Peel at the end of August restored Lord Stanley, who had been colonial secretary under Grey seven years before, to his old post. Sir Charles Bagot, a former undersecretary of the Foreign Office who had served as minister to Paris, Washington, St. Petersburg, The Hague, and Vienna, and had refused the governor-generalship of India, was named governor-general of Canada in October, but did not reach Kingston until the following January. He was chosen to fill Charles Buller's prescription of 'a humane just man who will have the liberality and good sense to raise up those whom we have been forced to put down in Canada.'[43]

Lifelong Tory that he was, Bagot nevertheless evinced from the moment of his arrival no such intention as Sydenham had displayed of identifying himself completely with one party and flatly opposing the other. Stanley's instructions to him were of a very different order.

You cannot too early, and too distinctly, give it to be understood that you enter the Province with the determination to know no distinctions of National origin, or Religious Creed; to consult, in your Legislative capacity, the happiness and (so far as may be consistent with your duty to your Sovereign and your responsibility to her Constitutional advisers) the wishes of the mass of the Community; and, in your Executive capacity, to administer the Laws firmly, moderately, and impartially . . .

In Civil matters, it must be your policy to seek to withdraw the Legislature, and the Population generally, from the discussion of abstract & theoretical questions, by which the Government of Canada, in former times, has been too often and too seriously embarrassed, to the calm & dispassionate consideration of practical measures for the improvement and advancement of the internal prosperity of the Province. In maturing measures of this description, you will endeavour to avail yourself of the advice and services of the ablest Men, without reference to distinction of local party, which, upon every occasion, you will do your utmost to discourage; and, in framing them for the consideration of the Provincial Legislature, you will endeavour to present them in the form in which they are most likely to be favourably received by the House of Assembly.[44]

Six weeks after his arrival in Canada, Bagot assured Stanley that there was 'scarcely anything to fear' from 'internal disaffection or disloyalty.'[45] Sydenham, suspicious of the French, had been somewhat disturbed by 'the great deal of uneasiness' which prevailed in Lower Canada, when the Anglo-French difficulties of 1840 over Egypt and Syria had caused the circulation of rumors of a French invasion of Canada.[46] But the new governor judged that there was much to dread from party feeling, and that 'the error of previous governments in Canada, has been the narrowness of the foundations on which they have been based . . . an attempt to govern by a single party and to confer on them the whole patronage and power of the Government has invariably united all parties in opposition, and has led to the defeat of the Government in the popular branch of the Legislature.' Thus:

The chief opponents of the Government during the last Session were first the French Canadians—secondly a portion of the (so named) Compact party, and thirdly the ultra popular Section of the Upper Canadians. These parties, though differing entirely on all questions of principle, repeatedly united for the purpose of defeating or obstructing the Government on individual measures.[47]

Bagot immediately set about breaking up this alliance by judicious distribution of patronage. Morin, Huot, and Mondelet were made judges, while Cherrier and Fisher were made Queen's Counsels. So much for securing the support of some leaders of the French party; Bagot judged the masses could be brought around without difficulty:

So long as Lord Sydenham continued in the government the personal feelings which they cherished against him as the author of the Union, might probably have kept them in opposition—but that difficulty removed, the peculiarity of their position on this Continent, and their habits and feelings would, I should think, lead them to ally themselves with the Government. Surrounded and outnumbered by a race of British descent, speaking a different language, following a different creed—bred up under a different system of law, and possessed at the same time of an energy of character and habits to which they can lay no claim, the French Canadians can scarcely avoid seeing that the natural Post is an alliance with the Government, and that by such an alliance alone can they hope to maintain their peculiar laws and privileges.

Bagot thus foresaw the role the French Canadians were to play a few years hence, when it was the English Canadians who sought to break the British connection, and also the reasons which still make the French Canadians today more determined, in the last analysis, to preserve that connection than their English-speaking fellow citizens, as insurance for their national survival.

In a later letter Bagot amplified his views of his own position and policy:

When I left England, I had an opinion which five months residence in this Country has much tended to confirm, that, as Governor of it, I was about to be placed in a very peculiar position—a position in which my Predecessor did not, and my Successor could not stand; but upon the careful maintenance of which, at this moment, might depend the future well being and tranquillity of the Colony. I felt that, in fact, I was the first Governor who was called upon to put practically into operation, and endeavour to give effect to the great measure of the Union, and to work out the experiment of fusing and identifying so far as might be possible, the very discordant elements to be reconciled by that irrevocable & unalterable Act—

The means which Lord Sydenham had resorted to, in order to carry and complete the measure, may have been absolutely necessary—but they involved a public, and something very like a private quarrel on his part with the whole mass of the French Inhabitants of Lower Canada— and it would have been totally impossible for *him* ever again to conciliate them, or indeed ever again to have met, with any prospect of success, another Parliament in this Country.—He therefore could not have effected the object.—I think that my successor would have quite as little chance of being able to do so.—He could not, as I accidentally can, treat *his* advent as a new starting point—a new era—and a new chapter in the history of the Country.—When the time should come for his arrival, he would most assuredly find that, if the opportunity had been lost upon the first establishment of the Union, of endeavouring to do away, all the old-party exclusions and differences, which had existed previously to it, it would be late too for him to make the attempt—that the Country had relapsed into its old divisions and subdivisions—and that the moment had passed, in which he could hope to extend, with safety, the patronage of the Government to all parties equally without reference to past estrangements, and to take from all sides the best and fittest men for the public service.[48]

Early in his administration Bagot set about taking 'from all sides the best and fittest men for the public service.' He named Vallières de Saint-Réal, the defender of the *habeas corpus* against Colborne, chief justice of the district of Montreal, and the educational reformer Dr. Jean-Baptiste Meilleur as the first superintendent of public instruction for Lower Canada. These appointments did much to make the new governor popular with the French Canadians, and Bagot's visits to Montreal and Quebec in the spring of 1842 both strengthened his position with the people and gave him some first-hand acquaintance with French-Canadian opinion. He also visited Toronto, and named Francis Hincks inspector-general of public accounts, a post for which the Upper Canadian Reformer had been selected by Sydenham, who admired his financial ability. Hincks had gradually been won around to the government which he had originally denounced, and so his appointment was criticized by both Reformers and Tories. The Tories were given a sop of satisfaction by the nomination of Henry Sherwood as solicitor-general to replace Baldwin.

But the government was still made up of heterogeneous elements, and it lacked the support of the assembly. The Tories were now more strongly opposed to the government than ever, since a Tory governor had made evident his failure to share their prejudices. The Reformers of both the French and English camps had increased in numbers, and under the leadership of Lafontaine and Baldwin they were more determined in their opposition than before. The Lower Canadian Reformers now numbered twenty-five, forming part of a clear and well-disciplined majority, while Lower Canada was represented in the ministry by two Tories and one convictionless creature of the government, all of whom were English.

Bagot consulted with Harrison and Draper, two of the government leaders, and they both expressed the opinion that the support of the French Canadians must be obtained by giving them a larger share in the administration. Confronted with this situation, Bagot wrote to Stanley:

> I am nevertheless fast arriving at the persuasion, that the moment is come when this question must be determined one way or the other, and this Government must be carried on, either in professed exclusion of, and defiance of the Canadians of French origin, or by their admission to such a share in it, as they may be contented to receive, and the Mother Country may deem it safe and reasonable to give them. . . .
> It is impossible to conceal from oneself that the French members of the Assembly possess the power of the Country and whoever directs that power, backed by the most efficient means of controlling it, is in a situation to govern the Province most effectually.[49]

Bagot knew that the admission of the French Canadians to a share in the government was in opposition to Durham's ideas, Sydenham's practice, and Stanley's policy; but he found no other solution to the problem. The essential connection between patronage and parliamentary government had once more been demonstrated.

With the assembly meeting on September 8, there was no time to wait for Stanley's authorization to reverse the policy which had been followed since the Rebellions of 1837–8. Bagot summoned Lafontaine to two interviews on September 10 and 11, during a weekend adjournment of the debate on the speech from the throne, and offered him the attorney-generalship of Lower Canada, as well as the right to nominate an English solicitor-general and a French commissioner of Crown lands. Lafontaine requested time to consult with his friends, and insisted on the inclusion in the ministry of Baldwin, who had resigned the year before when the French Canadians were left out; on the naming of another French-Canadian minister; and on the resignations of Draper and Sherwood, with whom Baldwin could not sit.

The debate was put off another day, and then opened on the 13th by Draper, who protested his belief in responsible government and in the inclusion of the French Canadians in the administration. The Tory leader revealed that under Sydenham, whom he could not win to his view, he had twice offered his resignation in order to further it; and that during the last forty-eight hours he had again offered to withdraw, in order to pave the way for a reconstruction of the government, which must necessarily include Baldwin, the ally of the French Canadians. His proposals to Lafontaine had been rejected, but he still hoped to see the day when the principle of government in accordance with the will of the people would be loyally followed. The speaker then read a letter from Bagot to Lafontaine,[50] delivered just before the meeting of the House, in which the governor offered him the attorney-generalship of Lower Canada, and the choice of a solicitor-general for Lower Canada, of a commissioner of Crown lands, and of the clerk of the executive council. Baldwin was to receive the attorney-generalship of Upper Canada, while the replacement of the solicitor-general of Upper Canada was left open for discussion. Ogden, the present attorney-general of Lower Canada, and Davidson, the present commissioner of Crown lands, were to receive pensions in return for resigning. Lafontaine had refused this last-minute offer, principally on the score of the pensions; and Bagot had decided to make it public, in order to embarrass Lafontaine and to make known his liberal intentions to the rank and file of the Lower Canadian Reformers.

The assembly was stunned by these revelations; but Baldwin attacked the ministry and reproached Draper for requiring eighteen months to reveal his belief in responsible government, concluding with a motion of no confidence in the government. The debate became vigorous. Finally Lafontaine rose and began to speak in French. One of the Upper Canadian ministers asked him to speak in English; and Lafontaine made his famous reply:

I am asked to pronounce in another language than my mother tongue the first speech that I have to make in this House. I distrust my ability to speak English. But I must inform the honorable members that even if my knowledge of English were as intimate as my knowledge of French, I should nevertheless make my first speech in the language of my French-Canadian compatriots, if only to protest against the cruel injustice of the Union Act in trying to proscribe the mother tongue of half the population of Canada. I owe it to my compatriots; I owe it to myself.[51]

After this eloquent protest, Lafontaine went on to explain the negotiations with Bagot. Lafontaine stated that he had not given a flat refusal to the governor's offer, but had merely pointed out the obstacles to its acceptance. He paid tribute to Bagot's sense of justice and equity, and to Draper's public admission that his initial prejudices against the French Canadians had been overcome as he came to know them during the last session. Lafontaine joined with Draper in a demand for co-operation:

The two populations of Upper and Lower Canada have common interests, and they will end by sympathizing with one another. Yes, without our active cooperation, without our participation in power, the government cannot function in a manner which will re-establish the peace and confidence which are necessary to the success of any administration. Placed by the Union Act in an exceptional position as a minority in the distribution of political power, if we are to succumb, we shall succumb while making ourselves respected. I do not recoil before the responsibility I have assumed, since in my person the governor-general has chosen the individual by whom he wished to make known his liberal and just views towards my compatriots. But in the state of bondage in which the iron fist of Lord Sydenham tried to hold the French population, in the presence of the deeds that were attempted in this end, I have as a Canadian only one duty to fulfil, that of maintaining the honorable character which has distinguished our fellow countrymen and to which our most bitter enemies are obliged to render homage. This character, Mr. Speaker, I shall never dishonor!

The governor's letter and Lafontaine's speech swayed the Lower Canadian Reformers. Negotiations between the two were resumed, and an agreement was reached on the basis of Sherwood's resignation, while the question of pensions remained open. Lafontaine and Baldwin became the attorneys-general of Lower and Upper Canada; Morin commissioner of Crown lands, and Etienne Parent clerk of the executive council; and the rest of the cabinet was revised so that only one Tory remained in it. The cornerstone of responsible government was thus laid on the foundation of control of patronage by the elected representatives of the people rather than by the appointees of the Crown. For the first time since the conquest the French Canadians were given their full share in the executive branch of the government.

Bagot broke the news to Stanley in a somewhat defensive letter which made much of the happy results of this action:

I have united the voices of seven eighths of the House of Assembly in present support of the Government—some defection must be expected, but none by which the Govt. will be at all weakened. I have met the wishes of a large majority of the population of Upper Canada and of the British Inhabitants of Lower Canada. I have removed the main ground of discontent and distrust among the French-Canadian population; I have satisfied them that the Union is capable of being administered for their happiness and advantage, and have consequently disarmed their opposition to it. I have excited among them the strongest feeling of gratitude to the Provincial Government, and if my policy be approved by H.M.'s Govt. I shall have removed their chief cause of hostility to British Institutions, and have added another security for their devotion to the British Crown.[52]

In a confidential dispatch of the same date, he contrasted his policy with that of Sydenham, who had rejected the same advice which Bagot had accepted from his councillors:

> Towards the French Canadians his conduct was very unwise. He made enemies of them unnecessarily at a time when he should have propitiated them and diminished their objections to the Union. He treated those who approached him with slight and rudeness, and thus he converted a proud and courteous people, which even their detractors acknowledge them to be, into personal and irreconcilable enemies. He despised their talents, and denied their official capacity for office. In this respect he was mainly right; but there was the lesser reason for fearing their power when held in proper check, and for endeavouring further to weaken it by measures which will not stand the test of justice . . .
>
> It was only by dint of the greatest energy, and I must add the unscrupulous personal interference of Lord Sydenham, combined with practices that I would not use, and Your Lordship would not recommend, in addition to the promise of the Loan and the bribe of the Public Works, that Lord Sydenham managed to get through the session.[53]

Faced with a *fait accompli* which appalled Peel and Wellington more than himself, Stanley sent a reluctant official approval of Bagot's action, coupled with private assurance that 'I do not mean to blame you for the step you have taken; on the contrary, I believe it to have been inevitable and that sooner or later it would have been found necessary to admit the leaders of the French party to a share in the government.'[54]

Bagot did not exaggerate the general satisfaction in Canada at his action. Parent reported in *Le Canadien* the friendly sentiments expressed by long-standing enemies of the French Canadians, and commented: 'I should not be surprised after that to see *La Minerve* embrace the *Herald*, *L'Aurore* embrace the *Montreal Gazette*, and the *Fils de Liberté* embrace the partisans of Captain Thom.'[55] Only the Tories were unhappy: they supplied three of the five dissenting voices to the assembly's resolution of approval; and their Toronto organ, the *Patriot*, referred to Bagot's letter to Lafontaine in the following bitter words: 'No public document since the triumph of Wolfe until this day has been read in the provinces of British North America by the faithful subjects of the Sovereign of Great Britain with such intense sorrow and humiliation.'[56] In England *The Times* expressed its astonishment that Bagot had called to the executive council 'known advocates of secession' and 'notorious traitors,'[57] while Charles Buller approved the governor's act in the London

Chronicle. Stanley had difficulty in winning Peel and Wellington over to Bagot's 'inevitable' course, but a ministerial crisis was avoided. In February of the following year, during a debate on the matter at Westminster, Buller paid tribute to Bagot: 'Sir Charles Bagot has adopted the surest and wisest policy; he has conducted himself in the most praiseworthy and best possible manner.'[58] Such words in the mouth of Durham's secretary and the reputed author of the *Report* carried great weight, since Bagot had reversed one of the fundamental proposals of that document.

The validity of another conclusion of Durham's *Report*, already shaken by Lafontaine's election by an English constituency, was shattered by the unanimous election of Baldwin as the representative of Rimouski in Lower Canada, after he had been defeated in his own Upper Canadian riding by the outraged Tories. A more united Canada could scarcely be imagined than that in which the two heads of the government were elected from each other's section, regardless of ethnic and religious differences.* During the short session of 1842 several ordinances of the special council or of Sydenham himself were upset, including those gerrymandering the constituencies of Quebec and Montreal and re-organizing the Lower Canadian judiciary. A new election law eliminated many abuses.

A few days after the assembly was prorogued, Bagot became severely ill with heart trouble. The place he had won in French Canada is indicated by the fact that many Masses were said for his intention. After one period of recovery, his condition grew worse and he died on May 19, 1843. He was widely mourned in Canada, and *La Minerve* regretted that his death had prevented the celebration of the anniversary of his first visit to Montreal with a great popular ovation: 'Only a memory remains to us now of the great man who was the regenerator of the French Canadians; but this memory, deeply marked on our grateful hearts, will be an eternal monument in the bosom of the people which posterity will contemplate when many others have crumbled and disappeared.'[59]

5

Bagot was replaced as governor-general by Sir Charles Metcalfe, an Anglo-Indian civil servant who had been governor-general of India and governor of Jamaica. He was offered the post by Stanley in January 1843, and took office in Canada on March 30. He

* A sidelight on the thoroughness of that unity is supplied by a letter of 1844 in which Baldwin consulted Lafontaine about a Quebec school for his son Willcocks: 'I must not expose him to the miserable embarrassment that I labour under myself for want of French.' Baldwin's daughters were already being educated by the Ursulines of Quebec. PAC, Lafontaine Papers, Baldwin-Lafontaine, 14 August 1844.

began his difficult task without eagerness and with premonitions of failure: 'I have never undertaken anything with so much repugnance, nor with as little hope of doing well. All my plans and my hopes of happiness are disappointed; and such little reputation as I have been able to acquire is, I fear, exposed to shipwreck in the agitated waters of Canada.'[60]

Metcalfe, an adherent of the old school of colonial rule, was struck soon after his arrival in Canada both by the doctrine of responsible government, which held that the policy and the conduct of the governor should conform to the party views and interests of the executive council, and by the violence of Canadian party feeling. He approved of Bagot's admission of the French-Canadian party to power, although he regretted the manner and the circumstances in which it had been done. He announced his determination to recognize no difference between French and English, but he commented on the dominant self-interest of the French party, which 'works ceaselessly for the maintenance and the extension of its power and for the interests of the French Canadians. It may be able to combine with other parties, on the principle of reciprocity, in giving support in exchange for support; but its views are purely French Canadian and have for object, among others, the conservation of the French language and laws. It opposes energetically any attempt to anglicize the French Canadian population.'[61] He also regretted the exclusion of the Tories, for he felt 'much more sympathy for those who have been loyal than for those who wished to shake off the yoke of the Mother Country.'

From these original dispositions he soon progressed to feeling no sympathy whatsoever for 'the anti-British bitterness of the French party, or the egoistical indifference of the republican party,'[62] with whom he had to co-operate. He then evolved the idea of 'freeing himself of exclusive relations with this or that party, and of adopting the best measures, rendering equal justice to all, with councillors chosen in all the parties.' In short he set out to follow the course of George III and Bute, creating a governor's party. It was inevitable that he should come into collision with Lafontaine, who threatened to resign when Metcalfe refused to accept the advice of the executive council. The governor, with his strong faith in his own views and a resolution which approached pigheadedness, saw the question simply as 'whether the governor will be purely and simply an instrument in the hands of his council, or whether he will have the right to exercise his own judgment in the administration of the government.'[63] It was a major conflict between the old and the new order in colonial administration; for the matter in question was the vital one of patronage, the appointment of Colonel de Salaberry, a French-Canadian Tory, as provincial aide-de-camp.

At the time Lafontaine was not even aware of the seriousness with which Metcalfe viewed the matter.

The irritated governor took a firm hand with the executive council, and revealed his curious concept of responsible government in a dispatch of June 25 to Stanley:

I have not had any difficulties with the Council; I have been prudent, but without sacrificing what appears to be, in the present circumstances, the legitimate authority of the governor. I administer myself the affairs of the government by means of the secretaries; no order is given without my direction or my sanction. And only those matters are submitted to the Council which should be according to law or practice, or on which I wish to have the benefit of the advice or the local knowledge of the councillors. The Councillors have made no pretensions rendering necessary a counter exposition of principles, and it can almost be supposed that the unreasonable declarations previously made by some of them have been abandoned. I am not sure of it, however; and although I see no reason to anticipate an immediate rupture, I feel that it can happen any day.[64]

By August Metcalfe was finding even his version of Sydenham's system too confining, and was considering dismissing the council. 'chiefly because they are under the influence of party views, and would, if they could, drag me on with them in the same course . . . The meeting of the Legislature will probably allow me to see my position more clearly. It is at present far from certain that a change of councillors would produce any beneficial alteration in respect to the difficulty noticed, for any Council appointed on the principle of Canada Responsible Government would most probably have similar party views, and the same pressure on them from their partisans.'[65]

Metcalfe found himself faced with the highly distasteful prospect of party government:

It seems to be inevitable in free and independent States where Responsible Government exists; and the same causes are likely to produce the same results everywhere; but there is a wide difference between an independent State and a colony. In an independent State all parties must generally desire the welfare of the State. In a colony subordinate to an Imperial Government, it may happen that the predominant party is hostile in its feelings to the mother country, or has ulterior views inconsistent with her interests. In such a case, to be obliged to co-operate with that party, and to permit party government to crush those who are best effected, would be a strange position for the mother country to be placed in, and a strange part for her to act. This ought to have been considered well before the particular system which has obtained the name of Responsible Government was established. It is now, perhaps, too late to remedy the evil.

The 'Sultan of India,' as Metcalfe had already been nicknamed by one of the Upper Canadian ministers, nevertheless sought to remedy the evil—and to console the Tories—by creating a governor's party through arbitrary disposition of patronage; he named the Tory Sherwood speaker of the legislative council, and another Tory to a clerkship which Baldwin desired for a supporter. Lafontaine and Baldwin demanded an interview with the governor, and for two days tried to win him to their concept of responsible government, which postulated that the royal prerogative should be used only on the advice of the ministers. But Baldwin had thought out the cabinet system more clearly than had yet been done in England. Metcalfe found their views untenable; and they and all their colleagues of the ministry, save one, resigned on November 26, 1843.

A twelve-day political crisis followed, during which the action of the retiring ministers was supported by a vote of 46-26 and the assembly refused to accept a message from Metcalfe requesting it to pursue its labors. In the face of this opposition the governor prorogued the assembly on December 9; and four days later named Denis-Benjamin Viger and William Draper to the executive council. Viger, the ancient champion of the people and of the assembly's privileges, was won from his life-long principles by the opportunity to play at last the leading role which had hitherto always escaped him. In the agitation previous to 1837 he had been thrust out of the limelight by his young cousin Louis-Joseph Papineau, and after the Rebellion he had been eclipsed by Lafontaine, a former student in his law office. But the seventy-year-old Viger was not destined now to play a notable role. Metcalfe contented himself with three ministers, who remained without portfolio or function, while he himself both reigned and governed, still, curiously, protesting his belief in responsible government.

For nine months, until August 1844, Canada lacked all save a token ministry. Then, after endless negotiations, Metcalfe succeeded in breaking down the refusal of Lower Canada to participate in his administration. After the attorney-generalship had been refused by six Lower Canadians, an English lawyer from Montreal was found who would accept it, while Denis-Benjamin Papineau, a brother of the great tribune, was persuaded to become commissioner of Crown lands. In his desperation Metcalfe had even thought of offering a place in the ministry to the exiled Louis-Joseph Papineau, in order to secure Lower Canadian support. This preposterous scheme had fallen through, but the great agitator's brother had been won over through his close ties with Viger. By September the ministry was formed, and on its advice Metcalfe dissolved the hostile assembly. The elections were bitterly contested, with Lafontaine's followers campaigning on the principle of responsible government, 'as understood by the ex-ministers.'[66] Lower Canada gave the Reformers twenty-eight out of forty-two seats, with Viger defeated in two constituencies and his follower John Neilson vanquished by young Pierre Chauveau, who had turned from verse to the hustings. In Upper Canada, where the governor had used the war cry of loyalty to the British connection, the situation was reversed, with Baldwin's followers winning only eleven seats. The result gave the governor an overall majority of six, won by the most vigorous intervention on his part in the elections.

The dubious quality of Metcalfe's victory was soon evidenced when the assembly met on November 28 at Montreal, which had been chosen as the capital at the last session. The government candidate for speaker, Sir Allan MacNab, was elected by only three voices. Baldwin's reply to the speech from the throne, in which he called for censure of Metcalfe's unconstitutional government during nine months, was warmly praised in the *Journal de Québec*, recently founded by Joseph Cauchon, a new member. Lafontaine parried Sherwood's condemnation of the French Canadians—for blindly following their leaders without understanding political questions—with the pointed remark that when his compatriots went to the polls, 'they vote for one of the candidates, and not for the governor-general, as in Upper Canada.'[67] Baldwin's resolution was defeated by just six votes.

Despite the near deadlock, the assembly passed a number of important bills, including one remodeling into its present form the plan of local government established by Sydenham. This measure had been drafted by Morin during the preceding session, and was now carried by Papineau. Another Morin measure established the school system of Lower Canada on a basis of voluntary contribution rather than direct taxation at the will of appointed municipal officials, as provided by Sydenham's Common Schools Bill of 1841, which had remained inoperative in the face of general opposition and had merely provoked the foundation of independent schools. The clergy were given the right to vote, and conversion of lands from seigneurial tenure was encouraged. A bill providing £40,000 for payment of indemnities for losses suffered during the Rebellion in Upper Canada was passed, but Lafontaine called in vain for a similar measure applying to Lower Canada. Nevertheless, at the opening of the session he had succeeded in obtaining unanimous approval of an address to the Queen praying for a general amnesty for the rebels of 1837-8. This measure was not adopted until 1849, but in practice the government began to act on it earlier in individual cases.

Lafontaine's maneuvers for repeal of the Union Act's provision against the legislative use of French were forestalled by Papineau's proposal of an address to the Queen on this subject, to which Metcalfe reluctantly consented as a tactical measure to disarm the opposition. The necessity of such action was proved in February 1845 when the speaker, Sir Allan MacNab, refused to accept a motion drafted in French by the member for Lotbinière, and his decision was supported by a single vote, after Lafontaine and Morin had made eloquent protests against a law contrary to natural right.

Dissension broke out among the ministerial supporters on the law establishing the University of Upper Canada, the forerunner of the University of Toronto. When the session closed at the end of March, Metcalfe found that 'the germs of division and of weakness have been sown in part by the divergence manifested on the university question, in part by personal dissatisfaction, and finally by the lack of popularity of the members of the Executive Council.'[68] Faced with this situation, he noted a tendency of some of the Upper Canadian Tories to join with the French Canadians, and remarked: 'If I saw a probability that this combination could be realized in conformance with just principles and in a manner to constitute a strong government, free of all anti-British sentiment, I should be disposed to encourage it.'

6

During the summer of 1845 Draper, the leader of the Upper Canadian Tories, opened negotiations with René-Edouard Caron, president of the legislative council, with a view to an alliance between the Lower Canadian Reformist majority and the Upper Canadian Tory majority. Under the proposed agreement Viger and Papineau were to retire from the ministry, leaving their places free for Morin as president of the executive council and another French Canadian as attorney-general. Lafontaine could not be admitted to the ministry, in view of Metcalfe's hostility to him, but he was to be given a place on the bench. Caron communicated these proposals to Lafontaine on September 8.

In reply Lafontaine condemned Draper's proposal as 'a repudiation of the principle of responsibility, in so much as it is a question of applying it to Lower Canada.'[69] Instead of forming a new administration for Lower Canada constitutionally, a few French Canadians were to be added to the ministry:

From this moment those who enter thus into the ministry enter not as a result of constitutional right, not by the action of the opinion of their compatriots, but solely as a result of the favor, of the good will of the governor. From this moment, experience teaches us, they are without influence; they are no longer free agents, but only instruments in the hands of the governor, for evil as well as for good. If they possess some capacity and talent, they will use them sooner or later to cause division amongst us ... Above all, the French Canadians must remain united and make themselves respected in the Council and exercise there the legitimate influence which is their right. This will not happen when they are represented there only by passive instruments of the government, whatever their number, but rather when they are constitutionally represented there by a Lower Canadian administration formed in harmony with principles that public opinion does not disavow ... In the administration Lower Canada should have what is granted to Upper Canada; nothing more, but also nothing less.

Lafontaine thus outlined his concept of the French-Canadian political position, calling for equal rights, equal justice, and equal influence. Beside this goal, mere places were to be despised, and he renounced all claim to personal consideration:

I have often said, and I repeat it again, no consideration for me should prevent my political friends from forming part of an administration organized for Lower Canada according to the constitutional principles which ought to guide our conduct. I shall never serve as a means to divide my compatriots. If an administration is formed which merits my confidence, I shall support it wholeheartedly. If this administration does not have my confidence, but possesses that of the majority of my compatriots, I, not being able to support it, shall willingly retire from the House rather than to throw division in our ranks. If under the system of accepting places at all cost, there are persons who for personal and momentary advantage do not fear to destroy the sole advantage which constitutes our strength, our unity, I do not wish to be and I shall never be of this number.

In his reply to Draper, Caron formulated the theory of double majority: 'It has been stated as a principle that the direction of affairs should be between the hands of the two dominating parties in each section of the province, that the administration should no more direct Lower Canada by means of an Upper Canadian majority than it should impose a law upon the Upper Canadian majority as a result of the aid received from Lower Canada, and that no administration should survive unless supported by a majority in each section of the province.'[70] Lafontaine had not gone so far; he had merely recognized the possibility of a coalition government for the two sections. Such a system had already been discussed in *Le Canadien*.

Lafontaine advised Baldwin of what was afoot, and the latter replied:

I consider the principle itself inadmissible and wholly impractical. I can conceive that in the practical labor of legislation a certain deference should be paid to the views of the respective majorities in each of the provinces, and that no measure should be imposed on one or the other against the will of a considerable majority of the representatives of the interested province. But this does not justify in any fashion the principle of having a double cabinet, of which half depends for its support upon the confidence of the representatives of Lower Canada and the other half upon the confidence of the representatives of Upper Canada. This principle, I am convinced, is absolutely incompatible with the very nature of our political institutions, and in the end it will be found impracticable.[71]

Baldwin expressed his opinion that Draper's negotiation indicated a weakness in the government and a fear of losing its majority. This opinion no doubt was affected by the consideration of the disaster which would have overtaken the Upper Canadian Reformers if the coalition had taken place. But it fell through, because of Draper's delays and Metcalfe's illness, which caused his resignation. The governor was afflicted with cancer, and the progress of the disease had already cost him the sight of one eye and soon made it almost impossible for him to speak or eat. On November 26, 1845, after a stubborn struggle against his illness, he handed over the government to Lord Cathcart, the military commander, and returned to England. He died nine months later, the third governor of Canada to whom the office had proved fatal.

At the opening of the session in March 1846, Viger was savagely attacked during a debate on the reply to the speech from the throne, which contained a eulogy of Metcalfe to which Baldwin and the Reformers of both provinces took exception. At the request of the caucus of the Reformers, Lafontaine read the correspondence which had been exchanged between Draper and Caron and Caron and himself. The government was weakened by this revelation, and hardly managed to survive the session. The tension between England and the United States over the Oregon question made it easy, however, to pass a new militia bill, which evoked Etienne-Pascal Taché's much quoted phrase: 'The last cannon shot for the maintenance of English rule in America will be fired by a French-Canadian hand.' The Lower Canada school law of the previous year was revised at Dr. Meilleur's instance so as to rest upon a basis of obligatory rather than voluntary support, since the latter system had proved unworkable in the midst of the popular revolt against the new schools, known as the 'War of the Extinguishers.'[72] With subsequent amendments, notably in 1849, this statute (9 Victoria, Ch. 27) long remained the legal foundation of the Quebec school system. Another provision of the Union Act was eliminated when the imperial government agreed, in exchange for the assembly's vote of £70,000, to revoke the article enabling it to take a civil list of £75,000 from the Canadian revenues.

Viger and Papineau lost all popularity in debates on the Jesuit Estates and on financing of the administration of criminal justice in Upper Canada. Sherwood and Draper quarreled, and the government found itself in the minority more than once. After the prorogation in June 1846, Viger and Sherwood resigned, and during the summer efforts were made to constitute a stronger ministry. Caron and Morin were again offered portfolios, but refused them. Dissension and dissatisfaction were general in both Upper and Lower Canada when the Earl of Elgin was named governor-general in September 1846.

7

Lord Elgin, who was to have a greater influence than Durham on the development of Canada, was a descendent of Robert Bruce and the son of the British ambassador to Turkey who brought home the Elgin Marbles from the Parthenon, then threatened with destruction in the Greek Revolution. The new governor-general had gone in for gentleman farming on his Fifeshire estates, after a brilliant career at Eton and Oxford, where he had been a member of a notable group which included Canning, Newcastle, Sidney Herbert, and Gladstone. He had studied law without practicing it, passed some time in France, and then entered politics in 1841 as a member for Southampton. He was a Tory, but not of the traditional type; he thus defined his Peelite politics: 'I am a Conservative, not because I am hostile to progress, not because I refuse to repair what is worn out or to modify what is defective in our political structure, but because I am convinced that in order to remedy effectively one must be determined to preserve religiously.'[73] When the death of his father elevated Elgin to the peerage of Scotland and barred him from the House of Commons in the same year as he entered it, Stanley offered him the governorship of Jamaica. He had a notable career there, though the climate cost him the loss of his first wife.

When he returned to England in 1846, the fall of the Tories seemed to leave him without prospects of office; but Grey, the new colonial secretary, who was as liberal a Whig as Elgin was a Tory, offered him the Canadian governor-generalship. Before leaving for Canada in January 1847, Elgin married Grey's niece, the daughter of Lord Durham. Elgin was very conscious of the heritage which had thus fallen upon him, and soon after he arrived in Canada, he wrote his wife, who at first remained in England:

I still adhere to my opinion that the real and effectual vindication of Lord Durham's memory and proceedings will be *the success of a Governor-*

General of Canada who works out his views of government fairly. Depend upon it, if this country is governed for a few years satisfactorily, Lord Durham's reputation as a statesman will be raised beyond the reach of cavil. I do not indeed know whether I am to be the instrument to carry out this work, or to be destined, like others, who have gone before me, to break down in the attempt; but I am still of the opinion that the thing may be done, though it requires some good fortune and some qualities not of the lowest order. I find on my arrival here a very weak Government, almost as much abused by their friends as by their foes, no civil or private secretary, and an immense quantity of arrears of business. It is possible, therefore, that I may not be able to bear up against the difficulties of my situation, and that it may remain for some one else to achieve that object, which many reasons would render me so desirous to achieve.[74]

Like Durham, Elgin believed in the principle of responsible government, accepting party monopoly of patronage, and his faith in it was sufficiently sturdy to carry him through the trials which lay ahead. In July 1847 he outlined his concept of the proper role of a governor to Grey:

I give to my ministers all constitutional support, frankly and without reserve, and the best advice that I can afford them in their difficulties. In return for this, I expect that they will, in so far as it is possible for them to do so, carry out my views for the maintenance of the connexion with Great Britain and the advancement of the interests of the province. On this tacit understanding we have acted together harmoniously up to this time, although I have never concealed from them that I intended to do nothing which may prevent me from working cordially with their opponents, if they are forced upon me. . . . It is indispensable that the head of the Government should show that he has confidence in the loyalty of all the influential parties with which he has to deal, and that he should have no personal antipathies to prevent him from acting with the leading men.[75]

It was on this policy—very different from those of Sydenham and Metcalfe—that Elgin intended to act, although it meant reconciling himself 'to tread along a path which is somewhat narrow and slippery, and to find that incessant watchfulness and some dexterity are requisite to prevent him from falling, on the one side into the *néant* of mock sovereignty, or on the other into the dirt and confusion of local factions.'

Elgin was not alone in recognizing that he was the heir of Durham. At the opening of the session in June 1847, Baldwin and Lafontaine proposed an amendment to the address replying to the speech from the throne, which congratulated the new governor on his connection with Durham and expressed the hope that practical application would be given to the principle of responsible government which had been recommended in the *Report*. This motion provided Baldwin with an opportunity to indict the ministry for its lack of principles. In reply Draper, who was resigning as attorney-general of Upper Canada and accepting an appointment to the bench, defended his role as leader of the government. He affirmed his belief in responsible government, and stated that he had conformed to this principle while serving under Metcalfe. He postulated that patronage should be dispensed only on the advice of the ministers. Since it was on these very matters that the Reformers quarrelled with his administration, it is evident that the same words held different meanings for Draper and for Baldwin and Lafontaine.

But the leaders of the Reformers had more love for their chief opponent than for his henchmen, particularly the Lower Canadian ministers, whom Lafontaine thus flayed: 'You have sacrificed honor to the love of office; you have been mere instruments in the hands of your colleagues, you have sacrificed the country, and you will soon have your reward. One of you has already been expelled from the Council, and the other soon will be.'[76] These merciless words referred to the fall of Viger, and the impending retreat of D.-B. Papineau, who now was the sole French Canadian in Sherwood's ministry. Baldwin's amendment was defeated by only two votes. While the government's power thus rested upon a precarious basis in the assembly, the legislative council manifested signs of revolt, with Caron supporting Neilson's attack on the government for its lack of French-Canadian representatives. Somehow the ministry staggered through the short session, but it was clearly doomed.

Elgin had recognized its weakness upon his arrival, and had favoured the fruitless negotiations to induce Caron and Morin to enter the ministry. He had written to Grey: 'If new elements of strength are required to enable the Government to go on, I think it very advisable to give the French a fair opportunity of entering the Ministry in the first instance.' And he added this significant comment, which was to become one of the basic principles of his governorship:

I believe that the problem of how to govern Canada would be solved if the French would split into a Liberal and a Conservative Party and join the Upper Canadian parties bearing the corresponding names.—The great difficulty hitherto has been that a Conservative Government has meant Government of Upper Canadians which is intolerable to the French—and a Radical Government a Government of the French which is no less hateful to the British. . . . The national element would be merged in the political if the split to which I refer was accomplished.[77]

As Elgin foresaw, the ethnic conflict in Canada was to be greatly eased by the political collaboration of French and English.

The governor repeated his observation a month later, coupling with it a recognition of the indispensability of the French Canadians to any Canadian government: '. . . until the French break into political Parties and join British Parties with corresponding names, I do not think any strong and lasting administration will be formed. Their coherence enables them to organize a powerful opposition to any Ministry from which they are excluded, but it no less certainly provokes among the British both of Lower and Upper Canada a feeling of antagonism to one of which they form a part.'[78] At intervals down to the present L.-J. Papineau's concept of a 'national' or ethnic party has been revived in French Canada, but the results have been as unfortunate as Elgin predicted, for politico-ethnic division has been created without profit to the French Canadians. With such convictions, it cannot be doubted that Elgin encouraged the eventual decision of the tottering ministry to confront the country. Elections were held in December 1847, after a manifesto issued in the previous month by a Quebec Constitutional Committee of Reform and Progress, headed by Caron, had violently attacked the three-year-old government.

Unlike Sydenham and Metcalfe, the governor remained neutral in the electoral fray, not trying to form a governor's party. The ministry was roundly defeated. Only five or six of its supporters survived in Lower Canada, where Lafontaine was elected in two constituencies and the Reformers won a majority of thirty seats. In Upper Canada only sixteen supporters of the government were returned, while twenty-six adherents of Baldwin were victorious. From the Reformers' point of view, there was but one fly in the ointment: the old tribune Louis-Joseph Papineau, who had been permitted to return from exile in 1845 at Lafontaine's instance and who had been nominated in two counties and elected as member for Saint-Maurice, had issued an address to his electors in which he announced his support of the program of Lafontaine and Baldwin with certain reservations. This document discussed at length the constitutional issues for which Papineau had always fought and closed with the somewhat startling statement that he had been 'a disciple from my early youth of the school of Adam Smith, and ever the enemy of all monopoly and privilege.'[79] It was admirably summed up by Elgin, who transmitted it to Grey with these comments:

Considerable excitement has been produced by the appearance of a manifesto from the notorious L. J. Papineau who has been requested to represent two constituencies—This document is in a nolo episcopari strain—contains a pretty frank declaration of republicanism—expresses the writer's hatred of the British Government—his distrust of Responsible Government and concludes that the time has not come for his reappearance on the stage—Whether he will be elected or not is uncertain in the face of this quasi refusal—The French Liberals are a good deal disconcerted by the tone of this address—on the one hand they do not like to proclaim that their sentiments are at variance with those of this redoubtable chief who still has a hold on Canadian sympathies—on the other it is awkward to profess antimonarchical doctrines and a contempt for Responsible Government at the time when the said Responsible Government is likely to bring them into place—Besides it is doubtful whether Upper Canada liberalism may not be alienated by the assertion of such principles.[80]

After Papineau's election by acclamation, Elgin assigned his support to the 'considerable section of the French Canadians who take their political opinions from writers and speakers who derive their inspirations from the hoco[s]pocus of Yankeedom and democrats of France.'[81] And later in January 1848, after announcing his determination to call upon Lafontaine and Baldwin to form a government, Elgin suggested one difficulty which would beset them:

Notwithstanding the condemnation of my present council pronounced by the constituencies, I am far from thinking that their successors will have an easy task—M. Papineau who has more personal influence than any other individual in Lower Canada returns into public life with the avowed object of proving Lord J. Russell a deceiver, and Responsible Government a delusion and a snare. He hates Great Britain, and is believed to be somewhat jealous of those who have become the leaders of the French Canadians during his eclipse. If the system of Government established in this province works satisfactorily, his vocation is gone, and he is proved a false prophet. It will therefore be his object to prevent this result—on the other hand, I am disposed to believe, that with a certain class of the liberals of British origin, there exists a genuine preference for what they deem British or constitutional practise as opposed to Republicanism. Whether it will be possible to bring the views of these Gentlemen who look at our Institutions through an American medium into perfect harmony with those of British Statesmen sitting in Downing Street, may be doubtful—But there is obviously room for antagonism between those who hold that British Institutions rightly interpreted, are the best in the World, and those who are pledged to prove that they are among the worst.

Between these two political sections M. Lafontaine and his followers are now placed.—Circumstances, perhaps, conviction, will induce them for the moment to take rank with the latter——.[82]

The governor was no false prophet.

8

The session opened at the end of February, and the verdict of the people on the old government was immediately reflected in the election of the speaker. Sir Allan MacNab was rejected by a vote of 54–19, and Augustin Morin was then unanimously elected to the post. Baldwin proposed an amendment to the reply to the speech from the throne, declaring it to be essential that the government should have the confidence of the assembly and the people, and stating that the present advisers of the governor lacked this confidence. Elgin immediately replied that 'Always disposed to listen to the advice of the Parliament, I shall take without delay measures to form a new Executive Council.'[83] This answer proclaimed that responsible government had at last become a reality in Canada. Before Elgin's departure from England, he and Grey had agreed upon the extension to Canada of the system of full responsible government which had been worked out for Nova Scotia between the colonial secretary and Sir John Harvey. Its basic concepts, as laid down by Grey, were that 'any transfer which may take place of political power from the hands of one political party in the province to another is the result not of an act of yours but of the wishes of the people themselves,' and that 'it is neither possible nor desirable to carry on the government of any of the British provinces in North America in opposition to the opinion of its inhabitants.'[84] These instructions to the governor of Nova Scotia had been communicated officially to Elgin, and he had now acted upon them.

Lafontaine and Baldwin were called upon to form a cabinet and were given complete control of patronage. The new ministry included the two leaders as attorneys-general for their respective sections, Hincks as inspector-general of accounts, Taché as commissioner of public works, Aylwin and William Hume Blake as solicitors-general for Lower and Upper Canada, and Caron as president of the legislative council. Elgin observed to Grey that 'My present council unquestionably contains more talent and has a firmer hold on the confidence of Parliament and of the People, than the last. There is I think moreover on their part a desire to prove, by proper deference for the authority of the Governor General, (which they all admit has in my case never been abused), that they were libelled when they were accused of impracticability and antimonarchical tendencies.'[85] Grey, who had expressed his willingness to accept even L.-J. Papineau in the cabinet and who had been warned by Elgin that it might be necessary 'to accept as advisers persons who were denounced very lately by the Secretary of State and the Governor General as impracticable and disloyal,'[86] wholly approved Elgin's policy and actions, and added: 'It is most fortunate that you had a Ministry including some of the Leaders of the French party before the news of the French Revolution reached you.'[87] Elgin, some of whose family were in Paris when the disturbances of 1848 broke out and who as a Tory was appalled by the revolutionary fervor which was felt even in England at this time with the Chartist rising, agreed that it was just as well that a Canadian government with popular support had been formed before the European news arrived: 'There are not wanting here persons who might under different circumstances have attempted by seditious harangues, if not by overt acts, to turn the examples of France and the sympathies of the United States to account——'[88]

The veiled reference to Papineau, notoriously sympathetic to the French *Républicains rouges*, was not lost upon Grey. The old tribune had not been able to resist the strategic moment which had always summoned him to battle in the past, and when a vote of supply was called for at the end of the brief session, he protested against adjournment without taking measures to revise the system of representation upon the basis of population. In his first speech since re-entering the assembly, he developed the ideas contained in his address to the electors of Huntingdon in the previous December, stating his confidence in the new ministry and his willingness to support them in the full realization of responsible government, though he expressed his disbelief in this principle for Canada. The main measure he proposed was ill chosen, for the population of Upper Canada was rapidly overtaking that of Lower Canada and was soon to surpass it. But Papineau had been too long silent and too long out of the limelight which he loved almost as much as he loved to speak. After his return to Canada in the fall of 1845, loyalty to his brother Denis and his cousin Viger, then in office as Metcalfe's ministers, had kept him in obscurity. Before leaving Paris he had described Metcalfe's views and conduct as 'an undecipherable enigma,' but he had protested that 'agitation has never been a necessity for me; and it is less so than ever after the lapse of seven years.'[89]

Papineau's stay in France and his visits to Switzerland and Italy had made him highly sympathetic with the revolutionaries whose schemes bore fruit in the revolutions of 1848; he wrote to Roebuck shortly before leaving Paris: 'I am more than ever the impassioned friend of democratic liberties, the enemy of kings, nobles, and priests, everywhere leagued for the exploitation of the majority to the profit of their castes. With these sentiments I cannot live happily in Canada.'[90] Gloom had descended upon him, once he was back in Canada. In 1846 he found that 'the political state of the country

Merry-Making

Oil painting (c. 1860) by Cornelius Krieghoff. This Brueghel-like study of a gay evening at the celebrated inn of Jean-Baptiste Jolifou, much frequented by British officers driving out from the Quebec Citadel, provides an unmatched picture of French-Canadian *joie de vivre*. (John T. Ross Collection, Quebec.) (National Gallery.)

Notre Dame Church, Montreal

Built 1824-9 by John Ostell after plans by James O'Donnell of New York. This was
the first church in the gothic style in Quebec and its influence was ruinous to the
native architectural tradition. (I.O.A.P.Q.)

is more of a stench in my nostrils than it has ever been . . . Birth-place, old relatives, family interests chain me here like an oyster on the rock where I was born, but the intellectual life here is so lifeless, political life so detestable, that I shall live here unhappily.'⁹¹ He met with Lafontaine in the fall of 1845, and the younger leader informed his old chief of all that had happened since their last encounter at Saratoga Springs in June 1838, when both were fugitives from warrants for high treason. Papineau approved Lafontaine's policies at that time, when the younger man was in the opposition, ever the favorite position of the elder. When chided by his ministerial brother for having delayed his return home by a day, Papineau had replied: 'I wanted to wait for an opposition boat; I love the opposition so much.'⁹² The retirement of his cousin Viger in 1846 and of his brother Denis-Benjamin in 1847 at last freed him from the obligation of silence, and with a show of reluct-ance he re-entered political life.

Not all the Reformers viewed this step with pleasure; Joseph Cauchon commented thus:

For my part, I should be glad to see M. Papineau in the House, because his talents, if his opinions were not extreme, could be useful to us. In the contrary case, in order to spare blood and oppression to our compatriots, we would be obliged to react against him and to isolate him. But then he would place us in a false position by making us appear men opposed to the democratic ideas which invade the new world.⁹³

When Papineau's address appeared, Jacques Grémazie, brother of the poet and editor of the new *L'Ami de la Religion et de la Patrie*, defined the old tribune's program as 'war without mercy on the Tories and Reformers of Upper Canada who called for the Union Act; war on the mother country which granted it; blame for the Lower Canadian liberals who helped to make this mockery of respon-sible government function; and, finally, reproaches to the ex-ministers for having been too moderate.'⁹⁴ When congratulated by an English-Canadian friend upon his return on not having changed in appearance, Papineau had replied, 'I am always the same,'⁹⁵ and his political behavior indicated the truth of his remark. Under Grey and Elgin he adopted the same policy of implacable opposition which he had followed under Stanley and Aylmer; he was tempera-mentally incapable of any other attitude. Living in the past, he could not realize how much the situation had changed in his absence. In February 1848 he wrote gloomily to O'Callaghan: 'In a few years from now we shall stand in the same relation to Upper Canada as Ireland to England;' and again in April: 'All is glory, happiness, progress in the rest of the whole world; all is baseness, oppression, cowardly inaction or regression in Canadian society.'⁹⁶

Papineau's first speech in the new assembly brought a vehement reply from his ancient enemy Colonel Gugy, the loyalist leader of 1837-8, and all the old quarrels and all the old wounds were reopened once more, to the joy of the surviving Tories. But the younger Lower Canadian Reformers censured Papineau's speech; and Cauchon wound up with the brutal comment: 'Once I much admired his brilliant harangues, but I admire them no longer, for they lead to nothing . . . There are men who are mighty in destruction, but who have never raised anything on the ruins they have made.'[97] Elgin judged the old popular leader 'a dangerous man' who has 'much influence among the French Canadians; who remember that he cheered them on to the fight, and forget that he left them in the thick of it.'[98] It was not consoling to the governor that Papineau should suggest to his Canadian electors that they should 'give themselves the pleasure of traveling to the United States, to see how much more at ease the farmers there generally are; how much more they harvest on bad land than we do on good; why their poor farms sell ten times more dearly than our richer ones,'[99] at a time when the jingoistic *New York Herald* was rejoicing in the prospect of acquiring Canada, Cuba, and the British West Indies through the aid of revolutionary France.

While Elgin struggled to maintain the British connection under these difficulties, Grey was writing to him: 'To us except the loss of prestige (no slight one I admit) the loss of Canada would be the loss of little but a source of heavy expense and great anxiety.'[100] With wry humor Elgin replied:

I feel myself however, I must confess, somewhat in the position in which the master of one of those ricketty vessels which are sent to this quarter in quest of timber occasionally finds himself. By dint of much labor and watching he succeeds in conveying ship and cargo safely through the tempests and icebergs which assail him on the voyage out and home, and he is not a little disappointed, poor simple minded man! when on reporting his arrival, he hears the owners mutter to one another 'It would have been better for us if the whole concern had gone to the bottom, as we should then have realized the Insurance.' Much in the same light are exertions made to maintain and perpetuate the connexion between this Province and the Mother Country, likely, I fear, to be viewed:—for Canada is beginning to be reckoned, I shrewdly suspect, by most English politicians, a bad bargain at any price.

Nevertheless, so long as I am in charge, it is my duty, I presume, to steer by the old lights, and to endeavour to keep things together as best I can.[101]

Elgin was right about the attitude of the British government, despite Grey's disavowal of his personal belief in the new colonial doctrines, which were an outgrowth of the attempt to bring about what Elgin scornfully called 'the Free Trade Millenium.' The repeal of the Corn Laws and the Navigation Act had upset the old colonial theory; and 'Little Englanders' now dominated the House of Commons. The imperial government displayed a growing reluctance to carry the old colonial burdens, and proposed that Canada should bear the cost of its own defence and of the immigration which continued to pour into Quebec and Montreal thousands of sick and penniless wretches from Ireland, Scotland, and England itself. In discussing these matters Elgin had already observed to Grey:

If you attempt to redress the balance by requiring the Colony to bear burdens which she does not choose to bear, you engage in a contest of which the issues are by no means certain. The position of Canada as respects British sympathies and antipathies is most anomalous and cannot be measured by ordinary rules.— . . . The question practically present to men's minds is not 'Do we hate England enough to renounce our allegiance and to affront all the inconveniences and perils of separation'—but rather, 'Do we love her enough, is her connexion sufficiently valuable to us to induce us to refuse to clasp the hand which is stretched out to us by a great neighbouring and kindred nation, with whose prosperity and rapid advancement as contrasted with our comparatively slow progress we are constantly taunted by British Statesmen.'[102]

In the face of continued efforts of the British government to cut its commitments in Canada, Elgin gave a sharper warning to Grey of the results that might be expected from such a policy:

The present is not a favorable moment for experiments. British Statesmen, even Secretaries of State, have got into the habit lately of talking of the maintenance of the connexion between Great Britain and Canada with so much indifference, that a change of system in respect of military defence incautiously carried out, might be presumed by many to argue on the part of the Mother Country, a disposition to prepare the way for separation—Add to this, that you effected only a few years ago an Union between the Upper and Lower Provinces by arbitrary means, and for objects the avowal of which has profoundly irritated the French population—That still more recently you have deprived Canada of her principal advantages in the British markets.—That France and Ireland are in flames and that nearly half of the population of this Colony are French—nearly half of the remainder Irish![103]

Elgin detected a ground swell in Canada raised by foreign storms, and reported: 'M. Papineau is deeply chagrined by his present position and is doing all he can to create disaffection by evoking Irish and French sympathies.' In a later letter Elgin pictured 'Guy

Fawkes Papineau' waving a lighted torch among the 'combustibles' of French and Irish sympathies, also incited by Irish Americans against England. Elgin pleaded for revocation of the restriction on the official use of the French language, announcing his conviction of 'the impolicy of all such efforts to denationalize the French,' as 'causing the flame of national prejudice and animosity to burn more fiercely.' He also advanced a cogent political argument:

> You may perhaps *americanise*, but, depend upon it, by methods of this description, you will never *anglicise* the French inhabitants of the Province. —Let them feel on the other hand that their religion, their habits, their prepossessions, their prejudices, if you will, are more considered and respected here than in other portions of this vast continent which is being overrun by the most reckless, self-sufficient and dictatorial section of the Anglo-Saxon race, and who will venture to say that the last hand which waves the British flag on American ground may not be that of a French Canadian?[104]

A revealing light on the rapid constitutional evolution of Canada is shed by a liberal Tory governor-general's echoing of the one-time rebel Taché's phrase.

With anti-British feeling increasing among the English Canadians as a result of the mother country's new trade policies, and the warhawk General Lewis Cass nominated as the Democratic candidate for the American presidency, Elgin developed a growing conviction that 'The sentiment of French-Canadian nationality which Papineau endeavours to pervert to purposes of faction, may yet perhaps if properly improved furnish the best remaining security against annexation to the States.'[105] He observed shrewdly: 'Was it, think you, love for England or hatred for these *sacrés Bostonais* which stirred the French-Canadian mind in the Revolutionary war and again in 1812?'

With such considerations in mind, Elgin gave official support to the colonization movement launched by Bishop Bourget of Montreal —at the inspiration of the Abbé Bourassa, a brother of Papineau's son-in-law—despite the fact that Papineau had 'pounced upon this association as a means of making himself of importance in the eyes of his countrymen and of gratifying his ruling passion by abusing England.'[106] The clergy had at last become alarmed by the ever-increasing emigration from Quebec to the United States, which had begun early in the century, grew considerably during and immediately after the Rebellions of 1837-8, and in 1849 was estimated to have amounted to 20,000 people in the last four years. Elgin defined the clergy's object in launching the colonization societies as 'being to prevent the sheep of their pasture, (who now, strange as it may appear, emigrate annually in thousands to the

States, where they become hewers of wood and drawers of water to the Yankees and bad Catholics into the Bargain) from quitting their fold.' The former gentleman farmer sympathized with the colonization program:

No one object in my opinion is so important, whether you seek to retain Canada as a Colony, or to fit her for independence and make her instinct with national life and vigor, (a result by no means less desirable than the former in so far as the interests of Great Britain are concerned) as the filling up of her vacant lands with a resident agricultural population. More especially is it of moment that the inhabitants of French origin should feel that every facility for settling on the land of their Fathers is given them with the cordial assent and concurrence of the British Government and its Representative.

Elgin also judged it imperative to 'wrest from M. Papineau's hands a potent instrument of agitation,' to 'fill up the Frontier country with French—and the lands to the rear with British, who may retain their love of home and its institutions at a distance from American influences,' and to promote a movement sponsored by 'the Priesthood the most powerful influence in Lower Canada.'

The immediate results of Elgin's action were the retirement of Papineau to Montebello and the issuance by Bishop Bourget on June 17, 1848 of a pastoral letter, which closed thus: 'For we are all children of the same Father who is in Heaven; we all live under the same government which has no other end but the welfare of its subjects, and which must take its glory from ruling peoples speaking all the languages of the world; we all have the same rights; we are all members of the great family of the mighty British Empire; and finally we are all summoned to possess together the same land of the living, after we shall have finished our pilgrimage in this land of exile.'[107] From this time onward, the Church threw its full support behind colonization in the Eastern Townships, in the Saguenay-Lake St. John country where the first settlement of 1838 had been given new impetus by the lumber industry of William Price, and in the Saint-Maurice and Ottawa Valleys where the Baptist family and the Yankee Philemon Wright had founded a great timber trade in the opening years of the century. The French Canadians at last began to expand out of the original strip of settlement along the St. Lawrence, but the ever-increasing emigration to the States, where the industrial revolution caused continual calls for more labor, still was not checked.

Elgin was justified in depriving Papineau of any 'instrument of agitation,' for the latter continued to work upon the sympathies of both French and Irish Canadians, which were kept stirred up by sensational telegraphic reports from Europe of the doings of Lamartine in France, of the followers of O'Connell in Ireland, and of the Chartists in England. The old tribune addressed meetings at Montreal and Quebec, comparing the wrongs of Canada to those of Ireland and denouncing the Union Acts as the means of English oppression in both instances. He also published several manifestos in which he attacked the Reformers and Lafontaine. Splitting the party, he formed the *Parti démocratique*, a group of hotheaded young men, whose organ, the newly founded *L'Avenir* edited by Eric Dorion, echoed the old tribune's revolutionary views. A.-A. Dorion, L.-A. Dessaulles, Rodolphe Laflamme, Labrèche-Viger, and J. Daoust were his chief disciples.

The group, known as the *Rouges*, urged repeal of the Union, the extension of the elective principle to every branch of the government, inclined towards annexation, and invoked the principle of nationality, which they saw threatened by the Union Act:

Seduced, distracted after a fashion by its details, we have for a long time lost sight of the object of that measure, which, however, is every day recalled to our recollection by that invasion of ideas and institutions, foreign to our ideas and institutions, which renders each day the most desirable, in the midst of the confusion of institutions, that perfect labyrinth of laws, of manners and of language, which imposes upon us a double nationality, so as to render the one necessary, the other useless, that is to say, to make us lose ours and adopt the other . . .

Nationality is the vital principle of a people, and someone has said with truth that the silence of a people, is its death . . . We pray you tell us, then, whether one hundred thousand should abandon their prejudices, rather than six hundred thousand should give up their just demands. We only wish for one thing, the preservation of our Institutions, our language, our laws, and our customs.[108]

In reply *La Revue Canadienne*, Lafontaine's organ, asked:

Tell us, gentlemen of *L'Avenir*, you who weep so much over the ruins of the past, and over imaginary evils—tell us at what period of our history has the French-Canadian nationality been more brilliant, more honored, more respected, or has it occupied a higher position than it holds today? . . . Has it not been thanks to the ability, the tact, the firmness and the patience of its able representatives that it has gained more in a few years, than previously in half a century of combats?

. . . The Union was brought about with the object of ruining us! But the Union has saved us, and after powerful and well-directed efforts, after having won a position which permits us to avoid its inconveniences and evil consequences, after having obtained the political rights for which we have struggled for fifty years, now it is, that the devoted and generous gentlemen of *L'Avenir* raise their voices against it . . .

. . . But tell us, ye young and fiery apostles of French-Canadian nationality, what do you mean by the principle of nationality applied to the management of public affairs? . . . Is it, perchance, that famous principle of public action which has excited the French lately to drive from France all workmen of English or foreign origin? . . . It is not after our party has recruited its ranks from men of all origins, when our friends, the liberals of Upper Canada and those of Lower Canada of foreign origin, have made prodigious efforts to carry the elections and that together we have gained the most signal victory—it is not now that your appeal to prejudices and passions will have the least echo in the country.[109]

Here are expressed for the first time the opposed principles of two great French-Canadian political factions, which have survived to the present day: the ultra-nationalist extremists, resisting all change and all outside influences, and lapsing into racism; and the much larger conservative group which is willing to collaborate with English Canada but is as determined as the nationalists upon the survival of the French Canadians and their language, laws, institutions, and customs. Almost all French Canadians are extreme nationalists in their youth, as English-speaking youth inclines to liberalism or socialism; almost all grow out of this frame of mind and adopt a more moderate position as they grow older; but some never do, and with these men this book will henceforth be largely concerned, because they personify the social forces which differentiate French Canada from the rest of Canada, and of North America.

Then as now, the ultra-nationalists were a minority, and they were bitterly criticized by the moderates. Only *Le Canadien* joined *L'Avenir* in supporting Papineau's idea, while Cauchon's *Journal de Québec*, *La Minerve*, and *Les Mélanges religieux* made common cause with *La Revue Canadienne* in condemning them. Dr. Wolfred Nelson, now back in the assembly as a Reformer, attacked Papineau for personal cowardice, and denied the story that he had urged the tribune to flee at Saint-Denis in 1837. Bitter controversy was widespread in the press, but not as much dissension resulted among the Reformers as might have been expected; Cauchon informed Lafontaine that 'the friends of M. Papineau in all the great parishes which he had recently visited were as rare as ears of corn after the harvest.'[110]

9

While the French Canadians were threshing over old political straw, a commercial revolution was taking place which profoundly affected most English Canadians and radically altered their political principles. Peel's budgets of 1842-6, particularly that of the latter year, which upset the old colonial system of privileged markets in Britain for colonial products at the expense of the British consumer, have been aptly described as 'the British Revolution from the

British Empire.'[111] Most of the preferential duties were abolished, crippling the wheat trade, ruining the new Canadian milling industry, and severely depressing the lumber trade. The American Drawback Acts of 1845-6, which permitted the duty-free passage of foreign imports to Canada and of Upper Canadian products through American territory, broke the monopoly of the St. Lawrence and gave New York a vast advantage over Montreal. What was left of the Navigation Acts kept St. Lawrence freights much higher than American ones. Canadian hopes of draining the products of both Upper Canada and the Middle West through the St. Lawrence system to the profit of Montreal and Quebec collapsed before the new canals were completed in 1848, despite successive relaxations of the Navigation Acts, which were finally abolished in 1849. An imperial loyalty which had thrived on privilege wavered and broke when loyalty was no longer profitable. In May 1846 the *Canadian Economist* was moved to ask: 'How far the adoption of Free Trade principles in Great Britain, and as a consequence in the colonies, is compatible with the nature of the connection subsisting between them?'[112] The Welland Canal miller Jacob Keefer supplied an answer in blunter language to W. H. Merritt in April 1848: 'The sooner the connection between Gt. Britain and Canada is dissolved the better.'[113] Reciprocity or annexation seemed the only solutions of their difficulties to the English-Canadian commercial classes, caught in a graver depression than that of 1836-7, and burdened with 100,000 cholera-stricken Irish immigrants dumped upon their shores in 1847. The Irish famine, which had hastened the repeal of the Corn Laws and caused this exodus, gravely tried English-Canadian imperialism.

Elgin, who had considered the danger from the Irish more serious than that from the French, now turned his attention to the English Canadians. He had already remarked that 'the only real discontent existing is to be found among the commercial classes,'[114] although the Canadian farmer also demanded the repeal of the Navigation Laws, 'not as favor but Justice,' since he had been deprived of protection on his products. Now Elgin pointed out: 'As soon as the navigation of the St. Lawrence is thrown open, and the barriers which check the entrance of Canadian products into the States removed, a large amount of American enterprize will be attracted hither. Whether the said enterprize and its accompaniments will or will not in the long run drag the whole concern first commercially and at last politically into the Union I do not now stop to enquire.'[115] In reply Grey sketched out the dilemma in which the British government found itself, and revealed a curious hope he had of its solution:

If we refuse to afford all the facilities we can for commercial intercourse between Canada and her powerful neighbour we must certainly create discontent inconsistent with our retention of the Colony—if on the other hand we encourage that intercourse there is every probability that Canada ere long will be Americanized by the influx of Yankees—between the two I have no hesitation in preferring the latter, and if ultimately it should lead to the separation of these Provinces from the British Empire let us hope that this may take place by amicable arrangement instead of by war, and may lead to a division of the Union—British America with some of the Northern States forming one Nation and the Southern States another—This would be no such bad result and in the mean time our trade would prosper and emigration would flourish.[116]

In disapproving arrangements for reducing the English garrison in Canada and inducing the colony to accept the burden of its defence, Elgin pointed out once more the drift towards annexation:

Canada is already gravitating pretty surely towards the United States.— A great deal has been done to strengthen that tendency by recent changes in the Commercial Policy of Great Britain—A little more and the onus probandi will be cast upon those who contend that the connexion with England should be maintained— . . . But I would be very cautious of announcing the principle that Canada was expected to defend herself— She owes it mainly to her connexion with you that she is pretty sure in the event of a war to have for an enemy the only nation on earth who could be formidable to her.[117]

Meanwhile the warhawks of the American press, unsatiated by the conquest of Texas and California, were talking of taking Canada when they pleased. Elgin anticipated trouble when the Irish sympathizers in the States were organized and strengthened by recruits drawn from 'the disbanded miscreants who are now returning in hordes from Mexico with appetites whetted for all deeds of rapine and blood.' In these difficult circumstances Canada was split into three groups, none of which offered much comfort to the anxious governor:

Firstly we have the Irish repeal body—I need not describe them— You may look at home—they are here just what they are in Ireland. Secondly we have the French population—Their attitude as regards England and America is that of an armed neutrality—They do not exactly like the Yankees but they are the *conquered oppressed subjects* of England.—To be sure they govern themselves, get all the places, pay no taxes, and some other trifles of this description—Nevertheless they are the victims of British *égoisme*. Was not the union of the Provinces carried without their consent and with the view of subjecting them to the British? Papineau, their press and other authorities, are constantly dinning this into their ears, so no wonder they believe it——

Again—our mercantile and commercial classes are thoroughly disgusted and lukewarm in their allegiance, if not disaffected— . . . It is easy to shew that as matters now stand the faithful subject of Her Majesty in Canada is placed on a worse footing as regards trade with the Mother Country than the rebel over the lines. The moral to be drawn from this fact is by no means encouraging to friends of the British connexion.[118]

Moved by 'much sullen discontent' among the commercial class, Elgin encouraged the schemes of William Hamilton Merritt, the promoter of the Welland Canal, for increasing Canadian prosperity, remarking that: 'He is considered sanguine, speculative and not very safe—but on the other hand he is unquestionably a man of large views and it is of great importance to kindle hope in the Public mind.'[119]

But the discontent of the merchants continued to increase. Elgin made a sound analysis of its causes:

Stanley's Bill of 1843 attracted all the Produce of the West to the St. Lawrence, and fixed all the disposable capital of the Province in Grinding mills, Warehouses, and Forwarding establishments—Peel's Bill of 1846 drives the whole of this Produce down the New York channels of communication, destroying the Revenue which Canada expected to derive from Canal dues, and ruining at once Mill owners, forwarders, and merchants. The consequence is that Private Property is unsaleable in Canada, and not a Shilling can be raised on the credit of the Province. We are actually reduced to the disagreeable necessity of paying all Public officers, from the Governor General downwards, in debentures, which are not exchangeable at par. What makes it more serious is that all the prosperity of which Canada is thus robbed is transplanted to the other side of the lines as if to make the Canadians feel more bitterly how much kinder England is to the children who desert her than to those who remain faithful. For I care not whether you be a Protectionist or a Free Trader, it is the inconsistency of Imperial legislation, and not the adoption of one policy rather than another, which is the bane of the Colonies. I believe that the conviction that they would be better off if they were annexed is almost universal among the commercial classes at present; and the peaceful condition of the Province under all the circumstances of the time is I must confess often a matter of great astonishment to myself.[120]

The merchants of Montreal began to hold meetings and formed an association to protect Canadian manufactures. Their organ, the *Gazette*, proclaimed: 'We hope that the Association, instead of looking any longer for commercial privileges in the English market, will regard English manufactures in the same light as foreign productions, and will sustain the interests of Canada in opposition to those of any other country. We are Canadians, let us regulate our trade for our own benefit alone.'[121]

But the ministry in London was finding it difficult to carry the repeal of the Navigation Laws which the Canadian merchants demanded; and was able to do little for the project, which Elgin strongly supported, of a Quebec–Halifax railway, which was expected to break the new American dominance of the carrying trade. The disaffection of the merchants grew steadily, and what had long been a smouldering fire flared up with the passage of the Rebellion Losses Bill by the assembly early in 1849.

10

That body met in January 1849, and the opening of the session was marked by Elgin's delivery of the speech from the throne in both English and French. The proscription of French in the Union Act had at last been repealed, and the French Canadians rejoiced at this official recognition of their cherished tongue. Papineau came into open conflict with Lafontaine in the debate on the address. In four three-hour speeches he displayed his old vituperative eloquence in attacking the ministry on every point of their legislative program. He concluded by exclaiming: 'Since I have been back in this country, I have been led to examine matters and to study men, and on one side I can say that the Tories are better than I thought, and on the other the Liberals are far from being what I thought them. This Tory ministry, which I thought so evil, and this Liberal ministry, of which I hoped so much, have both deceived my hopes and my fears.'[122]

Lafontaine replied, suggesting dryly that his own greatest fault had been to obtain permission for Papineau to return from exile. Papineau had condemned him for accepting power and for not following his own policy of last-ditch opposition. But in reply Lafontaine asked:

Where would our compatriots be today? Where would be our language, which a governor proscribed by a clause of the Act of Union, against the spirit of the peace treaties? This tongue, the language of our fathers, would it be rehabilitated today, as it has just been in the most solemn manner in the House and the acts of the legislature? If in 1842 we had accepted the honorable member's system of exaggerated opposition, would we have been in a position to solicit, to press for, as we did, the return of our exiled compatriots to this country? If we had not accepted a place in the administration in 1842, would we have been in a position to obtain permission for the honorable member in question to return home? A permission to obtain which I did not hesitate to offer my resignation from the well-paid post that I then held, in order to overcome the reiterated refusals of Sir Charles Metcalfe. Yet here is a man who, obeying his ancient habit of pouring out outrageous insults, dares in the face of these facts to accuse me, as well as my colleagues, of venality, of a sordid love of office, of servility to power! To hear him, he alone is devoted to his country! I demand no gratitude from him; I demand it from no one; but since he calls himself so virtuous, I ask him to be just, and nothing more. Is he capable of being so? If I had accepted the system of exaggerated opposition where would the honorable member be today? He would still be in Paris, doubtless fraternizing with the red republicans, or the white republicans, or the black republicans, and approving in turn all the constitutions which succeed one another so rapidly in France.[123]

Lafontaine also pointed out that his party had obtained the revocation of the most unjust clauses of the Act of Union, those which proscribed the use of French and appropriated the revenue without consent. He stressed that in fact and in law 'the Act of Union had not made one and the same province of the two Canadas, but had only reunited, under the control of one and the same legislature, two provinces hitherto distinct and separate and which were to continue so for all other purposes; in a word, that there had been after the example of our neighbors a confederation of two provinces, of two states.'[124] On this basis Lafontaine refused to accept the principle, which Papineau urged, of proportional representation. In concluding he attacked Papineau once more, and warned him that his day was past:

He has the modesty to think that he is authorized to threaten us with what he calls the anger of the people. Let not the honorable member be deluded by ancient memories. Let him learn that if he wishes to threaten us, I defy him to realize his threats, and that when the time comes, I shall be ready to meet him at any time and any place, this man who never ceases to vaunt his virtue and his courage![125]

It was Lafontaine's greatest moment as a parliamentary orator— he rarely attained eloquence—and it was the virtual end of Papineau's political career. Only one French Canadian and two English Tories joined Papineau in supporting the amendments he had proposed. His only triumph was to prevent by his own vote the two-thirds majority necessary to increase the representation of each province to sixty-five members, as Lafontaine proposed. The main outlines of the present judicial system were established by another ministerial measure, and the electoral laws were reformed. Baldwin's project of a non-sectarian University of Toronto was finally approved; while the government offered subsidies for the construction of railroads, and petitioned the imperial parliament to hasten the revocation of the Navigation Acts.

II

But the main business of the session was the passage of the Lower Canada Rebellion Losses Act, a measure promised since Metcalfe's time. The bill aroused one of the most bitter debates in Canadian history. The Tories, who while in power had adopted a similar measure for Upper Canada, now attacked the Reformers' proposal both on principle and on the method of financing it from the general revenue. Sherwood fulminated: 'I know nothing in history so abominable as to address oneself to those who have taken arms for the defence of their country, and among whom a great number have lost their nearest and dearest relatives and friends, to recompense those who have been the cause of murders and bloodshed all over the land! I defy anyone to find a parallel in history ... To admit the principle that those who took arms or engaged in a rebellion must be paid, would be an open invitation to revolt.'[126] Sir Allan MacNab proclaimed in a fine fury:

The Union has completely failed in its purpose. It was enacted with the sole motive of reducing the French Canadians under English domination. And the contrary effect has resulted! Those that were to be crushed dominate! Those in favour of whom the Union was made are the serfs of the others! ... I warn the ministry of peril, this ministry which treats me like a rebel when all the acts of my life show that I have striven to be loyal; I warn it that the course it takes is likely to throw the people of Upper Canada into despair, and to make them feel that if they are to be governed by foreigners, it would be more advantageous to be governed by a neighboring people of the same race than by those with whom it has nothing in common, neither blood, nor language, nor interests.[127]

The impassioned Tory went so far as to attack Lord Grey, whom he accused of nepotism in appointing his nephew Elgin as governor.

In reply two Upper Canadian Reformers flayed the old Tory Family Compact which MacNab represented. Irish-born W. H. Blake, the most eloquent orator yet heard in Canada, called MacNab and his party 'the true rebels against the constitution and the country,' and told them:

Your loyalty is the love of power . . . This loyalty which is always ready to extend and fortify the prerogatives of the Crown, in restraining and limiting the liberties of the people, is not loyalty, but slavery. It cannot result in fortifying the ties which unite this country to England; on the contrary, it can only weaken the allegiance of the people of this province by depriving them of the rights of British subjects . . . That is not British loyalty; it is a bastard loyalty which in all epochs of history has provoked the revolt of humanity under the whip.[128]

MacNab challenged Blake to a duel; and the following day young John A. Macdonald also sent him a challenge, as he continued to flay the Tories. But the speaker intervened and made the offending members swear to keep the peace. Disorder outside the House could not be repressed, however, and MacNab, Gugy, and other Tories agitated at public meetings, at one of which Lafontaine was burnt in effigy.

Lafontaine attacked MacNab for calling the French Canadians 'foreigners,' and asked: 'Would the honorable member who prides himself on being a native Canadian be such if the French Canadians, at the time of the War of American independence, had not saved the Canadas for England by their valor and devotion? If it had not been for the courage of the French Canadians in 1775 and 1812, Canada today would be part of the American confederation, and the honorable member would not be here to play the role he plays.'[129] The bill was finally carried in the House by a vote of 47–18, and in the legislative council by 20–14. There remained only the royal sanction by Elgin, who was warned by the *Gazette* on March 30 that 'if he should commit the error of approving of this most unjust measure, it will be the cause of such a movement as this province has never witnessed since the first European placed his foot upon its soil.'[130] The Montreal *Courier* more forthrightly proclaimed: 'Let the parliament pass the bill, let the Governor sanction it if he pleases, *but while there is an axe and rifle on the frontier, and Saxon hands to wield them, these losses will not be paid.*'[131]

Meanwhile Papineau's followers condemned the measure for excepting convicted or banished rebels from receiving indemnities:

Liberals, *Patriotes* of '37 and '38, have not blushed to declare legal the judgments of the most iniquitous court that ever existed; they have not blushed to declare that their friends, in whose struggles they had participated, and who, less fortunate than they, could not escape vengeance; that those men to whose principles they agreed, have been justly punished; that their blood has justly flowed on the scaffold. Oh! if they have not blushed, the whole country will blush for them.[132]

Again *L'Avenir* warned the Reformers that they were doomed in an age of democratic revolutions:

'Liberal' means in our day nothing but 'democrat'; if not, it is a false or lying title, in which you muffle yourself up to deceive the people. If you are not a 'democrat,' the people will repudiate you because you are not one,—because you are striving to maintain monarchical and aristocratical institutions, in spite of democratic principles, which have found a footing in America, which they will never give up; a fulcrum from which they are raising Europe, which will have soon done justice to those impious governments which for centuries have degraded humanity, crushed nations under the weight of tyranny. The people will repudiate you, because in America public men must be democrats first of all, because privileges, monopolies, despotism, are venomous plants to which the climate of America is deadly. A third party will form itself, stronger because it will leave convictions, purer because it will soak itself in the ideas of liberty, equality and fraternity; and one which will crush you, Tories, and self-styled Liberals, which will grind you like powder, because you have attempted to check it. The future belongs to democracy; this is a profound truth, and specially so in America, and you will perhaps grasp it when the people tell you, as the perjured King of France was told,—'It is too late!'[133]

Professing the hope that 'no power may ever be abused to the point of provoking reflecting men to the contemplation of an alliance with a foreign power,' the Montreal merchants formed the British American League and on April 19 issued a manifesto which stated: 'It is evident, from the known character of our race, that patient submission to any ascendency founded on feelings of nationality alone, and not actuated by any generous or progressive principle, never has been, and never will be for any length of time, endured by Britons.'[134]

Hoping the agitation would die down, Elgin delayed as long as possible the royal sanction to the Rebellion Losses Bill, but when he finally sanctioned it on April 25, 1849, he was booed in the House and exposed to a storm of rotten eggs and stones from a well-dressed English mob when he emerged from the Parliament Building. An extra of the *Gazette* termed him 'the last governor of Canada' and called for a racial uprising: 'Anglo-Saxons! you must live for the future; your blood and your race will be henceforward your supreme law, if you are faithful to yourselves. You will be English, if you no longer may be British.'[135] The meeting announced by the *Gazette* took place that evening on the Place d'Armes, and when the crowd of some 1,500 had been roused to fury by violent addresses, some one cried: 'To Parliament!' The mob burst in upon the assembly; some 'gutter Cromwell' proclaimed the dissolution of the 'French parliament'; another stole the mace; and the chamber was sacked and set on fire. Drafts from windows broken by a shower of stones whipped up the flames, and soon the whole building was ablaze. For several days Montreal was ruled by an English mob, which sacked Lafontaine's and Nelson's houses, damaged that of Hincks, and broke the windows of the *Pilot*, the sole English government organ.

Three days after the fire, the assembly, sitting under military protection, adopted an address to Elgin, expressing its indignation at the outrages. MacNab and Papineau both opposed the measure.

When the assembly's representatives went to the Chateau de Rame-zay, which served as Government House, to present this address, it was necessary to read the Riot Act and clear the streets with bayonets. Elgin was stoned as he emerged to return to his residence at Monklands. He was also expelled from membership in many of Montreal's select social organizations by the outraged English Canadians. Petitions were circulated for his recall and for disallowance of the obnoxious bill.

The governor kept calm, despite all manner of provocation; he judged that 'The whole row is the work of the Orange Societies, backed by the commercial men who desire annexation and the political leaders who want place.'[136] He refused to make use of the troops or to swear in French Canadians, the only loyal part of the populace, as special police to keep order. He wrote Grey, 'Of course all French Lower Canada is with us but the great object is to keep them quiet and to prevent collision between the races.'[137] In this he succeeded, despite the raging violence of the Tory press, which did not scruple to attack him personally for cowardice and double-dealing. MacNab and another Tory leader went to England to seek Elgin's recall and the repudiation of the Rebellion Losses Act; but despite Gladstone's advocacy of their cause, Elgin's conduct and the act were approved by a large majority in the imperial parliament. Lord John Russell, who had opposed colonial responsible government in 1837, now championed it and was supported by the same Whigs who had opposed it twelve years before. Thus on June 14, 1849, the British House of Commons proclaimed Canada's full achievement of responsible government, thanks to Baldwin and Lafontaine, two former rebels, and Elgin, the Tory nobleman who had become anathema to Canadian Tories.

The ultra-loyalist English Canadians of 1837 and 1838 now leagued themselves with discontented French-Canadian radicals in an open annexationist movement; the British American League met in convention at Kingston in July; and early in October 1849 they published a manifesto calling for 'an amiable and peaceful separation from the British connexion and a union under equitable terms from the great North American confederation of sovereign States.'[138] This document bore 325 signatures, of which by far the greater part were those of the leading English merchants of Montreal, although there was a sprinkling of French names drawn from among the followers of Papineau and *L'Avenir*. Such was the final result, as Elgin had anticipated, of the '£.s.d. view' taken by the self-professed loyalist organizers of the Kingston Convention, who in July had advocated protection of native industry, administrative economy, and Confederation of the British North American provinces as the remedies for Canada's ills.

Notes

[1] Kennedy, *Documents*, 376, Upper Canada Legislative Council Committee's Report, 11 May 1839.

[2] *Ibid.*, 377.

[3] Kennedy, 416, Russell-Thomson, 7 September 1839.

[4] *Ibid.*, 421-2, Russell-Thomson, 14 October 1839.

[5] *Ibid.*, 423.

[6] P. Knaplund (*ed.*), *Letters from Lord Sydenham to Lord John Russell* (London, 1931), 31-2, Russell-Thomson, 2 September 1839.

[7] A. Shortt, *Lord Sydenham* (Toronto, 1908), 197.

[8] Kennedy, 427, Thomson-friend, 20 November 1839.

[9] Knaplund, 36, Thomson-Russell, 25 November 1839.

[10] Kennedy, 427, Thomson-friend, 20 November 1839.

[11] Knaplund, 52, Thomson-Russell, 13 March 1847.

[12] Kennedy, 433-45, Union Act, 1840.

[13] *Ibid.*, 440 *n.*1.

[14] Knaplund, 45, Thomson-Russell, 23 January 1840.

[15] Chapais, IV, 305.

[16] J. Huston (*ed.*), *Le Répertoire national* (Montréal, 1893), II, 216-24.

[17] Kingsford, X, 534-5.

[18] Kennedy, 430, Thomson-friend, 12 December 1839.

[19] *Ibid.*, 449-50, Sydenham-friend, 1840.

[20] *Ibid.*, 449, Russell-Sydenham, 25 October 1840.

[21] Knaplund, 94, Sydenham-Russell, 27 September 1840.

[22] Kennedy, 457, Sydenham-brother, 28 August 1841.

[23] Quoted in *CHAR 1938*, 28, J. B. Brebner, 'Patronage and Parliamentary Government.'

[24] Knaplund, 97, Sydenham-Russell, 12 October 1840.

[25] PAC: Lafontaine Papers (transcripts from Saint-Sulpice), Hincks-Lafontaine, 12 April 1839; R. S. Longley, *Sir Francis Hincks* (Toronto, 1943), 51-2.

[26] PAC: Lafontaine Papers, R. Baldwin-Lafontaine, 26 November 1840.

[27] *Ibid.*, Hincks-Lafontaine, 9 September 1839; Longley, 54.

[28] *Ibid.*, Hincks-Lafontaine, 23 August 1840; Longley, 68.

[29] Knaplund, 121, Sydenham-Russell, 24 February 1841.

[30] *Ibid.*, 130, Sydenham-Russell, 10 April 1841.

[31] L.-P. Turcotte, *Le Canada sous l'Union* (Québec, 1871), I, 58-61; Chapais, V, 12-18.

[32] *Le Canadien*, 2 April 1841; Chapais, V, 21.

[33] *CAR 1883*, 168, Note B, Morin-Hincks, 8 May 1841.

[34] Knaplund, 120, Sydenham-Russell, 24 February 1841.

[35] *Le Canadien*; Chapais, V, 33.

[36] Knaplund, 48, Thomson-Russell, 13 February 1840; 141-2, Sydenham-Russell, 12 June 1841.

[37] Sydenham-Russell, 27 June 1841; Chapais, V, 33.

[38] Kennedy, 458, Baldwin's Resolutions, 3 September 1841.

[39] Shortt, 339, Sydenham-brother, 28 August 1841.

[40] *Ibid.*, 347, Ryerson in *The Christian Guardian*.

[41] Knaplund, 91, Sydenham-Russell, 16 September 1840; 93, Sydenham-Russell, 27 September 1840.

[42] *Le Canadien*, September 1841; Chapais, V, 67.

[43] *CHR 1927*, 43, P. Knaplund (*ed.*), 'The Buller-Peel Correspondence Regarding Canada, 1841,' Buller-Peel, 9 September 1841.

[44] Kennedy, 459, Stanley-Bagot, 8 October 1841.
[45] Ibid., 460, Bagot-Stanley, 23 February 1842.
[46] Knaplund, Sydenham, 97-100, Sydenham-Russell, 12 October 1840; 28 October 1840.
[47] Kennedy, 461, Bagot-Stanley, 23 February 1842.
[48] Ibid., 463-4, Bagot-Stanley, 12 June 1842.
[49] Ibid., 470, Bagot-Stanley, 28 July 1842.
[50] Ibid., 473-4, Bagot-Lafontaine, 13 September 1842.
[51] Chapais, V, 89; Lafontaine's whole speech, Ap. IV, 289-99.
[52] Kennedy, 476-7, Bagot-Stanley, 26 September 1842.
[53] Kennedy, 478-9, Bagot-Stanley, 26 September 1842.
[54] Kennedy, 486, Stanley-Bagot (private), 3 November 1842.
[55] Le Canadien, 21 September 1842; Chapais, V, 101.
[56] Chapais, V, 103.
[57] The Times (London), 15 October 1842; Chapais, V, 107.
[58] Hansard, III Series, LXVI, 7 February 1843; Chapais, V, 111.
[59] La Minerve, 22 May 1843; Chapais, V, 130.
[60] Chapais, V, 139-40, Metcalfe-friend, 22 January 1843.
[61] Chapais, V, 143, Metcalfe-Stanley, 25 April 1843.
[62] Chapais, V, 149, Metcalfe-Stanley, 25 June 1843.
[63] Chapais, V, 150, Metcalfe-Stanley, 12 May 1843.
[64] Chapais, V, 158, Metcalfe-Stanley, 25 June 1843.
[65] Kennedy, 492-3, Metcalfe-Stanley, 5 August 1843.
[66] Chapais, V, 191.
[67] A. Gérin-Lajoie, Dix Ans au Canada de 1840 à 1850 (Québec, 1888), 268.
[68] Chapais, V, 205, Metcalfe-Stanley, 13 May 1845.
[69] Ibid., 210, Lafontaine-Caron, 10 September 1846.
[70] Ibid., 214, Caron-Draper, September 1845.
[71] PAC: Lafontaine Papers, Baldwin-Lafontaine, 16 October 1845; Chapais, V, 215-16.
[72] Le Journal de Québec, 5 May 1846; Chapais, V, 226.
[73] Chapais, VI, 8.
[74] Kennedy, 501, Elgin-Lady Elgin, 1847.
[75] Ibid., 500-1, Elgin-Grey, 13 July 1847.
[76] Chapais, VI, 17-18.
[77] A. G. Doughty (ed.), Elgin-Grey Papers, 1846-1852 (Ottawa, 1937), I, 20, Elgin-Grey, 27 March 1847. In this and subsequent quotations from the Elgin-Grey Papers, Elgin's informal shorthand has been expanded, since it is obstructive to the reader unfamiliar with his style.
[78] Ibid., I, 28, Elgin-Grey, 26 April 1847.
[79] Ibid., I, 114, Papineau's 'Adresse aux Electeurs des Comtés de Huntingdon et de Saint-Maurice, 1847.'
[80] Ibid., I, 102, Elgin-Grey, 24 December 1847.
[81] Ibid., I, 117, Elgin-Grey, 7 January 1848.
[82] Ibid., I, 119, Elgin-Grey, 22 January 1848.
[83] Chapais, VI, 36-7.
[84] Elgin-Grey, III, 1022-3, Grey-Harvey, 3 November 1846.
[85] Ibid., I, 135, Elgin-Grey, 17 March 1848.
[86] Ibid., I, 123, Elgin-Grey, 5 February 1848.
[87] Ibid., I, 138, Grey-Elgin, 14 April 1848.
[88] Ibid., I, 139, Elgin-Grey, 27 March 1848.
[89] APQ: Fonds Papineau, XI, 544, Papineau- ——, 15 October 1844.
[90] Ibid., 545, Papineau-Roebuck, 16 July 1845.
[91] Ibid., 547, Papineau-O'Callaghan, 12 May 1846.
[92] Chapais, VI, 47.

[93] *Le Journal de Québec*, 13 November 1847; Chapais, VI, 47–8.

[94] *L'Ami de la Religion et de la Patrie*, 24 December 1847; Chapais, VI, 48.

[95] Gérin-Lajoie, *Dix Ans*, 314–15.

[96] APQ: XI, 547a, 548, Papineau-O'Callaghan, 22 February 1848; 19 April 1848.

[97] Gérin-Lajoie, 481; Chapais, VI, 53.

[98] *Elgin-Grey*, I, 134, Elgin-Grey, 17 March 1848.

[99] *Ibid.*, I, 115, Papineau's Huntingdon address, 1847.

[100] *Ibid.*, I, 125, Grey-Elgin, 22 March 1848.

[101] *Ibid.*, I, 141–2, Elgin-Grey, 9 April 1848.

[102] *Ibid.*, 1, 12, Elgin-Grey, 2 March 1848.

[103] *Ibid.*, I, 144–5, Elgin-Grey, 26 April 1848.

[104] *Ibid.*, I, 149–50, Elgin-Grey, 4 May 1848.

[105] *Ibid.*, I, 195, Elgin-Grey, 29 June 1848.

[106] *Ibid.*, I, 191–2.

[107] *Ibid.*, I, 200, Bourget's pastoral of 17 June 1848.

[108] *Ibid.*, I, 152–3, *L'Avenir*.

[109] *Ibid.*, I, 156–8, *La Revue Canadienne*.

[110] PAC: Lafontaine Papers, Cauchon-Lafontaine, 23 June 1848; Chapais, VI, 64.

[111] Innis & Lower, *Select Econ. Docs.*, II, 316.

[112] *The Canadian Economist*, 30 May 1848; Innis & Lower, II, 347.

[113] Innis & Lower, II, 357, J. Keefer-W. H. Merritt, 19 April 1848.

[114] *Elgin-Grey*, I, 182 & *n.* 2, Elgin-Grey, 6 June 1848.

[115] *Ibid.*, I, 204, Elgin-Grey, 5 July 1848.

[116] *Ibid.*, I, 208, Grey-Elgin, 27 July 1848.

[117] *Ibid.*, I, 217, Elgin-Grey, 2 August 1848.

[118] *Ibid.*, I, 224, Elgin-Grey, 16 August 1848.

[119] *Ibid.*, I, 250, Elgin-Grey, 19 October 1848.

[120] *Ibid.*, I, 256, Elgin-Grey, 16 November 1848.

[121] *Ibid.*, I, 285; *Montreal Gazette*.

[122] Chapais, VI, 70.

[123] *Ibid.*, VI, 74–5.

[124] *Ibid.*, VI, 77.

[125] *Ibid.*, VI, 79.

[126] *Ibid.*, VI, 96.

[127] *Ibid.*, VI, 97.

[128] *Ibid.*, VI, 99–100.

[129] Chapais, VI, 103.

[130] *Montreal Gazette*, 30 March 1849; *Elgin-Grey*, I, 337.

[131] *Montreal Courier*, ———; *Elgin-Grey*, I, 336.

[132] *L'Avenir*, 24 February 1849; *Elgin-Grey*, I, 342.

[133] *L'Avenir*, 3 March 1849; *Elgin-Grey*, I, 343.

[134] *Elgin-Grey*, I, 348 *n.*

[135] *Montreal Gazette*, 25 April 1849; Chapais, VI, 108.

[136] *Elgin-Grey*, I, 350; Elgin-Grey, 30 April 1849.

[137] *Ibid.*, I, 352, Elgin-Grey, 5 May 1849.

[138] *Ibid.*, IV, 1490. The signatures, elsewhere usually omitted, are here given, as well as the document in full.

[139] *Ibid.*, I, 441–3 *n.*, 'Address to People of Canada' of British American League, 31 July 1849.

CHAPTER VI

THE EMERGENCE OF A NATION—II

(1849-67)

IT HAD taken only ten years for the French Canadians to rally from the death sentence pronounced upon their nationality by Lord Durham's *Report* and the Act of Union. Under the sage leadership of Lafontaine their constitutional resistance had been so successful that they had gained undisputed political power. The disgruntled francophobe press now railed against French domination, protesting when the Eastern Townships were brought under the same legal system as the rest of the province that 'the obvious intention of that majority, composed of Frenchmen, aided by traitorous British Canadians, is to force French institutions still further upon the British minority in Lower Canada.'[1] The rebels of 1837-8, both English and French, now held office and were supported by the British government, while the former loyalists proclaimed their revolt: 'When French tyranny becomes insupportable we shall find our Cromwell . . . When we can stand tyranny no longer, it will be seen whether good bayonets in Saxon hands will not be more than a match for a mace and a majority.'

Both ethnic groups had now resorted to rebellion when dominated wholly by the other; the great achievement of the next two decades was to be the working out of a partnership of English and French which guaranteed the rights of both. Thanks largely to Elgin's leadership, the threat of annexation to the United States was averted by the establishment of reciprocity of trade, which did much to cure the economic ills of Canada; thanks largely to George Etienne Cartier,[2] the French Canadians were led to support the project of the Confederation of British North America into a Canada which was to be both French and English. Papineau's old lieutenant had broken with his former chief on the question of republicanism and annexation: Cartier was convinced that the French Canadians were monarchists by religion, by custom, and by tradition. Thanks largely to him, an English-French Canadian solidarity was achieved, as a result of which it was definitely settled that the continent was to be divided between two powers, rather than to be a political entity; and that one power was to be bicultural.

I

The nature of the new Canada then in the making was fore-shadowed by the decision of the legislature, after the Montreal riots, to meet alternately at Toronto and Quebec. After his Montreal experiences, Elgin favored the measure, for as he wrote Grey:

> You find in this city I believe the most Anti-British specimens of each class of which our community consists—The Montreal French are the most Yankeefied French in the Province—the British, though furiously anti-Gallican, are, with some exceptions, the least loyal—and the commercial men the most zealous annexationists which Canada furnishes—It must I think do great mischief to the members who come from the other parts of the Province to pass some months of each year in this hotbed of prejudice and disaffection——[3]

Though the self-styled loyalists had issued a proclamation to the 'Britons of the City of Toronto, Britons of the Home District,' urging them to 'let your eggs be stale and your powder dry' against the coming of Elgin, 'the political Judas Iscariot,'[4] it was decided that the legislature should go first to Toronto, to avoid the charge that the government was under French-Canadian influence.

Elgin travelled through Upper Canada during the autumn of 1849 on a courageous goodwill tour from which he returned with the firm conviction, as he informed Grey, that *'Canada cannot be saved unless you force the selfish scheming Yankees to concede reciprocity.'*[5] The annexationist English press of Montreal bewailed the loss of the seat of government, but the Tory *Daily British Whig* of Toronto told them to 'keep their breath to cool their porridge,' for it was:

> . . . the wretched selfishness of the Montrealers . . . caused the removal of the Seat of Government from Western Canada; from amid an Anglo-Saxon race, to place it within the control of French Oligarchists and their Helots. Had the Government remained at Kingston, or at any place within the limits of the upper province, the Franco-Canadians never would have attained and exercised that arbitrary power which has been the exciting cause of all the late political troubles and riots. A war of races might have existed, as it now does, but it would have been a defensive war on the part of the Eastern Canadians . . . From such evils the province, in future, will be protected, while legislation takes place in an educated land, and among free men. The Radicals may rule over us, and they will, but our rulers will be Anglo-Saxon Radicals, and not aliens to us in blood, language, and religion.[6]

It was to be a long time before the French Canadians would produce a racism as virulent as that which permeates this statement, which also reflects the powerful sectionalism that has remained almost as much of a factor in Canadian politics as the basic ethnic division.

2

Elgin now put aside the ethnic question and turned his attention to the economic matters which were of growing importance as Canada felt the impact of the industrial revolution. He was in close relations with William Hamilton Merritt, the promoter of the Welland Canal and the advocate of reciprocity as a solution for Canada's ills, who had been president of the legislative council and now became commissioner of public works. Elgin assured Grey that if reciprocity were obtained, 'Canada will remain attached to England though tied to her neither by the golden links of protection, nor by the meshes of old-fashioned Colonial office jobbing and chicane.' Otherwise, he feared that 'the closing period of the connexion between Great Britain and Canada will be marked by incidents which will damp the ardor of those who desire to promote human happiness by striking shackles either off commerce or off men.'[7] The repeal of the English Corn Laws and timber duties by the Little Englanders now in the saddle at London had brought commercial disaster upon the English-Canadian merchants, who promptly abandoned their traditional loyalism and sought a preferential market in the United States through annexation. Elgin thought a British preferential trade agreement with the United States was the only means of saving Canada from annexation. This project did not find particular favor at the Colonial Office, for Lord Grey was one of the new doctrinaire free-traders with little regard for the fate of the colonies.

Though the annexationist press continued to insult the governor, Elgin contented himself with dismissing from office militia officers or magistrates who signed manifestos calling for annexation to the States. Elgin refused to concur with Grey in making a distinction between separation with a view to annexation and separation with a view to independence. The colonial secretary considered the former an act of treason, the latter a natural and legitimate step in progress. Elgin protested: 'If you say that your great lubberly boy is too big for the nursery and that you have no other room for him in your house, how can you decline to allow him to lodge with his elder brethren over the way when the attempt to keep up an establishment for himself would seriously embarrass him?'[8] The governor-general also found it difficult to take strong measures against the annexationists in Canada, when Lord John Russell was proclaiming at Westminster:

I anticipate indeed with others that some of the colonies may so grow in population and wealth that they may say—'Our strength is sufficient to enable us to be independent of England. The link is now becoming onerous to us—the time is come when we can, in amity and alliance with England, maintain our independence.' I do not think that time is yet approaching. But let us make them, as far as possible, fit to govern themselves—let us give them, as far as we can, the capacity of ruling their own affairs—let them increase in wealth and population, and whatever may happen, we have the consolation of saying we have contributed to the happiness of the world.[9]

Elgin judged that this anticipation of the severance of the British connection would have a deplorable effect in Canada, and he considered it unnecessary.

In a remarkable anticipation of the idea of the Commonwealth of Nations and the present status of Canada within its framework, he wrote:

Here for instance, where the vicinity of the U.S. exercises so great an influence, it is, I think, possible, that the time may come when it may be expedient to allow the Colonists to elect their own Governors, to reduce their civil lists to the starvation point, &c, England withdrawing all her forces except 2,000 men at Quebec and being herself represented in the Colony by an Agent—something like a Resident in India—If yr. agent was well chosen and had a good status I am not sure but that the connexion might be kept up under such an arrangement quite as well and as profitably for England as under the present—One thing is however indispensable to the success of this or any other system of Colonial Government—You must renounce the habit of telling the Colonies that the Colonial is a provisional existence.—You must allow them to believe that without severing the bonds which unite them to Great Britain they may attain the degree of perfection and of social and political development to which organized communities of freemen have a right to aspire.[10]

He reported that Robert Baldwin, whom he thought 'of more importance to the connexion than three regiments,'[11] was deeply moved by Russell's speech, and had remarked:

But is it not hard upon us while we are laboring through good and evil report to thwart the designs of those who would dismember the Empire that our adversaries should be informed that the difference between them and the Prime Minister of England is only one of time? If the British Government has really come to the conclusion that we are a burden to be cast off whenever a favorable opportunity offers, surely we ought to be warned.[12]

It is clear that Elgin echoed Baldwin's sentiments.

3

At the outset of the new session in May 1850, a motion in favor of breaking the tie with Great Britain was roundly defeated, with only Papineau and six diehard Tories supporting it. Sir Allan MacNab continued his intemperate attacks on Lafontaine and the ministry, and finally drew upon himself the reproaches of his fellow Tory, Colonel Gugy, who remarked that he could no longer follow the leadership which had led to the Montreal disorders: 'When I saw the House of Assembly in flames, I said to an influential conservative who was near me, "In these flames are consumed the hopes of the conservative party." In fact, I think this party will never return to power.'[13]

The ministry carried almost all before it, since the opposition was hopelessly divided among incompatible groups: some fifteen Tories, five or six dissident Reformers known as 'Clear Grits,' and the declared annexationists. The Clear Grits, who favored the application of the elective principle to all offices, universal suffrage, the secret ballot, biennial parliaments, free trade, direct taxation, secularization of the clergy reserves, and other measures considered radical at the time, had broken away from the conservative Liberalism of Baldwin, as a similar Lower-Canadian group, the *Rouges*, was soon to do from that of Lafontaine. The ministry carried all its measures except Lafontaine's renewed proposal to increase the representation, which failed to win the necessary two-thirds vote. Free trade and reciprocity between the provinces of British North America were encouraged in one law which foreshadowed Confederation, while the vexed Upper-Canadian question of the clergy reserves was referred to the British parliament.

Of much more concern to Lower Canada were Lafontaine's resolutions leading to the abolition of seigneurial tenure. This measure, which had once been favored by the anti-French forces of the province, now had the backing of the *habitants*. A commission of enquiry had been appointed in 1841 and had made its report in 1843, but no action had as yet been taken. Lafontaine urged the abolition of seigneurial tenure with proper compensation to the landlords as a measure against revolution:

In justice to the two interested parties, it is time to destroy the evil which is so much complained of. I am convinced that the *seigneur* ought most to fear too long a delay of a remedy. Delay gives new occasions for the propagation of principles which tend to overturn society. There comes a time when the people say, 'It is too late.' In this case, as the *seigneurs* form the smallest number, they may expect to lose everything without compensation . . . But I hope never to see the day when society, when the whole country, will be demoralized. I see the march of events: it is the struggle of the masses against the few. The masses are beginning to become indignant. Time ought not to be lost. But if seigneurial tenure is to be effectively and really ended, let us all work together, *seigneurs* and *censitaires*, and if the *seigneur* gives the example of good will, it will be so much the better.[14]

But the question of seigneurial tenure was not settled at this session, though a committee was appointed to study the question and report upon it.

Oddly enough, the *seigneur* who did not display the goodwill for which Lafontaine called was none other than Papineau. The old champion of the rights of the people, the idol of the Lower Canadian democrats, whose organ *L'Avenir* denounced feudal tenure as a shameful relic of an abhorred past, was also the *seigneur* of Montebello and had no intention of renouncing his privileges. He rose to defend the wisdom and justice of seigneurial tenure, and denounced the demagogues who agitated the people in favor of its abolition. He proclaimed proudly: 'I am a great reformer in the matter of necessary political changes, but I am a great conservative in the matter of preservation of the sacred right of property.'[15] This curious mixture of political radicalism and economic conservatism was to become a tradition among French-Canadian leaders. Those who bewail most loudly the trampling underfoot of the rights of the people are often, like Papineau himself, members of the élite, aristocrats by temperament, taste, and training. The American democracy which Papineau preached was an exotic growth largely foreign to the French-Canadian tradition, reinforced at this period by renewed contact with France. Thanks to the intellectual reaction in Canada to the European revolution of 1848, American democracy never took root in French Canada, whose society still remains today a rigidly hierarchical structure, though lately somewhat shaken by movements from the long-submerged masses.

The course of the session, which closed in August, bore out Elgin's opinion that 'Bringing the French Canadian Members to this fine progressive well farmed Country, and placing them for a time in the midst of a British population who though they may have some John Bullish prejudices, do not cherish towards them the jealous antipathies of Montreal, gives in my opinion a chance to the Province and the Union which nothing else could have given—.'[16] French and English acted together in coping with the most pressing questions of each section; annexationism lost strength as prosperity returned with a sudden rise of prices and trade, an increase of exports and imports, the freeing of the navigation of the St. Lawrence, the development of close economic relations with the United States, the completion of the canals, the construction of railroads, the colonization movement, and an abundant harvest. Elgin paid tribute to the role played by the French Canadians: 'The Ministry supported by the French (whose tendencies when they feel that they are treated fairly, not as aliens but as genuine subjects of the Queen, are, as I always assured you, decidedly anti-revolutionary) have been able to resist the destructives.'[17] He added, after assigning to personal spite and selfishness the radicalism of the dissident Upper Canadians: 'Candor compels me to state that in these respects the conduct of the Anglo-Saxon portion of our M.P.P's, contrasts most unfavorably with that of the Gallican.'

Elgin took this opportunity to review developments in Canada since the Rebellions and to make another of his accurate forecasts:

The result of the policy which I have pursued with yr. concurrence and support has been briefly this—The French have been rescued from the false position into which they have been driven, and in which they must perforce have remained so long as they believed that it was the object of the British Govt. as avowed by Lord Sydenham and others to break them down and to ensure to the British race, not by trusting to the natural course of events but by dint of management and statecraft, a predominance in the Province—To eradicate from the mind of a people naturally prone to suspicion a belief of this kind when deeply engrained was no easy task, but the startling events of last year and above all the furious assaults directed by the mob and Press of the so called British Party against the Queen's Representative have accomplished the object. The French are restored to their normal condition and are therefore an essentially conservative element in the Canadian compound. Accident, or rather I believe I should say the artifices of Imperial Policy, have connected them politically with the liberals of Upper Canada—They are unwilling to break this connexion and they will adhere to it as long as a moderate liberal Party exists in this section of the province—If clear Gritism absorbs all the hues of Upper Canadian liberalism the French, unless some interference from without checks the natural course of events, will fall off from them and form an alliance with the Upper Canadian Tories.[18]

In the fall of 1850 Elgin was troubled by the prospect of Lafontaine abandoning public life at the end of the current parliament: 'I do not altogether approve of a man of his age and with his influence leaving public life, but the fact is that the French Canadians are generally (with the exception of Papineau) quiet sort of people, and Lafontaine's health is not very good. His desire for retirement arises I think partly from health and partly from disgust at the worrying and turmoil of office—.'[19] Elgin grew more and more convinced that the French Canadians would line up with the Upper Canadian Conservatives as the Clear Grits became more anti-French. Boulton, one of the Grits' chief spokesmen, proclaimed at a public dinner that 'the negroes are the great difficulty of the States and the French Canadians of Canada,' a sentiment which Elgin correctly judged as 'likely to stick in the gizzard of a rather sensitive and suspicious people.'[20] This consideration has not prevented the sentiment from being echoed down to the present day.

4

The new session opened calmly in May 1851, and was notable only for the presence of William Lyon Mackenzie, the leader of the Upper Canada Rebellion in 1837-8, who had defeated George Brown of the *Toronto Globe* in an election in which the latter made vain use of the 'No Popery' cry, in connection with the re-establishment of the Catholic hierarchy in England. The legislature was more concerned with economic matters at home than religious ones abroad. The St. Lawrence commercial system, with its dangerous navigation, high insurance rates, and limited supply of grain and high freights, was still losing ground to the New York one, which enjoyed lower insurance and freight rates, as the chief outlet for North American grain. Canada's trade with the United States increased more rapidly than that with Britain and became far more important than it had ever been before.

Since Canada found itself in the unhappy position of having completed some $20,000,000 worth of canals just as the rise of the railways lessened their importance, the legislature showed interest in Hincks' proposal to construct various roads, which were later consolidated as the Grand Trunk and the Intercolonial. In 1849 the annexationists mourned that Canada had only 50 miles of railway; but by 1854 2,000 miles were under construction and 800 already completed. $40,000,000 was spent on this program, and 20,000 men were given work in the summer of 1854. The railroads brought a large influx of foreign capital, mostly British. The legislature also turned its attention to the vexed question of the clergy reserves, which the imperial government had referred back for their decision. Lafontaine failed again to carry his project of increasing the representation, and it was still Papineau's vote which defeated the measure.

The far-sighted Merritt proposed a meeting of delegates of the British North American provinces to consider a constitution for a future confederation, but won only seven votes for this resolution. It was to be sixteen years before a majority would favor this project, proposed in the past by English administrators and now first brought to the attention of the Canadian parliament by a member of its government. The committee on seigneurial tenure made its report, and a group headed by its chairman Louis Drummond, the solicitor-general for Lower Canada, and including Cartier, Chauveau, and Cauchon, pressed for immediate action on the question. Lafontaine opposed a hasty settlement, and finally got his way, despite a sharp debate.

On June 30 Robert Baldwin, who had been able to defeat an attack on one of his judicial measures only with the aid of the Lower Canadian Reformers in the face of a revolt headed by Mackenzie, and who had also been embittered by the growing hostility of the Clear Grits, announced his resignation on the grounds that his party lacked confidence in him. Lafontaine declared that he, too, would resign after the session, and expressed his regret at Baldwin's action: 'I had at least hoped not to be separated until the end of my political career from my honorable colleague, to him I have been united not only by common principles but by the bonds of a close friendship.'[21]

Baldwin was only forty-nine; Lafontaine only forty-four, but they were both prematurely worn by their joint ten years' struggle to win responsible government for Canada, and so the great ministry resigned, closing one of the most notable epochs of Canadian parliamentary history. Grey wrote to Elgin: 'I am very sorry indeed you have lost Lafontaine from your Cabinet, he seems to me to have had more of the Gentleman about him than any other of the public men of Canada.'[22] Lafontaine himself, at a farewell public dinner in Montreal, gave some final advice to his compatriots: 'In retiring from public life I do not see without displeasure the attempts which are being made to divide those of my origin, and to array them against each other; but from my experience I may tell you that such efforts will not be successful. The common sense of our countrymen will prevent that; should it be otherwise, the fault and suffering will be theirs.'[23] Unfortunately this good advice was not taken, and much of the best of French-Canadian intellectual energy was long to be wasted in futile internecine bickering. Politics might well be considered the opium of the French-Canadian people, and over-indulgence in the vice has cost them dear.

5

The intellectual energy of the French Canadians was beginning, however, to find other outlets than politics. In the 1840's and 1850's there was a notable stirring in the cultural field which was not to be matched for almost a century, thanks to the tide of intellectual reaction which became dominant when Quebec found itself on the defensive in the new Confederation which it was only reluctantly brought to accept in 1867. French Canada responded vigorously to the challenge of Durham's contemptuous remarks about its culture in his *Report*, which merely echoed the long-standing opinion of the English merchants and officials of Quebec and Montreal.

In 1828, when young François-Xavier Garneau was a clerk in the Quebec law office of Archibald Campbell, he had been taunted by one of his English fellow clerks on the score of the constitutional struggle then raging in the assembly under the leadership of Papineau and Viger. The young Englishman had said: 'What is the use of all this quibbling, in this country conquered by our arms and which even has no history?' Garneau replied: 'I shall write the history which you do not even know exists. You will see that our ancestors yielded only when outnumbered. And then, "what though the field be lost, all is not lost." There are defeats which are as glorious as victories.'[24]

The son of a carriage-maker and innkeeper, Garneau had early attracted the notice of François-Joseph Perrault, the extraordinary former fur trader who became an educational reformer, establishing along Lancasterian lines the Quebec primary school which the boy attended, as well as writing legal and historical textbooks. Perrault, whose post as clerk of the Court of King's Bench enabled him to study and compile a manual of Canadian history, offered the boy, who lacked funds for the classical college course, a place in his office; and after two years there Garneau decided to become a notary. He apprenticed himself to Archibald Campbell, who did not allow his thriving practice and his extensive financial concerns to stop him from taking a lively interest in literature and science. Campbell opened his library to his serious young clerk, who thus became familiar with the chief English, French, and Latin poets and historians. After three years of self-education young Garneau accompanied a friend of Campbell on a journey to the Maritime Provinces, the United States, and Upper Canada, which helped to broaden his outlook. In 1830 Garneau passed his notarial examination, and having fulfilled his contract with Campbell by a year's further service in his office, set out for Europe in 1831 with $240 in his pocket, to visit, as he said, 'the cradle of genius and civilization to which America owes all that it is.'[25]

After passing a week in London seeing the sights, he went over to Paris, which was then celebrating the first anniversary of the accession of Louis-Philippe, the Citizen-King. It was the Paris of Lamartine, Victor Hugo, and Musset, of Thiers and Guizot, of Lamennais and Lacordaire—a very different world from that which Garneau had known in Quebec. Upon his return to London, he obtained the post of secretary to Denis-Benjamin Viger, then the assembly's agent in England. For a year Garneau drafted petitions to the colonial secretary, and correspondence to Papineau and Neilson, gaining an intimate knowledge of French-Canadian politics and also meeting such notables as William Lyon Mackenzie, Arthur Roebuck, and John McGregor, who came to call upon Viger. He also fell in with the Polish refugees whose meetings were frequented by O'Connell, the Irish patriot who was the friend of all oppressed peoples. With a natural sympathy for minorities under foreign rule, Garneau was drawn into the current of nationalism then undermining the old order in Europe. His studies in the British Museum were supplemented by visits to political meetings and the House of Commons, where he heard the debate on the Reform Bill. Thus Garneau obtained a thorough understanding of the workings of the British parliamentary system. This busy life was interrupted in the fall of 1832 by a two-weeks vacation in Paris with Viger and Amable Berthelot, and then resumed until May 1833, when Garneau took ship for Quebec. He returned greatly influenced by his two years in Europe: a democrat in politics, with a strong faith in the peaceful evolution possible under the English parliamentary system; a romanticist in literature, much influenced by Lamartine; and a Catholic of the liberal school of Lacordaire, Montalembert and Mgr. Dupanloup. He had resolved to serve his country with his pen.

Back in Quebec Garneau resumed practice as a notary to earn a living, but devoted much of his time to writing, first contributing verse to Etienne Parent's *Le Canadien* and then launching, at the end of 1833, his own short-lived *L'Abeille Canadienne*. In the following year, that of Bédard's 92 Resolutions, Garneau abandoned literature for politics, and as secretary of the Quebec Constitutional Committee played an active role as a speaker and writer on the issues of the day. The next year saw little work from his pen, probably because of the illness and death of his mother, and his own courtship and marriage. But in 1836 Garneau, inspired by Guizot and Augustin Thierry, set about studying the history of Canada. During this and the following year he published in *Le Canadien* descriptions of the famous battles fought on Canadian soil. His avocation interfered with the demands of his profession, and to meet the needs of a growing family he gave up notarial work and became a cashier in an English bank. The Rebellion of 1837 enlisted his poetic talents in the *Patriote* interest, while the succeeding years of reaction drove him back to pure literature. He published the best French-Canadian verse of the period in *Le Canadien*, and then in 1840, with Etienne Parent and under the leadership of John Neilson and Edouard Glackmeyer, he threw himself into agitation against the Act of Union. In 1841, he launched another short-lived publication, *L'Institut*, devoted to science, industry, and literature.

After its collapse, he turned once more to his original determination to rally the French Canadians in this crucial hour by writing their history, in order 'to re-establish,' as he later wrote to Elgin, 'the truth which has been so often disfigured and to repel attacks and insults . . . on the part of men who wish to oppress and exploit them at the same time.' His aim, as he defined it for Lafontaine, was 'to impress upon this nationality a character which would make it respected in the future.'[26] Thus, at thirty-two, Garneau finally began his life work. He was a self-trained historian, but his masters were great men. Guizot taught him the importance of exact documentation. Thierry gave him the notions of atavistic survivals and of racial antagonisms; Montesquieu convinced him that environment and the popular will shape the evolution of a people. Raynal bolstered his liberalism; and Michelet taught him that the people constitute a collective being with an evolving soul. He was French Canada's first scientific historian, using original sources, analyzing and criticizing them, and declaring the truth as he found it.[27]

Garneau abandoned his cashier's position in favor of the post of French translator of the assembly, which gave him the leisure he needed for his researches. In 1842 he published a study on Jacques Cartier which appeared as his first book, after first being published in Le Canadien. In 1844 his friend Glackmeyer obtained for him a sinecure as Quebec City Clerk. Finally in August 1845 the first volume of his Histoire du Canada depuis sa découverte jusqu'à nos jours appeared. It was well received, although some ultramontanes criticized what they called its gallicanism as 'anti-Catholic and anti-Canadian,' and gave Garneau, as he himself remarked, a 'terrible reputation with vestrymen and sextons.'[28]

Before publishing his second volume in April 1846, Garneau made a trip to Albany to examine the Brodhead Papers, which were copies of official French documents in the Paris archives dealing with colonial history. These papers were under the care of Dr. O'Callaghan, Papineau's colleague in 1837, now historian of the State of New York, who was sympathetic to Garneau's purpose and gave him every aid. Soon after his return to Canada, Garneau consulted the transcripts which Papineau himself had brought back from Paris, in the hope of writing the history of the country in whose political development he had played such an active role. Papineau had one of the best historical libraries in Canada at his home at Montebello—Parkman took pains to consult it in 1856—and he had much in common with Garneau, whose 'love of historical truth' and whose 'independence in stating it' he admired.[29] For his part Garneau had nothing but respect for the great tribune, whose ardent supporter he had been up to 1837. The first great statesman and the first great historian of French Canada had frequent discussions after this first meeting, from which Garneau emerged with four precious volumes of Paris transcripts.

The third and final volume of his history, which stopped at 1792, appeared in 1848, arousing more attention in France than in Canada. It was reviewed most favorably in the *Revue Encyclopédique* of Paris by Isidore Lebrun, who considered Garneau a 'fellow Norman' and who had published a book on Canada in 1833.[30] The assembly then voted a grant of $1,000 to further Garneau's labors, and in 1849 he was made a member of the Lower Canadian council of public instruction. Thus honored at home and abroad, he was less exposed to the criticism of the ultra-orthodox, who in any case had been largely won over by his affirmation in his third volume of the solidarity of religion and nationality in French Canada. Then Bishop Signay of Quebec completely disarmed the opposition by throwing open to him the diocesan archives, one of the richest sources for the history of New France. Garneau became one of the notables of French Canada, and was sought out by such distinguished visitors as the French academicians Marmier and Ampère in 1848 and in 1851. The French historian of Acadia, Rameau de Saint-Père, maintained a correspondence with him long after returning to France; and when Commandant de Belvèze came sailing up the St. Lawrence in 1855 in the frigate *La Capricieuse* on a goodwill mission, one of his first requests was to be introduced to the historian of Canada.[31]

Despite the constant threat of epileptic attacks, Garneau did not rest upon his laurels, but continued his researches in order to revise the completed portion of his work and to carry the story down to 1840. Elgin opened the official correspondence of the governors-general to him, and in this pioneer period of American historical studies other great new stores of material were being uncovered from day to day by a host of students. A second edition of the *Histoire* was published in 1852, and was hailed by both Théodore Parie in the *Revue des Deux Mondes* and by Orestes Brownson in the *Quarterly Review* of Boston. Brownson congratulated the author on having written without bias or prejudice, and with a constant respect for principles and truth. This was high praise from the difficult doctor, a zealous Catholic convert who did not hesitate to lecture bishops on theology. Garneau became the leading spirit of the *Institut Canadien* of Quebec, which numbered among its members the poet Crémazie, whom Garneau inspired with his own love and knowledge of French-Canadian history, Pierre Chauveau, Jean-Charles Taché, and the elder Philippe Aubert de Gaspé, who favored the historian with his own rich recollections of three-quarters of a century. In 1854–5 Garneau published in *Le Journal de Québec*, an account of his youthful European tour, but his harsh words about former *Patriotes* who had become ministers under the Union and his evident republicanism aroused criticism, which made him suppress

La Pérade Church

Built in 1855, obviously under the influence of Notre Dame in Montreal whose towers were built in 1841 and 1843. A disastrous venture in a style foreign to Quebec's tradition, and an example of the *folie de grandeur* which was to burden many a small community with a cathedral instead of a church. (I.O.A.P.Q.)

Pigeon Hunt

Oil painting (1853) by Antoine-Sebastien Plamondon, the first French Canadian to receive formal art education in Europe. Thanks to small boys' guns and farmers' flails, the once multitudinous passenger pigeon soon became extinct. (I.O.A.P.Q.)

the subsequent publication in book form of these *Voyages en Angleterre et en France (dans les années* 1831, 1832 *et* 1833).

As Garneau grew older and more conservative, and as he felt the powerful conformist influences of Quebec society, he decided to revise his history and modify its tone, as well as to incorporate in it the results of new researches and discoveries. In 1859 he published a third edition of the history, the last which he prepared himself, although he left materials for a fourth edition at his death in 1866. The 1859 edition was subjected to clerical censorship and lacks the ardor and the vigor of the earlier versions. Unfortunate as this revision was on literary and historical grounds, it cleared Garneau's name of the charges of anti-clericalism and free-thinking, and firmly established him as the national historian of French Canada. His history, which has never been surpassed by any French Canadian though in part outmoded by time, became the 'national bible.' Its assertions of the essential relationship between 'our language, our laws, and our customs' and between faith and nationality have become French-Canadian dogmas. Garneau's preoccupation with ethnic and cultural survival, natural enough in the 1830's and 1840's, still haunts the French-Canadian mind, long after survival has been assured.

6

Garneau may fairly be considered the father of French-Canadian literature, although there had been isolated efforts before his time. The most notable of his precursors was Michel Bibaud, who edited a long series of short-lived periodicals, beginning with *La Bibliothèque Canadienne* in 1825, which provided a forum for Canadian writers. Bibaud's chief work was a history of Canada, intended as a reply to William Smith's ultra-Loyalist account, which first appeared serially in these magazines and was later brought out in three volumes in 1837, 1844, and 1878. A Bureaucrat, Bibaud was bitterly opposed to the *Patriotes* and biased in favor of the Chateau Clique. His ponderous history, which is often a mere undigested collection of documents, was completely put in the shade by Garneau's interpretive work.

Bibaud also tried his hand at poetry, producing in 1830 a volume of very dreary and pedestrian verse, whose classical inspiration is evident in its title, *Épîtres, satires, chansons, épigrammes*. This book, dedicated to Boileau and imitating him closely, is chiefly notable for the four satires against avarice, envy, laziness, and ignorance, which first appeared in the newspaper *L'Aurore* from 1815 to 1819. To Bibaud's mind these were the chief vices of the French Canadian, and he devoted his life to a crusade to banish at least one of them, ignorance, from Quebec. He began as a teacher, and then shifted in 1813 to journalism, which remained his chief occupation for thirty years. He founded no less than two newspapers and four reviews, all of which followed the same pattern: chapters of his history of Canada, articles on geography and scientific subjects, extracts from the European and American press, and comments on Canadian politics, education, and letters. Not content with this effort, he edited popular manuals, made translations, and encouraged his contemporaries to undertake similar labors for the enlightenment of the people.

Bibaud had a strong moralistic strain—the preface of his history begins: 'All men ought to desire to know the history of their country and their nation'[32]—and in his verse he set himself up as a Canadian Cato, condemning the faults of his countrymen. Bibaud's zeal and industry were greater than his talent: he himself admitted that he was 'more rhymer than poet.'[33] This self-judgment is surely just, since he found twenty-six rhymes for 'Quebec'. The much-revised history never became either readable or authoritative, despite his best efforts. His place is as a transition figure in the shift of French-Canadian expression from journalism to literature and history. Bibaud was a voice in the cultural wilderness, calling the French Canadians to greater creative effort.

One of Bibaud's most faithful collaborators was his schoolmate, the antiquarian Jacques Viger, who began his career as editor of *Le Canadien* in 1808-9. In 1810 he compiled his '*Néologie canadienne*,' a lexicon of Canadianisms. During the War of 1812 Viger served as a lieutenant in de Salaberry's *Voltigeurs*, keeping an interesting diary, '*Mes Tablettes de 1813*,' which Bibaud published in the second and third volumes of the *Bibliothèque Canadienne*. After the war Viger entered the municipal government of Montreal, becoming the first mayor of the city in 1833. He was an antiquarian by avocation and in the tradition of the *cahier*-keeping *philosophes* compiled a series of forty-four notebooks and scrapbooks, which he called '*Ma Sabre-tache*.' These contain copies of documents, reports, manuscripts, maps, plans, statistics, and other materials for the history of Canada, frequently annotated by Viger; as well as autographs, paintings, watercolors, and prints concerned with the same subject. Viger became an authority consulted by all concerned with the history of Canada, though he published only an account of the '*Régime militaire*' (1760-4) and two papers on Montreal history. He saved from destruction much valuable material which might well have perished before the belated foundation of Canadian archives. He was the first of a line of amateur archivists and antiquarians, tireless researchers rarely ready to write, who have done yeoman service for the cause of history in Quebec.

Viger's immediate successor in this role was his friend Georges-Barthélemi Faribault, a government clerk and translator from 1822 to 1855, who devoted his spare time to collecting books and manuscripts concerned with the history of Canada. In 1837 he published a pioneer bibliography of Canadiana, his *Catalogue d'ouvrages sur l'histoire de l'Amérique et en particulier sur celle du Canada, de la Louisiane, de l'Acadie et autres lieux ci-devant connus sous le nom de Nouvelle-France.* Faribault's first collection of more than 1,600 volumes was lost in 1849, when the Parliament Buildings at Montreal were burned by the mob. Two years later Faribault, who at sixty had promptly set to work to replace the loss, was sent to Europe by the government to complete his task. His second collection consisted of nearly 2,000 volumes, of which 700 were lost when the government building in Quebec burned in 1854. Having thus seen the fruits of his labor twice destroyed, Faribault retired in broken health to private life; but before his death in 1866 he had built up another collection of Canadiana, including 400 manuscripts, 1,000 books, and an album of maps, plans, and pictures.[34]

In 1837 appeared the first French-Canadian novel, the younger Philippe Aubert de Gaspé's *L'Influence d'un livre*, a romantic tale of black magic on the lower St. Lawrence. The rather thin plot is eked out by the inclusion of many legends of the region, which echo the beliefs and superstitions of the early settlers. In 1844 Joseph Doutre, later a leading *Rouge*, published his *Les Fiancées de 1812*, a highly melodramatic story in which true love triumphs over all obstacles. Doutre was only nineteen when his work appeared, while de Gaspé produced his at twenty-three. Both books have all the faults of youthful efforts, but they mark a considerable advance on the sketchy short stories and legends which began to appear in 1827 as the newspapers became more literary in tone, and which have been preserved in Huston's *Répertoire National*, the first anthology of French-Canadian literature, which was published in 1851. But the first really notable work in fiction was Pierre Chauveau's *Charles Guérin*, published anonymously in 1846 in the *Revue Canadienne* and then under its author's signature as a book in 1853. When his novel first appeared, Chauveau had just begun the political career which was to lead him to the premiership of Quebec. Since literature was then regarded as a mere pastime—a young man could be dismissed with a 'he does nothing—he writes'[35]—he deemed it best to conceal his connection with the work, lest he be branded as a ne'er-do-well. But the tale won acclaim in France, and as ever since in a provincial culture, this latter consideration was decisive as far as French-Canadian opinion was concerned.

Charles Guérin is a realistic novel on a theme which was to become all too familiar with the years: the plight of the classical college graduate faced by the congestion of the professions, the only role in life for which he was prepared. Chauveau's statement of the problem in 1846 has been echoed again and again down to the present day:

In French Canada one must be doctor, priest, notary, or lawyer. Outside of these four professions it seems that there is no salvation for the young educated Canadian. If by chance one of us had an invincible distaste for all four; if it was too painful to him to save souls, mutilate bodies, or lose fortunes, there remained only one course for him to take if he were rich, and two if he were poor; to do nothing at all in the first case, to exile himself or to starve to death in the second.[36]

Charles Guérin plans to enter the priesthood; then, when financial ruin threatens his widowed mother, thanks to the machinations of an unscrupulous Protestant Channel Islander,[37] he turns to the study of law. During a country holiday he falls in love with a farmer's daughter. But once back in Quebec City and in his own world of the élite, he falls under the spell of the Channel Islander's daughter. While thus blinded by love, he is tricked by her father into signing away his heritage, so that his whole family is reduced to misery. His mother dies during a cholera epidemic, and he is forced to give up his studies. The once scorned country girl is now an heiress; she and Charles marry and become colonists in the undeveloped region of Quebec.

The tale is well constructed and moves rapidly; Chauveau's style, modeled on that of Chateaubriand, is pleasant. He makes skillful use of Canadianisms in the mouths of his rustic characters, without wearying the reader with them. But the great merit of the book is the clear picture of the times which it supplies, and its enunciation of certain themes which were to become traditional in French-Canadian literature. Such is the dilemma which confronts the young man educated only for the professions in a country where the professions are always overcrowded; the gulf between the élite and the *habitants*, often crossed of necessity because the superior commercial ability of cultural aliens forces members of the élite from their privileged position; the hymning of the rural life as the salvation of the French Canadians. In later life Chauveau became the second superintendent of public instruction, and like his predecessor, Dr. Jean-Baptiste Meilleur, he sought to liberalize the traditional educational system of Quebec in the light of European and American developments, giving more place to practical and vocational training. But the strength of tradition in Quebec and of French-Canadian resistance to change are evidenced by the fact that novels of recent years are still concerned with the same themes as *Charles Guérin*, though a century has passed.

7

Antoine Gérin-Lajoie was another of the early French-Canadian writers who helped to establish the tradition from which Quebec authors have not deviated until recent years. The eldest of the sixteen children of a *habitant* family of Yamachiche, Gérin-Lajoie made his mark at the Collège de Nicolet, where at eighteen he wrote a three-act tragedy, *Le Jeune Latour*. This play, strongly inspired by the tradition of Corneille, was based upon a legend of the early days of Acadia, which was revived by Michel Bibaud in his *Histoire du Canada*. Its hymning of the faithfulness to France of the younger Latour, who refused to follow his turncoat father's course in the days of the privateering Kirkes, made it a great success when first performed at the college exercises, and won publication for it in 1844 in *L'Aurore des Canadas*, in *Le Canadien*, and finally in a brochure dedicated to the governor-general, Lord Metcalfe, who rewarded the young author with $25 and his compliments. While still a student, Gérin-Lajoie also wrote one of the most popular French-Canadian songs, *Un Canadien errant*, which admirably expressed the yearning homesickness of the political exiles of 1837–8. Upon his graduation from Nicolet in 1844, Gerin-Lajoie journeyed to New York to learn English, but failing to find employment as a teacher of French—the English-speaking prejudice, fostered by Frenchmen, against French Canadians in this capacity had already developed—he was forced to return ingloriously homeward after seventeen days, instead of the two years on which he had planned.

Back in Montreal he found that his literary reputation brought him only a $2-a-week position as Ludger Duvernay's assistant on *La Minerve*. In the spring of 1845 he became secretary of the Saint-Jean-Baptiste Society which his employer had founded; and several months later he was chosen president of the *Institut Canadien*, a literary and scientific society which served as a center for young intellectuals after its foundation in 1844. His health was unable to withstand the burden of his largely unremunerated patriotic labors, and in 1847 he resumed the study of law, his first choice of a profession. But his initiation into political life as a parliamentary correspondent soon led him back into politics as the secretary of Augustin-Norbert Morin, the founder of *La Minerve* and speaker of the assembly from 1848 to 1851. The violence of political debates in the era when Lafontaine's and Papineau's followers were at one another's throats soon disgusted the timid and scrupulous Gérin-Lajoie with political life. Failing to win success at the bar, to which he was admitted in 1848, he gladly accepted a post as copyist and paymaster in the Department of Public Works when the French

Canadians first received a share of patronage. With the exception of a few months, the rest of his life was passed as a civil servant in varying capacities.

But as early as 1849 he confided to his journal his disgust with the various white-collar occupations which had fallen to his lot, and his idealization of the rural life:

I have returned to my project of going to live in the country as soon as possible . . . Oh, if only I were a farmer! . . . He does not become rich by beggaring others, as lawyers, doctors, and merchants sometimes do. He draws his wealth from the earth: his is the state most natural to man. Farmers form the least egotistical and most virtuous class of the population. But this class has need of educated men who can serve its interests. The educated farmer has all the leisure necessary to do good; he can serve as guide to his neighbors, counsel the ignorant, sustain the weak, and defend him against the rapacity of the speculator. The enlightened and virtuous farmer is to my mind the best type of man. [38]

Thus the atavistic call of generations of *habitants* was deeply felt while at the same time Gérin-Lajoie wrote a popular *Catéchisme politique* published in 1851, and in 1852 spent some months at Boston in order to improve his English and to prepare a study of the political, social, religious, and industrial development of the United States. The agrarian theme announced in his journal took more than a decade to ripen, while Gérin-Lajoie earned his living first as translator for the House of Commons and after 1856 as assistant parliamentary librarian. In the latter capacity he prepared the first catalogue of the Parliamentary Library, published in 1857–8. During the stay of the government at Toronto, Gérin-Lajoie became an intimate of Etienne Parent, then deputy provincial secretary of Lower Canada, and married his eldest daughter in 1858.

When the government moved to Quebec in 1859, Gérin-Lajoie fell in with the literary group which made Octave Crémazie's bookshop on the Rue de la Fabrique its headquarters. Here came Gérin-Lajoie's father-in-law, Parent; his professor of history at Nicolet, Abbé J.-B.-A. Ferland, then giving at Laval, the first French-Canadian university (1852), a popular course on the history of the French regime which was inspired by Garneau's work; and Garneau himself in all the glory of his last years. There were also the younger men who launched in 1860 the literary movement known as the Patriotic School of Quebec: Dr. Hubert LaRue, the brilliant young scientist just beginning his teaching career at Laval after studies at Louvain and Paris; Joseph-Charles Taché, the journalistic collaborator of Pierre Chauveau in the satiric *Les Guêpes Canadiennes* and the author of a study of the Confederation question (1850) and of a sketchy account of Canada, written for the Paris Exposition of

1855; and Abbé Henri-Raymond Casgrain, who had been inspired by Garneau's work to popularize Canadian history and to 'create,'[39] to use his own term, a Canadian literature.

In 1861 Gérin-Lajoie joined with LaRue, Taché, and Casgrain in launching *Les Soirées Canadiennes*, a monthly magazine announced as a 'collection of national literature.' The motto of *Les Soirées* was a quotation from Charles Nodier, the author of the original *Trilby*, 'Let us hasten to tell the delightful tales of the people, before they have been forgotten,' and the magazine sought to record the folklore of the pre-literary period in Quebec. LaRue was a man after Gérin-Lajoie's heart: a great popularizer of scientific knowledge who applied on his Ile d'Orléans farm the theories he taught at the university and expounded in a series of manuals for the common man; an intellectual who nonetheless shared Gérin-Lajoie's cult of the *habitant* as the best type of French Canadian. LaRue and Taché contributed folksongs and popular legends to the magazine, thus continuing the vein opened by Abbé Casgrain in 1860 with his *Légendes Canadiennes*, which recounted old Canadian customs. Taché's specialty was the life of the lumberjacks and the tall tales told in their shanties (*chantiers*); while LaRue devoted himself to the *habitants* of his beloved Ile d'Orléans and Casgrain, the heir of an old seigneurial family of the Lower St. Lawrence, romanticized the rich folklore of that region. Under such influences Gérin-Lajoie wrote his *Jean Rivard, le défricheur*, which appeared in *Les Soirées* during 1862.

Gérin-Lajoie himself called this work 'a little tale which will scarcely please the young literary men, but which I have written for the public good.'[40] He was impelled by love of his country and concern for the future of the French Canadians to preach a return to the land, and the necessity of hard work and frugality guided by education. He evoked the great tradition of French-Canadian history in his epic of young Jean Rivard, who having finished his studies and having little capital beyond his robust health, his love of independence and of outdoor life, and a desire to serve his country, rejects the usual alternatives of seeking his fortune in the city or of emigrating to the States, and undertakes the hard life of a colonist in the wilderness of the Eastern Townships. Here Jean Rivard, with the aid of a single companion, clears a farm for himself, and establishes a home for his sweetheart. Thanks to his example, a new parish is born and an outlet is established for the surplus population of the old settlements along the St. Lawrence, from which a significant number of young men were already in the 1860's beginning to drift away to the mill towns of New England, there to be absorbed into the American melting pot and lost to French Canada. Gérin-Lajoie's book is at once a colonist's guide, an inspirational sermon, and a sociological treatise.

It is not a conventional novel, as the foreword makes clear: 'This is not a romance, and if anyone seeks marvellous adventures, duels, murders, suicides, or amorous intrigues, no matter how uncomplicated, I advise him in friendly fashion to seek them elsewhere. In this tale will be found only the true and simple history of a young man without fortune, born to a humble state, who knew how to raise himself by his own merit to an independent position and the first honors of his country.'[41] But despite Gérin-Lajoie's abandonment of the whole apparatus of romantic fiction, then the delight of the French-Canadian élite, the author's passionate sincerity and his ability to give an epic quality to his account of his hero's struggle with the wilderness made the book at once a classic. Far better than *Charles Guérin*, it succeeded in accomplishing the author's purpose of 'encouraging our Canadian youth to turn towards the agricultural career, instead of encumbering the professions of lawyer, notary, and doctor and the counters of merchants, as it increasingly does, to the great detriment of the public and national interest.'[42]

It met with such popularity that Gérin-Lajoie was urged to continue the tale, which he did in *Jean Rivard, économiste*, published in *Le Foyer canadien* (an offshoot of *Les Soirées*) in 1864. The second part of this epic of colonization carries on the history of Rivard's settlement as it develops into a prosperous town, while the hero becomes in turn mayor, militia major, justice of the peace, and finally member of parliament, from which exalted dignity he finally retires in order to find happiness again on his own land, after revealing the secrets of his success and laying down the principles of successful colonization. More clearly than in the first book, Jean Rivard is revealed as Gérin-Lajoie himself, no farmer but an intellectual in love with rural life. The author thus established a literary vein which was to be worked and reworked by many French-Canadian leaders in later generations, urban intellectuals themselves but sincerely convinced that the salvation of their people lay in the land. *Jean Rivard* remains essential reading today for those who would understand the French-Canadian mind, with its distrust of the urban industrial civilization of the rest of the continent, which it cannot reconcile with its own patriarchal rural tradition.

8

The role of Octave Crémazie in launching the Patriotic School of Quebec has been somewhat overshadowed by the fact that bankruptcy forced him into exile in 1862, just as the movement got well under way, while his colleague Abbé Casgrain remained in Quebec and became the leading spirit of the group and finally its historian. But Crémazie really shares with Garneau the fatherhood of French-Canadian literature, and the slim body of his work constitutes one of its cornerstones. Casgrain, who maintained a correspondence with the exiled poet which reveals how great Crémazie's influence was upon his own critical ideas, and finally collected and published Crémazie's works in 1882, under the auspices of the *Institut Canadien*, himself judged that 'No one had a greater part in the literary awakening of 1860 than he.'[43]

Crémazie was descended from a Languedoc forebear who came to Canada in 1759, in the last days of New France. This heritage, in a land where genealogy is taken with tremendous seriousness, may have had something to do with the poet's preoccupation with the theme of faithfulness to France. Befriended as a student at Laval by the Abbé Jean Holmes, the great Vermont-born educational reformer and preacher of Quebec in the 1830's and 1840's, Crémazie early became a dweller in the world of ideas, as familiar with English, German, Italian, and Spanish literature as with French, and even learning Sanskrit. Of necessity he earned his living in the family bookstore, which after 1846 served the Upper Town of Quebec as a storehouse for the French Romantic writers of the school of 1830. His mind was less concerned with trade than with his studies and with the Hugoesque verses which he composed mentally, long before he put them on paper. In later years he regretted the way of life which had been forced upon him by the impossibility of earning a living in Canada as an intellectual, and complained bitterly that it had made him 'a bad merchant and a mediocre poet.'[44] But it is clear from Casgrain's biographical account that the attraction of Crémazie's astonishing erudition drew the literary men of Quebec to the dim backroom of the bookstores where this poet, physically disguised as a stolid bourgeois with 'all the virtues of an epitaph,'[45] held forth to his chosen friends, and made of the casual circle a coherent literary group.

Crémazie published his first verses in 1854, hymning the Anglo-French alliance in the Crimean War as an example for Canadians, 'children of these two races of which the whole world bears the noble traces.'[46] With ardent patriotism, he opposed annexationism and proclaimed that the French Canadians would revive the memory of Chateauguay and support the British flag if their country should be threatened by American ambition. In August of the following year, during the goodwill visit of the corvette *La Capricieuse*, which brought the French flag to the St. Lawrence for the first time since the Conquest, Crémazie wrote his 'Vieux Soldat Canadien,' one of his best known and most typical poems. It is based upon a legend of an old soldier of Montcalm who, remaining confident until his death that France would return to Canada, had visited the ramparts of Quebec during the great days of Napoleon, awaiting the sight of the French flag in the river, and had died expressing his belief that his son would see the great day when the French came back. Crémazie imagines this veteran and all the old Canadians roused from their graves by the sound of French cannon, and welcoming the display of the French flag from the ramparts of Quebec. In a final address to the sailors of *La Capricieuse*, the poet urges them to report that the Canadians had cherished the memory of France and conserved their heritage; that their heart still belonged to France, if their allegiance was to England.

It was long a carefully nourished legend in Quebec that the visit of *La Capricieuse* marked the resumption of cultural relations with France for the first time since the Conquest, and that romanticism then first crossed the seas and began to supplant the classicism of the eighteenth century French-Canadian tradition. This theory has been completely demolished by a close study of the French-Canadian press after 1800, which reveals that most of the Romantic authors and their books were well known in Canada only a few years after they made their mark in France. Rousseau was read in Canada as early as 1795; Bernardin de Saint-Pierre, the author of *Paul et Virginie*, as early as 1802; Chateaubriand by 1817; Béranger as early as 1829. Lamartine's and Victor Hugo's poems were first offered for sale in Canada in 1837, and the former, with his love of the country and his cult of the native heath, became the most popular of the Romantics with the French Canadians, and almost an obsession by the 1850's. The novels of Hugo, George Sand, the elder Dumas, Eugène Sue, and even Balzac were imported by the booksellers of Montreal and Quebec within a few years, and in some cases a few months, after their appearance at Paris.

It is true that the book-buying public in Canada was not large; but the Romantic authors reached a much greater audience, since they were put under contribution by the editors of the Canadian newspapers, which were also literary reviews. Lamartine and Victor Hugo were to be found in the pages of *La Minerve* by 1829 and 1831; Lamartine and Chateaubriand in *Le Canadien* by 1834. The editors picked and chose their selections carefully to avoid wounding the pious susceptibilities of their readers: the more indecorous features of Romanticism were slighted. French and French-Canadian literature were mingled from the outset. The youthful verses of Garneau appeared side by side with those of the great Romantics in the pages of Parent's *Le Canadien*, which more than any other newspaper of the period encouraged Canadian writers. In the 1840's the journals were full of Chateaubriand, Lamartine, and Hugo, as well as translations of Walter Scott; and in the late 1850's the early verses of Crémazie and Pamphile Lemay rubbed shoulders with those of their avowed masters.

The visit of *La Capricieuse*, then, did not introduce Romanticism to Canada, where since 1800 the authors most in demand in the bookstores had been, in order of popularity, Voltaire, Bossuet,

Bourdaloue, Fénelon, Fléchier, Massillon, Molière, Racine, La Fontaine, Corneille, Madame de Sévigné, Boileau, Rousseau, Bernardin de Saint-Pierre, and Chateaubriand; and where La Fontaine, Lamartine, Rousseau, Chateaubriand, Béranger, Voltaire, Bernardin de Saint-Pierre, and Victor Hugo, in that order, were most often pillaged by editors seeking to enrich their journals with borrowed jewels.[47] But *La Capricieuse* did bring to Canada a noteworthy collection of French books and pictures, with which Louis Napoleon endowed the *Instituts Canadiens* of Quebec, Montreal, and Ottawa, founded in 1847, 1844, and 1852. Thus the masterpieces of modern French literature were made available to a much larger audience than the small number who could afford to buy the books for themselves.

The coming of *La Capricieuse* and the great public demonstrations which everywhere greeted its captain, the Commandant de Belvèze, also ended the coldness which had existed between the ancient mother country and its former colony ever since the French Revolution. A distrust of the new France had been instilled into the French-Canadian mind by the considerable number of emigré clergy who settled in Quebec after the Revolution; and this distrust, coupled with the ultramontane tradition established in the days of Bishop Laval, had tended to make Rome rather than Paris the intellectual capital of French Canada. The Revolution of 1848, despite its influences upon the largely discredited Papineau and his disciples among the young republican *Rouges* of *L'Avenir* and *Le Pays*, did little to alter the sentiments of the masses, carefully guided by their conservative monarchist leaders, both lay and clerical. But the Anglo-French Alliance of 1854, sealed by the exchange of state visits by Queen Victoria and Louis Napoleon in 1855, opened a new era of good feeling between the ancient and modern mother countries of Canada.

Louis Napoleon, whose North American imperialism was to develop six years later into the tragic Mexican adventure of Maximilian, took the opportunity thus afforded to open relations with French Canada. These relations were professedly commercial, but Commandant de Belvèze was ordered not only to report on 'the commerce, transport, agriculture, and industry' of French Canada, but also on 'the political, moral, religious, and military situation'[48] of the country. The only portion of this report which has ever been made public was de Belvèze's description of his reception; and considering the coolness which developed between the British authorities in Canada and de Belvèze, resulting in his reprimand by the French government at the request of London, it is possible that de Belvèze revealed the ambitions of his imperial master a little too clearly while in Canada.[49] Old seadogs are not the best diplomats—the commandant found making speeches to an English governor and a French and Catholic people 'an acrobat's job' —and in any case de

Belvèze's reception was so enthusiastic as to excuse some indiscretion. His role was made more difficult by the appearance of J.-G. Barthe's *Le Canada reconquis par la France* (Paris, 1855), with a preface by Enre de Carondel suggesting the cession of Quebec to France.

De Belvèze's own description of his visit, written to a friend in France from Cape Breton Island on his homeward voyage, is a curious document, revealing a cynicism which contrasts strangely with Crémazie's impassioned idealization of his mission:

Capricieuse, Sidney, Aug. 29, 1855.

My dear friend:

As you will not be obliged to answer this letter, I am pleased to recall myself to your memory and that of your good family, and to give you some details of my strange peregrinations. First of all, we are well, I as well as Waresquiel, and I think, with God's help, that towards the month of November favoring winds will bring us safe and sound to our beautiful France, the finest country in the world.

I arrive from Canada where I have made the most marvellous journey which can be described. Imagine the banner of France reappearing after a century's absence in our ancient colony and finding there the memory and the love of the old mother country dormant at the bottom of men's hearts, and the explosion of this sentiment bursting out everywhere, even among the English population, which, thanks to the alliance, also had to celebrate by frantic hurrahs the arrival of the representative of 'the mighty ally of their gracious sovereign' (such was their expression for your humble friend). Thus I made a princely progress across 800 leagues of rivers, lakes, and railroads, passing under I know not how many triumphal arches, finding night and day the civic fathers awaiting me at the entrance of their towns, address in hand, and finding myself, poor wretch, obliged to reply to all that by *beautiful* and *good* speeches that later must be paraphrased mercilessly at banquets, in toasts, etc., etc. What an excessive outlay of oratory I made in these three weeks!! Twenty addresses to reply to, more than fifty speeches to make, one of them on the Champs de Mars (at Montreal) before 10,000 people, while mounted on a carriage like Mangin of comic memory, and all to the accompaniment of saluting cannons, fireworks, etc. If I did not die of indigestion, I was apt to die of vanity; happily my stomach and my common sense saved me from both fates. When I read to Madame de Waresquiel the hyperbole-stuffed articles of the newspapers of Saint-Pierre with regard to my august person, I count on giving her one of those laughing fits with which I used to supply her in my best days. The fact is that I fulfilled there, as one of these worthy journals said, the function of a sovereign who visits his states, and I assure you it is a gruelling profession, and that I prefer that of the Parisian bourgeois.

I went from Quebec to Niagara Falls, following always the waterways; I returned by the river, descending the rapids, a marvellous spectacle of which one will never get an idea in Europe. I even descended one of the great rapids of the Saint-Maurice in a birchbark canoe, like an Iroquois. It would take a book to tell you the details of this marvellous voyage, and I have the materials with which to spin yarns to you during many evenings. I hope that your uncle will take some interest in these accounts, so different from what may be seen in our country. I have had an unhoped success from the political and commercial point of view, and I return from this country, where antagonisms always grate upon one another, without having indisposed anyone, a feat of which the difficulty was such that no one believed it could be accomplished. But, my very dear friend, no one is a prophet in his own country, and while here one exclaims, 'Fortunate France, which possesses such men!' (always hyperbole), at home batches of rear-admirals have been named and I am left aside. What's to be done? I have now behind me enough proof so that no one, not even myself, has the right to consider me an idiot. If then the Navy does not wish to make anything of me, or do anything for me, one must console oneself for it with: *Exegi monumentum* . . . I can do no more than rest on my laurels.[50]

The Commandant de Belvèze flattered himself somewhat unduly on the success of his mission, at least in one respect, for the U.E.L.-minded governor-general, Sir Edmund Walker Head, took offence at the enthusiasm which the visitor evoked among the French Canadians, and his protests to London had the effect of ruining de Belvèze's career. Crémazie flayed the governor's attitude in his poem 'Sur les Ruines de Sébastopol,' written at the close of the year, which hymned the Anglo-French victory in the Crimea and poured out an extravagant eulogy to France, 'home of glory and land of genius,'[51] whose joys and sorrows were always echoed on the shores of the St. Lawrence by her ever faithful sons. It is clear that the governor-general fell into the error, so frequently repeated since by ultra-loyal English Canadians, of taking the French Canadians' professions of sympathy with France too seriously and of conceiving that they were more French than Canadian. De Belvèze urged his government to cultivate 'the remains of our nationality, not with an intent of absorption and conquest, but in the interest of our political and commercial relations,' but he thought independence or annexation would drown French-Canadian nationality. The France to which French Canadians profess loyalty perished in 1789, but the language barrier and the long survival of both French and British cultural colonialism in Canada have encouraged mistaken notions about the Frenchness of French Canada.

The true nature of French-Canadian faithfulness to France is revealed clearly in Crémazie's later work, which owed much of its inspiration to Garneau. It is best exemplified in his most famous poem, 'Le Drapeau de Carillon,'[52] which tells of an old soldier of Montcalm's who cherished the white banner of Louis XV's France, after 'the Canadian heroes had been betrayed but not conquered,' and bore it to Versailles, in the hope of persuading the 'weak Bourbon' to come to the aid of his lost colony. But the Voltairean-minded courtiers asked of what value 'some acres of snow' were to the king, whose sole devotion was to pleasure; and the old soldier returned sorrowfully homeward, seeking his last resting place on the hill of Caril-lon (Ticonderoga), where he planted once more the banner which had there won eternal glory. In a powerful closing passage Crémazie hymned the old French flag as 'a living witness of the glorious exploits of a warrior race' and 'the radiant relic of a great epoch,' around which the French Canadians should rally, with the sacred tradition of its memories ruling their hearts and guarding their tongue and their faith from all attacks.

In another poem written in the same year (1858) on Canada, Crémazie formulates the French Canadian's love of his own land, on whose enchanted shores France had left an immortal mark. This lyric closes with a significant expression of French-Canadian isola-tionism:

> Happy he who knows this land, happier he who inhabits it,
> And, never leaving to seek other climes
> The shores of the great river where fortune placed him,
> Knows how to live and to die where his fathers sleep. [53]

Crémazie might eulogize Napoleon in 'Un Soldat de l'Empire,' but it was as the hero who revived the great tradition of France in the days of Louis XIV's empire. As the poet's talent developed, he displayed a growing fondness for Canadian themes, turning from them only occasionally, as when he hailed French intervention in behalf of the Papacy in the Italian Revolution of 1859-60. His only two poems not devoted to his favorite themes of love of Canada and faithfulness to France are the melancholy 'Les Morts' and the morbid unfinished 'Promenade de Trois Morts,' which is more reminiscent of Théophile Gautier than of Victor Hugo, Crémazie's chosen model.

9

In the fall of 1862 financial catastrophe forced the poet-bookseller to flee to France. He wrote no poetry there, save a few occasional verses in honor of Hector Bossange, a former Montreal bookseller, and his wife, who befriended the exile, broken in both mental and physical health. But from time to time Crémazie wrote Abbé Casgrain, who sought him out when visiting Paris and once found employment for him as Parkman's copyist in the archives. [54] These letters constitute a notable literary testament which has been too much neglected. Writing to his mother and his brothers, Crémazie expressed his homesickness and his disillusionment with the France which he had hymned so lovingly while in Canada. He found the French peasant far less fortunate than the *habitant* of Quebec; he thought the expedients of Louis Napoleon's opposition would be ridiculous in America, where there was freedom of assembly and of the press; though he judged that the eloquence of Thiers put that of the Canadian orators into the shade. In 1870 he remained confident almost to the end that France would overcome the Prussians— it is interesting to note that he thought that through religious bias England and even the French Protestants favored Protestant Prussia, and that the conquest of Catholic France would be 'the beginning of the end of the Latin race.'[55] He kept a 'Journal of the Siege of Paris' which bears witness to his gradual disillusionment in France's military might, and closes with the hope that, this hard lesson learned, it might once more be possible to speak of *Gesta Dei per Francos*.*[56]

With the establishment of the Commune at Paris in 1871, Crémazie completely lost his faith in the French. He considered them degenerate: 'Without religious beliefs, without fixed political principles, having respect neither for family or woman, having abused all material possessions during the twenty years of the Empire, which was an epoch of well being and richness previously unknown in the country, the French have lost all which constitutes the strength and honor of a country, all, even to the love of country.'[57] When his brother in Quebec informed him that a political charge of gallicanism had been made against the law faculty of Laval, he replied with bitterness: 'Here it is "liberty"; at home it is "true principles" which aid the ambitious to rise to power.' He found himself agreeing with Louis Veuillot that 'the immortal principles of '89 have caused more harm to humanity than all the tyrants whose names are consecrated by history to the malediction of their peoples'; and he vowed that if Louis XIV 'of despotic memory' should return to earth, he himself would cry with all his strength: 'Long live the great king! Down with liberty!' Like a true French Canadian, he was a monarchist sympathetic to republican principles, a contradiction in terms which can only be explained by the course of British constitutional development in Canada.

In his correspondence with Abbé Casgrain, Crémazie wrote the first noteworthy French-Canadian literary criticism. His critical sense was better developed than that of the enthusiastic propagandist of the Patriotic School of Quebec; and he was personally familiar, in a way that the socially-privileged Abbé could not be, with the obstacles which beset the path of the French-Canadian writer. He deplored the tendency evident in *Le Foyer Canadien* to print only established French-Canadian writers, and to give place to well known French authors instead of encouraging unknown young Canadians. When Casgrain published an ardent article on the literary movement in Canada, Crémazie checked him with some sober reflections:

* 'God's great deeds are done by the French.'

MM. Garneau and Ferland have already, it is true, supplied a granite base for our literary edifice; but if one bird does not make a spring, two books do not constitute a literature. All that has been produced by us, beyond these two great works, seems to me to have no chance of survival. Who will read ———— in fifty years? And if I may speak of myself, who will think of my poor verses in twenty years?

We have then only two noteworthy works, the monuments raised by MM. Garneau and Ferland. In poetry, in fiction, we have only second-class works. Tragedy, the drama, are still to be born. The cause of this inferiority lies not in the rarity of men of talent, but in the disastrous environment provided for the writer by the indifference of a population which has as yet no taste for letters, at least for works produced by native sons.

Canadian writers are placed in the same situation as those of the Middle Ages. Their pens, unless they engage in politics (and God knows the sort of literature that we owe to the tirades of political pundits), cannot suffice for their least needs. When a young man leaves college, his greatest ambition is to have his prose or his verse inserted in some journal. On the day that he first sees his name emblazoned at the foot of an article of his making, he believes himself called to the highest destinies; and he dreams that he is the equal of Lamartine, if he devotes himself to poetry; of Balzac, if he has attempted the novel. And when he passes under St. John's Gate, he takes good care to bend, lest he bump his head. These foolish vanities of youth soon vanish before the daily cares of life. Perhaps he continues to work for a year or two; then one day his voice is silent. The need of gaining his daily bread has imposed upon him the harsh necessity of devoting his life to certain arid occupations, which will blight in him the sweet flowers of the imagination and break the intimate and delicate fibers of poetic sensibility. How many of your young talents have produced flowers which promised magnificent fruit; but their fate has been like those of certain fruits of the earth. A frost came which chilled forever the fire of their intelligence. This wintry wind which freezes sparkling spirits is the *res angusta domi* of which Horace speaks; it is the need of daily bread.

Under such conditions it is a misfortune to have received from heaven a portion of the divine fire. Since one cannot earn one's living by the ideas which boil in one's brain, one must seek employment, which is nearly always contrary to one's tastes. The most usual result is that one becomes a bad employee and a bad writer. Permit me to cite myself as an example. If I had not received at birth, at least the taste, if not the talent, for poetry, I should not have had my head stuffed with fancies which made me enter upon commerce as a means of existence, never as a serious end in life. I should have broken myself in entirely to business, and today I should have an assured future. Instead of that, what has happened? I have been a bad merchant and a mediocre poet.[58]

Crémazie criticized Casgrain for virtually giving away *Les Soirées Canadiennes*, while the review's writers went unpaid. He insisted upon the necessity of the artist being properly rewarded for his work, and urged the foundation of a joint stock company to underwrite a magazine which would pay its authors decently until it was established in the popular taste. He pointed out that capital was constantly poured into enterprises which were much more risky, and which lacked the merit 'of contributing to preserve our tongue, the second guardian of our nationality, since religion is the first.'[59] He singled out the lack of French-Canadian literary criticism, then represented only by the same sort of logrolling as was the lot of the hatter or dressmaker who bribed an editor. In urging Casgrain to deal out condemnation as well as praise when writing of French-Canadian literature, he observed: 'No one is better gifted than you to create literary criticism in Canada.' He summed up his views with the reflection that 'so long as our writers find themselves in the same situation as at present, Canada can indeed have, as in the past, literary accidents from time to time, but she will not have a national literature.'

In another letter Crémazie was roused to reflections on French-Canadian society by Casgrain's news that Les Soirées Canadiennes' circulation had dwindled to a few hundreds, while Le Foyer had had two thousand subscribers to start with. He denounced Quebec's 'society of grocers.'[60] By this term he meant the professional men whose intellectual interests were limited to their profession, for whom knowledge was only a tool: 'In such natures petrified by routine, thought has no horizon. For them, French literature does not exist after the eighteenth century.' The masterpieces of foreign literatures were completely unknown and of no concern to them; how should they be interested in an infant literature?

Patriotism should perhaps take the place of a taste for letters in influencing them to encourage all which tends to preserve the language of their fathers. Alas, you know as well as I that our 'wealthy and educated gentlemen' understand love of their country only when it appears in the form of railroad and goldmining shares promising fat dividends; or again when it offers the prospect of political honors, appointments, and above all chances for 'jobs.' With such men you will make good fathers, having all the virtues of an epitaph; you will have aldermen, churchwardens, members of parliament, even ministers, but you will never succeed in creating a society which may be called literary, artistic, and I may even say patriotic, in the fine and larger sense of the word.[61]

As proof of his conclusion, Crémazie pointed out that in his bookselling days it was not these pillars of society but a few students and young priests who bought works of real value and devoted their slim savings to the masterpieces of literature. It seemed to him that there was nothing to do but await better days; and he suggested that the neglected young poet Fréchette might well paraphrase Musset and write: 'I have come too soon into too young a country.'[62]

Though Crémazie thought himself finished as a poet at 39, he deplored the absence of Fréchette, Lemay, and Alfred Garneau, the poet son of the historian, from the pages of *Le Foyer*; and he criticized the custom of devoting each number to a single work instead of to a variety of material, although he praised Ferland's historical studies, Gérin-Lajoie's *Jean Rivard*, and Casgrain's biography of Garneau, which were thus published, as worthy of appearance in the great European reviews. He urged Casgrain not to fill up his pages, in default of native talent, with secondary, if doctrinally sound French writers; suggesting that it was better to let his readers suck the marrow bones of such 'lions' as Hugo, Musset, Gautier, Sainte-Beuve, Guizot, and Merimée, than those of such 'hares as' the Vicomte Walsh, the darling of the Bourbon-minded Faubourg Saint-Germain.[63]

In a noteworthy passage he treated the difficulties which beset the development of French-Canadian letters:

The more I reflect on the destiny of Canadian literature, the less chance I find for its leaving a mark in history. Canada lacks its own language. If we spoke Iroquois or Huron, our literature would live. Unfortunately we speak and write, after a sufficiently pitiful fashion, it is true, the language of Bossuet and Racine. Say or do what we will, we will always remain only a simple colony from the literary point of view; and even if Canada became an independent country and made her flag shine in the sun of nations, we should remain nonetheless simple literary colonials. Look at Belgium, which speaks the same tongue as us. Is there a Belgian literature? Unable to compete with France in beauty of form, Canada might have conquered a place among the literatures of the old world, if among her sons had been found a writer capable of initiating Europe, before Fenimore Cooper, to the grandeur of our forests, to the legendary exploits of our trappers and voyageurs. Today, even if a talent as powerful as that of the author of *The Last of the Mohicans* were revealed among us, his works would produce no sensation in Europe, for he would commit the irreparable wrong to be second, that is, too late. I repeat, if we spoke Huron or Iroquois, the works of our writers would attract the attention of the old world. This masculine and nervous language, born in the forests of America, would have the native poetry which delights the foreigner. One would be overcome by admiration for a novel or a poem translated from the Iroquois, while one does not take the trouble to read a book written in French by a colonial of Quebec or Montreal. For twenty years translations of Russian, Scandinavian, and Roumanian novels have been published each year in France. If these same works had been written in French, they would not have found fifty readers.

A translation has this to be said for it, if a work does not seem to deserve its reputation, one consoles oneself with the reflection that it must be magnificent in the original.

But what does it matter, after all, that the works of Canadian authors are not destined to cross the Atlantic? Are we not a million Frenchmen forgotten by the mother country on the shores of the St. Lawrence? Is it not enough to encourage all those who hold a pen to know that this little people will grow great, and that it will always guard the name and memory of those who have aided it to conserve intact the most precious of all treasures, the tongue of its fathers?

It should be thus with the Canadian writer. Renouncing without regret the beautiful dreams of echoing glory, he should regard himself as amply rewarded for his labors if he can instruct and charm his compatriots, if he can contribute to the conservation of the old French nationality on the young soil of America.[64]

Crémazie even had the ability, very rare among poets, of being able to criticize his own work soundly. He recognized that his widely hailed 'Drapeau de Carillon' had little literary value, and owed its success to its idea rather than to its form. With bitter truth he laid down the recipe for success as a French-Canadian poet: 'Rhyme "glory" with "victory" a certain number of times, "ancestors" with "glorious," "France" with "hope"; mingle with these rhymes some sonorous words like "religion," our "fatherland," our "tongue," our "laws," the "blood of our fathers"; warm the whole over the flame of patriotism, and serve hot. Everyone will say that it is magnificent.'[65] He recognized that his unpopular 'Les Morts' was a better poem than 'Drapeau de Carillon,' but remarked that only Chauveau had singled it out for notice. He confessed his literary creed:

As for me, while admiring the masterpieces of the seventeenth century, I love with all my heart the Romantic school which has given my soul the sweetest and purest pleasures it has ever known. And still today, when melancholy enwraps my soul like a mantle of lead, the reading of a meditation of Lamartine or of a *Nuit* of Alfred de Musset give me more calm and serenity than I should find in all the tragedies of Corneille and Racine. Lamartine and Musset are men of my time . . . Romanticism, after all, is only the legitimate son of the classics; but since ideas and customs are no more in the nineteenth century what they were in the seventeenth, the Romantic school has of necessity had to adopt a form more harmonious with modern aspirations, and it is in the sixteenth century that it has sought the elements of this new form . . . We should still be obliged to raise altars to Romanticism, if it had no other merit than to have delivered us from mythology and tragedy . . . This whole war that is declared on realism is absurd. What is this monster which makes so many worthy souls wroth? It is the 1789 of literature which necessarily followed the 1789 of politics; it is all the things scorned without reason by the privileged class of the classical school, which now come to claim their place in the literary sun; and be assured it will know how to win that place just as well as the serfs and the proletarians in the political world.[66]

Despite Crémazie's protestations, Casgrain judged that the poet's patriotic verses alone were original; that such was the secret of his success and his best claim to future fame, and that he would live as the father of French-Canadian national poetry. Casgrain was a better prophet than critic, and his verdict has withstood the test of time. Because of its nationalist content, Crémazie's verse, like Garneau's history, has survived, while the work of other pioneer French-Canadian writers has fallen into neglect. In a lyric passage Casgrain recalls the tremendous impression made upon him and his fellow students by the work of the two founders of French-Canadian literature, which revived the memory of past glories and hymned the beauties of the land in which they dwelt: 'Those who then were of an age to appreciate the delights of literature can still reveal what enchantment there was in the voice of this Canadian bard, standing on the rock of Quebec, and chanting in accents sometimes sonorous and vibrant like those of a trumpet in battle and sometimes plaintive and tearful like the harp of Israel in exile, the glories and the griefs of our native land.'[67]

But despite the enthusiastic reception of Crémazie's work, only a few interested themselves in him after his flight to France, chief among them being his clerical friends of the Seminary of Quebec. A committee sought to appease his creditors so that he might return home, but its efforts came to nought, and the exiled poet drudged out his life in France in such occupations as the kindness of friends provided for him. After sixteen years of an exile which weighed heavily upon him, Crémazie died at Le Havre in 1879. His last address was the Rue Bernardin de Saint-Pierre. It was not unfitting that the father of French-Canadian romanticism should perish in a street which commemorated the author of *Paul et Virginie*.

10

The dominant figure in Canadian public life from 1855 to 1867 was George Etienne Cartier, who looked to the future rather than to the past. Though he was loyally supported in Upper Canada by John A. Macdonald, Cartier as leader of the large Lower Canadian bloc was the real head of the Macdonald-Cartier ministries which held power until 1862, and a major figure in the coalition government of 1864-7. Macdonald's own greatness became evident only at Confederation, and was not fully revealed until after the death of his colleague Cartier. From 1835 until his death Cartier played a prominent role in the great movements of his time, and took a leading part in the solution of all the great political questions after the attainment of responsible government in 1848. Cartier had greater influence in the assembly than any other political leader from 1855 to Confederation, both through his own driving energy and lobbying ability, and the weight of his well-controlled following when Upper Canadian political groups were badly split. Though Lower Canada was not much interested in the clergy reserves question, Cartier brought its support to the government in the settlement of the matter which so vexed Upper Canada; while the abolition of seigneurial tenure, the codification of Quebec law, and the judicial and administrative reforms of the period were peculiarly Cartier's achievements.

Confederation owed more to him, perhaps, than to any other single man; for without him it would have been impossible. The expansion of Canada to the West was largely his work, as was the settlement of the first Riel Rebellion and the extension of the language and school rights of the French Canadians to Manitoba in 1870; and he closed his parliamentary career, as he had opened it, by advocating the construction of railroads, the links of steel which bind Canada together. He was the third of the great line of French-Canadian statesmen, but unlike Papineau and Lafontaine, he was also a leader in the English-Canadian world, a world in which business loomed ever larger as the years passed. In the end, like so many French Canadians who have grown into a larger Canadianism, he lost much of his influence over his own people, but their debt to him is almost unreckonable.

Heredity probably played some part in Cartier's career as the first French-Canadian public man to think in economic terms and to assume a leading role in the industrial civilization which was beginning to develop in both Canada and the United States in the middle years of the nineteenth century. He was the offspring of three generations of merchants, who had successfully engaged in the import and export trade at Quebec and in the Richelieu Valley. Through his grandmother he was allied with the clergy, whose support played a vital part in his rise to political power as the golden mean between the 'no popery' Grits and the godless *Rouges*. The Cartiers had prospered so greatly in their dealings, first in salt and fish, and then in wheat, that his vivacious father, one of the founders of the Bank of Montreal and of the St. Lawrence and Lake Champlain Railway, was able to devote most of his time to pleasure and hospitality, rather than to the commercial pursuits for which he was trained. The Cartiers belonged to the comfortable merchant-*rentier* class of Quebec, living in the villages in almost as much state as the great seigneurial families but also closely tied to the *habitants*, since they were landowners as well as traders.

Young George Etienne inherited from his father only a measure of gayness and fondness for song; his business sense can be traced back to his grandfather and great-grandfather, the founders of the family fortune; while from his pious mother he derived the religious and patriotic principles which were reinforced by his education at the Sulpician Collège de Montréal. He graduated from the *collège* in 1831, and at once entered upon the study of law in the office of Edouard Rodier, the noted advocate and *Patriote* orator. Admitted to the bar in 1835, he set about the creation of a practice, though a good measure of his time was devoted to patriotic activities in this period of political agitation. He was active in the Saint-Jean-Baptiste Society founded in 1834 by Ludger Duvernay, and was its first secretary and many years later its president. His deeply patriotic 'O Canada! Mon pays! Mes Amours!' was composed especially for the first banquet of the society, and was sung on that occasion by Cartier himself.

At twenty he opened his political career by supporting Papineau and Robert Nelson in the elections of 1834. His patron Edouard Rodier took a leading role in organizing the *Fils de Liberté* early in 1837, and if Rodier was one of their favorite orators, Cartier was their bard. His 'Avant tout je suis Canadien' was the marching song of the *Fils de Liberté*, and 'Petit Georges' was a familiar figure at their reunions. With Chevalier de Lorimer, who perished on the scaffold for his part in the 1838 Rebellion, Cartier was joint secretary of the Montreal Permanent Central Committee of the *Patriotes*. When the rebellion broke out at Saint-Denis, not far from Cartier's birthplace at Saint-Antoine, he served as Wolfred Nelson's aide and distinguished himself by his courage in crossing the Richelieu under fire to bring reinforcements to the victorious *Patriotes*. After the defeat at Saint-Charles and the collapse of the Richelieu rising, Cartier took refuge with friends at Verchères, while Nelson and other leaders fled over the border to the States. A convenient rumor, whose origin is sometimes assigned to Cartier himself, got about that he had perished of cold and hunger in the woods while seeking to escape. Etienne Parent mourned his passing in *Le Canadien* thus: 'He was a young man endowed in the highest degree with qualities of heart and mind and before whom a brilliant career opened,'[68] an observation which supports Parent's reputation for prophetic foresight.

Early in 1838, when Cartier's hiding place became known, he was forced to flee over the border, joining the other refugees first at Plattsburg, N.Y., and then at Burlington, Vt., where his associate in the Saint-Jean-Baptiste Society, Ludger Duvernay, launched *Le Patriote Canadien* on August 7, 1839, and printed Papineau's brief and tendentious *Histoire de l'insurrection*. Cartier, however, returned to

Montreal after the disallowance of Durham's amnesty, which had excepted him and twenty-three other leaders of the rising, and forbidden their return to Canada under pain of capital punishment. When Robert Nelson's ill-starred 'invasion' of November roused the *Patriotes* once more, Cartier was one of those upon whose head a price was put by Colborne. But he took no part in the second rising, having perhaps been led by his lifelong Sulpician friends to see that the clergy was right in condemning opposition to the constituted authorities, a view which he later recognized as 'the only one that offered some chance of salvation for the French Canadians.'[69] Cartier never apologized for his activity in 1837; years later he held that the cause of the *Patriotes* was just, though he censured the course of the political leaders of the time. To his mind the rising 'was caused by the actions of a minority which desired to dominate the majority and exploit the government in its own interests. . . . The events of 1837 have been misinterpreted. The object of the people was rather to reduce this oppressive minority to nothingness than to bring about a separation of the province from the mother-country.'[70]

Somewhat disillusioned by his early political experiences, Cartier devoted himself to his profession after his return to Montreal, and gradually won a notable position at the bar.[71] He became a constitutional Reformer and as such a follower of Lafontaine, but he refused his leader's requests to stand for parliament in 1841 and 1844. Though he devoted his energies chiefly to attaining an independent position in his profession, he nevertheless followed politics closely, taking heart at Lafontaine's appointment as attorney-general in 1842 and campaigning in 1844 against D.-B. Viger, the onetime *Patriote* who had become a pliant tool of Sir Charles Metcalfe. As a private citizen Cartier worked for the attainment of responsible government; and after being elected as member for Verchères in 1848, he supported Lafontaine in the latter's great duel with Papineau. Like his chief, he broke with the hero of the *Patriotes*, who now opposed the Union, denounced responsible government and came out for independence.

Papineau had lost all faith in Britain and monarchical institutions; while his former disciples Lafontaine and Cartier now upheld the British connection, and fought the annexation movement supported by the Montreal merchants and Papineau's ardent young *Rouge* followers. Lafontaine was the dominant figure of the transition period, but Cartier was a man of the future. In later years he expressed his belief that 'Papineau was justified in combatting the oligarchy then in power, but I have never approved the attitude that he took with regard to commercial affairs, nor his opposition to measures fit to favor the progress of the country.'[72] It was not without significance that Cartier's first speech in parliament was in support of a petition of the St. Lawrence & Atlantic Railway Co. for public aid in the completion of its proposed line linking Montreal and the ice-free harbor of Portland, Maine. Cartier's lifelong policy was to be 'a policy of railroads,'[73] and its fulfilment assured the creation of modern Canada.

His mind ran in the same grooves as those of the progressive English Canadians of the day, although in both person and temperament he was a true French Canadian. Small of stature, vigorous and lively of manner, terse and rapid of speech, quick in retort and tireless in labor, a man who did not suffer fools gladly but could be the soul of cordiality and urbanity, gifted with a charm and gaiety which drew his political enemies to him in leisure moments, Cartier was a human chameleon whose rapid changes of mood often hid from the casual observer his basic virtues of tremendous powers of work, courage, will power, and firmness of principle.

The commercial mind which he had inherited from his merchant forbears, no doubt developed by his legal practice in Montreal during the great transition period of the St. Lawrence trade, made him from the first the parliamentary spokesman of the transportation interests. When he entered the assembly, that body was considering the question of providing funds for the completion of the Welland Canal, begun in 1837. Cartier, who had perhaps devoted more study to such matters than any other public man of the period, supported the motion strongly, attacking the shortsighted local opposition to the project in Quebec:

> It is claimed that the expense will be for the benefit of Upper Canada and will bring to its door the agricultural products of the West which travel by Lake Huron and Erie; but it will do the like for Lower Canada! It will be the same with all the routes opened to communicate with distant parts. Remember that commerce always wishes to reach the sea. In our case all must end in the St. Lawrence. The Americans understand that. They have dug the Erie Canal across the land. Shall they surpass us? Yes, since we do not wish to compete with them. Nevertheless, the thing is simple for us. I say to Mr. William Hamilton Merritt that his creation of the Welland Canal is a monument which will perpetuate his memory and I urge the House to lend a final hand to the completion of this great national work.[74]

As late as 1864, when his forecast for the Welland Canal had been realized and the project of enlarging it was under discussion, Cartier not only supported the measure but urged the opening of the Ottawa River to navigation, with a Georgian Bay canal to shorten the Chicago–Montreal route and thus to offset the proposed New York ship canal.

But Canada had the fault of launching its canal program too late, and bringing it to a conclusion just as the American railroads provided a new and more serious competition to the great waterway of Canada. Cartier was among the first in Canada to see that the coming age was to be that of the railroads. In August 1846, when Canada's sole railroad was the ten-year-old line running from Montreal to St. Johns, Cartier spoke at a public meeting in Montreal under Lafontaine's chairmanship in favor of a line linking that city with Portland. He called upon all classes to support the project as he did, by buying shares on that occasion:

In the present age it is impossible for a country to enjoy great prosperity without railways. . . . Well, let us resolve to have our railways in order to join them to those of an enterprising people separated from us by an imaginary line, by a line which becomes only too visible, alas, when we contrast our apathy and our laziness with the incessant activity, the feverish energy, and the enterprising spirit of our neighbors. The United States can serve as an example to the peoples of America and even to those of Europe. . . . I should point out also that each city which has the advantage of being the terminus of a railway sees the value of its property double; witness Buffalo, Albany, Boston, New York, Philadelphia, Baltimore, and a great many other cities. There is no doubt that the same future awaits Montreal. . . . I shall not attempt to discuss whether this railway ought to be built, for this question has been treated by those who spoke before me. I shall content myself with saying the prosperity of Montreal depends upon its position as entrepôt of the commerce of the West, that the changes in the Corn Laws have endangered this trade; and that we cannot conserve it if we do not have the best means of transport from the Western waters to the Atlantic by our canals and by this railway. . . . I then invite all those who are present to come and take shares according to their means—first of all for their own profit, and then out of patriotism, for love of our country ought to make us work for its greater prosperity. I address myself to Canadians of all origins: Americans, French, and English, let us be united and march together towards our destiny. But above all let us not blush on this occasion to take our enterprising neighbors for models. Our connection with them will have a good effect; we shall know better their customs, habits, and their civilization; we shall be in a better situation to concern ourselves with the business relations that we will consequently have with them. [75]

Again at Montreal in 1849 Cartier spoke in favor of the railway:

We have an exceptional opportunity to attract foreign capital. . . . Look what New York has done. . . . She is at the head of American trade, but to obtain this position, she has not feared to go into debt to the amount of $25,000,000. It was necessary for her to have faith in herself, in her spirit of enterprise, and to discount the future. . . . The time has come to belie our reputation as apathetic men, without energy and spirit of enterprise. Let these epithets cease to be attributed to the Canadian name . . . Montreal is destined to become the great entrepôt of the West, but without railways and canals, it will be impossible for it to attain the glorious position which will make it one of the chief centers of the continent.[76]

As a member of parliament he supported the Guarantee Act of 1849, which provided for government assistance to the Great Western, St. Lawrence & Atlantic, and the proposed Halifax & Quebec line (soon known as the Intercolonial). Again in 1851 he backed the Hincks government's project of the Grand Trunk (Lévis-Hamilton). Cartier sponsored the acts of 1852 which incorporated the Grand Trunk and provided government guarantees for it; in 1853 he fathered the bill for the Victoria Bridge at Montreal, and the Amalgamation Act which permitted the Grand Trunk to take over the local lines already constructed. Cartier was the storm-center of this legislation, which roused furious protests from the cautious and the shortsighted; but firm in his faith in this 'national enterprise,' he triumphed over all opposition. He proclaimed publicly: 'I build for the future,' and privately this jingle was often in his mouth:

> L'heure viendra. Sachons l'attendre.
> Bientôt nous pourrons la saisir.
> Le courage fait entreprendre
> Et l'adresse fait réussir.*[77]

Again in 1854–6, and 1861–2 he promoted the interests of the Grand Trunk, of which he became the legal adviser in 1853, through legislation which provided guarantees, loans, or reorganization for the great project which met with many difficulties not all unavoidable.

Cartier's public part in aiding the construction of the Grand Trunk, of which he was admittedly the solicitor in Canada East (as Lower Canada was now known), was criticized at the time and has been criticized since, but it is not always recognized that other leading members of the successive governments of the time were more intimately involved with the company than he, and that despite all criticism Cartier was maintained as chairman of the Parliamentary Railway Committee from 1852 to 1867. He was the ablest politician and the only French Canadian in the Hincks, Galt, Merritt, Watkin, Keefer, Andrews group who created Canada's rail-road system, without whose existence 'the union of British North America would have been a farce.'[78] Cartier played a notable part in increasing Canada's fifty miles of railroad in 1850 to more than 3,000 by 1869, with vast expenditures which stimulated industry, gave employment to thousands, and attracted immigration. Not

---

* The time will come. Know how to await it.
Soon we shall be able to seize it.
Courage leads to undertakings,
Cleverness makes them succeed.

only was he the strongest parliamentary supporter of the Grand Trunk and the Intercolonial schemes, but he also played a major role in the chartering of the Canadian Pacific in 1871. In fact his part in that enterprise brought on his political ruin. His interest in the development of transportation was not confined to railroads alone, for in 1860 he encouraged by a subsidy the establishment of the Allan Steamship Line, linking Quebec in summer and Portland in winter with Great Britain; and to the close of his career he remained an advocate of further development of the canal system. The communication network of modern Canada owes much to Cartier, who through the force of his leadership brought Lower Canadian support to the far-sighted projects of a few English Canadians. And without the ties which the railroads and the canals supplied between the provinces, Confederation would have been both unattainable and unworkable.

It is clear from Cartier's record in public life that he was primarily a statesman, and not, as his enemies often proclaimed, merely a spokesman of the great interests and a lobbyist. But if Papineau was an idealistic statesman who in the end was betrayed by his own idealism, Cartier was a practical politician who eventually fell victim to his practicality. Though Cartier was by temperament an autocrat who loved to exercise absolute power,[79] he knew how to restrain his political ambitions. Just as he twice refused Lafontaine's pleas to enter the assembly in the 1840's, so he twice refused cabinet posts in the Hincks-Morin government of 1851-4. He met offers of the solicitor-generalship and the commissionership of public works with the very 'Anglo-Saxon' response that the salaries were not adequate enough to justify him in abandoning his flourishing legal practice. In 1854 he was defeated by three votes for the speakership of the House as being 'too friendly to the Grand Trunk'[80] according to William Lyon Mackenzie. But though public office held no overpowering attraction for him, politics was in his blood. He took an active part in forming the alliance of the conservative Liberals of Lower Canada with the moderate Conservatives of Upper Canada in the MacNab-Morin government in that same year. And in 1855 he was induced to become provincial secretary of Lower Canada, when Etienne-Pascal Taché succeeded Morin as head of the Lower Canadian section of the ministry. While seeking the necessary new mandate from his electors of Verchères for this office, Cartier was bitterly attacked by the young *Rouges*, who regarded the conservative Liberals' alliance with the Upper Canadian Tories as a betrayal. But Cartier was re-elected by a slim margin; and launched an important program of educational reform before he became attorney-general for Canada East, when the government was reorganized as the Taché-Macdonald ministry in 1856.

The great alliance of Macdonald and Cartier as the real leaders of Upper and Lower Canada was thus formed. The fact was recognized in the following year by the reorganization of the cabinet into the Macdonald-Cartier ministry. In the elections which followed Cartier won an overpowering majority in Lower Canada, being himself triumphantly re-elected in Verchères, though he lost the Montreal seat which he also contested. Macdonald was left in a minority in Upper Canada and thus dependent upon his colleague for the survival of the government of which he was the titular head. Until Confederation Macdonald had neither the support nor the influence which Cartier wielded in the assembly. Their government fell on July 28, 1858 when the Upper Canadian Liberal George Brown carried an anti-government motion against the adoption of Ottawa as the capital. The Brown-Dorion government which succeeded resigned on August 4 after a vote of non-confidence in the assembly, and Cartier was called to the prime ministership, with virtually the same cabinet as had held office under the Macdonald-Cartier regime.

This government took office on August 6, with the ministers exchanging portfolios, in order to avoid the necessity of seeking re-election under an act of the previous year. The following day, in what became known as the 'double-shuffle,' they resumed their old offices. This somewhat dubious proceeding, inspired by Macdonald, was frankly admitted by Cartier in the assembly to be designed 'to meet the requirements of the law and at the same time to prevent any unnecessary elections.'[81] The incident reveals Cartier's mastery of practical politics, for the government so questionably born was sustained against the objections of the opposition and had no difficulty in finding support for its program. Two notable items of its policy were the encouragement and protection of native industry and the consideration of a federal union of British North America. To Cartier's government belongs the distinction of first proposing administrative action on these two major matters, which A. T. Galt had made conditions of his entrance into the cabinet. Cartier showed such vigor and ability as prime minister that his government held office for nearly four years, an unusually long term in this disordered period of Canadian politics.

Though Cartier immediately took action on the question of Confederation, going to England that fall with Galt and John Ross to confer with the imperial authorities on the matter, that initiative bore no immediate fruit in the face of the apathy of the Maritimes. It was otherwise with other government measures. The future seat of government was fixed at Ottawa, thanks to Cartier's insistence, and A. T. Galt's protective tariff was adopted. Cartier's proposal of 1857, as attorney-general, of a measure for the codification of the civil law and civil procedure of Lower Canada was implemented by the formation in 1859 of a committee of jurists to perform the task, which was finally completed in 1864. At the same session in which this notable project was launched, Cartier had also sponsored legislation for judicial decentralization, the freer institution of new parishes, and the introduction of French civil law into the Eastern Townships, thus unifying the legal system of Quebec. And in 1859 Cartier passed the final measure in the long struggle to extinguish seigneurial tenure in Lower Canada, a struggle in which he had been active since 1850. Though credit for this reform belongs chiefly to Lafontaine and Lewis Thomas Drummond, Cartier took a prominent part in the final stages. The temper of his mind is well revealed by his comment when reviewing the whole question in April 1859: 'It has been said that the feudal system introduced by the kings of France, and later modified by special law, greatly contributed to assure the settlement of the country. I believe so, but this institution has had its day, and we have the satisfaction of being able to suppress it without the least trouble or the least effusion of blood.'[82] Here Cartier's essential conservatism and sense of tradition, coupled with a progressive outlook and a strong faith in gradual rather than revolutionary reform, are made clear.

Cartier's firmness in defending the rights of his own people, despite the fact that many of them regarded him as a traitor, is revealed by his vigorous opposition to the Upper Canadian Liberals' demand for representation by population. Like Lafontaine, Cartier held that the Union Act of 1840 was a compact or treaty whose basis could not be changed.[83] When the Union was established, each province had been given equal representation in the legislature, despite the fact that Lower Canada then had 600,000 inhabitants to Upper Canada's 400,000. This measure had been approved by English Canadians, though it had aroused much dissatisfaction among French Canadians. In 1852 the population of Upper Canada first surpassed that of the lower province, and agitation in favor of representation according to population was immediately launched in Upper Canada. This movement, whose most vigorous leader was the radical Liberal, or 'Clear Grit,' George Brown, grew rapidly. In 1856 it received the support of Antoine-Aimé Dorion, the chief of the Lower Canadian radicals, though he preferred formation of a federal union of the Canadas to reform of the existing order. In 1859 a great Reform Convention was held at Toronto, and a resolution was adopted to the effect that the Union was a failure and that only a government based upon 'Rep by Pop' would be acceptable to the people of Upper Canada. Appeals to London and even to Washington were threatened by the more hotheaded leaders. The agitation was stimulated by the revelation of the 1861 census that Upper Canada now had 300,000 more population than Lower Canada.

Cartier had fought the 'Rep by Pop' movement from the beginning, involving himself in many bitter brushes with George Brown, who spared neither French Canada nor its leaders in his attacks upon the government. In reply to the latter's war cry of 'No French domination,' Cartier observed in 1861: 'The Union in my view rests on the principle that the two provinces coexist with equal powers, and that neither should dominate over the other in parliament.'[84] Again he remarked: 'Lower Canada and Upper Canada are united by the St. Lawrence, by railways and canals, and each of the two sections is absolutely necessary to the prosperity of the other. I feel no hostile sentiment towards anyone; I am ready to render justice to Upper Canada as well as to Lower Canada, in maintaining the Union.'[85] He was already envisaging a greater confederation, but until it should be achieved, he believed in continuing the Union on the basis of equality. In this policy he was loyally supported by Macdonald, who had outgrown his youthful devotion to the rabid sectionalism of Sir Allan MacNab.

The Cartier government successfully resisted the Liberals' effort to make representation by population a panacea for Canada's ills and survived the bitter party warfare of the 1861 session, only to fall in May 1862 on the question of the reorganization of the militia system. The outbreak of the American Civil War and the *Trent* incident of 1861,[86] with its threat of a war between Great Britain and the United States which would probably be fought in Canada, caused the government to bring in a bill providing for an active force of 50,000 men and the expenditure of a million dollars. This measure, sponsored by Macdonald, was defeated by a majority of seven, with thirty-seven of the fifty-eight Lower Canadian members voting against it. Cartier for the first time thus lost the support of his province, with many of his closest followers objecting to the measure on the grounds of its cost. The ministry resigned, with Cartier consoling them with the face-saving reflection that 'we fall on a measure designed for the protection and defense of our country, a measure which we believe necessary to put Canadians in a state to enjoy freely their political institutions beneath the glorious flag of Old England.'[87] They were succeeded by the moderate Liberal government of John Sandfield Macdonald and Louis-V. Sicotte. This ministry survived reorganization in the following year as the Macdonald-Dorion government, only to collapse in March 1864. A Liberal-Conservative ministry was then formed under the leadership of Etienne-Pascal Taché and John A. Macdonald, but it lasted only three months.

The old double-majority system of the Union had completely broken down; four ministries had fallen in three years, two general elections had been held, and the parties still remained deadlocked with none able to maintain itself in office. Canada's constitutional difficulties were no nearer a solution, and all British North America feared that the massed strength of the Union Army might be turned against her after the defeat of the Confederacy, with which Great Britain and Canada had actively sympathized. The Confederate raid on the town of St. Albans, Vermont, from a Montreal base, and the freeing of the participants after their arrest upon their return to Canada, awoke a wave of resentment in the North. The consequent war talk caused Henry Adams to write from London, where he was aiding his father in the American Legation, 'This Canadian business is suddenly found to be serious, and the prospect of Sherman marching down the St. Lawrence and Farragut sailing up it, doesn't just seem agreeable.'[88] Cartier, as attorney-general for Canada East, handled this delicate international case with great adroitness. But in February 1865, Bennett's *New York Herald* was calling for annexation: 'Peaceably if possible, forcibly if necessary.'

At this crucial moment George Brown startled everyone by combining forces with John A. Macdonald and Cartier in a coalition government under the neutral leadership of Taché. The coalition's purpose was to bring about Confederation as soon as possible. Brown paid public tribute to the part played by Cartier in making possible this alliance with his opponent of fifteen years' standing. Meanwhile New Brunswick, Nova Scotia, and Prince Edward Island had determined to hold a convention at Charlottetown in September to consider a union of the Maritime Provinces. This movement was British in origin, and it aimed both at strengthening the Maritimes against Canadian 'aggression' and increasing their bargaining power. For the leading spirit was Charles Tupper of Nova Scotia, who foresaw a union of all British North America in the not distant future. To Charlottetown the Canadian government sent a delegation composed of Macdonald, Cartier, Brown, Galt, D'Arcy McGee, Hector Langevin, William McDougall, and Alexander Campbell. Macdonald, supported by Cartier and Brown, proposed to the convention the advantages of a union of all the British North American Provinces. After two days the Canadian delegation retired, urging that the convention should suspend consideration of a Maritime union and adjourn to Quebec to consider the broader scheme.

This plan was adopted, and the Quebec Conference met on October 10, 1864, under the presidency of Sir Etienne Taché, the prime minister of Canada. The other French-Canadian delegates were Cartier, Langevin, and Jean-Charles Chapais. The meeting was held behind closed doors, and the minutes are scant, and un-satisfactory. But it is clear that Cartier played a major role in the gathering as the representative of Lower Canada, which numbered more than a third of the total population of the proposed con-federation and which was the essential geographical and economic link in the scheme. It was Cartier, as the spokesman of French-Canadian particularism, who determined the initial decision that the union should take a federal rather than a legislative form. Macdonald, who presented to the conference an outline of the contemplated federation, himself favored a legislative union. But in discussion of the subject he found that both Lower Canada and the Maritimes wished to preserve their separate individualities, and so a federal union was decided upon. Macdonald carried his point, however, by following Galt's idea of 1858 in reserving to the federal government all powers not specifically granted to the separate provinces, so that in theory the Canadian federation was the exact opposite of the American one, then racked by civil war fought in the name of states' rights. In American constitutional terms Mac-donald was a Hamiltonian, while Cartier was a Jeffersonian, as far as provincial autonomy and minority rights were concerned.

Cartier succeeded in establishing Quebec as the pivot of repre-sentation in the proposed federal parliament, while the principle of representation by population was at last consecrated by law. Both Upper and Lower Canada were made happy by settlement of the question, for Quebec was guaranteed a constant and fixed number of representatives, while the other provinces were to have as many representatives in proportion to their population as the number sixty-five bore to Quebec's population. After some difficulty in settling the financial basis of Confederation, the conference adjourned on October 28, having passed seventy-two resolutions which were to form the basis of the new constitution.

Cartier, who had already expressed his confident hope in the formation of 'a great confederation which will be to the benefit of all and the disadvantage of none'[89] in an address to a public dinner on September 8 after the Charlottetown meeting, and had evoked at a later Halifax banquet 'a great Anglo–American power,'[90] stretching from the Atlantic far westward, made a still more notable speech on October 28 at the banquet given by the citizens of Mon-treal to the delegates at the conclusion of the conference. He justified the final form of the project as the best assurance of com-mercial prosperity and the best insurance against annexation, and as supplying equal protection for both races and their interests:

I have been told that in Lower Canada there exists a strong opposition to this project because the English-speaking population will find itself at the mercy of the French population. Why, I answer, should the English born in Lower Canada yield to such arguments? Let them reflect that if the French have a majority in the provincial government, they will in their turn be in a large minority in the federal government. The French population, in confiding their interests to a federal government, give proof of their confidence in our English fellow-countrymen. Is it too much to ask of the English that they should rely on the liberality and the spirit of justice of the French race in the local government? . . . For my part I am ready to admit openly today that the prosperity of the two Canadas is principally due to the spirit of enterprise of the English race. But why should they oppose the establishment of a provincial government in which the French-Canadians will be represented in accordance with their number? In any case I do not hesitate to proclaim that I will never suffer, as long as I am minister of the Crown, an injustice being done, under the constitution or otherwise, to my countrymen, whether English or Catholics. I will never permit my compatriots, the French-Canadians, to be unjustly treated, because they belong to a different race and religion from the people of Upper Canada.[91]

Cartier observed that the proposed central government would control all general interests, while the provincial governments would have power over local affairs and properties: 'Under the new system Lower Canada will have its local government and almost as much legislative power as formerly.'[92] He concluded by stressing that Confederation represented no destruction or even weakening of the tie with Great Britain: 'I am for confederation because I believe that the establishment of a general government will give even greater force to that tie which is dear to us all.'[93]

Meanwhile Eric Dorion, *Rouge* member from Drummond-Arthabaska, published the Quebec Resolutions in his newspaper, *Le Défricheur*, and campaigned vigorously against Confederation as a centralization of power which would be disastrous for Quebec and provincial autonomy. At Cartier's instigation *La Minerve* replied to Dorion's campaign, warning Quebec against dangerous isolation. Most of the leading Lower-Canadian papers supported Confederation, but with no great enthusiasm. French Canada's elder statesmen opposed the measure. Papineau saw in it 'the same defects as in preceding regimes, and additional ones which are particular to it.'[94] C.-S. Cherrier came out of retirement to oppose it before the *Institut Canadien-Français* at Montreal in February 1865. Public meetings and petitions against Confederation were organized by Médéric Lanctôt, the head of the law firm which employed young Wilfrid Laurier, and the founder of a secret society, the Club Saint-Jean-Baptiste, to fight the scheme. A host of pamphlets appeared, the most notable anti-Confederation one being the work of Charles Laberge, while Joseph Cauchon produced the strongest plea in its favor.[95]

Although the task of sponsoring action on the resolutions of the Quebec Conference fell to John A. Macdonald as leader of the government in the House when the legislature met in February 1865, while the nominal prime minister, Sir Etienne Taché, sponsored a similar bill in the legislative council, Cartier supported his colleague with a three-hour speech—one of the most notable efforts of a man who made no pretensions to oratory—on February 7, the day after Macdonald had introduced the measure. Outlining its provisions and advocating its advantages, Cartier traced the whole history of the Confederation movement, defending the measure itself and replying to the attacks which had been made upon him personally. He pointed out that the Cartier-Macdonald government of 1858 had proposed the project, which thus could hardly be called a surprise measure. The deputation to London in that year which he had headed had consulted with the imperial authorities, but of the Maritime Provinces only Newfoundland was then ready to confer on the subject. He traced his conflict with George Brown over representation of population, which he had opposed 'because of the danger of conflict between the two sections, . . . not with the intention of refusing Upper Canada justice, but simply to prevent Lower Canada from suffering injustice.'[96] Then he remarked: 'I do not fear that the rights of Lower Canada will in any way be placed in peril by the project of Confederation, even though in a general legislature the French-Canadians will have a smaller number of representatives than all other nationalities combined. The resolutions show that, in the questions which will be submitted to the Federal parliament, there will be no more danger to the rights and privileges of the French Canadians than to those of the Scotch, English or Irish.'[97]

Having thus reassured his countrymen, Cartier proclaimed that Confederation was the alternative to absorption in the United States. Disunited, the British provinces could not defend themselves against American aggression. Canada was the largest, wealthiest, and most populous province of British North America, but it lacked access to the sea during the winter, and for that vital necessity of its trade it was dependent upon the United States. He blamed the opposition among the English of Lower Canada to Confederation on their desire to throw Canada into the American union, and assigned the same aim to the *Rouges*. He traced the story of American efforts to win Canada in the past, and stressed the loyalty of the French Canadians in 1775 and 1778. Then he remarked: 'While the American union had divided against itself, the Canadians, who have the advantage of seeing republicanism in operation for a period of eighty years, of perceiving its faults and vices, have been convinced that purely democratic institutions cannot assure the peace and prosperity of nations, and that we must unite under a federation so formed as to perpetuate the monarchical element.'[98] He pointed out that the 'five different groups inhabiting five separate provinces' had the 'same commercial interests, the same desire to live under the British Crown.'[99] But the unity brought about by Confederation would be a unity of diversity:

If we unite we will form a political nationality independent of the national origin and religion of individuals. Some have regretted that we have a distinction of races, and have expressed the hope that, in time, this diversity will disappear. The idea of a fusion of the races in one is utopian; it is an impossibility. Distinctions of this character will always exist; diversity seems to be the order of the physical, moral, and political worlds. As to the objection that we cannot form a great nation because Lower Canada is chiefly French and Catholic, Upper Canada English and Protestant, and the Maritime Provinces mixed, it is completely futile. . . . In our confederation there will be Catholics and Protestants, English, French, Irish and Scotch, and each by its efforts and success will add to the prosperity, the might, and to the glory of the new federation. We are of different races, not to wage war among ourselves, but to work together for our common welfare.[100]

Fired by this noble vision, the practical Cartier for once was too idealistic as he looked to the future. He foresaw a 'happy spirit of emulation' arising from the contact of French and English, so that the 'diversity of races' would 'contribute to the common prosperity.'[101] With a Catholic minority in Upper Canada and a Protestant minority in Lower Canada, while the two communions balanced one another in the Maritimes, he foresaw no possibility of the arbitrary infringement of a minority's rights by either federal or provincial governments. He pointed out the strange bedfellows among the opposition to the project, with the *Rouges* lying down with the English: '*The True Witness*, a Catholic journal which opposes the project, is of the opinion that if it is adopted the French Canadians will be annihilated, whilst its confrère in violence, the Protestant *Witness*, assured us that it will be the Protestants who will suffer.'[102] He brought the force of clerical support to bear: 'Those of the clergy who are high in authority, as well as those in humbler positions, have declared for Confederation, not only because they see in it all possible security for the institutions they cherish, but also because their Protestant fellow countrymen, like themselves, are also guaranteed their rights. The clergy in general are opposed to all political dissension, and if they are favorable to the project, it is because they see in Confederation a solution to the difficulties which have so long existed.'[103] He concluded by urging the necessity of seizing this favorable opportunity to adopt Confederation:

'We know that the approbation of the Imperial Government is assured. If, therefore, Canada adopts these resolutions, as I have no doubt it will, and if the other British North American colonies follow its example, the Imperial Government will then be called upon to accord us a central government established on a broad and solid basis, and provincial governments under whose protection will be placed the persons, the properties, and the civil and religious rights of all classes of society.'[104]

It was Cartier's great plea which finally won a slim majority of French-Canadian support for the project, by a vote of 27 to 21. His calm words of tolerance and practical logic were offset by the reply of Antoine-Aimé Dorion, the *Rouge* leader, who thought Confederation of all British North America premature at this time, though he had earlier favored a confederation of the Canadas to break the existing deadlock. He denounced the proposal of a nominated instead of an elected upper house and the support pledged to the construction of the Intercolonial Railway. The type of confederation he favored would give the largest powers to the local governments and only delegated authority to the central government. He considered the Confederation scheme as a plot of the Grand Trunk, and denounced the conservative tendencies of the whole project: 'With a Governor-General appointed by the Crown; with local Governors also appointed by the Crown; with Legislative Councils in the General Legislature and in all the provinces nominated by the Crown, we shall have the most illiberal Constitution ever heard of in any country where constitutional government prevails.'[105]

In the isolationist tradition Dorion saw no need for the creation of military or naval forces: 'The best thing Canada can do is to keep quiet, and to give no cause for war.'[106] It was absurd 'to speak as a means of defence of a scheme of Confederation to unite the whole country extending from Newfoundland to Vancouver's Island,'— this was the first reference to extension of Confederation to the Pacific—'thousands of miles intervening, without any communication, except through the United States or around Cape Horn.'[107] When Cartier interrupted to state that an interoceanic railway was to be built, Dorion denounced the suggestion as an extension of the Grand Trunk line for the benefit of English capitalists. He saw an intention to convert the proposed federal union eventually into a legislative union, which Lower Canada would never tolerate:

The people of Lower Canada are attached to their institutions in a manner that defies any attempt to change them in that way. They will not change their religious institutions, their laws and their language for any consideration whatsoever. A million of inhabitants may seem a small affair to a philosopher who sits down to write out a constitution. He may think that it would be better that there should be one religion, one language and one system of laws, and he goes to work to frame institutions that will bring all to that desirable state; but I can tell honorable gentlemen that the history of every country goes to show that not even by the power of the sword can such changes be accomplished. . . . I know that there is an apprehension amongst the British population in Lower Canada that, even with the small power that the local government will possess, their rights will not be respected. How, then, can it be expected that the French population can anticipate any more favorable result from the general government, when it is to possess such enormous powers over the destinies of their section of the country? Experience shows that majorities are always aggressive, and it cannot be otherwise in this instance.[108]

Finally, Dorion concluded, if the project of Confederation should be adopted 'without the sanction of the people, the country would never cease to regret it.'[109] He had put his finger on a weak spot, for the few farsighted statesmen who sponsored the measure were perfectly aware that there was no popular enthusiasm for it, and that if the scheme were to succeed under existing political conditions, it must be rushed through the legislature without the appeal to the people which Dorion urged.

Henri Joly, the Swiss-born deputy for Lotbinière who later became a Liberal premier of Quebec, supported Dorion's opposition to the measure. Oddly enough, considering his background, he stressed the historical weakness of federations, and denounced the project as fatal to the French-Canadian nationality.[110] He called Cartier a traitor who had sacrificed his people to his own ambition and interest. Another notable opposition speaker, J.-F. Perrault, reviewed the record since 1760 and predicted a constant French-Canadian struggle to maintain their rights and liberties under Confederation, which he considered 'the political suicide of the French race in Canada' and a 'scheme of annihilation specially prepared for our destruction.'[111] The arguments of the *Rouges* were not without effect. One of Cartier's followers, Henri Taschereau, was led to part company with his leader because to his mind the project lacked sufficient guarantees for the rights of the French Canadians.[112] Fear for a future in which French Canada would be at the mercy of an English majority broke down party lines. Throughout the consideration of the project in 1864 and 1865 Cartier was bitterly attacked on the platform and in the press of Lower Canada—with Eric Dorion's *Le Défricheur* reinforced by a paper called *L'Union Nationale*, founded by L.-O. David and L.-A. Jetté to campaign against both the project and Cartier personally. This onslaught fatally weakened Cartier's hold on French Canada, and he may be said to have made a greater personal sacrifice than any other father of Confederation in carrying the project through.

While Cartier was being attacked by his compatriots for sacrificing the interests of his province, he was also engaged in meeting the objections of the English minority in Lower Canada with a pledge to guarantee their rights. He reiterated his assurance 'as a Catholic and as a member of the Canadian Government, that when the measure for the settlement of the local government of Lower Canada comes before this House for discussion it will be such as to satisfy the Protestant minority of Lower Canada.'[113] John Rose, one of the English-speaking members for Lower Canada, had already paid tribute to Cartier's notable tolerance by saying that 'in the whole course of his public life there has not been a single act on his part, whether of executive, administrative, or legislative action, tinged with illiberality, intolerance, or bigotry.'[114] Cartier answered the objection that the French Canadians were left at the mercy of the English majority in the federal parliament by pointing out that in case of unreasonable opposition they could break up the administration by retiring: 'When the leader for Lower Canada shall have sixty-five members belonging to his section to support him, and command a majority of the French Canadians and British from Lower Canada, will he not be able to upset the government if his colleagues interfere with his nominations to office?'[115] Dorion replied that nobody would care if he did retire, since 'there would be a sufficient number of English members to carry on without him.'[116] But Cartier expressed his confidence that the spirit of fair play and justice of the English members of the government would assure fair treatment for the minority in the federal parliament, and pleaded for a similar confidence on the part of the English minority in Quebec. The language question under the new order was made clear by Macdonald's statement that the continued use of the French language was one of the principles of Confederation, while Cartier added that the rights of English in the Lower Canada legislature would also be guaranteed, so that 'the use of both languages would be secured by the Imperial Act.'[117]

Despite all the arguments and explanations of a month and a half of debate, A.-A. Dorion, who with his brother Eric, Holton, Joly, Dunkin, and J. S. Macdonald, led the opposition, remained firm in his position. The opposition took new heart when the pro-confederation government of New Brunswick was defeated early in March, while Nova Scotia and Prince Edward Island backed out of the project. Macdonald and Cartier pressed for a vote, despite the fact that it now appeared that the project would be merely a confederation 'of the two Canadas,'[118] as François Evanturel, the editor of *Le Canadien*, called it. The government's position in the face of these setbacks was that the measure should be passed and then the imperial government could be induced to bring pressure to bear upon the Maritimes to accept it. A.-A. Dorion summed up the gloomy state of mind of the *Rouges* and French-Canadian popular opposition to the project thus:

I am opposed to this confederation in which the militia, the appointment of judges, the administration of justice, and our most important civil rights will be under the control of the general government, the majority of which will be hostile to Lower Canada, of a governor-general vested with the most ample powers, whilst the powers of the local government will be restricted first by the limit of the powers delegated to it, by the veto reserved to the central authority, and further by the concurrent jurisdiction of the general authority or government. Petitions with more than 20,000 signatures attached to them have already been presented to this House against the scheme of confederation. Numerous public meetings have been held in nineteen counties in Lower Canada and one in the city of Montreal. Everywhere this scheme has been protested against and an appeal to the people demanded; and yet in defiance of the expressed opinion of our constituents we are about to give them a constitution, the effect of which will be to snatch from them what little influence they still enjoy under the existing law. We are about, on their behalf, to surrender all the rights and privileges which are dearest to them, and that without consulting them. It would be madness—it would be more, it would be a crime. On these grounds I shall oppose the scheme with all the power at my command, and insist that under any circumstances it shall be submitted to the people before its final adoption.[119]

But Macdonald and Cartier succeeded in forcing the vote on March 10, 1865, when the House agreed to the Quebec Resolutions by a vote of 91 to 33, with 21 of the dissenting votes French Canadian. The measure had already been approved in the legislative council on February 20 by a 45–15 vote, with 6 French Canadians opposing it. The *Rouges'* campaign against Confederation was continued until the British North America Act was passed by the British parliament in March 1867. At the Westminster Palace Conference in London in December 1866 Galt secured a guarantee of minority educational rights in both Quebec and Ontario. But Dorion's and Perrault's objections to Confederation have often been re-echoed in French Canada through the years, and some of their dire predictions have come true, while some of Cartier's optimistic views have been discredited by developments. The greater Canada was not created without sacrifices by all who helped to make it, and its survival has been threatened by the failure of later leaders to live up to the liberal spirit of the fathers of Confederation.

Notes

[1] Kennedy, 502, Elgin-Grey, 30 April 1849. The quotations are from the *Montreal Courier*, as reprinted in the *New York Commercial Advertizer*, 5 April 1849.

[2] Cartier was named after George III. His signature usually follows the English spelling or is abbreviated to 'Geo.' See G. Malchelosse (*ed.*), *Sulte: Mélanges Historiques* (Montréal, 1919), 88, Ap., Note I.

[3] *Elgin-Grey*, II, 465, Elgin-Grey, 3 September 1849.

[4] *Ibid.*, II, 463, Proclamation to Britons of the City of Toronto, August 1849.

[5] *Ibid.*, II, 525, Elgin-Grey, 25 October 1849.

[6] *Ibid.*, II, 531, *Daily British Whig*, 26 October 1849.

[7] *Ibid.*, II, 534, Elgin-Grey, 8 November 1849.

[8] *Ibid*, II, 612, Elgin-Grey, 23 March 1850.

[9] *Ibid.*, II, 608 n., *Hansard*, III Series, CVIII, 567, Russell, 8 February 1850.

[10] *Ibid.*, II, 609, Elgin-Grey, 23 March 1850.

[11] *Ibid.*, II, 585, Elgin-Grey, 28 January 1850.

[12] *Ibid.*, II, 610, Elgin-Grey, 23 March 1850.

[13] Chapais, VI, 152-3.

[14] *Ibid.*, VI, 169-70.

[15] *Ibid.*, VI, 172.

[16] *Elgin-Grey*, II, 670, Elgin-Grey, 31 May 1850.

[17] *Ibid.*, II, 706, Elgin-Grey, 2 August 1850.

[18] *Ibid.*, II, 707.

[19] *Ibid.*, II, 745-6, Elgin-Grey, 22 November 1850.

[20] *Ibid.*, II, 746.

[21] Chapais, VI, 205.

[22] *Elgin-Grey*, III, 900, Grey-Elgin, 2 October 1851.

[23] *Ibid.*, III, 904.

[24] G. Lanctot, *François-Xavier Garneau* (Toronto [1925]), 1-2.

[25] *Ibid.*, 12.

[26] *Ibid.*, 29.

[27] G. Lanctot, 'L'Oeuvre historique de Garneau', in *Centenaire de l'Histoire du Canada de François-Xavier Garneau* (Montréal, 1945), 18-9.

[28] *Ibid.*, 24; Lanctot, *Garneau* (1925), 33.

[29] M. Wade (*ed.*), *Journals of Francis Parkman* (New York, 1947), II, 517-8; Lanctot, *Garneau*, 34.

[30] Lanctot, 36; Garneau, 'Voyage en Angleterre et en France,' in *La Littérature canadienne* (Québec, 1863), I, 250-1.

[31] Lanctot, *Centenaire*, 106.

[32] M. Bibaud, *Histoire du Canada* (Montréal, 1843), I, 2.

[33] C. Roy, *Nos origines littéraires* (Québec, 1909), 234.

[34] Faribault's collection, like Viger's 'Saberdache,' is preserved in the Seminary Archives, Laval University, Quebec City.

[35] P.-J.-O. Chauveau, *L'Instruction publique au Canada* (Québec, 1876), 322.

[36] Chauveau, *Charles Guérin* (Montréal, 1853), 2.

[37] Large Channel Island firms, the Robins and Le Boutilliers, took over the fisheries of the Gulf of St. Lawrence after the Conquest and soon monopolized both them and the supply trade. Young Jerseymen, known as '*les Jersiais*,' were sent out to the Gaspé and Cape Breton coasts to serve as traders and company storekeepers, setting arbitrary prices for fish and supplies. They were disliked by French Canadians as foreign exploiters and French Protestants, like the earlier Swiss officials who were also allied with the English conquerors and cut across the

racial-religious line. On the Jersey monopolists, see Innis & Lower, *Select Econ. Docs., 1783–1885*, 700.

[38] L. de Montigny, *Antoine Gérin-Lajoie* (Toronto, 1925), 13.

[39] Abbé C. Roy, *L'Abbé H.-R. Casgrain* (Montréal, 1925), 1170.

[40] A. Gérin-Lajoie, *Jean Rivard, le défricheur* (Montréal, 1874), Préface.

[41] *Ibid.*, 2.

[42] *Ibid.*, vii.

[43] H.-R. Casgrain (ed.), *Les Oeuvres complètes d'Octave Crémazie* (Montréal, 1882), 10.

[44] *Ibid.*, 22.

[45] *Ibid.*, 13.

[46] *Ibid.*, 100.

[47] S. Marion, *Les Lettres canadiennes d'autrefois* (Ottawa, 1944), IV, 140–2.

[48] Commandant de Belvèze, *Lettres choisies, 1824–75* (Bourges, 1882), 135.

[49] Marion, IV, 110.

[50] Belvèze, 150–2, Belvèze-Rohault de Fleury, 29 August 1855.

[51] *Oeuvres de Crémazie*, 106; PAC: 173F, 88–9, 64, Belvèze, 'Mission de la Capricieuse au Canada,' 1 November 1855.

[52] *Oeuvres de Crémazie*, 128, 136–7.

[53] *Ibid.*, 138.

[54] M. Wade, *Francis Parkman* (New York, 1942), 411.

[55] *Oeuvres de Crémazie*, 234, 238, 244.

[56] *Ibid.*, 469.

[57] *Ibid.*, 508–9.

[58] *Ibid.*, 20–2.

[59] *Ibid.*, 24, 25.

[60] *Ibid.*, 30.

[61] *Ibid.*

[62] *Ibid.*, 32.

[63] *Ibid.*, 39.

[64] *Ibid.*, 40–2.

[65] *Ibid.*, 43

[66] *Ibid.*, 51.

[67] *Ibid.*, 62.

[68] J. Boyd, *Sir George Etienne Cartier, Bart* (Toronto, 1914), 62.

[69] Boyd, 64 n.

[70] J. Tassé, *Discours de Sir Georges Cartier, Bart* (Montréal, 1893), 2.

[71] *CHAR 1938*, 70–8, J. I. Cooper, 'G. E. Cartier in the Period of the 'Forties.' Cartier's first law partner was his brother Damien, who prepared the cases which Cartier argued in court. George declared that Damien had a much better head (Boyd, 416). Then Lafontaine and Amable Berthelot took George into partnership. After their return to the bench, Cartier was joined by F.-P. Pominville, who became the dominant figure in the firm of Cartier, Pominville, & Bétourney from 1855 to Cartier's death, as the latter became more preoccupied with political life. It was one of the first Montreal law firms to specialize in guiding English businessmen through the unfamiliar mazes of French civil law.

[72] Tassé, 423.

[73] *Sulte: Mélanges*, IV, 15, 'Les Oeuvres de Cartier.'

[74] *Ibid.*, 12–3.

[75] Tassé, 6–8.

[76] *Ibid.*, 17–8.

[77] *Sulte: Mélanges*, 15.

[78] W. L. Grant, in *Canada and Its Provinces* (Toronto, 1914), V, 5–6; quoted Boyd, 167 n.

[79] Tassé, 402.

[80] Boyd, 107.

[81] *Ibid.*, 117.

[82] *Ibid.*, 142; Tassé, 194.

[83] Boyd, 176.

[84] *Ibid.*, Tassé, 258

[85] *Ibid.*, 147; Tassé, 278.

[86] Two Confederate emissaries, Mason and Sliddell, were seized on a British mail steamer intercepted by a U.S. warship. They were later released at the demand of Great Britain. See L. B. Shippee, *Canadian-American Relations, 1849–1874* (Toronto, 1939), 116, 126, 128.

[87] *Ibid.*, 129; Tassé, 309.

[88] W. Ford (ed.), *A Cycle of Adams Letters, 1861–65* (Boston, 1920), II, 238–9, H. Adams-C. F. Adams, Jr., 30 December 1864; *New York Herald*, 11 February 1865, cited J.-O. Mousseau, *Contre-Foison* (Montréal, 1867), 16.

[89] Tassé, 391.

[90] *Ibid.*, 395.

[91] *Ibid.*, 405–6.

[92] *Ibid.*, 407.

[93] *Ibid.*, 407–8; Boyd, 208–9.

[94] R. Rumilly, *Histoire de la Province de Québec*, I, 36.

[95] Joseph Cauchon, *L'Union des Provinces de l'Amérique Britannique du Nord* (Québec, 1865).

[96] *Parliamentary Debates on the subject of the Confederation of the British North American Provinces* (Quebec, 1865), 54.

[97] *Ibid.*, 54–5.

[98] *Ibid.*, 59.

[99] *Ibid.*, 60.

[100] *Ibid.*

[101] *Ibid.*

[102] *Ibid.*, 61–2.

[103] *Ibid.*, 62.

[104] *Ibid.*

[105] *Ibid.*, 255–6.

[106] *Ibid.*, 257.

[107] *Ibid.*, 263.

[108] *Ibid.*, 264.

[109] *Ibid.*, 268.

[110] *Ibid.*, 360–2.

[111] *Ibid.*, 613.

[112] *Ibid.*, 894.

[113] *Ibid.*, 932. Cartier's first pledge, *ibid.*, 411.

[114] *Ibid.*, 408.

[115] *Ibid.*, 571.

[116] *Ibid.*

[117] *Ibid.*, 944, 955.

[118] *Ibid.*, 71.

[119] *Ibid.*, 694–5.

CHAPTER VII

GROWING PAINS

(1867–96)

THE QUESTION of survival for the French Canadians was brought more to the fore by Confederation than at any time since the Conquest. Durham had counted on absorbing French Canada by uniting it with Upper Canada. His policy had failed because of the collaboration of French and English Reformers in the winning of responsible government. This collaboration greatly eased the tension between the two ethnic groups after the crises of 1837–8 and 1849. But with Confederation Quebec was united first to three and then to six English-Canadian provinces; and despite Cartier's arguments that the French Canadians' position was strengthened by a fixed federal representation and the attainment of their own Quebec legislature, both the *Rouges* and his own Conservative followers feared assimilation in the great English-speaking mass of which they had become a central part.

The French Canadians had outnumbered the English at the outset of the Union, and to their numerical strength some of their success in resisting the assimilative purpose of the Union must be assigned; but now they formed less than a third of the new Canada, a proportion which has declined slightly down to the present day.[1] The defensiveness aroused by this fact was enough to breed a strong spirit of reaction which contrasts strangely with the progressive spirit of the 1830's, 1840's, and 1850's; and the development of this reactionary spirit was greatly furthered by the immediate infringement and violation of Confederation's guarantees of minority rights and privileges. Confidence in the newly achieved partnership of French and English was undermined at the outset of the period, and in two decades' time the relations between the two groups had once more reached a state of major crisis.

The conflict was heightened by certain general trends, by no means confined to Canada, which were the legacy of the American and French Revolutions. In 1776 and 1789 the right of sovereignty was first attributed to the people. By 1848 this principle, and the derivative belief that each ethnic group or nation possessed the right of sovereignty, had wrecked the false reactionary European order established by the Congress of Vienna at the close of the Napoleonic wars. Nationalism was the most considerable political force in the nineteenth century, and the great historical process which began in 1776 has continued to our own day, which has seen nationalism locked in mortal combat with a new version of the older principle of internationalism. French Canada became involved in this historical process through two channels, one French and the other Roman. That the French Canadians had become North Americans and wholly distinct from the French of France was witnessed by the fact that far the more important channel was the Roman one. This fact affected the course of events in Canada during the first thirty years of Confederation, and involved the French Canadians in the European struggle between ultramontanism and liberalism, an outgrowth of the conflict between the old and new orders caused by the rise of nationalism.

For the first time since the days of Bishop Laval, Church and State were in open conflict in Canada. Among a people so religious and so politically-minded as the French Canadians, this struggle could not fail to be of extreme bitterness; and among a people who had confused, thanks to their history, racist and nationalist ideas with religious ones, it was inevitable that the major issues of the day, the ethnic conflict, the realignment of political parties to meet the new situation created by Confederation, and the relations of Church and State, should become intricately involved in a tangle which defied the talents of statesmen and canonists alike. The struggles of this period have left a deep mark on the French-Canadian mind, and out of them was born the ultranationalism which has attracted more attention outside Quebec than anything else connected with the French Canadians.

This nationalism, as befits the circumstances under which it arose, sometimes uses religion for political ends, and sometimes politics for religious ends, and in either case arouses the antipathy of English-speaking North Americans, whose cultural tradition is largely based upon the separation of Church and State. This antipathy in turn strengthens the French-Canadian minority complex, which is based upon the acute consciousness of the fact that they constitute a political minority which represents only 30 per cent of the population of Canada, and a cultural minority which represents less than 2 per cent of the neighboring Anglo-American group. As in the case of the inferiority complex of the individual, whose feelings of inadequacy cause him to adopt the arrogant and aggressive attitudes which are a form of defence mechanism, so the minority complex produces similar manifestations which intensify the conflict between the majority and the minority. Thus the first thirty years after Confederation were crowded with racial, cultural, and religious conflicts. Yet the period ended with Canada governed for the first time by a French-Canadian Catholic who was the prophet of an unhyphenated Canadianism, blending the old loyalties into a larger one—a Canadianism whose attainment is not yet complete today, when even the larger nationalism must yield to internationalism if a troubled world is to find peace.

I

Since Confederation marked a new beginning for French Canada, an account of its state at this period is demanded. The census of 1871 gave Quebec a population of slightly over a million, of which more than three-quarters was French.[2] The French Canadians were thus numerically dominant in their homeland, but they were outnumbered two to one in the new Dominion of Canada, despite growing groups in Nova Scotia, New Brunswick, Ontario, and in the Red River colony in the West.[3] Their actual influence in Quebec was less than the population figure indicates: the countryside, occupied by 85 per cent of the population, was predominantly French; but the cities were more English than French, and the control of trade and industry was largely concentrated in the hands of the English who had launched them, while labor was predominantly French.

Quebec City, whose population of 59,699 was 40 per cent English, was on the eve of a decline from the peak of prosperity reached during the previous decade, for the old dominance of the St. Lawrence waterway had been shattered by the completion in 1860 of the Grand Trunk Railway, which ran south of the river from Rivière-du-Loup to Montreal and thence to Sarnia in Ontario. Quebec continued to rely on the river, and was only linked with this railroad at Lévis across the St. Lawrence in 1884. Until the north shore line linking Hull, Montreal, Trois-Rivières, and Quebec was opened in 1879, Quebec was left without direct rail connections to the east and west, although a Lévis-Richmond line, connecting with the Montreal-Portland route, was built in 1852. Even before the building of the railways, the port of Quebec had gone into decline with the deepening of the St. Lawrence channel. In summer the steamers which replaced sailing ships could easily continue on to Montreal instead of halting at Quebec, while in winter the railroad linked Montreal with the ice-free harbor of Portland when the St. Lawrence was closed for five months.[4] The changing times not only paralyzed the port of Quebec, but they ruined one of its oldest industries, shipbuilding, which had supported half the population; for ships were now built of steel and Quebec lacked both iron and coal. The square-timber trade, which in its heyday had filled the river at Quebec for ten miles on both shores with rafts of logs and the basin with as many as 350 ships in a single season, had fallen upon evil days with the loss of British preference and demand. [5] Ruthless cutting had also almost exhausted the best of the forests of the Saguenay and Saint-Maurice in sixty years, while Montreal better served the booming Ottawa Valley trade.

With the rise of Montreal, the down-river ports were eclipsed. Quebec was left with its small industries—35 tanneries, 8 foundries, assorted woodworking establishments, and several breweries—which employed at best a thousand men. [6] It was becoming a town which lived off Church and State, for it remained the administrative center of the Church and the provincial capital, though it lost the federal government in 1867 and the English garrison in 1871. Trois-Rivières, a town of 7,570 without any major industry since the exhaustion of the white pine timber of the Saint-Maurice, and left aside by the railroads, also stagnated. Ever since the days of the California gold rush in 1849, it had contributed a notable number of its enterprising young men to the swelling tide of emigration to the States. Sorel, with its 5,636 people, was in decline as the railroads reduced the importance of the Richelieu–Lake Champlain water route; but its shipbuilders, boatmen, and longshoremen could at least find employment in the foundry, brickworks, and other small industries which flourished there, relics of the industrial-minded Englishmen and American Loyalists who had made Sorel, or William Henry as they called it, the most Anglo-American of the old Quebec towns.

On the other hand, Montreal, profiting by the brisk development of Upper Canada, had a rapidly growing population which numbered 57,715 in 1851, 90,323 in 1861, and 115,000 in 1871. [7] Inspired by Cartier and his farsighted English business friends to meet the competition of New York, Boston, and Portland, and to maintain itself as the terminus of the Great Lakes–St. Lawrence trade, Montreal began to deepen the St. Lawrence ship channel to twenty feet in 1844. A port commission created in 1851 improved the harbor facilities, so that the first transatlantic ship reached Montreal in 1857 and the number of ships entering the port more than doubled in thirty years time, reaching 500 in 1867, while the value of imports rose from $19,000,000 in 1865 to $28,000,000 in the following year. [8] By 1867 Montreal had become the metropolis of Canada and its port completely eclipsed Quebec as the center of the British import and export trade. Agricultural exports exceeded forest products by 1861. [9] Five to six hundred new houses were built each year to shelter the growing population attracted by the sixty-odd manufacturing establishments beside the Lachine Canal. Linked to the south shore and the eastern section of the Grand Trunk by the Victoria Bridge, over which trains had run since 1861,

Montreal was becoming a great rail center as well as the natural hub of the waterway system. The Grand Trunk was the biggest business in the Canada of its day, and employed more men than any other Canadian enterprise. Its warehouses for grain and other freight, its shops, and its offices all were at Montreal, which also became the banking center of Canada after the failure of the two leading Ontario banks in 1866 and 1867.

But the men who held the reins of power in Montreal were largely English Canadians—indeed the population was still more English than French in 1861, and the squalid narrow streets of the old French quarter contrasted strangely with the magnificent English country estates built on the slopes of Mount Royal by the magnates of the fur trade, whose descendants had become merchants, bankers, and industrialists. The well-to-do English lived west of St. Lawrence Main, the well-to-do French to the east, between St. Catherine and Sherbrooke Streets; and each group gave a certain flavor of its own to these new quarters of the city. Working-class villages had grown up about the factories along the Lachine Canal, and in both these new settlements and in the old quarters filth and refuse, floating on a sea of mud from October to May, filled the streets. Montreal, like New York, was growing too rapidly to concern itself with the amenities, and the unshorn aspect of both cities shocked visiting Europeans, unaccustomed to new cities. In all the province Montreal's only rival in prosperity was Sherbrooke, where textile and paper plants and a host of small industries were giving this center of the Eastern Townships the same aspect as the booming New England mill towns on which it was modeled. Sherbrooke nearly doubled its population between 1871 and 1881.[10]

All this economic activity, which characterized the coming of the industrial revolution to Quebec, was reflected in an alteration of French-Canadian society. Yet that society, because of its traditional conservatism and a resistance to change bred by the struggle to preserve the French-Canadian way of life, was not as greatly affected as the English-Canadian world which welcomed the industrial age, while the French resisted it because its pioneers were cultural aliens. From 1851 to 1881 there was a decline in domestic employment, as the old self-sufficient rural world was invaded by the new products of the cities; a slight increase in the professional class which provided services for the industrial world; and a large increase in the agricultural, commercial, and industrial classes.[11] Agricultural competition from the American Middle West hit both Upper and Lower Canada about 1850 and eventually forced technical improvement and diversification of crops. The hidebound tradition of Quebec agriculture led to much distress among the *habitants* and to the emigration of their sons before the system was finally changed.

Resistance to industralization at home and to emigration to the States led to strong support of the colonization movement launched in 1849, though with the development of large-scale grain culture in Ontario, Quebec turned in the 1870's from wheat to dairy farming for a cash crop beyond the subsistence provided by its traditional small-scale mixed farming. The old pull of the towns offset the increase of the agricultural class, and the exhaustion of the best land of the St. Lawrence seigneuries was an obstacle which no amount of encouragement of colonization by Church and State could overcome until obsolete agricultural methods were abandoned toward the end of the century. The province was glutted with cheap labor, as the former employees of the shipbuilding and timber trades desperately sought new work in the midst of the Great Depression which began in 1873; this situation and the absence of any govern-ment control over wages and working conditions made gross. ex-ploitation of labor possible for the industrial pioneers.

An ever-increasing number of French Canadians, faced with such conditions at home, passed over the border to the New England states where the industries launched during the first half of the century had swollen until their demands for labor were insatiable. At first the migratory movement was seasonal, with the French Canadians replacing at harvest time the native farming population which had been drawn to the mills by the lure of cash wages; then the French established a foothold in the brickmaking industry which was developed by the expansion of the mill towns; and finally they entered the mills themselves, where their large families gave them an economic advantage in an industrial era founded on the wretchedly paid dawn-to-dusk labor of women and children as well as men.[12] A later movement of population followed the west-ward course of the lumber trade which cut its way across the con-tinent in record time, exhausting the forests as it went. Emigration to the States remained at first largely transient, for most of the emigrants planned to return to Quebec after they had saved enough money to free the family farm from debt or to establish themselves in comfort on new land; but more and more of them found the freer way of life and the higher standard of living sufficiently attractive to hold them permanently. They founded 'Little Canadas' which were French-speaking islands in the New England towns.

Some of the most enterprising brought back to Quebec the knowledge of manufacturing processes which they had acquired in the States and established small industries in their native province. This development was particularly marked in Quebec City in the 1860's, where French Canadians gradually became dominant as management as well as labor in the newly established shoe industry, the foundries, the wood and metal-working shops, and the declining shipbuilding trade. They maintained and increased their hold on the tanneries and lumber mills, as the keener English Quebeckers followed the movement of capital towards Montreal, and the remainder abandoned industry in favor of banking and other financial pursuits in which their access to English credit and capital favored them. The first French president of the Quebec Chamber of Commerce was elected in 1871, while two years later 7,300 workers were employed in industries dominated by French Canadians. The slack of unemployment caused by the decline of the timber and shipbuilding trades was thus largely taken up, but there was little further expansion during the Great Depression which afflicted Canada generally for the next two decades.

With the rise of the saw-log and lumber industries, there was a major displacement of population westward from the Quebec-Montreal region, and a minor one eastward along the lower St. Lawrence. The headquarters of the timber trade shifted from Quebec to Montreal, for steamships, railroads, and the greater transportability of the new staples eliminated the old seasonal drives down the river system to the Quebec timber coves. Despite the establishment of small sawmills at Montmorency in the 1860's and at Batiscan, Montmagny, and Chicoutimi in the 1870's, the great development was in the Ottawa and Gatineau Valleys at Hawkesbury, Hull, and Chelsea. By 1881 the Ottawa timber and lumber trade, which at its peak in 1863 employed 15,000 men in the forests, 10,000 at the mills, and some 25,000 in exporting from Quebec, was petering out, as that of the Saint-Maurice had by 1873 and that of the Saguenay by the 1860's.[13] Towards the end of the century the new pulp and paper industry, which made use of forests already gutted of the best timber and lumber, was founded at Trois-Rivières and shortly afterward launched in the Saguenay-Lake St. John region and in the Ottawa Valley. This soon became the first industry of the province in which nearly all the wood was cut and half the paper made from it was manufactured.[14] The development was part of a shift from extractive industry to manufacturing which characterized the Quebec economy at the turn of the century, despite the continued exploitation of Chaudière River gold and of the Thetford asbestos deposits discovered in 1877 and developed after 1885.[15] Decentralization of manufacturing was fostered by the extension of the railroad network during the period. Trois-Rivières was linked to Arthabaska in 1865; Montreal to Sorel in 1882; Quebec to Lake St. John in 1888; and Gaspé to New Brunswick and Quebec in 1898.[16]

The economic development of this period was accompanied by a social development which held the seeds of a radical alteration in the character of French-Canadian society which is still being

M

worked out today. French-Canadian labor, bred in the agricultural tradition of dawn-to-dusk work for little cash return, or in the hard life of the timber trade, was slow to follow the lead of English workers who organized unions soon after their arrival in Canada, though these were only legalized after long opposition in 1872. From the French regime the *Québecois* had inherited the guild tradition—there were guilds in the tanneries and among the carpenters of New France[17]—but being hard-working, thrifty, and accustomed to obey orders and to a lower standard of living than his English compatriots, he was slow to show interest in the aggressive Anglo-American unions which sprang up about the middle of the century. These were frowned on by the clergy as 'dangerous secret societies.'[18] In any case the former shipbuilder or lumberjack, faced with the prospect of starvation if he did not find a job, was not inclined to stand upon the rights of labor, while the newly industrialized *habitant* had lost none of his traditional individualism in the transition from rural to urban life.

Of the new national and international unions, only the Knights of Labor were conspicuously successful in penetrating Quebec, despite the differences of Anglo-American and French-Canadian mentalities; and after their initial success in 1881 they encountered determined opposition from the Church as a secret society of dubious principles and finally disappeared from Quebec after Cardinal Taschereau condemned them in 1886.[19] The Catholic syndicates, launched in the 1890's on the inspiration of *Rerum Novarum* and favoured by the deeply-felt need of the French Canadian for his own social organizations in order to avoid absorption into the Anglo-American world, checked the growth of Quebec locals associated with the Canadian Trades and Labor Congress established in 1886.

The union movement in Quebec was met by united opposition from the French-Canadian élite and the Anglo-American economic overlords: the Church opposed the materialistic and socialistic outlook of the labor leaders and their threat to its dominance in the social field; the politicians successfully appealed to ethnic loyalty to curb the political threat presented by the movement; the professionals benefited by acting as middlemen between the economic overlords and the masses; and the employers fought a development which threatened an industrial system based upon low labor costs.

The profound individualism of the French-Canadian character also did not offer a fertile field for development of the union ideal. Generally speaking, the French-Canadian worker was slow to turn against his traditional leaders and to lose his hierarchical view of society. He was willing to pay the price of being distinctively French and Catholic in an industrial system dominated by the Anglo-American Protestant world which encircled Quebec. Though he sometimes protested when exploitation was too flagrant, he was much more apt to rebel at attempted alterations of his traditional ways than at long hours, low wages, and poor working conditions. The French-Canadian worker was bred in a desperately hard school: the fur trade, subsistence agriculture, and lumbering had given him an endurance and a patience under hardship rare among North American workers, although poor nutrition and sanitary standards had made him less productive than British or American workers.

2

These epoch-making alterations in the Quebec economy had a profound influence upon the French-Canadian mind, which tended then as now to look at every new development primarily from an ethnic point of view, particularly when the changes were coupled with English assertions of dominance in the political world. It is not without significance that the most bitter clashes of French and English opinion developed in Montreal and Trois-Rivières, where English economic influence was dominant, while French-dominated Quebec City remained serene and largely unaffected by the great conflicts of the period. The French Canadians, involved despite themselves in an industrial economy alien to their tradition, tended to assert their Frenchness and to contest stubbornly any infringement of their rights under Confederation. This assertion of their separateness also involved an assertion of their Catholicism, since the concept of French-Canadian nationality had become inextricably involved with religion. This aggressive Catholicism was also excited by the effort after 1850 of English Canadians to break up the French-Canadian cultural group by a militant missionary effort centering in the Montreal region, and by attacks on the Catholic Church from sources outside Quebec. This Protestant onslaught merely increased the religio-ethnic cleavage which it sought to break down.

Cultural relations with France, which had been renewed in the 1850's and industriously cultivated by Napoleon III, were greatly strengthened by French intervention against the Italian nationalists in 1860, when Rome was held for the Pope by a French garrison, and when Garibaldi's renewed onslaught in 1867 was checked at Mentana by the Papal Zouaves, who were largely French. Two French Canadians and one English Quebecker served with the Zouaves in their early days, while in 1867 Bishop Bourget of Montreal decided to raise a contingent of Canadian Zouaves, although the Pope had only appealed for financial aid and not for volunteers. The Bishop's personal following of zealous priests and laymen, always to the fore in French and Catholic matters, preached a holy war from the pulpit and in the press. In February 1868, 135

volunteers, chosen from 564 with more regard for their moral than
military qualities, set out from Montreal after three days of public
ceremonies. Their flag, designed by Papineau's son-in-law, the
artist Napoléon Bourassa, had been solemnly blessed; Bishop
Laflèche of Trois-Rivières had preached them a stirring sermon on
the Church militant and the Christian as a soldier; and Bishop
Bourget had administered an oath by which the volunteers bound
themselves to bring no stain upon Catholicism or their country,
with 'whose honor and glory you are charged.'[20] While at home
Bishop Bourget and the young Conservative orator Adolphe Chapleau continued to preach a crusade, the volunteers were greeted in
Paris by the ultramontane journalist Louis Veuillot as a 'band of
crusaders.'[21] The fact that they never saw action, thanks to the
collapse of Garibaldi's movement, diminished none of the Zouaves'
fervor, and on the third anniversary of their departure they organized the Union Allet—named after their colonel—which became
a center of ultramontane activity and still persists today, while the
Zouave uniform is affected by parish guards who add color to
church celebrations.[22]

The effect of the Papal Zouave episode was to widen the gap
between French and English in Canada, for Garibaldi was a hero
to the English-speaking world, and defending the temporal power
of the Papacy was not a popular course in North America outside
Quebec. Bishop Laflèche's discourse at the departure of the Zouaves,
which he had been unable to finish because of emotion, was later
published. It opened the public phase of the ultramontane-liberal
conflict. For Bishop Laflèche added to the ancient battles of the
Church against paganism, Arianism, Protestantism, and Voltairean-
ism, the contemporary struggle against rationalistic liberalism, born
of the principles of Voltaire and Rousseau and of the French
Revolution. He drew a black and white opposition between liberalism and Catholicism, and called upon French Canada to fulfil its
'Providential mission of maintaining and spreading the Kingdom
of God in the New World' by avoiding all contamination from
liberalism.[23] This discourse aroused considerable agitation among
the Liberals of Quebec, who were divided into a small and very
radical group known as the *Rouges* under the leadership of Louis-
Antoine Dessaulles, Joseph Doutre, and Rodolphe Laflamme, and
a larger and more moderate one made up of those who reconciled
their politics with their religion, and relied upon the sympathies
of pro-Liberal Archbishop Taschereau of Quebec and of Laval
University, in the face of a general alliance of the clergy with the
Conservative Party. The conflict thus opened was to continue on
many fronts until the close of the century, leaving an indelible
mark on the French-Canadian mind.

3

Since the 1830's two radically opposed currents of ideas had been flowing through French Canada. They are commonly called ultra-montanism and liberalism, although both are misnamed, for French-Canadian ultramontanism had a strong nationalist and even racist bent more characteristic of gallicanism than of its historical opposite, while French-Canadian liberalism was very different from its European namesake condemned by Pope Pius IX in the *Syllabus of Errors* (1864). The semantic confusion caused by applying European terms to North American movements of different origins and purposes envenomed the struggle between these two rival currents of ideas. The original leader of the ultramontane movement was Bishop Ignace Bourget, who became the second bishop of the new diocese of Montreal in 1840, after serving as vicar-general since its foundation. The Bishop sympathized with the *Patriote* movement of 1837–8; and in the diocese of Montreal the ecclesiastical author-ities, with the exception of the Sulpicians, took a much less firm stand against the movement than did those of Quebec, with their tradition of strict loyalism which had won for the Church virtual establishment under English rule—a status far more favorable than that attained under the gallican French regime.

After the Rebellions, under the Union which was intended to deprive the French Canadians of their separate nationality, Bishop Bourget, a zealous, energetic, authoritarian, and very Roman-minded prelate, was the dynamic force in providing every bulwark for that nationality which came within the province of the Church. His enthusiastic followers did not always stop at these limits, which in any case were a matter of dispute at the time.

In the first decade of his possession of the see, Bishop Bourget established no less than ten religious orders in his diocese, bringing many of them from France and creating others in Canada. Among the teaching orders were the Jesuits, the Oblates, the Holy Cross Fathers and Brothers, and the Clerks of St. Viator, who exercised a strong conservative influence on the French Canadians in their reaction against the French Revolutions of 1830 and 1848. French support of the Papacy against the Italian Republicans of 1848 and 1860 strengthened the tendency of these clerics and their lay disciples to identify themselves with the French ultramontanes, whose spokes-man was the zealous convert Louis Veuillot, editor of *L'Univers*. In particular the Society of Jesus, favored by Bishop Bourget and benefiting by the prestige of its achievements in New France, exercised a growing influence through its intellectual attainments and its identification with the promulgation of the dogma of the

Immaculate Conception (1854), with the condemnation of post-French Revolution ideas in the *Syllabus of Errors* (1864), and with the assertion of papal infallibility in matters of faith and morals (1870). The Jesuits were considered to be exceedingly close to Rome. Bishop Bourget befriended them and modeled his new cathedral on St. Peter's, while the more liberal Sulpicians fell out of favor and the vast single parish of Notre-Dame-de-Montréal, which they had held since 1657, was threatened with division by the bishop.

At this period many elements in the Catholic Church at large, in reaction to the blows dealt it by the French and Italian Revolutions, swung to a highly conservative position which clashed with the dominant ideas of the non-Catholic world, then deeply affected by the dynamic heritage of 1789. This Catholic conservatism hardened into reaction as a result of the plight of the Papacy, beset by successive nationalist assaults on its temporal power in Italy. Pius IX himself reflected this development by his gradual abandonment of his early liberal ideas for highly conservative ones. While ultramontanism was anti-nationalistic in Europe, it was combined with an aggressive nationalism in Quebec, in the fervor of French-Canadian reaction to the assimilative program of the Union.

The ultramontane doctrine of the supremacy of Church over State and the nationalist doctrine of vigorous defence of French-Canadian rights both held the seeds of religio-political conflict. This conflict was long postponed by the excellent personal relationship between the dominant figure of the hierarchy, Bishop Bourget, and the political master of Quebec, George Etienne Cartier, both of whom were deeply conservative and authoritarian by nature. Then Cartier's legal advocacy of the cause of his old teachers, the Sulpicians, in opposition to the Bishop's desire to divide the parish of Montreal, brought about a coolness which favored subsequent open clashes between the two men. For all his reliance on clerical support in politics, Cartier was gallican-minded, and when in 1870 the Church became active in politics on its own account, Cartier fought the development as bitterly as any *Rouge*.

The opposing current of ideas, present in the French-Canadian mind ever since the American Revolution, was furthered by the writings of Lamennais and Lacordaire in 1830, which notably influenced *Patriote* thinking in 1837. When Papineau returned in 1845 from exile in France, he introduced the advanced democratic ideas which had subsequently been developed by these and other French intellectual leaders, who were ultramontanes in 1830 and radical liberals in 1848. Papineau himself, however, was rather more influenced by the tradition of English liberalism and by the development of that tradition in the United States. His democracy was always more North American than European, but many of his fiery young *Rouge* disciples mingled French and American doctrines in their thinking. After the split of the French Canadians in the late 1840's into Liberal-Conservatives and Liberals, the *Rouges*, in their republicanism, often flirted with annexationism. Like the English Canadians of 1849, who wanted to be English at the cost of being British, the *Rouges* were willing to cease being Canadian in order to remain French. As Lamennais broke with the Church because of what he considered to be a conspiracy of kings and priests against the people, while Lacordaire reconciled his republicanism with his Catholicism and died 'a penitent monk and an impenitent liberal,'[24] so the small group of *Rouges* who in 1847 launched the republican *L'Avenir* (named after Lamennais' and Lacordaire's organ of 1830) and its more moderate successor *Le Pays* in 1852, followed different paths. That of Lacordaire was made difficult for them by the rigid authoritarianism of Bishop Bourget and his still more inflexible disciple Bishop Laflèche. As the English-Canadian Tories had long supplied proof, a colonial culture is narrower than its model, and some French Canadians became more French than the French and more Catholic than the Pope.

The *Rouge* group, filled with the spirit of 1848, was not content with uphill political and journalistic action in a French Canada which was either becoming too preoccupied with business or too reactionary to care for new ideas. They became dominant during the 1850's in the *Institut Canadien* of Montreal, which in the absence of universities had been founded in 1844 to provide an intellectual center for French-Canadian graduates of the classical colleges. The *Institut* maintained a library and reading room; held debates and lectures; and provided a free forum for that fervent discussion of general ideas so dear to young French-Canadian intellectuals. Despite the foundation of two rival institutions, *L'Oeuvre de bons livres* and the Sulpician *Cabinet de Lecture*, whose establishment under clerical auspices was inspired by Bishop Bourget, the Montreal *Institut* and others modeled on it throughout the province grew rapidly until 1858, when the bishop first took formal steps against it. It numbered some 700 members in 1857.

The leading figures were Dr. Louis-Antoine Dessaulles, a nephew of Papineau and like him a radical democrat of seigneurial background; Joseph Doutre, an able lawyer who was one of the editors of *L'Avenir* and one of the founders of *Le Pays*, a prophet of the Enlightenment and a mortal enemy of Cartier; Eric Dorion, the *enfant terrible* brother of Antoine-Aimé Dorion, the *Rouge* chief, and the founder of *L'Avenir* and *Le Défricheur*; and Charles Laberge, a lawyer who followed the elder Dorion in politics but broke with him over his alliance with the francophobe George Brown of Ontario. These radical-minded young men preached with various nuances the dawn of a new era of free speech and thought which was not at all to the taste of Bishop Bourget, who was disturbed by vigorous Protestant proselytizing in Montreal and by the *Institut's* tolerant attitude toward non-Catholic opinion.

So in the spring of 1858 the Bishop issued three pastoral letters, in the first of which he deplored the rise of irreligiousness in Canada as evidenced by 'bad books, lying publications, and irreligious discourses.' Members of literary societies were warned against 'books contrary to faith and morals.'[25] Now the *Institut's* library contained such books as Voltaire's works, Lamartine's *Voyage en Orient*, Pascal's *Provincial Letters*, Montesquieu's *Spirit of Laws*, Florente's *History of the Inquisition*, Montaigne's *Essays*, Sismondi's *History of the Italian Republics*, and Lamennais' *Paroles d'un Croyant*, while its sixty-odd journals ran the gamut from *Les Mélanges religieux*, the Bishop's organ, to the militantly Protestant *Witness*. After a meeting at which a majority of members decided that the *Institut* was capable of judging the morality of its library for itself, some hundred dissident members, headed by Edouard Fabre and Labrèche-Viger, resigned on the grounds that the *Institut*, which had been founded solely for French Canadians, now opened its library to all, and that it spread 'absurd moral, religious, and national ideas.' The dissidents, supported by the bishop, opened the short-lived *Institut national*, while the original body refused to recognize the authority of the *Index* on gallican grounds, and protested that its library was 'exclusively composed of moral books . . . suited to nourish the heart and to develop the intelligence,' and had never contained 'books of an obscene or immoral character.'[26] In reply Bishop Bourget issued another pastoral on March 30, invoking the authority of the Council of Trent on the question of episcopal jurisdiction in matters of censorship, and declaring that books listed in the *Institut* catalogue of 1852 had been condemned by the *Index*. Two months later he denounced 'bad newspapers,' defined as those 'whose belief and morality are contrary to those of the Faith.'[27] This utterance was clearly directed against *Le Pays*, the *Rouge* organ directed by Dessaulles, then a dominant figure in the *Institut*. Dessaulles later claimed that he twice wrote the Bishop for an explanation without receiving a reply.

Hostilities between Bishop Bourget and the *Institut* then lapsed for a few years, although the bishop threw his influence behind rival organizations under clerical control. Then in 1863 a committee, composed among others of Joseph Doutre and young Wilfrid Laurier, waited upon the bishop and in an attempt at reconciliation asked him to indicate the 'reprehensible works' in the library catalogue which they left with him. Bishop Bourget returned the catalogue without comment six months later, thus insisting upon formal submission to his authority before making peace. Meanwhile he had issued a pastoral letter on December 25, 1863, pointing out in apocalyptic terms the 'dangers of the times in which we live, the dangers from the men among whom we live, and the dangers of the errors in the environment in which we live.'[28] He also called for great vigilance lest impious books and bad newspapers should spread dangerous doctrines among Catholics. In March 1864 the *Institut* declared itself to be devoid of doctrine, although it carefully banned pernicious teachings and 'anything which might wound the religious sensibilities of some of its members.'[29] After another fruitless interview with the bishop, a group of members appealed to Rome and made charges against the bishop, who defended himself by sending to Rome a collection of pamphlets published under the *Institut's* auspices.

As a result of these steps, in 1868 the *Institut's* yearbook was put on the *Index*, an extraordinary measure, while the Provincial Council of the hierarchy again denounced impious and immoral books, libraries which contained both good and bad books, and certain harmful newspapers. The faithful were forbidden to own, edit, write for, or circulate the latter, while 'every true patriot' was called upon not to read them.[30] Meanwhile Papineau had emerged from his retirement at Montebello to contribute his prestige to the beleaguered *Institut* by giving a lecture under its auspices in December 1867, in which he maintained the thesis that solid convictions could only be arrived at by a free examination of the facts. This was taken as a declaration of open war by the bishop, and Montreal became the scene of a battle between the liberal and reactionary outlooks. Under the heavy pressure exerted by the bishop, Dessaulles openly defied episcopal authority, while stoutly maintaining his Catholicism. Doutre declared himself an agnostic.

During these years the aging Bishop Bourget had received wholehearted support from the ardent young Grand Vicar of Trois-Rivières, Louis-François Laflèche, recalled from the Red River missions after twelve years to become first superior of the Séminaire de Nicolet and later administrator of the diocese, which he was to head from 1870 to 1898. After the papal defeat at Castelfidaro in 1860, Abbé Laflèche delivered a passionate sermon in favor of the temporal power of the Papacy, hymning Lamoricière and his Zouaves. In 1866 Laflèche, now grand-vicar, published his *Quelques considérations sur les rapports de la société civile avec la Religion et la Famille*. In this adaptation to French Canada of the ideas of Rohrbacher, who as an apologetic Church historian had dealt crushing blows to French gallicanism after parting company with the more radical Lamennais in 1832, his disciple laid down the basic principles of French-Canadian nationalistic ultramontanism:

I. A nation is constituted by unity of speech, unity of faith, uniformity of morals, customs, and institutions. The French Canadians possess all these, and constitute a true nation. Each nation has received from Providence a mission to fulfil. The mission of the French-Canadian people is to constitute a center of Catholicism in the New World.

II. Authority derives from God. The best form of government is a moderate monarchy (the Church and the family are examples of it); the most imperfect is democracy. Liberalism commits the fundamental error of seeking to build society on other than religious principles. Electors not only exercise a right; they fulfil a duty for which they are responsible before God. The priest thus has a right to guide them.

'It is an error condemned by reason, by history, and by Revelation to say that politics is a field in which religion has no right to enter, and in which the Church has no concern.'[31]

In a Saint-Jean-Baptiste Day address to the French Canadians of Ottawa in this same year, Grand Vicar Laflèche advanced the doctrine, destined to become a dogma of French-Canadian nationalism, that whoever lost his language lost his faith. He also referred to the necessity of learning English as 'the heaviest tax imposed upon us by the Conquest,' and urged his auditors: 'Let us pay it loyally, but let us pay only when necessary.'[32] He denounced the idea that only political states constituted nations, and maintained that the French Canadians, like the Irish and the Indians, remained a distinct nation despite the fact that they were ruled by a foreign government. He insisted on the solidarity of family, nationality, language, and faith as the basis of French-Canadian nationhood; an analysis which is still the basis of nationalistic thinking in French Canada, despite the fact that the idea that faith is dependent upon language is totally foreign to true Catholicism, which is supranational.

Laflèche's doctrines were naturally opposed by the leading spirits of the *Institut*, who then dominated the Liberal Party in Quebec. Their position was gravely weakened when the *Institut* yearbook of 1868, containing an eulogy of free thought and annexationist speeches by Dessaulles and Horace Greeley of the *New York Tribune*, was condemned by the Holy Office in July 1869 and put on the *Index*. In a pastoral letter issued from Rome, where he had gone for the Vatican Council, Bishop Bourget announced this decision and proclaimed that it was forbidden, under pain of being deprived of the sacraments, to be a member of the *Institut* while it taught perverse doctrines, or to read or possess the condemned yearbook.[33] Gonzalve Doutre, a Papal Zouave brother of Joseph Doutre and a professor of law at McGill, went to Rome in a vain effort to upset the condemnation and to invoke restraint of Bishop Bourget's high-handed ways. While Doutre was at Rome, the *Institut* met and protested its innocence, and its Catholic members accepted the condemnation. But the refusal of some members, led by the gallican-minded Dessaulles, to bow to the storm provoked new episcopal thunders. The 1869 yearbook was in turn condemned by Rome in 1870, while the bishop again denounced 'promoters of such dangerous errors.'[34]

Then what had been hitherto a French-Canadian family quarrel became a national and international *cause célèbre* with the death in November 1869 of the printer Joseph Guibord, a member and former vice-president of the *Institut*. Bishop Bourget had decreed that those who persisted in membership in the *Institut* after its condemnation should be deprived of the sacraments and Christian burial. Some weeks before his death Guibord, who had not been a practising Catholic in recent years, had called a priest to his bedside, but, refusing to renounce the *Institut*, had not received the last rites of the Church. In accordance with the bishop's order, the Sulpician *curé* of Notre-Dame refused to perform any religious ceremony for Guibord and stipulated that his body should be buried in the unconsecrated part of the cemetery, reserved for those who died outside the Church. In short, he expressed his willingness to grant civil burial, but refused Christian burial. Guibord died on a Thursday, and his funeral was set for Monday by his friends, fellow-members of the *Institut*. After their request for Christian burial had twice been refused by Curé Rousselot, the corpse was carried on Sunday afternoon to the Catholic cemetery of Côte-des-Neiges. When the caretaker refused to accept it without authority from the *curé*—Catholic burials were never performed on Sundays or in the afternoon—the funeral proceeded to the Protestant cemetery, where Guibord's body found a temporary resting place.

The following Wednesday suit was brought against the *curé* and churchwardens of Notre-Dame in the name of Guibord's illiterate wife, Henrietta Brown, who later gave evidence that she had had no desire to sue and that legal action was taken on the initiative of her husband's friends. Rodolphe Laflamme, one of the leading spirits of the *Institut*, appeared as her lawyer in the case, which was heard by Judge Charles Mondelet, the defender of the Rebellion prisoners in the 1839 trials whose independence of spirit was further indicated by the fact that he had married outside the Church. Louis-Amable Jetté, Laflamme's brother-in-law and a moderate *Rouge* though a fervent Catholic, was the advocate of Notre-Dame. Both lawyers were at the outset of brilliant legal and public careers which carried Laflamme to the federal cabinet and Jetté to the lieutenant-governorship of Quebec and membership in the Alaska Boundary tribunal. Laflamme was soon reinforced by Joseph Doutre, and Jetté by Francis Cassidy, an Irish Catholic founder of the *Institut*, and

F.-X.-A. Trudel, who was to become famous as the lay leader of the ultramontanes under the mocking title of 'Grand Vicar' Trudel.

With this array of legal talent, carefully chosen on both sides with regard to personal positions and views, the trial soon departed from the matter in question and became a public debate on gallicanism *vs.* ultramontanism, free speech *vs.* authoritarianism, French law *vs.* English law, canon law *vs.* civil law—in essence, State *vs.* Church. The lawyers wandered from the Council of Trent through the Inquisition to St. Bartholomew's Massacre, from the capitulations of the Conquest through the Quebec Act to the constitutions of 1791, 1840, and 1867. The whole conflict of the *Institut* with Bishop Bourget was fought once more in open court, and the attention devoted to the trial by both the French and English press made it a focus of the religio-political controversies of the day. Judge Mondelet, who exhibited during the trial a partisan attitude which made plain his gallican and liberal sympathies, delivered judgment on May 6, 1870, condemning the parish to provide burial within the Catholic cemetery within six days and to bear all costs of the trial.[35]

This sentence was reversed on September 30, 1870 by unanimous decision of the Court of Appeals, on the grounds that the civil courts had no jurisdiction in ecclesiastical cases; that gallican law had never been in force in Canada; and that priests of the Catholic Church were entirely independent of civil tribunals in the exercise of their ministry.[36] On December 2 an appeal was carried to the Queen's Bench Court, which on September 7, 1871 sustained the judgment of the Court of Appeals, after its English presiding justice had sharply rejected Doutre's motion that Catholic judges be barred from the bench for this case.[37] Appeal was then taken to the Privy Council in the name of the *Institut*—the widow Guibord having meanwhile died—and Doutre and Jetté went to London to argue the case. By a judgment rendered on November 28, 1874, the parish was ordered to bury Guibord in the Catholic portion of the cemetery and to pay costs amounting to $6,000. The Privy Council held that during the French regime canon law had been subject to the Gallican Liberties and that a right of appeal from ecclesiastical decisions to the civil courts had been recognized. It maintained that this right had been continued by the Quebec Act, and that since the *Index* had never been recognized in France or Canada, Guibord was free of any valid ecclesiastical sentence barring him from Christian burial.[38]

Thus, after six years of litigation and agitation, September 2, 1875 was set by Joseph Doutre for the burial of Guibord by court order in the Catholic cemetery lot already occupied by his wife's grave. The triumphant Doutre went beyond the terms of the judgment and demanded that burial be accompanied by the ordinary religious ceremonies, under pains of damages and interest. All

Montreal and much of Canada was up in arms over the Guibord case, and both the mayor and chief of police were warned by Bishop Bourget to take measures against possible popular outbreaks on the day set for burial. While a turbulent crowd excited by the ultramontane press gathered at the Catholic cemetery, Guibord's body was removed from the Protestant cemetery and the coffin, covered with a British flag, was placed in a hearse surmounted by a cross. The funeral procession of a dozen carriages and some thirty people then proceeded to the open gates of the Catholic cemetery. Pushing aside the guards stationed there, the crowd closed the gates against the funeral procession. The caretaker, summoned by a bailiff to open the gates, declined to do so, protesting that he could do nothing against the opposition of the crowd. The mayor, summoned by telegram, arrived with police reinforcements after Doutre had retired to the Protestant cemetery with the body amid some stone-throwing and a growing hue and cry.

A few days later Bishop Bourget issued a circular letter urging the people to be calm and to offer no opposition to Guibord's burial. He added that the grave would be placed under interdict, and hence would be 'morally separated' from consecrated ground.[39] During the following month Doutre brought suit against *Le Nouveau Monde*, the ultramontane organ blamed for raising the agitation, and against the parish for refusing burial. Though both suits were thrown out of court, Doutre succeeded in extracting the costs of previous litigation from the parish, and these were paid under protest by the *curé*. Meanwhile an armed guard had been established over the Protestant cemetery, and a violent newspaper controversy broke out.

Finally, on November 16, after the *curé* of Notre-Dame had once more refused Christian burial and protested against this violation of the laws of the Church, the liberties of Catholics, and the sanctity of the cemetery by the enforced burial of Guibord in consecrated ground, the body was carried from the Protestant cemetery to the Catholic one under the protection of 1,235 soldiers, Mayor Hingston, and Judge Coursol. The *curé* assisted as a civil officer at the burial, but the only ceremony was a prayer by some of Guibord's friends. The grave was filled with cement and scrap iron as a precaution against desecration, and then guards were placed over the final resting place of the troubled corpse of Joseph Guibord. His epitaph was pronounced by Bishop Bourget in a pastoral letter published on the day of burial. The bishop rejoiced that calm had prevailed despite provocation; reaffirmed that the grave would be forever separate from consecrated ground; and concluded: 'There reposes a rebel who has been buried by force of arms.'[40]

4

The persecution of the *Institut Canadien* and the Guibord case cannot be understood without reference to the political history of the period. The *Institut* was not only a literary society; its leaders were also the leaders of the *Rouge* party, and they revolted against Bishop Bourget's authority in part because of the open alliance of the hierarchy with the Conservative Party. Since the *Rouges* believed in the new republican ideas which in Europe had endangered the position of the Church, the French-Canadian hierarchy was naturally inclined to ally itself with their political opponents. The new democracy of the nineteenth century had no appeal for the clergy, who were alarmed by the increase of official corruption and election disorders at home and by civil strife in Europe. Democracy was also tainted for them by its derivation from the suspect intellectual fathers of the French Revolution, and by the fact that its disciples went to still greater extremes than the leaders of the unsuccessful Rebellion of 1837–8, which had endangered the survival of French-Canadian nationality. The *Rouges* openly advanced the doctrine of the separation of Church and State—a doctrine repugnant to the Catholic tradition, which holds that such separation may be tolerated but not approved—and they gloated over the republican successes in Europe, which deeply distressed the innately conservative and monarchist French-Canadian clergy, who at this period identified themselves more closely with Rome than at any time since the days of Bishop Laval. The *Rouges* also were sympathetic to American ideas, ever distrusted by the clergy, and inclined to annexationism, which the clergy thought would doom French-Canadian Catholicism.

With the breakdown of the Union government in the early 1860's, the clerical leaders tended to throw their support behind Cartier in the project of Confederation, though not always enthusiastically—Laflèche, for instance, regarded repeal of the Union as impossible, legislative union as 'the extermination of our institutions and nationality'; and Confederation as the only solution 'which offers us a plank of safety.'[41] Possibly because of his difference with Cartier over the division of the parish of Montreal, Bishop Bourget contented himself with a neutral acceptance of Confederation, while the other bishops of the province supported it more warmly and thundered against the *Rouges* who opposed it. With the *Rouges* openly annexationist and opposed to the temporal power of the Church, it was easy for the bishops to view the political contest, as Laflèche did, simply as a 'struggle between good and evil.'[42]

Confronted with the prospect of an ever-diminishing minority position in Canada under Confederation, the French Canadians recoiled upon their own distinctive tradition, whose European bulwarks were also threatened at this period both in France and Italy. In 1870 Quebec was more French and Catholic than it had been since the heyday of New France. During the next thirty years French Canada turned more and more to the ancient mother country:

It established transatlantic contacts with France; it travelled in France for pleasure, for tourist and commercial purposes; it sent its sons to study in France; it read French periodicals and books; the textbooks which it used were for the most part published in France; it received Frenchmen as visitors, lecturers, preachers, and consuls; its newspapers cited the French press copiously; it sought French honors.[43]

One of the most notable French influences upon Quebec was that of *L'Echo de la France*, a review of science and literature founded by Louis Ricard in 1865, which familiarized Quebec with the writings of Mgr. Dupanloup, Montalembert, Père Félix, Père Hyacinthe, Lacordaire, Thiers, Berryer, Lamartine, Veuillot, Victor Hugo, Guizot, and Victor Cousin.

The renewal of ties between France and Quebec which had been fostered by Napoleon III in the 1850's and 1860's was furthered by the profound sympathy felt in Quebec for France when the Third Empire fell before the Prussian assault in 1870. In his unpublished memoirs Abbé Casgrain vividly describes the reaction in Quebec to the disasters of 1870:

The echo of these frightful disasters, brought by the telegraph and re-echoed by the newspapers, spread grief and consternation among the French population of Canada, which had remained profoundly attached to its mother country despite more than a century of separation. We were at first incredulous at the news of the first defeats; France, it was said, might suffer some reverses, but that she should fall, completely beaten down, demolished, and reduced to helplessness at the feet of an enemy whom she had already conquered, seemed implausible. The sad reality nevertheless had to be accepted. Stupor yielded to discouragement, to grief, to lamentation. It was as if each Canadian family mourned some of its members fallen on the fields of carnage where France left part of itself. The present generation cannot imagine the spiritual state in which we lived during this terrible year. We were hurt in the most sensitive and most intimate parts of national feeling. No more illusions were possible; we marched from humiliation to humiliation. Nevertheless, if we bent our heads at the sight of such great misfortunes, we raised them with pride to protest indignantly when cowardly detractors dared to raise their voices to insult conquered France.[44]

The Quebec clergy, which included some French emigrés of 1848, pronounced that France was undergoing the judgment of God for its sins, and the unusually vivid northern lights in the fall of 1870 were taken as divine portents of the disasters of which tidings continued to come from abroad. The news of the French surrender and Napoleon's capture, of the Paris Revolution and the proclamation of the Republic, was received by grief-stricken crowds in Quebec. Relief funds for French prisoners and refugees were raised with enthusiasm. Gambetta's determination to carry on the war, Thiers' policies, and the rise of the Commune were opposed in a Quebec which followed the lead of the French clergy. Almost to a man the French Canadians espoused the cause of the Comte de Chambord, the royalist leader.

For all the intense sympathy felt in Quebec for afflicted France, a lasting distrust of the Republic became part of the French-Canadian mind, and from it stemmed a growing conviction, encouraged by royalist-minded French priests and nuns who emigrated to Quebec, that the French Canadians were a people chosen by Providence to carry on the true French and Catholic tradition, uncorrupted by liberalism and republicanism. After 1867 the Sulpician *Cabinet de Lecture*, which made more of French than French-Canadian literature and introduced Mgr. de Ségur's anti-Masonic tracts, helped to develop a tendency to blame France's woes and Quebec's prospective dangers on the influence of Freemasonry, an idea which by the 1890's became an obsession with ultramontane journalists. This trend reached its height in 1895 with the publication of Jules-Paul Tardivel's *Pour la Patrie*, a novel which foretold an Orange Order plot to seize the Dominion government and to exterminate French Canada.

The development of emphasis on Quebec's Frenchness was accompanied by an intensification of French-Canadian Catholicism during the same period. The ultramontane leaders of the Quebec hierarchy, Bishops Bourget and Laflèche, were among the most ardent supporters of the dogma of papal infallibility, which was promulgated on July 18, 1870 by the Vatican Council. Bishop Laflèche wrote from Rome to his grand vicar that April: 'Protestantism has directly attacked the Church by rejecting its authority . . . Gallicanism, more hypocritical, has pretended to have a certain respect for the Church while exerting itself above all to attack it in its constitution.'[45] To him the providential moment had arrived to crush gallicanism—by which he meant any State opposition to the Church—and Protestant inroads on Catholicism. A month later he wrote again to Grand Vicar Caron: 'The dogmatic definition of the infallibility of the Sovereign Pontiff is the great remedy which God in His mercy has prepared to cure the frightful social evils of our time.'[46] Both Bishop Bourget and Bishop Laflèche returned from Rome with their ultramontane tendencies reinforced, and with new fervor to oppose the development in Canada of the political liberalism which had brought revolution to Italy and France. Both they and Bishop Taché of St. Boniface, who had been recalled from the Vatican Council by Cartier in January 1870 to aid the government in settling the Riel question,* evinced a tendency to extend Papal infallibility to the episcopate, while their zealous disciples extended it on down to the humblest *curé*. The way was thus paved for the bitter conflicts between Church and State which ensued for thirty years.

The old alliance between the hierarchy and the Conservatives was soon threatened by several developments. Bishop Bourget discovered that he could get little aid from Cartier, the political overlord of Quebec as well as the French-Canadian leader at Ottawa, in his campaign to divide the parish of Montreal. Cartier was loyal to his older teachers, the Sulpicians, whom he served as attorney in their legal proceedings in this matter, and he was too gallican-minded to take political orders from Bishop Bourget, who wanted legislative support for his plan. Then the federal government refused to disavow the New Brunswick law of 1871 which abolished the separate schools of that province, where the French Canadians formed a large minority. Using as an excuse the danger of infringing provincial rights and thus setting a precedent which might later be turned against Quebec, the ever-temporizing Sir John A. Macdonald managed to resist French-Canadian pressure for remedial action by Ottawa as provided for in the B.N.A. Act (Sec. 93, 3 & 4), and instead suggested recourse to the courts. Thus the question dragged on for years, envenoming the relations between Church and State and arousing ethnic antagonism. The government's course in regard to the Riel question also weakened its alliance with the hierarchy.†

These differences played a major part in the formation of a 'Catholic Program' by a group of fervent ultramontane followers of Bishops Bourget and Laflèche before the provincial elections of 1871. This remarkable document opened with a declaration of allegiance in principle to the Conservative Party, 'the defender of social authority' and the 'only one offering serious guarantees to religious interests.'[47] But party loyalty should not prevail over religious interests in such questions as marriage, education, the establishment of parishes, and the keeping of vital records, and members of parliament considering such laws were obliged 'to change and modify them as the Bishops of the Province might request, in order to harmonize them with the doctrines of the Roman Catholic Church.' Therefore the elector should follow these rules in voting:

1. If the contest is between two Conservatives, it goes without saying that we shall support the one who accepts the program we have just outlined.

* Cf. Chapter VIII, p. 401.   † *Ibid.*, 404–7.

2. If on the contrary it is between a Conservative of any shade whatever and an adept of the Liberal school, our active sympathies will be given to the former.

3. If the only candidates who come forward in a constituency are both Liberals or oppositionists, we must choose the one who will accept our conditions.

4. Finally, in the event that the contest is between a Conservative who rejects our program and an opportunist who accepts it, the position would be more delicate. To vote for the latter would be to imperil the Conservative Party, which we wish to see powerful. What decision should we make between these two dangers? In this case we would advise Catholic electors to refrain from voting.[48]

This attempt to set up a Catholic party within the Conservative Party was the work of a group of laymen which included F.-X.-A. Trudel, the defender of Notre-Dame in the Guibord case; Adolphe-Basile Routhier, an ultramontane writer and future judge; Testard de Montigny, the dean of the Zouaves; and Siméon Pagnuelo, Bishop Bourget's lawyer in the matter of the division of the parish. These were men of the bishop's 'New School,' and their model was Louis Veuillot. They met at the Montreal house of Alphonse Desjardins, owner of the ultramontane organ *Le Nouveau Monde* and host of the fugitive *Métis* leader Louis Riel, and in the presence of Canon Godefroy Lamarche, censor of that paper which had been established in 1864 at the instigation of the bishop. Bishop Laflèche's followers were represented by Magloire McLeod, editor of the *Journal de Trois-Rivières*, which reflected Laflèche's views as thoroughly as *Le Nouveau Monde* did those of Bishop Bourget. The Catholic program, written by Routhier, was approved by the two bishops and published in *Le Journal* on April 20, 1871.

The federal and provincial Conservative leaders, Cartier and Cauchon, immediately complained to the hierarchy about this attempt to form a Catholic party; and Archbishop Taschereau, the new bishop of Quebec, issued on April 24 a circular to his clergy and a statement to the press condemning the program as contrary to the regulation of the Fourth Council of Quebec against clerical intervention in politics, and as having 'the serious inconvenience of having been formulated without any participation of the episcopate.'[49] He persuaded his colleagues of Rimouski—Bishop Langevin was the brother of Cartier's aide Sir Hector—and of Saint-Hyacinthe to do likewise. This anti-ultramontane group of the hierarchy feared that the formation of a Catholic party in Quebec would provoke the formation of an inevitably stronger Protestant party in Canada at large, as well as a conflict between Church and State. But Bishops Bourget and Taché formally assured Trudel on June 6 that they fully approved the program, and thus the public was made aware of the disunity of the episcopate on the matter. In the provincial elections of June, only one programist, Trudel, was elected; and the Conservatives held their own by comparing their *Rouge* opponents to the *Communards* of Paris who had shot their archbishop and burnt the Tuileries, though a handful of new Liberal members, among them young Wilfrid Laurier, were elected.

Placed more strongly than ever under the disapproval of the Church, some of the moderate Liberals under the leadership of Louis Jetté attempted to get out of the impossible position into which the Catholic Program had forced them by forming a new *Parti National*, which was simply the old Liberal Party shorn of its extremist *Rouge* elements and its anti-clerical tradition. *Le National*, the organ of the new group, proclaimed:

> We are a national party because we are attached to our nation above all, and because we have pledged our unswerving loyalty to Canada above the whole world, Canada against the world ... *Le National* will be a political and non-religious paper, but as the special organ of the Catholic population and in conformity with the opinions of the journal's directors, when occasion arises we shall concur with Catholic opinion; and we repudiate in advance anything which may inadvertently be overlooked in the hasty editing of a daily paper, in order to protest our entire devotion and our filial obedience to the Church.[50]

But the *Parti National* seemed as heretical to the obdurate ultramontane bishops as its forebear; and its only notable triumph was Jetté's victory over Cartier in Montreal East, despite the active aid of Sir Hugh Allan's brawny longshoremen and all the prestige and power of the Conservative leader.

Cartier, already much weakened by the Bright's disease which later brought about his death, was subsequently elected for Provencher in Manitoba, after Riel had been induced to give up the seat. But the older leader never regained his former power. His health drove him to London for medical care, and there he labored fitfully on the Manitoba Act. He died in April 1873, some months before the mounting rumors of Conservative corruption culminated in the Canadian Pacific scandal, which drove his colleague Macdonald from office. Clear proof was supplied that Sir Hugh Allan had furnished $350,000 to Conservative campaign funds, at the demand of Cartier and Macdonald, in hope of obtaining the contract for the proposed transcontinental railroad.

This downfall of the federal regime which had held power since Confederation was paralleled by that of the Conservative provincial government in 1874 after the Montreal tanneries scandal, but neither event did the Liberals much good in Quebec, for Boucher de Boucherville, a programist, formed the new provincial government and was supported by clerical influence in the 1875 election.

With the approval of Bishops Bourget and Laflèche, the ultra-montanes hammered away at the Liberals as disciples of a doctrine condemned by the Pope and as Canadian counterparts of the French *Communards* who were now enacting anti-clerical legislation. When the Swiss Protestant Liberal leader, Henri Joly de Lotbinière, offered to resign to avoid embarrassing his colleagues because of his faith, his followers would have none of it, since the ultramontanes could be no more opposed to a Protestant Liberal than to a Catholic one.

5

What has been called the 'Holy War' in Quebec's political annals was now in full swing. On one side stood the ultramontanes, backed by Bishop Bourget, who had thus approved the Catholic Program in a circular to his clergy:

> I am very happy to see the formation of a group which is heartily attached to the teaching of the Holy See, which approves all that the Pope approves and condemns all that the Pope condemns; which consequently rejects liberalism, false philosophy, rationalism, indifferentism, and all the monstrous errors which like venomous serpents creep into the ranks of society. This group prides itself on following in all points the teaching of the Church, and its members prove by their deeds that they are sincere.
>
> This group is already composed of a good number of Catholics notable by their position in the various ranks of society, and above all of ardent and devout young men. We are happy to number among them several of our Zouaves, who consecrate their pens to the defence of the Holy See, since they are no longer able to use their swords to guard the Holy City. . . . These young men belong to good families . . . in several years they will be scattered through the legislature, the magistracy, and in other important positions. . . .[51]

At Bishop Bourget's right hand stood Bishop Laflèche, still more 'Roman' and rigid than the leader whose place he was to fill when illness and old age forced the elder man into retirement in 1876. Both men were conservative by nature; finding the Conservative or '*Bleu*' Party increasingly unresponsive to their influence as its power grew, they encouraged the ultramontane or '*Castor*' wing of that party which grew up under their domination.

The rest of the Quebec hierarchy took very different attitudes toward politics, with Archbishop Taschereau of Quebec, who possessed Liberal leanings, making no secret of his opposition to the proceedings of Bishops Bourget and Laflèche. This opposition in part reflected the ancient rivalry between Quebec and Montreal, for Quebec resented the rise of Montreal as the new center of the province. Bishop Larocque of Saint-Hyacinthe sought to remain neutral in the quarrel, while Bishop Langevin of Rimouski opposed the division of Conservative forces represented by the ultramontane development, out of loyalty to his brother, now Conservative leader after Cartier's death. Bishop Guigues of Ottawa favored strict neutrality in political matters. Aside from the major question of the relations of Church and State, another source of division among the hierarchy was the desire of Bishop Bourget, at the instigation of the Jesuits and with the backing of Bishop Laflèche, to establish a Catholic university at Montreal. This institution would destroy the educational monopoly enjoyed by Laval, of which Archbishop Taschereau had been rector before his elevation to the episcopate.

The rumored division of the hierarchy was made manifest at the celebration of Bishop Bourget's golden anniversary as a priest, which was marked by three days of tributes to the man who was already considered a saint by his devoted followers. For the moment his enemies were willing to relax their opposition and to pay honor to a distinguished career, and all his colleagues gathered in Montreal for the occasion. The climax of the celebration was a Pontifical Mass at Notre-Dame, where the ailing bishop, too ill to officiate himself, was enthroned on a dais which had served for the coronation of Charles X of France. This dais, like the sermon, was supplied by the Jesuits, who delighted to honor the bishop who had enabled them to regain so much of their ancient influence in Canada. The preacher was an Alsatian Jesuit, Père Braun, an extreme ultramontane theologian who was at loggerheads with the Abbé Benjamin Paquet, the leading Laval theologian.

Before a congregation which included all the bishops of Quebec and many from Ontario, as well as notables of the political world, Père Braun launched into a fervent promulgation of the extreme ultramontane position, framed in terms of eulogy for Bishop Bourget's war against gallicanism and liberalism:

The Church does not submit bills, projected laws, to the government; but a law which is already an obligation of conscience. It is not for the government to revise these laws, to discuss them, or to change them; it has no jurisdiction.

The Church can request the government to grant civil sanction to its laws, but this sanction adds nothing to the right of the law, but merely facilitates it.

The Church alone possesses the right to judge ecclesiastical cases, to dispose of matrimonial cases, and to prescribe the formalities therefor. The Church enjoys these immunities, and whoever dares to interfere is guilty of sacrilege.

Governments often aid in the establishment of parishes, but as a favor and not as a right, and they enjoy this right only when it is given them by the Holy Father. If the government should presume to aid in the establishment of parishes without the permission of the Holy See, it would be guilty of an act of sacrilege.

Such are the truths which your pastor has caused to triumph. They assure the submission of the State to the Church, and the State dependent upon the Church will be submissive to God. . .

At the moment we may see throughout Europe Catholics vying with one another, with the encouragement of the Holy See, to fight those who seek to hamper the liberty of the Church, and to elect to office those right-thinking men who promise to defend the rights of the Church.

Similarly on many occasions the Bishop of Montreal has exhorted the faithful to vote for men who are determined to fight error and to protect the Church and its rights . . .

[The directors of *Le Nouveau Monde*] have accepted the task of defending the truth and serving as champions of the rights and liberties of the Church.

And may you, brethren, be always one with your bishop in the battles against error. As a general guides his army, your pastor leads you . . . Remember that he has caused to triumph the infallibility and independence of the Church, the subordination of the State to the Church.[52]

This discourse uttered in the church of the Sulpicians, whose struggle with the bishop over the division of the parish of Montreal was not yet ended, struck at Cartier and Langevin and the judicial proceedings in the Guibord case. It was an open declaration of war, and it was so taken by the supporters of Archbishop Taschereau and the other anti-ultramontane bishops, already irritated by an earlier sermon by the Abbé Alexis Pelletier, who had taken refuge in Montreal after being silenced for a Jansenist campaign against the teaching of unexpurgated classical literature at Laval.

A journalistic war promptly broke out, waged by clerics and laymen alike; and the skirmishing took on new vigor when a bill providing for the establishment of a Jesuit university at Montreal was introduced in the Quebec Legislature in November 1872. Bishop Bourget had already twice applied to Rome for sanction of this project. His request had twice been denied by the Congregation of the Propaganda at the instigation of Archbishop Taschereau, who opposed the plan on the grounds that the small number of students and the great expense involved justified only one university in the province. Quebec rejoiced at the spectacle of the 'Roman' Bishop of Montreal appealing from Rome to the legislature, while accusing the Quebeckers of gallicanism. Bourget and Taschereau exchanged correspondence, which the Archbishop closed by the terse comment: '*Roma locuta est, causa finita est*' ('Rome has spoken, the case is closed').[53] This correspondence was published, and every member of the legislature received copies of letters supporting Taschereau from the bishops of Rimouski, Saint-Hyacinthe, and Ottawa. The 'Holy War' had become a public issue. In December 1876 Archbishop Taschereau and the Rector of Laval left for Rome, where they were soon followed by Bishop Laflèche and Père Braun. Each party there urged its views on the vexed questions of the division of the parish of Montreal, of the university, and of the Catholic Program. Rome sanctioned the new parishes, maintained its opposition to a second university, and refrained from pronouncing on the religio-political question.

That question remained a cause of grave scandal and dissension. At the Provincial Council of the hierarchy in 1873 Archbishop Taschereau had opposed a motion by Bishops Bourget and Laflèche for a warning against liberalism with the comment that there were no liberals in the condemned Catholic sense in Quebec. Subsequently the Liberal Party won the federal elections of 1874 but lost the provincial ones of 1875, against the opposition of most of the clergy, who were disciples of the two ultramontane bishops and great readers of *Le Nouveau Monde.* Some of the defeated Liberals, represented by François Langelier of the Laval law faculty, applied to the courts for annulment of the elections they had lost, on the grounds of undue influence exercised by the clergy in the Conservative interest. The clergy closed ranks under this attack, which coincided with the last flare-up of the Guibord case and a new onslaught of sensational revelations by the renegade priest Charles Chiniquy, who had turned the evangelical fervor which had made him Quebec's apostle of temperance and a leader of the Illinois emigrants to the service of the Protestant Missionary Society's campaign against Rome and all its works. [54]

Thus, at the Provincial Council of the hierarchy in September 1875, Archbishop Taschereau was induced by his ultramontane colleagues to join in a joint pastoral letter which firmly supported Bishop Bourget on the Guibord question and pronounced a strong warning against Catholic liberalism:

Distrust above all that liberalism which wishes to cover itself with the fine name of 'Catholic' in order to accomplish more easily its criminal mission. You will recognize it easily from the description which the Sovereign Pontiff has often given of it: (1) the endeavour to subordinate the Church to the State, (2) incessant attempts to break the bonds which unite the children of the Church with one another and with their clergy, (3) the monstrous alliance of truth with error under the pretext of reconciling all things and avoiding conflicts, (4) finally, the illusion, or at times the hypocrisy, which conceals a boundless pride under the mask of religion and of a fine assurance of submission to the Church. . . . No one, therefore, may in the future with good conscience be permitted to remain a Catholic liberal. [55]

The joint pastoral also condemned the views that religion had nothing to do with politics; that religious principles were not to enter into the discussion of public affairs; that the clergy's functions were confined to the church and the sacristy; and that in politics the people should practice moral independence. The bishops pronounced that priests had the same political rights as other citizens, and that there were political questions in which they might and should intervene in the name of religion. The Liberals, who had appealed to the courts against clerical intervention in the elections, were warned that it was for the Church to decide when it should thus raise its voice; and the Conservative press, which had attacked Laval for harboring such creators of scandal as Langelier and Flynn, was also warned that institutions under the protection of the bishops should not be called before 'the incompetent tribunal of public opinion.'[56] In both cases complaints should have been made to the hierarchy, rather than to the courts or in the press. In an accompanying circular letter, the clergy was warned against too free intervention in politics without consultation with the bishops. In his private circular Bishop Bourget added this bit of advice, which extended the new dogma of papal infallibility to the lowliest *curé*: 'Let each say in his heart, "I hear my *curé*, my *curé* hears the bishop, the bishop hears the Pope, and the Pope hears Our Lord Jesus Christ."'[57]

Such counsels, coupled with ultramontane pamphlets which sought to demonstrate the perfect identity of Canadian and European liberalism, threatened the Liberal Party, then in power at Ottawa, with extinction in Quebec. Archbishop Taschereau was approached by moderate Liberals of the Jetté, Langelier, and Laurier school, who urged an official distinction between condemned Catholic liberalism and permitted political Liberalism. A collective pastoral was required to remedy the injustice done by a collective pastoral, but Bishop Laflèche flatly opposed such a step and was supported in his stand by other bishops. Meanwhile in two federal by-elections in Charlevoix in January 1876, Hector Langevin triumphed by announcing that he had the support of the clergy, by parading his pontifical decoration, and by stressing the fact that he was the brother of the bishop and of the grand vicar of Rimouski. Under the adroit management of Israel Tarte, the Conservative organizer who later became famous for his observation that elections were not won by prayers, but who for some years did not hesitate to make use of the spiritual arm in politics, the 'Holy War' was carried onto the electoral battlefields. Some *curés* told their congregation that a Liberal vote involved mortal sin. One observed that the Conservatives ('*Bleus*') carried the blue banner of the Pope, while the Liberals ('*Rouges*') bore the red flag of Garibaldi, and asked his auditors on whose side they wanted to be when they died. It was noted in reporting this incident that 'Garibaldi does not enjoy a good reputation in this parish.'[58]

The growing tendency towards clerical intervention in elections, which culminated in such incidents as these, had already provoked an attack on ultramontanism by Lucius Seth Huntington, the Liberal representative of the English Eastern Townships, who had bared the Pacific scandal. In a by-election at Argenteuil in December 1875 Huntington denounced his English Protestant fellows in Quebec for their blind support of the Conservative Party, and called upon them to make common cause with the French Liberals against the ultramontane threat to freedom. These words aroused comment in the House at Ottawa, where Prime Minister Alexander Mackenzie repudiated his supporter's action in raising the religious issue, while the Conservative Sir Alexander Galt endorsed it. Sir John Macdonald, as chief of the Conservative opposition, privately remarked that the best course was 'to use the priests in the next election, but be ready to fight them in the Dominion parliament,' and urged the outraged English Quebeckers to remember that 'ultramontanism depends upon the lives of two old men, the Pope and Bishop Bourget.'[59] In the end the English Protestants of Quebec wisely abstained from the French-Canadian family quarrel, but the English press of Montreal never failed to single out with alarm the more extreme ultramontane utterances.

Indeed, they alone in Quebec could do so with impunity in the prevailing intellectual climate. The moderate Liberal L.-O. David, after seeing his *Bien Public* banned in parish after parish, abandoned journalism and took refuge from the ultramontane storm as a translator at Ottawa in May 1876,* after criticizing the later pastoral letters of Bishop Bourget which 'stirred prejudices, encouraged bad faith, and excited a certain number of priests who needed to be restrained.' He added: 'There are parishes where since that time the pulpit has become nothing but a tribune for violent political harangues. It would appear that there is no longer but one crime in the world, but one mortal sin, that of voting for a Reform candidate, of receiving a Reform journal which questions the infallibility of Sir John and M. Langevin.' He warned that in the end such abuses would become intolerable to a Catholic people, 'and then indifference towards religion and hatred towards the priest [will] produce revolution.'[60] The still more moderate Laurier in December 1875 expressed to an English-Canadian colleague reluctance at his prospective elevation to the federal cabinet, for 'from that moment my quietness and happiness will be gone. It will be a war with the clergy, a war every day, every moment . . . I shall be denounced as anti-Christ. You may laugh at that, but it is no laughing matter to me.'[61]

*Thus establishing the subsequently well-worn precedent of French Canadians finding security from provincial pressures in federal employment. This tradition accounts for some of Quebec's chronic distrust of Ottawa.

The semantic confusion which identified English political Liberalism with Continental social liberalism seemed to be beyond clarification until Laurier addressed the *Club Canadien* of Quebec on 'Political Liberalism' on June 26, 1877. Laurier, who had been driven from Montreal to Arthabaska by threatened tuberculosis, had seen his newspaper, *Le Défricheur*, whose editorship he had taken over from Eric Dorion, forced to the wall by Bishop Laflèche, as he had seen the *Institut Canadien* collapse under Bishop Bourget's assaults. A veteran of the religio-political persecution waged by the ultramontanes, he well knew the prejudices which his party had to overcome if it were ever to win power in Quebec:

I know that in the eyes of a large number of my fellow countrymen, the Liberal party is a party composed of men of perverse doctrines and dangerous tendencies, pressing knowingly and deliberately towards revolution. I know that in the eyes of a portion of my fellow countrymen the Liberal party is a party of men with upright intentions, perhaps, but victims and dupes of principles which are leading them unconsciously but fatally towards revolution. In short, I know that in the eyes of another and not the least considerable portion, perhaps, of our people, Liberalism is a new form of evil, a heresy carrying with it its own condemnation.[62]

Grouping all the charges against the Liberals in two principal propositions that 'Liberalism is a new form of error, a heresy already virtually condemned by the head of the Church,' and that 'a Catholic cannot be a Liberal,'[63] Laurier made his reply to the ultramontanes, which is one of the great landmarks of French-Canadian intellectual history.

At the outset he denied that political Liberalism was identical with condemned Catholic liberalism, and pointed out the consequences of this identification:

Either we would be obliged to abstain completely from taking any part in the management of affairs of state, and then the constitution—that constitution which was granted to us for our own protection—would be no more than a dead letter in our hands; or we would be obliged to take part in the management of affairs of state under the direction and to the profit of the Conservative Party, and then, our action being no longer free, the constitution would again be a dead letter in our hands, and we would in addition have to bear the ignominy of being regarded by the other members of the Canadian family composing the Conservative Party as tools and slaves.[64]

He blamed the confusion of political Liberalism with Catholic liberalism on French Canada's lack of experience with representative institutions; and on the fact that Quebec studied the history of the Continent, where 'the history of liberalism has been written in letters of blood,' rather than that of England, 'the classic land of liberty.'[65] Condemning the popular attribution of the 'Conservative' label to everything good and the 'Liberal' one to everything bad—revolt, anarchy, and disorder—Laurier cited Macaulay's definition of the two opposed ideas:

Everywhere there is a class of men who cling with fondness to whatever is ancient and who, even when convinced by overpowering reasons that innovation would be beneficial, consent to it with many misgivings and forebodings. We find also everywhere another class of men, sanguine in hope, bold in speculation, always pressing forward, quick to discern the imperfection whatever exists, disposed to think lightly of the risks and inconveniences which attend improvements and disposed to give every change credit for being an improvement.[66]

Dismissing the charge that Liberalism involved republicanism, Laurier remarked: 'the form matters little; whether it be monarchist or republican, the moment the people exercise the right to vote, the moment they have responsible government, they have the full measure of liberty.'[67] Citing Junius' remark that 'Eternal vigilance is the price of liberty,' Laurier commented that a representative monarchy lends itself better to this vigilance than a republic.

Then he went on to declare that both ideas which formed the basis of parties were theologically 'indifferent,' both 'susceptible of much good, as they are also of much evil.'[68] He made a moving confession of his own faith in Liberalism:

I am one of those who think that everywhere, in human things, there are abuses to be remedied, new horizons to be opened up, and new forces to be developed.

Moreover, Liberalism seems to me in all respects superior to the other principle. The principle of Liberalism is inherent in the very essence of our nature, in that desire for happiness with which we are all born into the world, which pursues us through life, and which is never completely gratified this side of the grave. Our souls are immortal, but our means are limited. We constantly gravitate towards an ideal which we never attain. We dream of good but never realize the best. We only reach the goal we have proposed for ourselves, to discover new horizons opening up which we had not even suspected before. We rush on towards them, and those horizons, explored in their turn, reveal to us others which lead us on ever further and further.

This condition of our nature is precisely what makes the greatness of man, for it condemns him irrevocably to movement, to progress: our means are limited, but our nature is always perfectible, and we have the infinite for our arena. Thus there is always room for improvement of our condition, for the perfecting of our nature, and for the attainment of an easier life by a larger number. Here again is what in my eyes constitutes the superiority of Liberalism.[69]

Laurier contrasted the treatment of human aspirations in England, where reforms had been brought about without violence, with that on the Continent, where repression had produced social explosions. He cited the great English Liberals: Fox, O'Connell, Grey, Brougham, Russell, many of them aristocrats sacrificing their own privileges for the good of the people; and quoted Macaulay's triumphant account of the passage of the Reform Bill, which deprived him of his seat for a rotten borough.

Such were the models, the principles, the party of the Canadian Liberals, who were not to be identified with the liberals of France, Italy, and Germany, who 'are not Liberals; they are revolutionaries: in their principles they are so extreme that they aim at nothing less than the destruction of modern society. With these men we have nothing in common; but it is the tactic of our adversaries always to assimilate us to them.'[70] He then traced the history of the Canadian Liberal Party, pointing out that until 1848 all French Canadians had belonged to it. Then, when Papineau returned from European exile, 'a generation of young men of great talent and still greater impetuosity of character'[71] forsook Lafontaine's leadership for that of Papineau, and soon went farther than their leader did. Laurier characterized the program of *L'Avenir* as 'calling for a complete revolution in the province,' and remarked: 'The only excuse for those Liberals was their youth. The oldest of them was not more than twenty-two years of age.'[72] Their enthusiasm for the wave of revolution in Europe brought down upon them 'merciless war' from the clergy and opposition from the English Canadians— the latter being 'friendly to liberty, but also friendly to the maintenance of order.'[73]

The *Rouges* initiated all the reforms achieved during the next twenty-five years: the abolition of seigneurial tenure, judicial centralization, colonization; but they got no credit for these measures and no recognition was made that their youthful rashness had been replaced by 'calmer and more thoughtful ideas.' Meanwhile the Lafontaine Liberals merged with the Conservative Party and became the forebears of the ultramontanes of today. Of them Laurier remarked:

If M. Cartier were to come back to earth today, he would not recognize his party. M. Cartier was devoted to the principles of the English constitution. Those who take the lead today among his old partisans openly reject the principles of the English constitution as a concession to what they call the spirit of evil. They understand neither their country nor their time. All their ideas are modeled on those of the reactionaries of France. They go into ecstasies over Don Carlos or the Comte de Chambord, just as the Liberals admired Louis Blanc and Ledru-Rollin . . . I accuse them of judging the political situation of the country not according to what is happening in it, but according to what is happening in France. I accuse them of wanting to introduce here ideas which are impossible of application in our state of society. I accuse them of working laboriously and unfortunately all too efficaciously to degrade religion to the simple proportions of a political party.[74]

Laurier declared that he had 'too much respect for the faith in which I was born to ever use it as the basis of a political organization.' Then he went on to voice the first of his many warnings against parties organized on a religious or ethnic basis:

You wish to organize a Catholic party. But have you not considered that if you have the misfortune to succeed, you will draw down upon your country calamities of which it is impossible to foresee the consequences?

You wish to organize all Catholics into one party, without other bond, without other basis than a common religion; but have you not reflected that by that very fact you will organize the Protestant population as a single party, and that then, instead of the peace and harmony now prevailing between the different elements of the Canadian population, you throw open the doors to war, a religious war, the most terrible of all wars?[75]

To Laurier's mind the only justification for French-Canadian attacks on liberty was that 'liberty, as it has been generally understood and practised in France, has nothing very attractive about it. The French have the name of liberty, but they have not yet had liberty itself.'[76] Liberty in Canada was not the liberty of Auguste Barbier, but the liberty of Tennyson's 'In Memoriam.'

To the charge that the Liberals sought to relegate the clergy to the sacristy and to prevent them from teaching the people their duties as citizens and electors, Laurier gave this classic definition of his position on clerical intervention in politics:

I maintain that there is not one Canadian Liberal who wants to prevent the clergy from taking part in political affairs, if they wish to do so.

In the name of what principle should the friends of liberty seek to deny to the priest the right to take part in political affairs? In the name of what principle should the friends of liberty seek to deny to the priest the right to have and express political opinions, the right to approve or disapprove of public men and their acts, and to instruct the people in what he believes to be their duty? In the name of what principle should he not have the right to say that if I am elected, religion will be endangered, when I have the right to say that if my adversary is elected, the State will be endangered? Why should not the priest have the right to say that if I am elected, religion will inevitably be destroyed; when I have the right to say that if my adversary is elected, the State will go into bankruptcy? No, let the priest speak and preach as he thinks best; such is his right, and no Canadian Liberal will dispute that right.

Our constitution invites all citizens to take part in the direction of the affairs of the State; it makes no exception of any person. Each has the right not only to express his opinion, but to influence, if he can, by the expression of his opinion, the opinion of his fellow citizens. This right exists for all, and there can be no reason why the priest should be deprived of it. I am here to speak my whole mind, and I may add that I am far from finding opportune the intervention of the clergy in the domain of politics, as it has been exercised for some years. On the contrary I believe that from the standpoint of the respect due to his character, the priest has everything to lose by meddling in the ordinary questions of politics; still his right to do so is indisputable and if he thinks proper to use it, our duty as Liberals is to guarantee it to him against all denial.

This right, however, is not unlimited. We have no absolute rights. The rights of each man in our state of society end precisely at the point where they encroach upon the rights of others.

The right of interference in politics ends at the point where it encroaches upon the elector's independence.

The constitution of the country rests upon the freely expressed wish of each elector. It intends that each elector shall cast his vote freely and willingly as he deems best. . . .

The law watches with so jealous an eye over the free expression of the elector's opinion as it really is that if in a constituency the opinion expressed by a single elector is not his real opinion, but an opinion forced upon him by fear, fraud, or corruption, the election must be annulled.

It is therefore perfectly legitimate to alter the elector's opinion by argument and all other means of persuasion, but never by intimidation. As a matter of fact, persuasion changes the elector's conviction, intimidation does not. When by persuasion you have changed the elector's opinion, then the opinion he expresses is his own; but when by terror you force him to vote, the opinion he expresses is yours; remove the cause of his fear and he will then express another opinion, which is his own.

Now it will be understood that, if the opinion expressed by the majority of the electors is not their real opinion, but an opinion forced from them by fraud, threats, or corruption, the constitution is violated and you do not have government of the majority but government of a minority. Well, if such a state of affairs continues and is repeated, if after each election the will expressed is not the real will of the country, once more you do violence to the constitution; responsible government is no longer anything but an empty term; and sooner or later, here as elsewhere, the pressure will culminate in explosion, violence, and ruin.

But people are not wanting to say that the clergy have a right to dictate to the people its duties. I simply answer that we are here under the government of the Queen of England, under the authority of a constitution which was granted to us as an act of justice, and if the exercize of the rights which you claim is to have for effect the impeding of the constitution and our exposure to all the consequences of such an act, then the clergy themselves would not want it.

I am not one of those who parade themselves as friends and champions of the clergy. I say this, however: like most of my young fellow countrymen, I have been reared among priests and among young men who have become priests. I flatter myself that I have some sincere friends among them, and to them I can and do say: see if there is under the sun a country where the Catholic Church is freer or more privileged than it is here. Why then should you by claiming rights incompatible with our state of society, expose this country to agitations of which it is impossible to foresee the consequences?[77]

After this forthright demarcation of the rights of the clergy and of citizens, Laurier closed with an eloquent apostrophe to free British institutions which had enabled the French Canadians to remain French and Catholic under the British flag, 'which floats tonight over our heads, without a single British soldier in the country to defend it, its sole defence resting in the gratitude which we owe it for our freedom and for the security we have found under its folds.'[78]

It was this speech which made Laurier, an undistinguished minister without portfolio, a national figure; and adherence to the views expressed in it was to put him at the head of the Canadian government in 1896, after half a century marred by the bickerings of smaller men who made political capital of differences of origin and religion, and almost wrecked Confederation on those reefs which beset the course of a nation made up not of one people but of two.

6

Relief for the situation against which Laurier made his eloquent protest had already begun to come from several quarters. In May 1876 Archbishop Taschereau, realizing that the condemnation of Catholic liberalism threatened to provoke a serious anti-clerical movement, issued a pastoral letter in which he put the two parties on the same footing and urged the electors to make calm inquiry into the merits of opposing candidates.[79] Though the archbishop asserted that his new pastoral did not revoke the joint one of 1875, it was taken by both the Liberals and the ultramontanes as a repudiation of the latter. Bishop Laflèche and Canon Lamarche went to Rome to voice their differences with the archbishop on the religio-political difficulties in Quebec, on which Cardinal Franchi, the prefect of the Congregation of the Propaganda, had requested Taschereau's views. While Rome heard the rival arguments, Judge Routhier, the drafter of the Catholic program and Langevin's former political aide, dismissed Langelier's petition for the annulment of the Charlevoix by-election, on the ultramontane ground that the clergy were immune from questioning or control by the State of their actions on such moral questions as voting. Routhier made a distinction between temporal influence, which was forbidden by law, and spiritual influence, which was legitimate. The case was appealed to the newly established Supreme Court of Canada, whose unanimous judgment, to the effect that undue influence had been exerted and that the election was consequently void, was delivered by Mr. Justice Taschereau, brother of the archbishop, who threw out Routhier's distinction.

While the appeal was in progress, the Superior Court of Quebec annulled an election in Bonaventure, where two *curés* had threatened to refuse the sacraments to Liberal voters. This judgment was written by Judge Casault, a professor of law at Laval; and Bishop Langevin, whose diocese included the constituency, insisted to Archbishop Taschereau that Casault must either retract or be deprived of his academic position. This request was backed by Bishop Laflèche, and Archbishop Taschereau referred the question to Rome, which eventually upheld the judge. To Rome the Liberals under Joseph Cauchon's leadership now also appealed for judgment on the ultramontane charges against them. While this appeal was under consideration, the bishops issued a joint declaration on March 26, 1877, protesting against the Supreme Court's decision and requesting a suitable remedy.[80] A telegram from Rome, warning the hierarchy against a pronouncement on the question, was received after the circular had been issued. There, after Canon Lamarche had offered the ultramontane arguments and the Abbé Benjamin Paquet had refuted them as Archbishop Taschereau's representative, it had been decided to send an apostolic delegate to Canada to investigate the situation which had filled the Vatican's offices with petitions and counter-petitions.

Bishop Conroy of Ardagh, the Irish prelate appointed to this mission, was instructed to eliminate the division among the Quebec bishops, the root of the troubles. It was likewise suggested to him that another cause of the difficulties was 'interference of the clergy in politics without sufficient care for pastoral prudence'; and that 'the Church, in condemning liberalism, did not intend to strike each and every political party which happened to be called Liberal, since the decision of the Church applied to certain errors opposed to Catholic doctrine, and not to any political party, and that consequently those did wrong who without further basis declared condemned by the Church one of the parties in Canada, i.e., the party known as Reformist, a party formerly warmly supported even by some bishops.'[81] Bishops were counseled to observe the greatest reserve about politics, 'having regard particularly to the danger of provoking a violent war against the Church, when Protestants were already uneasy and irritated against the clergy on the score of the latter's undue influence in political affairs.' The apostolic delegate arrived at Quebec in May 1877, visited Montreal and Ottawa, and then returned to Quebec, where he established himself—in order to preserve neutrality—in a country house on the Sainte-Foye Road, where he was besieged by ultramontane and Liberal spokesmen.

His views remained unknown until at his instigation the hierarchy issued a joint pastoral on October 11. This pronouncement made the distinction, as Laurier had done in his speech on 'Political Liberalism' in June, between political and Catholic liberalism, and declared that the Holy See's censures against Catholic liberalism were not to be applied to any particular political party.[82] In an accompanying circular to the clergy, they were reminded that 'The decree of the Fourth Council of Quebec forbids you implicitly to teach from the pulpit or elsewhere that it is a sin to vote for any particular candidate or party; even more is it forbidden to announce that you will refuse the sacraments for this cause. You are never to give your personal opinion from the pulpit.'[83]

Confronted with this ultimatum, Bishop Laflèche's organ, *Le Journal des Trois-Rivières*, bitterly observed: 'The year 1877 could be designated as the special epoch of concessions to liberalism and of cowardice, the epoch of the triumph of Catholic liberalism.'[84] In the like manner the *curés* who read *Le Nouveau Monde's* reflections on the circular viewed Bishop Conroy's mission as 'unfortunate for true principles.'[85] With that self-righteous fervor which sometimes makes French Canadians more Catholic than the Pope, the double rebuke by Rome of ultramontane pretensions through the Conroy mission and the Casault decision was not taken to heart. It was some years before the declaration which Bishop Conroy had inspired and which he hoped would restore peace to Catholic Quebec achieved its end.

The pronouncement did not immediately halt the use of religious means for political purposes. Forced to seek re-election by his elevation to the Mackenzie cabinet, Laurier was defeated in Drummond–Arthabaska—in Bishop Laflèche's diocese—on October 27, after a bitterly contested campaign in which his opponents made use of all the old ultramontane charges against the Liberals. The *curés*, somewhat checked in their Conservative zeal by the circular, followed a course which left the voters in a state of mind exemplified by one *habitant* who told his *curé*: 'I cannot vote for M. Laurier, for you tell me that if I vote for a Liberal, I shall be damned; I cannot vote for M. Bourbeau, for you tell me that if I do not follow my conscience, I shall be damned; I cannot vote for neither, for you tell me that if I do not vote at all, I shall be damned. Since I must be damned anyway, I'll be damned for doing what I like. I am going to vote for M. Laurier.'[86] Laurier was subsequently elected in Quebec East—in Archbishop Taschereau's diocese—in November, but his defeat in his own region left him with a certain bitterness against his opponents.

The same tactics were employed by the Conservatives in the provincial elections of May 1878, in which the Liberals under the Swiss Protestant Joly won a bare majority in the face of opposition from the *curés* in many counties. It was in this election that the memorable device was invented of indicating discreetly from the pulpit the right way to vote by the observation that Heaven was *Bleu* and Hell was *Rouge*.[87] And in the federal elections of September the Liberals went down to defeat in Quebec, where they were to remain in opposition until 1896. The obstinate self-righteousness of the ultramontanes, undaunted by Roman counsels of moderation and exploited by unscrupulous Conservative leaders, was so strong that the sudden death of Bishop Conroy on his way back to Rome was greeted as a clear intervention of Providence.[88]

7

The battle between ultramontanism and liberalism continued to rack French Canada for another twenty years. But essentially the outcome of that battle was determined by the election of Leo XIII to the Papacy in 1878. The new Pope's reign was to see the achievement of peace with the civil power, after the Catholic reaction under Pius IX against the new democratic nationalism. The duel between Archbishop Taschereau and Bishop Laflèche and between the two schools of thought they headed continued with the bitterness only possible in a deeply Catholic country, but each time that Rome was consulted, the decision went against the ultramontanes, whose obstinate conviction of the justness of their cause finally led them to the brink of rupture with that Holy See whose defenders and supporters they proclaimed themselves to be. The battle was fought on many fronts and produced such a wealth of literature, both public and private, that a book could be devoted to it alone. Only the main outlines of the endless bickering within the Church in Canada, which at this time gave Rome more trouble than the rest of Christendom combined, can be traced here.

One of the major quarrels was the question whether French Canada should have one university or two. Since 1843 there had existed at Montreal a medical school founded by English Protestants, which gradually became French and Catholic as the city did and as the rival McGill Medical School developed. It was known as the Victoria School because of its affiliation for degree-granting purposes with the Methodist Victoria University of Cobourg, Ontario. Bishop Bourget, under whose control the school was, planned to make it part of the Catholic university which he wished to establish in Montreal. Its doctors supplied the medical service of the Hôtel-Dieu and other Catholic institutions. Its directors were ultramontane in outlook, and resisted Bishop Conroy's effort to affiliate the institution to the Montreal branch of Laval. They were moved both by the old rivalry between Montreal and Quebec, and by their pious suspicion of the Laval Medical School, whose faculty included several English Protestants rumored to be Freemasons, a damning disability in the eyes of Bishop Bourget's supporters.

The agreement worked out under the supervision of Bishop Conroy and confirmed by Rome broke down in 1879. The Montreal doctors then appealed to Rome, while Laval opened a rival medical school in Montreal. The Hôtel-Dieu remained loyal to Victoria, and closed its doors to students of the new school, of whose legal right to existence there was some doubt under the terms of Laval's royal charter. On this point the Victoria spokesmen consulted the federal minister of justice and the Crown law officers in England, the latter supporting their case. The university question inevitably became one of Montreal against Quebec, of Conservatives against Liberals, in the religio-political atmosphere of the day; and cries of liberalism, gallicanism, and insubmission were raised in the press and in pamphlets, despite the instructions of Bishop Fabre, Bishop Bourget's peace-loving successor, that the matter was not to be publicly discussed.

Thus the issue became involved in the 'Holy War,' which had been revived by the contesting of the Berthier election of 1878 on the grounds of undue influence. The Liberals now boasted a Montreal organ, *La Patrie*, founded in 1879 by the radical *Rouge* Honoré Beaugrand, in whose pages the poet Louis Fréchette hymned Republican France, despite the Republic's blatant anti-clericalism. The times were indeed changing, and further evidence of the fact was provided by the introduction into the federal house by a Quebec Conservative of a bill which liberalized the marriage laws. Bishop Laflèche, whose basic article of faith was that the State had no concern with schools, charitable institutions, marriage legislation, or differences involving a priest, ordered the sponsor of the bill to withdraw it. The latter refused, but the bill was stopped in the Senate by the ultramontanes Trudel and Bellerose. Then, after a trial rich in scandal, the Berthier election was annulled on November 30, 1880 by unanimous decision of the Supreme Court.

While radical Liberals rejoiced at having 'muzzled the clergy,' Bishop Laflèche—fresh from a visit to St. Boniface, where he had advised the French *Métis* that if they remained grouped around their clergy, no one could disturb them—wrote a series of articles on 'Undue Spiritual Influence' for *Le Journal des Trois-Rivières*.

These articles took high ultramontane ground on the relations of Church and State, and proclaimed that the law against the exercise of undue influence must be repealed or amended, since it attacked the liberties of the Church. L.-O. David, back in the provincial fray as editor of *La Tribune* of Montreal after the Liberal downfall at Ottawa, objected that recourse to the courts was the only remedy for a defeated candidate, since an appeal to the clerical authorities could not restore his lost seat. Bishop Laflèche republished his articles in pamphlet form, thus adding a new ultramontane text to the *Syllabus of Errors*, the Catholic Program, and the joint pastoral of September 1875.

Both Laval's attempt to obtain legal authorization for its Montreal branch and Bishop Laflèche's measure against the undue influence law were submitted to the provincial legislature in 1881. Bishop Laflèche refused to join the other bishops in supporting the Laval measure, while Archbishop Taschereau advised his colleagues after consultation with Premier Chapleau, who feared that such a measure would arouse Protestant feeling, that he felt it useless to insist upon revocation of the undue influence law. Bishop Laflèche's proposal was then dropped, despite complaints from some ultramontanes that the existence of a Catholic party would have prevented such cowardice on the part of the Conservative government.

But the 'Holy War' broke out again with renewed vigor on the university question, despite Bishop Fabre's demand that his diocesans submit to the twice-expressed will of Rome that the Laval Medical School be maintained in Montreal. *Le Nouveau Monde*, rigid in its pro-Montreal and anti-Laval views for all its ultramontane pretensions, presumed to question the bishop's right to halt discussion of public affairs. Bishop Laflèche authorized Senator Trudel, attorney for the Victoria School, to make public a letter in which he expressed his disagreement with the bishops who had endorsed the Laval School. From his retirement at Sault-au-Recollet, Bishop Bourget wrote an endorsement of the opposition measure which was published in *Le Nouveau Monde*. Archbishop Taschereau then accused Bishop Bourget of undermining the authority of his successor and of the other bishops—indeed, in so many words, of exercising 'undue influence'—and when the retired bishop replied, closed the correspondence with a sharp reflection on 'letters publicly addressed to the diocesans of Montreal, counselling them to resist the will of their bishop and of the Holy See.'[89]

Such an attitude towards the old ultramontane leader, already canonized in the minds of his followers, made for bitter feeling between his cohorts and those of the archbishop. Once more Laval was accused of tolerating dangerous principles, of neglecting philosophy for the natural sciences, and abandoning its traditions for 'pretended modern progress.'[90] The Laval bill was carried through the assembly and the legislative council with both Conservative and Liberal support, amid a rain of petitions and counter-petitions and scandalous personal reflections. No sooner was it passed than Senator Trudel departed for Rome to plead the cause of Victoria, where he was soon followed by eighty-two-year-old Bishop Bourget. Both emissaries attacked Laval as being under the influence of Freemasons. But they had already been forestalled at Rome by Bishop Racine of Chicoutimi and Grand Vicar Hamel of Quebec, supporters of the Archbishop. Both parties were received by the Pope, who sustained Laval after the case had been heard by the Propaganda.

The official communication of Rome's opinion on September 13, 1881 was accompanied by a renewed warning against confusing political and Catholic liberalism, and the bishops were instructed to consult the Holy See before seeking repeal of the undue influence law. This decision, loyally accepted by Bishop Fabre and accompanied by Archbishop Taschereau with a warning against 'discussions which excite men's minds to the detriment of religion and public affairs,'[91] was greeted with joy by the Liberals. *L'Evénement* of Quebec did not neglect to turn the sword in the ultramontane wound by observing:

As to the Honorable M. Trudel, his religious mission seems to be ended. Rome decidedly does not wish a lay prelate among us. She does not desire that beside the orthodox Church a Church more orthodox still should establish itself. We must content ourselves with the religion of our fathers.[92]

When Archbishop Taschereau pressed his advantage and called for a joint declaration by the hierarchy against journalists who disobeyed the Holy See by attacking Laval, Bishop Laflèche first signed, then withdrew his signature and announced his departure for Rome to explain his objections. He was coldly received there by Leo XIII, who said that there was nothing further to be discussed and that his presence was not necessary at Rome, where the band of self-styled 'defenders of Montreal' had become wearisome to the Holy See. A communication to this effect from Cardinal Simeoni, the new head of the Propaganda, to Archbishop Taschereau was published at Quebec in January 1882.

Le Nouveau Monde took great offense, and did not scruple to blame both the Archbishop and the Cardinal for this insult to 'a bishop and priests whom the good Catholics of Canada have learned to venerate for their piety and devotion to the Holy See.'[93] Frédéric Houde, its proprietor, resigned rather than retract this statement at the request of Bishop Fabre. The ultramontanes had become so self-righteous, so full of a sense of mission, that they insisted upon going their own way regardless of the opposition of their bishop, of the hierarchy as a whole, of the Propaganda, and of the Holy Father himself. The Liberals did not fail to point out the humorous spectacle afforded by those who protested in the name of religion against complaints of clerical intervention in elections, but did not hesitate to make complaints against the Archbishop of Quebec and the Sacred Congregation of the Propaganda. On February 5 Archbishop Taschereau issued a pastoral which stressed the fact that the Propaganda had settled the university question once for all, and that no good Catholic could attack an institution protected by the bishops and the Holy See, particularly when such attacks were based on the fact that Laval had not condemned a political party which neither the hierarchy nor the Holy See wished to condemn. The freedom of electors to vote for either parties was again declared. [94]

Though the provincial elections of December 1881 had been contested by Conservatives and Liberals, in reality four parties were now involved. The Conservatives had with difficulty kept within their ranks the ultramontane group headed by 'Grand Vicar' Trudel, which threatened to revive the Catholic Program and to set up a Catholic party. Faced with this revolt, Chapleau was considering a coalition with the moderate Liberal Honoré Mercier, who found the radical Liberals headed by Beaugrand as embarrassing as Chapleau did the ultramontanes. The ultramontanes grew more and more discontented with Chapleau's dependence upon Sénécal, the ex-Liberal railroad promoter who now footed the Conservative party's bills and was rumored to pay himself well for his pains; they did not hesitate to make political capital of the fact that Chapleau had a Protestant wife, and hence might be considered a Freemason. From the French monarchists whom they so much admired, the ultramontanes had adopted the practice of seeing Masons and Masonic plots everywhere, and no one in French Canada was more adept at this game than Jules Paul Tardivel, who in 1881 launched his ultramontane La Vérité at Quebec.

Tardivel, born of a French father and an English mother in the United States, had been educated at Saint-Hyacinthe, whose seminary he entered at the age of sixteen, not knowing a word of French. With the zeal of a convert to a heady doctrine, Tardivel espoused the ultramontane cause, serving as a sounding-board at Quebec for the views of Bishop Laflèche and Trudel. He tended to be more French than the Séminaire de Québec and more Catholic than Archbishop Taschereau. He pursued Laval with charges of Masonry borrowed from his idol Louis Veuillot, finding the dark hand of the Grand Orient not only in the medical and law schools,

but in the very household of the archbishop. At the outset *La Vérité*
contented itself with a crusade against Sunday trains, but gradually
it turned to heresy-hunting on a higher plane. So intoxicating was
the ultramontane doctrine that Tardivel did not hesitate to point
out that Rome could err, when the decision on the university
question was announced:

> The Laval question is a question of fact, and without being a heretic
> or even a bad Catholic, one can say that the Pope is mistaken on this
> question. The question of indulgences is a question of doctrine, which
> is very different. In doctrine the Pope is infallible, he cannot err; but
> it is to expose our holy religion to the laughter of the impious to maintain
> that the Pope cannot err when it is a question of particular facts.[95]

And the still more official ultramontane organ, Bishop Laflèche's
Journal des Trois-Rivières, proclaimed: 'It is certain that for one
reason or another the Holy See can be led into error, above all for
a certain time, on questions of fact and questions of doctrine.'[96]
The Liberal press fell with glee upon such views in the mouths of
those who had proclaimed themselves the best Romans of them all.

Bishop Laflèche, whose fighter's temperament was daunted neither
by reverses nor rebuffs, remained at Rome despite the chilly atmosphere, compiling a memorandum on 'The Religious Troubles in
Canada,' which was printed both at Rome and in Canada in 1882.
Convinced as he was that gallicanism, liberalism, and nationalism
were the 'fundamental errors of the epoch,' and that liberalism in
particular was nothing short of a 'plague'[97] spread by the Masons, he
summed up the history of the politico-religious struggle in Canada
under three heads: the political question, the question of undue influence, and the university question. This sixty-page presentation of the
thesis that 'Canadian liberalism, by its anti-social tendencies, by its
hatred of the Church, and by its perverse principles, differed in no
respect from European liberalism,' supported by a hundred pages of
evidence and a rain of letters to Cardinal Simeoni, was little short of an
indictment of Archbishop Taschereau and the Séminaire de Québec,
where the 'subtle errors' of liberalism had penetrated 'like the
serpent into the Garden of Eden.'[98] Bishop Laflèche concluded his
memorandum: 'Thus all the most clear-sighted minds, both among
the clergy and the laity, are frightened, and all agree that unless
Providential aid enables us to check this fatal movement, we advance rapidly along the revolutionary paths of France and Belgium,
and we shall fall sooner than is thought into the same abyss.'[99]
To him it was clear that Freemasonry inspired the attack on the
Church in Canada as elsewhere; and he viewed with alarm the
influence of the French press on Quebec, whose native literature was

still in infancy. This ultramontane preoccupation with Masonic intrigue and with the dangers of French cultural influences was to become a lasting part of the French-Canadian mind, thanks to twenty years' harping on the theme by Trudel and Tardivel in *Le Nouveau Monde* and *La Vérité*.

Bishop Laflèche finally returned from Rome in May 1882. His friends Bishops Bourget and Taché endorsed the position he had taken in his memorandum, which Archbishop Taschereau refuted in a counter-memorandum which found favor in Rome. Bishop Moreau of Saint-Hyacinthe issued in November a circular to his clergy against encouragement of a new ultramontane organ launched by Senator Trudel with the support of Bishops Bourget and Laflèche, but against the desire of Bishop Fabre. Under this fire, the ultramontanes abandoned the proposed title of their new paper, but not the project itself. On January 23, 1883 the first number of *L'Etendard* appeared. It was to become the organ of the new Catholic party known as the 'Castors' ('Beavers'), and its course was foreshadowed from the first by its campaign against the big three of the Conservative Party in Quebec, Chapleau, Sénécal, and Mousseau. Chapleau was considered to be a Mason by Bishop Laflèche, and the ultramontanes complained that under his regime the interests of country and party had become secondary to those of 'The Great Man.'

Meanwhile there had been another epistolary battle between the archbishop and Bishop Laflèche, in which the former had summoned the latter to prefer his charges against Laval before the Superior Council of the university, while the latter refused to do so and rested upon his episcopal right to complain directly to Rome. The archbishop published the correspondence, having been assured by Cardinal Simeoni that Laflèche's charges were regarded in Rome as 'vague and without proof.'[100] A new decree of the Propaganda, accompanied by a pastoral letter from the archbishop, was read in all the churches of Quebec on March 25, 1883.[101] The former ordered that all attacks against Laval and its Montreal branch should cease, while the latter underlined the point that violation of the decree meant disobedience to the Holy See, of which an unfortunate example had been given for the last seven years elsewhere than in the diocese of Quebec.

While the irreconcilables of Victoria appealed once more to Rome, rumors came from thence that the diocese of Trois-Rivières was to be divided, with its richer portion south of the St. Lawrence to be established as the new see of Nicolet. Such a division was popularly regarded as a punishment and humiliation for Bishop Laflèche by his enemies. His friend Bishop Taché of St. Boniface wrote to Archbishop Taschereau a protest which he desired should be passed on to the hierarchy of Quebec. Replying that Bishop Taché seemed to regard Bishop Laflèche 'as a martyr whose executioners were (1) the majority of the bishops of the province, (2) the Sacred Congregation of the Propaganda, (3) the Sovereign Pontiff himself,'[102] the archbishop refused to circulate the letter.

Bishop Laflèche set off once more for Rome, while his aroused supporters went so far as to accuse Grand Vicar Hamel of Quebec of sympathy with Masonry, on the grounds that when Rector of Laval he had informed Rome that the Masons on the medical school faculty were 'Protestant doctors, very worthy citizens, for whom Freemasonry was in Quebec only a mutual aid society, without hostility to Catholicism.'[103] The ultramontanes of the Quebec *Cercle Catholique*, headed by Dr. Landry, made much of this scandalous tolerance. Dr. Landry refused to retract his charges, and was deprived of his honorary professorship at the university, while Tardivel defended him in *La Vérité*, which was promptly banned from the seminary, the university, and the archbishop's household. On June 1 the archbishop published a pastoral against secret societies, in which he ordered that since membership in them carried the penalty of excommunication, accusations of being a Mason, made against Catholics to anyone except the ordinary of the diocese, were forbidden; and that violations of this regulation would be considered cases of conscience whose absolution was reserved to the archbishop, his grand vicar, or priests designated by him.[104] Dr. Landry's son Philippe promptly denounced this pastoral to Cardinal Monaco of the Inquisition. Rome, finding itself swamped by a flood of petitions, protests, and denunciations from Quebec, decided once more to send an apostolic delegate to investigate the situation at first hand. Pending his coming, the suppression of the Victoria School was to be suspended.

This success heartened the *Castors*, who fell upon Chapleau's successor Mousseau with renewed vigor when he sought a provincial seat that fall. 'The Great Man' was called to his follower's aid, and on September 6 at Saint-Laurent Chapleau broke definitely with the ultramontanes by making this formal attack upon them with all his fiery eloquence:

What is a *Castor*? Is it a question of that intelligent and industrious animal who, along with the maple leaf, serves us as a national emblem? No, our opponents are not patriotic enough for that. What, then, is a *Castor*? The urban worker calls by this name those who make great pretensions and cannot do much, the braggarts and parasites of the trade. In the country those little black beasts who live in bands upon the surface of stagnant waters, spreading an odor than which there is nothing less agreeable, the water skunks, are also called *Castors*.

Are these typical of the tribe of *L'Etendard*? Political *Castors* are a little like that, and something still less good. Their party includes all the ambitious mediocrities who cannot come to power by the ordinary ways, all the disappointed ones, and a good number of hypocrites who pretend to be religious and conservative in order better to ruin the great Conservative Party and to destroy among the people true religious spirit, whose fundamental basis is respect for authority and love of neighbor.

For the rest, they have only one trait of resemblance to the true beaver. They do their work with mud; they destroy the sluices of good mills to make their dens; and are useful only when their hides are sold.

The opposition raised against us by these men would not be important, if it were not for the character which they have given to what they call their political mission. They have wrapped themselves in the mantle of religion, and in this disguise they have succeeded in deceiving a number of honest folk whom it is difficult to undeceive.

.   .   .   .   .

It is time to rip off the mask. There is no worse exploitation than religious exploitation. No one has the right to employ for his personal ends the great and powerful sentiment which dominates all others in this fine country of Canada.

In a country where there are so many sincere Catholics, it is easy to win followers in the name of religion. But woe to him who uses religion as a footstool![105]

The indictment was a telling one, but the course of the *Castors* has continued to be followed down to the present day by unscrupulous politicians who do not hesitate to make use of Quebec's profound religious feeling for political purposes.

Back from Rome trooped the rival petitioners as the court of appeal was shifted to Canada by the arrival at Quebec in October 1883 of the apostolic delegate, Dom Henri Smeulders, a Belgian Cistercian abbot. The ultramontanes were determined to win from him a canonical inquest into all the religious difficulties. Dr. Landry took it upon himself to circulate a petition in favor of this step among the clergy of the diocese of Quebec. The Christmas preacher at the Basilica of Quebec, the Grand Vicar Legaré, in the presence of the archbishop and Dr. Landry and Tardivel, who were wardens of the church, censured the latter:

We shall have the desired peace when all laymen confine themselves to their roles. It is truly strange that here and there in our Canadian society men arise who take upon themselves the mission of lording it over the Church. Do we not see them arrogate to themselves the right to concern themselves with all the questions which are primarily the concern of the Pope, the bishops, and the clergy?[106]

The *Castors* replied to this discourse, which caused quite as much excitement as Père Braun's ultramontane sermon of 1872, by publishing a pamphlet entitled '*La Source du mal de l'époque au Canada,*' credited to the Abbé Pelletier, which blamed the religious troubles on Archbishop Taschereau and his followers.

The delegate was overwhelmed with pleas, written and verbal, from the rival parties on the question of ultramontanism *vs.* liberalism, of Victoria *vs.* Laval, of the division of the diocese of Trois-Rivières, and of all the endless quarrels which had arisen between the adherents of two rival currents of ideas. The supporters of each sought to obtain exclusive control of the schools; and so the Victoria-Laval quarrel was duplicated on the secondary-school level by a bitter dispute between the Ecole Jacques Cartier of Montreal and the normal school which Bishop Laflèche, an opponent of lay instruction, proposed to establish at Trois-Rivières; and on the primary-school level by differences between the Christian Brothers and the Montreal School Commissioners. Dom Smeulders established himself at Montreal in the motherhouse of the Oblates; he visited Bishop Bourget in his retreat at Sault-au-Recollet, and he received the counsel of Archbishop Taché, who came east to defend his friend Laflèche. The latter was persuaded to renounce his request for a canonical inquest, and was then assured that the apostolic delegate regarded the division of his diocese as neither necessary or useful.

When this announcement was made, Bishop Laflèche took heart and insisted on a canonical inquest, while Archbishop Taschereau departed for Rome, where the ultramontane *Journal de Rome* was making much of lurid pictures of Masonic intrigue in Canada painted by the Jesuit Père Hamon ('Jean d'Erbrée') in *L'Etendard* and *La Vérité.* French-Canadian pride was injured by unfavorable foreign comment, and Bishop Fabre denounced 'those who, moved by one knows not what motive, sow false alarms in our ranks.'[107] But the ultramontanes felt a new confidence, and Senator Bellerose flatly contradicted his bishop in the third of the anti-Masonic memoranda which he presented to Dom Smeulders, while Bishop Laflèche issued a circular to his clergy recommending sermons against the plague of Freemasonry. Archbishop Taschereau did not waste time at Rome; on May 31 the cardinal prefect of the Propaganda informed Dom Smeulders that the question of the division of the diocese had been reserved for decision in Rome.

Bishop Laflèche had already announced the decision of the delegate in his favor, and the position of Dom Smeulders was gravely weakened by this repudiation. Despite his dismay at the news from Rome, Bishop Laflèche made a fighting speech at the fiftieth anniversary of the Montreal Saint-Jean-Baptiste Society in June; it was on this occasion that he condemned the mania for speaking English and observed: 'I am well enough pleased to meet compatriots who speak English badly.'[108] Again on July 4, the 250th anniversary of the founding of Trois-Rivières, the Bishop discussed the close alliance between Church and State throughout Canada's history; called for the return to the Church of the Jesuit Estates; denounced Free-masonry and proclaimed once more the French and Catholic mission of his people. Meanwhile his supporters deluged Rome with petitions against the division of his diocese, maintaining that such a step would be a 'moral disaster . . . interpreted as the condemnation of the doctrine of the Bishop of Trois-Rivières.'[109] Laflèche himself requested of the Propaganda that full reparation be made by the Archbishop of Quebec and the Bishop of Chicoutimi for injustice done him and his diocese.

Rome finally spoke on the university question on August 23. Its decision was virtually a complete victory for Laval, since Laval, including its Montreal branch, was recognized as the sole Catholic university, which all bishops were directed to aid and support; the failure of the fusion of the Victoria and Laval medical schools was deplored, although Victoria was permitted to remain *in statu quo*; and Laval was to be aided by a province-wide ecclesiastical tax.[110] New trouble broke out in Montreal when Bishop Fabre ordered the submission of all parties to this decision, and an ultramontane representative of Victoria soon departed for Rome. But the ultra-montane cause was failing fast; on October 5 Rome announced that the principle of the division of the diocese of Trois-Rivières was confirmed, though the actual division was not to take place until the coming of a new apostolic delegate.[111] In short, Dom Smeulders, who had been won over by the ultramontanes, was virtually repu-diated by Rome. He somewhat pointedly left Quebec for Trois-Rivières the day Archbishop Taschereau returned from Rome, and in December he quit Canada after a mission of fourteen months. He was feted in defeat by the ultramontanes, although he had solved none of the difficulties which had brought him to Canada.

The ultramontanes continued to fight for control of education, but Bishop Laflèche's attempt to annex the normal schools to the classical colleges was defeated in the Council of Public Instruction at the instance of Archbishop Taschereau, who also succeeded in making his own candidate head of the Ecole Normale Laval. The Catholic Committee of the Council continued to reject the textbooks of the Christian Brothers, and the ultramontane press denounced the lay members of the Committee—viewed inevitably as Masons and friends of free-thinking France—for their efforts 'to destroy our old Christian usages and to substitute for them the principles of modern, that is to say revolutionary, pedagogy.'[112] Bishop Laflèche again opposed the provincial government's attempt to strengthen state medical control of the insane asylums as based on 'the fatal principle of the omnipotence of the State with which the Revolution over-turned the religious institutions of our former mother country.'[113]

In May 1885 the nomination of Bishop Cameron of Antigonish, Nova Scotia, as the new apostolic delegate was announced. His function was not to investigate but to execute the decree of division. It was rumored that Bishop Laflèche would go to Rome once more to make a last effort against the division of his diocese. Archbishop Taschereau informed him that he had consulted Cardinal Simeoni, who had replied: 'It is inopportune that Bishop Laflèche come to Rome now.'[114] While the funeral of Bishop Bourget and the silver anniversary of the Séminaire des Trois-Rivières provided occasions for ultramontane rallies, it was announced that Archbishop Taschereau's Roman representative, Abbé Gravel of Saint-Hyacinthe, had been named bishop of the new see of Nicolet. Bishop Laflèche was assured by Cardinal Simeoni that the division of the diocese had not been provoked by any discontent with him at Rome, but kind words could not conceal the blunt logic of events. His followers made extravagant statements, saying among other things that Barabbas had been preferred to Jesus; but Bishop Laflèche himself submitted, though not with good grace, for he refused to assist at the enthroning of the new bishop. But on the urgent advice of Archbishop Taché, Laflèche's pastoral announcing the division of the diocese contained neither complaints nor reproaches. If there was any doubt in men's minds that the ultramontane cause was finished, it was remedied the following year when Archbishop Taschereau was made the first Canadian cardinal and Bishops Fabre of Montreal and Duhamel of Ottawa were named archbishops, while Bishop Laflèche was passed over.

He was to fight on for 'the true principles' as he saw them until the end of his life in 1898. As late as 1891 Laflèche was still capable of thundering with youthful vigor:

Poor France! What remedy is powerful enough to cure her of the terrible revolutionary sickness which has crept even into the sources of her religious life? Great remedies are needed for great evils! She will continue to be the land of massacres so long as she does not vomit up the last drop of gallican and liberal poison and return squarely to the Catholic fold, socially, politically, as well as individually.[115]

The authoritarianism and apocalyptic sense of modern evils which Laflèche shared with Bishop Bourget were deeply rooted. The world was changing and the bishops were no longer listened to as they had been in the heyday of the 'Holy War.' While Laflèche dutifully accepted the new order which forbade clerical intervention in politics, he remained resolute in his lifelong principles:

One must pray much for our poor people, who are prey to a crowd of demagogues who endeavor to inculcate them with revolutionary doctrines without even being aware of it themselves, because of their ignorance of the questions with which they concern themselves. These are blind men, who will lead our people to the abyss, if the latter do not regard the guidance which their first pastors give them.[116]

But the divergence between the hierarchy and the French-Canadian people on the Riel question had weakened the traditional influence of the bishops and permitted the rise to leadership, despite their opposition, of such Liberals as Mercier and Laurier, whom Laflèche unquestionably regarded as 'demagogues.'

8

While the dominant literary school of this period devoted itself to piously hymning the French-Canadian past and the traditional values of Quebec society, certain new currents of thought became evident in the intellectual ferment of the 1860's, 1870's, and 1880's. A spirit essentially gallic but without precedent in French Canada, save for Lahontan and the elder Pierre de Sales Laterrière, began to examine the contemporary scene when Arthur Buies launched his weekly, *La Lanterne*, in September 1868. Born in Montreal of a Scottish father and a French-Canadian mother, Buies was early orphaned and was brought up by two aunts at Rimouski on the lower St. Lawrence, where he seems to have imbibed an overdose of the independence of spirit for which its people are noted. Educated at the seminaries of Quebec, Lévis, and Nicolet—all of which he left at the request of the authorities—Buies went to Paris to complete his studies. Finding that academic life palled upon his restless and undisciplined temperament, Buies left Paris to become one of Garibaldi's Redshirts in 1860, while most French Canadians were denouncing these revolutionaries with pious fervor. But military discipline was no more to his taste than the academic, and Buies soon deserted and returned home, imbued with republican and Bohemian notions very foreign to Quebec. He studied law and was admitted to the bar, but soon turned to journalism, serving as one of the editors of the *Rouge* organ *Le Pays*.

With a temperament that brooked no mastery, even his own, Buies then launched a series of shortlived personal organs which drew down upon him ecclesiastical censure, for his impatience with hypocrisy, conventionality, and reaction spared no one and nothing. In 1868 the prospectus of *La Lanterne*, whose title echoed both the cry of the French Revolution and Diogenes' search for honesty, announced flatly:

I enter into open war with all stupidities, all hypocrisies, all infamies; that is, I take upon my back three-quarters of mankind, which is a heavy burden.

There are two sorts of imbecile: those who know it and those who do not. The latter are the worse; they write *La Minerve's* reports. As for the others, they console themselves with the prospect of the Kingdom of Heaven.[117]

Buies' chief targets were Conservatism and ultramontanism, the latter of which he flayed mercilessly with such comments as 'False piety always seeks to exhibit itself, because it is not what it appears.'[118] He remarked of one of Bishop Bourget's ceremonious progresses: 'I knew a time, which is not ours, when people were better Catholics than they are today, although they paraded it less.'[119] He spared neither cabinet ministers nor the influential Jesuits nor the Pope himself, commenting ironically on the spectacle of the Pastor of Christendom waging war. He attacked the clerical-Conservative alliance, clerical censorship, and clerical domination in general, blaming the reactionary tendency of close alliances between Church and State for the situation that 'in most Catholic states, revolution is permanently to be found beside the established order.'[120] Banned and persecuted by Bishop Bourget, *La Lanterne* succumbed in March 1869, to be succeeded by *L'Indépendant* (1870) and *Le Réveil* (1876), which were equally shortlived. Buies' talent was that of a pamphleteer and columnist, and his 'chronicles' for journals of such widely assorted opinions as *Le Pays*, *L'Opinion Publique*, *La Minerve*, and *Le National*, which were later collected in book form, provide a valuable commentary on the events of the time, whose satire is warmed by Buies' strong affection for French Canada.

In his own special way, which was that of the lone wolf and maverick, of the rebel against the established order, Buies was one of the Patriotic School of Quebec, although its godly members would have recoiled in horror at the thought. He was less blinded by sentiment than they, and by nature more keen-sighted and realistic. Buies is a serious writer beneath his mockeries and gibes at the great of his day, whose frailties he singled out unerringly. He had no love for pomposity and authoritarianism, whether found in such politicians as Cartier and Hector Langevin, or in such churchmen as Bishops Bourget and Laflèche; and he was a master of the witty and malicious gossip which is one of Quebec's little-celebrated but most notably French traits. Buies' matter was not limited to trivialities; as early as 1871 he deplored the misguided optimism dominant in the colonization movement, which resulted in tragedy for many colonists and vast waste of time and money in futile attempts to develop unsuitable regions, which had been chosen simply as blank spaces on the map which might be made French and Catholic. Not only did he describe the summer resorts of his beloved lower St. Lawrence, with sharply etched accounts of the

social differences between French and English, but he explored
the virtually unknown Saguenay, Gaspé, and Matapédia regions.
He carried his patriotism even into the field of transportation: the
railroads, particularly the Canadian Pacific, suffered from his
attacks, while the largely French-operated St. Lawrence steamers
found favor in his eyes.

As befitted a self-christened 'advanced *Rouge*,'[121] he delighted in
the brilliant red wagons used to distribute *Le Pays* in the countryside,
and he mourned over the death of Papineau in 1871. But his political
thinking was not merely partisan. The perverse streak in him noted
with ironic amusement that Canadian attachment to England grew
as England showed an increasing willingness to free herself of
Canada. In 1872, alone among the French-Canadian writers of the
day, he was concerned with the rise of unions, wage problems, and
emigration from the country to the cities, for he saw that Canada
was becoming an industrial country, while his contemporaries
preached a return to the obsolescent rural life. He also wrote
intelligently on the plague of alcoholism in Quebec—he himself
was not immune from it—but criticized the total abstinence movement which had been launched by the Church.

Writing a far more vigorous and lively French than most of his
contemporaries, Buies deplored the corruption of his mother tongue
by the anglicisms in use among lawyers and merchants, to whose
growing cultural pretensions he opposed the fact that purer French
was spoken in the country than among the urban élite. He considered that the genius of the language had been lost in Quebec,
and many Frenchmen have since agreed with him. He censured
the mania for 'having written a book, no matter what, no matter
why,'[122] which developed in the self-conscious attempt to create a
French-Canadian literature. To him, 'any real literature is impossible in a country where the sciences and arts are neglected,' and he
added bitterly: 'Our people are not willing to do difficult intellectual
work; they have not been trained for it.' In general he agreed with
Abbé Casgrain's ideas on French-Canadian literature; though he
singled out for particular praise only Garneau, Etienne Parent, Pierre
Chauveau, the journalist Oscar Dunn, and Dr. LaRue.

Despite his interest in the advancement of his own people, whom
he well served by drawing their attention to scantily-settled regions
of the province, he deplored the narrow racist outlook. On Dominion
Day 1877 he observed: 'While Canada is only a colony, there will
be no Canadian nationality; there will be French, English, Scottish,
Irish races, all hailing their respective mother countries, but they
will never mingle under the common name of Canadians, because a
Canadian nation cannot exist where there is no independent Canadian state.'[123] To him the French Canadians were the only true

Canadians; and this was in large measure true in a day when English Canadians were hopelessly colonial-minded, and their leaders often deserted Canada for England after obtaining eminence or wealth in the New World.

Buies' lifelong difficulties were partly personal, the result of a temperament not adapted to life in a closely knit and narrow society; but they also arose in part because he was a man far ahead of his time. Only when his restless energy and graphic pen were enlisted by the dynamic Curé Labelle to publicize the colonization move- ment of the 1880's and 1890's did Quebec find a place for this highly gifted son who refused to follow the ordained pattern of French-Canadian life, and who added insult to injury by irreverent comments on that pattern. Buies' career was symptomatic of the deep ferments at work in French-Canadian life at this period.

Buies was anything but typical of the writers of this epoch, however, most of whom devoted themselves to following the lead of the School of Quebec and concentrated on history. In 1871 and 1872 Louis-Philippe Turcotte published *Le Canada sous l'Union*, a history more notable for its minute detail than its penetration. From 1870 onward Benjamin Sulte published a host of historical monographs, which were synthesized in his *Histoire des Canadiens français* (1882–4). Sulte was more of an antiquarian than a historian at this period, and his works were carelessly written and constructed; but they have considerable charm and reflect a more independent point of view than most writings of the period. Narcisse-Eutrope Dionne was a meticulous researcher whose most notable productions were a monograph on Champlain and a bibliography of Canadiana. L.-O. David produced a series of biographies and historical sketches which are more lively than accurate. His *Les Patriotes de 1837–8*, written with the enthusiasm of an inveterate *Rouge* for the *Patriote* cause, is his best work. Mgr. Cyrien Tanguay published an ex- exhaustive *Dictionnaire généalogique des Familles canadiennes*, which despite its errors is an invaluable compendium for historical workers and the forerunner of a flood of later genealogical studies. The Abbé Charles-Henri Laverdière admirably edited three classic historical texts in his *Oeuvres de Champlain*, *Relations des Jésuites*, and *Journal des Jésuites*. He was a pioneer of rigorously accurate historical work. The Abbé Hospice-Anselme Verreau published many mono- graphs on Montreal history and edited a notable collection of docu- ments on *L'Invasion du Canada en* 1775, which appeared in 1873.

The most notable poet of the period, Louis Fréchette, reflected the main currents of the time in his work, and was involved in many of the main movements. He was born at Lévis, across the St. Lawrence from Quebec, in 1839, but ran away from his step- mother at the age of thirteen and found employment as a telegrapher in northern New York. He returned to Canada to finish his studies at the Quebec and Nicolet seminaries, and then studied law at Laval. Meanwhile he became interested in poetry under the influence of Crémazie, then holding forth in his Quebec bookshop. Fréchette's first book, *Mes Loisirs* (1865), clearly reflects Crémazie's influence. Fréchette set about the simultaneous practice of law, journalism, and poetry in his native Lévis, but failing in all three, he sought his fortune in Chicago, where from 1866 to 1869 he published his annexationist *Voix d'un Exilé*, which included bitter attacks on the conditions which made it necessary for young Canadians to leave home for the States. This work was later bought up and burnt after Fréchette became the unofficial laureate of Quebec. In 1871 Fréchette returned to Canada and entered politics. After twice having been an unsuccessful candidate, he was elected to the federal parliament in 1874, where he served until the Liberal downfall in 1878.

He published *Pêle-Mêle* (1877) and *Fleurs Boréales et Oiseaux de Neiges* (1879), winning a prize from the French Academy in 1880 for these poems on the themes of France and Canada, family and friendship. He was the first French-Canadian writer to be thus honored by the Academy, and so acquired enormous prestige in Canada. His *Légende d'un Peuple* (1887) was published in Paris and dedicated to 'la France.' Sounding as it did the patriotic chords which had made Crémazie famous, it reinforced Fréchette's standing as the laureate of French Canada. This eloquent evocation of notable passages in the history of Quebec in the manner of Victor Hugo was probably his best work. In 1891 Fréchette published another volume of verse, *Feuilles volantes*, but after that, with the exception of the poetic drama *Véronica*, he contented himself with revising his early poems and writing casual prose works, such as his *Originaux et détraqués* (1892) and *La Noël au Canada* (1900), which were popular studies in folklore. As dean of French-Canadian letters, he gave readings of his verse in Quebec and New England. Installed in a comfortable mansion in St. Louis Square in Montreal, he waged polemical warfare with the ultramontane Judge Routhier and his rival William Chapman, who accused him of plagiarizing Hugo. A three-volume definitive edition of his works, illustrated by Henri Julien, was published at Paris in the year of his death, 1908. With Fréchette, literature finally became respectable in Quebec.

Fréchette's most notable poetic rival was Pamphile Lemay, who did not achieve the same popularity but produced better work in his *Les Vengeances* (1875), a novel in verse, and *Les Gouttelettes* (1904), a collection of sonnets. Lemay was a countryman by birth and taste, and was the first French-Canadian poet to hymn rustic life, founding the *terroir* school which has continued down to the present day. Librarian of the Quebec Legislature from 1867 to 1892, he found leisure to write his own poetry and to translate Longfellow's *Evangeline*, as well as to produce a series of undistinguished novels and a translation of William Kirby's *Golden Dog*, a sentimental romanticization of Quebec life in the days of New France which has given many English-speaking people a false picture of old Quebec. Lemay was a patriot as well as a lover of the countryside, and thus carried on the tradition of Crémazie. With William Chapman's first book, *Les Feuilles d'Erable* (1890), a younger poet carried the rhetorical tradition of Crémazie and Fréchette to the breaking point in writing on patriotic and religious themes. His attack on Fréchette in *Le Lauréat* (1892) shows his critical talents, as well as his polemical power. A contemporary, Nérée Beauchemin, published his first verses in *Les Floraisons matutinales* in 1897, but despite the immediate success of 'La Cloche de Louisbourg,' a poem in the tradition of Crémazie, remained silent until the publication of his *Patrie intime* in 1928 revealed that the poetic patriot of the '90's had become one of the finest French-Canadian lyricists writing in the *terroir* tradition.

Most of the prose writers of the period were less distinguished than the poets. Joseph Marmette and Napoléon Bourassa wrote popular romantic historical novels, while Faucher de Saint-Maurice, a Dumas musketeer who by some error of Providence found himself on the shores of the St. Lawrence, devoted himself to casual but well-written descriptive sketches of Quebec life and the retelling of old legends, after serving under Maximilian in Mexico as a young man and exploring the Lower St. Lawrence by boat. His *A la brunante*, a collection of legends, was the prose counterpart of Ernest Gagnon's *Chansons populaires du Canada*, a collection of the old French folksongs which had survived in Quebec, as medieval English songs did among the mountaineers of Kentucky. The Abbé Léon Provancher carried on the popular scientific work of Dr. LaRue with his *Flore canadienne* (1862) and his *La Faune entomologique du Canada* (1877–89), compilations largely borrowed from American sources which helped to correct the French-Canadian tendency to confuse the North American environment with the European one of their French models. But as yet there was no true scientific writing in Quebec, and botany and geology were cultivated merely as avocations by a few amateurs.

The literature of 1860–1900 indicated a slow awakening to intellectual maturity of a people who had long lingered in a semi-primitive social state. So much intellectual energy was expended in the religio-political struggles of the period that there was little left for purely intellectual pursuits. The cultural colonialism produced by the renewal of close relations with France favored imitation rather than originality, while French-Canadian writers and painters were foredoomed to play second fiddle to those of France. The general preoccupation with religious and patriotic themes which characterizes the work of writers of the School of Quebec and their disciples reflects the fact that this literature was largely produced by members of the ecclesiastical and political élite, the only French Canadians who could afford to write when literature was an avocation rather than a profession. This élite was largely reactionary, and looked back at the past through romantic glasses, rather than forward to the future or closely at the present.

The enthusiastic reception given to the Bourbon pretender to the throne of France, the Comte de Paris, and his brother the Duc d'Orléans during the summer of 1890 indicates the temper of the times. Only three incorrigible *Rouges*, Fréchette, Honoré Beaugrand, and Raoul Dandurand, protested against the plans for a civic reception at Montreal, and the Conservative journalist Thomas Chapais dismissed them as 'the three Brutuses.' The ultramontanes outdid themselves in paying honor to the Bourbon princes, who were officially received at both Montreal and Quebec, and did not fail to pay homage to Bishop Laflèche at Trois-Rivières. Beaugrand redeemed republican honor by sending a telegram to President Carnot, and Dandurand was given the Legion of Honor, presumably for his legendary feat of crying '*Vive la République, Monsieur!*' as the Comte de Paris passed by.[124] A period of cultural colonialism was to end with Mercier almost succeeding in making Quebec an economic as well as a cultural province of France. It remained for Laurier to awaken French Canada to a larger Canadianism and for Henri Bourassa to spur its sense of particularism in the years to come.

Notes

[1] The population of Lower Canada in 1844 was 697,084, while Upper Canada's in 1840 was 432,159, according to the nearest comparable census figures, *Canada Year Book, 1922–23* (Ottawa, 1924), 142. The first census of the united Province of Canada in 1851 showed 60,000 more English-speaking than French Canadians, out of a population of nearly two millions. (Turcotte, *Canada sous l'Union*, II, 164). Massive emigration from Britain had strengthened the English-Canadian group—it is estimated that 428,000 emigrants from Ireland alone came between 1838–49 (Desrosiers & Fournet, *La Race française en Amérique*, 167)—though many of the newcomers continued on to the United States, immediately or after a short period. French-Canadian emigration to the United States from 1831 to 1844 is estimated by Sulte, *Histoire des Canadiens-français, 1608–1880* (Montreal, 1882–4), VIII, 132, at 40,000, and increased from that date onward. Although there are no U.S. census figures for French-speaking Canadians before 1890, when 302,496 were reported, it is probable that 50,000 had gone to the States by 1850, and

another 50,000 by 1860. R. H. Coats & M. C. Maclean, *The American-Born in Canada* (Toronto, 1943), 29-34. Langlois estimates 48,742 by 1851, and 86,615 by 1871. *Histoire de la Population canadienne-française* (Montréal, 1934), 174.

The French Canadians formed 31.07 per cent of the population in 1871, 30.03 in 1881, 30.71 per cent in 1901, 28.51 per cent in 1911, 27.91 per cent in 1921, 28.22 per cent in 1931, 30.27 per cent in 1941, 30.8 per cent in 1951, and 30.4 per cent in 1961. *Canada Year Book, 1934-35*, 123; *ibid.*, *1945*, 104; *ibid.*, *1952-53*, 149; and *ibid.. 1965*, 107. Their higher birthrate has been offset until recent years by massive immigration (see Langlois, 265-6, for annual totals, 1867-1933).

³ *Ibid.*, 167. The outlying groups have steadily increased, and by 1941 almost a quarter of the French Canadians lived outside Quebec (Langlois, 169 and *Canada Year Book, 1945*, 105-6).

⁴ R. Blanchard, *L'Est du Canada Français* (Montréal, 1935), II, 221-2.

⁵ *Ibid.*, 202-3.

⁶ *Ibid.*, 224.

⁷ *Ibid.*, 219-20.

⁸ Innis & Lower, *Select Econ. Docs., 1783-1885*, 489, 497.

⁹ *Ibid.*, *Select Econ. Docs., 1783-1885*, 455-7; M. Q. Innis, *An Economic History of Canada* (Toronto, 1935), 185.

¹⁰ *Canada Year Book, 1922-23*, 172.

¹¹ M. Q. Innis, 21.

¹² See E. Hamon, *Les Canadiens-Français de la Nouvelle Angleterre* (Québec, 1891).

¹³ Innis & Lower, *Select Econ. Docs.*, II, 513.

¹⁴ M. Q. Innis, 268.

¹⁵ Innis & Lower, II, 583-4.

¹⁶ *Ibid.*, 496.

¹⁷ N. J. Ware & H. A. Logan, *Labor in Canadian-American Relations* (Toronto, 1937), vi.

¹⁸ *Ibid.*, xviii.

¹⁹ *Mandements de Québec*, N.S., I, 554-7, Taschereau's pastoral, 19 April 1886; *ibid..* IV, 633-5, joint pastoral of 4th Provincial Council, 14 May 1868.

²⁰ R. Rumilly, *Mgr. Laflèche et son temps* (Montréal, 1938), 43.

²¹ Rumilly, *Histoire*, I, 138.

²² *CHAR 1950*, 20-9: Léopold Lamontagne, 'Habits gris et chemise rouge.'

²³ Rumilly, *Laflèche*, 44.

²⁴ H. S. Lear, *Lacordaire* (London, 1899), 223.

²⁵ *Mandements de Montréal* (Montréal, 1887), III, 356, Bourget's pastoral, 10 March 1858; T. Hudon, S.J., *L'Institut Canadien de Montréal et l'Affaire Guibord* (Montréal, 1938), 58.

²⁶ Hudon, 59-60, refers to the Institut National which was founded in 1852. See Léon Pouliot. S.J., 'L'Institut Canadien de Montréal et l'Institut National,' RHAF, XIV, 4 (mars 1961).

²⁷ *Mandements de Montréal*, VI, 38, Bourget's pastoral, 30 March 1858; Hudon, 60; *Mandements de Montréal*, III, 401, Bourget's pastoral, 31 May 1858; Hudon, 62.

²⁸ *Mandements de Montréal*, III, 427, Bourget's pastoral, 25 December 1863; Hudon, 64.

²⁹ Hudon, 65.

³⁰ *Mandements de Québec*, N.S., I, 628, 4th Provincial Council pastoral, 14 May 1868.

³¹ Rumilly, *Laflèche*, 26-7.

³² *Ibid.*, 28.

³³ *Mandements de Montréal*, VI, 48, Bourget's pastoral, August 1869; Hudon, 74.

³⁴ Hudon, 76.

³⁵ Hudon, 109-12.

[36] Hudon, 114.

[37] Hudon, 114–5.

[38] Hudon, 123–31.

[39] *Mandements de Montréal*, VI, Bourget's circular, 3 September 1875; Hudon, 135.

[40] *Ibid.*, Bourget's pastoral, 16 November 1875; Hudon, 147.

[41] Archives, Séminaire de Trois-Rivières, Fonds Laflèche, Laflèche-Boucher de Niverville, 2 March 1864.

[42] *Ibid.*, Laflèche-Abbé Boucher, 9 September 1867.

[43] *CHAR 1945*, 58–9, Abbé A. Maheux, 'Le Nationalisme canadien-français à l'aurore du XXᵉ siècle.'

[44] *Ibid.*, 59.

[45] ASTR, Laflèche-O. Caron, 27 April 1870.

[46] *Ibid.*, Laflèche-O. Caron, 27 May 1870.

[47] Skelton, I, 129; Rumilly, *Histoire*, I, 177–8. Skelton's version is a poor translation.

[48] *Ibid.*,

[49] *Mandements de Québec*, N.S., I, 37, Taschereau's circular, 24 April 1871.

[50] *Le National*, 24 April 1872; Skelton, I, 131–2.

[51] Rumilly, *Laflèche*, 65–6, Bourget's circular, 19 March 1872.

[52] *Ibid.*, 69–70.

[53] *Ibid.*, 76.

[54] The career of Charles Chiniquy, one of the few apostate priests in French-Canadian history, has been neglected and deserves further study, for he was a great force for both good and evil in his two careers. Chiniquy was born at Kamouraska in 1809, the son of a notary and the grandson of the Basque pilot who guided Admiral Saunders' fleet upriver in 1759 in the expedition against Quebec. Orphaned at an early age, he was educated at Nicolet thanks to an uncle and to the director of the *collège*. After ordination in 1833, he served as vicar at Saint-Charles, Charlesbourg, and Saint-Roch, the working-class quarter of Quebec. He was named *curé* of Beauport in 1838, and of Kamouraska in 1842, after launching his crusade against strong drink. For this work he received a papal blessing in 1841 and encouragement from Mgr. Forbin-Janson, the peripatetic Bishop of Nancy. His *Manuel des Sociétés de Tempérance* (Québec, 1844) sold 4,000 copies in six months—an unprecedented sale for a new book at this period in Quebec—and he became a great national hero.

Scandal involving a woman, however, forced his resignation from his parish and his departure from the diocese of Quebec in 1846. He then entered the newly opened Oblate novitiate at Longueuil, and after fourteen months resumed his temperance crusade in the diocese of Montreal. He was credited with inducing 2,300 to sign the pledge at Longueuil, and 10,000 more in other parishes. In eighteen months he covered one hundred and twenty parishes and converted 200,000 to temperance. The second edition of his *Manuel*, published at Montreal in 1847, sold 6,000 copies in a year and a half. But once more he fell into trouble with women, and after several warnings from Bishop Bourget, was deprived of his clerical faculties in 1851. He then went to the French-Canadian colony in the Kankakee country south of Chicago. Two hundred families from Canada followed him there in response to his letter in *Le Canadien* of September 22, 1851, which offered assurance that those who were forced to emigrate would not have to give up French-Canadian ways if they joined him there. In 1852 he returned to Canada to lead others to Illinois, and by 1856 he claimed that his parish numbered 6,000 souls. Chiniquy had become involved with difficulties with his bishop, however, and was put under interdict by Bishop O'Regan in 1856, and excommunicated shortly thereafter when he defied the interdict. The Bishop of Quebec sent his grand vicar, Mgr. Mailloux, to Illinois to combat Chiniquy and the schism he had created at Ste. Anne. Chiniquy sought reconciliation in 1856 and again in 1858, but further scandalous conduct called forth another excommunication in 1858.

He then became a Presbyterian, carrying some of his flock with him, and under the auspices of the Protestant Missionary Society visited Canada, England, Scotland, India, and Australia, preaching and lecturing against Catholicism. His best-known work of this second period is *The Priest, the Woman, and the Confessional*, a highly sensational work which appeared in the *Witness* of Montreal, as it served the purposes of the Protestant crusade against Catholicism. In a pastoral of March 19, 1875, Bishop Bourget forbade reading of the *Witness* and once more condemned Chiniquy (Rumilly, I, 345-6). The work was reprinted in Toronto in 1944 by Pastor Shields, the modern exponent of that tradition. Chiniquy died at Montreal in January 1899, publishing in the *Montreal Gazette* on January 10 his 'Testament,' which expressed his hatred and defiance of Catholicism once more. Le Jeune, *Dictionnaire générale du Canada*; biographical notice by Hector L. Langevin, in *Manuel des Sociétés de Tempérance* (Montréal, 1849); M. L. Hansen & J. B. Brebner, *The Mingling of the Canadian and American Peoples* (Toronto, 1940), 129-30. See Marcel Trudel, *La véritable figure de Chiniquy* (Trois Rivières, 1955).

⁵⁵ *Mandements de Québec*, N.S., I, 320-36, joint pastoral, 22 September 1875; Skelton, I, 135-6.

⁵⁶ *Ibid.*, 330; Rumilly, I, 380.

⁵⁷ *Mandements de Montréal*, VII, 299, Bourget's circular, 1 February 1876; Skelton, I, 136-7.

⁵⁸ Skelton, I, 137; Rumilly, *Laflèche*, 95.

⁵⁹ Skelton, I, 139.

⁶⁰ *Ibid.*, 140-1.

⁶¹ *Ibid.*, 141.

⁶² U. Barthe, *Wilfrid Laurier on the Platform* (Quebec, 1890), 52.

⁶³ *Ibid.*, 54.

⁶⁴ *Ibid.*, 55.

⁶⁵ *Ibid.*, 57

⁶⁶ *Ibid.*, 59.

⁶⁷ *Ibid.*, 59.

⁶⁸ *Ibid.*, 60.

⁶⁹ *Ibid.*, 61-2.

⁷⁰ *Ibid.*, 67.

⁷¹ *Ibid.*, 68.

⁷² *Ibid.*, 69.

⁷³ *Ibid.*, 70.

⁷⁴ *Ibid.*, 71-2.

⁷⁵ *Ibid.*, 72.

⁷⁶ *Ibid.*, 73.

⁷⁷ *Ibid.*, 75-8.

⁷⁸ *Ibid.*, 79.

⁷⁹ *Mandements de Québec*, N.S., I, 403-9, Taschereau's pastoral, 25 May 1876.

⁸⁰ *Ibid.*, II, 10-13, joint circular, 26 March 1877.

⁸¹ Conroy's instructions published by Taschereau, *Mandements de Québec*, N.S., II, 271, Taschereau's circular, October 1881; Rumilly, *Laflèche*, 118-9.

⁸² *Mandements de Québec*, N.S., II, 52, joint pastoral 11 October 1877; L. David, *Histoire du Canada depuis la Confédération* (Montréal, 1909), 152; Simeoni-Taschereau, 13 September 1881; Rumilly, *Laflèche*, 123.

⁸³ *Mandements de Québec*, N.S., II, 47, joint circular to clergy, 11 October 1877.

⁸⁴ *Le Journal des Trois-Rivières*; Rumilly, *Laflèche*, 124.

⁸⁵ Rumilly, *Laflèche*, 128.

[86] Skelton, I, 212-13.

[87] *Ibid.*

[88] Rumilly, *Laflèche*, 133.

[89] Rumilly, *Histoire*, III, 75–80; *Laflèche*, 152.

[90] Rumilly, *Laflèche*, 156.

[91] *Mandements de Québec*, N.S., II, 265; Taschereau's circular, 7 October 1881.

[92] *L'Evénement*, October 1881; Rumilly, *Laflèche*, 161.

[93] *Le Monde*; Rumilly, *Laflèche*, 171.

[94] *Mandements de Québec*, N.S., II, 286–96, Taschereau's pastoral, 2 February 1882.

[95] *La Vérité;* David, *Histoire*, 162.

[96] *Journal des Trois-Rivières*; David, *Histoire*, 161–2.

[97] ASTR: Fonds Laflèche, 'Diverses oeuvres MSS,' Laflèche-Leo XIII on 'Humanum genus,' (1884). The encyclical was published by Cardinal Taschereau in May 1884, *Mandements de Québec*, N.S. II, 404-28.

[98] Rumilly, *Laflèche*, 176-7.

[99] *Ibid.*, 177.

[100] Simeoni-Legaré, 10 January 1883; Rumilly, *Laflèche*, 189.

[101] *Mandements de Québec*, N.S., II, 349–56, Taschereau's pastoral, 19 March 1883, Propaganda degree, 27 February 1883.

[102] Taschereau-Taché, 1 May 1883; Rumilly, *Laflèche*, 196.

[103] Rumilly, *Laflèche*, 198.

[104] *Mandements de Québec*, N.S., II, 366–70, Taschereau's pastoral, 1 June 1883.

[105] Rumilly, *Laflèche*, 208-9.

[106] *Ibid.*, 213.

[107] *Mandements de Montréal*, X, 5, Fabre's pastoral, 22 May 1884; Rumilly *Laflèche*, 225.

[108] Rumilly, *Laflèche*, 228.

[109] L. Desilets, *Exposé sommaire* (Rome, 1884); Rumilly, *Laflèche*, 232.

[110] Rumilly, *Laflèche*, 233.

[111] *Ibid.*, 235.

[112] *Ibid.*, 245.

[113] *Ibid.*, 249.

[114] Taschereau-Laflèche, 26 May 1884; Rumilly, *Laflèche*, 251.

[115] ASTR: Fonds Laflèche, Laflèche-Abbé Arcand, 21 October 1891.

[116] *Ibid.*, Laflèche-Curé Tessier, 5 March 1892.

[117] *La Lanterne* (Montréal, 1884), I, 'Aux Lecteurs.' This reprint was condemned by Archbishop Taschereau on 8 November 1886 (*Mandements de Québec*, N.S., II, 591–2).

[118] *La Lanterne*, I, 'Aux Lecteurs.'

[119] *Ibid.*, I, 4.

[120] *Ibid.*, I, 53.

[121] A. Buies, *Petits chroniques pour 1877* (Québec, 1878), VI.

[122] *Ibid.*, XI.

[123] *Ibid.*, 36.

[124] Rumilly, *Histoire*, VI, 163 n. 1.

CHAPTER VIII

RIEL, THE WEST, AND MERCIER

(1818–97)

THE STRIFE in Quebec in the years between 1867 and 1896 which was heightened by developments in the West, was remote at the outset of the period and dominated national life at its close. The same period saw the birth and death of hopes of building a new Quebec in the West, upon the foundations laid in the days of the fur trade, under both the French and English regimes.

I

The Red River colony had depended on Quebec for its religious organization since 1818, when Bishop Plessis answered Lord Selkirk's request for missionaries by sending out the Abbés Norbert Provencher and S.-J.-N. Dumoulin. With them went a few settlers from Quebec, also requested by the noble colonizer. These new-comers joined the French-Canadian and *Métis* (half-breed)[1] employees of the fur trade settled about the missions of St. Boniface and Pembina, after the absorption of the North West Company by the Hudson's Bay Company in 1821 left many without work. At the outset the Selkirk colony was two-thirds Scottish, with the remaining third made up of German Swiss veterans of the Régiments de Meuron and de Watteville which had served in the War of 1812, French Canadians from Quebec, and veterans of the fur trade.[2] As the years passed, the French, who tended to follow a semi-nomadic hunting life, came to equal in number the Scottish and English settlers, who inclined more to agriculture. Because of this ethnic mixture the colony was described as 'a little Quebec.'[3] But the *Métis*, both French and English, increased far more rapidly than the pure-blooded whites, and developed a sense of nationality of their own, with Indian blood acting as a tie which offset ancient French and English differences.[4]

The West was more of a British frontier than a Canadian one at this period, since after 1821 it was controlled and supplied from Britain through Hudson Bay, rather than over the barrier of the Laurentian Shield north of the Great Lakes, or by the roundabout and difficult route from Canada through the States. The English group in the colony, including the Hudson's Bay Company men who dominated both trade and government, the Anglican mission-aries, and a few settlers, was the most influential; the group of Scottish settlers the most homogeneous; and the French-Canadian and *Métis* group the most numerous.[5] Aside from the officials, the French Canadians had the closest economic relation to the Hud-son's Bay Company, since they were largely nomadic trappers, *voyageurs*, and buffalo hunters who supplied the pemmican which was the basic ration of the fur trade. For this reason they were more restive under the company's monopoly than the agricultural Scots. Then from the North-Westers' bitter trade wars with the Hudson's Bay Company the French *Métis* had acquired a tradition of enmity to the latter; while from their Indian forbears they had inherited the belief that the West was their land, and that its natural resources were theirs, despite the company's strict regulations against unlicensed fur-trading. Gradually the *Métis*, both French and English, developed a sense of unity.

They called themselves the 'New Nation.'[6] Accustomed to choosing their own leaders, Indian-style, and to acting together with disciplined unity for the purposes of the buffalo hunt, the *Métis* grew increasingly restive under the regulations of the Hudson's Bay Company officials of Assiniboia, and in 1849 this unrest exploded into virtual rebellion.[7] When Guillaume Sayer was charged with illicit fur-trading before Recorder Adam Thom—who had been rewarded by Lord Durham for his services in 1839 with this office—a group of *Métis* under Scottish leaders invaded the courtroom and won the acquittal of Sayer by intimidation. Jean-Louis Riel, grand-son of the famous *coureur de bois* Lagimodière and himself the miller of St. Boniface, was the most influential figure among the French *Métis*, thanks to the prestige of his two years as an Oblate novice and his later industrial training in Montreal. He was generally believed to be the leading spirit in the agitation over the Sayer case and in the demand for free trade which was then expressed, though he remained behind the scenes of the courtroom drama in 1849.

The isolated little world of the Red River was gradually drawn into the life of the continent. There was an annexationist agitation in 1845–6, occasioned by the focusing of American expansionism on the Oregon boundary dispute, but its development was checked by a force of English troops who garrisoned the colony from 1846 to 1848.[8] In the West as in the East the Church threw its weight behind loyalty to the British connection, and the Abbés Blanchet and Demers were sent from the Red River to the Oregon settlements at the request of the imperial authorities to offset the influence of American missionaries in the latter regions. Again from 1857 to

1861 a small force of the Canadian Rifles was stationed at Fort Garry to guard against Fenian raids and to offset the annexationist movement in Minnesota inspired by James Wickes Taylor, then a special agent of the United States Treasury, who reported to the Governor of Minnesota in 1860 that 'the frontier, hitherto resting upon the sources of the St. Lawrence and the Mississippi, is soon to be pushed far beyond the International frontier by the march of Anglo-Saxon civilization.'[9] During the 1840's and 1850's the Red River region, which had previously been tied to eastern Canada only by the dependence of its missionaries on Quebec and Montreal, gradually became a bone of contention between Upper and Lower Canada. George Brown, the francophobe and anti-Catholic editor of the *Toronto Globe*, aroused English-Canadian interest in the West and preached annexation of the Red River colony to Canada. In this cause he was aided by the like-minded William McDougall, whose *North American* was soon absorbed by the *Globe*. Both men wanted to make the West an extension of English Upper Canada, with a view to dominating French Canada.[10] Quebec, whose interest in the West had been stirred by the reports of the missionaries whom it supported and largely supplied, naturally opposed this program, which increased its chronic sense of insecurity.

With the project of Confederation already under discussion, Canadian pressure was brought to bear in London against the renewal of the Hudson's Bay Company charter in 1857; and in that same year a committee composed of George Brown and Joseph Cauchon was appointed by the Canadian legislature to consider Western affairs. Canada took the view that the Hudson's Bay Company title to the North-West was invalid,[11] and, as its own expansionism developed, became somewhat concerned at the extension of American economic influence in the Red River region, which was linked to the United States by steamer in 1859 and by rail shortly afterward, when the railroad reached St. Paul. The Hudson's Bay Company itself began to import supplies by this route rather than by the traditional York Factory one. The authority of the company declined after the renewal of its charter was refused in London. The company's officials were left in the forlorn position of a lame-duck American president, obliged to round out his term of office after defeat at the polls.[12]

In this situation Canadian and American annexationist parties grew up among the new settlers at Fort Garry, the English settlement about the Hudson's Bay post across the river from St. Boniface, the *Métis* and French Catholic center; while the older settlers agitated for Crown colony status. The American party received backing from Minnesota, and Taylor reported on December 17, 1861: 'The

Americanization of this important section of British North America is rapidly progressing. Unless the British Parliament acts promptly . . . I shall confidently expect a popular movement looking to independence or annexation to the United States.'[13] Two Canadians, William Coldwell and William Buckingham, founded in 1859 the first newspaper, the *Nor'Wester*, which was the organ of the Canadian party.[14] In 1862 John Ross, a Scottish *Métis*, claimed that the 'New Nation' wanted responsible government, while J.-L. Riel denied it. Meanwhile the Canadian authorities, proceeding on their convenient view that Assiniboia had no legal government, provided for the admission of the North-West Territories into Confederation at the Quebec Conference of 1864, without consulting the wishes of the people of the region.[15] When this news reached the Red River, it was proposed that one French and one English delegate should be sent to London to express the popular demand for Crown colony status.[16]

Resentment of highhanded eastern determination of the fate of the West continued to grow along the Red River. A short-lived 'Republic of Manitoba' on the pre-annexation Texan model[17] was set up in January 1868, with Thomas Spence, a newly arrived English-Canadian disciple of D'Arcy McGee as president, while negotiations were still pending in London between the Hudson's Bay Company and the British and Canadian governments over disposition of the territory. The move was probably intended to aid the Canadian case by proving that the company had lost control of the Red River colony.[18] A plague of grasshoppers produced considerable economic distress along the Red River that same year, which sharpened the local opposition to the wholly illegal Canadian roadbuilding party under John A. Snow which had been sent into the region by William McDougall as a joint relief and political measure.[19] The paymaster of this party was the poet Charles Mair, whose Red River letters were published by the *Toronto Globe*. The following summer Canadian surveyors under Colonel J. S. Dennis proceeded to run their lines without regard to the river-strip holdings of the old settlers, and with a show of racist contempt for the *Métis*. The population at this period numbered about 10,000, predominantly *Métis* and almost equally divided between English and French. Despite the urgent representations of Governor Mactavish, Colonel Dennis, and Bishop Taché—who warned Cartier at Ottawa in July 1869 and Cartier and Hector Langevin at Quebec in September on the eve of his departure for the Vatican Council—that trouble was brewing in the West, the land schemes of the Canadian government were deemed more important than the protests of 10,000 'half-castes,'[20] as Sir John Macdonald contemptuously called the *Métis*.

The long negotiations carried on by Cartier and Macdonald with the Hudson's Bay Company finally came to an end. The company's deed of surrender of November 19, 1869, was to take effect with the transfer of the North-West Territories to Canada on December 1, when the latter was to pay £300,000, in addition to making land grants and other privileges to extinguish the company's claim. Under the Act for the Temporary Government of Rupert's Land, passed in June 1869 without consultation of the Red River people, Canada was to have both federal and provincial powers in the Territories, since the proposed governmental organization provided only for an appointed governor and council, whose members did not have to be residents. This was a backward step politically, for the old Council of Assiniboia had included local representation (on a roughly equal French and English basis since 1855);[21] and further popular agitation against absentee control arose.

William McDougall, already unpopular with the colonists for his heavyhanded expansionist activities, was appointed lieutenant-governor and dispatched by way of Chicago and St. Paul to the Red River, where he was to take office after the transfer of title on December 1. His council included Joseph-Norbert Provencher, nephew of the pioneer missionary bishop of the Red River and a former editor of *La Minerve*, Cartier's Conservative organ in Montreal; but for the rest was as militantly 'Anglo-Saxon' and Protestant as McDougall could have wished. The new government was frankly despotic, for Macdonald wrote Charles Tupper that McDougall 'will be for the time Paternal despot, as in other small Crown Colonies, his Council being one of advice, he and they, however, being governed by instructions from Headquarters.'[22] Joseph Howe, shortly to become Dominion Secretary of State, paid an unofficial visit to the Red River to assuage the rising unrest there, and found that discontent was general. The company officials felt that they should have received a share of the £300,000; the English were dissatisfied at not being consulted about the transfer; and the French were uneasy because of the appointment as governor of the francophobe imperialist McDougall.

2

The mounting unrest came to a head in October 1869. On the 11th, Louis Riel, the twenty-five-year-old son of the leader of the French *Métis* in 1849, who like his father enjoyed great prestige among his people because he had been educated for the priesthood in Montreal, thanks to Bishop Taché and the Masson family of Terrebonne, broke up a survey party which was running its lines without regard to the holdings of the French settlers. On October

20 the *Métis* assembled and elected a provisional government modeled on their organization for buffalo-hunting, with the Scottish *Métis* John Bruce as president and young Riel as secretary. Their aim was to win recognition of their rights by Canada before the territory changed hands. Father J.-J. Lestanc, a Frenchman like many of the Oblate missionaries in the West, who was acting as vicar-general in the absence at Rome of Bishop Taché, refused to intervene with Riel at the request of the old Council of Assiniboia, on the grounds that the *Métis* were justified in urging their grievances upon the government. Father Lestanc did not admire Riel, however, and was opposed to any resort to violence or unconstitutional means of protest; while the Canadian missionary of Rivière-Sale, Father N.-J. Ritchot, was known to favor direct action by the movement, which he supported; and the Fenian seminarian William O'Dono-ghue of St. Boniface was for radical measures, even the annexation to the States for which enthusiasm was being fostered in Minnesota by James Wickes Taylor, who was now simultaneously an agent of the State Department and of Jay Cooke.[23] The English settlers, though not threatened like the French on the score of language and religion, met on October 19 and refused to adopt an address of welcome to McDougall. But their attitude was one of willingness to wait and see how the new regime worked out, rather than of resistance to the establishment of Canadian government.

Riel was summoned to appear before the Council of Assiniboia on October 25, and there defended the actions of the *Métis* as being in the interest of the whole colony. He expressed satisfaction with the present government and objected to 'any government coming from Canada without their being consulted in the matter.'[24] Behind this opposition lay the *Métis* fear of being crowded out of their own country by the mass immigration from Ontario which McDougall had been promoting in the *Globe*. On November 2 Ambroise Lépine, the only other French *Métis* among the six officers of the provisional government, and a party of armed *Métis*, escorted McDougall and two of his council out of the country when he attempted to cross the frontier, after he had been warned on his arrival at Pembina on October 30 not to do so.[25] This incident has been responsible for the use of the term 'rebellion' in connection with the *Métis* rising; but it is difficult to justify the term, since McDougall was simply a private citizen and the Red River country not Canadian territory until the anticipated transfer took place. On October 30 the acting governor of Assiniboia, Mactavish, had written McDougall urging him to wait at the frontier.[26] On the same day that McDougall was deported in the name of the provisional government, Riel seized Fort Garry, thus forestalling a similar move by the Canadian party headed by Dr. Schultz and Colonel Dennis, the head of the surveying party which included a number of hot-headed expansionists.[27] Colonel Dennis had written McDougall on October 27, warning him that trouble was brewing, and subsequently planned a *coup d'état* to bring him in by force.[28] On November 6 Riel called upon the eleven Scottish parishes to choose representatives to meet with the French *Métis* on November 16.

In the face of these developments the acting governor of Assiniboia, Mactavish, issued a mildly-phrased proclamation on November 16, protesting against the provisional government's actions and urging 'lawful constitutional' action.[29] He then advised McDougall to return to Canada. On November 22 A. B. Bannatyne recommended that the English settlers should combine with the French, and a joint plan was formed to supplant the old council by a new popular one, which would enter into negotiations with the Canadian government. Riel, who had become the dominant figure in the provisional government by this time, first agreed to this proposal and then rejected it, while on November 23 his followers seized the provisions and cash at Fort Garry and interrupted free communication in and out of the fort. Though the French *Métis* had so far taken the lead in the actions of the provisional government, by the end of November the English and Scottish half-breeds were drilling to defend their rights if need be against the Canadian authorities.[30] There was no need to do so, for the intimidated McDougall simply crossed the frontier once more on December 1, issued a proclamation[31] which was invalid since the transfer to Canada had not taken place as scheduled and he was unsworn as governor, and then promptly returned to the States. There he found a letter of November 20 from Macdonald instructing him that he was entering 'a foreign country' and that he was not to attempt to force his way in.[32] Colonel Dennis, who had constituted himself McDougall's advisor and who had been given a curious commission as 'Lieutenant and Conservator of the Peace,'[33] was characterized as 'exceedingly injudicious.' And finally Macdonald had refused on November 27 to accept transfer of the territory from the Hudson's Bay Company in its disturbed state when he learned of the resistance to McDougall.

Though Ottawa marked time, events along the Red River did not. Colonel Dennis, at the head of some seventy Canadians and as many more Indians, had planned a rising on December 2 which McDougall thought would succeed in putting down the provisional government of the *Métis*. This scheme advanced no further than the seizure of the Lower Fort on December 1, for the Colonel found his followers undependable. His movement broke up on the 9th, after Riel had issued on December 5 a 'List of Rights'[34]—most of which were conceded in the Manitoba Act of the following year—and had seized some leaders of the Canadian party at Dr. Schultz' house on the 7th and imprisoned them at Fort Garry. In defiance of McDougall's proclamation, the provisional government flew its own fleur-de-lis and shamrock flag from its headquarters at the fort. The Canadian party had already displayed a flag of their own—the Union Jack with 'Canada' embroidered on it. [35]

Macdonald, who had previously refused to take the *Métis* agitation seriously, reached late in November the correct conclusion that 'the resistance of the half-breeds evidently is not against the sovereignty of Her Majesty or the government of the Hudson's Bay Company, but to the assumption of the government by Canada.' [36] He promptly sent out two unofficial emissaries, Father J.-B. Thibault, a missionary with twenty-seven years' service in the region, and Lieutenant-Colonel Charles de Salaberry, the son of the hero of Chateauguay. Donald Smith, recommended to Macdonald by George Stephen as a good agent because of his experience in the region as a Hudson's Bay official, was also sent out to buy off the insurgent leaders. Riel was to be offered a post in the new territorial police; two *Métis* were to be included in the new council, two-thirds of which was to be elected from the settlement; land titles were to be adjusted; and secret funds were made available, as Macdonald blandly put it, 'to construct a Golden Bridge over which McDougall can pass into the country.' [37] But McDougall's actions of early December anticipated the arrival of the emissaries and compromised their efforts. Macdonald promptly repudiated the acts of McDougall and Dennis when he learned of their course and refused to accept title to the region when it was a state in insurrection. By a royal proclamation of December 6 the *Métis* were urged to lay down their arms, and an amnesty was promised to all who did so. [38]

Meanwhile Riel had become more highhanded with success. He assumed the presidency of the provisional government on December 29, two days after Donald Smith and Father Thibault reached Fort Garry, and made it difficult for them to get a hearing from the people. His sentiments remained distinctly British—there is evidence that he refused offers of aid in money, men, and arms from American annexationists [39]—but he was inclined to use the threat of annexation as a club to force the Canadian government to grant the *Métis*' demands. [40] Father Thibault and Colonel de Salaberry met with the council on January 13, but Smith, posing merely as an old Hudson's Bay man without official status, did not win a hearing from the suspicious *Métis* until after a split developed between Riel and another *Métis* leader Léveillé on January 19. Smith then read his instructions and the royal proclamation at public meetings of the settlers, calling for 'union and entire concord among all classes.' [41] The explosiveness of the situation had largely evaporated by this time. Most of the French *Métis* who had taken up arms dispersed by

Fort Garry

Photograph by Hine. This stronghold and base of the Hudson's Bay Company played the key role in the Riel rising of 1869–70. It was seized by Riel early in the struggle and served as his capital. Here Donald Smith and Bishop Taché made their appeals, here Thomas Scott was shot, and here General Wolseley made his headquarters. In six months the Fort flew five flags—those of the Hudson's Bay Company, of Riel, of the Fenians, of Canada, and of the United Kingdom. (Public Archives of Canada.)

Cathedral and Convent, Saint-Boniface

Photograph by Hine of the birthplace of Catholicism in the West. Saint-Boniface, across the Red River from Fort Garry, was the cultural center of the *Métis*. (Public Archives of Canada.)

January 22, while three days later a convention of twenty English and twenty French representatives met and adopted a bill of rights, whose nature was moderated through Smith's influence on January 29 and 31.[42] A formal provisional government headed by Riel was established on February 10, and by all the evidence it received *de facto* recognition from Ottawa pending the arrival of a new governor. This government appointed a three-man delegation to Ottawa, composed of Father Ritchot representing the French *Métis*, Judge John Black for the English *Métis*, and Alfred H. Scott for the American and English settlers.

Unfortunately, just at this juncture when the unrest was subsiding, the hotheaded Canadian party determined to achieve by force a conclusion of the troubles, although one was well on the way to attainment through negotiation. A group at the English settlement of Portage la Prairie, incited by the lurid tales of Charles Mair and Thomas Scott, one of Schultz' followers who had escaped from Fort Garry on January 9, determined to make a raid on the fort and rescue the other prisoners. A party under the leadership of Major C. A. Boulton descended on Fort Garry during the night of February 14, but, having received a promise of peace from Riel if they disbanded, went off to Kildonan without taking action.[43] A *Métis* named Parisien, who had been picked up by Boulton's party, escaped from them and shot an English settler named Sutherland, who he thought was pursuing him, at Kildonan the following day. Boulton's party was then rounded up by Lépine and imprisoned at the fort.

Boulton was 'court-martialled' by the provisional government and sentenced to be shot, but his life was saved by Smith's intervention in his behalf. Smith was unable to do as much for the troublesome Thomas Scott, who on March 4 came to the end of a stormy career in the West—which had opened with his attempt to murder Snow, the surveyor in charge of the Canadian party to which he was attached—when he was shot, after a drumhead 'court-martial' presided over by Lépine. His anti-*Métis* activity in December, his escape in January, his role in provoking Boulton's raid and the subsequent bloodshed, and his rumored physical and verbal assaults on Riel while in prison all affected the verdict.[44] Scott's death has been called 'a judicial murder,'[45] but it seems rather to have been a vigilante execution in the tradition of the West, where people customarily took the law into their own hands in default of established institutions of law and order.

Bishop Taché returned to the Red River five days after Scott's death, having been urgently summoned from Rome by the Canadian government, which at last was willing to accept his advice. In interviews at Ottawa with Macdonald, Cartier, Howe, and the

o

governor-general during February, the Bishop received assurances
—at least so he thought—that the insurgents would receive the
promised amnesty.[46] Under his influence and the promise of an
amnesty the colony quieted down rapidly, although Riel displayed
distrust of his lifelong protector and treated him as an agent of
the Canadian government.[47] The remaining prisoners were set
free by the insurgents on March 16, and two days later Donald
Smith took his departure. The annexation movement collapsed.
At Bishop Taché's instigation, the Union Jack replaced the provisional government's flag at Fort Garry on April 23,[48] after Riel
had proclaimed peace on April 9. The insurgents continued to
govern with the tacit consent of Ottawa until the new governor
should arrive.

The execution of Scott, a member of the Orange Order, was used
by the expansionist 'Canada First' movement in Ontario to arouse
a violent agitation which exploited ethnic and religious hatred.
Scott's blood was shed on many a platform, and the 'traitor French
priests' of the Red River were denounced, although the clergy had
been Ottawa's most effective ally in quieting the Red River troubles.
When Father Ritchot and Alfred Scott arrived in Toronto on their
way to Ottawa as delegates of the provisional government, they
were arrested on April 11 on a provincial warrant taken out by
Thomas Scott's brother, though they were quickly released when the
Crown refused to prosecute. The arrest embarrassed the federal
and imperial authorities, who were trying to restore calm and feared
that a long drawn-out trial would encourage American intervention.[49] The delegates brought with them a new *Métis* bill of rights,
whose chief provisions were embodied in the Manitoba Act adopted
on May 12 as a result of extended negotiations between the delegates and Macdonald, Cartier, and the governor-general. This
act gave Manitoba the same organization of responsible government
as the old provinces, except that the public lands were reserved to
the dominion in exchange for land grants to the *Métis* in extinguish-
ment of their Indian title. Denominational schools and the existing
educational rights and privileges of Protestant and Catholic
minorities were given definite safeguards. Both English and French
languages were to be used for governmental purposes.[50] In short,
the Manitoba Act provided for the establishment of a new Quebec
in the West.

The long-delayed transfer of title to Canada took effect on July
15, 1870. The new lieutenant-governor, Adams G. Archibald,
accompanied by a military force under Colonel Garnet Wolseley,
made up mainly of imperial troops but including a battalion from
Quebec and another from Ontario, was to set out from Port Arthur
for the Red River on that date. The expedition's purpose, conceived

in aroused Ontario as 'suppression' of a 'rebellion' which had already ended, actually was to ensure against another such fiasco as McDougall's inglorious adventure and to prevent any new rising against Canadian authority.[51] The imperial government refused to send troops until reasonable terms had been granted the Red River settlers.[52] Wolseley reached Fort Garry on August 24 without any other difficulty than that provided by the arduous overland route. Wolseley had paved his way with a proclamation of his peaceful objects and assurance that his force represented no party either in religion or politics, and would afford equal protection to the lives and property of all races and creeds.[53] The force occupied Fort Garry without incident, for Riel and the other insurgent leaders, alarmed by Canadian threats of vengeance, fled on its arrival. So calm was the situation that the imperial troops left five days later, in order to return as prearranged to a Canada threatened by Fenian raids before the season closed their path, although the Canadian militia battalions remained.[54]

The Canadian party in the settlements, swollen in numbers by new immigrants, raised an agitation for reprisals which was ignored by Wolseley during his brief stay and later by the new lieutenant-governor, though Donald Smith issued warrants for Riel and some others.[55] This group celebrated the establishment of Canadian rule by a persecution of the French *Métis* which culminated in the killing of Elzéar Goulet, in which two members of the Ontario Rifles were involved. They were not brought to trial.[56] The Ontario Rifles organized an Orange lodge which had 200 members by 1872 and which alienated the English as well as the French *Métis*.[57] Governor Archibald reported to Macdonald on October 8, 1871, that 'many of·the French half-breeds have been so beaten and outraged by a small but noisy section of the people that they feel as if they were living in a state of slavery.'[58] He added that the newcomers from Ontario 'seem to feel as if the French half-breeds should be wiped off the face of the globe.' Despite such treatment Riel and Lépine, at the governor's request, raised a force of some 300 *Métis* to meet the threat of Fenian raids from Minnesota in October 1871. This body was publicly reviewed and thanked by Archibald for its loyalty, a proceeding which led Riel and Lépine to assume that Ottawa had decided to overlook their part in organizing the provisional government.[59]

3

After the creation of the new province of Manitoba, the Red River colony passed through a period of rapid transition. The division between old and new settlers prior to the insurrection was replaced by an ethnic and religious division which was a by-product of the rising.[60] The old way of life was destroyed by the advent of newcomers who were interested in agriculture rather than buffalo hunting, and who were inclined to gallophobia, thanks to the agitation aroused by the death of Scott. Though the white settlers did not outnumber the *Métis* for some time after 1870, French political influence in the province was lost by a gerrymander in 1874, which upset Cartier's and Bishop Taché's efforts to maintain a French balance of power, bolstered by such Quebec notables as Joseph Royal, Joseph Dubuc, Marc-A. Girard, Alphonse Larivière, and H. J. H. Clarke,[61] and by the encouragement of immigration from Quebec. Joseph Cauchon became the second lieutenant-governor and Cartier himself sat in the dominion parliament as member for Provencher, after his defeat in Montreal East in 1872, thanks to the withdrawal of Riel, who was contesting the seat in the first Manitoba election. Cartier's death in 1873 removed from Ottawa the last strong supporter of French interests in the West, for Hector Langevin's talents were of a lesser and more provincial order than those of his chief.

The swelling Orange agitation over the murder of Thomas Scott led to the arrest of Lépine in 1873 and his condemnation to death the following year, despite an eloquent defence by Adolphe Chapleau, the rising Conservative orator, whose legal fee was paid by Franco-Americans stirred by their compatriot's plight. At the intercession of Bishop Taché, who protested vigorously against the government's repudiation of its promises of a general amnesty,[62] Lépine was reprieved by the governor-general, and his sentence was commuted to two years' imprisonment and the loss of his civil rights. Riel, who like Lépine was paid to take refuge in the States in 1872 by Macdonald and Cartier, acting through Bishop Taché,[63] was re-elected in 1874 to parliament to fill Cartier's Manitoba seat. Risking seizure for the $5,000 reward which had been placed on his head in Ontario, he appeared at Ottawa, hurriedly took the oath and then disappeared. Such a storm arose that he was expelled from the House and later formally declared a fugitive from justice. A Royal Commission appointed in 1875 to investigate the question of whether or not an amnesty had been granted to the insurgents, reported that the execution of Scott was the act of a *de facto* government accepted by the people of the Red River and recognized by the Canadian and imperial authorities; that Bishop Taché and the delegates of the provisional government believed themselves authorized to promise to the insurgents in 1870 a full and complete amnesty, on the strength of the verbal and written promises of Macdonald, Cartier, Langevin, and Howe, made with the knowledge and consent of the governor-general and the imperial government; and that Governor Archibald's appeal to Riel and Lépine in 1871 for aid against the Fenians presupposed that they were not liable to arrest and punishment for their previous actions. [64]

Acting on this report, the government declared a general amnesty for all those who had taken part in the rising, with the provision that Riel, Lépine, and O'Donoghue were to be banished for five years. Lépine, released from prison in 1876, settled at Batoche on the Saskatchewan, where, as also at Duck Lake and Saint-Laurent, many of the *Métis* migrated after being driven from their old homes along the Red River by the tide of Ontario immigration. [65] Riel, who had become mentally unstable and had developed a sense of divine mission, took refuge from the persecution to which he was subjected with the ultramontane leader Alphonse Desjardins in Montreal. Desjardins was forced to put Riel in the Longue Pointe Asylum in 1875 and again in the Longue Pointe and Beauport Asylums from 1876 to 1878 under the names of Louis David and La Rochelle. In 1874 Riel prepared for Desjardins a *Mémoire sur les Causes des Troubles du Nord-Ouest et sur les Négociations qui ont amené leur Règlement aimable*, which was printed by *Le Nouveau Monde*. This account blamed the Canadian government for causing the rising in the first place, and then for failing to fulfil its promises. In the midst of the debate on the amnesty Riel was idolized by the ultramontanes in Montreal, and on two occasions in 1875 and 1876 was encouraged in his sense of mission by Bishop Bourget. [66] He went to the United States, arousing interest in the *Métis* cause in such Franco-American centers as Plattsburg and Keeseville, New York, Manchester and Nashua, New Hampshire, Worcester, Massachusetts, and Woonsocket, Rhode Island. In October 1875 Riel went to Washington to see Major Edmund Mallet, the Franco-American Civil War hero and politician, who had become the unofficial representative of his compatriots. Riel vainly sought a post in the Indian Bureau and proposed a plan for the annexation of Manitoba before succumbing to another period of madness, which led to his return to Canada by friends in February 1876. After his release from Beauport in January 1878, he went to Keeseville, New York, and then drifted westward, reaching St. Paul in 1879 and spending a year in the Franco-American community of St. Joseph, Dakota Territory. He finally settled at the Jesuit mission of St. Peter, Montana, after marrying a French *Métis* woman and becoming a school teacher and an American citizen in 1883, though he continued to play *Métis* politics. [67]

4

The North-West Rebellion of 1885 was largely a sequel and repetition of the Red River troubles of 1869-70, though in the second instance the rising was against unquestioned authority. The French and Scottish *Métis*, who made up most of the population west of the new province of Manitoba, began to petition Governor Laird of the North-West Territories and Ottawa as early as 1874, for their semi-nomadic culture was threatened by the westward advance of agricultural civilization and the decline of the buffalo. An 1877 ordinance restricting the buffalo-hunting upon which *Métis* life was based was followed by the rapid disappearance of the beast from the Saskatchewan country, thanks to the ruthless slaughter of the migratory herds by American hunters seeking buffalo robes. As the telegraph and the Canadian Pacific Railway advanced across the plains, bringing settlers in their wake, the buffalo retreated southward over the frontier and the *Métis* were left in sad straits, prey to land speculators who often robbed them of their homes.[68] Their chief grievances—the government's failure to meet their claims for land scrip and to supply aid in making the transition from semi-nomad to agricultural and commercial life—went unheard in an Ottawa which was preoccupied with vast land-grant schemes devised to lessen the heavy financial burden of railroad construction.

Once more Eastern expansionists were little concerned with the rights of Western pioneers; once more trouble arose out of the government's decision to survey lands after the American square section system, without regard for the Quebec-type riverstrip holdings of the *Métis*.[69] One of the North-West missionaries, Father Vegreville of Saint-Louis-de-Langevin, made urgent representations to Ottawa in 1884 about the need to consider existing land divisions.[70] Captain Deville, the Chief Inspector of Surveys, worked out a compromise between the chosen plan of survey and the *Métis* wishes, but this solution of the difficulty was buried, thanks to red tape in the Ministry of the Interior and to the unwillingness of English-speaking land agents in the West to take extra trouble to meet the wishes of the French-speaking pioneers of the country.[71] With the language difficulty increasing the misunderstanding resulting from the inability of the largely uneducated *Métis* to grasp the complexities of surveying and land regulations drawn up in Ottawa by lawyers unacquainted with the country, new unrest developed.

Its growth was fostered by Ottawa's interminable delay in answering *Métis* petitions. Supporting memoranda from Governor Laird, Archbishop Taché, and the Anglican Bishop McLean in 1878-9 finally were answered in 1881.[72] Archbishop Taché visited Ottawa in 1882 to intercede for his people without success. In the following year Father Leduc and one B. Maloney conveyed the settlers' resolutions to Ottawa, where they won a hearing, though no action was taken on the matters complained of. Finally, in the spring of 1884, a committee was formed by the 'people of Saskatchewan,' under the presidency of William Cromartie and the secretaryship of Louis Schmidt, to take action.[73] A delegation, headed by Gabriel Dumont and composed of Moise Ouellet, James Isbister, and Michel Dumas, was sent 800 miles across the border to seek out Louis Riel in Montana, and to urge him to return to Canada and lead the popular movement.[74] Riel, who was now dreaming of establishing a new half-breed nation in the West, decided to spend the summer in Canada, urging his own Manitoba land claims against the Dominion government, as well as those of the Saskatchewan settlers.

Upon his arrival in the North-West in July, Riel took the lead in agitation for righting of the settlers' wrongs. According to the account furnished to Governor Dewdney by Father André of Prince Albert,[75] his proceedings at first were quiet and orderly, and he won the support not only of the *Métis*, among whom his prestige was great, but also of most of the whites and Indians. Riel advocated free grants to the *Métis* of the lands they occupied; the elevation of the districts of Saskatchewan, Alberta, and Assiniboia into provinces, or at least provision for their representation in parliament; and the amendment of the land laws to further more rapid settlement of the country. Father André warned the government against interfering with Riel as long as he remained quiet, while other informants urged that he should be arrested and the agitation nipped in the bud. Charles Mair, the poetic Canada Firster, who had been a propagandist for the expansionists in the Red River troubles, came East every six months from 1883 to 1885 to warn the government that new trouble was brewing and that action should be taken on the settlers' grievances;[76] but the agitation was nonetheless allowed to run its course.

As Riel became more influential, he displayed aberrations in religion and politics which led the priests of the North-West to consider him mad and to bar him from the sacraments.[77] Father André finally became convinced that it would be well to get him out of the country; and was present at negotiations late in December 1884 between representatives of the government and Riel, during which the *Métis* leader offered to return to the States in exchange for a payment of $35,000 which would cover his personal land claims, while promising that in return he would use his influence to make the *Métis* drop their claims.[78] Until the outbreak of actual rebellion, the government refused to meet the *Métis* demand for land scrip, and contented itself with increasing the North-West Mounted Police force and trying to bribe the *Métis* leaders. Louis Schmidt was made an assistant land agent; Isbister and Dumas were offered posts as Indian agricultural instructors; and Gabriel Dumont was given a lucrative ferry license.[79] Riel was undoubtedly correct in assuming that the government was willing to bribe him once more, but he seems to have overjudged his market value in the midst of the mounting irresponsibility he displayed in word and deed during the winter.

During January and February Riel held secret meetings whose tendency was no longer towards constitutional action but rather towards armed rebellion. When the opposition of the clergy became more active with this development, he turned against the priests, proclaiming that 'the Spirit of God was in him' and that 'Rome had fallen.'[80] On March 17 a provisional government was established at Saint-Laurent, with Riel as president and Dumont as adjutant-general.[81] On the following day Riel seized the church at Batoche, overriding the protests of Father Moulin, whom he jestingly dismissed as a fellow 'Protestant,' and took some prisoners.[82] On March 21 he issued an ultimatum to Major Crozier, who commanded the Mounted Police at Carlton and Battleford, requiring him to surrender the police posts and to retire from the country, under threat of 'a war of extermination.'[83] This ultimatum, which was never delivered but served as the basis of negotiations between representatives of the insurgents and the authorities, was signed 'Louis "David" Riel, *Exovede*' and issued in the name of 'the Provisional Government of the Saskatchewan,' whose council was called the 'Exovedat,' for Riel insisted that his own and their authority was merely as 'members of the flock.'[84]

Riel's religious mania, the product of his native religiosity, a sense of mission, and a persecution complex, had become dominant: he proclaimed himself a prophet called to protect the oppressed nationalities of the world, attacked Archbishop Taché and Bishop Grandin of Saint-Albert, and denounced the authority of the Pope.[85] According to his cousin Charles Nolin, who later quarrelled with him and turned state's evidence, Riel had brought from Montana a book written in buffalo blood which described his mission as 'to destroy England and Canada . . . and also to destroy Rome and the Pope.'[86] Riel talked incoherently of dividing the lands of the North-West into sevenths among the pioneer whites, the Indians, the French *Métis*, the Church, and Crown lands;[87] on another occasion the Italians, Poles, Hungarians, Bavarians, Irish, and Belgians were each to have a seventh, after Riel had raised support for the *Métis* among these immigrant groups in the States.[88] He saw the West as the new home of immigrants of all nationalities from the Old World.[89] As proof of his divine mission to bring about these ends, Riel produced encouraging letters written to him in 1875 and 1876 by Bishop Bourget, whom he proposed to make 'Pope of the New World.'[90]

Thus Bishop Bourget's ultramontanism and messianic nationalism, the *Métis* concept of themselves as a 'New Nation,' the problems of European nationalism and of large-scale immigration in the States, were curiously intermingled in Riel's increasingly troubled mind. He alternated between respect for the clergy and the view that he had a divine right to direct them; he evolved new dogmas and proposed changes in the liturgy; he took to calling himself 'Elias' or 'David.' In the face of such behavior the clergy decided that he was irresponsible in matters of politics and religion; they judged charitably that 'he was insane, otherwise he would have to be too big a criminal.'[91] Both the priests and his followers found that he was excited by opposition, and became even wilder in word and deed when contradicted or checked. The record provides an almost classic case of paranoia, coupled as these symptoms were with a persecution complex, for the proud and sensitive Riel had never forgiven Sir John Macdonald for his banishment from parliament and his exile.[92]

With their religious and ethnic emotions aroused by Riel's ravings, and excited by the rumor that five hundred Mounted Police were being sent into the region, the *Métis* were now ready to take up arms. A party of thirty *Métis* and five Cree Indians on March 6 prevented a party of Prince Albert loyalists from bringing into Carlton some government supplies from Duck Lake. When the loyalists returned with Major Crozier and the police and opened fire on the insurgents, the unarmed Riel rushed about with a crucifix in his hand, urging his followers to reply 'in the name of God the Father, God the Son, and God the Holy Ghost.'[93] The police, no match for Gabriel Dumont and his veteran buffalo hunters in the snow, despite their superior numbers, were forced to retire, leaving twelve dead behind them. The North-West Rebellion had begun in grim earnest. Riel sought to win the sympathies of the English settlers, protesting that 'this quarrel was with the Government and the police and the Hudson's Bay Company,' and hinting that American aid would be given to the insurgents.[94] He also promised that he would keep the Indians quiet if the settlers remained neutral. With Custer's massacre by the Sioux fresh in men's minds, it was fear of the Indians joining their half-breed brothers that turned the English settlers of the North-West against Riel and led the government to organize a large military expedition to put down the insurrection. Riel proceeded to recruit his following among the *Métis*, to enter into the endless negotiations required to win Indian support, and to fortify in rough and ready fashion the *Métis* settlement at Batoche. But if, as seems probable, he hoped that the rising would follow the same course as that of 1869–70, and that he would achieve the *Métis*' ends without further bloodshed, he was very much mistaken.[95]

The North-West was no longer isolated from eastern Canada, as it had been fifteen years earlier when eight months passed before Ottawa could support its authority with military force. Thanks to the new telegraph system, which ran as far west as Edmonton and Calgary, the government was kept in close touch with the situation as it unfolded. Major-General Frederick Middleton, the English commander of the Canadian militia, left Ottawa by train on March 23, the day the government ordered the formation of an expeditionary force. He reached Winnipeg, the old Fort Garry, on the morning of the 27th and left that same night with the Winnipeg Rifles (90th Battalion) for Qu'Appelle, almost due south of the disaffected area. The Canadian Pacific Railway had been completed from Winnipeg to Calgary, although there was a hundred miles of unfinished line through the Laurentian Shield north of Lake Superior. Riel had probably gambled on the inability of the government to bring in troops from the East without long delay, and also that no action would be taken while the prairie still lay under the snow and mud of late winter and spring. But thanks to the energy and zeal of the Canadian Pacific officials, headed by William Van Horne, who were anxious to oblige the government so that more public funds might be made available for completion of the line, a force of 3,293 men was carried westward during the last weeks of March and the first few days of April. The men rode in coaches and sometimes in open flat cars where the rails were laid, and were transported in sleighs or marched over the unfinished sections of the line. The troops came chiefly from Ontario and Quebec, although one Nova Scotian battalion made the journey from Halifax to Winnipeg in three weeks, and an additional 1,600 men were drawn from Manitoba and the North-West Territories themselves.[96] It was the first purely Canadian military effort, for no force of British regulars was involved, and great enthusiasm was roused in the young nation by lurid telegraphic accounts of Indian outrages and the movements of the defenders of the country. In Ontario the departing militiamen were hailed as crusaders against the rebel French and Indians; while in Quebec, which supplied a third of the eastern troops, a wave of patriotism swept aside all feeling of kinship with the *Métis* or sympathy for their plight.[97]

The widespread Indian rising whose threat had caused the government to raise so imposing a force failed to materialize, although Big Bear's band of Crees massacred two Catholic missionaries and five officials and traders at Frog Lake on the North Saskatchewan on April 2 and forced the surrender of Fort Pitt on April 15, while Poundmaker's Crees and Stoneys committed isolated outrages at the end of March and besieged Battleford during April. General Middleton's small army, which vastly outnumbered the 600–700 insurgents, was divided into three columns and struck before the *Métis* and Indians had time to complete their organization. During April General Thomas Bland Strange, a retired English officer who had taken to cattle-ranching near Calgary after training the Canadian artillery, moved north from that point to Edmonton, and then down the North Saskatchewan to the smoking ruins of Fort Pitt, where a juncture was made with the eastern columns. The second column, under Colonel William D. Otter, marched north from Swift Current to the relief of Battleford, where it was joined by Middleton's force coming up the Saskatchewan. Middleton was accompanied by press correspondents and his well-publicized exploits have unjustifiably overshadowed Strange's remarkable ten-day march through 200 miles of wilderness.

Middleton set out from Qu'Appelle on April 6 against Batoche, the *Métis* stronghold. On April 24 he was halted at Fish Creek on the South Saskatchewan, and lost 10 killed and 40 wounded out of his 350 men to a handful of *Métis* under Gabriel Dumont, who neatly trapped the general in an ambush which made skillful use of folds in the ground.[98] On May 6 Middleton left his camp at Fish Creek after waiting for reinforcements, and with 700 men proceeded against Batoche, which he took on May 12 after four days' fighting in which he lost 8 killed and 46 wounded. The *Métis* losses were estimated at 51 killed and 173 wounded.[99] Riel, who had threatened to massacre his prisoners if Middleton shelled the women and children in the town, gave himself up on May 15 to two scouts, producing a note in which Middleton called upon him to surrender and promised protection until his case was considered by the government.[100]

With Riel's surrender—not capture, as the triumphant Middleton telegraphed to Ottawa—the *Métis* resistance subsided. Old buffalo guns were no match for Gatlings and artillery, no matter how skillfully used. The remainder of the campaign, which lasted until July, consisted of the vain pursuit of Big Bear, for Poundmaker surrendered ten days after Riel was reported 'captured.' The Indians and their *Métis* allies vanished like the will-o'-the-wisp before the cumbersome military columns, which vainly attempted to adapt parade-ground training to campaigning in the bush. General Strange was filled with admiration for the Quebec soldiers—'the plucky little French Canadians pulled 9-pr. guns, horses and all, right through the muskegs. They are fine little fellows, marching many of them barefoot, singing their old chansons. There was no flinch about them in fighting either, they bore the brunt of it such as it was.'[101] But General Middleton infuriated Strange by maintaining that the French-Canadian troops had marched no farther than the other troops—Strange protested 'they have marched four times as far as any other regiment except Winnipeg Light Infantry of my force also'—and by praising only the English Canadians who had fought at Batoche.[102]

The North-West Rebellion cost Canada 38 men killed and 115 wounded among soldiers and Mounted Police, while the military expenses amounted to nearly $4,500,000—two-thirds of which was incurred after the end of hostilities.[103] The Hudson's Bay Company, which had furnished supplies, land transport, and river steamers for the army, filed a claim for $1,737,032, while the Canadian Pacific billed the government for $852,231.32.[104] But without the Hudson's Bay Company's knowledge of the country and the railroad's transportation skill, the expedition might have come to grief. The cost in national unity proved in the event to be incalculable.

5

Ethnic antagonism had largely been latent while French and English troops campaigned together in the North-West, although the *Toronto News* had urged on May 18 that Riel be strangled with the French flag—'the only service which that rag can render in this country.'[105] But it broke out in the East when Riel was brought to trial for high treason at Regina on July 20, while the returning troops were receiving tumultuous receptions at Toronto, Montreal, and Quebec.

Under the provisions of the North-West Territorial Act of 1880, Riel was tried by an English magistrate with an associated French justice of the peace before a six-man jury of English settlers and merchants.[106] The Crown counsel had received instructions from the Deputy-Minister of Justice at Ottawa.[107] Only two or three French Canadians were included in the panel of thirty-six jurors selected by the magistrate.[108] The Crown challenged one Irishman and the defence five Englishmen.[109] Christopher Robinson and B. B. Osler of Toronto, and Tom Chase Casgrain of Quebec were the leading counsel for the Crown, while F.-X. Lemieux, Charles Fitzpatrick, and J. N. Greenshields were counsel for the prisoner. The political aspect of the trial was increased by the fact that the prosecution was made up of Conservatives and the defence of Liberals. Fitzpatrick first took issue on constitutional grounds with the jurisdiction of the court, seeking to have Riel tried in Ontario or British Columbia, rather than in the aroused Territories. When this plea was rejected, Lemieux and Fitzpatrick obtained an adjournment of a week in order that witnesses for the accused might be obtained. During this adjournment Riel's English secretary, William Henry Jackson, was tried, found insane in half an hour, and committed to an asylum, from which he escaped to the States, seemingly with the connivance of the authorities.[110] Jackson claimed that he shared Riel's responsibility and thus was exposed to the charge of treason.

Among the witnesses called by the defence were Gabriel Dumont, Michel Dumas, and Napoléon Nault—two of the *Métis* leaders who had urged Riel to return and his Montana cousin—Dr. François Roy of the Beauport Asylum, where Riel had been confined in 1876–8 and which had become a political issue in recent months; Dr. Daniel Clark, superintendent of the Toronto Asylum; and Dr. Arthur Vallée, a leading Quebec physician. Riel's request for the presence of the deputy-minister of the Interior, with official documents and the petitions filed by the *Métis*, was denied, as was his request for his papers, which had been seized at Batoche by General Middleton and which were used with telling effect by the Crown. Among them was his American naturalization certificate. Anticipating a plea by the defence that Riel as an American citizen could not be charged with treason, the Crown had framed its charge of treason on six counts, on three of which he was charged as a British subject, and on three as a resident of Canada, with armed revolt at Duck Lake, Fish Creek, and Batoche.[111]

Driven from its preliminary arguments of unconstitutionality and Riel's American citizenship, the defence devoted most of its attention to proving that Riel was insane. Unfortunately for this contention, Dr. Roy, the only medical witness with any real acquaintance with Riel's mental condition, who pronounced him irresponsible and of unsound mind,[112] became entangled in linguistic difficulties under Osler's ruthless cross-examination, while Dr. Clark of Toronto and Dr. Wallace of Hamilton refused to pronounce Riel incapable of distinguishing between right and wrong, though they thought him of unsound mind.[113] Dr. Jukes, the Mounted Police surgeon, flatly pronounced him sane.[114] Riel himself, who in the early stages of the trial tried to cross-examine the government witnesses and was told that he must either repudiate his counsel or keep silent, in his two remarkable addresses to the court at the end of the trial denied the plea of insanity upon which his defence had rested.

He spoke with remarkable if confused eloquence, calling himself the 'founder of Manitoba' and 'prophet of the New World'[115] and clearly revealing his religious mania as he recapitulated his career and his dream of the West as a haven for the oppressed nationalities of Europe, in which the ancient opposition between Catholics and Protestants would be overcome. He mentioned many things which the government would have wished unsaid, including the details of his dealings with Macdonald and Cartier after the first rising, the provocative role of the Mounted Police in 1885, the failure to give first Manitoba and then the North-West Territories real representation at Ottawa, and the administration's broken promises to the *Métis*.[116] Although he turned against the clergy—even against his lifelong protector Archbishop Taché—and made heretical statements,[117] his deep religiosity was very manifest in a moving plea which is quite as effective despite its imperfect English as Bartolommeo Vanzetti's. He concluded with a request to be tried before a full jury and to be examined by a medical commission, for the Crown's implication that he was shamming insanity pricked his intellectual pride. After a seven days' trial, the jury brought in a verdict of guilty, with a recommendation of mercy.[118] On August 1 Justice Richardson sentenced Riel to be hanged on September 18 at Regina.

Riel's counsel appealed to the Queen's Bench Court in Manitoba, which unanimously confirmed the verdict early in September,[119] and then to the Privy Council, which refused to hear the case on October 22.[120] Meanwhile an agitation arose in Ontario for immediate execution of a double traitor[121] and Quebec was swept by a great popular movement which demanded that Riel be reprieved as the irresponsible victim of the government's maladministration of the North-West. The Quebec press cited Jackson's easy fate and compared it with that allotted to Riel, with the observation: 'If madness is an excuse for an Englishman, it ought to be one for Riel, even if he is a *Métis*.'[122] Riel defence committees had been organized as early as June in Montreal and Quebec. Their sponsor was L.-O. David, who considered Riel a spiritual heir of the *Patriotes* of 1837. Thanks to his efforts, protest meetings began to be held throughout the province, with the watchword 'Riel must be saved.'[123]

During July, before the trial began, the Liberal leaders Blake and Laurier had attacked the government. Blake tabled seventy-six *Métis* petitions of grievances, while Laurier accused the government of treating the *Métis* as the Russians did the Poles.[124] Although Archbishop Taché and most of the Western clergy warned against mistaken sympathy with Riel, Quebec was won to his cause by Father André's account of the distress of the *Métis* after they had been ruthlessly pillaged by Middleton's English-Canadian troops.[125] Gradually the question became not one of Riel's guilt or innocence, but the execution or pardon of a compatriot. This development of ethnic feeling determined Chapleau's decision not to resign from the federal cabinet and to form a French-Canadian party. He and his French colleagues were denounced by Quebec, while petitions rained upon Ottawa from all quarters of French Canada, from Manitoba, the North-West, the United States, and even from England and France.[126] The great majority of them urged mercy, although the Ontario Orangemen and the English settlers of Regina recommended that the sentence be executed. While the government allowed three successive stays of execution until every avenue of appeal had been exhausted, and appointed a medical commission composed of Dr. Jukes, Dr. F.-X. Valade of Ottawa, and Dr. Lavell of Hamilton, who decided early in November that Riel was not legally insane,[127] the decision had already been made, in the words attributed to Sir John Macdonald, that 'Riel must swing.'[128]

In the last analysis the decision not to show the same mercy to Riel as to the other convicted rebellion prisoners was based upon political necessities. English-Canadian feeling had risen to the explosive point as French pressure for Riel's pardon grew stronger. Even General Strange, an old friend of the French Canadians, was moved to write Henri Joly:

> How sad and silly it all seems—after sending those brave battalions to the front—to start in with this childish twaddle about hanging a cur of a self-interested conspirator who has twice brought this country to rebellion and at last let loose savage Indians to murder White Men and even Priests. The idea that because a criminal is half-French it is to stop the sword of justice is outrageous. I would rather join in a war of extermination between French & English than to submit to live in a Country where such monstrously insolent pretensions were put forward by a part of the population.[129]

Macdonald decided that he could better afford to lose a few seats in Quebec than to have English Canada turn solidly against him. So after the governor-general in council had refused to alter the sentence on November 12, Riel was duly hanged at Regina on November 16.

While in prison and visited daily by priests, he had repeatedly renounced his religious heresies only to relapse into them once more. On August 5 he made a formal abjuration of his errors to his confessor, Father Vital Fourmond, in a moving and revealing document:

To Rev. Father Vital Jesus, Mary, Regina Prison, August 5, Fourmond, my director Joseph, 1885. Feast of Our Lady of conscience save me of the Snows

Archbishop Bourget told me: ' God, Who has always directed and assisted you, until the present time will not abandon you in the greatest of your trials for He has given you a mission which you must accomplish in all respects.' My director of conscience tells me that my misfortunes and errors arise from my misunderstanding of my mission. The religious principle which made me have so much confidence in the word of Archbishop Bourget logically leads me to have the same confidence in the interpretation which the approved priest, my director of conscience, gives me of the episcopal word of Archbishop Ignace Bourget of blessed memory.

Renouncing then, all the special interpretations that I have made of my mission which my confessor and director does not approve, I re-enter the bosom of the Catholic, Apostolic, and Roman Church by making the following declaration:

Father, my confessor, my director of conscience, please remit all my sins, all my faults, and all the consequences of my deeds; all my offences and all the consequences of my offences, whether with regard to God and the Faith, whether with regard to society, or my neighbor, or myself.

Witnesses: V. Fourmond, priest   Your poor penitent,
L. Cochin, O.M.I.   Louis Riel, or Louis 'David' Riel[130]

On August 31 Father André, the Oblate superior, in describing Riel's fantastic visions in prison, remarked:

Although his opinions upon religion are greatly erroneous, I do not hold him responsible and do admit him to receive the sacraments. And for all that, he often renews the errors which he has retracted and which he again retracts when I point out to him his heresies as contrary to the dogmas taught by the Holy Catholic Church. On the day following such a retraction, he talks to me more ardently than ever about his revelations and his communications with some angel who honors him with a nocturnal visit.[131]

And in the end, at the instigation of Archbishop Taché, who was convinced that this black sheep of the *Métis* flock was irresponsible, though a criminal, Riel was buried in the shadow of the cathedral of St-Boniface on December 12, under the guard of *Métis* who carried his coffin six miles from his family home to the church. It was not an unsuitable resting-place for the brilliant and unstable prophet of the West which had begun there and which was there to fulfil some of his fevered dreams.

6

Riel was not allowed to rest in peace. The agitation in Quebec against the execution of a French Canadian summarily condemned by an English judge and jury became a political revolution. The minority group of the assembly, which had in March 1885 censured the federal government for settling by force a disturbance which had been occasioned by its own culpable neglect, became an overpowering majority as Quebec public opinion rose against Sir John Macdonald and the French-Canadian ministers, Sir Hector Langevin, Sir Adolphe Caron, and Adolphe Chapleau, who had refused to break with their leader, though privately they opposed his course in the matter. The ministers were burnt in effigy as Quebec mourned Riel.

On November 22 the greatest mass meeting ever held in the province took place on the Champs de Mars at Montreal, where Conservatives and Liberals alike voiced violent protests and adopted resolutions severely condemning the government. *La Presse* had

Louis Riel

Drawing from Major Powell's scrapbook. As this contemporary portrait indicates, Riel had little Indian blood and was no wild *Métis* buffalo hunter. (Public Archives of Canada.)

Ojibway *Métis*

Photograph by Hine of a typical *Métis* buffalo hunter, posed with his carefully cased gun before a wigwam made of buffalo rugs. (Public Archives of Canada.)

Parliament Building, Quebec

Built 1878-84, after plans by Eugène Taché, a better cartographer than architect. The tradition of exotic imitation, launched by Notre Dame in Montreal, was now dominant and the French-Canadian architectural tradition was forgotten. (I.O.A.P.Q.)

sounded the warcry on the day after Riel's execution: 'Hence-forward there are no more Conservatives nor Liberals nor Castors. There are only PATRIOTS AND TRAITORS.'[132] For once the Quebec press ceased its habitual political axe-grinding and united in a unanimity to which was flatly opposed the equally rare unanimity of the English press, summed up by a Toronto dispatch of November 17 thus: 'A general sentiment of satisfaction prevails.'[133] Three platforms had been raised on the Champs de Mars, around which gathered a crowd of forty or fifty thousand, and from them orator after orator held forth. The three great speeches of this day in which a people voiced its indignation were made by the Liberal Laurier, who with a rare vehemence proclaimed: 'If I had been on the banks of the Saskatchewan, I, too, would have shouldered my musket'; by the ultramontane Trudel, who compared Riel to Christ and Joan of Arc; and by Honoré Mercier who won the leadership of French Canada at this moment of crisis with his opening words:

Riel, our brother, is dead, victim of his devotion to the cause of the *Métis* of whom he was the leader, victim of fanaticism and treason—of the fanaticism of Sir John and some of his friends, of the treason of three of our people who sold their brother to keep their portfolios.

In killing Riel, Sir John has not only struck a blow at the heart of our race, but above all he struck the cause of justice and humanity, which represented in all languages and sanctified by all religious beliefs, begged mercy for the prisoner of Regina, our poor brother of the North-West.[134]

Mercier called for the formation of a national party, uniting all those who were outraged by Riel's death, to drive Macdonald's government from office and to preserve the French-Canadian soli-darity created by this crisis. The crowd enthusiastically adopted the 'Resolutions of the Champs de Mars'[135] which had been previously drafted to embody Mercier's ideas.

The agitation in Quebec, which Macdonald had dismissed as 'a blaze of straw,'[136] spread like a forest fire, with assemblies in each parish adopting resolutions based upon those of the great meeting at Montreal, and with anti-ministerial demonstrations taking place throughout the province. Trudel and others wanted a national movement in which the old party lines would be preserved, except for the Riel matter and national questions; but Mercier succeeded in imposing his doctrine of a racial party founded on the newly made grave of Riel. Quebec rallied like one man to the defence of the outlying minority groups. Riel was enshrined as a national hero and a saint despite his treason and his heresies, and despite the resolute opposition of the Quebec hierarchy, whose attitude had been promp-ted by Archbishop Taché and who became increasingly alarmed by a movement which began to take on revolutionary tendencies, with public disorders, the burning in effigy of the federal ministers, and the singing of the *Marseillaise*.[137]

As a former missionary in the Red River Country, Bishop Laflèche was sympathetic to the *Métis*. In 1875 he had proposed a protest in Quebec against the federal government's treatment of them, but now he refused to support Mercier's movement. In May 1885 he wrote one of his *curés*:

> The news from the North-West is very sad.
> This spark, which would have been so easy to extinguish with a few drops of justice, is going, perhaps, to cause a disastrous conflagration.
> For years the *Métis* and savages have been treated in an unworthy manner by brutal agents, and scandalized by a police more immoral than the savages.
> The Ontario Orangemen are capable of setting fire to the four corners of the country to satisfy their hatred against Riel and to hang him.
> . . . for the *Métis*, the question is clear: they must conquer or die.[138]

But his friend Archbishop Taché assured him during this same month that Riel was a 'miserable madman and a fanatic.'[139] And however strong his sympathy for the *Métis* Laflèche remained convinced that no good could come from Liberal sources and refused to make common cause with his lifelong enemies on the Riel question. He remained silent while the fury at Riel's execution mounted in Quebec, and by 1886 Trudel and Tardivel found themselves on the opposite side of the political fence from the bishop who had been so long the guiding spirit of the *Castors*.

While Trudel and Tardivel expressed pious horror that the bishops should support the 'Orange Freemason' Macdonald, Laflèche assured one of his *curés* that the *Parti National* had 'worked great evil' in his diocese, and that the troubles in the North-West were not 'purely a political question.'[140] He reported that he had consulted an Ontario bishop on the respective merits of Macdonald and Blake and of the two parties which they headed, and his conclusion was that 'for us there is no great distinction to be made between one and the other.' At long last Bishop Laflèche had learned the advantages of a united front among the hierarchy, and he stood squarely beside Archbishop Taché and Bishop Grandin on the Riel question, as he wrote the federal member for Trois-Rivières in January 1887:

> I share entirely the views of Archbishop Taché, which are also those of Bishop Grandin. All the world will agree that these venerable prelates are the most competent judges of the matter. Besides, it seems evident to me that a movement too violently and imprudently aroused by political passions becomes more and more dangerous . . . In this sort of question the bishops can be regarded as the most competent judges

The history of our country shows us that the Canadian people has never had cause for regret in having followed in difficult circumstances the advice of the bishops, but on the contrary the country has gravely suffered when their wise guidance has been rejected.[141]

Party as well as caste loyalty no doubt played some part in Laflèche's attitude toward the Riel agitation, for in traditionally Conservative Trois-Rivières, a marriage between a Conservative and a Liberal was referred to as a 'mixed marriage.'

Under the goad of Mercier's burning eloquence, heard in all regions of the province as he tirelessly sought to break down old party lines and to unite the people under his leadership, the movement was only checked, not halted, by the opposition of the hierarchy, the English Liberals, Chapleau and his friends, and Laurier, who was alarmed at the growing isolation of Quebec from the rest of Canada. At the Champs de Mars meeting the latter had been swept by the wave of public indignation from his lifelong conviction that the formation of a Catholic or French-Canadian party would be suicidal for his people, since it would unite the English Protestants against them and pave the way for a war of religion or race. Once that party began to take form, Laurier withdrew his support from Mercier.

The beginnings of this English reaction which Laurier anticipated had already been produced by the Quebec agitation. On November 23 the *Toronto Mail* published an editorial in which it warned the French Canadians, 'now seeking to compel us to recognize their right to suspend the operation of the law when a representative of their race is in the toils,' that 'rather than to submit to such a yoke, Ontario would smash Confederation into its original fragments, preferring that the dream of a united Canada should be shattered forever, than that unity should be purchased at the price of inequality.'[142] Two days later the *Mail* told Mercier and his friends that 'if the cabinet should fall as a result of the intrigues of French influence, if such is the fruit of Mr. Mercier's programme, in that case, as Britons, we believe that the Conquest will have to be fought over again. Lower Canada may depend upon it, there will be no new treaty of 1763. The victors will not capitulate next time.'[143] To these utterances of the *Mail*, which was considered the chief mouthpiece of the government, but at this moment was running quite as free of political harness as the ministerial organs in Quebec were on the other side of the question, were added the observations of the *Orange Sentinel*: 'Must it be said that the rights and liberties of the English people in this English colony depend upon a foreign race? . . . The day is near when an appeal to arms will be heard in all parts of Canada. Then, certainly, our soldiers, benefiting by the lessons of the past, will have to complete the work they began in the North-West.'[144] Such statements only furthered Mercier's game by in-creasing the ethnic tension, which was also added to by an English attempt to enforce vaccination to check a severe smallpox epidemic in Montreal, and by the failure of two Channel Island firms, Charles Robin & Co. and LeBoutillier & Brothers, which had monopolized the fisheries and supplying of Gaspé, and whose collapse brought on disorders among the unemployed and starving fishermen, long restive under exploitation by these foreign French-speaking Protestants.

When parliament met at the end of February 1886, the first clash on the Riel question occurred in the Senate, where censure by govern-ment supporters of the raising in the press of racial and religious prejudices was opposed by followers of Mercier. In the House early in March the Conservative Philippe Landry offered a motion ex-pressing profound regret at Riel's execution, which had the effect of embarrassing the Liberals, who were divided on this question, although agreed on the government's responsibility for the execution. Archbishop Taché appeared in the visitors' gallery during the debate which followed, and counseled the French-Canadian Conservatives who consulted him not to vote against the government. This well-meant effort to quell the storm was taken in Orange quarters as new proof that Rome was running Canada.

Relief for the ever-growing tension was provided by Laurier's speech in the House on March 16. He denied the *Mail's* charges and forswore Mercier's suicidal policy of forming a French-Canadian party, but he indicted the government for its long neglect of the *Métis*' grievances: 'What is hateful . . . is not rebellion but the despotism which induces that rebellion; what is hateful are not the rebels but the men, who having the enjoyment of power, do not discharge the duties of power.'[145] He did not consider Riel a hero: 'At his worst he was a subject fit for an asylum; at his best he was a religious and political monomaniac.' But he attacked the fairness of the trial and the difference in the treatment of Jackson and Riel. Singling out the root of the Ontario agitation, he observed: 'The death of Scott is the cause of the death of Riel today';[146] and he argued that mercy rather than revenge should have been the guiding principle of the government, as in the United States after the Civil War. He concluded with an eloquent call for mercy to the remaining rebellion prisoners in the name of liberty and justice, which had been won at last for the *Métis* by those who had already suffered martyrdom: 'I say that their country has conquered with their martyrdom, and if we look at that one fact alone, there was cause sufficient, independent of all others, to extend mercy to the one who is dead and to those who live.'[147]

Political friends and foes alike hailed this first great English speech of Laurier. The *Montreal Star*, a Conservative organ, dubbed him the 'silver-tongued Laurier,' while his Liberal colleague Blake ironically referred to his speech as 'the crowning proof of French domination,'[148] since by it Laurier had added the palm for parliamentary eloquence in English to his reputation as the ablest French orator in the House. Blake himself made one of his greatest efforts in this debate, speaking for five hours as he indicted the government for negligence and as he piled up proof of Riel's insanity and precedents against holding madmen responsible for their acts.[149] But in spite of these notable speeches by the leading Liberals and the general weakness of Conservative replies, the government was sustained by a large majority, as Macdonald had foreseen, with losses among the Quebec Conservatives offset by support from Liberals from the English-speaking provinces. The vote gave evidence that the Riel question had become an ethnic rather than a party or a sectional one. It was to ease the ethnic tension that Laurier discussed the question at Toronto the following December, in the same terms that he had used at Ottawa. Quebec, however, turned against its Conservative government, since it placed party loyalty before ethnic considerations. The provincial administration crumbled before Mercier's assault in the October elections, and in January 1887 his *Parti National* took power.

7

A whole generation in Quebec was filled with emotional hatred for all things English by the Riel affair, while the gallophobia and 'no-popery' agitation aroused by it in Ontario were fed by the course of Mercier's administration and sustained by conflicts over the rights of the French language and of separate schools in the West. Mercier, who had won power by invoking the gibbet of Regina at ninety political meetings and had built his government on Riel's grave, did much to further the division between French and English in 1885 and to make it permanent. Faced with the political necessity of maintaining the coalition which the Riel crisis had forged between French-Canadian Liberals and Conservatives, Mercier disregarded the solemn warning which Laurier had given him in the Ottawa debate on Riel's execution:

It would be simply suicidal for the French Canadians to form a party by themselves. Why, so soon as the French Canadians, who are in the minority in this House and in the country, were to organize as a political party, they would compel the majority to organize as a political party, and the result must be disastrous to themselves. We have only one way of organizing parties. This country must be governed and can be governed only on questions of policy and administration.[150]

But Mercier had discovered how easy it was to organize a party in Quebec on the basis of nationality, and he attempted to govern by using the emotions conjured up by the words 'national,' 'French,' and 'Catholic,' rather than by the reasoned arguments demanded by questions of policy and administration. At the outset of his regime he seemed to take heed of Laurier's warning; speaking at Saint-Hyacinthe at the end of his government's first session, he reaffirmed its character:

National in its conception, national in its birth, this government was to be national in the basis of its organization, in the affirmation of its ideas and aspirations. The government is truly national; I hasten to add that it must remain national; it is our duty and intention to preserve this character which is its strength and which associates many honest citizens, weary of the ruinous conflicts of the past and anxious not to see them recommence.[151]

But he added: 'The *Parti National* will respect and cause to be respected the rights of the Protestant minority in this province. We wish to live in peace with all races, all creeds. We shall give justice to all, even to those who refuse the like to us.'[152]

Despite such fair words, it was not difficult for Mercier's enemies to use his nationalism to turn the English Canadians against him; and Mercier himself, lacking Laurier's understanding of the English mentality or caring less for its reactions, soon lost caution as power made him domineering. The incorporation in 1887 of the Jesuits, who had educated Mercier at their Collège Sainte-Marie in Montreal, did not cause much comment in the English-speaking world, although some English Quebeckers were disgruntled by the spectacle of the legislature receiving delegates of the Jesuits and of Cardinal Taschereau, who opposed the measure in the interests of Laval, and that of politicians discussing the fine points of theology and canon law. But when Mercier went to New York in search of a loan and there received the honors appropriate to the head of a state; when Mercier summoned an inter-provincial conference—the first held since Confederation—in October 1887 at Quebec and induced the delegates of five provinces (Prince Edward Island and British Columbia abstained from attendance) to reaffirm vigorously the principle of provincial autonomy; and finally when Mercier, unsuccessful in New York, went to Paris to obtain a loan from the Crédit Lyonnais and to Rome to consult the Holy See on the Jesuit Estates question, the English Canadians began to take alarm at this provincial premier whose watchword was 'national' and who acted like the ruler of an independent state. Dark rumors of Mercier's plan to set up a French-Canadian state began to go the rounds.

Mercier's actions did nothing to dispel these suspicions. In New York, on the eve of sailing for France, he had closeted himself in the rectory of the French-Canadian church with Bishop Grandin of Saint-Albert and Gabriel Dumont, the *Métis* 'general' in 1885. In Paris Mercier was given a royal reception and the Legion of Honor, and in his speeches stressed Quebec's ties with France; in Rome he was received in private audience by the Pope. His success abroad in winning popularity and in achieving his commercial and diplomatic ends greatly strengthened his position in Quebec, which felt itself honored through the honor paid to its premier; but Mercier's doings were entirely too French and Catholic for English-Canadian taste.

The vague fears thus aroused were strengthened by Mercier's vigorous opposition to the imperial federalism favored by the new governor-general, Lord Stanley, and the Imperial Federation League, whose English-Canadian nucleus had been active in the suppression of the rebellion and in the persecution of the *Métis*. Mercier attacked imperialism at the Windsor Hotel in Montreal in 1888:

It is proposed to impose upon us a political regime which through conscription could scatter our sons from the icefields of the North Pole to the burning sands of the Sahara; an odious regime which would condemn us to pay an arbitrary tax of blood and money, and tear our sons from us, in order to cast them into remote and bloody wars which we could neither prevent nor stop.[153]

Having thus stamped himself as 'disloyal' in the minds of the colonial-minded English Canadians of the day, Mercier went on to arouse new opposition by appointing the Curé Labelle deputy-minister of the new Department of Agriculture and Colonization, which he himself headed. It was the first time in America that a priest had held important public office, and the innovation found no favor in the eyes of those who believed in the complete separation of Church and State, as the great majority of English Canadians did. But it was sound Quebec politics, for the Curé Labelle was a popular figure whose devotion to opening up new regions and whose dynamic leadership had made him a hero of his people. The appointment did much to confirm the favor with which Mercier was viewed by the lower clergy after his stand on the Riel question. Only the Bishops of Trois-Rivières, Montreal, and Ottawa remained resolute in their conviction that salvation was only to be found in the Conservative Party.

In June 1888 Mercier announced to the Quebec Legislature that he had come to an agreement with Père Turgeon, representative of

the Holy See and the Society of Jesus, for the settlement of the ancient
Jesuit Estates question. Since 1831, when the imperial government
finally turned over the estates to the Canadian government, their
revenues had been used for the original purpose, the support of education. With Confederation the estates came into the hands of the
Quebec government, which used the revenue for the support of both
Catholic and Protestant institutions. When the Jesuits returned to
Canada in 1842 at the invitation of Bishop Bourget, they urged their
claim to their ancient property; and as they rose rapidly in influence,
they became more insistent about the matter. In 1884 the ultramontane Ross administration had attempted to settle the question,
but negotiations had come to nothing in the face of the opposition of
Archbishop Taschereau and Laval University, who maintained that
the proceeds of the estates should be divided among the Catholic
schools rather than assigned to the Jesuits, who were active in the
agitation to establish a rival university in Montreal. Mercier solved
this complicated question by offering $400,000—much less than the
value of the estates, which had been placed as high as $2,000,000—
in return for the renunciation of further claims. The division of this
sum was to be left to the Pope. $60,000 was to be granted to the
Protestant schools which had previously received a share of the
revenue from the estates. Although two English Protestants raised
some objections, they subsequently withdrew them; and the bill was
passed unanimously by both houses in the Quebec Legislature. But
Mercier's invocation of Papal action—in order to assure a lasting
settlement in the face of divided clerical opinion in Quebec—raised
the specter of 'papist aggression' in Ontario, which by its demand
for federal disallowance of the measure aroused once more the ethnic
and religious division engendered by the execution of Riel. The
cries of 'no popery' and 'French domination' were sounded by the
Equal Rights Association, headed by leading Orangemen. [154]

The storm thus raised, reflected as it was by protests in the
Toronto Globe, *Mail*, and *World* against 'Roman Catholic aggression,'
could not be ignored by Sir John Macdonald, although he decided,
after casting a political balance-sheet, to refuse to yield to the
Ontario Orangemen, rather than to cement Mercier's hold on
Quebec. A debate on the Jesuit Estates Act was held in the House
at Ottawa in March 1889, when Colonel William E. O'Brien moved
a resolution for disallowance on the grounds that act was *ultra vires*,
violated the separation of Church and State, represented 'the
usurpation of a right by a foreign authority,' and through its
'endowment of the Society of Jesus, an alien, secret, and politico-
religious body, the expulsion of which from every Christian community wherein it has a foothold has been rendered necessary by its
intolerant and mischievous intermeddling with the functions of civil

government, is fraught with danger to the civil and religious liberties of the people of Canada.'[155]

The artificial character of the attack on the Jesuit Estates Act was indicated by the fact that it originated in Ontario, which was not affected by the measure, despite acceptance of the act by Quebec Protestants. An editorial in the *Toronto Mail* gives the case for the Ontario crusade:

If the British and Protestant element in Quebec will not save itself, we must try to save it for our own sakes. That the abandonment of Quebec to the Ultramontane and the Jesuit will be the death of Canadian nationality is clear enough. But Ontario will not be safe. Our eastern gate has already been opened by the perfidious hand of the vote-hunting politician, and French and Roman Catholic invasion is already streaming through. The French priest, it is true, cannot formally import into Ontario his Church establishment and his system of tithes. But this matters little, if he can thrust out the British population and plant in its room a population which will be under his sway, and from which he can wring practically any payments which he thinks fit. The assessor, moreover, will be his creature, and he will be able to distribute the burden of local taxation between the faithful and the heretic pretty much at his pleasure. He will, to all intents and purposes, detach eastern Ontario from the British and Protestant civilization of which it now forms a part, and annex it to the territory of the French race, which is also the dominion of the priest. No distortion of facts by sophistical rhetoric, no hypocritical protests against race feeling will hide from us either the gravity or the imminence of this result.[156]

The most notable speeches in support of the O'Brien motion were those of Clarke Wallace, Grand Master of the Orange Order, and D'Alton McCarthy, the head of the Imperial Federation League. The three men, who had founded the Equal Rights Association, covered the same ground according to their varying ability, all protesting that they had no wish to arouse religious antagonism, all making an historical indictment of the Jesuits and of their claim to the Estates, and all viewing the Mercier measure as a threat to the Queen's supremacy and the rights of freeborn Englishmen. But in the face of the statement by C. C. Colby, the oldest English Quebec member, that 'There never was a minority in any country treated with more generosity than the Protestant minority of the Province of Quebec'[157]; of the coldly legal argument by Sir John Thompson, the Catholic Minister of Justice, against disallowance; of Laurier's and Sir William Mulock's deprecation of such invitations to racial division; and of Sir John Macdonald's bland dismissal of the resolution with an anecdote, the Orange onslaught collapsed. The O'Brien resolution found only a handful of supporters—the 'noble thirteen.'

But the agitation raised outside the House by the Equal Rights Association continued unchecked, and brought about a worse state of feeling between French and English than had existed since the height of the Riel affair.

In September 1889 Laurier went to Toronto to speak on the Jesuit Estates question, once more using the same language in Toronto as in Quebec and again pleading for an inclusive rather than a hyphenated Canadianism. This courageous invasion of the citadel of 'no popery' was not without effect, contrasting as it did with the Conservative strategy of being militantly Catholic in Quebec and militantly Protestant in Ontario. Laurier's behavior on these occasions did much to make him a national figure, and played no small part in his elevation to the leadership of the Liberal Party in 1887 and his victory in the elections of 1896.

Mercier, however, took a different course. With the same impetuous energy which he had devoted to settling long-standing provincial questions, he replied on Saint-Jean-Baptiste Day 1889 to attacks from without the province by proudly reaffirming Quebec's French and Catholic tradition:

As the authorized representative of Quebec . . . with the consciousness of the responsibility attached to my words, I declare in the name of all of us that we have remained and shall remain Catholic and French. Love of the religion and of the nationality of our fathers is stamped upon our hearts, and no one, not even the most potent of tyrants, can take this love from us.

This province of Quebec is Catholic and French, and it will remain Catholic and French.

While protesting our respect and even our friendship for the representatives of other races and other religions, while declaring ourselves ready to give them their legitimate part in everything and everywhere, while offering to share with them as brothers the immense territory and the great resources that Providence has put at our disposition; while desiring to live in the most perfect harmony with them in the shadow of England's flag and under the protection of a sovereign dear to all, we solemnly declare that we shall never renounce the rights which are guaranteed to us by the treaties, the law, and the constitution.

These treaties, this law, this constitution give us the right to remain Catholic and French . . . We are now two million and a half French Canadians in America, proud of our past, strong in our present, and confident in our future; we care little for the threats of our enemies . . .

When we vanish, we shall say to the generation called to succeed us: 'We are Catholic and French, and when you, our successors, vanish in your turn, you must say to the generation which will replace you: "We die Catholic and French!"' This will be our testament and theirs; the supreme last will of an heroic people, transmitted from father to son, from generation to generation, until the end of time.[158]

Mercier, better than any orator French Canada has produced, could evoke the deepest currents of national feeling. That feeling was also honestly his, but he played upon it for political purposes. Attacked on the right by Conservatives and on the left by advanced Liberals, he followed this declaration of fidelity to the French-Canadian tradition with an eloquent appeal for French-Canadian solidarity:

We are not as strong as we should be, because we are divided. And we are divided because we do not grasp the dangers of the situation. Our enemies are united in their hatred of the French homeland; and we are divided in our love of this dear homeland.

Why? We do not know. We are divided because the generation which preceded us was divided. We are divided because we have inherited the titles of *Rouges* and *Bleus*; because human pride bids us call ourselves Liberals or Conservatives; because it is good to have a name and a title on the pretext of having principles; because it is fashionable to defend principles, above all when they are attacked.

Let us break with these dangerous traditions; let us sacrifice our hatreds on the altar of the homeland, and on this day of patriotic rejoicing, in the name and for the prosperity of this province of Quebec that we love so well, let us clasp hands like brothers, and let us swear to cease our fratricidal strife and unite.

Let your rallying-cry in the future be these words, which will be our strength: ' Let us cease our fratricidal strife and unite!'[159]

Laurier, upon this same occasion—the dedication of the monument to Jacques Cartier and Brébeuf at Quebec—sounded a different note:

We are French Canadians, but our country is not confined to the territory overshadowed by the citadel of Quebec; our country is Canada, it is the whole of what is covered by the British flag on the American continent, the fertile lands bordered by the Bay of Fundy, the Valley of the St. Lawrence, the region of the Great Lakes, the prairies of the West, the Rocky Mountains, the lands washed by the famous ocean whose breezes are said to be as sweet as the breezes of the Mediterranean. Our fellow-countrymen are not only those in whose veins runs the blood of France. They are all those, whatever their race or whatever their religion, whom the fortunes of war, the chances of fate, or their own choice have brought among us, and who acknowledge the sovereignty of the British Crown . . . The first place in my heart is for those in whose veins runs the blood of my own veins. Yet I do not hesitate to say that the rights of my fellow-countrymen of different origins are as dear to me, as sacred to me, as the rights of my own race, and if it unfortunately happened that they were ever attacked, I would defend them with just as much energy and vigor as the rights of my own race . . . What I claim for us is an equal share of the sun, of justice, of liberty; we have that

share, and have it amply; and what we claim for ourselves we are anxious
to grant to others. I do not want French Canadians to domineer over
anyone, nor anyone to domineer over them. Equal justice; equal
rights . . . Cannot we believe that in the supreme battle here on the
Plains of Abraham, when the fate of arms turned against us, cannot we
believe that it entered into the designs of Providence that the two races,
enemies up to that time, should henceforth live in peace and harmony?
Such was the inspiring cause of Confederation.[160]

These two different concepts, which might be called the provincial
and the national, or the French-Canadian and the Canadian, were
to diverge increasingly in the years to come, and to divide the
French Canadians. Their respective popularity has varied with the
circumstances of the time. It is one of the tragedies of Canadian
national life that in moments of division between the ethnic
elements, in times of crisis, either political or economic, French
Canada is most apt to recoil upon itself, to wrap itself in its distinctive tradition, and to ease its sense of insecurity by asserting its
Frenchness and its Catholicity, thus increasing the resentment of
English Canadians that Canada is not a homogeneous nation whose
people think and react alike in national emergencies. But the
French-Canadian reaction is a natural one in the case of a minority
group whose sense of insecurity leads it to indulge in brash talk to
dispel its own fears.

8

Mercier reached the apogee of his career in his Saint-Jean-
Baptiste Day speech at Quebec in which he voiced the feelings of a
people scattered over North America. His words read like a declaration of war to the Ontario Orangemen, who in August established a
Montreal branch of the Equal Rights Association, the Protestant
Protective Association, to 'protect' their brethren of Quebec, and
who renewed their attack on the Jesuit Estates Act by calling for its
review by the courts. Mercier maddened them still more in November when he attended the Catholic Congress of Baltimore, where he
was the guest of the Jesuits, hobnobbed with the hierarchy, and
proclaimed: 'We have returned to the Church, through the Jesuits,
the possessions of which they were despoiled by the same George III
who wished to despoil you of your rights and liberties.'[161] Taillon,
the leader of the Quebec Conservatives, protested against 'the war
of race and religion inaugurated by M. Mercier,'[162] but the Protestant Liberal Joly approved the Jesuit Estates Act, despite his
differences with Mercier on the Riel question. Mercier himself
sought to reassure the alarmed Protestants by a gift of $10,000 to
the University of Toronto, which had suffered in a fire, and by
telling Alexander Cameron, the member for Huntingdon, that he

had no intention of replacing the Union Jack on the Quebec citadel by the Tricolor. Mercier also published an English pamphlet, *An Answer to the Equal Rights Association* (Quebec, 1890), containing the correspondence between himself and the president of the Association, and also Robert Sellar's 'Disabilities of Protestants in the Province of Quebec' and his own reply to this document. The pamphlet served as an answer to the Equal Rightists' attacks on the French Canadians, and reinforced Mercier's standing with his own people. The latter was also greatly strengthened by the transmission from Rome through the Curé Labelle of the Holy See's thanks to Mercier for his services to the Church.

Mercier was returned to office with a larger majority in the provincial elections of June 1890, despite the opposition's attacks upon himself and his disciples on the basis of the McGreevy and Whelan graft scandals. He characterized the result as a victory for provincial autonomy and for his railroad development policy. He announced his intention of furthering agriculture and colonization, of attracting foreign capital to develop Quebec's natural resources, of repatriating Franco-Americans, and of seeking commercial reciprocity with the United States. He dreamed of bringing about the downfall of his arch-enemy Sir John, but in the federal elections of 1891 Macdonald was returned to office despite the majority of fifteen Liberal seats which Mercier supplied in Quebec to Laurier.

Mercier endorsed a note for $10,000 to pay the expenses of contesting elections, and then departed for Europe in search of a $10,000,000 French loan. Soon after his departure, several opposition papers were put under severe pressure by Mercier's aides, amid protests against 'Caesar Mercier' and 'the Quebec Autocrat.' Israel Tarte carried his charges against Thomas McGreevy to Ottawa, where their hearing by the House was interrupted by the death of Macdonald in June. Meanwhile Mercier was making a royal progress through Europe, being decorated by the French President, the Belgian King, and Pope Leo XIII, who made him a papal count. His visit to Rome, where he sought the creation of a Franco-American bishop for his exiled compatriots, did him no good either with English Protestants or with the Quebec hierarchy, who resented the presumption of a layman meddling with ecclesiastical matters. The European money market proved tight, but Mercier raised a $4,000,000 loan in Paris and succeeded in interesting French capitalists in Quebec, before his triumphant return to a province which had been flattered by his reception in Europe.

But scandal broke out immediately upon his return. Mercier had approved the transfer of the contract for the Baie des Chaleurs Railway to a new syndicate, which, it was revealed, had paid a commission of $100,000 to Ernest Pacaud, the Liberal treasurer. And

Pacaud had paid off the $10,000 note endorsed by Mercier and had supplied him with $5,000 when he ran short of funds in Paris. Tarte's charges had also resulted in the resignation of Sir Hector Langevin as Minister of Public Works at Ottawa, and the launching of a wave of demands for reform. Public opinion dictated that the Lieutenant-Governor of Quebec should first limit Mercier's powers and then appoint a Royal Commission to investigate the Baie des Chaleurs scandal. On the strength of the commission's report, Mercier was dismissed from office on December 16. The lieutenant-governor, a Conservative, called upon the Conservative ex-premier, Charles de Boucherville, who had been dismissed from office by the Liberal Letellier de Saint-Just in 1878, to form a new government. Mercier denounced the lieutenant-governor and the Royal Commission for their political partisanship, and promised to seek a new mandate from the people. But the new administration uncovered further scandals, and pressed the attack upon the Mercier regime. Laurier showed personal sympathy for Mercier, but referred to the Baie des Chaleurs episode as 'an unfortunate transaction which must be condemned without hesitation, which cannot be defended.'[163]

In the elections of March 1892, which followed a bitter winter campaign to the cry of 'A bas les voleurs!' only seventeen partisans of Mercier were elected, and Mercier himself barely retained his own seat. The press hailed the downfall of the Mercier regime as 'the punishment of a band of brigands who bled the province for four years.'[164] Mercier saw the verdict as the victory of 'calumny over the constitution,' and announced his return to private life. At the end of April Mercier and Pacaud were called before the Quebec Assizes on charges of misappropriating public funds, and were held for trial. Arthur Buies wrote a virtual epitaph for the fallen leader in La Patrie, which concluded thus: 'He had in his hands the most brilliant role which has ever been given to a Canadian statesman; he had a whole people behind him and a glorious role to fill; his vanity, his egotism, and his absolute absence of moral sense lost everything.'[165] Mercier was ill, and by June he was bankrupt to the tune of $83,163. At his trial in October he was found not guilty, and aroused sympathy by the way in which he had aged under affliction. During the winter session of the legislature he forced his enemy Tom Chase Casgrain to disavow a charge that he had embezzled $30,000 of public funds.

On April 4, 1893 Mercier addressed a crowd of six thousand at the Parc Sohmer in Montreal on 'The Future of Canada.' This was rumored to be his political swansong, and his partisans gathered as of old for the occasion. He defended himself against the charges of anglophobia and disloyalty:

I am not an anglophobe. I admire Englishmen and I love English-women, but England leaves me indifferent, nearly cold. I admit that she has done us some good, but I believe that she has done us more harm than good, and that if we, especially we French Canadians, have pros-pered, it is not her fault. We have contributed much to the fortune of her merchants and manufacturers, as we have always paid generously the governors whom she has sent us. If some of them insulted us, and said that we were an inferior race, we never threw rotten eggs at them, as the English Tories did to Lord Elgin . . .

Thus, all accounts balanced, we owe nothing to England; and we shall separate from her when the majority, regularly consulted, so wishes, without remorse of conscience, without a broken heart, and even without shedding tears. . . .[166]

He weighed the relative merits of the present system, of imperial federation, of annexation to the States, and of independence, observ-ing that Confederation had outlived its time. He blamed Canada's failure to make as much progress as the United States on its false political position. Supporting his position by the statements of Englishmen favorable to colonial emancipation, he came out for independence. With something of his old eloquence he concluded his two-hour speech thus:

Standing as a free man on American soil, I defend the sacred cause of my compatriots, whatever their race or religious belief, and I ask for all colonial emancipation and liberty . . .

In undertaking this considerable task which I have imposed upon myself, I wished to show you what our country could be, this Canada, dear to all our hearts. I have done all that I could to open up new hori-zons for you, and by making you see them, push you towards the realiza-tions of our natural destinies. You have colonial dependence, I offer you independence; you have shame and misery, I offer you fortune and prosperity; you are only a colony ignored by the entire world, I offer you the opportunity of becoming a great people, recognized and re-spected among free nations.

Men, women, and children, it is for you to choose; you can remain slaves under colonial status, or become independent and free, among other peoples who invite you to the banquet of nations.[167]

The meeting ended in a triumph for Mercier and for his doctrine of independence, but there was no political aftermath. Mercier had dreamed of raising the people with the cry of independence as he had raised them in the days of the Riel affair.

But that outburst of feeling had exhausted the emotions of French Canada for the time being, and the public mood had changed. There was now more response to Laurier's academic eloquence than to the impassioned melodramatics of Mercier. Laurier's stock was rising steadily, and he was very conscious of being the leader of a party which was both French and English. His watchwords were conciliation and unity, and Mercier's last appeal to the French Canadians was dismissed as a personal one, unsupported by the Liberal Party. So Mercier took his doctrine of independence to the United States, where he aroused much enthusiasm in the Franco-American centers.

In the Quebec legislature that fall, after his administration had undergone many attacks, he improvised despite his failing health a two-hour apologia, which closed thus:

You have ruined me, you sought to dishonor me, and now you wish to walk on my corpse. Well, here is that corpse! Look at it; look it in the face, for it rises before you to say: You have taken from me all that I possess in the world, even to my library, my beloved books which I amassed during thirty-five years—all has been sold, save my honor. And be assured that I shall defend my honor like a lion, alone against you, were you a hundred or a thousand.[168]

Taillon, who had attacked Mercier bitterly, rose and shook his hand after this speech. During the rest of the session Mercier continued to be the soul of the opposition, but in the summer of 1894 diabetes forced him to give up legal work and to take to his bed. As he lay dying the new Liberal leader Laurier made a triumphant tour to the Pacific Coast, as if to symbolize the triumph of the larger nationalism. But Laurier and many others came to the bedside of the dying Mercier, among the rest his old adversary Chapleau. The end came on October 30. Some twenty-five thousand people paid their respects to the dead leader as he lay in state, and countless thousands attended the funeral, the most impressive seen in Montreal since Cartier's. Notables and rank and file alike did honor to one who, despite all his faults, incarnated the spirit of French Canada, and whose influence was to remain a lasting force in the French-Canadian tradition. Mercier's revival of the old cry of 'Gesta Dei per Francos' and his messianic pronouncements of the providential mission of the French Canadians were to find echoes in the years to come.

9

Despite his dislike for the 'demagogues' who had won the leadership of the people away from the bishops in the course of the 'Holy War,' Bishop Laflèche shared one great nationalist idea with Honoré Mercier, while he was the new master of Quebec. Laflèche, too, dreamed of the development of a French-Canadian state on the banks of the St. Lawrence, with the French Canadians of Quebec reinforced by the exiled Franco-Americans of New England. In the 1870's, like the other bishops, he had fought the exodus from depressed Quebec, and had encouraged Curé Labelle in his colonization movement with this remarkably foresighted estimate of the resources of Quebec:

The direction that you give your activity in the work of colonization is certainly most patriotic, and the good Lord will lavish His most abundant blessings upon it. The valleys of the Ottawa and of Lake St. John offer a vast field for our surplus population, and it is there that they must be guided. The Saint-Maurice valley offers little advantage for agriculture. Its arid and rocky soil contains few assets for agriculture, and it will be difficult to form prosperous parishes there. By way of compensation, it is rich in minerals and in timber, and the waterpower to work these raw materials is plentiful and powerful. Agriculture and industry, then, join in Providence's plan to make our country prosperous and happy. As industry must follow agriculture, you walk in the paths of Providence by giving the latter all the impetus possible through the colonization of our most fertile lands.[169]

But with Canada racked by the ethnic division of the Riel affair, Bishop Laflèche talked unguardedly to Curé Biron of West Springfield, Massachusetts, who quoted him in the Franco-American press as saying that Confederation was only a house of cards which would soon collapse, and then the 800,000 Franco-Americans of the States must aid the French-Canadians 'to protect ourselves against Anglo-Saxon hatred.'[170] Therefore the exodus from Quebec could no longer be considered a disaster. Bishop Laflèche denied that he had said that Canada would be annexed by the States, as Curé Biron claimed, but declared that on the contrary he had said that part of the United States would annex itself to an independent French state. By guarding their faith and their customs, the Franco-Americans could further this development, which might have been the design of Providence in causing the exodus. This concept of an independent French state, which has ever remained dear to French-Canadian ultranationalists, thus seems to have been the joint idea of Mercier and Laflèche, born of the bitter aftermath of the Riel affair and of the bishop's dismay that Canada was going the way of other nations in which the Church was not dominant over the State.

At this period a wave of anti-Catholicism in New England, aroused by the sudden realization of the great numbers of immigrants of largely Catholic stock, had thrown the Franco-Americans back upon their distinctive traditions. Ferdinand Gagnon, one of their best-known leaders and also the paid repatriation agent of the Canadian government, had aroused much Yankee opposition by his cry of 'Be loyal, yes, but be French always!'[171] Such

P

utterances, combined with national conventions which reunited Franco-Americans and French Canadians, and the constant comings and goings of Canadian mission priests and cultural envoys among the Franco-American colonies of New England, caused alarm among the thinning stock of Yankees. A lingering Puritan prejudice against the faith of some three hundred thousand Franco-Americans was not diminished by aggressive defence of their right to preserve their own language and traditions in their new home. English-Canadian immigrants took a leading role in rousing nativist sentiment. On December 28, 1889 the Boston *British-American Citizen* printed an editorial based upon the fear that a French annexation of New England was being plotted:

Romanism is already a terrible power in our country. It dominates New York, and exercises a considerable influence in many cities and towns of New England. But to this Roman force must be added the French ultramontane power, which we have completely ignored up to now. Reflect, American patriots, the French Jesuits have conceived the project of forming a Catholic nation out of the province of Quebec and New England, and this project of making New England French Catholic has already taken proportions capable of alarming the most optimistic. The French number more than a million in the United States, and in all probability 350,000 in New England. They fill your factories, buy your farms, introduce themselves into your legislatures, and exercise there a powerful influence. The number of their children is unimaginable for Americans. These children are kept away from the public schools, in order to receive an education entirely similar to that they would have received in Quebec. They are told that by learning English they will lose their mother tongue, their nationality, and their religion. They are kept a distinct alien race, subject to the Pope in matters of religion and of politics. Rapidly they acquire the right to vote; in certain places they already have an absolute majority, while in many others they balance their enemies. Soon, united to the Irish, they will govern you, Americans; or rather the Pope will govern you, for these masses recognize him as master.[172]

Thus the religio-political strife of Quebec was echoed in the States, where the Franco-Americans had been awakened to a consciousness of their ethnic origin by the execution of Riel and by the opposition they provoked by insisting upon remaining a people apart. But after a 58 per cent increase of the French-Canadians in the States between 1890 and 1900, the tide of immigration from Quebec dwindled away with the opening of the Canadian West and the industrialization of Quebec. Meanwhile the earlier immigrants had become Americanized, as was witnessed by the decline of the conventions, of the Franco-American press, and of the insistence on maintaining separateness.[173] Those of their sons and grandsons who have returned to Quebec have been among the most bitter opponents of the ultranationalist school which still dreams of that French-Canadian state whose emergence Bishop Laflèche regarded as possibly within the plans of Providence.

10

The political fortunes of the Conservative Party were greatly embarrassed after Macdonald's death in 1891 by the fact that many of those engaged in the struggle for the leadership were also leaders in the Orange crusade against 'French domination'—which was really a crusade, as Dr. Skelton has pointed out, against French-Canadian equality.[174] The anti-French agitation which was aroused by the Riel affair continued with the demand for disallowance of the Jesuit Estates Act in 1889. The Equal Rights Association, formed in June 1889 by the same 'noble thirteen' who had voted for disallowance against an overwhelming majority of both parties, was led by D'Alton McCarthy and other leading imperial federalists. The Liberal government of Ontario was attacked for allowing the use of French in the schools of eastern Ontario, but anti-French measures were pressed hardest in the federal House. In February 1890 McCarthy introduced a bill to abolish the use of the French language in the legislature and courts of the North-West Territories, after having made a tour during the previous year through Manitoba and raised an agitation there which revoked the language and scholastic guarantees of the Manitoba Act and raised a question which brought about the downfall of the Conservative regime at Ottawa in 1896.

Meanwhile the nominal leadership of the party changed hands rapidly, with the Catholic and Orange wings of the party alternating in power, and all unity shattered by their bitter differences. No one then or since has been able to repeat Macdonald's feat of reconciling the irreconcilable year in and year out. As in all governments which had held power too long, corruption was rife; and Israel Tarte's revelations of graft in the Public Works Department brought about the downfall of Sir Hector Langevin, who had been slated to succeed Sir John Macdonald as leader. Further Liberal charges of corruption were countered by Conservative revelations of the Baie des Chaleurs Railway scandal in Quebec. With the electors becoming convinced that one party was as crooked as the other, the Conservatives managed to increase their majority from twenty-odd to sixty in the by-elections of 1892, but after that date they steadily lost ground.

Meanwhile Laurier knitted the Liberals together by speaking trips which made him known all over Canada and by a national convention at Ottawa in June 1893, the first ever held by any party. The Liberal program of lower tariffs and reciprocity with the United States gained in popular favor as time went on, and as leader of the opposition Laurier was able to avoid committing himself on the Manitoba school question, which became increasingly embarrassing for the government. The Conservative Party was torn apart by the question, which divided its support from the Catholic hierarchy and the Orange Order. When the government finally decided upon a remedial bill against the Manitoba anti-French legislation, Laurier was able to take his stand as the supporter of the Liberal doctrine of provincial rights, while promising to win better terms for the minority from the Liberal government of Manitoba.

Laurier resisted the intense pressure put upon him by the Catholic hierarchy to support the government measure, and made a moving statement of principle which reassured his English Protestant followers:

I am here the acknowledged leader of a great party, composed of Roman Catholics and Protestants as well, as Protestants must be in the majority in every party in Canada. Am I to be told, occupying such a position, that I am to be dictated the course I am to take in this House, by reasons that can appeal to the consciences of my fellow-Catholic members, but which do not appeal as well to the consciences of my Protestant colleagues? No. So long as I have a seat in this House, so long as I occupy the position I do now, whenever it shall become my duty to take a stand upon any question whatever, that stand I will take not upon grounds of Roman Catholicism, not upon grounds of Protestantism, but upon grounds which can appeal to the conscience of all men, irrespective of their particular faith, upon grounds which can be occupied by all men who love justice, freedom, and toleration.[175]

Laurier held that the federal government had the power to interfere in Manitoba, but should not do so until all the facts had been investigated and until all means of conciliation had been exhausted. He moved the six months' hoist, and the government defeated that motion by little more than half its normal majority. Sir Charles Tupper's attempt to jam the remedial bill through second reading was met by a filibuster in which rebellious Tories took a leading part. Finally the bill was abandoned. Elections followed in June 1896, with Tupper leading the Conservatives at the head of a cabinet whose ultramontane representation had been strengthened.

The Quebec hierarchy issued a collective pastoral on May 16 which said that the Manitoba school question was primarily a religious one, and while disavowing any intention to side with any political party, ordered that 'all Catholics should vote only for candidates who will formally and solemnly pledge themselves to vote in Parliament in favor of the legislation giving to the Catholics of Manitoba the school laws which are recognized as theirs by the Privy Council in England.'[176] The Vicar-General of Quebec, Mgr. Marois, pronounced it mortal sin to vote Liberal, while Bishop Laflèche condemned Laurier's stand as 'the most categorical affirmation of the liberalism condemned by the Church' and pronounced that 'a Catholic cannot under pain of sinning in a grave matter vote for the chief of a party who has formulated so publicly such an error.'[177] The clergy supported the Conservative candidates even in cases where the Liberals signed the required pledge. Against the solid opposition of the clergy, broken only by the neutrality of Bishop Emard of Valleyfield, Laurier could only rely on Quebec's pride in its native son and in Israel Tarte's organizing ability. Quebec, given the choice of following its bishops or electing the first French-Canadian prime minister of Canada, voted more than three to one for Laurier. It was thanks to this Quebec majority that the Liberals took power and kept it for fifteen years.

Laurier's first task as prime minister was to settle the Manitoba school question. Negotiations between Ottawa and Winnipeg were made easier by the fact that the Liberals held power in both capitals, and that Laurier was pledged to the use of 'sunny ways' rather than the big stick. The Laurier-Greenway Agreement—actually made by Israel Tarte and Clifford Sifton—met with favor in moderate quarters when it was announced on November 19, 1896, though it was denounced by both the Manitoba Orangemen and by Archbishop Langevin, who was supported by most of the Quebec bishops. The days of the 'Holy War' were recalled as the leading Liberal journal of Quebec, *L'Electeur*, was banned in a pastoral letter signed by Archbishop Bégin of Quebec, Bishop Laflèche, Bishop Gravel of Nicolet, Bishop Blais of Rimouski, and Bishop Labrecque of Chicoutimi.[178] The paper was condemned for disrespect to the hierarchy, for criticizing clerical intervention in education, and for reproducing a pamphlet by Laurier's intimate friend L.-O. David, *Le Clergé canadien, Sa Mission, et Son Oeuvre*. In this work David, outraged by the hierarchy's support of the Conservatives on the school question, criticized the policy of the hierarchy from their opposition to the *Patriotes* down to the present day, while professing his faith in a less political Catholicism. The same five bishops sought and won condemnation of the pamphlet at Rome, where it was put on the *Index* in December 1896.

But the Liberals stood firm against this assault on the party in Quebec. They won a contested election involving undue influence in Champlain, where the *curés* had declared it mortal sin to vote for a Liberal; and in the Bonaventure by-election of March 1897 the Liberal candidate, J.-F. Guité, refused to sign the pledge exacted by Bishop Blais to vote against the Laurier-Greenway Agreement. Guité was elected by double the previous Liberal majority, after his statement: 'I am a Catholic, and in all questions of faith and morals I am ready to accept without restriction the decisions of the Church. In all political questions I claim the freedom enjoyed by every British subject . . . I cannot before God and my conscience renounce the freedom of exercising my privilege as a member to the best of my judgment.'[179]

In addressing the *Club National* of Montreal in December, Laurier clarified his own position and restrained the anti-clericalism of such inveterate *Rouges* as Honoré Beaugrand, who had proclaimed in *La Patrie* after the banning of *L'Electeur* a struggle to the death between the government and the hierarchy. Laurier spoke thus to the young Liberals:

Let me give you a word of good counsel. During your career you will have to suffer many things which will appear to you as supreme injustices. Let me say to you that you should never let your religious convictions be affected by the acts of men. Your convictions are immortal. Their foundation is eternal. Let your convictions be always calm, serene, and superior to the inevitable trials of life. Show to the world that Catholicism is compatible with the exercise of liberty in its highest acceptation; show that the Catholics of the country will render to God what is God's, to Caesar what is Caesar's.[180]

And in a personal letter to Beaugrand, who was forced to sell *La Patrie** by clerical pressure, Laurier made a revealing statement of their differences: 'I am a liberal like yourself, but we do not belong to the same school. I am a disciple of Lacordaire.'[181]

Because of the difficult position in which the Quebec Liberals stood after the election of Laurier, an appeal to Rome was launched. Abbé Proulx of Saint-Lin, an old friend of Laurier who had stood by him on the school question, and the Chevalier Drolet of Papal Zouave fame were dispatched to Rome, where Archbishop Langevin likewise hastened to support the hierarchy's stand. Abbé Proulx carried semi-private credentials from Laurier, urging a statement of doctrine from Rome 'which would have the effect of bringing regrettable abuses to an end, maintaining peace and harmony in our country, and reassuring the consciences of Catholics.'[182] In a letter to Drolet at Rome, Laurier regretted the prospect of a war of religion in Canada and the attacks which had been made upon him at Rome, but said that his religious convictions had not been shaken 'by the attacks of those whose mission it is to preach Christian charity.' He added: 'It is a singular thing that these violent acts,

* The paper was purchased by Israel Tarte's sons.

this ignorance of conditions in our own country, this war to which we are going to be exposed, far from estranging me from the Church, draw me closer to it. I feel how superior religion is to all that often is done in the name of religion.'[183]

To support the unofficial envoys went a petition to the Pope from forty-five Catholic Liberal members of Parliament, urging a renewal of Pius IX's prohibition of clerical intervention in politics. But Abbé Proulx found himself outweighed at Rome by the opposition of all the Quebec hierarchy except Bishop Emard, and returned home in December. Meanwhile the bishops prepared a collective pastoral against the Laurier-Greenway Agreement. So Laurier sent his solicitor-general, Charles Fitzpatrick, and Charles Russell, the son of the English chief justice, supplied with letters from Cardinal Vaughan and the Duke of Norfolk and legal opinion from Edward Blake, to Rome to argue the Liberal case and to urge the sending of an apostolic delegate.

The appointment of Mgr. Merry del Val, a thirty-two-year-old confidential chamberlain of the Pope and a schoolmate of Russell, soon followed. Mgr. del Val arrived in Canada in March 1897, and spent several months consulting with the Quebec and Ontario bishops and clergy, and many leading laymen, both Catholic and Protestant. Bishop Laflèche made the mistake of patronizing the young delegate, whose Spanish temperament did not take kindly to the old ultramontane leader's presumption. Laurier soon achieved friendly terms with the delegate, and without any public statement pressure was exerted which ended the 'Holy War.' In May the Liberals swept the provincial elections in Quebec. The bishops had been ordered to suspend all action pending Rome's decision, and Abbé Proulx happily expressed the opinion that 'the number of mortal sins in this country will be diminished by at least one.'[184]

Leo XIII's encyclical *Affari vos*, given at Rome on December 9, 1897 and issued in Canada a month later, justified the hierarchy's protests against the 'unjust' Manitoba law of 1890, which had persecuted Catholic education, and called the Laurier-Greenway Agreement 'defective, imperfect, insufficient.' But it stated that in seeking complete justice, 'the rules of moderation, of meekness, and of brotherly charity were not to be lost sight of,' and meanwhile Catholics were urged that 'wherever the law or the situation or the friendly disposition of individuals offer them some means of lessening the evil and of better averting its dangers, it is altogether becoming and useful that they make use of these means and draw from them the utmost possible advantage.' The provincial plan of improving public instruction was pronounced 'great and noble,' and Catholics were urged to make their schools rival the most flourishing in methods and efficiency.[185] Though the encyclical made neither camp wholly happy, and consequently was twisted to suit the ends of each, it did put a final end to the 'Holy War.' Concessions were duly made on either side, and when the new Liberal premier of Quebec, F.-X. Marchand, sought to achieve the old Liberal goal of putting the schools under government control, he was blocked by the pressure exerted upon Laurier by Archbishop Bruchési of Montreal, who was also an advocate of 'sunny ways.' Liberalism had been restored to good standing in Catholic Quebec, but in the process it was largely purged of its traditional anti-clericalism.

Cartier's dream of another Quebec in the West was doomed forever by the flood of multi-national immigration into that region under the Laurier regime. But Riel's dream came true, as the West became the new home of the poor and oppressed of Europe. The growing dominance of English Canadians in the West, the reaction to the Riel troubles, and the desire to force assimilation, deprived the western French Canadians of the constitutional guarantees for their language and their schools which Cartier had carefully written into the Manitoba Act. The Laurier-Greenway Agreement was the first of a series of compromises in the matter of educational rights in the West which embittered French-Canadian feeling and furthered the development of a provincial nationalism in Quebec.

The French Canadians became convinced that they stood on a basis of equality with their English compatriots only in Quebec, despite their constitutional guarantees, and that their brethren in the West were oppressed by the English majority. The question of the rights of the minority groups in the West has remained a thorn in the flesh of French Canada down to the present day, and the only hope of healing this old wound lies in English-Canadian acceptance of the doctrine that Canada is a bilingual and bicultural nation, and that the rights of the French language are not confined to Quebec. Some evidence that this hope may be realized lies in the growing tendency of English Canadians in the West to regard Riel as a regional hero rather than as a French traitor.

Notes

[1] The *Métis* ('mixed') people were the human result of the French tendency to go native when trade or exploration took them to the Great Lakes or beyond, where 'neither *curé* . . . nor Jesuit nor governors existed,' as Denonville put it. M. Giraud, *Le Métis canadien: son rôle dans l'histoire des provinces de l'Ouest* (Paris, 1945), 312. Despite the opposition of Church and State and, in the case of some tribes, of the Indians themselves, the number of mixed unions increased and by 1871 the offspring of French and Indians numbered 9,810. The *Métis* supplied much of the personnel of the fur trade in the West. They remained distinct from the French Canadians, unlike the halfbreeds of Quebec, for the children of these western unions were usually assimilated into the mother's family and reared as

savages. But they remained a group apart from both whites and Indians and there was no great unity between the French *Métis* and the smaller number of English or Scottish halfbreeds who originated in the Hudson's Bay Company posts.

² A. S. Morton, *A History of the Canadian West to 1870–1* (London, n.d.), 645, 581.

³ Morton, 802.

⁴ *Ibid.*, 651; Giraud, 533–4, 255–6.

⁵ Morton, 803–5.

⁶ Giraud, 612; Morton, 'The New Nation,' in *TRSC 1939*, 137–45.

⁷ Giraud, 920–1. *Métis* unrest, due to poverty and dissatisfaction with the Hudson's Bay Company monopoly, led to risings in 1815–16, and near insurrections in 1826–7. Giraud, 550–93, 727, 742.

⁸ Morton, 812; Giraud, 790–1.

⁹ Morton, 827–9; T. W. Blegen, 'James Wickes Taylor,' in *Minnesota History Bulletin*, I (Nov. 1915), No. 4, 170–1. In 1856 Colonel C. F. Smith, U.S.A., ordered the *Métis* to stop crossing the border on their annual buffalo hunts, which aroused the Sioux (Morton, 825; Giraud, 828).

¹⁰ Morton, 836–7.

¹¹ Morton, 844–5.

¹² Morton, 852.

¹³ J. W. Taylor, 'Relation between the United States and Northwestern British North America,' *37th Congress, 2nd Session, House Executive Documents*, X, No. 146, Serial 1138; Blegen, 175.

¹⁴ Morton, 854–6.

¹⁵ Kennedy, *Const. Doc.*, 542, Quebec Resolutions, No. 10. This provision became No. 11 of the Westminster Palace Resolutions, and Sec. 146 of the B.N.A. Act, 1867. Kennedy, 611, 633. The Canadian delegates who waited on the colonial secretary on 15 February 1865 declared: 'It appears that nothing deserving the name of "government" exists in the populated portion of the territory known as the "Red River Settlement"' (Morton, 862).

¹⁶ Morton, 863.

¹⁷ G. F. G. Stanley, *The Rise of Western Canada* (London, 1936), 57; Blegen, 179. Taylor proposed the annexation of Western Canada in the absence of a transcontinental Canadian railway and of a Great Lakes seaway. J. W. Taylor, 'Commercial Relations with British America,' 12 June 1866; *39th Congress, 1st Sess., House Ex. Docs.*, No. 128, Serial 1263; Blegen, 178–9.

¹⁸ Morton, 864–5.

¹⁹ *Ibid.*, 866.

²⁰ *Ibid.*, 870–1.

²¹ *Ibid.*, 667.

²² *Ibid.*, 874.

²³ Blegen, 187–8.

²⁴ Morton, 880.

²⁵ *Ibid.*, 881–2.

²⁶ *The Canadian North-West* (Can. Archives, No. 9, Ottawa, 1915), II, 884–7.

²⁷ Morton, 882–3.

²⁸ *Ibid.*, 881, 888–91; *Can. North-West*, II, 881–2, Dennis-McDougall, 27 October 1869.

²⁹ *Ibid.*, 884–8, 882–3; *Can. North-West*, II, 890–2, Mactavish's proclamation, 16 November 1869.

³⁰ *Ibid.* 887.

³¹ *Can. North-West*, II, 893–5, McDougall's proclamation, 1 December 1869.

³² J. Pope, *Memoirs of Sir John A. Macdonald* (Toronto, n.d.), 407–9, Macdonald-McDougal, 20 November 1869.

[33] *Can. North-West*, II, 896–8, Dennis' Commission, 1 December 1869.

[34] *Ibid.*, 891–2.

[35] A. G. Morice, O.M.I., *History of the Catholic Church in Western Canada* (Toronto, 1910), II, 34.

[36] J. Pope (ed.), *Correspondence of Sir John A. Macdonald* (Toronto, n.d.) 106–7, Macdonald-J. Rose, 23 November 1869.

[37] Morton, 887.

[38] *Can. North-West*, II, 900–1, royal proclamation, 6 December 1869; 908–13, Howe-McDougall, 24 December 1869.

[39] Morice, II, 13–14, Taché-Gov.-Gen., 23 July 1870, *Northwest Committee Evidence*, 42.

[40] Morton, 896–7.

[41] *Ibid.*, 900–2.

[42] *Ibid.*, 903; Stanley, 96, 108.

[43] Morton, 904.

[44] *Ibid.*, 907–9.

[45] *Ibid.*, 908.

[46] *Ibid.*, 910.

[47] Morice, II, 56.

[48] *Ibid.*, II, 58–9. Cf. Morton, 911.

[49] Morton, 912; Stanley, 117 n. 36 and 37.

[50] Kennedy, *Const. Docs.*, 640–4, the Manitoba Act, 1870. Section 22 provided: 'In and for the Province, the said Legislature may exclusively make laws in relation to Education subject and according to the following provisions:

(1) Nothing in any such Law shall prejudicially affect any right or privilege with respect to Denominational Schools which any class of persons have by Law or practice in the Province at the Union:

(2) An appeal shall lie to the Governor-General in Council from any Act or decision of the Legislature of the Province, or of any Provincial Authority, affecting any right or privilege of the Protestant or Roman Catholic minority of the Queen's subjects in relation to Education.

(3) In case any such Provincial Law, as from time to time seems to the Governor-General in Council requisite for the due execution of the provisions of this section, is not made, or in case any decision of the Governor-General in Council on any appeal under this section is not duly executed by the proper Provincial Authority in that behalf, then, and in every such case, as far only as the circumstances of each case require, the Parliament of Canada may make remedial laws for the due execution of the provisions of this section, and of any decision of the Governor-General in Council under this section.'

Section 23 provided: 'Either the English or the French language may be used by any person in the debates of the Houses of Legislature, and both of these languages shall be used in the respective Records and Journals of these Houses: and either of those languages may be used by any person or in any pleading or Process, in or issuing from any Court of Canada established under the British North America Act, 1867, or in or from all or any of the Courts of the Province. The Acts of the Legislature shall be printed and published in both those languages.'

[51] Morton, 916–17; Giraud, 1111 n. 3.

[52] Morton, 911–12.

[53] *Ibid.*, 917.

[54] Stanley, 143; C. P. Stacey, *Canada and the British Army, 1846–1871* (London, 1937), 239.

[55] Morton, 919; Giraud, 1112.

[56] Morton, 910–20; Stanley, 165; Giraud, 1111.

[57] Morice, II, 64; Giraud, 1112–13 and n. 8.

[58] Morton, 920, Archibald-Macdonald, 9 October 1871.

[59] Morice, II, 72–3.

[60] *CHAR 1940*, 46–7, R. O. MacFarlane, 'Manitoba Politics and Parties after Confederation.'

[61] *Ibid.*, 49–50; Giraud, 1117.

[62] PAC: Macdonald Papers, North-West Rebellion, III, 104, 108; Giraud, 113–15.

[63] *Epitome of Parliamentary Documents in connection with the North-West Rebellion, 1885* (Ottawa, 1886), 221, Riel's testimony.

[64] Mgr. A. Taché, *L'Amnestie* (Montréal, 1874); *Encore l'amnestie* (n.p., 1875).

[65] Stanley, 174.

[66] PAC: Riel Papers, Canada Public, Dept. of Justice, Riel Rebellion, Vol. 61, No. 3, Bourget-Riel, 14 juillet 1875, Bourget-Riel, 2 janvier 1876.

[67] J. A. Jonasson, 'The Background of the Riel Rebellion,' in *Pacific Historical Review*, III (Sept. 1934), 3, 278.
   In 1878–9 his friend Father Fabien Barnabé of Keeseville, N.Y., sought to find a job for Riel in New York or the West. By June 7, 1879 Riel was planning to leave St. Paul for Dakota or Montana, and Father Barnabé had recommended him to Archbishop Ireland of St. Paul as a founder of Catholic colonies on the frontier. The Jesuits of Fort Benton and St. Peter's Mission, with whom Riel later became on friendly terms, discouraged his political activities, but nonetheless he sought to organize the American *Métis* and vote them in a bloc for the Republican Party in 1882. Riel was indicted for this in 1883, but the case was dropped. J. K. Howard, *Strange Empire* (New York, 1952), 319–22, 334–50.
   Riel also interested himself in Indian affairs and was accused of planning an invasion of the North-West Territories to return to the Indians and *Métis* the lands which the whites were occupying (Giraud, 1195).

[68] Giraud, 1163.

[69] *Ibid.*, 1179–94.

[70] *Epitome*, 323–4, V. Vegreville-E. Deville, 19 janvier 1884.

[71] *Ibid.*, 324–5.

[72] Morice, II, 166.

[73] *Ibid.*, 167–8.

[74] *Epitome*, 386–7, 'Report of the Delegates'; 387–8, Riel delegates, 5 June 1884.

[75] *Ibid.*, 383–4, André-Dewdney, 7 July 1884; 388–9, André-Dewdney, 21 July 1884.

[76] G. T. Denison, *Soldiering in Canada* (Toronto, 1906), 262–3.

[77] Morice, II, 172.

[78] *Epitome*, 383, Inspector Howe-C.O., N.W. Police, 24 December 1884; 112, Charles Nolin's evidence; 147, Father André's evidence.

[79] Giraud, 1208.

[80] *Epitome*, 99, George Ness' evidence.

[81] Morice, II, 173.

[82] *Epitome*, 96, George Ness' evidence.

[83] *Ibid.*, 51, Riel-Crozier, 21 March 1885.

[84] *Ibid.*, 197, Riel.

[85] *Ibid.*, 99–100, George Ness; 141, Thomas Sanderson; 149, Philip Garnot.

[86] *Ibid.*, 124, Nolin.

[87] *Ibid.*, 105, Henry Walters.

[88] *Ibid.*, 216, 222–3, Riel; 56, Willoughby; 125, Nolin; 150, Garnot.

[89] *Ibid.*, 193, Riel.

[90] *Epitome*, 149, Garnot; 193, Riel. These letters were in the possession of the Crown at Riel's trial.

PAC: Riel Papers, Canada Public, Dept. of Justice, Riel Rebellion, Nos. 3 and 4, Bourget-Riel, 14 juillet 1875, 2 juin 1876. The relevant passages are as follows:

No. 3—'God, who has always guided and aided you until now, will not abandon you in the strongest of your prayers, *for he has given you a mission which you must accomplish in all respects* . . . you will work ceaselessly for the honor of the Faith, for the salvation of souls, and the good of society.' (Italics added.)

No. 4—'For my part I pray God, who is all good and all merciful, not to abandon you and to guide you in all your ways, *so that you shall never wander from the path which Divine Providence has traced out for you for our greatest good and that of your country and people*. One must hope and ask that the time of mercy arrive for this desolated country and this people afflicted and visited with different calamities which aggravate its misfortune; but the Faith, which is its only consolation in its hardest tests, will raise it sooner or later from this state of oppression in order to cover it with honor and good. Be blessed then of God and men and have patience in your woes.' (Italics added.)

These are classic examples of the messianic religious dynamic of French-Canadian nationalism. They were strong medicine for a disturbed mind.

[91] *Epitome*, 146-8, Father André; 151-3, Father Fourmond.
[92] *Ibid.*, 107, Hillyard Mitchell.
[93] *Ibid.*, 139, Sanderson.
[94] *Ibid.*, 111, Thomas Jackson.
[95] *Ibid.*, 171, Captain Young; 174, General Middleton.
[96] Dept. of Militia and Defence, *Report Upon the Suppression of the Rebellion in the North-West Territories, and Matters in Connection Therewith, 1885* (Ottawa, 1886), Frontispiece, 'The North-West Field Forces.'
[97] R. Rumilly, *Histoire*, V, 21.
[98] *Report*, 21.
[99] *Ibid.*, 35-7, 33.
[100] *Ibid.*, 33.
[101] Archives seigneuriales de Lotbinière, T. B. Strange-H.G. Joly, 20 June 1885.
[102] *Ibid.*, Strange-Joly, July 1885.
[103] *Report*, xi.
[104] *Ibid.*, 68.
[105] *Toronto News*, 18 May 1885; Rumilly, V, 36.
[106] *Epitome*, 4, Memorandum of Minister of Justice, 25 November 1885.
[107] *Ibid.*, 12, Campbell-Robinson, Osler, Burbridge, Casgrain, Scott, 20 June 1885.
[108] *Ibid.*, 13, jury list.
[109] *Ibid.*, 48.
[110] Rumilly, V, 63.
[111] *Epitome*, 14-16. The charge against Riel was brought by Alexander David Stewart, chief of police of Hamilton, Ontario.
[112] *Ibid.*, 154-5, Dr. Roy.
[113] *Ibid.*, 161, 163, Dr. Clark; 164, Dr. Wallace.
[114] *Ibid.*, 168, Dr. Jukes.
[115] *Ibid.*, 195, 197, Riel.
[116] *Ibid.*, 220-1, 224, 195, 198, 215, 217-19, Riel.
[117] *Ibid.*, 195-7, Riel.
[118] *Ibid.*, 213, verdict.
[119] *The Queen vs. Louis Riel* (Ottawa, 1886), 176-98, Queen's Bench Court Appeal.
[120] *Ibid.*, 199-202, Privy Council judgment.
[121] Skelton, I, 308.

[122] *La Presse*, 2 août 1885; Rumilly, V, 64.

[123] Rumilly, V, 66.

[124] *Ibid.*, V, 55–6.

[125] *Ibid.*, V, 43, 68–9.

[126] *Epitome*, 235–87, petitions.

[127] Stanley, 450 *n*. 11, gives the full text of the medical reports, not printed in *Epitome*, 1–2.

[128] Skelton, I, 312.

[129] ASL: T. B. Strange-H. G. Joly, 10 decembre 1885.

[130] PAC: Riel Papers, Canada, Miscellaneous Docs., XIV, 1660–1938, 73, Riel-R.P. Vital Fourmond, 5 août 1885.

[131] *Queen vs. Riel*, 204–5, Father André-F. X. Lemieux, 31 August 1885.

[132] *La Presse*, 17 novembre 1885; Rumilly, V, 111.

[133] *Ibid.*, 113.

[134] *Ibid.*, 121, Laurier, Trudel; 123, Mercier.

[135] *Ibid.*, 125–6, Champs de Mars resolutions.

[136] *Ibid.*, 99, Macdonald.

[137] Rumilly, *Laflèche*, 269.

[138] ASTR: Laflèche-Abbé Boucher, 5 mai 1885.

[139] Rumilly, *Laflèche*, 267, Taché-Laflèche, 26 mai 1885.

[140] ASTR: Laflèche-J.-O. Prince, 14 fevrier 1887; *La Minerve*, 14 mars 1887; Rumilly, *Laflèche*, 282.

[141] Rumilly, *Laflèche*, 278–9, Laflèche-H. Montplaisir, 17 janvier 1887.

[142] *Toronto Mail*, 23 November 1885; J. Willison, *Sir Wilfrid Laurier & the Liberal Party* (Toronto, 1903), 450–1 *n*.

[143] *Toronto Mail*, 25 November 1885; Rumilly, V, 119; Skelton, I, 316.

[144] *Orange Sentinel*, Skelton, I, 316–17.

[145] Skelton, I, 321.

[146] *Ibid.*, 322.

[147] *Ibid.*, 323.

[148] *Ibid.*, 323, 325.

[149] *Ibid.*, 326; Rumilly, V, 55–6.

[150] Barthe, *Laurier*, 256.

[151] Rumilly, *Honoré Mercier* (Montréal, 1936), 325.

[152] *Ibid.*, 326.

[153] *Ibid.*, 339.

[154] *Ibid.*, 353.

[155] *A Complete and Revised Edition of the Debate on the Jesuit Estates Act* (Ottawa, 1889), 3.

[156] *Toronto Mail*, 14 March 1888; *ibid.*, 14.

[157] *Ibid.*, 57.

[158] Rumilly, *Mercier*, 363–4.

[159] *Ibid.*, 365.

[160] Barthe, 527–8. Retranslated in part.

[161] Rumilly, *Mercier*, 375.

[162] *Ibid.*, 377.

[163] *Ibid.*, 467.

[164] *Courrier du Canada*, 9 mars 1892; *ibid.*, 479.

[165] *Ibid.*, 489.

[166] *Ibid.*, 518.

[167] *Ibid.*, 519–20.

[168] *Ibid.*, 526.

[169] ASTR: Fonds Laflèche (1848–9, 1862–84), Laflèche-Curé Labelle, 18 novembre 1879.

[170] *La Minerve*, 30 janvier 1889; Rumilly, *Laflèche*, 294.

[171] E. Hamon, *Les Canadiens Français de la Nouvelle-Angleterre* (Québec, 1891), 70.

[172] *Ibid.*, 134.

[173] M. Wade, 'The French Parish and *Survivance* in Nineteenth Century New England,' in *Catholic Historical Review*, XXXVI (July 1950) No. 2, 163–89.

[174] Skelton, I, 392.

[175] *Ibid.*, I, 475.

[176] *Mandements de Montréal*, XII, 196, Joint Pastoral, 16 mai 1896; Skelton, I, 482; Rumilly, VIII, 60.

[177] Skelton, I, 483; Rumilly, VIII, 62–3.

[178] Rumilly, VIII, 141.

[179] Skelton, II, 30.

[180] *Ibid.*, 31.

[181] *Ibid.*

[182] Skelton, II, 34.

[183] Skelton, II, 36 *n.*, Laurier-Drolet, 15 December 1896.

[184] Rumilly, VIII, 160.

[185] Skelton, II, 41–2; Rumilly, IX, 37. In most Quebec dioceses the encyclical was read from the pulpit along with a circular on education by Archbishop Bégin, reportedly written by Bishop Bruchési (Rumilly, IX, 42–3).

CHAPTER IX

IMPERIALISM *vs.* NATIONALISM

(1867–1904)

THE BOER WAR split open the cleft between French and English Canadians which had been developing since 1867, and created a deep division between them which has lasted until the present day. Behind this split and behind the internal conflicts which have already been recounted was the interplay of two great, opposed forces, Canadian nationalism and British imperialism. The ethnic division caused by the Riel Rising of 1885 and by the bitter disputes which ensued over the rights of the French language outside Quebec did much to align English Canadians largely in the imperialist camp and French Canadians largely in the nationalist one. But in fact Canadian nationalism in the post-Confederation period was English in origin, and in the last analysis ever since the Conquest the French Canadians have placed a greater reliance on the British connection than their fellow-countrymen, since it affords a certain security to a minority group which has lacked confidence in the goodwill of the majority.

Only in recent years have the French Canadians begun to realize that all English Canadians are not imperialists, and that indeed many of them are as much Canadian nationalists as any French Canadian. As the jingoistic 'Anglo-Saxon' imperialism of the turn of the century gradually lost its compulsive emotional force, the English Canadians have also learned that much was to be said for the French Canadians who fought it tooth and nail. But, as always in time of crisis, the ultraimperialists and the ultranationalists came to represent the ethnic groups of which they were in reality merely the extremist fringes. The conflict between nationalism and imperialism constituted one of the bitterest chapters in Canadian history, and has left lasting wounds which still hinder Canada's national development.

The conflict may well be considered a vicious circle, for as J. A. Hobson pointed out, 'Aggressive Imperialism is an artificial stimulant of nationalism in peoples too foreign to be absorbed and too compact to be permanently crushed.'[1] The 'pan-Anglo-Saxon' idea not only largely swallowed up early English-Canadian nationalism; it stimulated French-Canadian nationalism with its strong tendency toward isolationism, and thus largely defeated the chief purposes of its prophets. Canada was fortunate in being governed during fifteen crucial years of this conflict by a French-Canadian prime minister who possessed an equal devotion to the spirit of British political institutions and to the ideal of Canadian nationhood, and who was able to rally most of his compatriots behind his leadership. Despite the bitterness of the conflict, Laurier held office for a longer consecutive period than any Canadian prime minister had yet done. One of the darkest blots in the record of French and English relations might have been avoided if he had still been in power during the 1917–18 conscription crisis whose roots went back to the Boer War. But he was driven from office in 1911 by a momentary combination of the extreme nationalists and aggressive imperialists, political enemies on either side of the middle path he always favored. For French Canada, with its devotion to the leader principle, the conflict between nationalism and imperialism is largely the story of Laurier and Henri Bourassa, but the ideological background of their long duel has been too much neglected by both French and English Canadians.

I

The ebb and flow of imperialism is one of the remarkable features of nineteenth-century British history. At the outset the old mercantilism which had stimulated the conquest of the first British Empire in the previous century was still firmly in the saddle. Its rigorous application in Canada had much to do with the 1837–8 revolts, though it was already going out of fashion in England. But thanks to the efforts of Durham, Buller, and Wakefield, who were 'the truest Imperialists of their time,'[2] Canada did not go the way of the American colonies. Indeed, their disciple John Stuart Mill largely anticipated the modern view of the Empire as a commonwealth of autonomous nations.[3] The Colonial Reformers' twofold remedy of responsible colonial government and systematic colonization was only half applied to an ailing Canada, for after the great movement of the middle third of the century which populated Ontario, British emigration declined until 1897, while the Canadians had to achieve for themselves the responsible government which Durham had intended should be a primary feature of the new regime. In the face of rapidly rising Little Englandism, the Canadians also gradually acquired many of the powers which Durham had intended should be reserved to the imperial authorities.

Carlyle's cry of 'Why should not London long continue the All-Saxon home?'[4] was not at all typical of English opinion in the 1860's, although his chosen-people complex and his concept of 'Saxondom' were adopted by the imperialists of the '80's and '90's.

Far more representative were the views of Richard Cobden and John Bright, who favored 'this Confed. scheme, because I thought it was a step in the direction of an amical separation'[5] and believed that 'separation wd. be better for us & better for her,'[6] while from his snug berth in the Post Office Anthony Trollope preached Canadian rebellion and independence.[7] 'Mr. Mothercountry' at the Colonial Office hated to have his leisure disturbed by business from the colonies; parliament took no interest in colonial debates; and there was no real English public opinion on Canadian matters until indignation arose at the failure of the Canadian Militia Bill of 1862, which would have relieved the English taxpayer of some of his colonial burdens. So vast was the prevailing ignorance of colonial matters in England that the London *Times* came out flatly for Montreal as the new Canadian capital, under the impression that it was in 'loyal' Upper Canada.[8] Alexander Galt was able to assert Canada's financial autonomy in 1859 without rebuke from an apathetic Colonial Office,[9] while in 1866 Macdonald almost succeeded in his effort to have the new Dominion called the 'Kingdom of Canada,' in token of an independent relationship to the Crown which was not finally to win formal recognition until the Balfour Declaration of 1926.[10]

As far as the French Canadians were concerned, the Oxford don Goldwin Smith, then high in favor in political circles, voiced English opinion when he wrote in 1863: 'Our presence in Canada artificially preserves from absorption the French Canadian element, an antediluvian relic of old French society with its torpor and bigotry, utterly without value for the purposes of modern civilization.'[11] Smith ignored both the existence of a theory of French-Canadian nationality, and Lord Acton's dictum of the previous year that 'at the present day the theory of nationality is not only the most powerful auxiliary of revolution but its actual substance in the movements of the last three years.'[12] But Smith, like other early prophets of the new imperialism, was thinking in purely 'Anglo-Saxon' terms, conveniently ignoring the fact that a great part of the British Empire was not 'Anglo-Saxon.' For him, the dismemberment of the empire might be a step towards 'the moral federation of the whole English-speaking race throughout the world.'[13]

This, too, was the vision of Charles Dilke, later under-secretary of the Foreign Office, who visited and then described the English-speaking world in his *Greater Britain* (1869), a book with the revealing subtitle of 'Saxon Sketches.' In his preface Dilke confessed that his guiding idea was 'a conception, however imperfect, of the grandeur of our race, already girdling the earth, which it is destined, perhaps, eventually to overspread.'[14] He was thrilled by America, for there 'the peoples of the earth are being fused together, but they are run together into an English mould. . . . Through America, England is speaking to the world.' Dilke's 'Greater Britain' was to consist of America, Australasia, and India. French Canada was an obstacle to his scheme, for 'not only here, but elsewhere, a French "dependency" is France transported; not a double of the France of today, but a mummy of the France of the time of the "colony's" foundation.'[15] Passing northward into Canada from the United States, Dilke was depressed by the 'fog of unenterprise [which] hung over the land; roads were wanting, houses rude, swamps undrained, fields unweeded, plains untilled.'[16] Accustomed to the neat fields of a crowded England, Dilke, like the earlier emigrants of the British American Land Company and many another traveller, contrasted frontier country unfavorably with New England which had been pioneered a century or two earlier.

Dilke felt that 'in all history there is nothing stranger than the narrowness of mind which has led us to see in Canada a piece of England and in America a hostile country.'[17] He saw a little more clearly into the North American triangular relationship than those at home: 'That the Canadians hate the Americans can be no reason why we should spend blood and treasure in protecting them against the consequences of their hate. . . . Canada, perhaps, can defend herself, but we most certainly cannot defend her; we provoke much more than we assist.'[18] But it was to be some years before Canada recovered from her fright at the threats of a militant North to fulfil Manifest Destiny by the conquest of its northern neighbor, once the South was subdued; and some years before Canada resentfully realized that English sacrifices of her territory and rights nourished Anglo-American friendship.

The annexationist *Rouges* might have welcomed Dilke's observations on the political future of Canada, but his concluding view that 'Saxondom will rise triumphant from the doubtful struggle' with the 'cheaper races'[19] would have been gall and wormwood to them. The 'Anglo-Saxon' racism of which Dilke was the first popular spokesman nourished the swelling fervor of the imperialist movement until the Boers humbled English pride of race at the turn of the century. This British chosen-people complex, which steadily acquired more adherents as France lost its European hegemony and Britain filled an ever larger place in the world at large, came into head-on collision with the French-Canadian one nourished by the messianic nationalism of Bishops Bourget and Laflèche, Riel, and Mercier.

About 1870, the long dominant English anti-colonialism began to weaken. It was replaced by a new imperialism which was at first commercial in outlook, later political and militaristic, and finally became international rather than nationalistic in character. The roots of the new imperialism were many and diverse, but perhaps the most important factors in its evolution were the rise of the newly united Germany and Italy, the emergence of the United States after its Civil War as a world power, and the growing rivalry England began to experience as 'the workshop of the world' as other nations overtook her original lead in the industrial revolution. The powers launched a frenzied competition for colonies and colonial markets which made England value her empire more dearly and made her fear for her commercial supremacy.

The improvements of communications brought the colonies closer to the mother country, and made possible a greater unity of the empire. The new imperialists were among the leading backers of the Atlantic and Australian cables, of an imperial penny-post, of the 'all-red' line of communications which linked England with the East by way of British steamships and the Canadian Pacific Railway. As England's commercial supremacy was challenged by Germany and the United States, the slogan of 'free trade' gave way to that of 'fair trade,' a term which politely covered a reversion to the old mercantilism under a new system of preferential tariffs within the empire. With such factors at work, the rulers of Britain were pleased to discover that Canada's Confederation, hailed in the 1860's as a step towards emancipation, had increased rather than lessened 'a romantic attachment to the mother country.'[20] An overestimate of this sentiment and a neglect of the concurrent development of Canadian nationalism largely accounted for the failure of the Imperial Federalists.

The forerunner of this movement, which became so influential in the 1880's, was the Colonial Society, later known as the Royal Colonial Institute, which was founded in 1868 and began its meetings in the following year. At the outset it was a non-partisan group whose purpose was to overcome Little Englandism. At its inaugural dinner, attended by notables of the Colonial Office, Gladstone spoke of 'the noble tradition of the unity of the English race.'[21] Its spokesmen, under the leadership of Lord Bury, opposed the ideas of Goldwin Smith and other English colonial separatists with the slogan of 'United Empire.' The note of romantic enthusiasm for the imperial idea which was so marked a feature of the movement in its later stages and its true emotional dynamic was first sounded by the Australian P. F. Labilliere in 1869:

Englishmen at home and their sons in the colonies should not be foreigners to each other . . . My great desire is to show that the idea of dismembering the British Empire should not be entertained for a moment by any good Englishman or by any good colonial; that the union of the Empire is a sentiment or rather a sacred principle, in devoted loyalty to which we should vie with one another . . .

We have, hitherto, only seen England nursing infant nations. I believe, and ardently hope, that she is destined to retain under her mild sway her colonial children, long after they shall attain the maturity and strength of manhood. I am convinced that the existence of such a relation will not only be of vast moral and material advantage both to the parent nation and to the offspring nations, but will constitute an Empire more splendid than any the world has yet seen. [22]

This was the imperial vision which later inspired Kipling and Newbolt, the bards of empire. Fired by it, the Imperial Federalists in 1869 urged the colonial secretary, Lord Granville, to call a conference of colonial representatives to discuss the present unsatisfactory relations with the mother country. This suggestion was coldly rejected by the anti-imperialist Lord Granville, and its sponsors were dismissed as 'presumptuous busybodies' [23] by the colonial press. But they had succeeded at least in arousing English interest in the colonial question, which was brought to the fore by new agitation in favor of state-aided emigration to the colonies, as a remedy for unemployment resulting from the industrial depression of the period. Organized emigration became a favorite theme of the new imperialists and was to remain one, with the twofold object of relieving distress at home and of consolidating the empire.

The new gospel won the adherence of recruits more notable than the founders of the movement. Ruskin held up colonial expansion as the alternative to Mammon-worship for England: 'This is what she must do, or perish; she must found colonies as fast and as far as she is able, formed of her most energetic and worthiest men;—seizing every piece of fruitful waste ground she can set her foot on and there teaching these her colonists that their chief virtue is to be fidelity to their country and that their first aim is to be to advance the power of England by land and sea. . . .' [24] Less eloquent but more influential was the support of the Liberal politician W. E. Forster and of the historian J. A. Froude. Forster soon became one of the chief leaders of the movement, and his address on 'Our Colonial Empire,' delivered at Edinburgh on November 5, 1875, was one of the first statements urging closer imperial union. Froude advocated the imperialist program in 1870 and 1871; then lapsed into the anti-imperialism of the second Disraeli administration; and finally, after 1880, was closely associated with the Imperial Federation League.

Imperial federation was widely publicized by Edward Jenkins, a Radical social reformer, who was the leading spirit of the Westminster Conference on colonial affairs in July 1871. Arguing against the prevailing policy of drift in colonial relations, he concluded his opening address with evangelical fervor:

It is not necessary that we should dissolve this marvelous Empire, the upgrowth of an energy and sacrifice unrivaled in the history of races. It is not necessary that we should dismiss from our family circle that vast sisterhood of nations which has grown up under our parental care—. . . we must take our stand on the unity of our race, on the unity of our interests, on language, religion, laws, manners, customs, and a citizenship that are one. What God hath joined together let no man put asunder.[25]

Labilliere, who spoke on 'Imperial and Colonial Federalism' on this occasion, proposed that the central government should concern itself with defence and diplomacy, leaving commercial policy to the colonies. Other imperialists were not so wise, and aroused opposition in the colonies by their Anglo-centric ideas, according to which it was the colonist's duty to sacrifice his economic advantage to England's interests without receiving in return anything more than the moral satisfaction of being British.

The movement, which had been attracting more and more support from both Whigs and Tories, was taken under the wing of the Conservative Party in Disraeli's Crystal Palace speech of June 24, 1872. He accused the Liberals of attempting to, and nearly succeeding in bringing about, 'the disintegration of the Empire of England.'[26] Supporting colonial self-government, he nevertheless urged reservations to it:

But self-government, in my opinion, when it was conceded, ought to have been conceded as part of a great policy of Imperial consolidation. It ought to have been accompanied by an Imperial tariff, by securities for the people of England for the enjoyment of the unappropriated lands which belonged to the Sovereign as their trustee, and by a military code which should have precisely defined the means and responsibilities by which the colonies should be defended, and by which, if necessary, this country should call for aid from the colonies themselves. It ought, further, to have been accompanied by the institution of some representative council in the metropolis, which would have brought the colonies into constant and continuous relations with the Home Government.[27]

These measures—about whose adoption the Canadian imperialists and nationalists were to contend until well after the First World War—had been neglected by the British Liberals because they slighted the 'moral and political considerations which make nations great'[28] in their preoccupation with the financial burden of the colonies. Disraeli rejoiced that the disintegration of the empire had failed to take place, thanks to 'the sympathy of the colonies for the mother country.'[29] Reconstruction of the colonial empire was a policy adopted by Disraeli more in hope of 'dishing the Whigs,' however, than from any great personal conviction, for he had long regarded the 'wretched colonies' as 'a mill-stone round our necks.'[30]

Disraeli added little to the doctrine of imperialism, but he did correctly judge its popularity and promote the development of jingoism and of what Seeley called the bombastic school, which gloried in red spaces—no matter how empty—on the map and in an empire on which the sun never set. It was also in 1872 that Tennyson added a new epilogue to the *Idylls of the King* in which he hymned an 'ever-broadening England' and 'one isle that knows not her own greatness.'[31] Ten years later he was hailing imperial unity in the blatant 'Hands All Round,' and in 1886 he vented his imperialist sentiments in such vociferous verse as:

> *Sons be welded each and all*
> *Into one Imperial whole,*
> *One with Britain heart and soul!*
> *One life, one flag, one fleet, one throne!*
> *Britons, hold your own.*[32]

Like many another Englishman of the day, Tennyson was a nationalist who thought he was an imperialist, and it was because of this same confusion that the Imperial Federation movement failed.

The new imperialism fed on the fears aroused by the mounting armaments of Europe. In 1878 a Colonial Defence Committee was appointed, succeeded in the following year by a Royal Commission on defence which after sitting for three years recommended an imperial *Kriegsverein*. While the armament race did not become serious until Germany began to threaten Britain's mastery of the seas, there was recurrent talk about war for the next decade.[33] Renewed British colonial expansion, coupled with rivalry with a Germany and a France now seeking colonies, also served to nourish the imperialist spirit. The scramble for African and Asiatic colonies was on, with France and Germany challenging Britain's place as the great colonial power, and the third British Empire was in the making. The imperialism of the '70's, which had stressed the tightening of internal ties, now became expansionist and jingoistic, while trade rivalry and protective tariffs abroad tended to give an economic basis to proposals for unification of the empire. The cry of 'trade follows the flag' enlisted the support of both manufacturers and working people for the tremendous expansion of British territory which took place in the 1880's and 1890's, despite the fact that England's colonial rivals remained her best customers, while her colonies accounted for only one-third of her trade.[34] Acute depression in England in 1876-9, 1883-6, and 1893, coupled with vigorous competition abroad, created a fearful and panicky state of mind which also supplied an impetus for the new imperialism.

In 1883 John Robert Seeley popularized the new imperialism with his Cambridge lectures, *The Expansion of England*, which when published sold 80,000 copies in two years.[35] Though his ideas were permeated with a pan-'Anglo-Saxonism,' Seeley cared more for the state than for the race, unlike his predecessor Dilke. Thus, instead of accepting without alarm the prospect of the break-up of the empire, Seeley wished to preserve and strengthen its unity. In his study of the creation of the first British Empire in the eighteenth century he found the keynote of English history: a process of expansion of the English state. To him 'in that century the history of England is not in England but in America and Asia.'[36] From this dictum he evolved the principle that the colonial and European policies of England were merely different aspects of the same great national development.[37] He urged a new view of Greater Britain:

We must cease altogether to say that England is an island off the northwestern coast of Europe, that it has an area of 120,000 square miles and a population of thirty odd millions . . . When we have accustomed ourselves to contemplate the whole Empire together and call it all England, we shall see here too is a United States. Here too is a great homogeneous people, one in blood, language, religion and laws, but dispersed over a boundless space.[38]

This insular view that the empire was 'one in blood, language, religion, and laws,' with its convenient ignoring of the existence of the French Canadians, the Boers, and the native populations of the greater part of the empire, was to arouse much colonial opposition to Imperial Federation when the theory was applied in practical measures for strengthening the bonds of imperial defence and trade. Seeley, like most Englishmen for three decades to come, was ignorant of the existence of colonial nationalism, which blocked imperial federation until the basic concept of the third British Empire, unity in diversity, was evolved and the British Commonwealth of freely associated autonomous nations was made possible. Seeley was not an original thinker, but he gathered together in eloquent and logical form the arguments for closer imperial union and the retention of the colonies. By his emphasis on the importance of colonial expansion, he brought the colonial question to the fore in the public mind and paved the way for the Imperial Federation League which was launched in 1884.

2

Again it was the Australian Labilliere who took the leading role in founding a society for promoting imperial federation in July 1884. He formed a committee including Captain P. H. Colomb, Sir George Baden-Powell, W. E. Westgarth, J. Dennistoun Wood, and Frederick

Young to further the idea. The committee induced the Liberal leader W. E. Forster to preside over a non-partisan inaugural conference at the Westminster Palace Hotel on August 29, 1884, and to become the first chairman of the Imperial Federation League. The meeting was widely attended by English statesmen of both parties and representatives of colonies—among them James Bryce, Albert Grey (later governor-general of Canada), and D'Alton McCarthy—and received the support of many other influential figures, including Seeley. Among the speakers were Forster, W. H. Smith, a former first lord of the Admiralty; Sir Henry Holland, former under-secretary for the Colonies; Lord Rosebery; Edward Stanhope, former parliamentary secretary to the Board of Trade; Sir Charles Tupper, then high commissioner for Canada; Oliver Mowat, premier of Ontario; and W. Gisbourne, a former New Zealand minister. The resolutions prepared by Labilliere's committee went farther than the colonial spokesmen were prepared to go. Tupper refused to support the original resolution, which expressed a belief that federation or separation were the only alternatives for the empire. After much discussion, unanimous support was given a compromise resolution 'that, in order to secure the permanent unity of the Empire, some form of federation is essential,'[39] and that 'a society be formed of men of all classes to advocate and support the principles of federation.'[40]

At a second meeting on November 18, the Imperial Federation League was formally organized, with Forster as chairman, on the basis of the following resolutions:

That the object of the League be to secure by Federation the permanent unity of the Empire.

That no scheme of Federation should interfere with the existing rights of Local Parliaments as regards local affairs.

That any scheme of Imperial Federation should combine on an equitable basis the resources of the Empire for the maintenance of common interests and adequately provide for an organized defence of common rights.[41]

In the large general committee and smaller executive committee which were charged with the management of the organization, English representatives were preponderant, while the main colonial influence was Canadian. The League came into existence on a wave of imperialist sentiment, and the English press hailed its birth by expressing contempt for the school of Goldwin Smith and other Little Englanders.[42] The League embraced many shades of opinion, with some of its members out-and-out federalists, some interested in consolidation of the empire's military resources, some in preferential trade agreements, and some suspicious of any attempt to encroach upon colonial self-government. Forster himself summed up the situation thus:

> My own impression is that, at first, at any rate, we had better aim at concert among the governments rather than at an imperial parliament. Thanks to the steamship and the telegraph, time and space no longer make such concert very difficult; but distance does prevent a member from being fully in touch with his constituents. We must remember that in order to realise federation, we only want (1) an organization for common defence, and (2) a common foreign policy. Practically, great steps have already been made, not merely as regards defence—thanks to Australian aid—but as regards foreign affairs. I do not believe that any colonial secretary will in future venture to disregard any large self-governing colony in negotiating with any foreign government in matters affecting such colony. . . .[43]

Because of the diversity of aims of its members, the League largely confined itself to propaganda for the general concept of imperial unity. When it attempted to produce a definite plan of federation, it broke up, like the later colonial and imperial conferences for which it paved the way.

Though the first branch of the League was formed in Cape Town before the London organization took form, the Canadian branches played a particularly important part. The parent one was formed in Montreal in 1885 by D'Alton McCarthy and George Denison, with the backing of Archbishop O'Brien of Nova Scotia, Sir Leonard Tilley of New Brunswick, Sir John Schultz· of Manitoba, and Alexander McNull of Ontario.[44] It was a center of opposition to the depression-born annexation movement; and in its reliance on imperial preference as a means of combating annexationism, it differed from the League in England, which, with its Liberal chairman and many Liberal members committed to free trade, could not adopt such economic views. Other Canadian branches were formed at Ingersoll and Halifax in 1886, and at Peterborough, Victoria, and Ottawa in 1887. Toronto, the center of United Empire Loyalism, only boarded the bandwagon in 1888 when the Liberals favored commercial union to the United States. Brantford, St. Thomas, Port Arthur, and Orillia then followed Toronto's lead. Meanwhile branches were formed in Australia and New Zealand, where the League sent the Canadian Dr. George R. Parkin, a zealous imperial missionary whom Lord Rosebery called the 'bagman of Empire.'[45]

The League's monthly organ, *Imperial Federation*, was launched in January 1886, and a few months later Lord Rosebery succeeded Forster as chairman upon the latter's death. Rosebery took an active part in the League's work, and his moderate and compromising spirit did much to keep its unyoked horses headed towards a common goal. The League was responsible for the Indian and Colonial Exhibition of 1886, which displayed the varied resources of the empire. In July its executive committee, upon a motion of the Canadian Alexander A. McGoun which was supported by Sir Alexander Galt, the Canadian high commissioner in London, resolved that a deputation should call upon the prime minister or colonial secretary and urge the summoning of a conference of 'accredited representatives of the United Kingdom and of each of the self-governing colonies' for the following purposes:

(1) For placing upon a satisfactory basis the defence of the ports and commerce of the Empire in time of war.

(2) For promoting direct intercourse, commercial, postal and telegraphic, between the countries of the Empire in time of peace—and other means for securing the closer federation or union of all parts of the Empire.[46]

Peter Redpath of Montreal was one of the delegation which waited upon Lord Salisbury on August 11 and was favourably received. Some three months later the Colonial Secretary Stanhope, a leading member of the League, issued invitations to the first Colonial Conference, which assembled at London on April 4, 1887, under the chairmanship of Sir Henry Holland, one of the prominent members of the League and Stanhope's successor as colonial secretary.

The conference was epoch-making. For the first time responsible statesmen from the self-governing colonies had an opportunity to join with those of the mother country in common discussion of certain questions important to both. The conference was not merely a piece of pageantry designed to add to the effect of the celebration of Queen Victoria's Golden Jubilee. Such an assembly supplied a precedent which was not likely to be reversed in a land whose law was based upon precedent, and from Salisbury's opening remarks it was evident that the British Government regarded this meeting as 'the parent of a long progeniture.'[47] Stanhope had specifically excluded political federation from the agenda of the conference in his invitations, and Holland as chairman was very cautious in the debates on commercial union which took place at the insistence of Queensland and the Cape Colony.

The colonies were far more eager for closer imperial union than the mother country. The British delegates were reluctant to discuss the topic of imperial preference, because of the political danger attached to departure from the traditional doctrine of free trade; but they sought the assistance of the colonies in imperial defence, a question which had become urgent with the emergence of German and French naval rivalry. On the other hand the spokesmen of the

Cape, Victoria, and Queensland favoured closer imperial union through preferential tariffs and had little hesitation in falling in with the defence proposals of the Admiralty. Canada's representatives were scarcely spokesmen of national feeling: Sir Alexander Campbell, the lieutenant-governor of Ontario, called his country a colony and referred to himself as an Englishman, while Sir Sandford Fleming of Canadian Pacific fame was president of the new Ottawa branch of the Imperial Federation League. Neither, however, played a notable part in the proceedings. The Australian Alfred Deakin of Victoria was the leading spokesman of colonial nationalism at the conference, with his request 'that from this time forward, Colonial policy will be considered Imperial policy; that Colonial interests will be considered and felt to be Imperial interests.'[48]

But such views were hesitantly received by the English. Salisbury expressed the opinion that neither a *Zollverein* nor a *Kriegsverein* was yet possible within the British Empire, and brought forward the question of common action for mutual defence as the best field for present discussion and action. The chief feature of the concrete British proposals was that the Australians should undertake the local defence of certain points and strengthen the imperial fleet in Australian waters by the addition of a local force. The proposals also involved colonial contributions to a common imperial defence fund. Canada, which enjoyed the protection of two navies without cost, thanks to the British squadrons based upon Halifax and Esquimalt and the Monroe Doctrine, stood pat on the arrangement made at the time of Confederation whereby Great Britain assumed the responsibility of naval defence and Canada of that by land. Much was made of the value for imperial defence purposes of the Canadian Pacific Railway, completed the previous year. Beyond offering to provide men for the naval service from her Atlantic fisheries, Canada made no effort to go. J. H. Hofmeyr of the Cape Colony offered an argument later echoed in Canada when he said that the colonies must be granted some share or influence in the making of imperial policy before assuming defence responsibilities arising out of it: 'So long as no system of federation or government in which they (i.e., colonial governments) are represented has been hit upon or developed, so long they cannot be expected in duty bound to defend themselves against the European enemies of England.'[49]

But all the colonial spokesmen agreed that there was a common burden to be shared, and none declined outright to share it, although there was disagreement on the manner of doing so. It was Hofmeyr who most strongly advocated a proposal for a commercial union which would solve the problem of colonial contribution to imperial defence by means of an imperial customs tariff. The colonial secretary opposed the passage of a resolution by the conference in favor of this proposal, however, on the grounds that it was beyond the bounds set forth in Stanhope's invitation, and hence of the instructions supplied to the delegates by their own governments. For these reasons the Canadians had taken no part in the discussion. Canada also remained silent on the question of the negotiation of commercial treaties by the colonies, in which it already enjoyed a privileged position, thanks to Galt and Macdonald's efforts in 1859 and 1871. Only on the question of inter-imperial communications did the Canadian delegates take a notable part, with the result that the conference endorsed Sandford Fleming's claims for the Canadian Pacific and urged a cable connecting Canada with Australia.

Sir Samuel Griffeth of Queensland, who had raised the proposal of commercial union which Hofmeyr so ably advocated, expounded at the close of the conference his dream for the future: 'I think we may look forward to seeing this sort of informal Council of the Empire develop until it becomes a legislative body, at any rate a consultative body, and some day, perhaps, a legislative body under conditions that we cannot just now foresee; and that, indeed, meetings such as this will before long be recognized as part of the general governing machinery of the Empire.'[50]

3

Although in general it was true that in 1887 the colonial spokesmen were the most ardent advocates of imperial federation, while the British authorities were reluctant to consider any change in the existing order of imperial affairs and displayed a cautious attitude towards the concrete projects advanced by the imperialists, in Canada the situation was reversed. Canadian national feeling had been awakened at Confederation. Two groups stood apart from the new Canadianism: the French Canadians, who had only reluctantly been won to the support of Confederation; and the United Empire Loyalists, for whom Britain and the empire came before Canada. The Fathers of Confederation did much to foster a sense of nationality with their prophecies of a greater Canada stretching from sea to sea, and their willingness to sink ancient local differences to make their dream come true. D'Arcy McGee has been credited with having done more than any single person to establish faith in the possibility of a 'great northern nation' in America, and with having warmed into active life a patriotic love for the new nationality.[51]

The degeneration of party politics before Confederation brought a reaction in the form of the Canada First movement, which originated in Toronto in 1868, with William A. Foster, George T.

Denison, Henry J. Morgan, Charles Mair, and Robert J. Haliburton as its leading spirits. For these men the nation came before party. They were active expansionists and preached an Ontario crusade to open up the West. Mair's enthusiastic letters to the *Toronto Globe* from the Red River in 1868 attracted attention and were reprinted both in Ontario and in the Maritimes. While at Fort Garry, Mair enlisted the support of Dr. John Schultz, who joined the Canada First group in March 1869.[52] In December of the same year Schultz formed a Canadian party among the Ontario men at Fort Garry, but both he and Mair were seized and imprisoned by Riel. Their Canada First colleagues took a leading part in arousing the anti-Riel agitation in Ontario by exploiting the death of Thomas Scott, and forced the hand of the government in dealing with the situation. The fiery Colonel Denison disrupted the Manitoba negotiations of Cartier and Bishop Taché, and raised the war cry: 'Shall French rebels rule our Dominion?'[53] at a Toronto mass meeting on July 22, 1870. He and his colleagues formed a North-West Emigration Aid Society as a front organization for the Canada First group. It was under the auspices of this society that Foster published his *Canada First* pamphlet, which strongly evoked national pride and achieved a very wide circulation.

After the close of the first Riel affair, and in the midst of the anti-political reaction aroused by the Canadian Pacific scandal, the group founded a political party under the name of the Canadian National Association. Its platform, drafted by Foster and adopted in January 1874, called for consolidation of the empire and a voice in treaties affecting Canada; closer trade relations and eventual political connection with the British West Indies; an income franchise, secret and compulsory voting, minority representation; the reorganization of the Senate and the abolition of property qualifications for members of parliament; the encouragement of immigration and free homesteads; the improvement of the militia system under Canadian officers; and a tariff designed to encourage native industries. There was a division between the old guard of Canada Firsters and new adherents. Denison and his group were imperial federalists, but Foster and W. H. Howland favored an independent Canada. Howland's speech on December 6, 1873, at the first public meeting of the new party, in which he denounced 'toadyism to English aristocratic usages'[54] and English titles for Canadians, labeled the party as one favoring independence. Some of its members no doubt had that aim, but others sought the achievement of nationality within the empire by rounding out Canadian self-government. Still others were chiefly interested in commercial legislation of the sort later adopted under Macdonald's National Policy, which owed much to the ideas of the Canada Firsters. Most members were moved by anti-annexationist sentiment, and agreed with William Caniff that 'the history of the United States was prominently characterized by unswerving efforts to obtain possession of British America.'[55]

Howland took the leading part in the founding of the National Association and the National Club, but he could be attacked, as he was by Denison, as the son of an American, and hence hereditarily tainted with disloyalty. For political leadership, therefore, the Canada Firsters looked to Edward Blake and Thomas Moss, while invoking the name of the martyred D'Arcy McGee as their spiritual father. For two years they possessed a journal of their own in *The Nation*, an independent literary and political journal of high standard founded in 1874. Canada First supported Thomas Moss for election in West Toronto in 1873, despite the denunciation of the Conservative press, and with his success at the polls its hopes rose. Edward Blake was undoubtedly affected by the ideals of Canada First in his celebrated Aurora speech of October 1874, when he proclaimed that 'at no distant period the people of Canada would desire that they should have some greater share of control than they now have in the management of foreign affairs. . . . The time will come when that national spirit which has been spoken of will be truly felt among us, when we shall realise that we are four millions of Britons who are not free.'[56] But the *Globe* and the old-guard Liberals were as harsh in condemning Canada First ideas as the Conservative press. In January 1875 Blake set up an independent organ, *The Liberal*, but in May he re-entered the Mackenzie cabinet which he had quit soon after it took office in 1873, and *The Liberal* ceased publication. As minister of justice Blake sought to extend Canada's national powers and contributed much to English recognition of her national status. Tentatively he favored imperial federation as an ultimate goal.

Meanwhile Foster had proclaimed the aspirations of the more ardent members in his February 1875 address to the National Association in which he said:

We no more advocate Independence than we advocate the Day of Judgment. There are those among us who think, just as Mr. Gladstone, Mr. Lowe, Mr. Brown, Sir Alexander Galt, Mr. Blake and others think, that the relations of Canada to the Empire are proper subjects for discussion; that some day or other separation may or must come, and that now is the time at least to begin to prepare for it. England has been trying for years to make us stand upon our own feet. The troops have been withdrawn. We are allowed to legislate as we please and there is great dislike of interfering with our action. It would rather take us aback if at some early day we were made to strike out for ourselves without any preparation for the event. What must come is either Federation of the Empire or Independence.[57]

The regular party organs attacked this statement as treason, with the Grit journals displaying more vigor than the Conservative ones because the unity of the Liberal party was threatened by the popularity of these ideas in its radical wing.

Blake's return to Liberal orthodoxy broke the back of the Canada First movement. Its only other political leader, Moss, soon after quitted parliament for private life. Foster followed suit, for, like Caniff, he became convinced that 'a Canadian political party is an impossibility. No doubt, however, whichever party be in power will hereafter give more prominence to the views originated and urged by the Canadian Association during its brief existence.'[58] Unfortunately, however, neither the Liberals, who had adopted some of Foster's political ideas, nor the Conservatives, who had adopted his economic ones, abandoned the factional use of religious, racial, sectional, and class differences which the Association had decried as barriers to the achievement of national unity.

4

The protective tariff which had been one of the planks of the Canada First platform was put into force in 1879 by the Conservatives under the name of the National Policy. Alexander Mackenzie, as head of the Liberal Government which was defeated in 1878, had opposed protection and maintained the English Liberal tradition of free trade; but his successors in the leadership of the Liberal Party, Blake and Laurier, favored a moderate protective tariff. Laurier personally inclined towards free trade, but the *Parti National* in Quebec, like the Canada Firsters in Ontario, found it politically expedient to favor protection for native industry in the depressed 1870's. But in the 1880's, when Canada became economically stagnant, new economic policies were urged by sections of both parties. Imperial federation and imperial preference found favor in the Tory camp. Although Macdonald was present at the first meeting of the Imperial Federation League in 1884 and expressed sympathy with its aims, in 1888 he formally expressed his belief in the impracticability of anything like an imperial legislature,[59] and characterized as 'an idle dream'[60] the proposal to establish a uniform tariff throughout the empire. However, in 1890 he stated his desire 'that the connection between the mother country and the colonies shall be drawn closer, and that the large groups of colonies shall assume by degrees a position less of dependence and more of alliance.'[61]

Though Macdonald often proclaimed his British loyalty and made political capital of loyalist sentiment, in practice he restrained the enthusiasm of his more imperialist-minded colleagues. In February 1883 he cautioned Galt, then serving as the first Canadian high commissioner in London, against committing himself too much to the 'project of Imperial Federation, which, in my humble opinion, can never be worked out.'[62] The instructions given the Canadian delegates to the first Colonial Conference did not authorize support of either an imperial tariff or imperial defence. And in 1889, when Charles Tupper as Canadian high commissioner proposed at a London dinner of the Imperial Federation League that a new colonial conference be called and a policy of mutual preferential trade be adopted, he was warned by Macdonald to let it be known that he had spoken only for himself and not for Canada.[63] Tupper, somewhat disgruntled, replied to Macdonald that 'although you and two other members of the Government are on the council of the Imperial Federation League, I have stood somewhat aloof. I have not disguised the opinion that the difficulties in the way of a parliamentary federation were insuperable.'[64]

Macdonald, like the leading English politicians until the advent of Joseph Chamberlain, was content to praise the ideal of imperial federation while opposing any concrete scheme to that end. He was very much of an opportunist in his attitude towards imperialism. Macdonald was in his way a Canadian nationalist, as his fight for the adoption of the term 'Kingdom of Canada' at Confederation, his share in the Treaty of Washington (1871), his attitude towards the Sudan affair, and his refusal of various imperialist gambits all indicate. It was probably more political necessity than conviction that led him to fight his last election on the cry, 'A British subject I was born and a British subject I shall die.'[65] After the Riel affair of 1885 had inflamed English-Canadian racial feeling, Macdonald had to restrain the imperialist hotheads in his own camp who sought a holy war against the French Canadians on all fronts, regardless of the political necessities which shaped Macdonald's course. Only after his death did they win sufficient authority in the Conservative Party to align Quebec against it in a solid Liberal phalanx. Since that day the federal Conservative Party has never been a real force in Quebec.

Since imperial federation and imperial preferential trade found favor chiefly in Tory quarters, the Liberal party pursued two other alternatives to the Canadian dilemma. Many Liberals were sympathetic to the schemes of commercial or customs union with the United States which were advanced in the 1880's and 1890's. The prophet of this minority group was Goldwin Smith, the brilliant Oxford don who first abandoned England for the United States, and then the United States for Canada, where from his home in ultra-loyalist Toronto he preached the inevitability of the union of English-speaking North America. To him Canada was destined to become the Scotland of North America.[66] A larger group of Liberals favored independence, which had been preached by Galt and McDougall in the early seventies as the next step in national development after Confederation. In 1878 under Mackenzie and Blake Canada had won the right to self-government in domestic affairs and the right to make her own commercial treaties, and at the outset of his leadership of the Liberal Party Laurier spoke of his hopes for Canadian nationhood: 'The time is coming when the present relations of Great Britain and Canada must either become closer or be severed altogether. . . . If ever and whenever Canada chooses, to use the language of Lord Palmerston, to stand by herself, the separation will take place not only in peace but in friendship and love . . . But this is not the question of to-day.'[67] In 1889 and 1890 the young Liberals of Toronto favored complete independence, with the support of the *Globe,* which commented in February 1888 in connection with the Atlantic fisheries dispute:

So long as the Canadian people remain unwilling to assume the responsibility of independent nationality, so long must they expect to be despoiled by the United States with British consent and aid. . . . The truth is that the connection seriously embarrasses England and seriously embarrasses and injures Canada. So long as we insist upon retaining it, we cannot justly complain of suffering for the indulgence in a noble loyalty to a country five-sixths of us never saw.[68]

As an alternative to complete independence, the *Globe* also advocated that the empire should become a league of equal self-governing states under the Crown, thus anticipating the British Commonwealth of Nations born some thirty years later.

With free trade still in the saddle in Britain, Canada had little hope of winning a larger share of that market. Her other and more natural market was the United States, from which she had been largely shut out in 1866 by the termination of the Reciprocity Treaty of 1854 and to which she had since been unable to win greater access, though both Liberal and Conservative administrations had gone more than halfway to meet the Americans. Now, for the first time since the Civil War, the high-tariff Republican party was out of power, while American manufacturers were as anxious for new markets as were the producers of Canadian raw materials.

In 1887 Erastus Wiman, a Canadian who had made his fortune in the States and was interested in Canadian telegraph companies, proposed not mere limited reciprocity but complete free trade between Canada and the United States, with a common tariff against the outside world. Wiman owed the idea to Samuel Ritchie, an American capitalist interested in Ontario railways and the Sudbury ore deposits, and to Hezekiah Butterworth, his legal advisor, who was a member of Congress. Wiman's scheme was supported by Goldwin Smith and found favor in farming, mining, and lumbering circles in Canada. The movement centered in Ontario and received the support of the *Toronto Mail*, then in revolt against 'French domination' as a result of the Riel episode, and of the *Globe*, which thought commercial union would favor the development of national and imperial sentiment. Macdonald and Langevin, with their close ties to the protected manufacturers of Ontario and Quebec, were not interested in Wiman's proposal; but Tupper, hailing from the Maritimes which favored low tariffs, was in a different position. At Wiman's suggestion Tupper visited Washington in 1887 and consulted directly with Secretary of State Bayard, thus short-circuiting the customary triangular negotiations through London. He offered trade reciprocity in exchange for reciprocity of fishing rights. The subsequent Fisheries Treaty was killed in the United States Senate, but a precedent had been established for direct negotiations between Ottawa and Washington.

On the Liberal side, Laurier was not prepared to endorse commercial union, but favored the traditional Liberal program of reciprocity: 'I may say—and it is my actual policy—that the time has come to abandon the policy of retaliation followed thus far by the Canadian government, to show the American people that we are brothers, and to hold out our hands to them, with a due regard for the duties we owe to our mother country.'[69] But his lieutenant Sir Richard Cartwright came out flatly for commercial union, and was joined by David Mills and John Charlton, prominent Ontario Liberals. The sentiment in favor of commercial union was confined largely to Ontario, and at the first Interprovincial Conference at Quebec in October 1887 the delegates unanimously favored unrestricted reciprocity rather than commercial union. Nevertheless the movement for commercial union, supported as it was by some of the wealthiest men in New York, continued to develop. In March 1888 Cartwright proposed in the House a resolution calling for free trade between Canada and the United States in all manufactured and natural products. Laurier declared that he would have liked to make a similar bargain with Britain, but that it was impossible under her free-trade policy. Rejecting the sentimental appeals of the Conservatives for preserving the British connection at all costs, he said that this was a question of duty and not of sentiment: 'If I have to choose between the duty I owe to England and the duty I owe to my native land, I stand by my native land.'[70] Despite the vigorous support of the Liberals, free trade was rejected by the full Conservative majority in an April vote.

Subsequently, the Canadian advocates of commercial union were embarrassed by statements made during the presidential campaign in the United States that fall. Senator Sherman, chairman of the Foreign Affairs Committee, speaking in the Senate on September 18, 1888, favored commercial union as a step toward the political union which seemed to be manifest destiny. On September 26 the *Chicago Tribune* said that if Canada were ready neither for commercial or political union, 'her safety lies in not provoking the United States by unfair or unfriendly dealing, for when the provocation comes, Uncle Sam will reach out and take her in, in order to ensure quiet, and neither she nor her venerable old mother can prevent it.'[71] In December the *New York World* published a map showing Canada included in the United States. W. C. Whitney, Secretary of the Navy, said four armies of 25,000 men each could easily conquer Canada, while Ben Butler described annexation as Canada's fate: 'Peacefully, we hope; forcefully, if we must.'[72] With the defeat of Cleveland in the November 1888 elections, reciprocity became an impossibility in American politics, and the McKinley tariff bill of 1890 bore hardly on Canadian trade.

A group of prominent Republicans then seemingly sought to force political union or annexation by reducing Canada to economic misery. Among the leading members of the Continental Union League which was formed in New York in 1892 were Charles A. Dana, Andrew Carnegie, John Jacob Astor, Ethan Allen, Warner Miller, Edward Lauterbach William C. Whitney, Orlando B. Potter, Horace Porter, John Hay, Theodore Roosevelt, Elihu Root, Cornelius N. Bliss, Chauncey M. Depew, William Walter Phelps, General Henry W. Slocum, General Granville W. Dodge, Charles Francis Adams, Oliver Ames, Seth Low, Bourke Cochrane, Charles L. Tiffany, Nathan Strauss, and many others. In Toronto there was an allied Continental Union Association, with Goldwin Smith as honorary president, John Morrison as president, and T. M. White as secretary.[73] Wiman's most useful Canadian colleague was Edward Farrer, who as chief editorial writer of the *Toronto Mail* in 1887 played a leading role in the creation of commercial union sentiment, and in the summer of 1890 became chief editorial writer for the *Globe*.

Aside from glorification of 'the old man, the old flag, and the old policy,' the Conservative campaign in the 1891 election was based upon the charge that the Liberals were working directly for annexation. Damaging support was given this charge by Macdonald's exposure of a secret pamphlet written by Farrer for American consumption. This document outlined an American policy which would lead Canada to annexation by taxing Nova Scotian fishing vessels, by the suspension of the railroad bonding privilege, and by other preventive measures. Farrer was known to be intimate with Sir Richard Cartwright, and both Cartwright and Honoré Mercier were accused of intriguing with the annexationists in the States.[74] In his manifesto to the electors Macdonald grandly protested: 'A British subject I was born, a British subject I will die. With my utmost strength, with my last breath, will I oppose the "veiled treason" which attempts by sordid means and mercenary proffers to lure our people from their allegiance.'[75] Back of Macdonald stood the business interests of Canada, headed by the Canadian Pacific Railway, which needed the support of its traditional political ally for British loans to cover its extensions into the United States. Macdonald's majority was secured largely thanks to the Canadian Pacific, which returned a Conservative candidate in every constituency but one through which its main line passed.[76]

The Liberals made large gains in both Quebec and Ontario, despite the support won for Macdonald by his own flag-waving and by the drum-beating of such impassioned imperialists as Colonel Denison. But the Liberals' new strength was weakened by division, for the former leader Blake did not approve of the fiscal policy which had been adopted during his absence in England. He issued a manifesto against commercial union to his old constituency of West Durham, which was withheld at Laurier's request until after the election. In it Blake characterized the policy he would have preferred—a moderate tariff with restricted reciprocity—as impossible, an imperial *Zollverein* as outside the realm of practical politics, and commercial union as leading to political union. Though Blake also condemned Tory policy, the net result of his utterance was to give support to Tory charges against the Liberals. But with stagnant trade and continued mass emigration from Canada to the States, public faith in a protective tariff continued to decline, and the advocates of reciprocity and commercial union won more and more adherents.

In consequence the imperialists redoubled their efforts, and the Canadian members of the Imperial Federation League were delighted when the 1894 Ottawa Trade Conference of the self-governing colonies, with a non-participating British representative, passed a strong resolution in favor of imperial preference, coupled with a request to the British government to denounce the Belgian and German trade treaties which extended to those countries any preference Canada might grant to Britain. But the Canadian imperialists had long pressed their case farther than their British colleagues were willing to go, and thanks to the strength of the free trade interests in the parent Imperial Federation League, that body was dissolved in November 1893 without warning to the Canadian members. Those who had been responsible for the dissolution formed the Imperial Federation (Defence) Committee, with a program calling for cash contributions from the colonies to the Army and Navy. The Canadians were still in favor of a *Zollverein* rather than a *Kriegsverein*, and Colonel Denison was dispatched to England to urge that course. He succeeded in rallying enough preferential tariff-minded members of the old League to form a new body, which was inaugurated as the British Empire League in January 1895. At a subsequent meeting in March the Canadian League changed its name and affiliated itself with the new league.

5

The man who became colonial secretary in the new Unionist government of Lord Salisbury in 1895 personified the new imperialism which combined Anglo-Saxon racism, the doctrine of the white man's burden, and the need for new overseas markets. Joseph Chamberlain had begun his political career as a reformer concerned with local government in Birmingham. When he first entered national politics as a Liberal of radical socialist sympathies, he had opposed Disraeli's adventures in imperialism, but found himself hampered by the more conservative elements in the party. When Gladstone set out to repair by Home Rule the Irish economy which had been destroyed by agricultural depression, Chamberlain devloped a passion for the preservation of the empire. The Union was his form of United Empire Loyalism. He broke with Gladstone on Home Rule and gravitated toward the Conservative Party, which had always been the party of imperialism.

Partyless for the time being, he was appointed as head of the British delegation to the fisheries arbitration in Washington. During a holiday recess of the commission, Chamberlain was guest of honor at a dinner given by the Toronto Board of Trade on December 30, 1887. Responding to the toast of 'The Commercial Interests of the Empire,' he spoke of an idea with which he had become obsessed through the influence of Dilke and Seeley:

The idea is the greatness and importance of the destiny which is reserved for the Anglo-Saxon race—for that proud, persistent, self-asserting, and resolute stock that no change of climate or condition can alter, and which is infallibly destined to be the predominant force in the future history and civilization of the world . . . I am an Englishman. I am proud of the old country from which I come. I am not unmindful of the glorious traditions attached to it, of those institutions moulded by slow centuries of noble endeavour; but I should think that our patriotism was warped and stunted indeed if it did not embrace the Greater Britain beyond the seas—the young and vigorous nations carrying everywhere a knowledge of the English tongue and English love of liberty and law . . . I refuse to make any distinction between the interests

of Englishmen in England, in Canada, and in the United States . . .*
Our past is theirs. Their future is ours. You cannot if you would break
the invisible bond which binds us together . . . It may yet be that the
federation of Canada may be the lamp lighting our path to the federation
of the British Empire. If it is a dream—it may be only the imagination
of an enthusiast—it is a grand idea. It is one to stimulate the patriotism
and statesmanship of every man who loves his country; and whether
it be destined or not to perfect realization, at least let us all cherish the
sentiment it inspires. Let us do all in our power to promote it and
enlarge the relations and goodwill which ought always to exist between
sons of England throughout the world and the old folks at home.[77]

Having thus eloquently furthered the work of those in Canada who
were engaged in promoting imperial federation and in scotching
commercial union, Chamberlain returned to England.

He had become a convert to imperialism, and henceforward
devoted most of his attention to imperial affairs. In 1888 he advocated not only the preservation of the empire but its extension in
Africa, as essential to further 'the necessary work of colonization and
civilization' and 'to justify our position as a nation.'[78] His tour of
Egypt in 1889 crystalized his imperialism. Earlier in that year,
speaking of imperial federation, he said: 'Although I have never
seen my way to any practical scheme of Imperial Federation, yet I
do not deem that idea to be altogether beyond the reach of statesmanship. I hold it to be right and proper that we should do nothing
to prevent it; that we should do everything in our power to bring
it about; and as the first step to any such arrangement I am convinced that the perfection of our means of mutual defence stands in
the foreground.'[79] When Colonel Denison visited England in May
1890, he got a pledge from Chamberlain that the latter would
examine the policy of imperial preference, which was favored by
Canadian imperialists.[80] Chamberlain was already committed to
the doctrine that trade follows the flag, and that reducing the empire
would reduce British trade. To him, preservation and extension of the
empire were matters of economic necessity.[81] But as yet he was un-
convinced that Britain ought to sacrifice free trade to the undoubted
interest of the colonies in a commercial union of the empire.[82]

Five more years of expanding empire and contracting trade at
least partially converted him to the Canadian view that tariff reform
was essential to prosperity. Within a few months after taking office
as colonial secretary—a hitherto minor post which he chose 'in the
hope of furthering closer union between them (the colonies) and the
United Kingdom'[83]—Chamberlain sent a circular dispatch to the
colonial governors requesting detailed trade surveys:

* This observation was made in the midst of the greatest emigration from Canada to
the United States.

I am impressed with the extreme importance of securing as large a share as possible of the mutual trade of the United Kingdom and the Colonies for British producers and manufacturers, whether located in the Colonies or the United Kingdom . . . I wish to investigate thoroughly the extent to which, in each of the Colonies, foreign imports of any kind have displaced, or are displacing, similar British goods, and the causes of such displacement.

I am further desirous of receiving from you a return of any products of the Colony under your government which might advantageously be exported to the United Kingdom or other parts of the British Empire, but do not at present find a sufficient market there.[84]

This unprecedented inquiry, framed in businesslike terms new to the Colonial Office after Chamberlain had consulted with the Canadian high commissioner and the agents of the unfederated colonies of Australia and Africa, foreshadowed an attempt to realize the dream of imperial federation. It was the first step in that direction by the mother country after the colonies had urged such measures for over a decade.

Chamberlain outlined his scheme for an imperial *Zollverein* on March 25, 1896 at a dinner of the Canada Club in London. He sought to take advantage of the loyalism aroused by Cleveland's militant manifesto on Venezuela, by the Jamieson Raid, and by the Kaiser's telegram to Kruger, coupling imperial defence and imperial trade:

What is the greatest of common obligations? It is Imperial defence. What is the greatest of our common interests? It is Imperial trade. And these two are very closely connected. It is very difficult to see how you can pretend to deal with the great question of Imperial defence without having first dealt with the question of Imperial trade. . . . My proposition is that a true Zollverein for the Empire, that a free trade established throughout the Empire, although it would involve the imposition of duties against foreign countries, and would be in that respect a derogation from the high principles of free trade, and from the practice of the United Kingdom up to the present time, would still be a proper subject for discussion and might possibly lead to a satisfactory arrangement if the colonies on their part were willing to consider it . . . it would undoubtedly lead to the earliest possible development of their great natural resources, would bring to them population, would open to them the enormous market of the United Kingdom.[85]

Within the empire 'protection must disappear,' and then a council of the empire might be constituted on the basis of the *Zollverein*. Chamberlain declared that he spoke only for himself: 'I want, not to lay down a course of policy which must be followed, but I want to provoke discussion . . . To organize an Empire—one may almost say to create an Empire—greater and more potent for peace and

civilization of the world than any that history has ever known—that
is a dream if you like, but a dream of which no man need be ashamed.'
But many in England were as yet unwilling to abandon free trade,
and the colonies were equally unwilling to abandon protection.
Chamberlain urged his scheme upon the Empire Congress of Chambers of Commerce which met in London in June 1896, but the
Canadian delegates attacked free trade, while the British representatives characterized tariffs as tabu.

So discouraging was the reaction that Chamberlain abandoned
his scheme, and even doubted whether it was worthwhile to summon
a colonial conference. To him Canada was the bellwether of the
colonies, and Canada's new premier was a French Canadian who
stood at the head of a party committed to commercial union with
the United States rather than with Great Britain. There seemed
little hope of winning Laurier to a dream of a British *Zollverein*,
but Chamberlain exerted some pressure. At a meeting in September
1896 with Sir Richard Cartwright, Chamberlain said that reciprocity with the United States would be regarded as a great step toward
separation, while 'if the Canadian government proposed to reduce
their tariff generally, or at least to allow the mother country to share
any reductions which they might make to the United States, there
would be nothing but satisfaction on the part of the British Government and people.' Chamberlain backed his position with a threat to
halt his plan to subsidize a fast steamship service to Canada.[86]

Meanwhile he invited the premiers of all the self-governing colonies
to come to London for Queen Victoria's Diamond Jubilee as state
guests, at the head of picked contingents of colonial troops who were
to march in honor of the Queen. All the premiers accepted, and
then Chamberlain decided to hold a colonial conference whose purpose he defined as 'an interchange of ideas about matters of common and material interest, about closer commercial union, about the
representation of the Colonies, about common defence, about
legislation, about other questions of equal importance, which cannot
but be productive of the most fruitful results.'[87] This was a very
different attitude from the caution displayed by the British Government in organizing the 1887 Conference.

Meanwhile in Canada, rebuffed in their efforts to win commercial
union or tariff concessions from the United States early in 1897, in
the first budget of the new government the Liberals provided a tariff
which did not vary greatly from the National Policy which they had
denounced for eighteen years. For the sake of consistency it was
called a revenue tariff, but in reality it was protectionist, though
there was an over-all reduction of about 10 per cent in duties. A
special feature provided a minimum tariff for British goods, thus
pleasing both free traders and imperial preference advocates at home

and abroad. The Liberals sought to promote freer trade, particularly with Great Britain and the United States, but reciprocity with the latter country had been doomed first by the McKinley Tariff and then by the still higher Dingley Tariff of 1897.

As Canada emerged from the Great Depression which had afflicted it since the 1870's, with the rise in wholesale prices and the decline in transportation costs, it gained self-confidence. Annexation no longer seemed inevitable, and the unneighborly policy of the United States, carefully made the most of by imperialist spokesmen in Canada, strengthened national and imperial sentiment. In the Venezuela and Yukon incidents, the bumptious imperialism of the United States gravely offended the growing sense of Canadian nationalism. It was easy for this nationalism to take an imperialist channel for the moment, when American markets were barred and English markets stood open, absorbing a 57 per cent increase of Canadian exports in 1896, and when the celebration of the Jubilee in June 1897 served to focus pride of race and pride of empire. The gorgeous pageantry of the Jubilee provided an environment in which Joseph Chamberlain was to find it easy to lead to his way of imperialist thinking the delegates to the Colonial Conference.

Canada's course before the conference met in June, which John Hay characterized as that of 'a married flirt,' changed the whole imperialist movement. Her continuance of protection killed the notion of an imperial *Zollverein* with complete internal free trade. But her provision of a British preference aroused English enthusiasm for Canada. According to the *New York Times* correspondent, Laurier was expected to be 'the most conspicuous and the most popular of all the visiting premiers of the Empire.'[88] The Canadian move suggested to Chamberlain one that might be agreed upon by all the self-governing colonies. As he anticipated, all the colonial premiers supported the Canadian plan which he commended to the conference, and promised to introduce the necessary legislation. But for the rest there was little advance of Chamberlain's ideas, despite the overpowering hospitality which was lavished upon the guests. Laurier wrote home: 'I am not sure whether the British Empire needs a new constitution, but I am certain that every Jubilee guest will need one.'[89] The five sittings of the conference were held at intervals between June 24 and July 8, in the midst of a round of pageants, ceremonies, dinners, luncheons, balls, garden-parties, and country-house weekends.

As chairman of the conference Chamberlain tactfully expressed his desire 'rather to learn your views than to press ours upon you.'[90] The eleven premiers were the heads of their respective states, and were made imperial privy councilors. The assembly thus approximated an imperial cabinet. Chamberlain suggested the possibility of a 'great council of the Empire,' which might grow into a federal council, 'to which we must always look forward as our ultimate ideal.'[91] Laurier, singled out for special honor by being knighted against his will, caught up the idea of colonial representation in an imperial parliament and told the National Liberal Club that 'it would be the proudest moment of my life if I could see a Canadian of French descent affirming the principles of freedom in the parliament of Great Britain.'[92] Yet he and other colonial spokesmen voiced the view that 'colonies are born to become nations,' 'in a few years the earth will be encircled by a series of independent nations, recognizing, however, the suzerainty of England.' No concrete plans for an imperial council were realized.

In the matter of defence Chamberlain pressed for 'some adequate and regular system of contributions to sea-power'[93] and an interchange of troops between Great Britain and the colonies. The Australians agreed to continue their naval subsidy for the British squadron defending their home waters, but Canada made no response to a request from the Admiralty to open similar negotiations. Chamberlain's suggestion of an interchange of troops between Britain and the colonies was not taken up by the colonial spokesmen. Laurier, however, in a public speech observed in an unguarded moment of rhetorical excess: 'Let the watch fires be lit on the hills, and Canada will be the first to respond.'[94]

In the matter of commercial relations, Chamberlain implied that a full imperial *Zollverein* was impracticable for the present. Canada's introduction of the principle of preference had raised an international difficulty. By treaty Germany and Belgium had a right to commercial equality with Britain throughout the empire, and many other countries could claim the same privilege through the most-favored-nation clause. He suggested that the United Kingdom would not hesitate to denounce these treaties if such was the will of conference, and he implied that the other colonies should then follow Canada's example. All the premiers favored the denunciation of the treaties, and agreed to urge the cause of British preference at home. And at the final session the premiers adopted a resolution that conferences should be held at regular intervals, preferably triennially. Chamberlain made the most of this forerunner of a permanent imperial organization: 'That is the beginning of it—the beginning of a Federal conference.'[95] Before July was out, the British Government gave notice of its repudiation of the Belgian and German treaties, and thanks to Canada the empire was launched on a preferential tariff policy.

After his stay in England, Laurier paid a visit to France, Canada's other mother country. Through public speeches and private interviews he endeavored to improve the relations between Britain and

France which had been strained by colonial rivalry in Egypt and the Sudan.[96] Since his statement in England that he was 'British to the core,' had aroused criticism in France, he spoke eloquently of Canada's double loyalty: 'We are faithful to the great nation which gave us life, we are faithful to the great nation which has given us liberty.'[97] He urged a renewal of the close friendship that had bound France and Britain together in the Crimean War. He preached the possibilities of trade between France and Canada. And in a speech before the British Chamber of Commerce in Paris he clarified his ideas on the question of imperial organization:

It may be that this solution will be found in the great principle of imperial representation. The colonies of France are represented in her parliament. Our situation is very different. We have not merely local autonomy, but the most complete legislative independence. If, as the price of imperial representation, we had to renounce our autonomy, our legislative independence, we would have none of it. If imperial representation is to be the solution, it can only be as the complement and not as the negation of that which exists today.[98]

Once more he pictured a French Canadian representing Canada at Westminster. Privately he told French statesmen that Anglo-French goodwill was essential for the peace of the world and of Canada in particular. Having successfully fulfilled his role of unofficial ambassador, Sir Wilfrid passed on to Switzerland and Rome, where he had an interview with the Pope. And then, by way of France and Ireland he returned home, making a triumphant progress up the St. Lawrence and finding public opinion united in his favor. Only a few ultra-imperialists growled at his reference to Canada as a nation and urged more rapid realization of the goal of imperial unity.

6

The bill for Laurier's profession of imperialist sentiments at the Jubilee was soon presented. For all his business methods Chamberlain was an emotional imperialist who rated sentiment higher than interest as a governing factor.[99] His pride of race and sense of the British mission drove him onward in the path of expansion until war in South Africa became inevitable. Meanwhile he had quietly prepared the way for Canadian contribution to imperial 'defence' by the appointment in 1898 of Lord Minto as governor-general and of Major-General Edward Hutton as commander of the Canadian militia.

The new governor-general, a zealous soldier who was chiefly noted for having broken his neck in the Grand National and living

to tell the tale, had as Lord Melgund served as the governor-general's
military secretary in Canada from 1883-5. When in August 1884 his
friend General Wolseley asked Lansdowne for 300 *voyageurs* to serve
under Melgund in the Gordon Relief Expedition to the Sudan,[100]
Melgund had declined the command, which went to Major Frederick
Denison, but had personally enlisted 367 men, mostly French-
Canadian raftsmen, but including some English Canadians from
Ontario, and some Caughnawaga Indians, whom Wolseley had
particularly requested.[101] In this task Melgund had the hearty
co-operation of Adolphe Caron, the minister of militia. The five
officers who served with the *voyageur* contingent included Captain T.
Aumond, the Abbé Bouchard, a former missionary in Egypt, and Dr.
Hubert Neilson, John Neilson's grandson who was as much French
as he was English.[102]

Later in that same year Melgund served on a Canadian defence
committee, and early in 1885 he had prepared a memorandum on
preparations to be made against the anticipated Fenian raids on
Canada. Before the Sudan campaign came to a close, he was active
in the scheme of raising a Canadian contingent which at London's
suggestion was to serve in Egypt as an imperial force and not as
Canadian militia.[103] In the Riel Rising of that summer Melgund
was General Middleton's chief of staff. Macdonald, who had opposed the Sudan expeditionary force, nonetheless subsequently
offered Melgund the post of commandant of the Mounted Police;
and when he left Canada in the fall of 1885, told him: 'I shall not
live to see it, but some day Canada will welcome you back as
Governor-General.'[104] Now at Wolseley's instigation Minto was
named to the post by Chamberlain, whose imperialism he admired,
although he abominated Rhodes' 'dirty speculations'[105] in South
Africa. Laurier judged Minto thus: 'When he came to Canada
first, he was absolutely untrained in constitutional practice, knew
little but horses and soldiering, but he took his duties to heart, and
became an effective governor, if sometimes very stiff.'[106]

General Hutton was one of the best-known of Wolseley's younger
disciples, and had organized a co-operative defence plan for the
Australian colonies. As one of the school of soldiers who had been
inspired by Wolseley to work out the problems of imperial defence, he
held strong views on the necessity of colonial participation. He had
been at Eton and seen service in Egypt with Minto, who agreed with
the policy that Hutton attempted to inaugurate, but thought it best
that he himself 'should not appear too military.'[107] After his first
few months in Canada Minto gave this report of Hutton to Wolseley:
'The country itself is very military in feeling, and he has struck a
right note, with the result that the people and the press generally
are on his side. . . . He really has put life into everything, is all over

the place organizing and inquiring, and entertains a great deal, feeding military, political, and civilian society with great judgment, and evidently excellent effect.'[108] If anything, Hutton was too successful, for his apostolic zeal brought him into conflict with the ministers, whose hand he frequently forced by speeches, interviews, and manipulation of the press. These minor difficulties were soon to create major ones.

Negotiations concerning Canada's share in a possible South African war began in March 1899, when the War Office and Admiralty raised through Minto the question of Canadian troops serving outside of Canada. In 1885 Sir John Macdonald had interpreted Section 79 of the Militia Act as meaning that Canadian troops could not be ordered outside of North America, though this interpretation was seemingly based upon his reluctance to sacrifice men and money 'to get Gladstone and Co. out of the hole they have plunged themselves into by their own imbecility.'[109] When Minto consulted Laurier and his cabinet on the question, they held that the imperial government had the right under the act to order Canadian troops anywhere in time of war, but for Laurier the decisive point was whether the troops were required for the defence of Canada, not whether the war was at home or abroad. In April the South African League Congress, an organization inspired by Cecil Rhodes, urged by cable the despatch by the British Empire League in Canada of a sympathetic resolution to the imperial government.[110] But Principal G. M. Grant of Queen's University, a leading figure in the League, sympathized with the Boers, as did such divergent Canadian public figures as Laurier and Goldwin Smith, and no action was taken at the time.

In July official and unofficial imperial pressure really began to be exerted on Canada. Chamberlain wrote to Minto on July 3 that war was probable and asked whether Canadian troops would be offered: 'Such a proof of the unity of the Empire would have a great moral effect and might go far to secure a pacific settlement. Is such an offer probable? If so, it should be made soon, but I do not desire that it should be the result of external pressure or suggestion.'[111] Minto promptly urged upon Laurier the adoption of the principle of Canadian participation in imperial wars by such an offer. Meanwhile a representative of the South African League and agent of Rhodes, J. Davis Allen, came to Ottawa in July from England. Through leading Canadian imperialists he agitated for the passage of a resolution expressing sympathy with the imperial government's efforts to obtain justice for British subjects in the Transvaal.[112] On July 13 Colonel Sam Hughes, an Ontario Orangeman, fervidly supported Canadian intervention in South Africa, citing Queensland's offer of troops.[113] Laurier yielded to pressure and on July 31

moved the requested resolution, which was seconded by George
Eulas Foster and passed unanimously by a fervid House which
then sang 'God Save the Queen.' This was the only parliamentary
action on the question. But Laurier refused to make the offer of
troops which the British government desired, writing Minto: 'The
present case does not seem to be one in which England, if there is
war, ought to ask us, or even expect us, to take a part; nor do I
believe that it would add to the strength of the imperial sentiment to
assert at this juncture that the colonies should assume the burden of
military expenditure, except—which God forbid!—in the case of
pressing danger.'[114]

But during August and September, thanks to the activity of
British agents which found expression in agitation for Canadian
participation by Hugh Graham's *Montreal Star* and the Conservatives under Sir Charles Tupper, public opinion in English Canada—
notably in Toronto, where Allen made great play with Milner's
despatches to Chamberlain[115]—was aroused against the Boers.
Sam Hughes offered to raise a regiment or brigade for South African
service, while other militia officers volunteered the services of their
battalions. When Hughes' offer was refused by the minister of militia,
he renewed it directly to Chamberlain. Meanwhile Minto and
Hutton worked out a plan for a Canadian contingent on September
5, offering the command to Major Oscar Pelletier, and turned the
project over to the minister of militia. Seemingly, Minto privately
sympathized as late as September 28 with Laurier:

From the point of view of a Canadian statesman I don't see why they
should commit their country to the expenditure of lives and money for
a quarrel not threatening imperial safety and directly contrary to the
opinion of a colonial government at the Cape. . . . Sir Wilfrid told me
the other day that if the question were reconsidered he should call a
Cabinet Council and ask me to be present. I hope he won't, for I should
be in a nice muddle—my chief at home thirsting for blood, all my friends
here ditto, and myself, while recognizing imperial possibilities, also
seeing the iniquity of the war, and that the time for colonial support has
hardly yet arrived.[116]

Hutton further alienated the cabinet by telling Richard Scott of
Ontario, who with Israel Tarte of Quebec headed the opposition to
participation, that if war came, public opinion would force the
government to send troops. Then on October 3 the *Canadian Military
Gazette*, an unofficial but authoritative publication, announced that
if war began in the Transvaal, the government would offer a force
from the militia, and gave the details of Hutton's scheme. Seemingly
this article was not the work of Hutton himself, but of an over-
zealous subordinate who shared his views. Laurier promptly denied

the statement as 'pure invention,' and said troops could not be sent without the permission of parliament.[117]

On the same day Chamberlain cabled Minto in the same terms used to the governors of colonies which had already offered contingents, proposing a detailed scheme of organization for Canadian units. The troops were to be integrated with the imperial forces, with no Canadian ranking higher than major. Minto urged Laurier to reconsider the question of an official contingent, thus anticipating Chamberlain's letter of October 4 which informed Minto: 'We do not intend to accept any offer from volunteers. We do not want the men, and the whole point of the offer would be lost unless it was endorsed by the Government of the Colony.'[118] Minto was in New York when the cable arrived, and Hutton in the North-West, while Laurier left Ottawa on October 7 to attend an international gathering in Chicago. After Laurier's return on the 12th—the date hostilities commenced in South Africa—the cabinet weighed its action for two days in the face of the agitation which had been aroused by publication of Chamberlain's cable.

Tupper and the opposition, moved by both imperialist emotion and thirst for office, attacked the government for its delay and its unwillingness to send a Canadian contingent, incidentally arousing anti-French-Canadian sentiment. For Quebec was unmoved by the wave of British feeling which had swept Ontario. *La Patrie*, the organ of Laurier's Quebec organizer Tarte, took its stand on the principle of no share in Britain's wars without a share in Britain's councils. The independent *La Presse* expressed the fundamental French-Canadian attitude toward foreign wars, which was later to cause two more major crises in Canada's national life: 'We French Canadians belong to one country, Canada; Canada is for us the whole world; but the English Canadians have two countries, one here and one across the sea.'[119] A smaller third group would have had no objection to unofficial participation by Canadian volunteers.

On October 13 the government reached a compromise, passing an order-in-council which did not authorize an official contingent but did undertake to equip and transport up to 1,000 volunteers. The order was ingeniously framed to avoid the difficulties with which the government was beset:

The Prime Minister, in view of the well-known desire of a great many Canadians who are ready to take service under such conditions, is of opinion that the moderate expenditure which would thus be involved for the equipment and transportation of such volunteers may readily be undertaken by the Government of Canada without summoning Parliament, especially as such expenditure, under such circumstances, cannot be regarded as a departure from the well-known principles of constitutional government and colonial practice, nor construed as a precedent for future action.[120]

In a letter of October 14 to Chamberlain, Minto thus explained Laurier's position:

> . . . though he thoroughly approves the action of the Imperial Government on South Africa and admits the undoubted necessity of war, he has not been inclined to admit the policy of this colony accepting pecuniary liabilities for the old country. He says it is contrary to the traditions of Canadian history. . . . He considers, however, that the acceptance of your offer to contribute to pay and transport of troops so minimizes the expense that the principle of non-acceptance of pecuniary liability is hardly departed from.[121]

Laurier himself publicly defended his course in a speech at Bowmanville, Ontario, on October 17: 'We as a government, and especially I as the head of the government, have in all these matters to think and go slowly and to act formally and with due consideration. For my part, so long as I have the honor to occupy my present post, you shall never see me carried away by passion or prejudice or even enthusiasm. I have to think and consider. I have to look to the right and the wrong. I have to see what will be the effect of any action that we take.'[122]

On the whole the government's course was supported throughout the country. But some Conservatives criticized Canada's unwillingness to shoulder the full burden of sending a contingent, while Henri Bourassa, a promising young Liberal protégé of Laurier from Quebec, resigned in protest from parliament on October 18, after the leading French-Canadian Liberals had abandoned under Laurier's influence the same attitude of non-participation which he held. In caucus, Bourassa asked Laurier whether he took account of Quebec's opinion and Laurier replied: 'My dear Henri, the Province of Quebec has no opinions, it only has sentiments.'[123] Tarte yielded to the party decision and supported the volunteer scheme, after winning the insertion of a no-precedent clause in the order-in-council. He was burnt in effigy at Toronto for maintaining that Canada was not obliged to participate in Britain's wars.

The first contingent, including a French-Canadian company raised with some difficulty at Quebec, sailed from Quebec on October 30, after being addressed by Laurier and Minto. Laurier told the men that they went to fight for the cause of justice, humanity, civil rights, and religious liberty.[124] Minto permitted himself the indiscretion of observing that 'the people of Canada had shown that they had no inclination to discuss the quibbles of colonial responsibility.'[125] The governor-general resented the charge that Chamberlain had attempted to maneuver Canada into the course he desired by accepting in his cable of October 3 an offer which had never been made. Somewhat tortuously, considering the pressure which had been exerted from Britain for months, he now wrote Laurier: 'I have always carefully explained to you that any offer from Canada must be spontaneous.'[126] Laurier for his part made the best of the position into which he had been forced: at his insistence the War Office arranged that the Canadian troops should form a unit, rather than being attached to British regiments as the Australians were.

A week after the first contingent sailed, the government offered to raise a second, but the offer was not accepted until the British disasters of mid-December. Early in the New Year Lord Strathcona (formerly Donald Smith) personally raised three squadrons of mounted infantry, known as Lord Strathcona's Horse. All told, Canada sent some 7,300 men to South Africa, only one-third of whom were in the official contingents.[127] In addition, a battalion was raised in Canada to garrison Halifax and thus to relieve a British regiment, the Leinsters, for active service. The contingents enlisted for a year, and many of the men of the first contingent were unwilling to prolong their service. In money Canadian participation cost the Dominion some $2,800,000.[128]

During the fall and winter the ever-zealous General Hutton proved even more of a thorn in the ministers' flesh than before. Finally he was accused of favoring Conservative interests in purchasing horses for army use. When interviewed by Laurier, he pleaded guilty 'only to have roused the latent military enthusiasm through all ranks of the militia, and having strengthened the innate feeling of patriotism towards the old country and the Empire, which already existed in all parts of the Dominion.' Laurier professed to see 'little difference between inculcating patriotism and arousing military enthusiasm, and party politics;'[129] and asked Minto for the general's recall. Minto defended Hutton, but said he would transmit the request to London with a covering letter expressing his opposition. Laurier said such action might result in the resignation of his government, while Minto advised Chamberlain that he did not 'admit any right on the part of any Government to expect me to refrain from commenting to you adversely on their action.'[130] On February 8, 1900 Hutton was ordered home for South African service, and sent in his resignation as commander in Canada.

In a despatch of April 17, Chamberlain expressed his disappointment 'that Ministers should have found themselves unable to allow General Hutton to complete the work he had begun,' and his own view that 'although the responsibility to Parliament must be maintained, it is desirable that the officer in command of the defensive forces in Canada should have a freer hand in matters essential to the discipline and efficiency of the Militia than would be proper in the case of an ordinary civil servant even of the highest position.'[131] But Laurier had won a victory for the principles of responsible government and Canadian autonomy by resisting an effort to make the English commander in Canada a political agent of the governor-general and of the colonial secretary for whatever colonial program they favored.

When parliament met in February 1900 the war and the coming elections were the dominant issues. The only new legislation increased the British preference from 25 per cent to 33⅓ per cent and was attacked by the Conservatives on the grounds that the government should have demanded a preference from Britain in return. Sir Charles Tupper led the Conservative attack upon the government for doing too little in the South African War, and doing that little late. One of his lieutenants remarked that Laurier 'had been first in the Jubilee parades, and last in the test of action.'[132] Tarte came under heavy fire in Ontario as a sympathizer with Bourassa and for his own utterances and La Patrie's editorials on the theme of 'no taxation without representation' in imperial affairs. The temper of the House grew hot, and there was much name-calling both in parliament and in the press. When Laurier replied to the attacks which had been so freely made upon him, he destroyed the Conservative argument that Canada should have borne all the cost of the Canadian contingents by showing that all the colonies had followed the same policy as Canada, which was that suggested by the British government. He reminded Tupper of the latter's earlier condemnations of imperial federation and imperial war expenses. As to the 'lukewarmness' with which he had been charged by Tupper, he spoke thus:

Sir, I have no hesitation in admitting that I was not enthusiastic for that war or any war. I have no sympathy for that mad, noisy, dull-witted, and short-sighted throng who clamour for war, who shouted 'On to Pretoria,' who complacently prophesied that General Buller would eat his Christmas dinner in the capital of the Transvaal. . . .

Whilst I cannot admit that Canada should take part in all the wars of Great Britain, neither am I prepared to say that she should not take part in any war at all . . . I claim for Canada this, that in future she shall be at liberty to act or not to act, to interfere or not to interfere, to do just what she pleases.[133]

Meanwhile the cleavage between the races, which Laurier had tried to avoid and which the Conservatives had fostered, bore fruit in Montreal on March 1 when McGill students celebrating the relief of Ladysmith besieged the offices of La Patrie, Le Journal, and La Presse and Laval's building and became involved in riots with the anti-war students of Laval. Rival contingents waved the Union Jack and the Tricolor, and for three or four days there was street fighting. The students were restrained by Archbishop Bruchési and

Principal Peterson of McGill and by the greater part of the press, although *La Patrie* and the *Star* accused one another of responsibility for the 'savage assaults' of the McGill students and the 'insults to the Union Jack' by the Laval students.[134]

It was against this background that on March 13 Bourassa, who had been re-elected by acclamation, made a three-hour speech in the House, proposing that 'parliament insist on its sovereignty and independence, refuse to consider the government's action a precedent for the future, and declare its opposition to any change in the existing relations between Canada and Great Britain, unless decided by parliament and sanctioned by the people of Canada.'[135] To him Canada was now threatened as a result of the government's action with ceaseless wars and unbearable burdens. Why had Canada taken part in this war? Because it was just? The British Liberals did not think so. Because it was necessary? Necessary to aid 40,000,000 to crush 400,000? Because public opinion demanded it? Every French-Canadian journal was opposed. Because of the action of other British colonies? The cable news had been manipulated by the English-Canadian 'yellow press' to make it appear that all the colonies had eagerly offered men, but in several Australian parliaments the issue had been closely contested and in one case carried only by the speaker's vote. The government claimed that no precedent had been created for Canadian participation in imperial wars, but 'the accomplished fact is a precedent,' as Chamberlain had made clear in his reply to the order-in-council authorizing a contingent, in which he hailed 'the desire thus exhibited to share in the risks and burdens of the Empire.'

Chamberlain and his fanatical disciples were leading Canada in a constitutional revolution of which no one could foresee the consequences. Such questions should be submitted to parliament, thoroughly discussed, and settled by plebiscite. Bourassa expressed his own attitude, describing himself as 'a Liberal of the English school,' 'a disciple of Burke, Fox, Gladstone.' No force could impose upon him opinions which were not his. He would support the government's general policy, because he believed it good; but he condemned it in this particular. His constituents had ratified his attitude and charged him to warn the cabinet against any further attempt to mortgage in advance the future of the country without its knowledge and without the consent of the people.[136]

In a reply to Bourassa on March 13 Laurier defended both his deference to public opinion and the justice of the war. He denied that Canada had been forced into the war by England:

No, we were not forced by England; we were not forced by Mr. Chamberlain or Downing Street to do what we did ... We acted in the full independence of our sovereign power. What we did we did of our own free will. . . . My honorable friend says the consequence will be that we shall be called upon to take part in other wars. I have only this to answer, that if it should be the will of the people of Canada at any future period to take part in any war of England, the people of Canada will have to have their own way.[137]

Then he agreed with Bourassa that if it were to be admitted that Canada should take part in all Britain's wars, there would have to be a new constitutional basis; Canada would have to say to Britain, 'If you want us to help you, call us to your councils.'[138] He warned Bourassa of the danger of a cleavage of the races if the government had not followed public opinion: 'A greater calamity could never take place in Canada. My honorable friend knows as well as any man in this House that if there is anything to which I have given my political life, it is to try to promote unity, harmony, and amity between the diverse elements of this country. I shall not deviate a line from the policy that I have traced out for myself.'[139] In conclusion Laurier spoke of the benefits he hoped for from Canadian participation:

The pride of pure patriotism, the pride of consciousness that that day it had been revealed to the world that a new power had arisen in the West. . . . The work of union and harmony between the chief races of this country is not yet complete. We know by the unfortunate occurrences that took place only last week that there is much to do in that way. But there is no bond of union so strong as the bond created by common dangers faced in common. To-day there are men in South Africa representing the two branches of the Canadian family, fighting side by side for the honour of Canada. Already some of them have fallen, giving to their country the last full measure of devotion. Their remains have been laid in the same grave, there to rest to the end of time in that last fraternal embrace. Can we not hope—I ask my honorable friend himself—that in that grave shall be buried the last vestiges of our former antagonism? If such shall be the result, if we can indulge that hope, if we can believe that in that grave shall be buried the former contentions, the sending of the contingents would be the greatest service ever rendered to Canada since Confederation.[140]

Only nine Quebec members, both Liberals and Conservatives, supported Bourassa's resolution that the action of the government created no precedent for future participation in Britain's wars, but his speech had only served to illustrate to English Canadians the difficulties that Laurier faced in Quebec. Three French-Canadian attitudes towards the empire developed during the debate: the colonial-minded, like T.-C. Casgrain, who favored moderate aid when ever Britain demanded it; those who looked forward to independence, like Dominique Monet, and wanted neither colonialism

nor imperial entanglements; and the rare imperial federalists, like
Tarte, who nevertheless opposed support of military policies which
they had no hand in shaping.

Laurier refused to commit himself to any position but guided himself by what seemed best for national unity under the circumstances.
When Chamberlain raised the idea of an imperial advisory council in
March 1900, Minto discussed the matter with Laurier and reported
to Chamberlain:

Sir Wilfrid's own inclination towards an imperial federation of any
sort is, in my opinion, extremely doubtful—in fact, though his recent
speeches appear to have been taken in England as enthusiastically
imperialist, I am convinced that they guarantee no such opinion. His
speech in the House was very eloquent, and the 'call us to your councils'
phrase appears to have been accepted as indicating a wish to be called—
the very last thing Sir Wilfrid would want, and the speech itself did not
justify that interpretation of it. He recognized the strong British devotion to the motherland existent here, and the imperial feeling at home
stronger perhaps than here, and got a chance for his great eloquence.
But I should say that seriously he is devoid of the British feeling for a
united Empire, that it has no sentimental attraction for him, and that a
closer connection with the old country he would consider from a utility
point of view and nothing more. He recognizes the fact that his Canadian
fellow-countrymen must follow the Anglo-Saxon lead, and will do his
best to educate them up to it; but I believe it to be much more with
the idea of the welding together of a Canadian nation than of forming
part of a great Empire . . . and though he has never actually said so to
me, I suspect that he dreams of Canadian independence in some future
age. He thinks the arrangement of tariff questions far more likely to
bring about imperial unity than any joint system of imperial defence;
the former may be made to appear magnanimous in an imperial sense,
but it would hardly be advocated by a colonial government except
in a belief in some practical gain to the colony from it, whilst the latter,
upon which the safety of trade must depend, probably appears before
the public merely as a direct increase in military expenditure to meet
an obscure danger not generally realized.[141]

Minto was singularly apt at reading Laurier's mind, as later developments bore witness. He considered Laurier 'far the biggest man in
Canada,' and realized that he expressed the 'strongest feeling of
Canadians,' 'a feeling of Canada's national independence,'[142]
ready to resent any imperial interference.

In the November 1900 elections Minto's observation was confirmed
by the gains which the Laurier government made. British victories
in Africa had eased the tension in Canada, but racial appeals were
still made by the Conservatives. Ontario accused Quebec of disloyalty, and the *Toronto News* threatened that British Canadians

would find means, through the ballot or otherwise, of 'emancipating themselves from the dominance of an inferior people that peculiar circumstances have placed in authority in the Dominion.'[143] Minto wrote home:

The writing of the leading Opposition papers in Ontario has been positively wicked, simply aiming at stirring up hatred of French Canada. It is perfectly monstrous. . . . I believe myself that the French Canadians are very much maligned as to their disloyalty. French Canada does not wish to be mixed up in imperial wars, and is lukewarm, but at home you do not call a man disloyal if he disapproves of the war. Here, if he is only lukewarm, and is a French Canadian, he must be a rebel.

Later he commented: 'I think pig-headed British assertiveness is much more to be feared than French sympathies.'[144]

In Quebec the Liberals urged French Canadians to stand behind a French and Catholic premier against the Ontario fanatics, while Sir Charles Tupper endeavored to prove in behalf of the Conservatives that Laurier was 'too English for me'[145] and that he himself deserved credit for smashing the Imperial Federation League. Israel Tarte, serving as the Canadian commissioner at the Paris Exposition, made speeches which were interpreted by the press in Ontario as attacks on British policy, and proclamations of independence and of pro-French sentiments, while in Quebec he was represented as advocating imperial federation. But Tupper's attempt to woo Quebec was not successful. Quebec went nearly solidly Liberal, while in Ontario Laurier lost fourteen seats in the larger cities and in the strongly Protestant constituencies which in 1896 had voted against Tupper's 'coercion' of Manitoba. The Maritimes were not distracted by the imperialist cry, which they regarded as an Ontario and Quebec question; they were pleased by the prospects of better British trade under the new preference; while the West, rejoicing in a novel prosperity, strongly supported the government under which it had arrived. But it was still Laurier's majority in Quebec which maintained him in power, and this fact stuck in the imperialists' craw. The *Toronto News* commented: 'It is an intolerable situation for English Canadians to live under French domination. . . . It is infinitely deplorable that the government remains in power by the massive vote of a section of the Canadian people speaking a foreign language and maintaining an ideal foreign to the dominant race in this country.'[146]

In March 1901 there was another flare-up of French-Canadian opposition to the Boer War when Bourassa introduced a resolution requesting the British government to make peace on the basis of independence for South Africa, and opposing any further despatch of Canadian contingents. Canada had the right to make her voice heard, he argued, since Canadian blood and money had been spent in a war not of her making. Laurier expressed his surprise that one who had been so opposed to sending troops should be so ready to send advice. In any case, the question of sending more men was academic, since the war was practically over. It was too late for independence, since the Boer territory had been annexed to the British domain by 'the terrible logic of war.'[147] Laurier looked forward to a South African confederation, 'united together under a federal constitution, under the British flag, and under the sovereignty of England,' and blandly added: 'Mr. Bourassa will agree with me that when they have the British flag over South Africa, they shall have that which has been found everywhere during the last sixty years under the British flag—liberty for all, equality, for all, justice and civil rights for English and Dutch alike.' Bourassa's resolution was defeated with only three votes in its favor, and the House sang 'God Save the King.'

7

The South African War altered the course of Canadian political life by introducing the new ideas of imperialism and nationalism into party strife. This was not a normal process, for as James Bruce observed: 'In Canada ideas are not needed to make parties, for these can live by heredity, and like the Guelfs and the Ghibellines of medieval Italy, by memories of past combats.'[148] But within and without the parties, an influential and determined group demanded closer union of the empire, with Canada having a larger share in the control and responsibilities of imperial policy. The Imperial Federalists and the war itself had aroused pride of race and jingoism in English Canada. There was much waving of the Union Jack in school and press, while the swelling tide of British immigrants, principally to the cities, strengthened the bonds between Canada and England.[149] Almost a billion and a half of British capital poured into Canada between 1900 and 1913, and consciously and unconsciously exerted an imperial influence.[150] Resentment of American economic and political imperialism was increased by the highhandedness of Washington on the tariff question, and in the fur-sealing and Alaska boundary disputes.

On the other hand there was a rapidly developing national consciousness brought about by the opening of the West and the industrial development of the East, which to some extent broke down the old provincialism. Laurier expressed this new nationalism when he called Canada 'the country of the twentieth century,'[151] suggesting that its role would be as great as that of the United States in the nineteenth. Canada's part in the Boer War was exaggerated and served as a stimulant of national pride, while on the other hand friction with English officers and loss of confidence in the War Office and in English military leadership strengthened national consciousness. French Canada, with its instinct for conservatism, on the whole was opposed to Canada's taking a more active role in the empire. A small group, however, headed by Bourassa, had begun to evolve a French-Canadian nationalism in reaction to the imperialist jingoism of English Canada during the Boer War. This nationalism was largely a reiteration of the doctrines of the Canada First movement in French-Canadian terms. Under the brilliant leadership of Bourassa it became an ever more formidable stumbling-block in Laurier's path and finally brought about his downfall.

In the early days of his premiership Laurier inclined towards imperialism, as his statements at the 1897 Jubilee bore witness. This policy was adopted in part to disavow the annexationist sentiments which the Conservatives had long charged against the Liberals; in part because British preference suited Canada's needs after the adoption of the McKinley and Dingley tariffs; and in part because Laurier sought to meet English Canada, then in the full flood of imperialist sentiments, more than halfway, in accordance with his desire to foster national unity. But Quebec's almost unanimous opposition to the South African adventure warned him of the dangers of yielding too much to Ontario's sentiments, and experience with British imperialist pressure cooled his interest in imperial federation. Gradually he evolved the concept of Canada as a nation within the empire, thus reconciling the ideals of nationalism and imperialism, and anticipating the modern concept of the British Commonwealth of Nations.

Preoccupied as he was by the problems of the South African War and of Australian confederation, Chamberlain neglected the development of Laurier's ideas, which was made evident at the Colonial Conference of 1902. With peace in South Africa and the coronation of Edward VII to provide the background of pageantry which had by now become conventional for these gatherings, Chamberlain summoned the premiers of the empire to meet in London in June and July. Judging that 'bloodshed has cemented the British Empire and the sense of unity is stronger than it has ever been before,' Chamberlain felt that 'the time has come when the defence of the Empire, and its military and naval resources, have become the common concern of the whole Empire and not of the Mother Country alone, and that joint action, or at least joint organization, with regard to this subject should be organized on a permanent footing.' He proposed the formation of an imperial council, 'acting as an advisory board to enquire into and report to the various governments on the subject of Imperial Defence.'[152]

Laurier, whom Chamberlain had thought of in 1897 as the bell-wether of the colonial statesmen, when sounded out by Minto, thought 'the arrangement of tariff questions far more likely to bring about imperial unity than any joint system of imperial defence.'[153] Chamberlain was reluctant to adopt preferential trade as a means of imperial unity—he still stood for 'free trade under the flag'—but in the face of colonial reluctance to organize an imperial council for defence, he gradually prepared to take his political life in his hands by supporting the plan the colonies favored for closer union of the empire. He was well aware of 'the strong feeling of independence which exists in all the self-governing colonies' and declared that 'I am almost afraid to make suggestions lest I should appear to presume, and I would greatly prefer that the initiative in any further movement towards closer union should be taken by the colonies.'[154]

A debate in the Canadian House in May 1902 on the government's reluctance to discuss political change or imperial defence at the impending conference made clear the new Canadian attitude. Laurier defended the government's position:

If it be intended simply to discuss what part Canada is prepared to take in her own defence, what share of the burden must fall upon us as being responsible for the safety of the land in which we were born, and to which we owe our allegiance, in which all our hopes and affections are centered, certainly we are always prepared to discuss that subject. Nor do I believe that we need any prompting on that subject, or that our attention should be specially called to it. . . . There is a school abroad, there is a school in England and in Canada, a school which is perhaps represented on the floor of this parliament, a school which wants to bring Canada into the vortex of militarism which is the curse and blight of Europe. I am not prepared to endorse any such policy.[155]

Robert Laird Borden, the new leader of the opposition, who thought that 'the ties that bind self-governing nations of the Empire would probably become closer, but that any change would be slow and gradual,'[156] made a cautious criticism of the government's attitude: 'I am ready to uphold as strongly as anyone the necessity of control by Canada of the expenditure of our public moneys and of the question of imperial defence relating to Canada. But, holding this view, I see no reason why we should not be open to discuss that question with the imperial authorities.'[157]

When the conference finally met, after a delay caused by the King's illness, Chamberlain found no response for his program of an imperial council, of definite pledges of naval and military contributions from every colony, and of union in trade. The conference expressed the opinion that the 'present political relation was generally satisfactory under existing conditions,'[158] and was unmoved by Chamberlain's citation of Laurier's earlier attitude of 'If you want our aid, call us to your councils' and his own statement that 'The weary Titan staggers under the too vast orb of his fate.'[159] A resolution was passed providing that the conference should meet regularly at not greater than four-year intervals, and expressing the desire to keep all parts of the empire in touch, not through a new body exercising direct control over the whole, but through a meeting of governments responsible to their own peoples.[160] Chamberlain's proposal of free trade within the empire found no friends: a resolution affirmed its impracticability, approved the principle of British preference, and recommended reciprocal preference for colonial goods.

Most of the discussion centered on the question of defence, on which the British authorities made a determined effort to take advantage of the imperial loyalty aroused by the South African War and of the precedent established by colonial participation. But the delegates were divided in their reactions to the defence schemes proposed by the War Office and the Admiralty. Canada and Australia jointly repudiated the suggested formation of special colonial forces 'set apart for general imperial service and practically under the absolute control of the imperial government' as 'objectionable in principle, as derogating from the powers of self-government enjoyed by them, and . . . calculated to impede the general improvement in training and organization of their defence forces.'[161] Australia promised a renewal and extension of her contribution to the British Navy, but Canada refused to make any offer of assistance other than its contemplated establishment of a local naval force. The smaller colonies agreed to provide money grants or aid to local naval reserves.

In a private interview Chamberlain, who never appreciated how little Laurier did compared with how much he eloquently said, learned the full measure of the Canadian differences with him on imperial policy. The Englishman expressed his surprise that Canada and Australia did not realize that strength and safety lay in union, and that self-respect did not make them wish to bear a fair share of the imperial burden. Laurier replied that the empire's strength lay in local diversity and freedom. Canada was prepared to bear her just burdens, when the safety of Britain or the whole empire was challenged, but he remarked that what Chamberlain called the empire's interest and the empire's policy were in most cases Britain's interest and Britain's policy. Canada had an immense domain to develop and was far removed from European quarrels; her interests were not those of Britain which constantly sought to extend her domain and to keep open the seaways. Moved by his Anglo-Saxon racism, Chamberlain made evident his impression that Laurier was 'a very imperfectly assimilated Englishman.'[162] Laurier then suggested that Chamberlain have a private interview with his English-Canadian colleagues, and Chamberlain found that they stood with Laurier: they were Canadians first and believed that the empire began at home. Chamberlain was disgruntled by his disappointed hopes and by what he called 'the icy wind from the Canadian snows,'[163] and when Lady Minto spoke to him of Laurier as 'a very great gentleman,' he replied sourly, 'I would rather do business with a cad who knows his mind.'[164]

Laurier had learned how to resist the unofficial blandishments which were coupled with official pressure in the imperialist campaign, and stood firm. Before the conference he refused a peerage,[165] and during his stay in England he was led into no such rhetorical excesses as had characterized his utterances in 1897, to his subsequent embarrassment. To the Constitutional Club he expounded the text, 'The British Empire was founded and must be maintained by the arts of peace more than by the arts of war'; at the Guildhall he maintained that 'The British Empire is a charter of freedom, united, prosperous; there is no need of organic changes; it would be a fatal mistake to force events'; at the National Liberal Club he proclaimed that 'The devolution of legislative power has been the bond of union of the British Empire.'[166] Though Laurier expressed the Canadian reaction to the imperial enthusiasm of the war years, he had not lost interest in imperial affairs. Privately he urged a policy of conciliation and self-government for South Africa upon Chamberlain and other English public men. When his health broke down after a summer crowded with public appearances and he sought treatment in Paris, he preached Anglo-French friendship to President Loubet and Foreign Minister Delcassé. Such mediation was needed, for French feeling had been much embittered against Britain by the Boer War. Laurier's share in bringing about the subsequent *Entente cordiale* was publicly acknowledged three years later by the French president.

Laurier returned home, greeted by triumphal receptions at Quebec and Montreal and finding general support of his stand at the conference, although the Conservative press criticized his 'negative' attitude. Laurier faced, however, a revolt in his own camp, for Israel Tarte had taken advantage of his absence and rumored serious illness to make a bid for power. As minister of public works, Tarte had become the apostle of a new doctrine: 'Outbuild the Americans in canals, harbours, ships; build a tariff wall as high as Dingley's.'[167] As Laurier's lieutenant and as an opponent of Canadian intervention in South Africa, Tarte held Quebec at his command; his protectionism now won him friends in the very Ontario circles which had so enthusiastically condemned his views on the war. Commercial self-interest had a persistent way of outweighing abstract principle in the latter province, where Tarte made a triumphant progress in September, delivering more than a hundred ardent protectionist speeches.

The Western Liberals and the official party press repudiated Tarte's campaign, but he was not called to book until Laurier's return in October. The prime minister promptly had two interviews with Tarte, demanding his resignation on the grounds that he had advocated revision of the tariff without consultation with his chief or his colleagues. On October 20 Tarte resigned, and when he spoke of his resignation, at a National Club dinner given that day in Toronto to Colonel Denison, the leading advocate of imperial preference, the cheering which had greeted him died away.[168] His new Ontario friends had little use for him when he ceased to represent their interests in the government. Tarte retired to the editorship of *La Patrie*, and within a few months lapsed back into the Conservative camp in which his checkered political life had begun.

The Colonial Conference of 1902 forced Chamberlain to abandon temporarily the political and military paths to his goal of United Empire. The plan of commercial union through a system of preferential tariffs, which the colonies had favored over his imperial *Zollverein*, now seemed the only feasible measure to strengthen the empire immediately. After the conference Canada added to the list of British products which received a preferential treatment of 33⅓ per cent; New Zealand granted a preference of 10 per cent on manufactures; the Cape Colony and Natal gave a preference of 25 per cent; and Australia announced its intention of granting a preference.[169] But the English cabinet, whose leaders were still devoted to free trade, made no move to provide in return the preferential treatment for colonial products which the conference had requested. After Chamberlain had made a South African tour and had aided in the formation of a customs union of the four colonies there, he returned to England early in 1903 to find that the war tax on grain, which he had hoped would be an entering wedge for a system of preferential duties, had been repealed. He could not persuade the cabinet to change its mind, and so in May 1903 began his own appeal to the people to support a policy of imperial preferential trade. This, he argued, would protect Britain's industries and give her bargaining power against other powers; preferential rates on colonial products would be met by preference for her manufactures; and a self-sufficient empire would be bound together so closely that political and military union must necessarily follow.

The motives for Chamberlain's decision to press his own program against the opposition of the cabinet and his party were mixed.

As colonial secretary he had become convinced that imperial union was necessary for the survival of the empire. He had sponsored the resolution of the conference of 1902 in favor of the preferential tariff, and he probably felt responsible to the colonies for Britain's doing its share in the program. His long-nourished desire to become prime minister also played a part. Until his split with Gladstone on Home Rule, he had been expected to succeed the 'Grand Old Man.' When Salisbury retired in July 1902, Chamberlain may well have hoped to replace him, but Balfour took office while Chamberlain was out of action as a result of an accident. In any case Chamberlain, though the strong man of the cabinet, was unacceptable to the Conservative Party as a Liberal Unionist. His best hope now lay in pursuing an independent policy and trying to win support for it and himself from the public. His decision split the cabinet, and on September 9 he offered to resign. At first Balfour did not accept his resignation, but six days later announced the resignation of two of the most ardent free-trade ministers. The following day two more like-minded members of the cabinet resigned, and the next day Balfour announced his acceptance of Chamberlain's resignation. In the reconstructed cabinet his son Austen Chamberlain became Chancellor of the Exchequer, and a free trader financial secretary of the Treasury, as Balfour attempted to straddle the issue by proposing a retaliatory tariff program. This policy pleased neither Chamberlain nor the free traders.

Chamberlain promptly organized the Tariff Reform League and took to the platform, advocating his policy in every quarter of Britain. He spoke as a missionary of empire: fiscal reform was secondary to the need to increase the solidarity of the empire. At Glasgow he urged:

. . . the realization of the greatest ideal which has ever inspired statesmen in any country or any age—the creation of an Empire such as the world has never seen. We have to cement the union of the states beyond the seas; we have to consolidate the British race; we have to meet the clash of competition, commercial now—sometimes in the past it has been otherwise—it may be again in the future. Whatever it be, whatever danger threatens, we have to meet it no longer as an isolated country; we have to meet it fortified and strengthened and buttressed by all those of our kinsmen, all those powerful and continually rising states which speak our common tongue and glory in our common flag.[170]

He appealed to the British public in the name of the eleven million colonists who were British in race, religion, and traditions and who wanted to unite the empire by commercial union. Contrary to the facts, he contended that the colonies were Britain's best customers, and that refusal to adopt the plan they favored would result in unemployment and lowered wages in Great Britain. Without imperial trade, Great Britain would decline and might become a fifth-rate power. The Little Englanders might argue that Britain's trade with the colonies was less than with foreign countries, but he was willing to lose foreign trade for the sake of an increase in colonial trade which would prevent the dominions from drifting away from the empire. For him the great imperial principle was 'to treat each other better than we are treated by any one else.'[171] His experience in the Colonial Office had convinced him that free trade was an anti-imperial policy and would end in the disruption of the empire. But Chamberlain's attack on free trade only served to unite the Liberals, while the Conservatives were divided by Balfour's compromise plan of retaliatory duties, which Chamberlain's followers reluctantly accepted in March 1905. Balfour was forced to resign in December 1905 and Campbell-Bannerman took over in a Liberal landslide. This public verdict marked the defeat of the imperial preference scheme in England and the last act in Chamberlain's career, for in July 1906 he suffered a paralytic stroke which kept him in retirement until his death in July 1914. French Canadians seldom realize that the man who personified imperialism for them never won support of his views from the British people at the polls.

In Canada his dramatic campaign had won warm support at the outset. The Toronto correspondent of the *Morning Post* noted on May 17, 1903, after Chamberlain's opening gun at Birmingham, that 'Canada has seldom before felt such unanimity over a proposed imperial policy, as that which greets the project of Mr. Chamberlain for the granting of trade concessions in the markets of Great Britain.'[172] The Liberal leaders were relieved that those who had criticized them for granting a British preference without exacting an equivalent were now disarmed; but they cautioned that it was for Britain to decide whether she wanted a protective tariff, and that in any subsequent agreements each country must preserve the right to change its course or withdraw. The Conservatives gave the proposal warm support, and George Eulas Foster, left without a seat in the House, went to England to aid Chamberlain in his campaign.

Then Canadian enthusiasm gradually waned, as it was realized that Chamberlain's policy meant a return to the old colonial system, with Canada permanently reduced to the role of producer of raw materials and consumer of British manufactures. The difficulties soon became apparent of reconciling business with sentiment, protection of expanding native industries with free trade for English manufactures, American reciprocity with preference for the colonies. Canada's manufacturers, generally Conservative, soon made evident their conviction that reduction of duties should only be granted to goods which Canada did not manufacture; and later they became so imbued with the Liberal faith in Canada's development that they 'were not prepared to admit that there was any article that could not at some point in Canada, and in time, be successfully manufactured.'[173] But the Imperial Federalists under Colonel Denison continued to support Chamberlain's policy, which they had in no small measure succeeded in forcing upon him.

Before the Conservatives lost power in England they made one last attempt at formal federation of the empire. Chamberlain's supporters were anxious to hold another colonial conference to supply proof of colonial support of his policy, while Liberal imperialists of the Asquith-Haldane group likewise favored closer union of the empire. Chamberlain's successor at the Colonial Office, Lyttelton, sent out a circular despatch in April 1905, proposing the establishment of an 'Imperial Council' with the same personnel as before, plus an added permanent commission to prepare agenda and to act on the instructions of the council and of the British and colonial governments. The proposal was welcomed by Australia, New Zealand, Natal, and the Cape, but flatly opposed by Canada. The Canadian ministers maintained that any change of title must originate with the conference itself; they preferred the old terminology, with its traditions of informal consultation, to the new, which indicated 'a formal assembly, possessing an advisory and deliberate character, and, in conjunction with the word imperial, suggested a permanent institution which, endowed with a continuous life, might eventually come to be regarded as an encroachment upon the full measure of autonomous legislative and administrative power now enjoyed by all the self-governing colonies.'[174] In a country where, thanks to massive immigration, 50 per cent of the population was now of non-British descent there were now many besides the French Canadians who disliked the imperial label or were neutral as regards imperial federation.

8

The decisive factor in Laurier's withdrawal from seeming support of imperial centralization was the mushroom growth of the nationalist movement in his own province of Quebec, the Liberal stronghold which assured his majority in the House. The nationalist leader was Henri Bourassa, who by his opposition to Canadian participation in the Boer War personified the French-Canadian reaction to the imperialist movement which had been active in Canada since the 1880's. The movement was also a reaction against the attempt of certain English Canadians since 1885 to make Canada a land of one tongue and one culture, and to treat the French Canadians as foreigners in their own country. Unfortunately for

Canadian national development, many of the leaders of the imperialist movement were also leaders in the anti-French movement;
their 'Anglo-Saxon' racism and appeals to British traditions fostered
the development of racist feeling in a Quebec which had been
aroused by the Riel affair. Attacks on the privileges of the French-
Canadian minorities in Manitoba and Ontario fostered a French-
Canadian group consciousness, a sense of 'racial and religious
separateness.'[175] Clifford Sifton's massive immigration policy
brought a steadily increasing flood of New Canadians—Ruthenians
and Doukhobors, Germans, Austrians, Americans, and finally a
stream of British immigrants, who soon outnumbered the Continental and American newcomers. Few of these immigrants were
French-speaking, and even some of those who were, like the Swiss
and Belgians, showed a tendency to assimilate to the English
Canadians. The French Canadians, remembering Sifton's anti-
French record in Manitoba, began to suspect a plot to swamp them
in an English-speaking Canada in which Quebec would have little
voice and importance.

Thus thrown back upon itself, French Canada began to assert
its Frenchness: in literature the Patriotic School of Quebec yielded
to the Literary School of Montreal, which found more of its inspiration in France than in Canada; the coming of religious orders
banished from France by the anti-clerical laws strengthened the
bonds of the French tradition in Quebec; each year the young men
in the classical colleges became more intent upon stressing their
Frenchness and their Catholicity; even the infant labor movement
developed national syndicates as rivals to the American international
unions, while opposition arose to the development of Quebec's
natural resources by English and American capital under English-
Canadian auspices. For some the new sense of separateness involved
merely an effort to maintain the faith and culture of French Canada
against 'Anglo-Saxon' encroachment, while freely collaborating with
English Canadians in building up a nation of dual culture. For a
more narrow-minded group, it meant a withdrawal within the shell
of an exclusive and isolated French and Catholic province. For
them nationalism was really provincialism, but the movement was
not provincial in outlook at the start.

The man who became the idolized leader of the nationalist movement was the grandson of Louis-Joseph Papineau, and like his
celebrated forebear combined an admiration for British institutions
with a passionate devotion to French Canada and a rebellious nature
which brooked no restraint of his opinions or actions. Like Papineau,
Bourassa was a brilliant orator and a poor politician, able to fire
the people with his own intellectual enthusiasm, but unable to
work with other men. Laurier once observed: 'Having known Mr.

La Chasse-Galérie

Oil painting (1906) by Henri Julien, the best-known French-Canadian artist of his day. He was famous for his political caricatures, but this illustration for the popular Quebec folk tale of the lumbermen who paddled home through the skies is his best-known work. (Quebec Provincial Museum.)

Quebec from Lévis

Oil painting (1920) by Maurice Cullen (1866-1934). This English-Canadian painter, born in Montreal, lived much abroad, but his Montreal and Quebec studies had as much influence in French Canada as the work of the Group of Seven did on English-Canadian art. (University Club, Montreal.) (Quebec Provincial Museum.)

Papineau, I can in some measure understand Mr. Bourassa; having known Mr. Bourassa, I can in some measure understand Mr. Papineau.'[176] The son of the artist Napoléon Bourassa and Azélie Papineau, Bourassa was born in Montreal in 1868 and privately educated. Before entering parliament in 1896 he spent some years on his grandfather's seigneury of Montebello, the center of the constituency of Labelle which he later represented.

Keenly intelligent, idealistic, widely read in both French and English and a powerful speaker in either tongue, unimpeachable in character, deeply religious, highly cultured, and charming in manner, Bourassa represented the best of the French-Canadian élite and was soon singled out as a promising disciple by Laurier, who thought it well that a politician should be a gentleman. Laurier sent him to Winnipeg in 1896 as an aide to Tarte in the negotiations for the agreement. Then Bourassa accompanied Tarte to the Pacific coast, and gained further first-hand knowledge of the West. It was Bourassa who drafted the petition of the Liberal members to Rome in October 1896, and who urged Mgr. Merry del Val's recommendations on the Manitoba schools in 1897 on the Manitoba authorities. In 1898 Laurier appointed him secretary of the Joint High Commission which met in Quebec in that year and in Washington the following one to discuss the questions outstanding between Canada and the United States. These experiences provided Bourassa with an admirable apprenticeship in domestic politics and in international affairs.

He made dismaying use of this training in the fall of 1899 when he broke with Laurier on the question of Canadian participation in the Boer War. Laurier respected the devotion to principle which motivated Bourassa's resignation from parliament on that issue, however, and bore his '*cher Henri*' no ill will. Their personal relations remained so close that Bourassa went to Laurier at the close of the session with the proposal that the no-precedent clause of the order-in-council should be embodied in a statute. Laurier suggested that Bourassa draft a resolution to this effect, but subsequently refused to propose the one which Bourassa duly prepared and submitted. The prime minister said that Bourassa was free to do so, however, though he himself probably would be forced to speak against it. In March 1900 Laurier did so crushingly, using the occasion to demonstrate to his English-Canadian supporters the difficulties he faced in Quebec which had forced him to take a middle-of-the-road course.[177] In replying to Bourassa's later attacks on the government's war policy Laurier never lost his temper or barred the path to a reconciliation. This reconciliation duly came when Laurier communicated to Bourassa the confidential report of the 1902 Conference which revealed the prime minister's opposition to Chamberlain's pressure for political and military union of the empire.[178]

Meanwhile Bourassa had expounded at length his views on the imperial question in a lecture, 'Great Britain and Canada,' given at the Théâtre National in Montreal on October 20, 1901, and published in both French and English in the following year. In the preface to the printed version Bourassa defined imperialism and gave a classic expression of French Canada's view of it:

British Imperialism—as opposed to British democracy, to British traditions, to British grandeur—is a lust for landgrabbing and military dominion. Born of the overgrowth of British power, bred by that blatant and stupid sense of pride known as *Jingoism*, it delights in high-sounding formulas:—'*Britannia rules the waves*' . . . '*Britons never shall be slaves*' . . . '*Trade Follows the Flag*' . . . '*What we have, we hold!*' . . .; to this last axiom, the Prime-Minister of Ontario has added:—'*and what we don't have, we take*' . . . which is now supplemented by public good sense by: '*when we can.*'

Having undertaken more responsibilities than she is able to stand, surrounded as she is by hostile or indifferent nations, the new Britain of Mr. Chamberlain is in sore need of soldiers and sailors to prop the fabric raised by her frantic ambition. Being actually denuded of troops at home, she turns in distress to her colonies. Realizing as they do that without practicing evasion they cannot possibly achieve their purposes, British rulers of today resort to deceit and bribery with colonial statesmen; they lull the incredulity and inflame the jingo feelings of the people of the colonies. Under miscellaneous names and variegated uniforms— Royal Rifles, Mounted Infantry, Strathcona Horse, Yeomanry,—they extort from us whatever they may get in the shape of human material for their army; even if they have to dangle before our eyes a few paltry advantages to be thrown as a sop to us whenever we get tired of this deadly game.

In short, MILITARY CONTRIBUTIONS FROM THE COLONIES TO GREAT BRITAIN, in men and treasure, but mainly in men, constitute British Imperialism.

. . . In England the taxpayer hears only of the great benefits to be gained by the Mother Country: she is going to be helped with colonial contributions to her army and navy—not only in time of need, but as a permanent military system that will save her from the dread of conscription. In the colonies, we are told that our free and voluntary sacrifices in the cause of the Empire in South Africa are bound to bring us incalculable advantages in trade and industry, in immigration from the British Isles, etc.

In Canada the same double game is carried on by politicians of all shades. In the English-speaking provinces, both parties run for the prize of 'loyalty'—each side claiming the credit of having done the most for Great Britain. Of sole devotion to Canadian interests, we hear no more . . . The only point in real dispute between both parties is which will eat the biggest piece of the jingo pie. All this, of course, does not prevent them from selling Canada wholesale to American railway magnates. In Quebec . . . it is no longer a question of which party has done more for Great Britain, but, the less done, the greater credit claimed. 'The government are selling us to Great Britain,' shout the Conservatives: 'put us back in power and save the country!'—'There is no such thing as imperialism,' retort the Liberals; 'it is an empty dream, kept up by a few eccentrics. We have permitted only a few men to go to Africa; had our opponents been in office, many more men would have gone and more money would have been spent. Keep our illustrious compatriot, Laurier, in power and be safe from Tory imperialism!'[179]

In this double game Bourassa saw a danger of a clash between French and English Canadians and a danger to the British connection, paving the way for ethnic feuds which would lead to annexation to the United States.

In the French edition of his pamphlet Bourassa defined anti-imperialism (which he here significantly called 'counter-imperialism') as 'to denounce these attempts and to fight them—not only between the pear and the cheese of special banquets, but in parliament, in the press, on the platform, everywhere, always, at the risk of one's peace, livelihood, glory, and even popularity. It is to manifest one's thought not only at the moment and the place where profit and applause may be earned, but above all where the adherents of jingoism make their muscles and their lungs felt.'[180] Since imperialism had back of it the majority, money, and influence, its adversaries must preserve their superiority in moral courage, sincerity, and perseverance. Bourassa blamed the popular blindness to the danger on French-Canadian intellectual laziness and on the 'Latin' tendency to refuse to believe in a social development until it was formulated on paper, while the 'Anglo-Saxon,' with less respect for logic and theory, altered constitutions and empires without using paper at all.

In the scholarly manner which characterized all his polemics, using an overpowering wealth of documentation, Bourassa sketched the position of Canada, with a constitution drawn from Britain but modified by certain American elements, and with an industrial life either English or American in its origin and operations. The majority of Canadians were of British stock, who were more English than the French Canadians were French—and occasionally more English than the English, since they were more recent comers and less absorbed into the North American way of life. Since materialism dominated that life, interest rather than sentiment would determine the future of Canada; and if interest drew the English Canadians towards the United States, 'those very same voices would be heard singing the glories of the "Stars and Stripes" which but yesterday were hurraying themselves hoarse over the visit of the heir to the throne of England.'[181] Bourassa deplored French-Canadian ignorance of the history of both 'Great Britain, which holds us, and of the United States, which waits to gobble us up.' He blamed it on Canada's lack of true nationhood since she entrusted her foreign relations to Britain, which admittedly had conducted them wisely until the rise of jingoism. Thus international politics and even British politics had remained unknown to Canadians, who were now ill prepared to direct their own course. Therefore he was led to outline the development of British imperialism.

Expansionism began with the industrial revolution, increased population, and religious controversies, which led the home-loving and insular Englishman to seek new markets and new homes overseas. The British Empire, unlike others of ancient and modern times, was not the fruit of a political or military idea, but was established and grew like the British constitution itself, without a plan, without official aid, and often in opposition to the wishes of government and people. The development of British imperialism within a century was illustrated by the change from official reluctance to take over India from the East India Company and the repudiation of Warren Hastings to the support of Rhodes' African adventure and the whitewashing of his character. Bourassa preferred Pitt to Wellington, and saw in him the 'great man of modern England,' because he governed England in accordance with its national temperament rather than under a policy of military adventure and conquest. The principle of decentralized power which was evolved in the American colonies became the strength of an empire larger and more widely scattered than any ever known. But the expansion of British power in India resulted in the creation of a professional army and civil service, which bred the social evils of militarism and the bureaucratic mind. India led Britain into the Chinese opium wars and the conquest of the Cape Colony, and America into the conquest of New France. To the old Irish question two new racial problems were thus added, 'Than which there are none more irritating, none more fraught with dangers and more difficult to solve.' When England attempted to force the American colonies to share the cost of their defence, they revolted, and their action, hailed by Chatham, checked the progress of imperialism in England.

But Canada was at first denied the privileges of self-government, to whose workings the American Revolution was wrongly imputed by Britain's rulers. Those privileges were finally granted 'with the sole view to safeguarding the interests of the Mother Country.' Bourassa held that to be rightly understood, the relations of Great Britain to the colonies must be studied in the light of the constant fact that the exclusive interest of Great Britain was the mainspring which moved her statesmen, whenever they had to modify the colonial status. After a fifty-year struggle Canada finally won responsible government and provincial autonomy:

To the statesmen who so nobly and manfully struggled, and with such unflinching tenacity, for the triumph of those principles of liberty, decentralization, respect to minorities, which were ever in the past the glory and the strength of Great Britain we do indeed owe—and England and the whole world with us owe—a debt of gratitude . . . What a noble spectacle it was to see this old soldier Wellington . . . entering his protest against the bill for the Union of the two Canadas, and thereby constituting himself—unconsciously perhaps—the champion of a weak offspring of the old French parent tree, at which he had struck so many a hard blow!

Yes, indeed, to such men as Gosford, Ellenborough, Brougham, Peel, Grey, Bright, Gladstone—to all those who, few though they be, were, out of a pure love of liberty, instrumental in securing and preserving to us political freedom—our admiration and our gratitude are due without stint.[182]

But the grant of responsible government was due only in part to these men; distance from Britain, their proximity to the United States, and the cost and dangers of military domination were important factors. And now the circumstances which favored Canada sixty years before had changed, while the disciples of her champions had been replaced in power in England by a new school of statesmen, linked to the men like Durham and Colborne who had sought to assimilate the French and to enslave the colony. Bourassa echoed the ancient warning: 'Eternal vigilance is the price of liberty.'

Then he showed how the triumph of free trade under Cobden, who abhorred both military and political imperialism, and distrusted colonial expansion, had favored Canadian liberty by introducing colonial decentralization as a first step towards separation. 'The colonies were given to understand that they were to be self-reliant and self-supporting, and that whensoever they thought fit to sever their connection with the motherland, no obstacle would be put in their way.' But imperialism revived with further expansion in India after the Sepoy Rebellion, resulting in the Afghanistan War, which in turn led to trouble with Russia. Similarly the occupation of Egypt led to the Sudan War and to friction with France. In South Africa were sown the seeds of militarism. The Cape was the sole British colony which had been acquired purely for imperial purposes, as a stronghold on the sea route to India. The attempt to rule it by the sword had caused the Dutch to revolt and to make the Great Trek to the north which resulted in the birth of the two Boer republics. Annexation of the Transvaal in 1879 under the imperialist government of Disraeli aroused hatred and suspicion of the British among the Boers. Then imperialism was momentarily checked by Gladstone's return to power.

But Home Rule split the Liberal party, and Chamberlain led the dissidents into the Tory camp, which was 'instinctively favorable to the autocratic and military government of the Empire.' Debarred from radical reforms at home by his Tory colleagues, Chamberlain stirred up national pride and evoked the prospect of a Cape-to-Cairo African empire. His schemes resulted in 'a war expenditure of half a billion pounds, another prospective expenditure of five hundred millions, seventy thousand men disabled, 200,000 soldiers held in check, the impossibility to find any more recruits, the stupidity of the British staff exhibited to the world, the military prestige of Great Britain destroyed.'

The Englishman was reluctant to tax his own necessities of life, imported from the colonies, in order to secure in return a favorable market for his products, increasingly shut out from the world market by protection and by German and American competition. Thus Chamberlain was unwilling to support publicly commercial imperialism, while the majority of the English people were still inclined to favor imperial decentralization and colonial autonomy. Great Britain now stood isolated from the world by her jingoism, with an army discredited by failure and a navy no longer able to dominate the seas against a rival alliance. Conscription at home spelt political ruin for the government which imposed it. The imperialist solution was an amalgam of military and economic imperialism, with the British taxpayer induced to pay a colonial preference, while in return the colonies were invited to fill up the ranks of the British army and navy. Bourassa concluded that whether or not the British taxpayer could be induced to grant a preference, 'the balance of profit will not be in our favor.' He deplored the growth in England of militarism, of brutal instincts bred by sports, and of a greed for gold which made English youth seek adventure and profit abroad while the moral and intellectual level of parliament declined.

Now, as in 1774, the colonies were to be taxed for the defence of the empire, though the tax was to be self-imposed rather than ordained by the British parliament. Such a program was favored by closer contact with the colonies and the existence of colonists avid for titles and honors; it was threatened by greater colonial freedom and democracy. Chamberlain proposed an imperial *Zollverein*, which was opposed by English taxpayers, in return for colonial military contributions. 'That the whole system rests on the idea of colonial military contributions, it cannot be questioned; all the rest—commercial reciprocity, political representation, judiciary appeal—all are mere accessories tending to secure the adoption of the principle and its permanent development.'

Bourassa paid tribute to Chamberlain's clever showmanship in launching his appeal in the midst of the pageant of the Jubilee in

1897, in arranging the Canadian tour of the Duke and Duchess of York in 1901, and in calling a new conference to meet on the occasion of the coronation of Edward VII. 'As at the time of the Jubilee, so upon the occasion of the Coronation, official representatives from the colonies will gather in London, who may easily be won over and fashioned into docile tools of the powers that be: a title to one, a medal to another, an opening in the House of Lords, kissing His Majesty's hand: few virtues are proof against such temptations.' Overcome by such attention, in 1897, Laurier had publicly pledged the aid of the colonies in the defence of the mother country; though Bourassa added: 'to my mind it never occurred to the Prime Minister of Canada that in so doing he was going beyond a hearty acknowledgment of England's generous hospitality —which was evidenced from his attempted opposition to the sending out of Canadian troops to South Africa.' But Bourassa warned that the English were not as fond as the Canadians of 'high-sounding formulas' and that they 'take words for what they mean.'

Chamberlain made the most of his opening, and sent out to the colonies governors and military commanders committed to fostering imperialism: 'Of this class Lord Minto and Col. Hutton are supreme types.' Minto disregarded the constitutional tradition established by Elgin and followed by all his successors, while Hutton 'made a boast of having smashed a Cabinet in Australia, and in the midst of his petty court of Rideau Club, in Ottawa, he declared that he was ready to repeat the same exploit in Canada.' Bourassa charged that 'it was in order to snatch from the Colonies, at a moment when the voice of reason is stifled by pride and passions, the tribute of Blood which until then he had been denied, that Mr. Chamberlain forced the South African War.'

He described the way in which the imperialist movement was organized by Rhodes through the South African League of Rand speculators, which bought the local press and supplied slanted correspondence to Tory and jingo papers in London. In Canada the *Montreal Star* served the same purpose. The Boers and their 'interesting victims, Cecil Rhodes & Co., were described under such colors as were best calculated to inflame the indignation of British subjects throughout the world.' Bourassa did not wonder that the blood of English Canadians had consequently become overheated. He spoke of the Ottawa mission of Rhodes' emissary Allen, who 'organized among members of Parliament a Committee of his League, wherein he introduced a few heads from every herd—I beg your pardon!—a few representatives of every political group: Grits, Tories, *Rouges*, *Bleus*, Senators, members of the House, past, present, and future Ministers of the Crown'; and stampeded them into a parliamentary resolution of sympathetic approval of

Chamberlain's policy. He charged that in July 1899 Hutton had urged Canadian militia officers to prepare for South African service, and that the *Star's* campaign in September for a Canadian contingent was 'inspired by Lord Minto and managed by General Hutton. In well-informed circles, Mr. Graham's trips to Ottawa were an open secret.' Thus the government yielded to 'intrigues and wire-pullings in high and low places.'

Bourassa disposed of the no-precedent question by stating that Chamberlain had boasted after receiving Canada's answer to the call for troops that he had 'at last secured the participation of the Colonies in the Wars of the Empire,' while the Canadian parliament had refused to ratify Bourassa's no-precedent resolution. He argued that 'from the fact of our contributing, whether directly or indirectly, whether permanently or accidentally, to the imperial exchequer, it necessarily follows that we should be represented in the Imperial Councils.' He rejected the solution of representation in the imperial parliament as out of the question after the experience of Irish members. Canadian democrats and Australian socialists would not be tempted from their principles by admission to the House of Lords. He denounced the suggestion of an imperial consultative council:

From our experience of the influence now exerted from afar by the British authorities over colonial ministers, it may safely be inferred that for the British Government to keep under the yoke men in close touch with them, and upon whom the whole weight of their favors and seductions could be brought to bear, would prove no difficult task. In all such issues as involved the interests of both the Mother Country and the colonies, the British government would never fail to secure a majority in the council, which would prove easier from the fact that the United Kingdom would long be represented by a larger number of delegates than the combined colonial representation.[183]

He anticipated that through the periodic '*ad limina*' visits of the colonial premiers and the influence exerted on the resident colonial agents, whose offices already had become 'so many branches of the Colonial Office,' the accomplished fact of an imperial organization would gradually be arrived at without direct action by parliament. He laid Lord Strathcona's imperialism to gratitude for his peerage, and suggested that the Canadian high commissioner in London should not be allowed to accept British favors. He denounced titles and decorations as means of political corruption, citing Lord Melbourne's explanation of his refusal of the Garter, 'that he did not see why he should be such a fool as to buy himself, when he could buy somebody else with it.'

Though the English middle and educated classes were opposed to imperialism, the British Liberal Party was split on the South African question and Chamberlain's policy was gaining ground in the absence of strong opposition leadership. Bourassa anticipated that the Australians would prove 'more strenuous opponents of imperialism than we are,' and he discounted New Zealand's loyalism as based upon a temporary need for British capital. He deplored the fact that in the Canadian house the sort of imperialism which had been laughed at, a few years ago, in the speeches of Alexander MacNeill, nicknamed the 'Father of the Empire,' was now cheered when it came from the leaders of both parties. The British Empire League of Dr. Parkin and Colonel Denison was now supported by many ministers and members of parliament. At the last meeting of the League Sir Charles Hibberd Tupper had favored colonial contributions to the imperial army and navy, and had been seconded by the Liberal Dr. Russell. In the summer of 1901 the *Globe* had come out for colonial contributions to imperial defence.

And in the strong Canadian party spirit and in the racial cleavage Bourassa found a two-fold opening for imperialism:

A mutual regard for racial sympathies on both sides, and a proper discharge of our exclusive duty to this land of ours, such is the only ground upon which it is possible for us to meet, so as to work out our national problems. There are here neither masters nor valets; there are neither conquerors or conquered ones; there are two partners whose partnership was entered into upon fair and well defined lines. We do not ask that our English-speaking fellow-countrymen should help us to draw closer to France; but, on the other hand, they have no right to take advantage of their overwhelming majority to infringe on the treaty of alliance, and induce us to assume, however freely and spontaneously, additional burdens in defence of Great Britain.[184]

He respected the English Canadian's love of his mother country, and expected the same respect for the French Canadian's love for France; 'but the only sure way of obviating fatal misunderstandings lies in a determination that we shall, both of us, French and English alike, look at all constitutional and political questions from a purely Canadian standpoint.'

Until a better understanding was reached between the races, Canada was not ready for independence. Even if it were, there would be danger in independence because of the strength of American imperialism and the threat of annexation. Eventual independence was the most acceptable solution of the Canadian problem for the French Canadian, but imperialism had embittered the relations between the races and under the absolute control of a Canadian parliament, 'our constitution would be exposed to terrible assaults, mainly directed against the French-Canadian minority, whose only refuge, under such circumstances, would be Pan-Americanism.'

Only if imperialism won the upper hand should immediate independence be risked. In conclusion, Bourassa warned against being carried away by enthusiasm or allowing ideals to be debased. He called for a deeper and broader patriotism less given to 'the worship of party leaders than towards the pursuit of principles and lofty ideals.'

9

In this first major public address Bourassa displayed an attitude towards imperialism which was at once Canadian and in accordance with the best traditions of English Liberalism. His ideas were not very different from those of Goldwin Smith, and indeed he was more reluctant to envisage the end of the British connection than the Toronto prophet of annexationism. But Bourassa's opposition to imperialism made him the hero of the young anglophobe French-Canadian students, who envisaged the formation of a new French-Canadian party which would not make concessions to imperialism, as Conservatives and Liberals alike had done. As Laurier's success gradually eclipsed the Conservative party in Quebec, Bourassa became the leader of those French Canadians, particularly the younger generation, who found the Liberal chief too willing to compromise with imperialism and the English Canadians. Bourassa's vanity was too great for him to reject the role that the students thrust upon him, and he did not strongly condemn their anti-English excesses, though these did not express his own position.

A group of young men in Montreal, headed by Louvigny de Montigny and Olivar Asselin, launched in 1900 a weekly paper called *Les Débats*, which made much of Bourassa's skirmishes in the House against war measures, condemned by the press of both old parties. In Quebec Armand Lavergne, the son of Laurier's Arthabaska friends, distributed *Les Débats* and Bourassa's speeches to a circle of Laval students, after the clerical authorities had moderated the tone of the aggressively nationalist *Semaine Religieuse*. At Saint-Jérôme, the Nantels launched a weekly, *La Nation*, with a program of seeking independence through constitutional means, and of opposing imperialism and the federal and provincial administrations. Occasionally *Le Pionnier*, formerly of Sherbrooke and now of Montreal, printed articles by the disciples of Bourassa, while the Conservative *Journal* sometimes defended the young Liberal who broke with his leader and his party on the war issue. For Frederick Debartzch Monk, the provincial chief of the Conservatives, son of an English-Canadian father and a French-Canadian mother, and professor of law at Laval University in Montreal, was more French than English in his outlook, and sympathetic to Bourassa's ideas. When in November 1901 the question of a third contingent for South Africa arose, Monk condemned imperialism and militarism in the face of the Ontario Tory press support of the move. Laurier followed the same course as before, with an order-in-council authorizing the recruiting of six hundred mounted infantry at the expense of the War Office.

The pamphlet publication of Bourassa's 'Great Britain and Canada' early in 1902 stimulated the growth of anti-imperialism in Quebec. When parliament met in February, and the *Toronto World* and the *Montreal Star* urged that Canada should pay the expenses of the third contingent, Bourassa demanded that correspondence between London and Ottawa on the recruiting of Canadians for South Africa should be produced in the House. He also offered an amendment on the speech from the throne, condemning American control of Canadian railroads, for he was on guard against both English military imperialism and American economic imperialism. He yielded to government pressure and withdrew the latter motion, as well as a later one on the Alaska boundary, though in that instance he accused Great Britain of sacrificing Canadian interests to her desire for American friendship. Again he pressed the government for the production of correspondence relative to the granting of imperial commissions to Canadian officers, and in doing so attacked the governor-general for interfering in Canadian affairs. Laurier and Monk, both realizing that Bourassa was becoming a threat to their leadership in Quebec, took a stiffer tone towards him. But his ideas continued to gain even wider support in Quebec.

Laurier checked the movement by producing the official correspondence in which he had refused to discuss political and military union of the empire at the forthcoming colonial conference. But Bourassa criticized the grant of a preferential tariff to Britain without return—to him, it looked as if imperialism meant that Canada should give everything and receive nothing—and he urged the government to be guided by Canada's interests in the commercial discussions to which Laurier had consented. Laurier yielded to imperialist pressure for a fourth contingent, but reassured his Quebec followers by the declaration that nothing but commerce would be discussed in London: 'Public works, colonization, railroad construction, and harbor development, there is the field in which our activity must be exercised and it would be criminal to devote a portion of the funds necessary for the accomplishment of these works to the purchase of cannon, rifles, and munitions of war'.[185] Bourassa was now exercising pressure on Laurier, almost to the same extent as Laurier had previously done on him.

Bourassa's lecture on 'Canadian Patriotism' at the Monument National in Montreal on April 27, 1902, was clearly designed to stiffen Laurier's new attitude of resistance to imperialist influence.

The nationalist leader stressed the fact that the French Canadians were first of all Canadian, sympathetic to France but reserving their chief love for Canada. Their resistance to imperialism was not born of hatred for the English nor of fidelity to France, but of their exclusive devotion to their own country. It would be easy to win applause by denouncing England and everything English, but he refrained from doing so, because he did not believe in arousing racial prejudice and because it would be unjust not to praise that which was good, and there were men in England with just ideas and generous souls. The French Canadians were bound to England and owed her a loyal and suitable fidelity. But they owed her neither bitterness nor gratitude. He urged his hearers to be conciliatory, tolerant, and generous to their English compatriots, and to exact the same behavior in return. 'Let us be neither servile nor insulting; let us win their esteem by being proud.'[186] But excited by the enthusiasm which he evoked, Bourassa himself aroused, by the bitter sarcasm to which he was given, the separatism of some of his disciples and the fury of English-Canadian Tories.

Unquestionably Bourassa's speech influenced the reply of the French-Canadian Chambre de Commerce of Montreal to the Toronto Chamber's resolution favoring imperialism and defence contributions. Montreal called for English tariff concessions in return for Canada's British preference; it asserted that Canada had done its part for imperial defence by building the Canadian Pacific and the Intercolonial, and in the future should reserve its resources for its own development. Laurier paid heed by his reply to Borden in the House on May 12, denouncing the imperialist school which wished to plunge Canada into the gulf of European militarism. At the beginning of June the Toronto congress of the Canadian Chambers of Commerce passed a resolution, originating with the English-Canadian Montreal Board of Trade, favorable to imperialism; but Laurier replied that the government intended no change in the existing political and military relations with Great Britain.

On June 19, 1902, after Laurier had sailed for London, Napoléon Garceau organized a nationalist manifestation at Drummondville, using Mercier's slogan: 'Let us cease our fratricidal strife and unite!' Of the seven speakers, the only two of the older generation, Louis Lavergne and Victor Geoffrion, counselled reliance on Laurier to check imperialism. Dominique Monet proclaimed that imperialism blocked the progress of Canada to its national destiny by raising obstacles to a single patriotism which would be neither French nor English. The nationalist movement had been criticized as being impractical and useless, but was it useless to combat the imperialism which imposed upon Canada an annual burden of ten to fifteen million dollars for defence of the empire? It had been argued that Laurier had taken a decided position on the question, but considering the great effort of the imperialists to influence the government, it was worthwhile to counterbalance this effort. Bourassa urged all, Liberals and Conservatives alike, to support the prime minister in his resistance to imperialism. Resolutions drawn up by Garceau were unanimously approved and cabled to Laurier in London. After proclaiming the participants' attachment to their nationality and to its constituent elements, faith, language, laws, and traditions, and their fidelity to the British Crown, the resolutions declared:

their fidelity to Canada, their only fatherland, to its constitution and liberties; they declare themselves ready to sacrifice their possessions and their lives to maintain national integrity, as their fathers had done in the past; but they refuse to accept modifications which would diminish the independence and autonomy of the Canadian people, to draw tighter the bonds which united Canada to the British Crown, and to assume towards the Empire obligations more onerous than those imposed by the constitution, with which Great Britain had declared itself satisfied.

Thus this convention approves the attitude that the prime minister has taken on this subject at the last session of the federal parliament and which he has declared must be maintained at the Colonial Conference soon to meet in London.[187]

This gathering was notable as the first occasion on which a nationalist political program was presented to a great popular meeting.

Bourassa's ideas received the sanction of Mgr. L.-A. Paquet, the noted theologian and orator of Laval, who in the chief address of the 1902 Saint-Jean-Baptiste celebration at Quebec, which celebrated simultaneously the fiftieth anniversary of the university and the diamond anniversary of the Quebec Saint-Jean-Baptiste Society, hymned 'the vocation of the French race in North America':

. . . We are not only a civilized race, we are the pioneers of civilization; we are not only a religious people, we are the messengers of the religious idea; we are not only submissive sons of the Church, we are, we ought to be, numbered among its zealots, its defenders, and its apostles. Our mission is less to manipulate capital than to change ideas; it consists less in lighting the fire of factories than to maintain and to make shine afar the luminous fire of religion and thought.[188]

This sermon of Mgr. Paquet provided a classic example of the messianic nationalism derived from Bossuet and De Maistre and widely expounded in French Canada, chiefly by the clergy, during the last half century. Abbé Casgrain and Louis Fréchette had frequently mentioned the providential mission of the French Canadians in their writings, and Bishop Laflèche, Judge Routhier, and a host of clerical orators had made it a commonplace of Saint-Jean-Baptiste Day sermons and orations.[189] With the renewal of close relations with France and the coming of refugees from the anti-clerical laws, De Maistre won a new dominance in French-Canadian thinking. Mgr. Paquet's warning against excessive industrialization and his call for the exertion of Quebec's intellectual influence outside the province fitted in with Bourassa's program. Canadian priests served in the Franco-American parishes of New England which Bourassa visited early in 1902, and many of them sought to link the expatriates with Quebec. And Quebec itself steadily drew more of its culture from France, although there were already those who rebelled against French intellectual influence, as well as against English political influence and American economic influence.

In June 1902 Bourassa wrote an essay in English, 'The French Canadians and the British Empire,' which appeared in the London *Monthly Review* and was subsequently published in a French translation in *La Nouvelle France* (Paris). He wished to explain to the English why his compatriots were opposed to British imperialism, and he did so in a frank and objective way. He pointed out the importance of the French Canadians as one-third of the population of Canada, the most important self-governing dominion, with their dominance in Quebec and growing importance in the Maritimes. He spoke of their higher birth rate and of the gradual reversal of the flow of emigration to the States. He admitted the comparative inferiority of the French Canadians in business, but stressed their pioneering and colonizing ability. In intellect and culture they were at least the equals of their 'Anglo-Saxon' neighbors, and they had made notable contributions to constitutional and legal progress in Canada. He concluded that they would continue to occupy a substantial position in Canada, to modify its policy, and gradually to augment their influence. They had made British institutions their own and reclaimed their rights with the same pride as all British subjects, but they were not ready to follow the British in an evolution which would lead to new obligations towards the empire.

After reviewing the history of the French Canadians, showing how they had struggled to win all the rights they enjoyed and paid their debt to Britain by twice preserving Canada for her, Bourassa outlined their present position. They were not driven by ambition and cupidity in either private or public life. They wished their English compatriots well and often had warm relations with individuals among them, though no sympathy for the English as a group. They desired no change in Canada's status, but if a change were necessary, they felt it should be in the interest of Canada at large. They were exclusively Canadian, while their English compatriots still spoke of England as 'Home.' They did not consider that the English Canadians had the right to make Canada more British than Canadian. Independence seemed to them their inevitable destiny, but they would make no move to break the English connection unless it was sought to tighten it. Recently French Canada had become more French in spirit, as the Americans had become more English, but neither sought reunion with the ancient mother country, and in fact there were more profound differences between the French Canadians and the French of France than between the Americans and the English. The French Canadians' intellectual and moral loyalty to France, their political loyalty to England, were both entirely subordinated to their exclusively Canadian patriotism.

They viewed imperialism not sentimentally but purely logically. For England they felt a reasoned affection; a mixture of esteem and distrust varying according to the time and the circumstances and modified by the education and temperament of each individual and his social milieu. For the empire they had no emotional feeling, since there was no link of blood or pride in imperial power and glory. They considered that they had settled their debt with England and owed nothing to the empire. They did not join the English Canadians in demanding special consideration in commerce, for they judged that for each favor it would be necessary to give compensation. Uncommercial-minded, they were not lured by the prospect of turning the empire into a gigantic business; they preferred to have Canada keep control of its own commercial policy and deal with all nations as its advantage dictated. Bourassa disposed of the argument that Canada owed sacrifices to Great Britain, since it had enjoyed British diplomatic services, by pointing out how costly to Canada this system had been. Since Britain refused to make sacrifices to preserve Canadian interests, why should Canada assume new obligations towards her?

Bourassa declared that the French Canadians had an aversion to militarism. Under British rule Canada had never involved England in a war, but had been twice invaded as a result of British policy. There was no foreseeable prospect of Canada needing the military aid of the empire, and she did not choose to be drawn into foreign conflicts in which she had no interest, such as the South African war. Canada was willing to provide for her own defence, but military imperial federation would offer new dangers without providing any compensation. Canada would be an inevitable victim in an Anglo-American war; and the French Canadians would not be willing to fight the almost equal number of Franco-Americans. He summed up the attitude of the French Canadians thus: 'Indifferent to commercial imperialism, hostile to military imperialism, we desire no organic change in our constitution, and we reject any project of imperial federation.'[190]

Annexation, though traditionally repugnant to the French Canadians, might be more popular if their autonomy was lost. Commercial union with the States offered a better prospect than an imperial *Zollverein*. The American economic invasion of Canada and the prospect of the reunion of the two branches of their race also were weakening the old aversion to annexation. Bourassa concluded that love of the soil and of their nationality had always been characteristic of robust and growing peoples; while the fever of exaggerated expansion and the thirst for domination had always been signs preceding the decadence of nations.

In this article Bourassa adopted the traditional Canadian tactic of using annexation as a threat to compel concessions by one major ethnic group to the other in time of crisis in their relations. In a foreword to the French version, he said that he himself was more opposed than ever to annexation, but he was forced to recognize that it was increasingly popular with his compatriots, as a result of English-Canadian imperialism and jingoism. If forced to choose between imperialism and annexation, he would accept the former without hesitation. But such was not the sentiment of the French-Canadian majority, and he foresaw annexation as the inevitable result of the imperialist movement.[191]

10

Before Laurier returned from London, the Australian delegates to the Colonial Conference passed through Montreal and were given a banquet by the Board of Trade on September 8, 1902. Lord Minto was present and spoke on imperial defence, while the Australians confirmed the popular impression that the question was far from dead. Bourassa, speaking at Labelle a few days later, replied to Minto, who had said that Canada would soon have to provide its own army and perhaps cooperate in the defence of the empire, by urging that 'We should keep our sons for ourselves, and before spending millions to make soldiers, ought to make colonists.'[192] Then he launched into a criticism of the federal government, which imported foreigners of all races to people the West but allowed Quebec to depopulate itself by emigration, and of the provincial government, whose blind policy of granting vast timber limits to lumber merchants had aroused the antagonism of land-hungry colonists. Bourassa had passed his youth among the pioneers and lumberjacks of his grandfather's seigneury, and he knew them and their needs. He made a moving plea for colonization, in which he took a growing interest as the development of the northern region of the province became more and more of an issue. Bourassa naturally espoused the cause of the colonists, who figured largely among his northern constituents, against the extension of the holdings of American lumber interests in the Témiscamingue country.

Bourassa was privately reconciled with Laurier after reading the confidential report of the 1902 Colonial Conference. Fielding won over other doubters of Laurier's anti-imperialist attitude in London by revealing to the press various documents, in particular a Canadian memorandum presented on August 11 which refused suggested support of the imperial fleet and army. It stated that the delegates' objections were not due to the expense involved, but to the fact that 'acceptance would be considered as an abandonment of the principle of colonial responsible government.' Canada proposed by perfecting its militia system 'to take upon itself, within its territorial limits, some of the functions which until now the imperial government has had to fulfil alone.'[193] Bourassa's reconciliation with Laurier was publicly revealed when at the opening of the session in February 1903 the former refrained from attacking the prime minister while criticizing Great Britain's sacrifice of Canadian interests in the constitution of the Alaska Boundary Tribunal.

Early in 1903 Bourassa published a French translation of Goldwin Smith's *Before the Tribunal of History*. In a foreword he pointed out that the French Canadians, in their almost unanimous condemnation of the Boer War, were supported by the English Liberals and many English Canadians who had commended his anti-war utterances. Despite the check suffered by Chamberlain at the 1902 Conference, aggressive imperialism was still a danger, and 'pan-Anglo-Saxonism' destined no happy lot for minorities and foreign races in the 'United Empire' it desired. He warned that hatred of England might become the common feeling of the French Canadians if England continued to follow an imperialist policy, 'blinded by jingoism and bent under the yoke of Mr. Chamberlain.'[194] But they were reassured by the opposition to imperialism of such men as John Morley, Viscount Bryce, Courtney, and Goldwin Smith himself: 'If we hate Mr. Chamberlain's Empire, we admire and love Gladstone's England.' If England became once more the classic land of liberty and freed Ireland and South Africa, the confidence of the French Canadians would be renewed.

Smith himself pointed out in a preface that the position of the French Canadians was similar to that of the Boers. He warned that the same party which had led Canada into aggression against a people who had never done her wrong would bring on other imperial wars in which Canada, and above all French Canada, had no interest. Forgetting his wonted anti-clericalism, Smith paid tribute to the 'impartial and dignified attitude' of the Catholic clergy, which during the Boer War had not sought popularity nor catered to the passions of the moment like their Protestant colleagues. And he expressed his happiness that his translator was the man who 'had not feared to affirm persistently the thought of his compatriots in the face of a violently hostile parliament.' The pamphlet itself was a vigorous attack on Chamberlain's policy and on the war itself from start to finish, and a demonstration of its uselessness. Smith concluded: 'If the existence and aspirations of a nationality are, as one has always believed, necessary to the well being and progress of men, it is a grave thing to destroy a nation. Those who, having at heart the interest and the honor of their country, wished to prevent the destruction of the South African republics have the satisfaction of feeling that they have not been accomplices in this act.'[195] By publishing a French translation of Smith's pamphlet Bourassa no doubt sought to buttress his own position by English authority, and perhaps to restrain the growing anglophobia of his student followers.

II

The nationalist movement now began to take definite form, as the younger generation rebelled against both the old parties. The group which had cut their teeth since 1900 as editors and contributors to *Les Débats* now founded *La Ligue Nationaliste* at a public meeting in Montreal on March 1, 1903. Its program, which had been submitted to Bourassa, had three main points:

1. For Canada, in its relations with Great Britain, the largest measure of autonomy compatible with the maintenance of the colonial bond.
2. For the Canadian provinces, in their relations with the federal power, the largest measure compatible with the maintenance of the federal bond.
3. Adoption by the federal government and the provincial governments of a policy of Canadian economic and intellectual development.[196]

The autonomy desired for Canada was three-fold: political, commercial, and economic. Under the first head the detailed program called for maintenance of political liberties, opposition to Canadian participation in the imperial parliament or in a periodic or permanent imperial council, consultation of parliament by the government in regard to colonial conferences, freedom to regulate immigration, production of all correspondence between London and Ottawa, restriction of appeals to the Privy Council, and the right of direct representation in international congresses. Under the second head, Canada should have the right to make and revise its commercial treaties with all countries, including Britain and its colonies;

and the privilege of naming commercial agents. The third called for non-participation in imperial wars outside Canada; resistance to all recruiting efforts made by England in Canada; opposition to the establishment of a naval school in Canada, with the aid and for the benefit of the imperial authority; command of the Canadian militia by a Canadian officer named by the Canadian government, and strictly Canadian training for the militia.[197]

This program was drafted by Olivar Asselin, who had been born in the Charlevoix countryside depopulated by emigration to the States. Asselin had been educated at Rimouski, and had then gone to New England at the age of seventeen, dazzled by the prosperity of two Franco-American schoolmates. After working as a grocer's clerk and as a mill foreman, he had embarked on a journalistic career with the Franco-American newspapers of Fall River, Woonsocket, Pawtucket, and Lowell, which was punctuated by military service in the Spanish-American War. Returning to Canada in 1900, he continued his journalistic career on the staffs of *La Patrie*, the *Herald*, *Le Canada*, and *Les Débats*, moving from one paper to another both from a desire to gain varying viewpoints on provincial politics and from temperamental instability. He became the private secretary of Lomer Gouin, the minister of colonization, and was briefly jailed in 1903 for assaulting Louis-Alexandre Taschereau in the Quebec Assembly after being verbally attacked by him.

Asselin then returned to journalism with *Le Journal*, *Le Canada*, and *La Presse*; but devoted much of his time to the new movement of which he was president, with Omer Héroux as secretary, and Armand Lavergne as organizer in the Quebec district. Like his master Bourassa, Asselin admired British institutions, made a distinction between 'imperialist adventurers' like Chamberlain and the 'lovers of liberty' like Campbell-Bannerman and Lloyd George, and sought to defend the French language and French thought in Canada. Endowed with great energy and an eager intelligence which led him to educate himself, by temperament a fighter and gifted with a talent for polemics which often fell into violence and sarcasm but were never dull, he was a notable recruit to the cause of nationalism.[198]

Another group of younger men, at first less politically-minded since they were still in the classical colleges of the Montreal region, had grown up since 1900. They gave their nationalism a more religious bent under the guidance of Abbé Lionel Groulx of Valleyfield, Abbé Emile Chartier of Saint-Hyacinthe, and Père Hermas Lalande, superior of the Jesuit Collège Sainte-Marie. Their 'Catholic Action' groups inspired by Montalembert and the Comte de Mun, were at first religious fraternities, but soon took on nationalist overtones.[199] They rallied around a French-Canadian flag of Catholic character, the so-called '*drapeau Carillon-Sacré Coeur*,' a mythical standard supposedly flown at Ticonderoga in 1758 but actually devised by a romantic abbé at the Seminary of the Quebec under the inspiration of Fréchette's poem and messianic nationalism.[200]

Following a suggestion of Jules-Paul Tardivel of *La Vérité*, Joseph Versailles of the Collège Sainte-Marie summoned a congress of delegates from the chief classical colleges to meet in Montreal on June 24, 1903, on the occasion of the unveiling of a statue of Bishop Bourget.[201] Before that meeting Laurier intervened with Archbishop Bruchési, fearing an Ontario reaction to the inevitable separatist demonstrations; and the Archbishop persuaded the young men to abandon the flag idea and to emphasize Catholic Action rather than nationalism.[202] The delegates agreed to form an *Association Catholique de la Jeunesse canadienne-francaise* (A.C.J.C.), with a permanent central office under the secretary Henri Bernard. The movement steadily grew, and as it grew became more nationalistic.[203] The A.C.J.C. was the nursery of twentieth century French-Canadian nationalism, and its confusion of religion and patriotism was carried into every walk of French-Canadian life by the heady indoctrination which the young élite received as it passed through its ranks.

The existence of the *Ligue Nationaliste*, like that of the A.C.J.C., was at first neither known nor noticed; but it soon came before the public as the imperialist campaign continued, reinforced by the return of the volunteers who had served in South Africa and by the appointment of Lord Dundonald, the hero of Ladysmith, as Canadian commander-in-chief. Dundonald followed the course of Hutton in seeking to stimulate imperialist sentiment in Canada. He found no official support for his pleas for more funds for the militia and for extensive fortifications on the American border, and gradually fell into the habit of publicly criticizing the government. His public speeches at Hamilton and Toronto, proclaiming the necessity of developing Canadian military spirit, caused Bourassa to request in the House that Dundonald be warned that Canada had responsible government, and would form its own policies. An Ontario member, A. H. Clarke, then expressed the opinion that distinguished Englishmen had the right to express their views freely in Canada without being attacked in the House. Laurier supported the right of Bourassa (who expressed an opinion which the prime minister shared but had kept to himself) and of all members of parliament to criticize freely the speeches of public servants.[204] On August 20 Laurier reinforced this anti-imperialist stand at the closing banquet of the Congress of the Empire Chambers of Commerce, which had been held at Montreal at the suggestion of Chamberlain and under the honorary presidency of Lord Strathcona in the hope of influencing Canada into imperialist paths. Senator George Drummond, president of the Montreal Board of Trade, had proposed a resolution asserting the duty of the colonies to participate in wars necessary to the defence of the empire, which was supported by a similar resolution of the Canadian Manufacturers' Association. The French-Canadian delegates, under the leadership of Napoléon Garceau and J.-X. Perrault, raised opposition, but finally adopted the Drummond resolution modified by a clause stating that Canada should itself decide the method and the extent of its participation. In the face of Minto's support of Chamberlain's projects at the dinner, Laurier declared: 'I should not yield an inch of our independence, should the destinies of the Empire be in danger.'[205]

Three days later the *Ligue Nationaliste* proclaimed its existence by holding at the Théâtre National a public protest meeting against the imperialist manifestations of the congress. Bourassa was the chief speaker. He described the congress as the work of Chamberlain, who would use its recognition of the principle of imperial defence as an argument to support his imperialist plans. But Canadian autonomy had been too hardly won and was too dear to be sacrificed to the views of Chamberlain and his Canadian representative, Lord Minto. The French Canadians' first duty was to Canada, to develop their country. To England they owed neither gratitude nor bitterness, since they had done more for her than she had for them. The French Canadians had preserved Canada for England, but they did not wish to be involved in war with all England's enemies. Bourassa urged resistance to imperialism, and 'the silencing of the voice of Rideau Hall, so that the people's voice might be heard.' Too close commercial relations with Britain were dangerous; Laurier's stated principle should be supported. Finally Bourassa said that he desired no break with England, but if there had to be a choice between a break and servile dependence, he favored the break: 'Rather independence than imperialism!'[206] These words brought down the house.

Bourassa's leadership in combating imperialism was praised by the next speaker, L.-A. Chauvin, former member for Terrebonne, who attributed to Bourassa the change in Laurier's attitude in the last three years. Garceau said a few words, and then Dominique Monet hotly proclaimed that the enemy had come within the gates of Montreal to deliberate, so that England might urge Canada to fight the Boers, the Irish, and the French. He urged the French Canadians not to forget that by Confederation they were only bound to defend their own frontiers. He called for the end of party strife and the union of all Canadians in the fight against imperialism. Three M.P.'s, Rodolphe Lemieux, J.-E. Léonard, and Charles Angers, declared by letter their sympathy with the purpose of the meeting and their opposition to political, commercial, and military union of the empire. Unanimously the assembly voted resolutions favoring a reduction of military expenses, a Canadian commander for the militia, Canadian consuls, and free negotiation of treaties; and finally declared:

> . . . the Canadian people has done in the past more than its duty to assure the maintenance of English power in America, refuses to impose upon itself new sacrifices for the organization and defence of the Empire, and affirms that the duty of the colonies in this respect is limited to the defence of their respective territories.[207]

The first effort of the *Ligue* was hailed by the French press as a major event. An account of Bourassa's speech was cabled to London, where according to the shocked *Star* it occasioned 'a certain surprise.'[208] Louvigny de Montigny dispatched to *Le Canada* of Paris an account of the *Ligue* and its meeting, giving its program, which thus was first published in France. Asselin, anticipating political repercussions, resigned as Gouin's secretary and became news editor of *La Presse*.

12

With elections in the offing, Israel Tarte now made a bid for leadership of the Conservative Party in Quebec and took to the platform. Dominique Monet challenged him to an '*assemblée contradictoire*' at La Prairie on September 19, with Monet speaking three-quarters of an hour, Tarte an hour and a half, and Bourassa three-quarters of an hour, with Tarte having ten minutes for rebuttal. Five thousand people came to hear this debate on imperialism between three leading spokesmen of the opposed schools of opinion. Monet attacked Tarte as the champion of economic imperialism, asked him why he returned to the party of the 'brigands and thieves' he had denounced in the days of Langevin, why he had not returned the money lent him by the Liberal Party for the purchase of *La Patrie*, and why he supported the policy of Chamberlain. In reply Tarte defended his departure from the Liberal Party on the grounds that he had the same right to preserve his liberty of thought and action as Monet and Bourassa. He said the tariff was not a Liberal or Conservative question, but a business one, and stressed the importance of the British market which annually absorbed $108,000,000 worth of Canadian agricultural products. Tarte declared that he had purchased *La Patrie*, not with Liberal funds, but with the loans of his own friends; and that he had refused to sell it to the Liberals after his departure from the cabinet. And finally he claimed that the development of the St. Lawrence route and of the port of Montreal was due to his efforts.

Then Bourassa launched a vigorous attack on the man who had initiated him into politics. Under an imperial tariff union, Canada would lose the right to make its own commercial treaties. It would be no longer 'Canada for the Canadians,' but 'Canada for England.' He pictured Tarte as the creature of Chamberlain, the statesman who had done most to violate colonial liberties and whose ultimate triumph would deprive the autonomous peoples of the empire of the right to govern themselves. Speaking of their collaboration in fighting against participation in the Boer War, he denounced Tarte for changing his stand on imperialism because of ambition:

> I voted and spoke against Sir Wilfrid Laurier when, in the fullness of his strength and of his prestige, he seemed to forget his duties to the Canadian people and to yield to the current of English imperialism; and you, M. Tarte, who condemned the African War as I did, who did everything to prevent Canada from participating in it, who were as 'anti-British,' as 'disloyal,' as I, you yielded to Laurier when he was in the best of health and obeyed the imperialist movement which you condemned. Oh, no; you did not resign then; your conscience permitted you to cooperate with a policy that you condemned. But when Laurier, ill, but showing himself firmer, more energetic, prouder of the rights of Canada than when he was well, you, sir, wishing to regain your popularity in the English provinces and to put yourself in the good graces of the great industrialist—while Laurier was in England, sick it is true, but standing up to Chamberlain—you abandoned him, and knelt before Chamberlain . . .
>
> As three years ago I fought Laurier, the partisan of Chamberlain, today I fight you, M. Tarte, because you have the sad honor to be the sole partisan of Chamberlain in the Province of Quebec.[209]

Thus the 35-year-old Bourassa crushed the 57-year-old Tarte, who had made and broken so many political careers and had been called the master of Laurier's administration. Tarte found no more effective answer to the onslaught than to match Bourassa's prophecy of the end of his career with a prophecy of a brilliant one for the young nationalist.

Bourassa, whose sorties against imperialism had been so embarrassing to Laurier during the Boer War, now justified the prime minister's refusal to read him out of the Liberal Party. Acting on his own account, as always, Bourassa had destroyed Tarte, who had become Laurier's most dangerous enemy in Quebec. Later that fall, when the Alaska Boundary Tribunal's award was announced, Bourassa used it as an argument in the House that in the future Canada must conduct her own international negotiations and have her own representative at Washington. This speech paved the way for Laurier's declaration that the time had come for the imperial parliament to concede to Canada the right to conclude her own treaties. The press, English and French alike, deplored England's concessions at Canada's expense in the Alaska affair, and supported the proposed step. Sifton, who had followed the work of the tribunal in London, expressed himself even more vigorously than Bourassa, and upon his return home denounced Chamberlain's mutual preference policy.

Bourassa was invited to speak in Toronto on November 9 on 'The Loyalism of the French Canadians.' Hailed as the spokesman of Quebec, he was widely interviewed. Goldwin Smith welcomed him at his home 'The Grange,' that shrine of maverick Liberalism, where the pair passed the night in talk. Under the chairmanship of James Hughes, the Orangeman brother of Colonel Sam Hughes, Bourassa expounded his topic very frankly. He deplored the fact that the English Canadians did not know the French Canadians as well as the latter did the former. His compatriots were not French, but exclusively Canadian in outlook, and hence anti-imperialist. While the English Canadian prided himself on loyalty to 'King and Country,' the French-Canadian's loyalty was to 'Country and King.' He opposed sending men to fight abroad when they were needed at home. Canadians should govern Canada and negotiate Canada's treaties. Finally he urged his audience to try and know the French Canadians better. Bourassa, praised in Toronto for his frankness and for having the courage of his convictions, followed up this speech with another at Woodstock, Ontario, on the spirit of the B.N.A. Act.

Then, upon his return to Montreal, he spoke at a meeting organized by the *Ligue Nationaliste* in honor of Charles Ramsay Devlin, a former Canadian M.P. for Ottawa, now representative of Galway in the British Parliament. Devlin spoke of Ireland's martyrdom; comparing the position of the Irish and the French Canadians, and urging them to be united in Canada. Bourassa paid tribute to Devlin and urged the solidarity of all the colonies; Canadians had both the right and the duty to request liberty for Ireland. Bourassa was rapidly becoming the man of the hour; he was widely spoken of as a possible minister of colonization in a reorganized provincial cabinet. But he aimed still higher, and seemingly expressed to Laurier his willingness to enter the provincial field as premier if given a free hand to form a government of his choice.[210] His willingness to begin at the top was not gratified.

Bourassa then went to Quebec on December 8 to expound the program of the *Ligue Nationaliste* in the provincial capital. An audience of six thousand gathered at the Manège Militaire, and the platform was packed with Liberal senators and M.P.'s. But Ernest Roy, who introduced Bourassa, said the meeting was neither Liberal nor Conservative in character. Asselin spoke briefly on the origins of the *Ligue*, and then Bourassa took the floor. He defined the *Ligue* as neither a revolutionary organization nor a prelude to a racial movement. He was opposed to imperialism as a Canadian, not only as a French Canadian; and he pointed out that his ideas had been applauded in Toronto, where they were shared by some Ontarians. It was not revolutionary to claim for Canada the right to conclude its own treaties and to direct its own foreign policy. 'Every time that a statesman, English or French, Conservative or Liberal, sacrifices Canadian interests to English ones, we shall fight him. Every time that a statesman, French or English, Liberal or Conservative, upholds the country's rights to absolute autonomy, we shall approve him.'[211]

Then Bourassa dealt with three main points: Canada's situation in the empire, the federal organization of Canada, and economic problems with particular reference to Quebec. It was clear that Quebec did not want political or military imperialism, and neither did the majority in Ontario. To the economic imperialism of which Lord Strathcona and Lord Minto had constituted themselves the heralds, he opposed the principle of the absolute autonomy of Great Britain and of each of the colonies in tariff and commercial questions. He urged that the federal subsidy should be divided fairly among the provinces according to their population. The federal government should aid colonization in the old provinces as well as in the West; newcomers in Quebec would replace those who had followed the frontier elsewhere, and they would stimulate by new methods the too traditional agriculture of French Canada. The federal government should vote funds each year for a program of colonization public works prepared by each province. Appeals in cases based upon provincial laws should not be carried beyond the courts of the province; the Supreme Court should decide only the interpretation of federal laws and cases involving citizens of different provinces. He saw colonization as the first and last duty of the Quebec government in the provincial field. He criticized the sales of timber limits as on too great a scale in the first place, and as too often made to speculators who stripped colonization lots of their wood and then abandoned them. He favored a law obliging American lumbermen to convert wood into pulp in Quebec factories. Waterpower rights should be rented rather than sold. This program was less to the taste of the leading provincial Liberals on the platform than Bourassa's anti-imperialism, but it was equally cheered by the students for whom Bourassa was a hero who dared to upset the political applecart in the interest of French Canada.

Laurier was less disturbed by Bourassa's heresies on provincial policy than by the anti-British tendencies of the *Ligue*. He remembered how England had been hooted by the students at the Devlin meeting, and he knew that Armand Lavergne, Bourassa's chief disciple in Quebec, was willing 'to throw the English into the St. Lawrence.'[212] He warned Bourassa of the danger of forming a French party in Quebec which would produce an anti-French-Canadian reaction in Ontario. Bourassa protested that the *Ligue* was purely Canadian and not anti-English, and sent Laurier the *Ligue's* program.[213] When an opening presented itself in Montmagny, Laurier proposed Lavergne as Liberal candidate, probably in hope of restraining him by bringing him under his own influence at Ottawa. Lavergne accepted the nomination after consulting Bourassa, but resisted the Liberal machine's effort to make him sign a pledge to approve all government measures. Laurier refused to be scandalized by such independence, and gave Lavergne the same indulgent leeway as he had long given Bourassa. But he recognized that he had provided himself with 'another thorn in the flesh'[214] by supporting Bourassa's disciple.

At the Théâtre National in Montreal on February 21, 1904, at a meeting called by the *Ligue Nationaliste* to celebrate Lavergne's election, Bourassa repeated the analysis of the *Ligue's* program which he had given in Quebec in December, and renewed the attack he had made three days earlier, before the Colonization Commission, on the existing system. He called for a separation of colonization areas from timber limits, and an end of alienation of the province's natural resources. With the growing industrial development of the province, it was significant that the nationalists were advancing an economic program as well as a political one.

At this same meeting Asselin announced the forthcoming establishment of a weekly paper, *Le Nationaliste*, which would be the organ of the *Ligue*, and absolutely independent of the old parties. The first number appeared on March 6, 1904, with two articles by Bourassa and others by Asselin, Omer Héroux, Louvigny de Montigny, and the poet Charles Gill. Asselin had the editorial collaboration of Jules Fournier, a brilliant young journalist of A.C.J.C. background whom he had encountered in the office of *La Presse*. The chief backers of the paper were G.-N. Ducharme and Edmond Lepage, whose aid Bourassa had enlisted with the following arguments:

Here are some young men who have talent, character, and ideas. They wish to escape from the sordid slavery that party journalism imposes on its workers. I am a party man—oh, not the most docile one—but I belong to a political party and I freely recognize that the parliamentary regime necessitates the organization and maintenance of two parties. Nevertheless, I believe it good that the parties—mine like the others— should be watched, criticized, and indeed scolded by a free press.

If party spirit here were what it is in England, the necessity of independent journals would be less imperative. In England, party discipline allows very great liberty of thought, speech, and even action. Here one must not only vote with one's party, but one must under threat of major excommunication write, talk, think, breathe, eat, and sleep according to the strict rules of *Rouge* or *Bleu* disciplinary protocol. This regime produces the moral and intellectual degradation of public men and the demoralization of popular thought and action. . . .

Our political parties, less and less divided by principles, dispute the victory, not to assure the triumph of an idea, but to gather the honors and profits of power. At bottom, under the cover of bitter battles which involve chiefly men and methods of administration, the two parties agree like thieves at a fair to manage all the great influences. Let the imperial authorities desire to impose upon us some action conformed to their wishes—as happened during the war in Africa—they seize upon the minds of the leaders, by seduction or fear; and immediately they have at their service the orators, the journalists, and the battalions of both parties; and any serious discussion of their projects is stifled. The great financial interests—railway contractors and directors, manufacturers, stock brokers and speculators, timber merchants, act in the same fashion and succeed marvelously in having their interests protected under all ministries. If one studies political developments at Ottawa and Quebec, one observes that this pernicious tendency is growing every day.

It is urgent that a press independent of parties, coteries, and financial syndicates arouse public opinion and put the people on guard against the dangers which menace our national integrity and economic stability.[215]

Bourassa made clear that he was 'neither founder, proprietor, director, nor editor of *Le Nationaliste*,' but merely a contributor who assumed responsibility only for the articles he signed. But it was also clear that he now had an organ and was now more redoubtable an influence in Quebec than ever before.

As might have been expected from the dominant influence of Bourassa at the start, *Le Nationaliste* was nationalist in a Canadian sense, not merely in a French-Canadian one. It was the first French-Canadian publication to escape from provincialism by adopting this position, and its establishment was welcomed by two of the leading English-Canadian nationalists, Goldwin Smith and John S. Ewart. In a letter to the editor dated March 13, 1904, Smith 'hailed with joy its apparition' and spoke of its important mission of reminding English Canadians that they were not the only inhabitants of a Canada 'which counts today among its citizens, aside from your compatriots, representatives of several different races.' He added: 'One should not expect that the non-British elements of our population should see without protesting their interests sacrificed to those of a political party in Great Britain whose ends, however glorious they may appear to those who pursue them, satisfy only British ambition.' Smith judged that the new journal could contribute to revealing this aspect of imperialism, and that it would introduce into 'the stifling atmosphere of our politics a little of the fresh air of patriotism and of youthful hope.'[216] In the paper Bourassa approved the views of John S. Ewart as those of the *Ligue* in a more accentuated form: 'The ideal of Mr. Ewart is a federation of sovereign states united by the sole bond of obedience to the same Crown. Mr. Ewart is more radical than I am. I do not find the position of Canada as humiliating as he paints it; and consequently I do not desire, for the moment, as complete a liberation as that which he calls for.'[217] But Bourassa asserted that Ewart's views were those of the majority of the English Canadians, and he called for the collaboration of English and French in enlarging the Canadian people's field of action.

13

The difference between Bourassa's nationalism and that previously known in Quebec was made evident in an exchange between Jules-Paul Tardivel and Bourassa soon after *Le Nationaliste* appeared. Tardivel's ultramontanism and anglophobia had developed into separatism, and his apocalyptic novel, *Pour la Patrie* (1895), one of the classic texts of the A.C.J.C.,[218] looked forward to the establishment of a French-Canadian state. In his organ *La Vérité* on April 2, 1904, he distinguished between his nationalism and that of the *Ligue*:

Our own nationalism is French-Canadian nationalism. We have worked for twenty-three years for the development of French-Canadian national sentiment; what we wish to see flourish is French-Canadian patriotism; for us our compatriots are the French Canadians; for us our fatherland is—we do not say precisely the Province of Quebec—but French Canada; the nation we wish to see founded at the hour marked by Divine Providence is the French-Canadian nation. These gentlemen of the *Ligue* appear to take their stand on another point of view. One would say that they wish to work for the development of a Canadian sentiment, independent of all questions of origin, language, and religion.[219]

In reply Bourassa paid tribute to Tardivel's career as a defender of the French-Canadian nationality, but suggested that this struggle had made him too suspicious of those who differed with him. He thus defined the nationalism for which the *Ligue* stood:

Our own nationalism is a Canadian nationalism founded upon the duality of races and on the particular traditions which this duality involves. We work for the development of a Canadian patriotism which is in our eyes the best guaranty of the existence of the two races and of the mutual respect they owe each other. For us, as for M. Tardivel, our compatriots are the French Canadians; but the English Canadians are not foreigners, and we regard as allies all those among them who respect us and who desire like us the maintenance of Canadian autonomy. For us, the fatherland is all Canada, that is, a federation of distinct races and autonomous provinces. The nation that we wish to see develop is the Canadian nation, composed of French Canadians and English Canadians, that is of two elements separated by language and religion, and by the legal dispositions necessary to the preservation of their respective traditions, but united in a feeling of brotherhood, in a common attachment to the common fatherland.[220]

When Tardivel replied, regretting that Bourassa should write elsewhere than in *La Vérité*, since one nationalist journal sufficed, and deploring the fact that *Le Nationaliste* excluded religious sentiments from its columns, he provoked a rude rejoinder from the youthful editors, who did not take Tardivel as seriously as Bourassa did.[221]

The old politico-religious nationalist school of Tardivel was carried on, however, by the formal foundation on March 13 of the *Association Catholique de la Jeunesse canadienne-française* (A.C.J.C.) under the presidency of Joseph Versailles and the guidance of the French Jesuits, with the watchword of 'piety, study, action.' To their second congress at Montreal in June 1904 they summoned all young French Canadians 'who believed in Catholicism and in its universal efficacy for the good of individuals and societies, in the French-Canadian race and its providential mission; of all who are aware of the dangers which beset our Catholic faith and our French-Canadian race.'[222] At first the organization had enlisted only the support of classical college students, but their announced purpose of study of national problems soon led them into the political field from which Archbishop Bruchési had sought to deflect them at Laurier's request.

In any case *Le Nationaliste* found an eager audience among their members, and Asselin hailed the A.C.J.C.:

The Catholic Association of French-Canadian Youth has bravely inscribed on its program the study of the political and social problems whose solution is demanded by the interest of the French-Canadian race; education, agriculture, colonization, trade and industry, the relations of capital and labor. Our young friends have understood that Catholicism is essentially a social work, and that according to the saying of one of our French colleagues, those peoples are destined to destruction who choose the hour when the enemy beats breaches in their ramparts to discuss whether the light which appeared on Tabor was created or uncreated. Immediately after the religious question—we read in the program of the Association—let us put the national question, studied in the light of the teachings of our history; providential mission of the French Canadians; aptitudes of our race; resources of our soil; our rights to its possession;

the necessity to remain faithful to our tradition and to preserve our distinct entity; our colonial obligations; our position in regard to other races and to the Liberal power; our rank among the nations with regard to education, commerce, etc.; a purely French-Canadian patriotism, an always greater autonomy; resistance to all attempts to absorb us; dangers of political partisanship; the Confederation Act; the French language; the religious liberty recognized by the constitution of the country.

There is nothing there that we do not approve wholeheartedly, with the reservation already made by M. Bourassa in his friendly response to M. Tardivel, to wit: that in our eyes French-Canadian patriotism is not incompatible with a larger patriotism extending to all the country discovered by our fathers.

The Catholic Association, along with the *Ligue Nationaliste* upholds the right of minorities to separate schools. [223]

Asselin sought to associate the new movement with the demand raised by the *Ligue d'Enseignement* [224] for reform of primary education, with support of colonization, and with conservation of natural resources—all causes dear to his group—and concluded by observing that the A.C.J.C. was clearly no mere 'pious confraternity,' since it was aware that 'a well-governed state is also one of the finest homages that can be paid to God.'

At the A.C.J.C. Congress in June, Bourassa made the principal address to the 500 delegates, and both the president's speech and the congress' resolutions had a strongly nationalist character. [225] Versailles resigned and was replaced as president by R.-A. Benoit. The A.C.J.C. launched a monthly bulletin, *Le Semeur*, under the editorship of Antonio Perrault. There was some evident distrust of exactly what 'action' might be intended by the A.C.J.C.; Archbishop Bruchési insisted upon the primary purposes of piety and study, but the Rector of Laval made evident his suspicion of the organization, which had been joyously hailed by Tardivel.

The new nationalism soon made itself felt at Ottawa. When the session opened on March 10, Tom-Chase Casgrain accused the government of supporting the *Ligue Nationaliste*, and asked whether its anti-British views had been incorporated in the Liberal program. Had not the Liberals selected Armand Lavergne? Bourassa replied that he was not a member of the *Ligue*, but saw nothing pernicious in its doctrine, which was supported by some Conservatives and was anti-imperialist, as Sir John Macdonald and Sir Charles Tupper had been on occasion. The *Ligue* members, like Bourassa and Sir Wilfrid Laurier, were Canadians who had only one country, Canada, a British land, but Canadian before it was British. The next day Bourassa asked why the Union Jack had replaced the Canadian flag on the Parliament buildings. The minister of public works replied that until now a constitutional error had been made in flying the flag of the merchant marine, but the error would be repaired as soon as a new flag was purchased.[226] Bourassa's position in this matter was scarcely understood by English Canadians, who did not see how one could profess to be British and yet object to the Union Jack. The flag question has remained vexed, with one English school swearing by the Union Jack, the French generally calling for the '*drapeau fleur-de-lisé*' (now the Quebec provincial flag) or the '*drapeau Carillon*' or some other distinctively Canadian flag, and the English generally fancying the Red Ensign. Though the Red Ensign with the Canadian arms on the fly had long been in unofficial use as the Canadian flag in 1904, it had not yet been officially adopted.

14

Imperialism suffered another check when a second Dundonald incident arose in June. The acting minister of militia, Sydney Fisher, had crossed off the name of a political opponent from the list of officers of a new militia regiment raised in the Eastern Townships. General Dundonald, already up in arms at the rejection of his advice in the drafting of the new Militia Act, spoke at a military banquet in Montreal on June 4 of this 'gross instance of political interference,'[227] and expressed his desire that 'the militia of Canada may be kept free from party politics.' Dundonald had long been courting the Conservatives, more sympathetic than the Liberals to his imperialist views. His conduct was attacked in the House on June 10 by Fisher and Sir Frederick Borden, and defended by Colonel Sam Hughes, who read a statement from Dundonald, and by Robert Laird Borden, the Conservative leader.

Laurier admitted the good motives of Dundonald, but questioned his discretion and urged him to remember that Canada had responsible government. In passing he referred to Dundonald as 'a foreigner—no . . . he is not a foreigner but he is a stranger,'[228] making one of his rare errors in English by using the equivalent of the French word '*étranger*,' which has both meanings. The Tories waxed indignant at a French Canadian describing an Englishman as a foreigner in Canada. Bourassa intervened in support of Laurier by stating that it was simply a question of a public servant making a speech in which he had used unjustifiable expressions about a member of the cabinet: 'Lord Dundonald and those who preceded him as commander of the troops never seem to have understood that the commander of the militia is a servant of the State . . . If the commander of the troops is of the opinion that the system applied by the Minister of Militia and the Canadian Parliament is defective, he had only two choices: to submit or to resign . . .'[229] Lord Minto agreed to Dundonald's immediate dismissal, though he disagreed with the government's support of Fisher, and signed the order-in-council of June 14 which relieved Dundonald of his functions. Dundonald had urged Minto to delay while he sought to appeal to public opinion, which he did through Sam Hughes, who got the *Ottawa Citizen* and other Conservative organs in Ontario to espouse the general's cause. The *Citizen* declared the country was tired of being governed by the Province of Quebec, and called upon Canadian Scots to avenge their distinguished compatriot.

The quarrel, which was really one between Fisher and Dundonald, was quickly turned for political purposes into one between Dundonald and Laurier, and thus one in which ethnic feeling could be aroused. When the question came up again in the House, Laurier declared firmly: 'So long as there is a Liberal government in Canada, the civil power shall rule the military power.'[230] He deplored the press' effort to describe his use of the word 'foreigner' as deliberately insulting and indicative of anti-British feeling. He made a statement of his high standards of political controversy, and concluded: 'If sixty years of what I believe to be, after all, an honourable life, a life which has certainly been one of loyal devotion to British institutions, is not a sufficient answer to such an insinuation, I will not attempt to make an answer.'[231] Up to his departure for England late in July Dundonald conducted an imperialist campaign, holding mass meetings in Toronto, Ottawa, and Montreal against the government's action, and urging his auditors, 'Keep both hands on the British flag.'[232]

This campaign had its aftermath in the Conservative opposition to the new Militia Bill, which provided that henceforward the commanding officer should be a Canadian and that the militia could be put on active service, 'anywhere in Canada and outside Canada, for the defence of this last.' A Conservative criticized the 'defence of Canada' clause and asked whether or not Canada was a part of the empire. Others saw in it a weakening of the British connection. On August 1 Sam Hughes burst out with the charge that the clause 'was inspired not by the Minister of Militia but by the member for Labelle.' Bourassa demanded a retraction. When Hughes in accordance with the rules of the House was forced to make a half-hearted one, he was interrupted by Armand Lavergne, who observed that 'all our population is faithful to England,' a statement which Hughes flatly denied.[233]

The Tories also opposed Honoré Gervais' proposal for the foundation in Montreal of a School of Higher Commercial Studies to train Canadian consular agents, picturing Laurier as being under Bourassa's anti-British influence and yielding to it. In fact Bourassa was inclined at this period to retire from politics and to become postmaster of Montreal. But Laurier thanked him for his services during the session in reply to Casgrain and Sam Hughes, and urged him to remain in parliament. Laurier wanted an offset to English-Canadian criticism of the guarantee of Catholic minority rights in the two new provinces of Alberta and Saskatchewan, which were to be set up in the North-West Territories after the forthcoming elections.[234] Bourassa promised to stay in politics, and began to prepare himself to argue the case of the minorities.

In Quebec Laurier, hailed as the conqueror of imperialism, had seemingly little to fear in the elections from the Conservatives or the Nationalists. Bourassa and Lavergne ran as Liberals with strong Liberal support, while only Charles Angers in Charlevoix and Asselin in Terrebonne appeared as independent nationalists. Dominique Monet had momentarily withdrawn from politics, hurt at being set aside in favor of Rodolphe Lemieux for the office of solicitor-general. Asselin and Bourassa, both hypercritical by temperament, had drifted apart, and Bourassa ceased to write for *Le Nationaliste.* It was the nationalist organ, however, that on October 16 first published the news of the sale of *La Presse*, previously an influential supporter of Laurier, in an intrigue by Mackenzie and Mann—the promoters of the Canadian Northern—to upset the Laurier government and its plan for the Grand Trunk Pacific, the chief national issue in the election.

Andrew Blair of New Brunswick, who had resigned from the administration after earlier opposition to its railway policy, was enlisted as political chief of the intrigue, which was organized by David Russell, a New Brunswick and Montreal speculator associated with Mackenzie and Mann, and J. N. Greenshields of Montreal, their lawyer. Hugh Graham of the *Star* and Arthur Dansereau of *La Presse* were also involved. The plot called for the purchase of *La Presse* and other Liberal journals, which were to oppose Laurier and reveal scandals in the administration, and the bribing of Liberal candidates in Quebec. Once the revolt was well advanced, the conspirators hoped to be able to dictate the railroad policy of the Conservative government they hoped to put into office.

But the revelations made by *Le Nationaliste* and *La Patrie*—for Tarte found the plot distasteful—indicating that the Mackenzie and Mann interests were involved in the purchase of *La Presse*, upset the scheme. Thomas Côté, Laurier's disciple on *La Presse*, balked at the publication of anti-Laurier articles. Robert Borden, the Conservative leader, refused to have Blair thrust upon him as prospective minister of railways and to have any part of the scheme. Laurier threatened to denounce the sale of *La Presse* to a group of English-speaking speculators, thus destroying its circulation, and party discipline was re-established over the Liberals who had been ready to desert their leader. Edward Farrer, as agent of Laurier, compiled a report on the intrigue and most of the information thus obtained was published in the *Toronto Globe* in December.[235] The conspiracy collapsed, and *La Presse* returned to the Liberal fold.

In the elections of November 3, 1904, the Liberals lost three seats in Quebec and increased their strength in Ontario. Except in Prince Edward Island, they swept the other provinces. Their majority in the House was nearly double that of 1896. If imperialism was to be identified with the Conservative cause, it had suffered a crushing defeat, for even the Conservative leader Borden was overwhelmed at the polls. Laurier had reached the zenith of his power, with his supporters, English and French alike, backing his growing nationalism as prosperity prevailed in the country and the West looked forward to even greater expansion with the construction of a new transcontinental railroad. No one rivaled Laurier in 1904 as the embodiment of the new Canada or matched his hold upon the hearts of Canadians, English and French alike. But in Quebec a groundswell of youthful nationalism was rising which threatened his dominance of his native province. The hero of the young nationalists was Henri Bourassa, not Sir Wilfrid Laurier.

Notes

[1] J. A. Hobson, *Imperialism* (New York, 1902), 10.
[2] C. A. Bodelsen, *Studies in Mid-Victorian Imperialism* (New York, 1925), 16.
[3] *Ibid.*, 19 n.
[4] *Ibid.*, 26.
[5] *Ibid.*, 33–4.
[6] *Ibid.*, 34.
[7] *Ibid.*, 37.
[8] O. D. Skelton, *Life & Times of Sir A. T. Galt* (Toronto, 1920), 232.
[9] *Ibid.*, 330–1.
[10] The term occurs in all the early drafts of the B.N.A. Act (J. Pope, *Confederation Documents*, 159, 181), and was altered at the instance of Lord Derby (J. Pope, *Macdonald*, 332).
[11] Bodelsen, 55.
[12] Lord Acton, *History of Freedom & Other Essays* (London, 1907), 276. The essay on 'Nationality' was written in 1862.
[13] Bodelsen, 56.
[14] C. W. Dilke, *Greater Britain: Saxon Sketches* (New York, 1869), preface.
[15] *Ibid.*, 57.
[16] *Ibid.*, 59.
[17] *Ibid.*, 67.
[18] *Ibid.*, 66.
[19] *Ibid.*, 346–8.
[20] Bodelsen, 80.
[21] *Ibid.*, 94.
[22] *Ibid.*, 99.
[23] *Ibid.*, 103.
[24] *Ibid.*, 105 n. 2.

[25] *Ibid.*, 115–16.

[26] *Ibid.*, 121.

[27] *Ibid.*

[28] *Ibid.*

[29] *Ibid.*

[30] *Ibid.*, 122.

[31] *Ibid.*, 124–5.

[32] *Ibid.*, 125.

[33] J. E. Tyler, *The Struggle for Imperial Unity 1869–95*, (London, 1938), 31.

[34] *Ibid.*, 36; B. H. Brown, *The Tariff Reform Movement in Great Britain, 1881–1895* (New York, 1943), 87.

[35] Bodelsen, 175.

[36] *Ibid.*, 156.

[37] *Ibid.*, 158.

[38] J. R. Seeley, *The Expansion of England* (London, 1883), 171.

[39] Bodelsen, 206–7.

[40] Tyler, 108.

[41] Bodelsen, 207.

[42] *Ibid.*

[43] Tyler, 110.

[44] Sir J. Willison, *Sir George Parkin* (London, 1929), 44.

[45] *Ibid.*, 85.

[46] Tyler, 113.

[47] *Ibid.*, 115.

[48] *Ibid.*, 120.

[49] Tyler, 126.

[50] *Ibid.*, 135.

[51] W. Caniff, *Canadian Nationality: Its Growth & Development* (Toronto, 1875), 7.

[52] G. T. Denison, *The Struggle for Imperial Unity* (London, 1909), 15.

[53] *Ibid.*, 42.

[54] Caniff, 16.

[55] *Ibid.*, 18.

[56] O. D. Skelton, *Life & Letters of Sir Wilfrid Laurier* (Toronto, 1921), I, 176.

[57] *Canada First: a Memorial of the Late William A. Foster, Q.C.* With an introduction by Goldwin Smith (Toronto, 1890), 80–1.

[58] Caniff, 18.

[59] Sir J. Pope (ed.), *Correspondence of Sir John Macdonald* (Toronto, 1921), 422–3, Macdonald-editor of *United Service Gazette*, 18 Sept. 1888.

[60] Sir J. Pope, *Memoirs of Sir John Alexander Macdonald* (Toronto, 1930), 581.

[61] Pope, *Correspondence*, 468, Macdonald-Machin, 4 April 1890.

[62] Skelton, *Galt*, 540.

[63] Pope, *Correspondence*, Macdonald-Tupper, 14 Aug. 1889.

[64] Sir C. Tupper, *Recollections of Sixty Years in Canada* (London, 1914), 249.

[65] Skelton, *Laurier*, I, 415.

[66] G. Smith, *Canada and the Canadian Problem* (London, 1891), 267.

[67] Skelton, *Laurier*, I, 363.

[68] *Ibid.*, 365.

[69] *Ibid.*, 376.

[70] *Ibid.*, 380.

[71] Denison, *Struggle*, 103; *Chicago Tribune*, 26 Sept. 1888.

[72] *Ibid.*, 104–5.

[73] *Ibid.*, 108–9.

[74] *Ibid.*, 110–16.

[75] Skelton, *Laurier*, I, 415.

[76] *Ibid.*, 418.

[77] J. Chamberlain, *Foreign & Colonial Speeches* (London, 1897), 6–13.

[78] *Ibid.*, 200.

[79] J. L. Garvin, *Life of Joseph Chamberlain* (London, 1934), II, 468.

[80] Denison, 146–7.

[81] Chamberlain, *Speeches*, 201–2.

[82] W. L. Strauss, *Joseph Chamberlain* (Washington, 1942), 62.

[83] Garvin, III, 5.

[84] *Ibid.*, III, 23–4.

[85] *Ibid.*, III, 179–81.

[86] *Ibid.*, III, 183–4.

[87] *Ibid.*, III, 185.

[88] Skelton, *Laurier*, II, 58.

[89] *Ibid.*, II, 67.

[90] Garvin, III, 187.

[91] *Ibid.*, 188.

[92] Skelton, *Laurier*, II, 72.

[93] Garvin, III, 188.

[94] R. Rumilly, *Histoire*, VIII, 202.

[95] Garvin, III, 192.

[96] Rumilly, VIII, 203.

[97] Skelton, *Laurier*, II, 81.

[98] *Ibid.*, 82.

[99] Strauss, 82.

[100] PAC: Governor-General's Numbered Files 162 (July–Dec. 1884), Vol. II, Colonial Office-Lansdowne, 20 Aug. 1884.

[101] *Ibid.*, 162-II, Lansdowne-Colonial Office, 21 Aug. 1884; I, Detachment Issue Sheets.

[102] *Ibid.*, 162-I, Lansdowne-Derby, 5 Sept. 1884.

[103] *Ibid.*, 114, Nos. 36–50, 9–19 Feb. 1885. Lansdowne reported to Derby on February 9 and 10 that General J. W. Laurie of Nova Scotia and Lt.-Col. A. T. H. Williams had offered to raise troops 'for active duty in defence of the Empire.' In reply Derby asked whether these offers were sanctioned by the Canadian government. Lansdowne indicated that the offer was probably illegal under Section 61 of the Canadian Militia Act, but that the Canadian government approved recruiting under the Imperial Army Act at British expense. He proposed a contingent of three battalions from the Maritimes, 'Old Canada,' and Manitoba. On February 19 Derby declined the offer for the present because of the delay involved, and suggested New South Wales' offer of men to serve in British units as a model. On February 20 the *Toronto Daily Mail* commented: 'The British Government of course would foot the bill . . . We cannot afford it; moreover there's no necessity for it.' An index of the impact of imperialism on English Canada in the next fifteen years is provided by the fact that such an attitude on the part of the French press in 1899 would have been promptly stamped as 'disloyal.'

[104] J. Buchan, *Lord Minto* (London, 1924), 82, 83.

[105] *Ibid.*, 105.

[106] Skelton, *Laurier*, II, 86 *n*.

[107] Buchan, 129.

[108] *Ibid.*, 130, Minto-Wolseley, 21 April 1899.

[109] Pope, *Correspondence*, 337–8, Macdonald-Tupper, 12 March 1885.

[110] Denison, 258.

[111] Buchan, 133.

[112] W. S. Evans, *The Canadian Contingent & Canadian Imperialism* (Toronto, 1901), 11–12.

[113] *Ibid.*, 13.

[114] Buchan, 134–5, Laurier-Minto, Aug. 1899.

[115] Denison, 260.

[116] Buchan, 136, Minto-Arthur Elliott, 28 Sept. 1899.

[117] *Ibid.*, 137.

[118] Garvin, III, 139.

[119] Skelton, *Laurier*, II, 96.

[120] *Ibid.*, 97.

[121] Buchan, 141, Minto-Chamberlain, 14 Oct. 1899.

[122] Skelton, *Laurier*, II, 98 *n.*

[123] Rumilly, VIII, 120.

[124] *Ibid.*, 139.

[125] Buchan, 143.

[126] Skelton, *Laurier*, II, 99.

[127] The great majority of these men were English Canadians, including many recent immigrants whose ties with the mother country were still close. Some French Canadians laid the foundations of their careers by espousing the unpopular imperial cause: Colonel Oscar Pelletier of Quebec was second in command of the first contingent, and Dr. Eugène Fiset, later deputy-minister of defence and lieutenant-governor of Quebec, was surgeon-major. The Quebec company included four French-Canadian non-commissioned officers and thirty-two privates. Colonel F.-E. Lessard accompanied the second contingent. G. P. Labat, *Le Livre d'or of the Canadian Contingents in South Africa* (Montreal, 1901), 155, 82.

[128] Skelton, *Laurier*, II, 101.

[129] Buchan, 146.

[130] *Ibid.*, 146–7.

[131] *Ibid.*, 148.

[132] Skelton, *Laurier*, II, 104.

[133] *Ibid.*, 104–5.

[134] Evans, 155; Rumilly, IX, 174–81.

[135] Rumilly, IX, 191.

[136] *Ibid.*, IX, 188–92.

[137] Skelton, *Laurier*, II, 106–7.

[138] *Ibid.*, 107.

[139] *Ibid.*

[140] *Ibid.*, 108–9.

[141] Buchan, 159–60, Minto-Chamberlain, March 1900.

[142] *Ibid.*, 158–9.

[143] *Toronto News*, quoted Skelton, II, 113–14.

[144] Buchan, 161–2, Minto-Arthur Elliott, Nov. 1900.

[145] Skelton, II, 114.

[146] *Toronto News*, 8 Nov. 1899; quoted Rumilly, IX, 261–2.

[147] Skelton, II, 110–13; Rumilly, X, 12–21.

[148] Buchan, 153.

[149] Immigration from the United Kingdom, which had averaged 11,000 annually since 1897, reached 50,000 in 1904 and 120,000 in 1908. Although the latter figure was unusually high, the annual total never dropped below 50,000 until 1910, and was over 100,000 for the four following years, reaching 150,000 in 1914. *Canada Year Book 1922–23* (Ottawa, 1924), 206. The total amounted to over a million by 1914.

[150] C. C. Tansill, *Canadian-American Relations, 1875–1911* (New Haven, 1943), 446.

[151] Skelton, *Laurier*, II, 47.

[152] Garvin, III, 129–30.

[153] Buchan, 160.

[154] Garvin, III, 129–30.

[155] Skelton, *Laurier*, II, 293.
[156] [H. Borden (*ed.*)] *Robert Laird Borden: His Memoirs* (Toronto, 1938), I, 82.
[157] *Ibid.*, 87.
[158] Buchan, 160.
[159] Skelton, *Laurier*, II, 294.
[160] *Ibid.*, 295.
[161] *Ibid.*, 297.
[162] *Ibid.*, 299.
[163] Rumilly, X, 125.
[164] Buchan, 205.
[165] *Ibid.*, 199.
[166] Skelton, II, 301.
[167] *Ibid.*, 177.
[168] Denison, 366-7.
[169] Strauss, 106.
[170] *Ibid.*, 109.
[171] *Ibid.*, 112.
[172] Denison, 347.
[173] Skelton, *Laurier*, II, 304.
[174] *Ibid.*, 305.
[175] *Ibid.*, 310.
[176] *Ibid.*, 312.
[177] Borden, *Memoirs*, I, 62-4.
[178] Rumilly, XI, 17.
[179] Henri Bourassa, *Great Britain and Canada* (Montreal, 1902), 4-5.
[180] H. Bourassa, *Grande-Bretagne et Canada* (Montréal, 1902), 3-4.
[181] Bourassa, *Great Britain*, 7.
[182] *Ibid.*, 17-18.
[183] *Ibid.*, 39.
[184] *Ibid.*, 45.
[185] Rumilly, X, 106.
[186] *Ibid.*, 108.
[187] *Ibid.*, 117-18.
[188] *Ibid.*, 120-1.
[189] *CHAR 1946*, 65-6, J.-C. Bonenfant & J.-C. Falardeau, 'Cultural and Political Implications of French-Canadian Nationalism.' An edition of this sermon for use in the classical colleges was edited by Canon Emile Chartier under the title of *Bréviaire du patriote canadien-français* (Montréal, 1925). *Ibid.*, 66 *n.* 27.
[190] H. Bourassa, 'The French Canadians in the British Empire,' London *Monthly Review*, Sept.-Oct. 1902.
[191] H. Bourassa, 'Les Canadiens Français et l'Empire britannique,' *La Nouvelle France*, II (Jan. 1903), No. 1, 7-8.
[192] Rumilly, X, 149.
[193] *Ibid.*, 167-8.
[194] G. Smith, *Devant la tribune de l'histoire* (Montréal, 1903), 8.
[195] *Ibid.*, 61.
[196] J. Gauvreau, *Olivar Asselin: précurseur d'action française* (Montréal, 1937), 24.
[197] Rumilly, XI, 14-15.
[198] Gauvreau, 14-22.
[199] L.-A. Groulx, *Une croisade d'adolescents* (Québec, 1912).
[200] *Le Drapeau National des Canadiens Français* (Québec, 1904).
[201] *La Croix* (Montréal), 10 May 1903; cited Groulx, *Croisade*, 233.
[202] Rumilly, XI, 84.
[203] Groulx, *Croisade*, 142-63.
[204] Rumilly, XI, 17.

[205] *Ibid.*, 19-21.
[206] *Ibid.*, 23-4.
[207] *Ibid.*, 23-7.
[208] *Ibid.*, 28.
[209] *Ibid.*, 33-44.
[210] *Ibid.*, 73-5.
[211] *Ibid.*, 78-83.
[212] Rumilly, X, 67-8, Laurier-Madame Lavergne, 29 Nov. 1901.
[213] Rumilly, XI, 85-6.
[214] *Ibid.*, 96.
[215] *CHAR 1945*, 70-1, *Le Nationaliste*, 27 March 1904. Abbé Arthur Maheux, 'Le Nationalisme canadien-français à l'aurore du XXᵉ siècle.'
[216] *Ibid.*, 65-6; *Le Nationaliste*, 20 March 1904.
[217] *Ibid.*, 71-2; *Le Nationaliste*, 17 April 1904.
[218] Groulx, *Croisade*, 179. Other favoured authors were Veuillot, Montalembert, Ozanam, Lacordaire, Henri Perreyve. Two books which influenced the movement politically were Père Berthe's life of Garcia Moreno and Nemours Godré's life of Daniel O'Connell.
[219] *CHAR 1945*, 68; *La Vérité*, 2 April 1904.
[220] *Ibid.*, 69; *Le Nationaliste*, 3 April 1904.
[221] *Ibid.*, 69; *Le Nationaliste*, 25 April 1904.
[222] Rumilly, XI, 125.
[223] *CHAR 1945*, 72-3; *Le Nationaliste*, 8 May 1904.
[224] The *Ligue d'enseignement* was founded by Honoré Gervais and Godfroy Langlois in November 1902 for the reform of Quebec's educational system. Under the inspiration of Langlois, who desired to laicize the system, it soon came into conflict with Archbishop Bruchési.
[225] Rumilly, XI, 158-60.
[226] *Ibid.*, 127-8.
[227] Skelton, II, 198-9.
[228] *Ibid.*, 199-200.
[229] Rumilly, XI, 146.
[230] Skelton, II, 201.
[231] *Ibid.*, 202 n.
[232] *Ibid.*, 202.
[233] Rumilly, XI, 151-2.
[234] *Ibid.*, 162-3.
[235] Skelton, II, 209-16.

CHAPTER X

NATIONALISM *vs.* IMPERIALISM

(1905–11)

T HE YEAR which saw Chamberlain's retirement from politics marked the ebb of the imperialist tide in Canada, and the rise of the nationalist tide in Quebec which had developed in reaction to bumptious jingoism. One appeal to racial solidarity provoked another, and the French Canadians reacted to 'Anglo-Saxonism' by reasserting their French and Catholic heritage with the aggressive spirit which is characteristic of Quebec when it is on the defensive. Two great achievements of Laurier's regime brought about the beginning of its decline. The massive polyglot immigration since 1897, which had peopled the West and added one-third to the nation's population, revived French Canada's fears for cultural survival. The rapid development of the West called for the creation of new provinces in the old North-West Territories. This step raised once more the question of minority rights, with its ethnic and religious differences whose power to disrupt Canadian national life Laurier knew only too well. For all his political adroitness and willingness to compromise, he could not avoid a bitter division of the nation and of his following, and with that division the eventual doom of his regime was assured.

I

As early as 1903 the Conservatives demanded the enfranchisement of the Territories, and thenceforward opposition papers began to agitate the school question in order to embarrass the government. During the 1904 campaign Laurier promised to introduce a measure creating new provinces if he were re-elected. Early in that year he wrote John S. Willison, who had declared in the *Toronto News* that the formation of new provinces was being delayed until after the election because the hierarchy demanded separate schools, that he anticipated the outbreak of 'bitter passions on both sides' and that it would be his lot 'to fight extremists and to place and maintain the question where it has been placed by the British North America Act.' Laurier urged Willison to remember that Confederation was a compromise and that the work of effecting union was far from complete: 'The work must be continued in the same spirit in which it was conceived, and I certainly indulge the hope that you and I will always find it easy to stand on that ground.'[1]

On February 21, 1905 Laurier introduced the Autonomy Bills, establishing the provinces of Alberta and Saskatchewan, which had been drafted by Charles Fitzpatrick, the minister of justice, after a conference with the territorial authorities, and after consultation through Bourassa with Mgr. Sbaretti, the apostolic delegate, on the school clause. The bills represented the views of Clifford Sifton, the Western leader in the cabinet, except for the school clause which was drafted after his departure for a rest in Florida. Sifton had already had differences with Laurier as a result of the latter's growing habit of presenting the cabinet with a *fait accompli*, and in particular had been irritated by being passed over for the justice portfolio in favor of Fitzpatrick. In introducing the bills Laurier dealt cautiously with the school question, urging the spirit of toler-ance in which Confederation had been achieved. Protection of minority rights was an essential feature of that compact. The principle had been reinforced by Edward Blake's definition of these rights in the North-West Territories Act of 1875, whose educational clause provided that, as in Ontario, the majority should establish such schools as they saw fit, while the minority had the right to organize separate schools and to share in public funds for education. The Act had been opposed by George Brown in the Senate, but had been passed by a large majority of both parties. The new bills provided for the continuation of this tradition. In conclusion Laurier made an appeal for fairness in carrying on the principle embodied in Confederation, whose value he illustrated by con-trasting sound conditions in Canada resulting from religious teaching in the schools with the social disorder in the United States where religion was banned in the public schools.[2]

In reply the Conservative leader, R. L. Borden, took the position that the school question and the control of public lands should be left to the people of the new provinces. In fact there was little criticism of the proposals in the West; but the Ontario Conservatives, under the leadership of Sam Hughes, W. F. Maclean, and Dr. Sproule, launched an opposition movement which was supported by the Orange Order. Dr. Carman, General Superintendent of the Methodist Church, called the measure 'reactionary, mad, monstrous, hideous, and oppressive,' while Presbyterian, Baptist, and other Pro-testant ministerial associations demanded its withdrawal. Goldwin Smith, always an opponent of close relations between Church and State, felt that it bound the new provinces to maintain and propa-gate Catholicism. Willison's *Toronto News* and the *Toronto Telegram* denounced this 'endowment of clerical privilege,' this 'fastening of the dead hand of denominational control' upon the new provinces.[3]

But the most serious reaction of all was a revolt within the Liberal camp. Sifton hurried back to Ottawa from Florida, and finding that the school clause scrapped all subsequent territorial educational provisions in favor of the 1875 status, promptly resigned as minister of the interior. He had previously advised Laurier that Western public opinion favored continuing the existing school system, which by the ordinances of 1892 and 1901, passed under the influence of D'Alton McCarthy, had put crippling restrictions on separate schools and had secularized the educational system. Sifton, the supporter of the Manitoba School Act and the prophet of a West which would be English rather than English and French, could hardly support the administration's policy. In addition he was at swords' points with Fitzpatrick, and the administration of his department was under fire. His resignation as minister of the interior was announced on March 1, while at the same time it became known that William Fielding, the minister of finance, also disliked the separate school clause and might resign. There were rumors of other prospective cabinet resignations, while the *Toronto Globe* urged that under the Liberal principle of provincial rights the educational clause must be opposed. The *Montreal Herald* and *Witness*, and Sifton's *Manitoba Free Press* also revolted. [4]

Laurier found himself in much the same position as Mackenzie Bowell in 1895 on the Manitoba school question, with his own party split and the opposition making the most of the division. He took a firmer stand in favor of minority rights than he had in 1896, perhaps because of Manitoba's and Ontario's insistence that Quebec should make all the sacrifices demanded for national unity. When Sifton announced his intention of resigning, Laurier replied that this distrust of him as a French Canadian and as a Catholic by Protestant Liberals suggested that he should resign as prime minister. [5] When this threat was ineffective and the agitation against the bill continued to rise both in the House and the press, Laurier called a meeting of the Quebec Liberals, and told them that it was necessary to compromise or lose power—power both to aid the minorities of the West and to enjoy the patronage which maintained their position. Only Bourassa and Lavergne opposed a compromise. Mgr. Sbaretti, bowing to the storm, informed Laurier that he would accept a compromise. [6]

Sifton, who headed the Liberal revolt in parliament, proposed to Laurier a compromise drafted by himself and negotiated with Fitzpatrick by H. M. Howell of Winnipeg as representative of the Western members. [7] The new educational clause, which replaced the original Article 16 when the Autonomy Bills came up for second reading on March 22, applied Section 93 of the British North America Act to the new provinces, as its predecessor had done, but modified by the Territorial Ordinances of 1901. After emphasizing that the minority provision of the British North America Act had been created at the instance of the Protestants of Quebec, Laurier explained the new clause as one avoiding the confusion and litigation which might arise under the original one. But Sifton, in supporting the compromise, flatly characterized the difference between the two clauses as that between a system of complete ecclesiastical control and one of secular control, with religious teaching after school hours. He hailed the new measure as one containing the essential principles of a national school system, free from 'the taint of ecclesiasticism.'[8] Borden confined himself to arguing on the provincial rights issue rather on that of separate schools. He said 'Let the minorities trust the majorities and the result will be the same as in Nova Scotia and New Brunswick,'[9] and moved not to defeat the bill, but for a resolution urging for the new provinces 'full powers of provincial self-government, including power to exclusively make laws in relation to education.'[10] Fielding stated his dislike for the principle of separate schools, but urged that the legal basis now provided did not justify a governmental crisis and a consequent struggle on religious lines.

When Bourassa rose in the House on March 28, fireworks were anticipated; but he contented himself with a statement of the French-Canadian and Catholic position, reserving for the third reading his criticism of the bill and an amendment to it. He spoke, as Rodolphe Lemieux had already done, of the role of French-Canadian priests and colonists in opening up the West to civilization. Their descendants deserved the same treatment that the Protestant minority received in Quebec. But the opposition found it natural to support the suppression of Catholic separate schools in the West, though they would denounce as infamous the suppression of the Protestant separate schools in Quebec. He urged justice to the French Canadians and the two million Catholics who dwelt in Canada. They should not be forced to conclude that their country was limited to Quebec, since they could not obtain justice in the English-speaking provinces.[11] Despite Bourassa's restraint, he did not refrain from referring to Dr. Sproule, Grandmaster of the Orange Order and a leader in the anti-French agitation, as 'chief of the Orange Hierarchy,' and from advising Sam Hughes, who had regretted that unlike most of the French-Canadian members he could not express himself in both languages, to take a course in the separate schools.[12]

The debate dragged on through April, with new fuel added to the fire by the Conservative charge that the government had been influenced by Mgr. Sbaretti. Maclean made rude references to the apostolic delegate and the Pope, and was rebuked by Bourassa, who referred to the 'clerical intervention' of the Protestant ministers of Ontario. The ablest Conservative speaker, George Foster, made a violent attack on the government's inconsistencies; but the influential Conservative Herbert Ames of Montreal supported the bill, while Frederick Monk attacked the myth that the Quebec voter was subjected to any greater clerical influence than his English-speaking fellows. Despite the opposition to the law of Archbishop Langevin of Saint-Boniface and Bishop Cloutier of Trois-Rivières, supported by *Le Nationaliste*, *La Vérité*, *La Semaine religieuse* of Quebec, and *L'Evénement*, which deplored the 'capitulation' of Laurier and urged 'Let us go down like men,' the French Canadians refused to unite against the measure and were gradually won over by the Liberal press.[13] The vote on the second reading on May 3 was carried by 140 to 59. Only one Liberal, a nephew of D'Alton McCarthy true to family tradition, voted against it, and ten Quebec Conservatives voted for it. In two Ontario by-elections, where the Conservative cry was to vote against 'Laurier, Sbaretti, and the Pope,' the Liberal candidates were successful; and when Frank Oliver was named to replace Sifton as minister of the interior, he was returned by acclamation in Edmonton, despite Toronto prophecies of revolt in the West.

Bourassa gave a foretaste of his promised future criticism of the bill at a meeting called by the *Ligue Nationaliste* on April 17, 1905 at the Monument National in Montreal. The *Ligue* and the A.C.J.C., now led by Antonio Perrault, were aroused by the issue, and looked to Bourassa for leadership. His disciple Lavergne and Auguste Noel of Edmonton, the fiancé of Lavergne's sister, urged Bourassa to exercise pressure on Laurier. Before speaking on the question, Bourassa studied it thoroughly. His address '*Les Ecoles du Nord-Ouest*,' was a model of scholarly polemic, tracing the historical development of the question and dissolving the fogs of legalism to lay bare the essential points. He began by calling the question 'perhaps the gravest' since Confederation, since it was a matter of providing a constitution for what promised to become half the Canadian nation. The dualism of the British North America Act of 1867 must be applied to the West if it were to become Canadian despite a vast foreign immigration, primarily American and predisposed to commercial union and perhaps even annexation. He asserted the right of the French-Canadian Catholic, whose forefathers had pioneered the West, to enjoy there the same rights which the English-Canadian Protestant enjoyed in Quebec. He announced his intention of analyzing the question justly and impartially, for this was 'one of those hours in which men and parties do not count, since religion, the country, and nationality were in danger.'[14]

Then he traced the development of Canadian educational law from the beginning of the Confederation movement, with Galt as representative of the Quebec English Protestants insisting upon a guarantee of minority rights, which had been interpreted by Lord Carnarvon as putting the Catholic minority of Upper Canada, the Protestant minority of Lower Canada, and the Catholic minority of the Maritimes upon a footing of perfect equality. Thus Section 93 of the British North America Act did not apply, as Borden claimed, only to Ontario and Quebec. This pact had been loyally kept by Quebec; at first it had been violated in the Maritimes but later fulfilled in spirit; and for the last ten years it had been violently attacked in Ontario by the Conservatives, whom Sir Oliver Mowat had firmly resisted. Turning to the North-West Territories, Bourassa pointed out that they were the common property of the whole Canadian people and their development had been brought about at the expense of all Canadian taxpayers. The French Canadians had the moral and legal right to insure the lot of the French and Catholic minority in the West, as that of the Protestant minority in Quebec had been safeguarded by Confederation.

Then Bourassa turned to the constitutional history of the West, paying tribute to Blake for his introduction into the Territorial Act of a guarantee of the minority's right to denominational education. The Senate had disregarded George Brown's objections to separate schools in 1875. Why had that parliament shown itself more broad-minded and superior in national spirit to that of 1905? Was it because of the fact that in 1875 the majority in the North-West was Catholic and the minority Protestant? Today, when the situation was reversed, there was a storm of protest when the government proposed to continue the principle laid down thirty years ago. Before D'Alton McCarthy's campaign against the French language and separate schools, the French Canadians of the North-West had enjoyed the same privileges as their compatriots in Quebec. Then the French language had been suppressed in 1891, and the school system secularized in 1892, under a law which Laurier had then said would have been called an 'act of the most infamous tyranny' if it had been directed against the Protestants of Quebec.

It was this very act which the government was now prepared to sanction as an 'honourable compromise.' Faced with such measures, the Catholics of the West had vainly sought justice from Ottawa under Section 93 of the British North America Act. But the government no longer needed the influence of the hierarchy, as it had had in 1869, and no satisfaction was forthcoming. The ordinance of 1901 completed the work of secularizing the separate schools. Bourassa pointed out that the offending territorial ordinances of 1892 and 1901 were illegal, since they violated the underlying

Territorial Act either in letter or spirit. He judged that the government's original bill would have passed without opposition except from Tory Orangemen, if it had not been for Sifton's resignation, which had created a panic in the administration. Laurier had been forced into the path of concession by some of his English colleagues and partisans, while the Quebec members had given him little support. Finally he capitulated and substituted the new clause, which Bourassa called the 'Sifton amendment.' But no concession could appease the fanatics who opposed the original clause: 'justice had been betrayed without benefit to the party.'

Bourassa thus characterized the difference between the two clauses thus: 'Article 16 perpetuates the principle of liberty consecrated in 1875. The Sifton amendment ratifies for all time the infringement of this principle made in 1892.' The latter assured the gradual suppression of Catholic and French education. In thirty-three school districts the Catholics, constituting the majority, were forced to establish public schools; in nine districts, where they constituted the minority, they had a right to maintain schools separate only in name. At any time the educational authorities could suppress the teaching of religion and French, yet the Catholics would be bound by compulsory attendance and taxation laws to support these schools. There was little hope of a federal remedial bill, and nothing in the history of the last thirteen years justified the reliance on the benevolence of the majority which the Conservatives urged. Under the regulations of the Department of Public Instruction, French could be taught only between 3 and 4 in the afternoon and religion from 3.30 to 4, while young children could be dismissed at 3. Either health, faith, or nationality had to suffer. Bourassa summed up by saying:

Such is this regime of liberty, this guarantee of our religious and national rights, that we are urged to accept under the name of an 'honourable compromise!'

In truth, the school system which Lord Kitchener has guaranteed to the Boers of Africa in making peace with them, is more just and liberal than that which it is desired to impose upon us in the West, upon us who have in Canada, and more particularly in these territories, which belong to us as much as to the English and Protestant majority, inalienable rights guaranteed by the treaties and by the constitution.

And because I refuse to accept this iniquity, because I denounce a state of things which so cruelly and odiously infringes the most sacred natural rights of my compatriots and coreligionists, I find myself termed an intransigent, a demagogue, a creator of disorder, a false friend, and a bad citizen.'[15]

He explained that he had not previously spoken against the amendment, because it was not yet formally before the House when he spoke on March 28. He hoped that the administration would keep its pledges and not persist in supporting the amendment when its effect was properly understood. He thus explained his appearance in Montreal:

It was in order that the situation should be clarified and this iniquity not consummated that I have come to demand the moral support of the people of this great city of Montreal—the very heart from which go forth the currents which animate the body of the Canadian nation—of this city where religious liberty reigns so splendidly, where Protestants and Catholics, English and French, you live in such admirable harmony, where each father sees his son grow up in the traditions dear to him, where each Christian mother has the consolation to think, in confiding her child to the public school, that he will find there support for the religious and national ideas she has imparted to him.

I wish that from this hall shall go forth a voice which will penetrate to the floor of the House of Commons and recall the representatives of the people to their duty.[16]

To the argument that Laurier and his colleagues should not be embarrassed, Bourassa replied: 'But it was not in abandoning Laurier to the enemies who surrounded him, more dangerous than his adversaries, that his true friends proved their devotion and affection; on the contrary, by fortifying him with the manifest expression of the desire that they should feel to maintain his individual prestige and his political strength by causing the principles he has himself laid down to triumph.' It was a mistake for the party press to oppose petitions to the House. It was a calumny on the great majority of English Protestants to maintain that the original bill could not be passed because of the fanaticism of the English population and its representatives in Parliament. He had not found the English Canadians fanatics when he spoke in Ontario in time of crisis. He cited the speeches of the Liberal Fisher, and the Conservatives Ames and Pringle, all Protestants, in support of the original bill. He protested against the acceptance of the Sifton amendment as an 'honourable compromise' in the spirit of the conciliation which ought to unite French and English:

Certainly conciliation is good, always and everywhere, and in our country necessary to the existence of our institutions and of our national organization.

But conciliation is never good, it is never possible, between two contrary principles, between truth and error, between justice and iniquity.

To search for the union of the two races of Canada, beyond the mutual respect that they owe to their respective rights, is to build the nation on a fragile foundation, to give it as cornerstone an element of ruin and destruction.

To wish to obtain the esteem, the confidence, and the goodwill of our English fellow citizens in sacrificing our incontestable rights, in consenting ourselves to the rupture of the national compact which guarantees these rights and in accepting thefts, infringements, and insults in the same manner as we welcome fair dealing, is to doom ourselves in advance to scorn and slavery.

The Englishman is proud and strong; he scorns baseness and cowardice, but he bows with respect to those who uphold, without insult and provocation, their rights, their honour, and their possessions.

It is in this spirit that Parliament should seek the solution of the problem that must be solved now.

It is in this spirit that the Fathers of Confederation conceived the charter of our liberties and of our autonomy; it will last only as long as our public men and the whole Canadian people conserve its essence and fundamental basis.[17]

In the actual delivery this speech was phrased more strongly than the printed version. Bourassa was always carried away by a crowd, when the crowd was carried away by his eloquence. He could fire a French audience to tumultuous enthusiasm with a closely thought and wrought address which would have left an English audience, less moved by oratory, somewhat cold. On this occasion he spoke as a leader, and created an effect which was not forgotten. He carefully refrained from breaking with Laurier, but he now stood at the head of a growing group which recognized his leadership rather than Laurier's. Laurier recognized the fact, writing to a friend:

I believe I shall pull through this difficulty, but I am not sure that I shall pull through, as you suggest, stronger than at the beginning. Matters are not going too badly at the moment in the English-speaking provinces. . . . But our friend Bourassa has begun, in Quebec, a campaign which may well cause us some trouble. . . .[18]

Laurier steered a middle course between that called for by Bourassa in Quebec and the opposite one urged by John Willison at a mass meeting in Massey Hall in Toronto on the same date. The middle way seldom arouses enthusiasm, and it was Bourassa's extreme position that won the support of French Canada's educated youth, which found his eloquence intoxicating, and of French Canada's clergy, which saw in him a defender of the Church. In the hierarchical society of Quebec such a following was not to be despised.

In the hope that agitation would die down, Laurier delayed the third reading of the Autonomy Bills, but by-elections fed the flames of anti-'papistry' in Ontario, and in turn aroused a French-Canadian reaction. The Conservative Party, because of the excesses of its Ontario champions, lost further ground in Quebec. Monk and

Bergeron sought to rally the *Bleus* with amendments to the bill, providing bilingualism in the legislatures and courts of the new provinces, and a school system similar to Quebec. But it was Bourassa who, in a three-hour speech in the House on June 28, best expressed French Canada's reaction. He repeated his arguments of April 17 in a calmer tone, appealing to the English-Canadian sense of justice and constitutionalism. He concluded by proposing, with the support of Lavergne, an amendment calling for the application of Article 93 of the British North America Act to the new provinces and the equality of public and separate schools in the distribution of public funds. Dr. Sproule replied to Bourassa, and the latter was also criticized by Rodolphe Lemieux for provoking quarrels between French and English. Lemieux compared him to his grandfather Papineau, who had attacked Lafontaine's conciliatory measures just as Bourassa did those of Laurier. After Lavergne had spoken in support of Bourassa, Dr. Sproule crossed the floor to shake hands with Bourassa and his disciple, amid the applause of the House at this gesture of goodwill from one who bitterly opposed their views. The tension of racial feeling was relaxed for the moment.

But Bourassa's amendment was supported only by himself and Lavergne, and five French-Canadian Conservatives, Monk, Bergeron, Léonard, Morin, and Paquet. Monk's and Bergeron's amendments received the same support, with Laurier, Lemieux, and Ernest Lapointe speaking against them. Laurier recognized the value of Bourassa's criticism, and used it as a wedge to obtain support from the Sifton group of an amendment proposed by Lamont of Saskatchewan, which guaranteed a half-hour of religious instruction in a sort of new Laurier-Greenway agreement. The bill then passed. But a new grievance had been added to the indictment of the French Canadians against the federal government, which had failed to uphold their rights in New Brunswick, Manitoba, and now the North-West. In his final speech Bourassa had revealed an emotional French-Canadian patriotism, rather than his former reasoned Canadian one, thus adopting the attitude of the majority of his followers. If a nationalism which was increasingly provincial in outlook gained ground markedly in Quebec after 1905, it was clear what had provoked it.

The excitement aroused in Quebec by the North-West school question died down during the summer. Then, on September 17, Lavergne addressed his electors at Montmagny to explain his stand. Bourassa supported him, and both refrained from largely blaming Laurier, but rather criticized the failure of his Quebec followers to support his original stand. Paquet, one of the five Conservatives who had backed Bourassa and Lavergne, expressed his pride in having been associated with them. A number of *Bleu* notables of ultramontane stamp attended the meeting, and the Conservative press supported the stand taken by Bourassa and Lavergne. The Liberal press criticized the two young members of parliament for aiding and abetting the Conservatives, and for being unrealistic extremists. There was little popular feeling to add new recruits to the nationalist flock, while the nationalists were divided by differences in principle between the *Ligue Nationaliste*, which put nationalism before religion, and the A.C.J.C., which put religion before nationalism. *La Vérité*, now edited by Omer Héroux, Tardivel's son-in-law who had broken with Asselin, quarreled with *Le Nationaliste*. While division reigned in the nationalist camp, Laurier's prestige was reinforced by overwhelming Liberal victories in the first Alberta and Saskatchewan elections that fall, after a campaign in which the Conservatives urged repeal of the school law as too favorable to Catholics and Archbishop Langevin consequently supported it and the Liberal candidates. Laurier's firm anti-imperialist stand in response to the proposed calling of an imperial council also raised his stock in Quebec.

2

With imperialism seemingly checked, Bourassa now found more frequent occasion to express his French-Canadian patriotism than the larger Canadianism which he had earlier advanced. When during the session of 1906 George Foster sought to discredit the government by attacking Sifton's administration of its immigration policy, Bourassa took the opportunity to criticize a system which peopled the West with a mixture of foreigners, neglecting prospective French and Belgian colonists in favor of Jews from Poland and Russia. The rapid increase of the Jewish population of Montreal had already aroused anti-semitism among the French Canadians,[19] and Bourassa thus gave expression to it. But he was more concerned with voicing Quebec's opposition to an immigration which promised to lessen French Canada's influence by counterbalancing its higher birthrate, and by the national danger which he saw in the new West:

> The East and the West of Canada are separated by a natural barrier which does not exist in the United States . . . Our national unity would be less endangered if there were in the North-West more French and Catholic Canadians, and even separate schools, and fewer of these thousands of strangers who have contributed nothing to the building of the country, who have made no sacrifice for the cause of national unity, and who if we ever had to pass through some fearsome test, would not associate themselves with it.[20]

He warned the government that the Sifton scandals might cause its fall, as other scandals had destroyed the Conservatives.

Again in June, when the government introduced the Sunday Bill desired by the Lord's Day Alliance headed by Dr. Shearer of Toronto, Bourassa criticized the government for yielding to agitators and putting a premium on 'hypocrisy, drunkenness, idleness and the vices that develop in any country where the attempt is made to make people virtuous by law, instead of relying on the individual conscience and the moral quality of the Church.'[21] Laurier took advantage of the opening to proclaim himself once more a follower of the middle path, attacked by extremists on either side; last year he had been accused of being dominated by Mgr. Sbaretti, this year by Dr. Shearer. In fact, the Catholic Fitzpatrick had drafted the bill, and it had been publicly approved by Archbishop Bruchési. But it was a puritanical measure which met with far more approval among the Protestant sects of Ontario and the Maritimes than in Quebec, which habitually enjoyed the freedom of a Continental Sunday after Mass.

The prospect of the extension of the notably cheerless Toronto Sunday to Quebec aroused public feeling. The *Ligue Nationaliste*, quite willing to settle old scores with Ontario fanatics, called a mass meeting in Montreal at the Champs de Mars on June 29, with Bourassa, Lavergne, and labor leaders as speakers. The meeting was intended to reveal public opinion, but the placards announcing it had already taken a stand. They read '*A bas l'hypocrisie!*', '*Vive la liberté!*' Ten thousand workers and small merchants of Montreal attended. Bourassa denounced the bill and a proposed compromise, which gave the provinces the right to make exceptions to it:

The citizens of Quebec respect the Lord's Day as much as anyone, but protest against a measure derogatory to the ancient customs of the province and infringing the civil rights and social organization which they have enjoyed, both under the French regime and the various constitutions which Great Britain has given them since the Treaty of Paris. . . .[22]

Bourassa concluded by submitting resolutions for the assembly's approval, petitioning parliament to respect provincial rights by submitting the application of the law in each province to the decision of the legislature. He was promised the support of Alphonse Verville, labor member for the Montreal constituency of Maisonneuve, in voting against the bill on its third reading. Bourassa's resolutions were voted by acclamation.

To his student following Bourassa now added that of labor, which was beginning to make itself felt in politics. He was attacked in the Liberal press for setting himself up in opposition to Archbishop

Bruchési as guardian of public morality, and in the House by Camille Piché, representative of the Montreal workers' quarter of Sainte-Marie, who saw in Bourassa's intervention a raid on his political preserves.

On July 6 Bourassa introduced an amendment to the Lord's Day Bill in accordance with the Champs de Mars resolution, and spoke three hours in its favor, heckled by Liberal interruptions. The amendment won the support of fifteen votes, among them those of Lavergne, Verville, Monk, Paquet, Bergeron, and Léonard. The agitation Bourassa had begun continued, with Quebec increasingly indignant at having Ontario's customs thrust upon her, and with the big industrialists joining the opposition to the bill. The latter made their influence felt in the Senate, which imposed amendments to the law embodying Bourassa's suggestions. Thus, while settling old scores with Sifton and the Ontario sectarians, Bourassa increased his political influence. He found himself for the first time in the company of the great English-Canadian interests, which were later to make a brief but effective alliance with him. And he came closer to an open break with Laurier, using his growing popularity in Quebec as a threat in his closing words of personal appeal:

Despite all that has passed between you and those who think as I do, I appeal to you to remember that the eyes of the Canadian people are fixed upon you tonight.

It is in your hands to decide whether you will give this Bill the stamp which will make it acceptable to the people of this country. You can do that, or you can refuse to do it. But I say again, we are not at present in the same condition that we were on some other questions that have caused so much difficulty in this country. We are not in the same circumstances that we were in the Manitoba school case, or the Northwest school case, or the Boer War, because in those days the government were obliged to adopt and to follow a uniform line of conduct. I think that the government were wrong then, but the people of Canada have judged that they were right. But the position today is not what it was then. Then you were forced as a government to adopt certain legislation and to follow one line of action. But that is not the case at present. You can adopt this legislation and give satisfaction at the same time to Quebec and Ontario. I repeat to the Prime Minister that when it is a question of choosing between Quebec and Ontario, when it becomes necessary to trample upon the feelings of Quebec or the feelings of Ontario, in such a case there must necessarily be a compromise, there must be give and take. On an occasion like this, when you can give to Ontario what it desires and when you can refrain from imposing upon Quebec what she does not desire, I appeal to the best feelings of the Prime Minister, I appeal to the principles he has proclaimed, to the conduct that he has followed ever since he began his career, and I say, do not minimize the authority of the voice that utters these sentiments to you. If anything personal has passed between us, let us ignore it; let us trample upon personal feelings. But I repeat to you that my voice tonight is not the echo of a single individual; it is the voice, not only of Quebec, but it is the voice of Ontario as spontaneously expressed in many of their newspaper organs; and it appeals to you that, while giving to Ontario what it wants, you do not impose upon Quebec what it does not want.[23]

This appeal to the people may have been rhetorical, but that fall Bourassa made one in all earnest by supporting an independent Liberal, Lorenzo Robitaille, in a by-election in Quebec County against G.-E. Amyot, the official candidate. The latter, a successful manufacturer, had been imposed by the party upon the constituency; Robitaille was a native son and represented the masses. In the campaign Amyot was supported by the Liberal leaders and the Liberal machine; Robitaille only by Bourassa and a few of his followers, with Asselin exercising his talent for verbal assassination in a little campaign sheet, *La Mitraille*. The culminating point of the campaign was a joint meeting at Beauport on October 20, for which 20,000 people gathered. First Bourassa and Lavergne joined Robitaille in addressing 6,000 of his supporters denouncing the Liberal practice of imposing candidates on the people and turning them into voting machines; while Lemieux and Prévost gave the endorsement of the federal and provincial governments to Amyot before a larger crowd nearby. Then Bourassa invaded Amyot's meeting and attacked him and his supporters for being servile followers of the party to which he himself gave his support—but not blindly.[24]

The election became a test of the leadership of Laurier and that of Bourassa, and the latter's candidate defeated the official Liberal. The Conservative press promptly hailed the beginning of the end of Laurier's supremacy in Quebec, while the Liberal papers denounced Bourassa as a demagogue who concealed personal ambition beneath professions of independence. But other independent candidates appeared, and Bourassa's following grew. The Liberal organs warned that if Quebec adopted Bourassa's strictly French and Catholic point of view, Ontario would follow Dr. Sproule, Sam Hughes, and W. F. MacLean in a strictly English and Protestant policy, with civil war as a result.[25]

In November Bourassa also supported Joseph Ainey, the labor candidate in Sainte-Marie, against Médéric Martin, the official standard-bearer. Bourassa defended the candidate of the international unions against charges of radicalism by expounding Leo XIII's approval of labor organizations and declaring that he had not denounced the international unions. Again he urged a revolt against party discipline in the interest of independent judgment. Carried away by his vehemence, he called his Liberal colleagues 'traitors' and 'vendus.' The Liberals made the most of the obvious incongruity of the intellectual aristocrat Bourassa supporting the growing labor movement. A coalition of nationalists and 'socialists' appeared too extreme to the electorate, and the official candidate was elected by a large majority.[26] But the Liberals had had a scare at the prospect of the insurgent nationalists being joined in the House by labor members who would doubtless have followed Bourassa's leadership after his intervention in the election.

When parliament met late in November, Bourassa criticized the government policy on immigration, but above all he sought to justify his previous departures from the party's official position and proclaimed his loyalty to true Liberal principles. Late in January Laurier, acting at the instigation of the party regulars who had been outraged by Lavergne's part in managing Robitaille's campaign, expelled his protégé from the party by depriving him of the patronage for his constituency. On February 5, 1906, Lavergne defended his course on the same grounds as Bourassa had done, saying that the people preferred independent men to slaves and voting machines. War between the Liberals and the nationalists was now more or less open. On February 25 Lavergne proposed a bill extending bilingualism to currency and postage stamps. The measure was gently killed by the government forces. Arthur Dansereau wrote condescendingly in La Presse that Lavergne was cutting his teeth, to which Lavergne replied that his bibulous critic was still on the bottle. But Lavergne won the support of Senator Philippe Landry, who had called for the use of French in the militia regulations. Bourassa was becoming something of a figure in the House, and when the Conservatives charged that the government members were given to 'wine, women, and graft,' he demanded a parliamentary commission of inquiry into the charge. His holier-than-thou attitude irritated the government's supporters, but he was supported by the Conservatives. Laurier defended the honor of parliament and the motion was rejected by the government majority. But Bourassa continued his attacks, and Le Nationaliste published a picture of the cabinet, with a frame suggesting the charges and a large question mark.[27] Laurier's partisans were outraged that he was included, for none of the many scandals engendered by the administration's long stay in office had touched the prime minister.

In April Lavergne and Bourassa launched a new attack on the government's immigration policy. Lavergne pointed out that the newcomers now numbered 37 per cent of the population and in another ten years might well represent half the population. He said Canada needed only English and French immigrants, and called for more of the latter. Bourassa protested against the tendency to swamp the French Canadians, and criticized the railway tariff which made it much more expensive for a French Canadian to reach the West than for a foreign immigrant. Robitaille joined in with a demand that the government make the same effort to recruit immigrants in France as in England. Bourassa criticized the fact that in the Canadian immigration bureaus he had visited in Europe, all the literature was devoted to the West. He urged that the East had the same right to receive immigrants, and urged Lemieux on his next visit to France to seek immigrants there and in Belgium. Lemieux contented himself with observing that Frenchmen had proved reluctant to emigrate, despite the efforts made by two Canadian agents. These criticisms of Bourassa expressed the feeling of his supporters, who feared that French Canada would lose its influence as its numbers were dwarfed by immigration, and who felt that there was a definite attempt to prevent French-Canadian expansion outside Quebec. Again Bourassa and Lavergne had an opportunity to pose as the defenders of Quebec when the Fielding resolutions, providing for a revision of provincial subsidies according to population, every ten years for the old provinces and every five for the West, came before the House. Bourassa protested against the inequality, and against the necessary modification of the British North America Act by the British parliament. The session closed with the nationalists having achieved only a nuisance value, but the three-man party nonetheless had made itself felt.

Their student followers had been somewhat restrained for the moment by an article in *Le Semeur* by Antonio Perrault, president of the A.C.J.C., which criticized 'men who believe, wrongly, that they alone possess, in all things, the monopoly of sound doctrine and of the good . . . not suffering that anyone think, speak, act differently from them, condemning without mercy anyone who does not have the upright mentality that these gentlemen believe they have.'[28] This article, written under the inspiration of a visiting French Dominican, Père Lemarchand, and approved by Archbishop Bruchési and Bishop Emard, was printed accompanied by reservations to its thesis by the A.C.J.C. chaplain, Père Hermas Lalande, S.J. The Jesuits, more inclined to political action than the Dominicans or the bishops, stood firm in the position taken by the chaplain, despite pressure from Archbishop Bruchési. Some of the Quebec members of the A.C.J.C. resigned on the advice of Bishop Mathieu, and Perrault summoned the annual congress to meet at the University rather than at the Jesuit Collège Sainte-Marie, as usual. Archbishop Bruchési attended and supported Perrault's stand. The nationalism to which many young priests were already given was not yet sanctioned by the hierarchy. Archbishop Bruchési and Bishop Emard also prevailed upon Archbishop Bégin of Quebec to postpone the announced establishment of an official Catholic daily newspaper under the editorship of the crusading Abbé Paul-Eugène Roy and the name of '*L'Action Sociale Catholique*.'

3

Meanwhile Laurier had gone to London for the fifth Colonial Conference, which met in London in April 1907. With Chamberlain, the great showman of empire, no longer at the helm, there was no pageantry or display. Laurier, the only delegate who had taken part in the Conferences of 1897 and 1902, maintained his announced opposition to the setting up of an imperial council. He yielded in the matter of a change of terminology for the gatherings, which were henceforward to be called 'imperial' rather than 'colonial' conferences. Everything associated with colonial status was becoming distasteful to the self-governing dominions, which pressed unsuccessfully for the transfer of their affairs from the colonial secretary's office to that of the prime minister. They won, however, official recognition of dominion status and of the equality of the several governments. Laurier declared 'We are all His Majesty's governments,' and his view was adopted in a resolution which described the conferences' business as considering questions 'between His Majesty's Government and His Governments of the self-governing Dominions beyond the Seas.'

Confronted with the Campbell-Bannerman's government's objections to imperial preference, the conference could do little but renew its resolution in favor of that principle. Laurier, however, did not renew his 1902 offer of increased preference to Great Britain in exchange for a Canadian preference in British markets. On the question of defence, the Liberal government, hoping for general disarmament as a result of the Second Hague Conference, scheduled for 1908, did not press the dominions. Australia favored creating its own navy rather than cash contribution to the imperial fleet, and Canada refused any defence contribution other than the contemplated establishment of a local naval force. Laurier approved the proposed 'All Red Line' of communication from Great Britain to Australia which had been evolved by Sifton and Strathcona, the Canadian high commissioner in London. This project called for fast steamer services on the Atlantic and Pacific, linked by four-day transcontinental trains, which would cut ten days off the time required to journey from London to New Zealand. The plan demanded an annual subsidy of a million pounds, of which Great Britain was to pay half, and Canada £325,000, with New Zealand and Australia making up the balance. A resolution favorable to the scheme was adopted by the conference, but in the face of the lukewarmness of the British government and the determined opposition of the threatened P. & O. Steamship Line, the project came to nothing.[29]

Upon his return from the conference in July, Laurier was faced with the task of remaking his cabinet, in which the portfolios of railways and public works were vacant. The former post he had offered to Sifton while both were in London.[30] The Westerner delayed his answer until his return home, and then sought to bring in three colleagues with him. Laurier wanted Sifton in the cabinet, but he did not want him as second-in-command and inevitable successor. The negotiations fell through. At the same time Laurier had some thought of appeasing the Quebec wing of the party by offering a portfolio to Bourassa. The nationalist leader had continued to gain in influence during Laurier's absence, and in Quebec he and his followers pressed a bitter attack on Jules Prévost, minister of colonization, and Adélard Turgeon, minister of lands and forests. Discontented Liberals and Conservatives rallied to Bourassa's support, and there were rumors that he might resign from the federal parliament and enter the provincial field at the head of an independent third party. The Gouin government considered this a real threat, and Laurier sounded out Bourassa's willingness to enter the federal cabinet through E. W. Thompson and Lavergne.[31] But Bourassa proved unwilling to join a ministry including Sifton. Thus, in both the West and Quebec, Laurier's position became increasingly less secure, after failure of these efforts to unite his divided followers.

Bourassa went his own way, and his path was indicated by the fact that he spoke August 5 under the auspices of the *Ligue Nationaliste* at Saint-Roch in Laurier's own county of Quebec East. Fifteen thousand people gathered to hear him, Lavergne, and Robitaille; but the meeting was broken up by a barrage of tomatoes, eggs, and stones from Liberal stalwarts directed by Louis-Alexandre Taschereau. The publicity given this affair did the Liberals no good, and Bourassa promptly began a speaking tour in the country, where various parishes offered a fair hearing. He presented what amounted to a provincial platform, denouncing the mismanagement of the province's natural resources and calling for reforms in the administration of justice, labor legislation, education, and colonization. Laurier refrained from expelling him from the party, but did make the statement that Bourassa's attitude was not approved by him and that Bourassa was 'not one of his best political friends.'[32] But Bourassa continued his campaign throughout the province, gaining adherents and larger audiences as he went. Finally, at Trois-Rivières on September 30, he called for the formation of a third party, 'which ought necessarily absorb the best elements of the two old parties.'[33] He had already invoked the example of Mercier in following the same course. Under his sustained attack, Prévost, Turgeon, and the provincial treasurer resigned early in October.

Prévost then challenged Bourassa to an '*assemblée contradictoire*' at Terrebonne. Speaking before the house of Curé Labelle, Bourassa invoked his memory and that of the colonists who had pioneered the North in order to provide for the expansion of the race and the enlargement of the fatherland. He denounced those who sold the natural resources of Quebec to Americans or Belgians for a song, and declared: 'I want the people's wealth to be kept for the people.' Prévost, speaking in his family stronghold, defended himself and called Bourassa's charges lies unworthy of Papineau's grandson. But in rebuttal Bourassa evoked the tradition of Papineau and of true Liberalism as his reason for condemning Prévost, Turgeon, and Gouin: 'If I have undertaken this campaign, it is to save the honor of the Liberal party; it is to snatch the old flag which they have torn and sullied.' Bourassa was acclaimed in the home town of his opponent.[34]

For his part, Turgeon challenged Bourassa to resign from the federal House, and to run against him in Bellechasse. Bourassa promptly accepted the challenge, and said farewell to Laurier, who dryly remarked: 'I regret your departure. We need a man like you at Ottawa . . . though I should not want two.'[35] Turgeon was supported by the Liberal organization; Lavergne improvised one for Bourassa, with the aid of Robitaille, N.-K. Laflamme, Joseph Rainville, Alleyn Taschereau, Napoléon Garceau and Ernest Tétreau. Asselin revived *La Mitraille* for the duration of the campaign; students came from Montreal and Quebec to aid their idol. But Bellechasse was a rural constituency, and the farmers remained attached to Turgeon, a farmer's son, despite the support Bourassa received from the clergy. Bourassa was defeated on November 4 by more than 700 votes. Laurier then sought to rally the rebel's followers to the old party, treating their chief not too unkindly:

No one recognizes Bourassa's talent more than I do. He has one capital defect, he does not know how to keep within bounds. It is impossible that there should not be differences of opinion among friends, but he fights his friends with the same violence as his enemies; he becomes intoxicated with his own words; he grows irritated if contradicted; in the end he overshoots his own mark and allows himself to be drawn along unconsciously from friendly criticism to open war. Just there is the origin of this bitter struggle he is carrying on with the provincial government. . . .[36]

Laurier offered to let Bourassa resume his federal seat without opposition, while the Conservatives volunteered to support him against a Laurier candidate. Bourassa declined both offers, preferring to follow provincial politics. He was in disgrace with the Liberals, and coldly treated by those Conservatives who had supported him when he held a federal seat.[37]

4

Bourassa was not left wholly without support, however. On December 21, 1907, the first number of *L'Action Sociale* appeared at Quebec, with Omer Héroux and Jules Dorion, two of his disciples, among the editors. The new daily was nominally independent in politics, but it soon exhibited *Castor* and nationalistic tendencies. In parliament Lavergne upheld the nationalist cause. He objected to the imperialist slant being given to plans for the forthcoming celebration of the three hundredth anniversary of the founding of Quebec by Champlain. The Prince of Wales and representatives of all the colonies had been invited; and Lord Grey, the imperial-minded governor-general who was one of Cecil Rhodes' executors, took a lively interest in the preparations. Lavergne protested that Champlain and his work were being lost sight of, and that the celebration was coming to be regarded rather as the apotheosis of Wolfe and the English Conquest. He went on to complain that the rights of the French language were slighted by the railway, telephone, and telegraph companies. Laurier spoke soothing words, while the Orangemen Sam Hughes and MacLean paid tribute to Champlain. Lavergne, with the aid of Monk, also continued Bourassa's criticism of the government's immigration policy, blaming on it the crime waves and anarchist activity now found in Montreal and other large cities. But Frank Oliver, the new minister of the interior, favored cosmopolitan immigration, as his predecessor Sifton had done.

Lavergne's call for bilingualism in the public services was supported by the circulation of petitions to that effect by the A.C.J.C., and which called a mass meeting at the Monument National on May 8, with Bourassa, Lavergne, and Verville as speakers. The organization was now in the hands of those who favored political as well as religious action. Lavergne spoke first, calling for a realization of the constitutional principle of bilingualism. He urged that party spirit should be forgotten in this effort to attain the common good of all French Canadians. Verville, president since 1904 of the Canadian Congress of Trades and Labor, supported the bilingual movement. Bourassa was received with wild enthusiasm by the audience, in which young people predominated. He congratulated Lavergne on his campaign in favor of French, and called it an opportune one, since national consciousness had suffered losses in recent years. It was only just that companies enjoying public subsidies should give the French language equal rights with English. The assembly adopted a resolution urging all public services in Quebec to employ both languages in all their relations with the public, and petitioning parliament to provide penalties for infringement of this policy. Raoul Dandurand, president of the Senate, urged a less aggressive tone, but was howled down by Bourassa's tumultuous young followers, who habitually pushed his demands for equality to the point of provocation. The rising generation was nationalist almost to a man, to the dismay of Laurier, Gouin, and other prophets of the middle way.

Bourassa believed that the time had come to found a nationalist daily, and planned to withdraw from politics for that purpose. But nationalists and Conservatives alike urged him to run against Lomer Gouin, the provincial premier, in Saint-Jacques. The Conservatives promised to help him to acquire a journal if he thus aided them against the Liberal chief. A tacit alliance was arranged whereby the nationalists and Conservatives would conduct separate campaigns, but the latter would present no rival in constituencies where a nationalist candidate was running. Bourassa began his campaign on May 8 at Saint-Lin, Laurier's birthplace, where he attacked the chief Liberal spokesman, Turgeon, and urged the electors not to allow Laurier's mantle to be used 'to wipe the floor of the Legislative Assembly, soiled by intriguers.' He expounded the nationalist program: 'We are going to spread throughout the province the ideas of independence, honesty, and patriotism.'[38] After Gouin and Taschereau, the two leading Liberals, had announced their intention of each running in two counties, Bourassa declared that he would contest both Saint-Jacques in Montreal and Saint-Hyacinthe. Lavergne resigned from the federal parliament to contest Montmagny. J.-E. Bédard was induced to run in Beauport against the official candidate. These were the most hopeful nationalist candidacies; Napoléon Garceau in Drummondville, Joseph Rainville in Verchères, and J.-R. Labelle in Iberville admittedly stood little chance of election.

Bourassa opened his Montreal campaign at the Monument National on May 25, before a house packed with what the Liberal press called 'the choirboys of the new pontiff.'[39] The applause was so great that three times he tried in vain to begin his speech. When finally he was allowed to speak he pointed out how within ten months 'two or three young men, supported by men still young, having at their disposition neither money, nor papers, nor places, nor patronage, but having feeling, thought, and principles, had succeeded in arousing the province and making it understand that Confederation was based on two principles: equilibrium between the two races and equilibrium between the federal and provincial powers.'[40] He separated provincial and federal affairs, urging his audience not to let Gouin take shelter under Laurier's mantle. Then he expounded his provincial program; sale of waterpower rights to the highest bidder, separation of colonization and lumbering areas, study of prospective laws by a legislative commission before debate in the assembly, creation of a permanent board for the adjustment of differences between employers and labor. In the educational field he deplored the excessive attention given to secondary and higher education while primary instruction was neglected, and he criticized the establishment of a school of higher commercial studies in a province which lacked technical schools for training artisans. Bourassa declared that there was nothing in this program to make English-Canadians uneasy, though he had been denounced for appealing to racial prejudices. He thus answered his critics:

I have made appeals to my race and I still make them. I make these appeals to my race in order that, conscious of its dignity, it may stand up straight and proud before others, not as an enemy, but to accept their hands.

I appeal to my race in order that in this province there shall be no more question of popular passions but only of honor and dignity, and in order that we may prove to our sister provinces that if we have remained at home, alone, without having perhaps as much wealth as others, the little that we have has sufficed to keep us honest and worthy of those who have preceded us.

I appeal to my race in order that it may understand that on Canadian soil the land is too large for one race to tread on the other and for one race to fuse with the other.

I appeal to my race in order that it may understand that we are united, Catholics and French, English and Protestants, not to fight and crush each other, but to work with a common mind to enlarge our country.[41]

This peroration brought down the house. Bourassa and his wife were taken in triumph to their home in a carriage drawn by students, at the head of a throng of 1,500 people. The Liberal press belittled the demonstration, but its significance could not be ignored. *L'Action Sociale* showed itself well disposed to the nationalist-Conservative coalition and assigned Georges Pelletier, a disciple of Bourassa, to cover his campaign at Saint-Hyacinthe.

Bourassa devoted most of his attention, however, to the contest in Montreal, where a joint Liberal-Conservative committee aided his old nationalist supporters: Asselin, Fournier, Paul-Emile Lamarche, and eager troops of students. A meeting on June 2 could not find room enough in the Théâtre National and paraded through the streets behind Bourassa to St. James' Market. Gouin's gatherings were not as enthusiastic, and one on June 4 was broken up by followers of Bourassa. On June 5 Bourassa held a special meeting for English voters, and then challenged Gouin to meet him on the following day, the last of the campaign, in an *assemblée contradictoire*. Gouin was willing, but the municipal authorities discouraged such a meeting, since feeling had risen so high. On the night of the election, when it was learned that Bourassa had defeated the premier by forty-three votes, the nationalist leader was met at Bonaventure Station upon his return from Saint-Hyacinthe and hauled homeward in a carriage drawn by students at the head of an impromptu parade which interrupted traffic for several hours, as it paused for speeches along the way. The triumphant nationalists' cry was 'Saint-Jacques has avenged Bellechasse.' Bourassa declared that this victory was only the beginning of a great national movement. In Saint-Hyacinthe, the result was a tie, subsequently decided in Bourassa's favor by a recount which gave him a majority of thirty-eight. Lavergne and twelve Conservatives were also elected, thus doubling the opposition to Gouin's government. The Liberals had done well, but Bourassa's prestige was immensely increased by his victory over Gouin in the latter's home district.

While the nationalist leader took a vacation in Europe, the imperialist forces exerted themselves at the Quebec tercentenary. A British naval squadron brought the Prince of Wales and a distinguished suite including Lord Roberts; a French squadron brought a mission including the Marquis de Lévis and the Comte de Montcalm; an American warship Vice-President Fairbanks. Laurier read an address in English to which the Prince replied in French. Quebec was packed with notables drawn from all over Canada and from Newfoundland, Australia, New Zealand, and South Africa. More than 20,000 sailors and soldiers were encamped about the city. For a week the celebrations continued, drawing the attention of the world to Canada, and particularly to French Canada. At the banquets French Canadians professed their loyalism and Englishmen expressed their sympathy with the French race. The premier of the province and the mayor of Quebec City were knighted; once more Laurier declined the offer of a peerage. But there were rifts in the lute: nationalists quarrelled with the imperialist flavor of the gathering, while imperialists protested at the number of Tricolors in evidence, and the ultramontane press muttered darkly that the French envoy was a Freemason.

During Bourassa's travels in France and Belgium he gave an interview to *La Gazette de France* in which he expounded the doctrines of the nationalist movement, explaining that one of its principal aims was to develop a more general Canadianism and thus to weaken English-Canadian antagonism to French Canada.[42] Meanwhile at home he was being suggested as chief of the provincial opposition, and Jean Prévost offered him alliance. He returned home on August 25, and first appeared in public on September 6, when he spoke with Lavergne at Montmagny. After the exchange of mutual compliments, Bourassa outlined a program in both federal and provincial affairs, stressing the danger of immigration and calling for a revocation of the colonization laws. He warned against the educational reforms preached by Godefroy Langlois and the *Ligue d'Enseignement.* In France, he said 'I saw a Catholic people governed by a handful of men without faith or patriotism, who imposed upon it a dangerous system of education.'[43] He thought such a system would endanger Quebec's Catholicism and thus its nationality.

At Saint-Hyacinthe on September 19 Bourassa announced that he had chosen to represent that county in parliament rather than Saint-Jacques. His choice of the less sure seat was admired by his youthful followers. As yet he had said nothing of his attitude in the impending federal elections. Finally he called a meeting at the Monument National on October 2, barely three weeks before the elections. With the assurance of an established leader he sketched out his program. He was not content with two or three seats in the provincial parliament; he was going to conquer the whole province, whose autonomy and proper place in Confederation he wished to assure. The first step was not to criticize Ontario and the other provinces, but to bring about reform at home. Once party spirit was replaced by public spirit, the province could be launched on a program of economic, moral, and intellectual development. He called for the aid of all, Conservatives and Liberals alike. He did not seek to lead Conservatives to Laurier or Liberals to Borden, and would remain neutral in the federal elections, except in particular cases.[44] To achieve his purpose he planned to establish a daily newspaper in Montreal and clubs throughout the province, whose dues would be used to meet electoral expenses and those of the paper.

As in 1907, Laurier confined his campaigning to Ontario and Quebec, urging the electors to rally to his 'white plume' on what was doubtless the last occasion he would appeal to the people. He stood on his record of having raised Canada in twelve years from the status of a colony to that of a great nation, and urged: 'Let me finish my task!'[45] He spoke no word against Bourassa, and Bourassa returned the compliment. In Quebec the Conservatives were too divided and too unorganized to be effective; elsewhere they charged scandals against the government. The Orangemen issued a pamphlet, 'The Duty of the Hour,' urging a vote against Laurier as a vote against clerical domination; but this effort did the Conservative cause as much harm as good. When the ballots were counted, Quebec and Ontario showed the same majorities for Laurier as in 1904, though there were many shifts in individual constituencies and the popular majority in Quebec was small. The Liberals lost much ground in Manitoba and British Columbia, and some in Novia Scotia. Their majority shrank from sixty-two to forty-seven, and outside Quebec the party held a majority of only four. With British Columbia in revolt against his Japanese policy and Manitoba becoming a Conservative stronghold under Robert Rogers, Laurier could not but be uneasy as the nationalist movement grew ever stronger in Quebec, the backbone of his power.

Bourassa supplied evidence of his growing influence when on February 25, 1909 he drew as large a crowd as Laurier had done on his last appearance at the Monument National to hear a declaration announced as 'perhaps one of the turning-points of the political history of our province.'[46] The audience was made up largely of French-Canadian businessmen and the chairman was J.-A. Vaillancourt, head of the Banque d'Hochelaga. Having won the support of youth, Bourassa now sought that of older men, particularly businessmen and teachers. The latter were already largely gained for his cause through the A.C.J.C. and its study groups in the classical colleges. A professor at the Collège Sainte-Marie, for instance, had formally approved in the classroom one of Bourassa's earlier lectures, and had commented that 'perhaps he was destined to change the political face of the country.'[47] At the Monument National Bourassa spoke in general terms, dismissing his program as familiar enough. He urged the necessity of a third party, now that the Liberals had lost their idealism and enthusiasm through long stay in office, and the Conservatives lacked the vigor to govern. Both parties had lost their principles and become mere coteries, 'syndicates of appetites.' A new group, with the life-giving principles of justice and honesty, was needed.

To found such a party, he appealed to men of goodwill in all groups and parties, 'in order that we may unite around the ideas which we believe necessary to the future of our province, around a program of economic reforms which we believe necessary to the development of our domain.' A true public opinion must be awakened in the province, like that which existed in England and which permitted English Liberals to vote against the Liberal government on a question of principle without being called traitors. This public opinion, once created or regenerated through a new party, clubs, and the proposed journal, would permit the establishment of a government which would conform to the ideals of the race and the main lines of the British tradition. This strong and honest government, backed by powerful public opinion, would solve social problems in the best possible fashion and would open more largely the sources of economic development. The English Canadians of Quebec need not fear this program and could collaborate in it. It was not an attempt at fusion or isolation, but one of association. Such was the course which the rising leader of Quebec urged, without sensationalism and without the verbal violence beloved by his younger followers, upon this staider audience. It won him new support, though the Liberal press dismissed it as mere rhetoric and as another proclamation of Bourassa's 'providential mission to regenerate the province of Quebec.'[48]

When the provincial session opened early in March, Tellier, the chief of the Conservative opposition, offered to share his office with Bourassa. The latter made a poor impression with his first speech, which he had neglected to prepare sufficiently, thinking the provincial legislature a small stage after the larger one at Ottawa on which he had already figured prominently. Gouin defended himself successfully and even carried the attack to Bourassa. Then, in support of a Conservative amendment to the speech from the throne, which outlined the opposition's program, Bourassa made a three-hour speech which was a *tour de force* of eloquent polemic. He resumed all his criticisms of the administration and the remedies he proposed. But once more Gouin rose above his diffidence and lack of eloquence to reply adequately to the newcomer who challenged his power. The session went its way, with Bourassa, Lavergne, and their new ally Jean Prévost seizing every possible opportunity to attack the government, and Gouin and Taschereau replying. The galleries were filled in the afternoon with students from the Quebec and Lévis seminaries, who came to hear and applaud their hero Bourassa.

In *Le Nationaliste* Olivar Asselin and Jules Fournier pressed their leader's charges of scandal with a vigor that often disregarded the decencies. When one day Taschereau warned Bourassa in parliament that he had about him 'bandits for whom the reputation of a neighbor did not count,' Asselin left the press gallery and struck Taschereau in the face as he left the Chamber. The journalist was promptly arrested and condemned to fifteen days in prison. His plight awakened sympathy among the nationalists, and Omer Héroux of *L'Action Sociale* likened him to one of the '*camelots du roi*' of the *Action française* movement, with their 'necessary violences.'[49] Thus began a long feud between Taschereau and Asselin, and between Taschereau and *L'Action Sociale*. The session closed with the Liberal administration forced into reforms along the lines favored by their opponents, and with a nationalist-Conservative alliance, with clerical backing, well-nigh cemented.

T

5

Meanwhile the navy question had arisen in the federal House, as a result of a March debate in the British Commons. The armament race in Europe, particularly keen between Britain and Germany since 1900, largely escaped Canadian attention until March 16, 1909, when in a debate at Westminster on the Admiralty estimates it was announced that Germany was speeding up her naval construction and by 1912 would attain equality in dreadnoughts with Britain. The Admiralty, Foreign Secretary Sir Edward Grey, and Asquith and Balfour all spoke of a crucial situation. In March the scare was so pronounced that the Liberal government, instead of reducing the naval estimates, increased them by provision for four more dreadnoughts; and in July, after pressure from the opposition, it added four more. In the first alarm Britain's very safety was pictured as being at stake, and there was an immediate response in Toronto and Winnipeg, where strong demands were made for the gift of a dreadnought by Canada to the British navy. The great Liberal organ, the *Globe*, on March 23 urged Canada 'to fling the smug axioms of commercial prudence to the winds and to do more than her share . . . Within the next two years the Colonies of Britain should be able to place three Dreadnoughts at the disposal of the Motherland, and they should do it. So far as Canada is concerned, such vessels would be under the control of the Canadian government, but that is only another way of saying that they would always be at the call of the Empire in every worthy cause and in every time of danger.'[50] There was an equally prompt anti-imperialist reaction in Quebec, which saw in the situation another imperialist attempt to force Canada's hand, as in 1899.

Nothing had as yet been done to realize the government's announced policy of setting up a Canadian Navy, beyond the taking over in 1905 of the bases at Halifax and Esquimalt when the British fleet was concentrated in home waters. Since the British government held out for a single imperial fleet under its control, while Canada took the position that she should provide for her own naval defence with a force under her control, the situation had remained a stalemate. There had been for some years an imperialist campaign in the English provinces in favor of Canadian contribution to the naval defence of the empire, which had been growing in strength. Early in the session of 1909, before the British scare, George Foster gave notice of a motion calling upon Canada to take action to protect her coastline and seaports. The opposition of Frederick Monk and other members of the Conservative party delayed the proposal, but on March 29 Foster opposed contribution to the British Navy and advocated a Canadian naval force, with an emergency gift of a dreadnought to Britain if the prime minister so desired. Laurier countered with a more specific resolution recognizing Canada's willingness to assume a large share of defence responsibilities, rejecting the policy of contribution, approving 'the organization of a Canadian naval service in co-operation with and close relation to the imperial navy,' and expressing Canada's belief in the necessity of Britain's naval supremacy and her readiness to co-operate with the imperial authorities.[51] This resolution was modified to meet Borden's criticisms by not completely ruling out the possibility of contribution in case of an immediate emergency and by approving 'speedy' organization of a Canadian naval force. It was then passed by unanimous vote, for parliament now boasted not a single Quebec nationalist.

The decision was approved by the Liberal press in Quebec, though even *Le Soleil* expressed forebodings at being led by force of events into the armament race. *L'Action Sociale* feared secret imperialism on the part of the government, and *Le Nationaliste* attacked the ministers as having 'sold out to England.'[52] Goldwin Smith wrote to Bourassa, urging him to renew his anti-imperialist campaign of 1899, but Bourassa was too much preoccupied with provincial matters. In June an Imperial Press Conference was held in London, and the British statesmen who addressed the gathering eloquently evoked the immediate danger of Britain's losing its vital mastery of the seas. Sir Hugh Graham of the *Montreal Star*, who had been knighted the previous year and was fuller than ever of imperial zeal, inspired an article which appeared in the *Star* on June 19, denouncing Laurier's naval policy as inadequate, and urging that Canada should follow the example of Australia and New Zealand and make a cash contribution to the British Navy, instead of herself constructing ships which would be 'mere children's toys.' The suggestion was promptly taken up by the Tory press of Ontario.

In July an Imperial Defence Conference was held in London, with Louis-Philippe Brodeur, minister of marine and fisheries, and Sir Frederick Borden, militia minister, as the Canadian delegates. The *Star* and the Tory press urged them to offer dreadnoughts to England; the *Globe* and the Liberal journals of Quebec beseeched them to maintain Laurier's stand; and the nationalist and ultramontane organs warned them to offer no contribution at all. At the conference the Admiralty called for a single imperial navy aided by contributions from the empire, but urged those dominions which insisted upon their own navies to form a 'distinct fleet unit.'[53] Since all the dominions favored separate navies, the Admiralty authorities prepared detailed proposals for the construction and maintenance of such units. The Canadians asked for and received two plans, one calling for an annual expenditure of three million dollars and the other of two millions. The report of the conference was to be kept secret until the government announced its naval proposals, which Laurier held off until January 1910.

Meanwhile the nationalist-Conservative alliance in Quebec had been tightened by the anti-imperialism evoked by the navy question. Jules Fournier, Asselin's associate on *Le Nationaliste*, followed him to jail in June for contempt of court in his comments on the case. Upon his release Fournier was hailed as a hero by the students, who saw in him an adversary of imperialism as well as a critic of the provincial government. On June 1 a banquet in honor of Mathias Tellier, the Conservative chief, was given at Joliette; it was attended by Bourassa, Lavergne, Asselin, and other nationalist leaders, as well as by their ex-Liberal ally Jean Prévost. Prévost hailed this 'coalition of the people' against the government's corruption, and Bourassa insisted upon its disinterestedness, proclaiming his willingness to retire from politics when its ideal was realized.[54] Fifteen days earlier Lavergne had attended a Borden banquet at Quebec. Bourassa's aide was unpredictable: to show his opposition to British control of the proposed Canadian Navy, he enlisted in the militia, now completely under Canadian control. The nationalists criticized Lord Grey's support of the imperialist navy campaign, and urged that the next governor-general should be a Canadian.[55] Ethnic feeling was already aroused by the divergence of opinion on the navy question; the *Quebec Chronicle* protested the flying of the Tricolor on local yachts, and said that 'if the Red Ensign is good enough for millions of British subjects all over the world and on all the seas, it should be good enough for some thousands of Canadians of French extraction scattered in the east of Canada.'[56]

In October the nationalist-Conservative coalition was confirmed by the appearance of Bourassa, Lavergne, Prévost, and Tellier on the same platform at Saint-Hyacinthe. Bourassa proclaimed the disinterestedness of the coalition: 'Above all, comes the general interest of the province of Quebec. We want the right to march in the same rank as the others in Confederation.'[57] In three by-elections in November only one nationalist-supported candidate was elected, while the candidate chosen by Bourassa to replace him in Saint-Jacques was defeated by the revived Liberal forces. The election was fought on provincial issues, though the nationalists and *L'Action Sociale* had already taken a stand on the navy question by adopting Bourassa's old principle of no obligatory participation in the wars of the empire. As early as June Asselin had published a pamphlet, '*La Défense navale de l'empire britannique,*' protesting against the Laurier-Borden naval measure and calling for Canadian autonomy or independence. The Quebec Conservatives were as strongly opposed to the government's naval proposal as the nationalists, and the most loyalist of them, Tom Chase Casgrain, urged Bourassa to campaign against Laurier's plan. Goldwin Smith wrote him: 'It is too bad that you are no longer at Ottawa; but your voice will be heard all the same.'[58]

Frederick Monk, federal leader of the Quebec Conservatives, took his stand against the naval proposal at a banquet at Lachine on November 8. He said a navy would be costly and useless, and that the Canadians, a small and poor people, should concentrate on developing their natural resources before assuming the crushing burden of militarism. The Conservative party was now split wide open, with Borden approving Laurier's position, Roblin of Manitoba calling for a direct contribution to the British Navy, and Monk opposed to both measures. When the federal session opened, the government tabled the blue book containing the official documents on the Imperial Defence Conference, and the naval program was revealed as calling for the immediate construction of three cruisers and four destroyers. Roblin denounced this 'tin-pot navy' and called for cash contributions or the gift of dreadnoughts. The Tory press, led by the *Star*, followed his lead. Borden wavered in his stand, but Sir Charles Tupper supported it. Laurier made a concession to Quebec by declaring that the Canadian fleet would not participate in imperial wars without the consent of the Canadian people.[59] But it was clear that once more public opinion in English Canada was flatly opposed to sentiment in Quebec, and that a political crisis was at hand.

It was in this atmosphere that Bourassa's independent journal *Le Devoir* first appeared, after an eighteen-month campaign for funds. There were some 500 small contributors, and one large one: G.-N. Ducharme, who made an initial investment of $10,000, later increased to $40,000. Some Conservatives, foreseeing a useful ally in the fight against Laurier, subscribed. The board of directors was made up of French-Canadian businessmen without political bias, and Bourassa controlled 51 per cent of the stock, in order to assure the editorial freedom of the paper. He was editor-in-chief, with Omer Héroux and Georges Pelletier leaving *L'Action Sociale* to become his associates. Asselin and the leading writers of *Le National-iste*—henceforward a weekly edition of *Le Devoir*—Jules Fournier, Tancrède Marsil, Léon Lorrain, and others made up the staff. Both the ultramontane element, for whom religion came before national-ism, and the liberal one, for whom nationalism came first, were thus included.

Bourassa himself thought of his journal as a center of national rather than Catholic action. In the first number, which appeared on January 10, 1910, he sketched out a program:

Le Devoir will support honest men and denounce rascals.

In provincial politics, we combat the present government because we find in it all the evil tendencies which we want to make disappear from public life: veniality, irresponsibility, cowardice, degrading and narrow party spirit.

We support the opposition because we find in it the opposite tendencies: probity, courage, firm principles, great largeness of views. These principles are admirably united in the personality of its leader, M. Tellier.

On the day when this group no longer follows the inspirations which guide it today, it will find us ready to fight it, as we fight the men now in power.

At Ottawa the situation is less clear.

The two parties are sinking into the same decline in which provincial politics lay some years ago.

Desire for the conquest or conservation of power seems to be their sole motive.

During the last ten years vital questions have demanded attention from our federal parliamentarians: the South African War and imperialism, the constitution of new provinces and minority rights, the construction of the Grand Trunk Pacific and the regulation of railways, foreign immigration and the settlement of the national domain.

By a sort of conspiracy, the two parliamentary groups connived to give each of these problems a solution in which right, justice and national interest have been sacrificed to opportunism, to party intrigues, or still worse to the cupidity of individual interests.

At the very hour that we appear upon the scene, parliament is deliberating a question of the highest importance, which is only a new episode of the imperialist movement: the construction of a Canadian Navy.

Shall we watch a repetition of the comedy of 1899? Will the Canadian people be the dupe of the machinations and miserable intrigues of parties?

The resounding discourse of M. Monk at Lachine gives us the hope that the dangerous and stupefying situation in which we rest will not continue.

The member for Jacques-Cartier can be assured of our support, if he maintains his attitude with firmness, logic, and perseverance.

In order to assure the triumph of ideas over appetites, of the public good over party spirit, there is only one means: to awaken in the people, and above all in the ruling classes, the sentiment of public duty under all its forms: religious duty, national duty, civic duty. Thus the title of this journal, which has astonished some people and caused some colleagues to smile.[60]

Thus from the start *Le Devoir* took an active political role. The expression of sympathy with the Conservatives in the first number was followed the next day by Bourassa's biting reference to the 'golden clouds' in which Laurier 'had veiled the betrayals, weaknesses, and dangers of his policy.'[61] It was clear that open nationalist warfare against Laurier was not far off.

Le Devoir, like *L'Action Sociale* was a journal of opinion addressed to a cultivated audience, not a commercial paper on the new American model addressed to the lowest common denominator of the population, a model increasingly followed by the rest of the French-Canadian press as yellow journalism proved profitable. The founding of *Le Devoir* was warmly hailed by *L'Action Sociale* and *L'Evénement*, which did not fear Montreal competition in the district of Quebec; the Liberal press greeted it sourly. The new paper opposed the Gouin government; it attacked municipal corruption in Montreal; and it espoused the cause of the newly founded Ontario *Association canadienne-française d'éducation*, which under the leadership of Senator Napoléon Belcourt undertook the defence of bilingualism in that province against the Irish clergy under Bishop Fallon. But Bourassa's chief interest at this time was the navy question.

On January 12 Laurier himself introduced the Naval Service Bill, providing for the creation of a permanent force, supplemented by a reserve and by volunteers on the same basis as the militia, with the exception that naval service was to be wholly voluntary. The force was to be under the control of the Canadian government, but in case of war might be placed under imperial control by order-in-council, subject to the approval of parliament, which was to be summoned within fifteen days, if not in session. Five cruisers and six destroyers were to be built, costing $11,000,000 if constructed in England, and $15,000,000 if in Canada, as was desired if possible; the annual budget was estimated at $3,000,000. In response to a question from Dr. Sproule, asking whether 'case of war' referred to war anywhere in the empire or in Canada only, Laurier replied: 'War everywhere. When Britain is at war, Canada is at war; there is no distinction. If Great Britain, to which we are subject, is at war with any nation, Canada is exposed to invasion; hence Canada is at war.'[62] He stressed the fact that there was no liability to service in the navy, as there was under the Militia Act. R. L. Borden approved the proposal, expressing his conviction that Britain would not engage in war without consulting the dominions, but urging that a Defence Committee made up of representatives from both British parties and the self-governing colonies should have some control over the imperial defence organization: 'If we are to take part in the permanent defence of this great empire, we must have some control and some voice in such matters.' He opposed the policy of contribution to the British navy in general, but urged a special emergency contribution under the present circumstances.[63] Monk, like Laurier, belittled the crucial nature of the present situation, which Borden had once more emphasized; and expressed his belief that Canada was unable to build and maintain a suitable navy. He called for a plebiscite on the question.

Bourassa at once attacked the bill and Laurier's declaration that Canada was at war when Britain was at war. In *Le Devoir* for January 17 he pointed out the consequences:

> Let the notion occur to a Chamberlain, a Rhodes, a Beers, to gold-seekers or opium merchants, of causing a conflict in South Africa or India, in the Mediterranean or the Persian Gulf, on the shores of the Baltic or the banks of the Black Sea, on the coasts of Japan or in the China seas, we are involved, always and regardless, with our money and our blood . . .
>
> It is the most complete backward step Canada has made in half a century.
>
> It is the gravest blow our autonomy has suffered since the origin of responsible government.[64]

Bourassa indicted Laurier for his weaknesses and betrayals from 1902 to the present 'national capitulation.' *L'Action Sociale* supported Monk's suggestion of a plebiscite and protested against the creation of a navy without an appeal to the people. In Montreal a lecture by Bourassa on military imperialism and the Navy Bill was announced.

The Monument National on January 20 was packed, with several hundred persons seated on the stage itself. Without oratorical preliminaries, Bourassa plunged into a discussion of the bill. Citing the example of the National Transcontinental Railway, he pointed out that the initial cost of the proposed navy would be dwarfed by later expenses. He criticized the bill for not limiting the navy to the defence of Canada, as the militia was by the law of 1904. He then listed twenty-three wars in which Britain had been engaged since 1812, of which he singled out five as the most serious, and asked when Canada had been threatened with invasion by the Russians, the Sepoys, the Sudanese, the Afghans, or the Boers. If he had a seat in the House, he would ask what possible threat there was to Canada from England's potential enemies, save the United States and Japan. He called Laurier's declaration a reversal of his stand in 1902 and 1907 and a constitutional heresy. If it were sanctioned, Canadian troops could be sent abroad whenever England was at war. It plunged Canada into the very 'whirlpool of militarism' which Laurier had once eloquently denounced.

The bill did not provide, as Laurier had promised, for a Canadian Navy under Canadian control, to be used for the defence of the empire only so far as Canada was concerned; but instead for one placed under imperial authority in all the wars of England. It was not a defence force, but one designed, as the Admiralty had wished, also for offence. No other empire had ever imposed upon its colonies the obligation of constructing a navy. Citing the example of the South African War, Bourassa denounced Borden's assurance that Britain would consult the colonies before making war as impossible under the existing regime. The reservation demanding the approval of parliament was worthless; either parliament would be stampeded, as it had been in 1899, or it would be presented with a *fait accompli*, since the fleet would remain under imperial control until the war's end.

Then Bourassa considered the questions of whether Canada needed a navy, whether England needed aid, and whether that aid was owed by Canada. The projected navy did not augment Canada's security but decreased it, since a young country could stand only so much military expense, and the cost of the militia had doubled within the last five years without providing an army adequate to defend Canada's frontiers. In wartime, Canada's maritime commerce could be carried on under a neutral flag without naval protection. Then railroads and canals, built or in prospect, called for the expenditure of 800 millions. Bourassa agreed with Monk that Canada could not bear an additional burden of military and naval expenses. He belittled the German menace, comparing it to the exploded French and Russian menaces of past years, and citing the evidence of Sir William White, long director of British naval construction, in the *Nineteenth Century Review* for April 1909, that there was no real basis for the naval scare. He pictured Britain's present plight as the result of her foreign policy since the end of the Napoleonic Wars, in which the colonies had never been consulted.

Was it Canada's duty to share the burden which Britain had imposed upon herself for her own glory and greatness? 'We Canadians owe all our blood, all our effort, all our consideration to the country that providence has given us. As British subjects, we owe to England only the preservation of that part of the Empire which has fallen to our share, with its inconveniences and its advantages. To depart from this path is to compromise the future of Canada without assuring the security of the Empire.'[65] He recited the long history of Britain's efforts to make Canada assume a larger share in imperial defence, and the stand taken by Mackenzie, Macdonald, Blake, Tupper, and Laurier up to 1907 in favor of local defence and against imperial centralization. Asquith, Dilke, and Lord Charles Beresford were on record to the effect that Britain could not reduce its defence burdens even if Canada left the empire. In the past Canada had been involved in two wars with the United States on Britain's behalf; as for the present and the future he cited Laurier's statement of March 1909: 'Canada has no quarrels with anyone; no desire to expand its territory; it occupies an isolated position; it has only one neighbor, with which it has lived in peace for more than a century.' Britain neither could nor would defend Canada against the United States, her sole possible enemy. Canada enjoyed the protection of the Monroe Doctrine, and if Britain protected the Canadian merchant marine, she did so because it was essential to her commerce. Sure of her supremacy at sea, Britain had rejected the American proposal to the Hague Tribunal that the commerce of belligerents should be regarded as neutral.

Canada owed no gratitude for British diplomacy, which had cost her dear, nor for British capital, which had been invested in Canada because it was profitable. The imperialists argued that Canada owed Britain a debt of gratitude for its liberty and British institutions. Bourassa refuted the contention:

Gentlemen, I highly appreciate this liberty; I love these institutions and you love them. But the essential part of British institutions is the preservation of the spirit of liberty and independence. I recognize that England has admirably governed its colonies, particularly since she decided to govern them no more. The great English Liberal school, more modest and less noisy than the Chamberlains and the Balfours, made the British Empire what it is, because it consolidated it in the liberty, independence, and autonomy of its colonies.

Yes, certainly I appreciate the liberty we have enjoyed since English Liberal principles triumphed, but, gentlemen, once more, need we deny our past?

England accorded us this liberty because those who preceded us in our path, less ardent to seek decorations from His Majesty, carried the fight for our rights to the foot of the throne.

We obtained this liberty because we knew how to conquer it; not only we French Canadians, but the patriots of Ontario as well as those of Quebec, the Mackenzies as well as the Papineaus: because we knew how to ask for it during seventy-five years with energy, calm, in the full awareness of our rights; because we knew how to be a strong people!

But we shall preserve this liberty only by guarding intact the tradition of national pride and not, after fifty years of autonomous government, by putting our flag at the feet of a Chamberlain or a Balfour.[66]

Then Bourassa considered the consequences of the bill, which he summed up as 'disastrous for Canada and fatal to the British Empire.' Canada would be drawn into all the wars of England, which had averaged one every four years in the past century. Canadian armament might provoke the United States to fortify the frontier. It would cause the abandonment of the theory that Canada was neutral in all British wars in which its interests and territory were not involved. It was absurd to pretend that Canada's entry into the 'whirlpool of militarism' was avoided since there would be no naval conscription—something which no country had adopted. He cited Laurier's denunciation in 1902 of Canada's entry into the European armament race as suicidal for the country, and his characterization of devoting money needed for public works to armaments as a crime. Imperial defence collaboration would lead to an imperial tariff, to an imperial council, to the full realization of Chamberlain's dream, which was impossible because the British Empire was separated by the seas, diverse in components, and autonomous in its parts. The result of the imperialist policy would be immediate rupture of the empire in hatred and conflict of interests, and the destruction of its ideal. Canadians were not Englishmen; every day they were becoming more Americanized, though the French Canadians' difference of language was 'the best safeguard of Canadian autonomy and of British institutions.'

There was no racial quarrel involved in this stand. Any of his arguments could have been addressed to an English-speaking Canadian, to a Protestant or a Catholic. The French Canadians were not isolated in their anti-imperialism, although there were no doubt many imperialists among the Anglo-Saxons, captivated by Chamberlain's great dream. He defended such rational and sincere imperialists as Stephen Leacock; such emotional and sincere imperialists as Colonel Denison. But he denounced those who were imperialists in their own financial interest and the snobbish imperialists who formed a little court about the governor-general at Rideau Hall and sought imperial decorations. He pointed out that there were also English-Canadian anti-imperialists such as Goldwin Smith, Adam Shortt, and the members of the Ontario Grange and of the Manitoba Grain Growers' Association. He denounced the opportunism of Laurier and Borden, and the conspiracy of both parties to sacrifice national interests to party intrigues.

Lord Grey had not caused Laurier's change of attitude by a *coup d'état* such as had been urged upon Minto in the case of General Hutton; but Grey, the disciple of Rhodes in South Africa and his executor, had privately done more for the cause of imperialism in Canada during the last two years than any Canadian politician had ever done. But since the cabinet had failed to remind the governor-general that he had no more right to play politics in Canada than the King had in England, the people should raise its voice. Parliament had no right to vote this law without appealing to the people, since it reversed the stand sanctioned at the polls in 1904 and 1908. 'Not in my name, but in the name of your sons, in the name of those who will bear the weight of this criminal policy, in the name of those who will pay the taxes which will weigh more heavily upon us, in the name of those who perhaps soon will embark upon these vessels to go and perish upon far-off seas, I ask you to unite with me in making known to Lord Grey, Sir Wilfrid Laurier, and Mr. Borden that before starting us on this path, they ought to explain their designs, make them known to the people, and obtain approval of their policy.'[67] Then Bourassa read a resolution, calling upon parliament to defer the bill until a plebiscite had made known the will of the people. He described it as 'neither a declaration of war nor the commencement of a revolution,' but as a resolution already adopted by the Grange of Ontario and the Grain Growers of Manitoba. The resolution was adopted amid vast enthusiasm.

6

Thus began the revolt against Laurier which eventually brought about his downfall. Bourassa's speech was published as a pamphlet, '*Le Projet de Loi Navale*,' and widely circulated throughout the province. *Le Devoir* printed a blank petition for a plebiscite, and lawyers, doctors, notaries, and many *curés* sought signatures for these petitions, which were forwarded to Monk at Ottawa. The French-Canadian Conservatives generally supported the nationalist campaign. Some Quebec Liberals showed signs of opposing the bill, and Laurier exerted his influence upon them, as he did on those Ontario Liberals who found the measure was not imperialist enough. The Liberal press in Quebec could only argue that the navy would not cost more than the announced figure, and that a plebiscite would set Ontario and Quebec at each other's throats.[68]

When the Navy Bill came up for second reading on February 3, 1910, Laurier defended it in one of his most notable speeches. The measure realized a policy announced to the country in 1902 and reaffirmed in 1907 and 1909. He called it the last link in the long chain since Baldwin and Lafontaine started Canada on the path to nationhood, with its rights and its obligations. He cited Kipling's definition of Canada's position:

> *Daughter am I in my mother's house,*
> *But Mistress in my own.*

The Conservatives were divided in their councils; they had offered no policy of their own, and many of them approved the government's proposal. Of course it had been severely criticized by those ultra-imperialists 'who carry abroad upon their foreheads imperial phylacteries, who boldly walk into the temple and there loudly thank the Lord that they are not like other British subjects, that they give tithes of everything they possess, and that in them alone is to be found the true incense of loyalty.'[69] Aside from Monk, who was utterly opposed to any measure of the sort, there were those Conservatives who criticized the government for not going far enough, who wanted an imperial navy supported by colonial contributions, or who wanted the Canadian Navy automatically to pass under imperial control in case of war, or who wanted an emergency contribution in addition to the proposed navy.

To these imperialist solutions Laurier opposed his own, saying that he was 'Canadian first, last, and always,' but that he was a 'British subject by birth, being convinced by tradition and conviction that under favor of British institutions my native land has obtained a measure of security and liberty which it could not have enjoyed under any other regime.'[70] The imperialists thought centralization essential to the maintenance of the empire; he believed that autonomy was. He traced the development of Canadian autonomy from Durham's time, and denounced the contention that it should be abandoned in naval matters. This question had been settled at the last colonial conference, and Australia had adopted Canada's plan of building her own navy. Lord Milner himself, the prophet of imperialism, had supported it in speeches at Vancouver and Toronto in October 1909.

Laurier then discussed the crucial point. He had declared that the 'navy will not go to war unless the parliament of Canada chooses to send it there.' This declaration had been attacked in Quebec, where it was said that Canada ought not to take part in England's wars under any circumstance, and in Ontario where it was said that Canada ought to participate in England's wars under all circumstances. He maintained that it was the function of parliament, which created the navy, to decide when and where it should go to battle. He had declared that 'if England is at war, we are at war,' and had been bitterly criticized in Quebec for thus proclaiming a principle of international law. It did not follow that Canada would always be attacked, nor that Canada should always take part in all the wars of England. That was for parliament to decide, according to the circumstances. England could afford to devote its resources to armament, but Canada had above all to devote herself to the development of the country. He warned the imperialists against compelling the colonies to contribute to England's armaments. Such a course had caused the revolt of the American colonies, and he cited Benjamin Franklin's answer at the bar of the House of Commons, when asked whether the colonies would contribute to the aid of England: 'As long as they are well treated, they will always be ready to defend her to the extent of their feeble means.' Today there was no danger of taxation without representation, but there was the same relationship between the autonomous colonies and Britain.

Laurier defended the provision for immediate mobilization of the fleet without parliament's previous consent on the grounds of the possible necessity of immediate action. Against the dreadnought agitation, he advanced Lord Charles Beresford's opinion that the colonies would do best to provide for the defence of their coasts and their merchant shipping by the construction of cruisers. He belittled the talk of emergency and the possibility of war; but if war should come suddenly, Canada could always aid Britain with funds, as Britain so often had aided her European allies in the past.

The proposal for a Canadian Navy had been before the country since 1902. Since then the population had grown half again as large and the national income had nearly doubled. Canada could afford a navy and needed one, just as Montreal needed a police force. In Quebec it was argued that Canada should not risk a single man or dollar to maintain British supremacy of the seas. But in this measure there was no compulsion to risk one's life for one's King; those who objected could sit at home and 'enjoy the security and comfort procured for them by the self-sacrifice of more generous men.'[71] Canada was a constitutional country and the will of the majority must rule; if parliament decided to mobilize the Navy, the minority must accept the decision. He evoked the military tradition of the French Canadians, and concluded that liberty was worth fighting and dying for. If Britain lost her supremacy, Canada and Quebec would lose their prosperity, so dependent upon British trade. Then he concluded with the argument that Canada could not stand still, and he urged it to go forward in the tradition of union, friendship, and brotherhood established by Lafontaine and Baldwin.

R. L. Borden, influenced by a revolt within his own party against his leadership, criticized Laurier's proposals for not following the recommendations of the Admiralty and for permitting the government to withhold cooperation with England in time of war. The heavy outlay would give no immediate or effective aid to the empire and no satisfactory results in Canada. No permanent policy should be adopted without an appeal to the people, and meanwhile Canada should make an emergency gift sufficient to enable the Admiralty to purchase or construct two dreadnoughts.[72] Monk, clearly inspired by Bourassa's arguments, denounced the bill as a surrender of autonomy, a capitulation to Chamberlainism, an involvement of Canada in the consequences of a policy in which she had little interest and over which she had no control. Parliament had no right to pass such measure, which modified Canada's autonomy, her international relations, her economic security, and perhaps the sacrifice of Canadian lives, without consulting the people. He then proposed an amendment to Borden's resolution, calling for an immediate plebiscite. Lemieux defended Laurier's middle-of-the-road policy, and urged his compatriots of Quebec to abstain from isolationism and to defend the rights granted them by the Quebec Act. The Liberals stood firm behind Laurier's proposal; the Conservatives attacked it on either English loyalist grounds or French-Canadian nationalist ones. Monk's amendment won the support of only 18 votes; Borden's of 74 against the government's 129.

The press sought to increase the division between French and English Canadians on the issue, or to minimize it, according to party affiliation. In *Le Devoir* Bourassa accused Laurier of sacrificing Canada to England; the *Toronto Mail and Empire* accused him of seeking to separate Canada from England. Bourassa hinted at a secret imperialist agreement between Laurier and Borden. *Le Canada* and *La Patrie* opposed a plebiscite as tending to align Quebec against the other eight provinces; *La Presse* straddled the question by organizing a poll, weighted in favor of Laurier, among its readers as to whether they favored Borden's, Monk's, or Laurier's policy. *Le Devoir* continued its petition campaign with clergy and brothers seeking signatures.[73] In a by-election at Drummond, contested by the provincial minister of lands and the nationalist Napoléon Garceau, the Liberal candidate was elected on March 5 by a sharply reduced majority after a campaign marked by much more discussion of the naval question than provincial matters.[74] Anglophobia was aroused in Quebec, while the *Toronto Mail* urged its readers to defend the Union Jack against Laurier and Quebec.[75]

The provincial session opened on March 15, and Bourassa was forced to leave Ottawa, where he had been following the navy debate from the press gallery, for Quebec. Once more he joined Lavergne and Prévost in attacks on the Gouin administration. Prévost introduced the navy question by condemning Taschereau for his loyalist speech at a *bonne entente* dinner in Toronto in December, which gave 'the false impression that the French Canadians were dying with envy to quit the shores of the St. Lawrence to offer their breasts to the enemies of England, to the spears of the Chinese or to the assegais of the Hottentots.' Prévost accused the provincial administration of depopulating Quebec by forcing some of its people into exile in the States or in the West, and of making the rest cannon-fodder.[76] The Orangemen of Ontario, already on the warpath against Quebec to the cry of 'One school, one language, one flag,' were aroused still further by such utterances, and by extracts from Bourassa's and Monk's speeches.

Their attacks increased the division between French and English Conservatives, though Borden defended the loyalty of the French Canadians, and said they merely differed from the English Canadians in their estimate of the situation.[77] Nonetheless Quebec Conservatives revolted against his leadership, while his Ontario followers urged the expulsion of Monk from the party. Borden's concession to the imperialists was sharply criticized in *Le Devoir*, and the Quebec Conservatives affirmed their loyalty to Monk. When they warned Borden that they would not attend the national convention scheduled for June, he cancelled the gathering. In the face of this divided opposition, the Navy Bill was passed on its third reading, April 20,

by a vote of 111 to 70. Despite the opposition of the Conservative
Landry and the Liberal Choquette, the bill passed through the
Senate without much breaking of party lines.

7

The anti-imperialist agitation did not die down in Quebec, however, with the passage of the Navy Act. The Conservatives held a
protest meeting on April 24 at Coteau Landing, and published a
manifesto in *L'Evénement* threatening a rupture of the coalition with
the Ontario Tories which Morin and MacNab had made in 1854.
Their program was close to the nationalist one, calling for protection
of minority rights, refusal of participation in wars without consultation of the people, the end of 'undesirable' immigration, and respect
of provincial autonomy.[78] On May 11 there was a manifestation in
honor of Monk at the Monument National, organized by a young
lawyer, Paul-Emile Lamarche. Monk maintained his constitutional
position:

I imagine that there are still some Anglo-Saxons in this country, and
that they will not tolerate being taxed indefinitely without having a
word to say in the making and control of wars to which their taxes are
devoted. I have not sought to isolate the province of Quebec, to align
it against the other provinces of Confederation . . . but I claim for every
group of British subjects, whatever its origin and its importance, the
right to say freely, on such a question as this, what it believes to be just
and true.[79]

Senator Landry promised Monk the support of all Quebec Conservatives. Bourassa, urging the necessity of forgetting party lines, won the
lion's share of applause.

The fight for the rights of the French language was also waged
vigorously. Aided by a campaign of the A.C.J.C., Lavergne's
proposal of compulsory bilingualism in the public services of Quebec
was adopted first by the municipal council of Montreal and then by
the provincial legislature. Under the influence of Senator Dandur-
and, Thomas Shaughnessy, head of the Canadian Pacific, persuaded
the Grand Trunk, the Montreal Light, Heat, and Power, the Bell
Telephone, and other great English-owned companies to accept the
measure rather than to fight it, as they at first proposed to do.

The growing national consciousness of the French Canadians
was also reflected by the establishment of the cult of Dollard, the
hero of a battle against the Iroquois at the Long Sault 250 years
before. The editor of the *Montreal Herald*, John C. Walsh, seems to
have been the first to call attention to the anniversary. The artist
J.-B. Legacé proposed a ceremony at the Place d'Armes, and a

Evening on the North Shore

Oil painting (c. 1920) by Clarence Gagnon (1881–1942). This Paris-trained Montreal painter had a passion for the simple life and magnificent scenery of the Charlevoix country between the St. Lawrence and the Saguenay. (Quebec Provincial Museum.)

Family Prayers

Monotype (c. 1933) from water color by Clarence Gagnon. Another illustration from *Maria Chapdelaine* which shows the deep piety of the French Canadian and the strong family tradition. (I.O.A.P.Q.)

Sugar-Making

Monotype (c. 1933) from water color by Clarence Gagnon. One of the illustrations to the magnificent Paris edition of Louis Hémon's epic of frontier life, *Maria Chapdelaine*. (I.O.A.P.Q.)

committee consisting of Legacé, the sculptor Philippe Hébert, the Abbé Philippe Perrier, and Emile Vaillancourt, was set up to organize a celebration on May 29. The A.C.J.C. anticipated the gathering by a congress at the Gésu on May 22, in which tribute was paid to Dollard. The gathering on the 29th was attended by the patriotic societies and a detachment of the 65th Militia Battalion. Bourassa was the chief speaker; he argued that the support given to the celebration by English Canadians foreshadowed better understanding and that Dollard could become a national hero for Canadians of both races. Archbishop Bruchési proposed the erection of a monument to the hero, and the A.C.J.C. at once started a fund, to which Lord Grey subscribed $100.[80]

Stimulated by their success, some young members of the A.C.J.C. obtained and published a list of members of the Lodge of Freemasons in Montreal. This exploit was hailed as happily in *Le Devoir*, more ultramontane in tone since Asselin and Fournier had broken with Bourassa and left the staff, as in *L'Action Sociale*. The politico-religious aspect of nationalism was increased by the tightening alliance between the A.C.J.C. and the nationalists. The provincial session closed in June, after Lavergne and all members of the Conservative opposition had supported Prévost's motion of censure against Taschereau for his loyalist statement at Toronto.

In this atmosphere the nationalists and Conservatives launched a joint campaign for the repeal of the Navy Act. The Liberals took the agitation so seriously that they published Lemieux's speeches in favor of the act in a pamphlet, to act as a counterweight to Bourassa's *Le Projet de Loi Navale*. The British government extended Lord Grey's term of office for a year, thus enabling him to continue his imperialist influence. But anti-imperialism in Quebec continued to grow. Monk, Lavergne, and Blondin held a meeting at Beauport on July 10, where Lavergne supplied the first evidence that this was to be a campaign against Laurier as well as one against the Navy Act. On July 17 Bourassa joined in the campaign at a meeting held at Saint-Eustache, before the church which bore the scars of English cannon-balls fired in 1837. On the previous day *Le Devoir* and *Le Nationaliste* had published resolutions drafted by Bourassa and to be proposed by him at Saint-Eustache. They declared the French Canadians' loyalty and willingness to defend Canada; their opposition to foreign wars without a voice equal to the mother country's in imperial affairs; the rights of the majority to determine Canada's course after deliberation by the people; and their censure of Taschereau's declaration, of the federal administration and its supporters, and of Borden and his followers. Monk's course alone was approved.[81]

At Saint-Eustache Monk recounted the rise of imperialism and the decline of opposition to it by the Laurier administration, which now surrendered responsibility to England. Though the Navy Bill had become law, the people could still have the last word by making known their opposition to it. Bourassa sketched political history since 1896, when he had held Laurier to be the 'champion of the tradition of autonomy.' Then in 1899 Laurier had begun to yield to imperialism by sending a Canadian contingent to Africa. Today Laurier travelled through the West, 'acclaimed by people who have done nothing to make our country what it is, while we, descendants of those who thrust back the forest, hunted wild beasts, loyally defended New France, then fought for the English flag against the revolting American colonies, have not the right to say to Laurier and Borden, who have cancelled with a pen stroke all our dearly acquired liberties: "You are only cowards and traitors who do not deserve well of your country."' Bourassa confessed that once he had loved Laurier, served him to the best of his strength, and believed in him. Then he launched into a denunciation of Laurier for coming to terms with Lord Grey, for betraying his followers, for leading the French Canadians into imperialism, for denying the Catholics of half the country the right to have their children taught the religion and the language of their fathers. 'I say that when a man, whatever his personal qualities, so violates the confidence and the love that a people have placed in him by betraying his own kind at one stroke, such a man is more dangerous to his religion, to his country, and even to the British Crown than the worst of Orangemen.'[82] Bourassa then read the resolutions, to which only three of the crowd of some 8,000 objected. He concluded with a fervent word of thanks: 'Not for us, not for M. Monk, not for your humble servant; I thank you in behalf of your people, your country, your fathers, and above all your sons.'

When the storm of applause died down, Prévost proposed Monk, who put his convictions before his ambition, as federal leader in place of Laurier, the Liberal who had become an imperialist and a militarist. Three Conservative speakers and a former Liberal then closed the meeting by promising Monk and Bourassa their support. Héroux hailed the Saint-Eustache meeting in Le Devoir as the inauguration of a new era. It was so indeed, since Laurier had been attacked in public without protest or indignation.

The campaign thus launched continued without notable opposition. Laurier spent the whole summer touring the West. Lemieux was abroad; Brodeur was sick; and the provincial Liberals were reluctant to risk their popularity on a federal issue. The defence of Laurier and the Navy Act was left to the editors of Le Canada and Le Soleil, whom Bourassa contemptuously dismissed as 'Laurier's domestics.' Meanwhile Bourassa strengthened his hold on the clergy, already sympathetic to him thanks to his opposition to secular schools and to the proposed nomination of an English-speaking bishop to the see of Ottawa. He took this stand: 'To bind the cause of the Church to that of the French race and tongue in Canada would be an error. To make the Church an instrument of Anglo-Saxon assimilation would be equally absurd and odious.'[83] Abbé Emile Chartier of Saint-Hyacinthe, one of the founders of the A.C.J.C., defended nationalism as being closer in its principles, in the eyes of youth, than any other political doctrine to the ideal and superior political principles which must be taught to students. With such views questioned only by faithful Liberals, with *Le Devoir* and *L'Action Sociale* the only newspapers permitted in the classical colleges, the rising generation was thoroughly indoctrinated with nationalist beliefs.

The campaign went on, with meetings at Saint-Henri and Saint-Hyacinthe, at which Bourassa moved the resolutions of Saint-Eustache, and vainly urged opponents of them to express their opposition in the face of almost unanimous support. On August 21 the nationalists held eight simultaneous meetings, while Bourassa journeyed to Halifax to expound before the Canadian Club a program which he wished to be national and not merely provincial. As usual he won the respect of an English-speaking audience by his knowledge of constitutional law, his courage, and his oratorical ability. But he was a little too ready to assume that applause meant agreement. On August 28 eight more meetings were held in Quebec. There was practically no opposition. Again on September 4, at Napierville, Bourassa drew a crowd of 5,000, not one of whom favored the Navy Act. When Laurier returned from the West to attend the Eucharistic Congress at Montreal, the revolt in Quebec against him was well advanced.

8

The Twentieth Eucharistic Congress, the first ever held in North America, assembled in Montreal on September 6, 1910. Present were the Cardinal Legate Vincenze Vanutelli, Archbishop Bourne of Westminster, Archbishop Ireland of St. Paul, all the Canadian hierarchy, and many bishops from Germany, France, Belgium, Holland, Ireland, and Spain, as well as a horde of pilgrims who temporarily doubled the population of the city, which had been specially decorated for the occasion. The provincial government gave a dinner to the legate on September 7, at which Sir Lomer Gouin expressed the eternal attachment of the French Canadians to the Holy See. The Congress divided into two sections, the French one meeting at Notre-Dame Church and the English one at St. Patrick's. Archbishop Bruchési endeavoured to avoid too much emphasis on the division, opposing the plan of the rector of St. Patrick's for a dinner for the English-speaking bishops by suggesting a banquet for all the bishops, at which he and the legate would preside.

Laurier, won over by his friend Bishop Mathieu to participation in the congress despite the risk of arousing Anglo-Protestant feeling, made a careful speech on September 9 on religious tolerance, freedom of worship, and legal guarantees, to which no exception could be taken. Remembering political anti-clericalism at home, the French visitors wistfully remarked that Canada was fortunate in having such leaders as Laurier and Gouin. On the afternoon of September 10 the A.C.J.C. assembled 25,000 young people at the Arena, where they were addressed by the legate and Archbishop Langevin, who spoke of his past struggles and future hopes for Catholic and French education in the West. Bourassa congratulated the audience on uniting their patriotism and their faith. After three delegates from France had spoken, Archbishop Langevin stole a march on Archbishop Bruchési by obtaining the legate's blessing for the Carillon–Sacré-Coeur flag, which the Montrealer disapproved as a separatist emblem.

But the great event of the congress was the meeting that same evening at Notre-Dame, from which the Blessed Sacrament was removed so that the church became merely an immense auditorium for the occasion. Archbishop Bourne startled the assemblage by arguing that since Canada was growing and peopling itself with people of different origins but who all spoke English, the Church must not give the impression that Catholicism was linked with the French language, if it were to hold or win the New Canadians. The Church must use the growing influence of the English language in Canada; English ought to be the vehicle of the Faith. In the future Catholicism must be linked to the English language. At the conclusion of this address, which clearly implied abandonment of the struggle for the French language outside Quebec, Archbishop Langevin privately urged Bourassa to reply. While Thomas Chapais and Judge Sullivan of New York spoke, Bourassa had an opportunity to consider the language question, which he had barely touched upon in his prepared speech.

When his turn came Bourassa glanced at his text and put it in his pocket, and then improvised an eloquent reply to the English archbishop's address. He promised that in the future as in the past Canadian priests would always supply the consolations of religion to the exiled sons of England and Ireland in the language of their fathers.

But at the same time permit me to claim the same right for my compatriots, for those who speak my language, not only in this province, but wherever French groups live in the shadow of the British flag, of the glorious Stars and Stripes, and above all of the maternal wing of the Catholic Church—the Church of Christ who died for all men and imposed on no one the obligation to deny his race in order to remain faithful to Him.

I do not wish, through a narrow nationalism, to say—that would be the contrary of my thought, and I do not say it, my compatriots—that the Catholic Church ought to be French in Canada. No, but say with me that among three million Catholics, descendants of the first apostles of Christianity in America, the best safeguard of the Faith is the conservation of the idiom in which during three hundred years they have adored Christ.

Yes, when Christ was attacked by the Iroquois, when Christ was denied by the English, when Christ was fought by all the world, we confessed Him, and confessed Him in our language.

The fate of three million Catholics cannot be indifferent, I am certain, to the heart of Pius X, or to the eminent Cardinal who represents him here.

But there is still more to say: Providence has wished that the principal group of this French and Catholic colonization should constitute in America a separate corner of the earth, where the social, religious, and political situation most closely approximates that which the Church teaches us to be the ideal state of society. We do not have union of Church and State in Canada; let us not oppose words. But we have in the Province of Quebec—I might say almost exclusively in the Province of Quebec—peace, good understanding between the civil and religious authorities. From this peace have derived laws which permit us to give the Catholic Church a social and civil organization which she finds in no other province of Canada, and in no other part of the British Empire.

Thanks to these laws, our dioceses are organized, our parishes founded . . . And the Church of Quebec, at peace in legal and material matters, has been able to give the fullness of its efforts to the apostolate; and this effort has been felt far beyond the diocese of St. Paul.

From this Province of Quebec, from this minute French colony, whose language, it is said, is doomed to disappear, have come three-quarters of the clergy of North America, who came to draw from the Seminary of Quebec or Saint-Sulpice the knowledge and virtue which distinguished the clergy of the great American Republic and the English-speaking clergy as well as the French-speaking clergy of Canada.

Your Eminence, you have visited our religious communities, you have gone to seek in the convents, hospitals, and colleges of Montreal the proof of the faith and works of the French-Canadian people. You would have to stay two years in America, to cross five thousand kilometers of country, from Cape Breton to British Columbia, and to visit half the American Republic, to trace the foundations of all sorts—colleges, convents, hospitals, asylums—which are the daughters of these mother institutions that you have visited here . . . Must one conclude that the Roman Catholics have been more zealous, more apostolic than the others? No, but Providence has wished that they should be the apostles of North America.

Let one beware, let one be carefully aware, of extinguishing this fire, with its intense light which has illuminated a whole continent for three centuries . . .

But, it is said, you are only a handful; you are fatally destined to disappear; why persevere in the struggle? We are only a handful, it is true; but in the school of Christ I did not learn to estimate right and moral forces by number and wealth. We are only a handful; but we count for what we are; and we have the right to live . . .

For nineteen centuries there has not been a Hebrew Pope, a Roman Pope, an Italian Pope, a French Pope, but the Pope, father of all the great Catholic family.

Let us go higher, let us go to Calvary; and there on that little hill in Judea, which was not very high in the world, let us learn the lesson of tolerance and of true Christian charity.[84]

There was a hush when Bourassa concluded; then the legate came and shook his hand, a gesture which he had not made in the case of the other speakers. Tumult broke loose. Hats and handkerchiefs were waved, bishops applauded with their feet instead of their hands; within and without the church people embraced one another. The Place d'Armes was filled with dancing, jubilant figures. Bourassa had made himself the hero of the French-Canadian people. The next day, as the procession of 100 prelates, 10,000 priests and religious, and 50,000 lay folk paraded through the streets to close the congress with Benediction at the foot of Mount Royal, the passage of Bourassa provoked demonstrations which dwarfed those aroused by Laurier. Quebec had found a new leader, to whom the Franco-Ontarians now turned for aid in their struggle for a French bishop of Ottawa and for bilingualism in their schools.

9

After the truce of the Eucharistic Congress, the fight against the Navy Act went on with renewed vigor. Bourassa's prestige was much enhanced by his defence of the French language at Notre-Dame, which was published in Le Devoir on September 26 as 'Religion, Langue, Nationalité.' At Farnham on September 17, to a largely Liberal audience, Bourassa again denounced Laurier's betrayal of Liberal principles and appealed for support in his campaign in their favor. He conjured up the prospect of future conscription as a result of Laurier's action, and won almost unanimous approval for the Saint-Eustache resolutions. A week later 8,000 people gathered at Grand'Mère to hear Bourassa, who once more warned of the danger of conscription. Meanwhile in Le Devoir he supported the Franco-Ontarians.

To an interviewer from the New York Herald at this time Bourassa defined nationalism as 'a doctrine and not a political party.' It was based on the familiar American constitutional principle of no taxation without representation. It was not anti-British, since Canada could best serve the empire by devoting herself to her own development. It was not a doctrine for French Canadians alone, but for all Canadians, since it tended to develop national spirit while assuring the French Canadians their right to exercise social and political influence in the country.[85] The *Manitoba Free Press* asked what flag Bourassa would substitute for the British flag. Bourassa replied in *Le Devoir*: 'As a Canadian and a British subject, I recognize only one flag, on which tradition and the sentiment of our era—that since 1867—placed the arms of the Canadian Confederation. This flag is at once the emblem of our allegiance and the mark of our relative autonomy.'[86] He said that he respected, without sharing, the wish of many of his compatriots for a special French-Canadian flag.

On October 10 Laurier himself tried to check the growing agitation in Quebec at a mass meeting at the Monument National under the chairmanship of Sir Lomer Gouin. Gouin hailed Laurier as one of the greatest Canadians; and young Athanase David, son of Laurier's old friend, L.-O. David, assured the prime minister that the youth of Quebec would do its duty under his banner when the time came, though it had been temporarily misled by the campaign against the Navy Act. Then Laurier began his speech, which was a vigorous attack upon the nationalists and a defence of his administration. He began by stressing the disunion of the Conservative party, which in the approaching elections would have as many programs as there were provinces. In British Columbia the government was attacked on the question of Asiatic immigration; in the Prairie Provinces on the tariff question, with a demand for a higher tariff. Also in Ontario the naval policy was attacked on the grounds that it led to the separation of Canada from Britain; while in Quebec it was attacked on the grounds that it would lead to the loss of autonomy and make Canada the slave of Britain.

In Quebec the disintegration of the Conservative party had begun long ago and its saner heads had joined the Liberals, driven out of their party by the violence of the intemperate ones who had seized control:

This violent section—you know it—comprises the Pharisees of Canadian Catholicism; those who have constituted themselves ostentatiously the defenders of religion, which no one attacked; those who handled the holy water sprinkler like a club; those who have arrogated to themselves a monopoly of orthodoxy; those who excommunicate right and left all whose stature is a little greater than theirs; those who seem to have for motive and instinct only hatred and envy; those who insulted Cardinal Taschereau when he was alive and who since his death have outraged his memory; those who made life bitter to Chapleau, the most brilliant figure whom the Conservative party has produced; those, finally, whom the people with their picturesque language designated and bedizened under the name of 'Castors.'[87]

To this group had rallied certain young Liberals, who, 'having nothing Liberal in their nature, after some ventures, found their true mentality among the Castors.' Such was the opposition today, which did not even respect the name of nationalist which it had given itself. At Montmagny, Monk and Lavergne had supported a Conservative candidate; at Farnham, Monk had appeared with Bourassa, who declared himself 'the only Liberal left today in the country.' 'They call themselves nationalists, Conservatives, Liberals, according to the character of the audience they address, with the intention of doing the most harm possible to the government and of achieving their goal of destroying the government.'[88]

After thus labeling his opponents Castors, Laurier sought to disprove their charges. Monk and Bourassa argued that he had reversed his position since 1902, but the fact was the Navy Act was in full conformity with the policy then announced, which Monk and Bourassa now said they had then approved. The law provided for the creation of a naval service which would remain completely under the control of the Canadian government. It did not provide for a contribution to the British Navy, nor for taking control away from the government, parliament, and people of Canada. In 1907 Laurier had maintained his position that Canada should develop its land and sea defences, but should conserve its autonomy in these matters as in all others. Now he was accused in Quebec of being a traitor to his country, and in Ontario of being a traitor to the empire. But such charges had come his way ever since 1896 for urging moderation upon extremists, who always replied with accusations of treason. He repeated the arguments used in the House as to the necessity of a navy, and refuted Bourassa's argument that Canada was not a nation: 'It is true that we are politically dependent upon England, but we are legislatively independent . . . we have become a nation without breaking the colonial tie.'[89]

He called Bourassa's charge of a Grey-Laurier conspiracy as baseless as that of a Laurier-Borden conspiracy, which Bourassa had abandoned when Borden turned against the Navy Act. Laurier was accused of being influenced by ambition for new honors, but neither the British nor the Canadian government could offer him any reward worth that which he had already received from the Canadian people; when he quit the prime-ministership, either at the will of the people or by his own desire, the only position worthy of his pride would be that of a simple citizen of Canada. He would accept nothing else, no matter what the honor might be. He compared the Navy Act with the Militia Act, which had been accepted without question; and pointed out that naval service was to be purely voluntary. He rebuked Bourassa for misrepresenting this fact. He dismissed the argument that the Canadian Navy would be constantly involved in Britain's wars by pointing out that the British Navy had fought no battles since Trafalgar, aside from Navarino, some engagements in the China seas, and the bombardment of Alexandria. And only the Canadian government, parliament, and people could put the Navy at the service of the King. He repeated that Canada was at war when Britain was at war, but that merely meant that 'we shall take part only when we judge it fitting to do so.'[90] Finally, the annual cost of the Navy would amount to only 3 per cent of the annual national revenue.

Once more Laurier promised that no one would be obliged to serve in the Navy who did not desire to do so. The nationalists had no right to forbid those who did wish to serve from doing so, as he had had no right to forbid those who wished to do so from serving in the South African War. His policy then had been approved by Monk. He did not fear the prospect of war; Canada had not had one for nearly a hundred years, and with the rise of democracy war was becoming less frequent, since the poor and humble suffered most from it. He hoped that as Germany became more democratic, it might form an *entente cordiale* with Britain, like that between Britain and France. Canada was not obliged to take part in any war, but if there should be a war in which the empire's naval supremacy was at stake, he himself believed that Canada should aid Britain with all its strength.

Laurier rejected the nationalist policy of forming a party composed exclusively of French Canadians as 'the contradiction of all our traditions. Our duty is to take part in the battles of our country to defend the rights not only of our province, but also the rights of the other provinces.'[91] In the past, when fighting for their rights, the French Canadians had not rested their case solely on the question of race; they had based it on the principles of truth and justice which appealed to all men's conscience, and thus they received the support without which they could not have succeeded. Papineau had been aided by Neilson and Wolfred Nelson; Lafontaine by Baldwin; Lafontaine and Baldwin by Samuel Blake in the matter of the Rebellion Losses Bill. Lafontaine, the greatest statesman that French Canada had produced, had preached the union of the Reformers of the two provinces in a spirit of peace, union, friendship, and fraternity. Laurier himself had been chosen the leader of a party in which his people were a minority, and when he had hesitated to accept the post, had been told that the Liberal party knew no distinction of race or religion. He had more sympathy for his own people, but the rights of other races were as sacred to him as the rights of his own.

He was accused of being a traitor to his race because he had permitted immigration in the West. In that policy Canada had followed the example of the United States in opening their territory to the whole world. For a hundred years the American star had shone in the firmament; he hoped that in the twentieth century the star towards which all regards would be turned would be the star of Canada. The West had been peopled; he would have liked to see a current of emigration from Quebec toward the West, but it had gone to the States instead. But this leakage had been checked by the development of industry in Montreal, thanks to the new market of the West. It was to Montreal and not the States that the surplus agricultural population of Quebec now went, so that Montreal had doubled in size in ten years. He defended the policy of reciprocity with the States, which would open up a rich market for Canadian goods and provide an inexhaustible source of prosperity. He summed up the results of his fourteen years in power as 'more harmony, more peace, more prosperity, more well-being, than in any previous epoch of our history.'[92] Whatever the result of the elections, he urged his auditors to be faithful to the principles of progress, liberty, tolerance, and justice which had insured this state of the nation.

This two-hour speech won Laurier an ovation from his audience of loyal Liberals, but cries of '*Vive Bourassa!*' disturbed the overflow meetings held outside the Monument National. The Liberal press said that the nationalists considered only Canada's interests, the imperialists only the empire's interests; but since Canadians were British subjects, the two interests should be reconciled as Laurier argued. Liberals of Quebec and Tories of Toronto joined to denounce Bourassa as an enemy of England and the English. The *Toronto World* wrote: 'M. Bourassa considers that his mission consists in kicking the English out of Quebec and reconquering Ontario.'[93] *L'Action Sociale* saw a vast plot to confine the French Canadians to Quebec, while Bishop Fallon of London attacked the Quebec nationalist organs for supporting the French-Canadian movement in Ontario. Bourassa took an opportunity to clear himself of the charge of disloyalty by urging the French Canadians to support the plan to erect a statue to Edward VII in Montreal.

A test of power between the followers of Bourassa and those of Laurier was soon provided by a by-election in Drummond-Arthabaska, occasioned by the appointment to the Senate of Louis Lavergne, a brother of Laurier's former law partner. His nephew Armand reported to Laurier that he had been asked to be a candidate in the constituency, and promised a fair contest.[94] Laurier himself presided at the Liberal convention which chose the official candidate, J.-E. Perrault, son of an old friend of Laurier, brother of the A.C.J.C. leader, and in his early days a nationalist, but now the pillar of the Arthabaska bar. Arthabaska was Laurier's own country, where he maintained a summer home and had many close friends. The constituency was too Liberal for a Conservative to stand a chance. The nationalists thought of nominating Armand Lavergne, who declined in the interests of his profession, and Napoléon Garceau, who had the handicap of being at odds with the clergy. In the end they settled upon a young farmer, Arthur Gilbert, whose election would represent a successful protest by the people itself. The Conservatives supplied organization and funds, the nationalists orators: Bourassa, Lavergne, Tancrède Marsil, Blondin, and all the rank and file.

The Arthabaska campaign really began in Montreal, where on October 20 Bourassa and Monk replied to Laurier. The students came to the meeting at the Ontario Rink in a procession preceded by a band, carrying a great portrait of Bourassa framed by the legend: 'The country before party.' Monk, in analyzing Laurier's speech, gave a stiff warning to Lord Grey: the governor-general should observe the fundamental constitutional rule that the King or his representative must refrain from political discussions. Bourassa devoted himself to refuting Laurier and sought to show that Laurier had indeed given ground to the imperialists since 1907. Lavergne attacked Lemieux and 'Laurier's valets' of *Le Canada*. Albert Sévigny concluded the evening with a speech which delighted the younger element of the audience. After the meeting the crowd paraded to the Théâtre National, where Lavergne spoke, and then to the University, where speeches by Lavergne, Sévigny, and others concluded an evening which had evoked far more enthusiasm than Laurier's meeting. [95]

Throngs of speakers descended upon the peaceful and lovely countryside of Arthabaska, and *assemblées contradictoires* abounded. One of the most notable was at Drummondville on October 27, when Monk, Bourassa, and Lavergne supported Gilbert, while Perrault was backed by Brodeur and three Liberal members of parliament. Brodeur and Henri Béland proved a team which could stand up to Bourassa and Lavergne. The Liberals maintained Laurier's contention that Canada, now become a nation, needed a navy. The nationalists denounced the government's adoption of a policy hitherto rejected by both parties; ridiculed the notion of Canada's having duties to England; and predicted that the Navy Act would lead to involvement in war, which in turn would lead to conscription. Borden's policy of financial contribution was also denounced. The Liberal candidate was reminded that he had approved the nationalist declaration of principles at Drummondville in 1902. Tancrède Marsil evoked the memory of English outrages at Saint-Eustache in 1837; Pierre Blondin said of the English flag, 'Our fathers had to pierce it with bullet holes to breathe the air of liberty.'[96] Men in uniform visited the farms and pretended to take a census of manpower, 'to have the lists ready when the Laurier Naval Act goes into force.'[97] The electors were told that 'To vote for Perrault is to vote for war; to vote for Gilbert is to vote for peace.'[98] The Liberal organizers relied too much on the constituency's record as a Liberal stronghold. But even Bourassa himself anticipated the election of Perrault and prepared an article for *Le Devoir* of November 3 explaining that the Liberal victory was due to 'drunkenness, debauchery, tumult . . . appeal to the lowest passions . . . under the serene eye and with the tacit and complacent connivance of the Right Honorable Sir Wilfrid Laurier, P.C., G.C.M.G., K.C., D.C.L., LL.D., etc.'[99]

In fact Gilbert was elected by a majority of 200; the constituency which had seen Laurier's first defeat in 1878 now gave warning of the downfall of his administration. The verdict was taken as a victory for Bourassa, who received more congratulations than the successful candidate, and as a defeat for Laurier. The prime minister's prestige suffered not only in Quebec but all over the country, because of the wide attention given to the election by the English-Canadian press. Ontario papers predicted an immediate revolt of the French Canadians against England, not realizing that the verdict represented merely a revolt against Laurier and imperialism.

The nationalist victory was celebrated at a meeting at the Ontario Rink in Montreal on November 9. The gathering was so large that the auditorium, the largest in the city, could not contain the throng, and the meeting was adjourned outdoors. The Conservatives had organized the affair, and aside from Monk and Bourassa all the announced speakers were *Bleus*. But after hearing Monk, the crowd called for the nationalists and the list of speakers was hastily revised.[100] Bourassa stressed the fact that he was not anti-British and that he was not conducting a war of races. He insisted: 'There is no more a conquering race nor a conquered race; there is no more here a right of the stronger and a right of the weaker; there are only the equal rights of two great races.'[101] Bourassa, greeted as warmly as ever Laurier had been in his heyday, challenged the prime minister to contest any great city constituency against him, 'to see whether the Canadian people is the slave of a man or whether it is in the service of a principle.'[102] The crowd paraded to the St. James Market, where Bourassa spoke again, and was reinforced by Jean Prévost, Tancrède Marsil, and other nationalists.

The attacks against Laurier now knew no limits; youth had the bit in its teeth and mocked its distinguished elders. Laurier felt obliged to write an article for *La Presse*, explaining once more that the Navy Act provided that parliament should control the fleet, and that conscription was not involved.[103] Lavergne carried the war into Ontario, where he had been invited by the students of the University of Toronto to expound nationalism on November 18. He closed his very restrained exposition with this appeal: 'I want to return to Quebec with a message of peace between the two provinces. I see the two great races working together in the future for the good of the country.' The following day he appeared in uniform as a captain of the Régiment de Montmagny and proclaimed: 'If Canada were attacked, the French Canadians would be the first to rise against the enemy, even if the enemy flew the French flag.'[104]

When the federal session opened on November 16, the Drummond-Arthabaska election had repercussions. Borden had censured the Conservative whip for congratulating Gilbert on his victory, but he himself could not refrain from taunting Laurier with his defeat. Laurier replied: 'There are defeats more honorable than victory. This victory was won not by loyal opposition, but by His Majesty's disloyal opposition.'[105] The Conservatives had joined the nationalists in making the people believe that the government was going to impose conscription. Monk proposed an amendment to the speech to the throne, regretting that it had made no mention of the government's intention to consult the people on its naval policy and on the general question of Canadian contribution to imperial armaments. Borden moved a sub-amendment, supporting the idea of a plebiscite, but stressing Canada's loyalty and willingness to fulfil its imperial responsibilities. Both amendments were defeated by large majorities.[106]

The administration undertook a Quebec campaign in support of the Navy Act. Special attention was given to St. Johns, where a provincial by-election was soon to take place. Despite the effort of the provincial Liberals to avoid the federal issue, the supporters of the opposition candidate succeeded in introducing the navy question. But Bourassa had gone abroad to study international politics, visiting London, Paris, and Rome, where he had a private audience with the Pope. The nationalists were left without a leader and without organization, while the Liberals made up for their overconfidence in Drummond-Arthabaska. The government candidate triumphed by a larger majority than before. The English voters, usually Conservative, supported the Liberal candidate, after his backers had represented Bourassa as an agitator who wished to free Quebec from English rule.

But in Paris Bourassa, interviewed by *La Libre Parole*, said that separatism was no part of his nationalism. If the tie with Britain were broken, it would be only because of the imposition of an imperialist regime, which would produce a quicker and more violent anti-British reaction among the English Canadians than among the French Canadians. The Canadian students in Paris, who likened Bourassa's ideas to those of Charles Maurras, and the *Ligue Nationaliste* to the *Ligue d'Action Française*, were contradicted by Bourassa, who found the French royalists 'narrow and sectarian.'[107] In Rome, where Bourassa had been preceded by Laurier's friend, Curé Côté of Arthabaska, Mgr. Merry del Val judged that 'Archbishop Bourne and Bishop Fallon had lacked judgment and tact, but M. Bourassa is a hothead,' and the Pope dismissed Bourassa's attempt to raise the language question with an assurance that justice would be done.[108]

Bourassa's prestige at home was reinforced by his encounters with leading figures of the London and Roman worlds, and when he returned to Montreal on January 13, 1911, he was greeted by 2,000 people at the station. When he went to Quebec for the provincial session, which had already opened with mocking regrets for his absence from Taschereau, he received an equally warm reception. The first anniversary banquet of *Le Devoir* was attended by 500 guests, headed by Monk, Tellier, and Jean Prévost. With the nationalist-Conservative alliance in the Province now firmly cemented, Bourassa journeyed to Ottawa to consult with Monk on the possibilities of a national alliance in opposition to the government's proposal of reciprocity with the United States.

10

The reciprocal tariff agreement with the United States introduced in parliament on January 26, 1911, by Fielding, had been worked out after nearly twelve months of negotiations, initiated at the request of President Taft. The protectionist Payne-Aldrich Tariff, enacted in 1909, had proved unpopular at home and a source of complications abroad. It carried penalties against those countries which discriminated against the United States. Canada's recent concessions to France, Germany, Italy, Belgium, and the Netherlands called for the application of the penalty clause against her, unless concessions were made to the United States. Early in 1910 two American representatives were sent to Ottawa to confer with Laurier and Fielding, and in March Taft met Fielding at Albany. Later Fielding and another Canadian minister went to Washington, and a compromise was worked out, whereby Canada made nominal concessions. With growing sentiment in favor of reciprocity in his own party and with the Democrats clamoring for it, Taft opened negotiations in October for a wider agreement, after announcing his conviction that 'these two countries, touching each other for more than three thousand miles, have common interests in trade and require special arrangements in legislation and administration.'[109] The negotiations were concluded at Washington in January 1911, virtually providing for a renewal of the Treaty of 1854. Complete free trade had been offered by the Americans, but refused by the Canadians, who also insisted that the agreement should take effect by concurrent legislation, which either country might modify at any time, rather than by an inflexible treaty. The reduction given to American imports could be extended to British imports. Essentially the agreement provided for the free entrance into the United States of all Canadian natural products, while American manufacturers benefited by a lower Canadian duty.

The agreement realized the goal of both Canadian political parties since the revocation of reciprocity in 1866. It met the desires of the farmers of Ontario and the West, who through the Grange and the Grain Growers' Association had been pressing for lower duties on manufactured goods. In December 1910, 900 Western farmers had invaded parliament to demand reciprocity. They urged a cause already won, for Laurier was sympathetic to the English Liberal tradition of free trade and Fielding had long favored a measure welcome to the Maritime Provinces, whose natural economic capital lay in New England rather than in central Canada. Reciprocity had offered a distraction from the political-religious question in 1896, and might once again relieve a menacing situation in Quebec.

At first the proposal met with general approval, with the Western Conservatives and the *Toronto News* and *Ottawa Journal* backing it. Borden's only criticisms were the possible danger to Canadian industries, the indefinite duration of the agreement and the possibility of dislocation of the Canadian economy if it were suddenly terminated, and its threat to the Conservative program of reciprocity within the empire. The Conservative camp was divided by support of the proposal in the West and opposition to it from protected Eastern industries. Protests were made from the Montreal and Toronto Boards of Trade, supported by the industrial, financial, and railway interests which benefited by an east-west flow of trade, rather than by a north-south one. Clifford Sifton, with the aid of Zebulon Lash, Mackenzie and Mann's lawyer, organized a revolt by eighteen Liberals of Toronto, all eminent in the financial world, who on February 20 publicly repudiated reciprocity. On the 22nd Sir William Van Horne announced that he was 'out to bust the damn thing,'[110] and most Canadian big business followed the lead of the influential former head of the Canadian Pacific.

Meanwhile the Conservatives had decided to fight the proposal. On February 10 Monk, true to form, criticized the haste with which the measure was being adopted and moved a resolution regretting that the opinion of the people had not been taken on the question. Borden took a firmer stand, criticizing the radical revision of the Canadian trade structure which had been built up since 1866. Free trade would lead to commercial union, and the Canadian people should not abandon their effort to build up a great nation under the British flag, when the battle was more than half won. But it was Clifford Sifton who, on February 28, made the strongest attack on reciprocity. He urged that the Liberals, who had abandoned reciprocity after the failure of the Joint High Commission in 1899, had no mandate to reverse the policy of protection which had since been in force. He showed how the agreement would injure such Canadian industries as meat-packing and milling, while the industrial development of Canada by American branch factories and pulp mills would be ended. Canada would become dependent upon the United States, and in the end might lose the American market as well as the British one, which would suffer under this agreement. In the long run the Canadian wheat growers and cattlemen would suffer by American control, while New York would gain the trade which now passed through Montreal. He opposed the proposal on patriotic grounds, and said it spelled 'retrogression, commercial subordination, the destruction of our national ideals, and displacement from our proud position as the rising hope of the British Empire.'[111] Borden soon became involved in negotiations with the dissident Liberals headed by Sifton, who urged a stronger attitude both towards the United States and towards Quebec.[112] These negotiations resulted in another revolt within the Conservative party against Borden's leadership, and the further alienation of Monk's followers.

Somewhat surprisingly, Bourassa generally supported reciprocity in a series of articles which appeared in *Le Devoir* from January 31 to February 7 and were reprinted in pamphlet form in both French and English.[113] He took the basic position of 'Canada first and Canada for the Canadians,' and then approved reciprocity as fostering agriculture and not harming Canadian industry. He saw no danger of political union in it, since Canada had attained nationhood under reciprocity from 1854 to 1866; and he expressed the belief that a 'measure of reciprocity, both broad and prudent, between Canada and the United States, is natural; it is in conformity with the political traditions and economic needs of Canada.'[114] Internal east-west trade would be little altered, while the export trade already enjoyed access to the American routes through the bonding privilege, and American railways already drained Canada's wealthiest regions. The development of the Georgian Bay Canal, which Monk desired instead of the creation of a navy, might favor the St. Lawrence route. Bourassa shared Monk's doubts as to whether the agreement was the most advantageous one which Canada could make, with reciprocity steadily growing in favor in the States. He questioned Laurier's trustworthiness and revived the memory of the Liberal annexationist movement in the 1880's and 1890's; but since this agreement was open to termination at any time, he saw no great danger in it. There was no sacrifice of true British interests, but it unquestionably sacrificed imperialist ones by blocking commercial union of the empire. On this ground Borden objected to it, ignoring the fact that Canada had a more natural market in the States than in the empire. The anomaly of the nationalist-Conservative alliance was made evident by the fact that Bourassa favored reciprocity on anti-imperialist grounds, while Borden opposed it on imperialist grounds.

Bourassa made evident his distrust of Laurier, whom he thought had been influenced in favor of reciprocity by the Asquith government and of the British Ambassador, James Bryce, at Washington, as he had been influenced in favor of the Navy Act by Lord Grey. At present the West favored reciprocity and Quebec was aroused against imperialism, so Laurier followed an opportunist course, which he might reverse if public opinion changed; therefore the nationalists reserved the right to change their stand. In the Quebec legislature in March Bourassa also urged the provincial authorities to consider the repercussions of reciprocity upon the paper and lumber industries; but it was clear that he was more interested in what was happening at Ottawa than at Quebec, and that he might once more enter the federal field.

At Ottawa reciprocity made heavy weather against growing Conservative opposition, and Laurier was forced in May to adjourn parliament for two months in order that he might attend the Imperial Conference scheduled for the end of the month. The Conference was chiefly notable for the effort of the Round Table school of imperialists to secure approval of some plan of imperial parliamentary federation. This proposal was made through Sir Joseph Ward of New Zealand, who, in addition to pressing for an imperial council of state, urged the creation of an imperial parliament with power over foreign policy and defence. Laurier rejected the scheme as 'utterly impracticable,'[115] and was joined in his opposition by Asquith of Britain, Fisher of Australia, and Botha of South Africa. Laurier also opposed an alternative scheme suggested by Harcourt, which proposed a standing committee composed of the colonial secretary and his under-secretaries, together with the high commissioners of the dominions. Through the Imperial Defence Committee, in which the dominions did not enjoy the same equality with the British as in the conference, confidential defence information was for the first time given to the colonial representatives.[116] But Laurier objected to an Australian motion that the British government should consult the dominions before signing treaties binding the empire. Giving advice implied backing that advice with armed strength; Laurier was opposed to centralization of policy, as well as centralization of defence. Indeed he won further freedom for Canada to free herself from old commercial treaties made by Britain which impeded her negotiations with the United States. By the end of the 1911 Conference it was evident that imperialism in Chamberlain's sense was dead; the empire was to be a league of equal nations making mutual arrangements by negotiation.

During Laurier's absence his enemies had been busy, both in French and English Canada. While Borden began a campaign in the West against reciprocity, on May 31 the nationalists held a mass meeting in support of Monk at the Ontario Rink in Montreal, as the initial step in a new drive against the Navy Act. Taillon read an address to Monk and assured him of support. Monk condemned imperialism, and without discussing the merits of reciprocity, criticized the government for adopting that policy and its naval one too quickly, without sufficient study and consultation of the people. Lavergne devoted himself to criticizing the immigration policy, while Paul-Emile Lamarche, a powerful speaker, supported Monk's stand. Bourassa attacked Laurier for his lack of principle, his opportunism, and his betrayals, and predicted the triumph of nationalism. This meeting drew down upon Bourassa and his allies new criticism from the Quebeckers, and the *Quebec Chronicle* announced that no English Conservative could accept an alliance with anti-British Bourassa. Within his own camp Bourassa met with opposition from Asselin and Fournier, who differed with his moderate attitude in the current Franco-Ontarian and Franco-American struggles against assimilation, and criticized his failure to exploit the Drummond-Arthabaska success. In *L'Action*, a little nationalist weekly founded by Fournier in April 1911, Asselin complained that 'M. Bourassa imagined that all parliamentary tactics and all the art of politics consist of speeches.'[117] But the defection of Asselin and Fournier did not check the growth of nationalism, which was now penetrating into Conservative and clerical circles where these hot-headed young men were not in good odor. When Lemieux undertook a speaking tour through Quebec in June in favor of Laurier's policies, the nationalists followed suit with opposition meetings. In early June there were meetings at Joliette, Nicolet,

Sorel, and Sainte-Scholastique, where Bourassa and Lavergne were supported by Tellier, Monk, and other Conservative orators. Lemieux and Bourassa made charges and counter-charges against each other, and the atmosphere grew bitter.

There was a truce for Saint-Jean-Baptiste Day, when the Montreal Saint-Jean-Baptiste Society held a banquet to manifest their sympathy for the persecuted French Canadians outside Quebec. Asselin savagely attacked Irish bishops who wished to anglicize the French Canadians, and urged his people to support only French-Canadian banks, insurance companies, and businesses, in order to increase their economic power. Bourassa expressed his sympathy for the minorities of Maine and Ontario, but counseled moderation:

> Before all and despite all, remain unalterably attached to the Catholic Church. The constituted authorities of the Church can err. The Pope himself can err. Whatever happens, never doubt Rome. At Rome you will end by finding justice. You will even find there indulgence for the excesses of word and errors of tactics which may escape you in the course of battle.[118]

And he urged his audience not to make the whole Irish race responsible for the iniquities committed by some of its members. The *Montreal Gazette* took alarm at the boycott of English business proposed by Asselin, and Bourassa was credited with his disciple's suggestion, which he himself repudiated. When a rumor came from London that at the conference Laurier had refused the participation of the navy in all Britain's wars, the *Quebec Chronicle* proclaimed: 'It is the voice of Laurier, but the hand of Bourassa.'[119]

The campaign was renewed by both government and opposition forces before Laurier returned to Quebec on July 10. At the ancient capital he claimed that he had adopted the same attitude at the conference as at earlier ones: 'the revindication of our rights and of our policy. This policy has triumphed, and we have succeeded in establishing a solid basis on which the Empire and all the young nations which make it up can grow great: each community, each society, each nation ought to govern itself, in taking account of its own public opinion . . . We are loyal subjects of the British Crown, but we shall never consent to being governed from London by Downing Street.'[120] Again at Montreal the following day there was a carefully organized reception for Laurier at the Champs de Mars.[121] But Bourassa was not impressed by these tributes to the old leader and by Laurier's well-worn arguments that he had made Canada a nation, and had followed a middle path which caused him to be attacked by imperialist and nationalist extremists. Bourassa held that Canada was not a nation since the decisions of its highest court were subject to appeal to the Judicial Committee of the Privy Council; and that Laurier was attacked by both imperialists and nationalists because his policy was neither imperialist nor nationalist. Bourassa concluded his series of articles on Laurier and the Imperial Conference in *Le Devoir*, which were reprinted in pamphlet form, by declaring: 'The power of the man of the golden mean, of the honorable compromises, of false "conciliation" solutions, evaporates like morning fog under a hot sun.'[122]

When parliament reassembled on July 18, reciprocity was pressed once more by the government. Fielding threatened that if the manufacturers succeeded in defeating the measure, 'then there will rise up in the Western country a storm-cloud no bigger than a man's hand, and the end will be a change in the fiscal policy of the country which the manufacturers will find much greater than anything they conceived of.'[123] But the opposition had grown stronger in Laurier's absence, and in the face of Conservative obstruction, Laurier had no recourse but to dissolve parliament and appeal to the country. The Conservatives' patriotic argument had gained new strength from indiscreet statements of President Taft and Speaker Champ Clark in support of the agreement. On two occasions Taft spoke of Canada as 'being at the parting of the ways'[124]—a statement which was twisted to suit Conservative purposes. On April 27 Taft said 'no such opportunity will ever again come to the United States. The forces which are at work in England and Canada to separate her by a Chinese wall from the United States, and to make her part of an Imperial band reaching from England round the world and back to England again by a system of preferential tariffs would derive an impetus from the rejection of this treaty.'[125] The president also wrote Theodore Roosevelt, in a letter made public on April 25, that reciprocity 'would made Canada only an adjunct of the United States.'[126] Champ Clark, speaking at Chicago, said: 'I hope to see the day when the American flag will float over every square foot of the British North American possessions, clear to the North Pole . . . That is the way things are tending now.'[127]

As in 1891, the Liberals found it difficult to convince Canadians whose emotional patriotism was aroused by such statements that limited reciprocity did not mean annexation, and that the argument of 'no truck nor trade with the Yankees' came oddly from bankers and railroad magnates closely tied to Wall Street and international corporations. The old United Empire Loyalist sentiment against the Yankees was revived, and Canadian national pride found it difficult not to retaliate for years of unfriendly American acts and restrictive tariffs. A Canadian National League was formed under the auspices of the eighteen rebel Liberals of Toronto; a nonpolitical Anti-Reciprocity League sprang up; and appeals were made to the British-born to keep Canada British. Sifton took an active part in the campaign, and his speech against reciprocity was widely circulated in the West. Upon the dissolution of parliament Sifton issued a manifesto to the people of Canada, restating his arguments against reciprocity.[128]

Laurier's election manifesto insisted that both parties had long sought reciprocity; that the arrangement now made had been criticized in the States as being too favorable to Canada; that the Conservatives had blocked debate in the House upon its merits, and hence had made necessary an appeal to the people. The alleged peril to the British connection was discounted; and it was argued that the arrangement would improve relations between all three countries, and would remove forever the possibility of war between the British Empire and the United States.[129] No mention was made of the naval question.

Borden's first manifesto also ignored the navy question and welcomed the appeal to the people, while condemning the government for the sudden dissolution of parliament. In a second manifesto on August 14, Borden deplored the reversal of Canada's traditional economic policy, and objected to reciprocity on the grounds that it would integrate the Canadian economy with the American one, and lead to commercial union with the United States excluding trade relations with the empire. It threatened the farmer and fisherman, left Canada's natural resources at the mercy of the American trusts, and discouraged Canadian industry. The Conservative platform provided for a reform of extravagant public expenditure, return of their natural resources to the Prairie Provinces, construction of a Hudson Bay railroad, government-controlled grain elevators, encouragement of the meat-packing industry, and other minor reforms. The Conservatives pledged themselves to 'maintain independent and unimpaired the control of our own affairs by the Parliament of Canada; a policy which, while affording no just cause of complaint to any foreign nation, will find its highest ideal in the autonomous development of Canada as a nation within the British Empire.' Borden concluded with a plea 'for the strengthening and not the loosening of the ties which bind this Dominion to the British Empire.'[130] In this manifesto he did not urge Canadian contribution to the British navy, but attacked the Laurier naval policy as costly, inefficient, and likely to result in 'the useless sacrifice of many lives.'

Borden had made a deal with the Quebec Conservatives, whereby the campaign in that province was left to Monk, who was now very much under Bourassa's influence. At a meeting in Montreal on August 1, the Conservative organizer Charles Beaubien achieved the agreement of the very imperialist Herbert B. Ames, the more moderate imperialist C. J. Doherty, the moderate nationalist Monk, and the very nationalist Bourassa to the common objective of defeating Laurier. Protectionist and imperialist big business was willing to use the nationalist movement to defeat reciprocity. In Quebec reciprocity was a minor issue, but the nationalists had roused a swelling and potent agitation against the government on the navy question.

Therefore funds began to flow into the nationalist war chest from Tory sources. One English Conservative from Montreal, who had violently attacked the nationalists as 'rebels and disloyal traitors,' now took out forty subscriptions to *Le Devoir*, and others followed suit.[131] The paper's capital was tripled; and Ernest Lapointe remarked: 'If I were given to the bitterness of the nationalists, I should say that M. Bourassa has opposed reciprocity since the capital of his paper has been increased by $200,000; I should say that M. Bourassa has been bought.'[132] Rodolphe Forget, whose interests had also been opposed by the Liberals, threw the support of his money and influence behind the nationalists. Sir Hugh Graham, whose *Montreal Star* had fought reciprocity from the outset, and his imperialist friends now backed them with money and influence. Bourassa stressed that the main issue was imperialism, while the Liberals sought to divert public attention from the navy question by concentrating on reciprocity, as a benefit to the farmers of Quebec. Thus Bourassa was soon drawn into criticism of reciprocity. *Le Devoir* found itself in the same camp as the *Star*, *Gazette*, *Chronicle*, *La Patrie*, and *L'Evénement*, opposed by *Le Canada*, *La Presse*, the *Herald*, the *Witness*, and *Le Soleil*. Borden's followers chose candidates only for the English seats of Quebec; elsewhere a free field was left to Monk and the nationalists.

Bourassa did not contest a seat himself, but in *Le Devoir* and on the platform he acted as leader in the district of Montreal, while Lavergne directed the campaign in the district of Quebec. Bourassa campaigned harder than any candidate, speaking at Fraserville on July 20, at Saint-Hyacinthe on July 30, at Saint-Denis on July 31, at Trois-Rivières on August 6. On August 13 Rodolphe Lemieux accepted his challenge to an *assemblée contradictoire* at Saint-Hyacinthe, the most memorable of the campaign. Thirty thousand people appeared, three times the normal population of the town. Lemieux, aroused by the attacks of *Le Devoir* and *Le Nationaliste*, accused the 'independent' Bourassa of having sought the postmastership of Montreal, the Canadian commissionership at Paris, and the deputy-speakership of the House; and blamed his hatred of Laurier on the fact that these offices had been refused him. Lemieux compared Laurier's work of peace and concord with Bourassa's work of hatred and envy; supported reciprocity; and once more stressed that the navy would be Canadian, not imperial, and that service in it would be voluntary, not compulsory. His final eulogy of Laurier did not arouse the usual storm of applause. Bourassa denied that he had sought the postmastership or the commissionership, and then turned to the political questions. He repeated Monk's criticism of reciprocity, but stressed that the question had been raised to bury the navy issue. But the navy question, the whole imperialist question, was far more important, since reciprocity would be adopted or rejected once for all at the next session, while the imperialist question would remain and rise again. He quoted Fielding to prove that the navy was primarily intended for imperial wars. He traced the history of the Navy Act and of the imperialist movement; and asserted that the law had been passed at the request of the imperial authorities. It did not expressly provide for conscription, but conscription would come when men were needed to man the ships. He concluded:

> The vote you give on September 21 will be a vote for the navy if you vote in favor of Laurier's candidates. It will be a vote against the navy if you vote in favor of independent candidates—whether they call themselves Liberals, Conservatives, or nationalists, provided that they are not tied hand and foot and support M. Monk in the House; M. Monk who has fought and will fight any government, Liberal or Conservative, which refuses to submit these questions to the free judgment of the people.[133]

And then he burst into an attack on Laurier: 'It is time for the people of the province of Quebec to prove to M. Laurier that if they admired him when he served the interests of the country well, today that he has prevaricated, today that he has duped us. . . .'

The rest was lost in a tumult raised by the Liberal followers of T.-D. Bouchard, a local Liberal leader, who were under orders to cover all attacks on Laurier. When Béland attempted to attack Bourassa, by accusing him of abridging his quotation from Fielding and of dishonesty in arguing that conscription would be imposed, another disturbance broke out; for the crowd was divided between partisans of Laurier and partisans of Bourassa. The crowd quieted in order to hear Lavergne, but his attacks on Lemieux were so lively that the latter rose and grappled with him. Then fights broke out in the audience, and the meeting dissolved in disorder. The English-speaking press reported the affair as a nationalist outrage.

Bourassa was defended in the *Gazette* by C. H. Cahan, a leader of the Montreal bar, who said that he had long shared the English prejudice against Bourassa as an enemy of England, but had learned that Bourassa judged Canadian policy from a Canadian point of view, which was just and wise.[134] The journalist John Boyd also published in the Tory *Toronto World* a favorable account of the true Bourassa, 'as eloquent in English as in French, of stainless reputation, of great moral energy, a sincere admirer of English institutions which he wishes to preserve while safeguarding Canadian autonomy.'[135] *Le Devoir*, now backed by St. James Street, with an audience made up of the French-Canadian élite and the students of the province, and exercising influence from New England to Western Canada, had become within a year and a half of its foundation a more influential organ than *La Presse* or *La Patrie*, despite their infinitely greater circulation. And through *Le Devoir* the clergy of Quebec was largely won to the cause of Bourassa. In vain L.-O. David protested to Archbishop Bruchési against 'the fatal error' made by the clergy in trying to bring about Laurier's downfall.[136]

Laurier did not underestimate the danger in Quebec and made no less than seven speeches in the province during August. He opened his campaign at Trois-Rivières on August 17, replying to Monk and Bourassa's speeches there ten days before. He urged that reciprocity would benefit the farmers of Quebec, and defended the navy on the grounds that a greater Canada required its protection, as a greater Trois-Rivières needed a police force. He denounced Bourassa's alliance with the Tories and Jingos of the English-speaking provinces, and upheld his own record. Elections were always as uncertain as a horse race or a cockfight, but 'If I had to bet, I should bet on the old game cock who for fifteen years has led the Liberal party to victory.'[137] At Sorel, whose shipyards might benefit from the building of a navy, Laurier for once found little opposition to his naval policy, and moved his old followers by the declaration that he would retire from politics if defeated.[138] At St. Johns he said:

I am branded in Quebec as a traitor to the French, and in Ontario as a traitor to the English. In Quebec I am branded as a Jingo, and in Ontario as a Separatist. In Quebec I am attacked as an Imperialist, and in Ontario as an anti-Imperialist. I am neither. I am a Canadian. Canada has been the inspiration of my life. I have had before me as a pillar of fire by night and a pillar of cloud by day a policy of true Canadianism, of moderation, of conciliation. I have followed it consistently since 1896, and I now appeal with confidence to the whole Canadian people to uphold me in this policy of sound Canadianism which makes for the greatness of our country and the Empire.[139]

But he could not arouse the wonted enthusiasm for his cause; Bourassa had monopolized the enthusiasm of Quebec, and even Laurier's long devoted followers could muster only respect for their old leader.

In Ontario Laurier waged an even more uphill battle. If in Quebec the young nationalists cried that he was betraying Canada to England, in Ontario the Conservatives proclaimed that he was betraying Canada to the United States. It was in vain that he belittled annexation talk by saying that he was willing to meet the Americans in business, but if they wanted to talk politics, they should keep to their side of the line and the Canadians would keep to theirs.[140] A whispering campaign against the French Catholic prime minister was pressed by the Orangemen, who maintained that the papal *Ne Temere* decree of 1907, which annulled marriages thereafter contracted between Catholics before a Protestant minister, invalidated all marriages not made before a Catholic priest.[141] Laurier had nothing to say in this question, which was a purely provincial one, and the civil code of Quebec had long recognized the impediments to marriage established by the Catholic authorities for Catholics and by the Protestant authorities for Protestants. But the Orangemen proclaimed in a fine frenzy that Canada was governed by the Pope through Laurier and the Province of Quebec, and backed their argument by citing his appearance and that of other officials at the Eucharistic Congress. J. S. Ewart's explanation in one of his 'Kingdom Papers'[142] that the *Ne Temere* decree affected only Catholics appeared too late and reached too few readers to offset the effect of the campaign. The manufacturers fought Laurier on the reciprocity issue; the imperialists on the navy question; and the old passionate loyalism of Ontario rose against him in response to Kipling's cabled warning, 'It is her own soul that Canada risks today'—despite the fact that Kipling's own soul was seemingly unendangered by the fact that most of his royalties were earned in the States. Throughout Ontario Laurier evoked few cheers and found many old friends missing at his meetings.

Bourassa pressed the attack on Laurier relentlessly in Quebec. He spoke on August 21 at Lachine, on the 26th at Joliette, the 29th at Bécancour, the 30th at Sainte-Scholastique, the 31st at Saint-Jérôme. Borden contented himself with a meeting at Montreal on the 29th in support of the English candidates, and another for the mixed population of Lake Megantic. Asselin, candidate in Saint-Jacques, announced his return to acceptance of Bourassa's leadership, and *Le Devoir* wished him well. On September 3 and 4 Bourassa spoke in his old county of Labelle, and on the 5th at Hull, in company with C. H. Cahan, who approved his program. On the 6th he spoke at Sainte-Rose, and on the 8th at the Monument National in Montreal in support of Asselin. On this occasion Cahan coined the slogan 'No Navy made in London; no reciprocity made in Washington,' while John Boyd announced in English that he, too, was a nationalist.[143] In the face of this effective campaign Laurier privately conceded that the Quebec cities were lost, but he hoped to win back the country districts.[144] The Liberal press began to paint dark pictures of what would result from a defeat of Laurier; his compatriots would be humiliated and Borden would take power:

> Then, instead of an essentially Canadian navy, over which England had no rights, we shall see the triumph of jingo imperialism, with participation in imperial wars and an endless string of dreadnoughts.
> Then, instead of the reciprocity which the Canadian farmer and worker have so long awaited, we shall remain in the *status quo* so keenly defended by the trusts.
> Then, instead of a French-Canadian prime minister, we shall have a prime minister who understands none of our aspirations and who has already promised to the voice of Toronto, i.e., to the voice of fanaticism, predominance in the councils of the nation . . . .[145]

But Sir Hugh Graham organized a literary bureau where highly paid journalists turned out a stream of articles, advertisements, tracts, and pamphlets for the Conservative press. Graham was reported to have spent more than $250,000 before the campaign was finished. The great industrialists warned their workers that reciprocity would close the factories. The Liberals derived some comfort from representing an election in which the millionaires William Price and Rodolphe Forget were Conservative candidates as a contest between the trusts and the people.[146] Organs of both parties embarrassed their opponents by recalling past statements which contradicted present positions: Bourassa was reminded of his support of reciprocity, and both he and Lavergne of their attacks on the Tories; while Laurier was reproached with abandoning his old autonomist position. William Randolph Hearst, an advocate of reciprocity, sent articles urging Canadians to support Laurier, and the nationalists protested at this foreign intervention in a Canadian election.[147]

At Laprairie on September 9, when the nationalist candidate was greeted by cheers for Laurier, Bourassa rose and said:

> Formerly I also cried hurrah for Laurier. But Laurier· has sacrificed his own in the West, Laurier protects the thieves and grafters, Laurier imposes upon us a costly navy, which will serve no purpose except to kill our sons in the wars of England. Laurier forces me today to choose between him and the country; I choose the country.[148]

The campaign grew increasingly bitter, with Asselin and Tancrède Marsil using ever more violent language. Laurier decided that his danger was greater in Quebec than in Ontario, and cut short his tour of the latter province to fight Bourassa. On September 11 he spoke at Victoriaville. On the following day, while Bourassa spoke at Verchères, Laurier at Beauceville denounced the insidious and dishonest tactics of the opposition and declared: 'The Imperialists of Toronto and the Nationalists of Quebec will never succeed in beating Laurier.'[149] On the 13th Laurier spoke at Montmagny, while Bourassa took the fight into the prime minister's county of Soulanges the following day. Meanwhile Laurier held forth in his old stronghold of Quebec at the Ménage Militaire, promising the city a new drydock and proclaiming once more that he was neither an imperialist nor an anti-imperialist, but a Canadian. He warned that the Borden-Bourassa alliance would lead to racial conflict and internal divisions, while under the Liberal standard, 'which shelters all races, there is room for all to live in harmony and peace, and to enjoy happiness.'[150] On the 15th, while Bourassa spoke against Lemieux at Marieville, Laurier and Lavergne held rival meetings at Rimouski. The young nationalist did not spare his former patron, and his violence attracted those who found Laurier too gentle for their taste. Rival partisans fought in the streets, as they did also at Trois-Rivières on the 17th. On the 16th Bourassa spoke at Acton Vale, while Laurier addressed a meeting at Grand'Mère. On the 17th Bourassa spoke at Victoriaville, and was greeted by the singing of a hymn, 'O Bourassa,' to the air of 'O Canada.' The Conservative leaders of the Eastern Townships provided free subscriptions to *Le Devoir* for all French voters of the region. Rehabilitated in Ontario public opinion through the efforts of the Toronto *World*, Bourassa received numerous invitations to speak there, but agreed only to abandon the Quebec campaign for a speech at Sudbury, the French center of Northern Ontario, on September 18, where he made two addresses, one in French and one in English.

Bourassa returned to Montreal in haste for a great meeting at the Ontario Rink on the 19th, the principal one of the nationalist campaign. It rivaled that of Laurier at the Parc Sohmer on the eve of his rise to power in 1896. Bourassa was supported by Boyd, Asselin, and Cahan; and his speech won an ovation such as Laurier used to receive. The crowd, too large for the largest hall in the city, would not cease applauding to allow the others to speak. A parade through the streets was improvised. One detachment headed by Asselin encountered Laurier about to take the train at Place Viger Station, and pursued him to his train. Meanwhile Bourassa spoke from a balcony of the Hotel Viger, and was greeted with the singing of 'O Bourassa.' The following day at Saint-Hyacinthe, the outraged partisans of Laurier under the leadership of T.-D. Bouchard stoned Bourassa's meeting and prepared an ambush at the station, which Bourassa avoided by boarding the train at the next stop. Meanwhile Laurier wound up his campaign in Quebec, where he had been attacked in his own district by Lavergne and where a scandal was caused by the sudden withdrawal of the opposition candidate just before the election. As the campaign closed, *La Presse* proclaimed that a vote for Bourassa was a vote for Borden, and a vote for Borden a vote for extreme imperialism. At Toronto the *Globe* reversed the slogan: 'A vote for Borden is a vote for Bourassa, and a vote for Bourassa is a vote for the break-up of this country.'[151]

On September 21, 1911, the Laurier regime went down to defeat before the united forces of the Conservatives and the nationalists. In Quebec the Liberal majority fell from 43 to 11, with one minister, Sidney Fisher, losing his seat. In Ontario the Liberals suffered a rout, with the Conservatives winning 72 seats and the Liberals only 14. Three ministers—Graham, Mackenzie King, and Patterson—lost their seats. The Maritimes returned 16 Conservatives and 19 Liberals; Fielding and Sir Frederick Borden were defeated. British Columbia went solidly Conservative and Manitoba strongly so. Only Saskatchewan and Alberta returned strong Liberal majorities. The majority in the House was exactly reversed, with the Conservatives now holding 133 seats to the Liberals' 88.

The outcome was hailed in Quebec as a nationalist triumph; in Ontario as an imperialist one. But Borden was escorted to Ottawa under the banner of 'One fleet, one flag, one Throne.'[152] The *Ottawa Citizen* rejoiced that the political center of gravity of Canada had been changed from Quebec to Ontario.

The new Conservative regime rested on the basis of a solid Ontario, just as the old had stood on a solid Quebec. By his fight against Laurier the nationalist Bourassa had delivered Quebec into the hands of an administration committed to imperialist paths and unsympathetic to the French Canadians. Thanks to the unscrupulousness of the campaign on both sides, Canada was already split by bitter ethnic division as one of the great crises of its national life drew near.

Notes

[1] Skelton, *Laurier*, II, 224-5 *n.*
[2] *Ibid.*, 226-8.
[3] *Ibid.*, 229.
[4] Rumilly, XII, 16-17.
[5] J. Dafoe, *Clifford Sifton in Relation to His Times* (Toronto, 1931), 291.
[6] Rumilly, XII, 20-2.
[7] Dafoe, 297.
[8] Skelton, II, 239.
[9] Borden, *Memoirs*, I, 146.
[10] *Ibid.*, 147.
[11] Rumilly, XII, 26-7.
[12] *Ibid.*, 27.
[13] *Ibid.*, 30, 37.

[14] H. Bourassa, *Les Ecoles du Nord-Ouest* (Montréal, 1905), 1-3.
[15] *Ibid.*, 25.
[16] *Ibid.*, 27.
[17] *Ibid.*, 28-9.
[18] Skelton, II, 247 *n.*, Laurier-J.-B.-A. Casgrain, 20 April 1905.
[19] Groulx, *Croisade*, 9.
[20] Rumilly, XII, 135.
[21] Skelton, II, 248.
[22] Rumilly, XII, 151.
[23] *Hansard, Commons Debates*, 6 July 1906, IV, 7332-3.
[24] Rumilly, XII, 173-6.
[25] *Ibid.*, 182.
[26] *Ibid.*, 182-6.
[27] *Ibid.*, XIII, 33.
[28] Rumilly, XIII, 43.
[29] Dafoe, *Sifton*, 327-32.
[30] *Ibid.*, 332.
[31] A. Lavergne, *Trente ans de vie nationale* (Montréal, 1935), 136-7; Rumilly, XIII, 73-5.
[32] Rumilly, XIII, 82.
[33] *Ibid.*, 92.
[34] *Ibid.*, 101-3.
[35] *Ibid.*, 105.
[36] PAC: Laurier Papers 3233, Laurier-Laflamme, 20 nov. 1907; Skelton, II, 313.
[37] Rumilly, XIII, 113-14.
[38] *Ibid.*, 139-41.
[39] *Ibid.*, 143.
[40] *Ibid.*, 144.
[41] *Ibid.*, 146-7.
[42] *Ibid.*, 163.
[43] *Ibid.*, 166.
[44] *Ibid.*, 172.
[45] Skelton, II, 265, 281.
[46] Rumilly, XIV, 17-18.
[47] *Ibid.*, 12.
[48] *Ibid.*, 20-3.
[49] *Ibid.*, 52, 55-6.
[50] Skelton, II, 319.
[51] Borden, *Memoirs*, I, 246.
[52] Rumilly, XIV, 73.
[53] Borden, I, 253.
[54] Rumilly, XIV, 77-8.
[55] *Ibid.*, 81; *La Patrie*, 24 juillet 1909.
[56] *Ibid.*, 82; *Quebec Chronicle*, 11 Aug. 1909.
[57] *Ibid.*, 85.
[58] *Ibid.*, 99, G. Smith-Bourassa.
[59] *Ibid.*, 98-100.
[60] Rumilly, XIV, 114-18.
[61] *Ibid.*, 118.
[62] Skelton, II, 327-8; full text in A.-D. DeCelles, *Discours de Sir Wilfrid Laurier de 1889 à 1911* (Montréal, 1920), 113-15.
[63] Borden, I, 269-74.
[64] Rumilly, XIV, 135, *Le Devoir*, 7 janvier 1909.
[65] H. Bourassa, *Le Projet de Loi navale: sa nature, ses conséquences* (Montréal, 1910), 16.

[66] *Ibid.*, 26.
[67] *Ibid.*, 37.
[68] Rumilly, XIV, 138.
[69] Skelton, II, 352–8; DeCelles, 95.
[70] *Ibid.*, 327; DeCelles, 104.
[71] DeCelles, 135.
[72] Borden, I, 280–1.
[73] Rumilly, XIV, 142–7.
[74] *Ibid.*, 149.
[75] *Ibid.*, 150.
[76] Rumilly, XV, 13–14.
[77] *Ibid.*, 17.
[78] *Ibid.*, 25.
[79] *Ibid.*, 28.
[80] *Ibid.*, 52–5.
[81] *Ibid.*, 70–1.
[82] *Ibid.*, 74.
[83] *Ibid.*, 80.
[84] *Ibid.*, 114–16.
[85] *Ibid.*, 136–7, *New York Herald*, 9 Oct. 1910.
[86] *Ibid.*, 137–8.
[87] Skelton, II, 337; DeCelles, 149.
[88] *Ibid.*, 338–9; DeCelles, 151.
[89] DeCelles, 164.
[90] *Ibid.*, 181–2.
[91] *Ibid.*, 192–3.
[92] *Ibid.*, 202.
[93] Rumilly, XV, 14, *Toronto World*.
[94] *Ibid.*, 146.
[95] *Ibid.*, 152–4.
[96] *Ibid.*, 157.
[97] Skelton, II, 339.
[98] Rumilly, XV, 157.
[99] *Ibid.*, 159.
[100] Lavergne, 174–5.
[101] Rumilly, XV, 161.
[102] *Ibid.*, 162.
[103] *Ibid.*, 103, *La Presse*, 7 oct. 1911.
[104] *Ibid.*, 165.
[105] Skelton, II, 339.
[106] Borden, I, 295–7.
[107] Rumilly, XV, 180–2.
[108] *Ibid.*, 183–5.
[109] Skelton, II, 367.
[110] *Ibid.*, 370.
[111] Dafoe, 364–8.
[112] Borden, I, 308.
[113] H. Bourassa, *La Convention Douanière entre le Canada et les Etats-Unis: sa nature, ses conséquences; The Reciprocity Agreement and its Consequences, As viewed from the Nationalist standpoint* (Montréal, 1911).
[114] Bourassa, *Reciprocity*, 12.
[115] Skelton, II, 340.
[116] G. Neuendorf, *Studies in the Evolution of Dominion Status* (London, 1942), 341.
[117] Rumilly, XVI, 57.
[118] Rumilly, XVI, 59–61.

[119] *Ibid.*, 62, *Quebec Chronicle.*
[120] *Ibid.*, 64.
[121] *Ibid.*, 65.
[122] H. Bourassa, *La Conférence impériale et le rôle de M. Laurier* (Montréal, 1911), 5.
[123] Skelton, II, 373.
[124] *Ibid.*, 375.
[125] Dafoe, 370 n.
[126] Borden, I, 319.
[127] *Ibid.*, 319–20.
[128] Dafoe, 371–2.
[129] Borden, I, 321–2.
[130] *Ibid.*, 322–5.
[131] Lavergne, 193–4.
[132] Rumilly, XVI, 75. Bourassa denied this charge at the fifth anniversary dinner of *Le Devoir* in 1915, recounting how he had refused to be bought by the Anti-Reciprocity League. *Le 5ᵉ Anniversaire du 'Devoir'* (Montréal, 1915), 29.
[133] *Ibid.*, 81–2.
[134] *Ibid.*, 84–5.
[135] *Ibid.*, 86, *Toronto World*, 26 Aug. 1911.
[136] *Ibid.*, 87.
[137] A.-D. DeCelles, *Discours de Sir Wilfrid Laurier de 1911 à 1919* (Montréal, 1920), 7.
[138] Rumilly, XVI, 90.
[139] Skelton, II, 380.
[140] *Ibid.*, 379.
[141] Rumilly, XVI, 105.
[142] J. S. Ewart, *The Kingdom Papers* (Ottawa, 1912), I, 121–32, No. 5, '*Ne Temere Decree.*'
[143] Rumilly, XVI, 97.
[144] Rumilly, XVI, 97.
[145] *Ibid.*, 98–9, *La Presse.*
[146] *Ibid.*, 100.
[147] *Ibid.*, 101.
[148] *Ibid.*, 103–4.
[149] *Ibid.*, 106.
[150] *Ibid.*, 107.
[151] Skelton, II, 379; Rumilly, XVI, 114.
[152] Rumilly, XVI, 118.

SELECTIVE BIBLIOGRAPHY

General Works

The standard reference guide, now badly out of date, is R. G. Trotter, *Canadian History: A Syllabus and Guide to Reading* (Toronto, 1934), which is supplemented by Robin W. Winks, *Recent Trends and New Literature in Canadian History* (Washington, 1959). *The Cambridge History of the British Empire*, Vol. VI: "Canada and Newfoundland" (Cambridge, 1930); Justin Winsor, *Narrative and Critical History of America* (8 vols., Boston, 1888-9); and R. G. Thwaites, *The Jesuit Relations and Allied Documents*, Vol. LXXI (Cleveland, 1901) offer guidance to the earlier literature. G. Lanctot, *L'Oeuvre de la France en Amérique du Nord; bibliographie sélective et critique* (Montreal, 1951); Philippe Garigue, *A Bibliographical Introduction to the Study of French Canada* (Montreal, 1956); and F. Dumont and Y. Martin, *Situation de la recherche sur le Canada français* (Quebec, 1963) are the most recent bibliographies. There is much useful guidance in H. P. Beers, *The French in North America: a Bibliographical Guide to French Archives, Reproductions, and Research Missions* (Baton Rouge, 1957) and *The French and British in the Old Northwest: A Bibliographical Guide to Archive and Manuscript Sources* (Detroit, 1964). F. M. Staton and M. Tremaine, *A Bibliography of Canadiana* (Toronto, 1934) covers up to 1867. The *Bulletin des recherches historiques* (Quebec), the *Review of Historical Publications Relating to Canada* (Toronto, 1897-1919), and the *Canadian Historical Review* (Toronto) deal with recent publications, as does the *Revue de l'histoire de l'Amérique française* (Montreal).

L.-M. LeJeune, *Dictionnaire général du Canada* (2 vols., Ottawa, 1931); C. Tanguay, *Dictionnaire généalogique des familles canadiennes* (7 vols., Montreal, 1871-90); W. S. Wallace (ed.), *The Macmillan Dictionary of Canadian Biography* (3rd ed. rev., Toronto, 1963); and J.-J. Lefebvre, "Le Canada; L'Amérique–Géographique, Historique, Biographique, Littéraire," Supplément du *Larousse Canadien Complet* (Montreal, 1955) are useful reference works.

Chapter I (1534-1760)

Primary Sources – Collections

The annual *Rapport de l'Archiviste de la Province de Québec* (42 vols., Quebec, 1922-64) contains many documents, primarily for the French regime, but recently for the nineteenth century. An index was published in 1965. The *Reports of the Public Archives of Canada* (Ottawa) also contain many documents, as well as calendars of the principal collections.

The following collections of documents are invaluable for the French period:

Akins, T. B. *Selections from the Public Documents of the Province of Nova Scotia* (Halifax, 1869).

Alvord, C. W. (ed.). *Cahokia Records, 1778-1790* (Collections of the Illinois State Historical Society, Vol. II, Springfield, 1907); *KasKashie Records, 1778-1790* (Collection of the Illinois State Historical Library, Vol. V, Springfield, 1909).

[Colbert] P. Clément (ed.). *Lettres, instructions, et mémoires de Colbert* (7 vols., Paris, 1861-73).

Collection de manuscrits contenant lettres, mémoires, et autres documents historiques relatifs à la Nouvelle France (4 vols., Quebec, 1883-5).

Doughty, A. G., and Parmelee, G. W. (eds.). *The Siege of Quebec and the Battle of the Plains of Abraham* (6 vols., Quebec, 1901).

Edits, ordonnances royaux, déclarations et arrêts du Conseil d'Etat du roi concernant le Canada (3 vols., Quebec, 1854-6).

French, B. F. (ed.). *Louisiana Historical Collections* (5 vols., New York, 1846-57).
—— *ibid.*, *Second Series* (New York, 1875).

Grenier, F. *Papiers Contrecoeur et autres documents concernant le conflit anglo-français sur l'Ohio de 1745 à 1756* (Quebec, 1952).

Julien, C. A., *et al.* (eds.). *Les Français en Amérique pendant la première moitié du XVIe siècle* (Paris, 1946).

Laverdière and Casgrain, Les abbés (eds.). *Le Journal des Jésuites* (Quebec, 1871).

Margry, P. (ed.). *Mémoires et documents pour servir à l'histoire des origines françaises des pays d'outre mer: Découvertes et établissements des Français dans l'ouest et dans le sud de l'Amérique septentrionale (1614-1754)* (6 vols., Paris, 1879-88).

Michigan Pioneer and Historical Society. *Historical Collections*, Vol. XXIV (Lansing, 1905), "Cadillac Papers".

O'Callaghan, E. B. (ed.). *Documents Relating to the Colonial History of the State of New York*, Vols. IX and X. (Albany, 1856 and 1858).

Pargellis, S. *Military Affairs in North America, 1748-1765* (New York, 1936).

Quebec Literary and Historical Society. *Historical Documents* (10 vols., Quebec, 1838-1921).

Têtu, H., and Gagnon, C.-O. (eds.). *Mandements, lettres pastorales, et circulaires des évêques de Québec* (8 vols., Quebec, 1887-93).

Thwaites, R. G. (ed.). *The Jesuit Relations and Allied Documents* (73 vols., Cleveland, 1896-1901).
—— *Wisconsin Historical Collections*, Vol. XVI (Madison, 1902), "The French Régime in Wisconsin, I: 1634-1727"; *ibid.*, II: "1727-48"; Vol. XVII (Madison, 1906), *ibid*; III: "1743-60".

Tyrrell, J. B. *Documents Relating to the Early History of Hudson Bay* (Champlain Society, Toronto, 1931).

Contemporary Narratives and Correspondence

[Amherst] J. C. Webster (ed.). *The Journal of Jeffrey Amherst* (Toronto, 1931).

[Boucher] Pierre Boucher. *Histoire véritable et naturelle des moeurs et productions du pays de la Nouvelle-France* (Boucherville, 1964).

[Bougainville] Edward P. Hamilton (ed.). *Adventures in the Wilderness: the American Journals of Louis Antoine de Bougainville, 1756-1760* (Norman, Oklahoma, 1964).

[Cartier] H. P. Biggar (ed.). *The Voyages of Jacques Cartier* (Ottawa, 1924).
—— *The Precursors of Jacques Cartier* (Ottawa, 1911).
—— *A Collection of Documents relating to Jacques Cartier and the Sieur de Roberval* (Ottawa, 1930).

[Champlain] H. P. Biggar *et al.* (eds.). *The Works of Samuel de Champlain* (Champlain Society, 6 vols., Toronto, 1922-36).

[Charlevoix] L. P. Kellogg (ed.). *Charlevoix' Journal of a Voyage to North America* (2 vols., Chicago, 1923).

———— J. G. Shea (ed.). *Charlevoix' History and General Description of New France* (6 vols., New York, 1900).

[Denys] W. F. Ganong (ed.). Nicolas Denys, *The Description and Natural History of the Coasts of North America* (Champlain Society, Toronto,1908).

[Dièreville] *Relation du voyage du Port Royal de l'Acadie* (Quebec, 1885).

[Dollier de Casson] R. Flenley (ed.). *Dollier de Casson's A History of Montreal, 1640-1672* (New York, 1928).

Franquet, Louis. *Voyages et mémoires sur le Canada* (Quebec, 1889).

[Hennepin] J. G. Shea (ed.). Louis Hennepin, *Description of Louisiana* (New York, 1880).

———— R. G. Thwaites (ed.). Louis Hennepin, *New Discovery* (Chicago, 1903).

[Kalm] A. B. Benson (ed.). *Peter Kalm's Travels in North America* (2 vols., New York, 1937).

[Knox] A. G. Doughty (ed.). *An Historical Journal of the Campaigns in North America for the years 1757, 1758, 1759 and 1760, by Captain John Knox* (3 vols., Champlain Society, Toronto, 1914-16).

[La Haye] Bernard de La Haye, *Journal historique de l'établissement des Français à la Louisiane* (New Orleans, 1831).

[Lahontan] R. G. Thwaites (ed.). *New Voyages to North America by the Baron de Lahontan* (2 vols., Chicago, 1905).

La Potherie, Bacqueville de. *Histoire de l'Amerique septentrionale* (4 vols., Paris, 1753).

[La Vérendrye] L. J. Burpee (ed.). *La Vérendrye's Journals and Letters* (Champlain Society, Toronto, 1907).

Le Beau. *Aventures du Sr. C. Le Beau* (Amsterdam, 1735).

[Le Clercq] J. G. Shea (ed.). Chrétien Le Clercq, *Establishment of the Faith in New France* (2 vols., New York, 1881).

———— W. F. Ganong (ed.). Chrétien Le Clercq, *New Relation of Gaspesia* (Champlain Society, Toronto, 1910).

[Lescarbot] W. L. Grant (ed.). *Marc Lescarbot's The History of New France* (Champlain Society, 3 vols., Toronto, 1907-14).

[Lévis] *Collection des manuscrits du maréchal de Lévis* (12 vols., Quebec, 1889-95).

Malartic, A. J. H. de Maures. *Journal des campagnes au Canada de 1755 à 1760* (Paris, 1890).

[Marie de l'Incarnation] Dom Albert Jamet (ed.). *Ecrits spirituels et historiques* (4 vols., Quebec, 1929-39).

Morin, Marie. *Annales de l'Hôtel-Dieu de Montréal* (Montreal, 1921).

Perrot, Nicolas. *Mémoire sur les moeurs, coutumes et reliques des sauvages* (Paris, 1864).

Pichon, Thomas. *Lettres et mémoires pour servir à l'histoire naturelle, civile et politique du Cap Breton* (La Haye, 1760).

[Pitt] C. S. Kimball (ed.). *Correspondence of William Pitt with Colonial Governors* (2 vols., New York, 1906).

Pouchot, Pierre. *Mémoires sur la dernière guerre de l'Amérique Septentrionale entre la France et l'Angleterre* (3 vols., Yverdon, 1781).

[Radisson] G. D. Scull (ed.). *Voyages of Peter Esprit Radisson* (Prince Society, Boston, 1885).

[Sagard] G. M. Wrong (ed.). *Sagard's Long Journey to the Country of the Hurons* (Champlain Society, Toronto, 1939).

Sagard-Théodat, Gabriel. *Histoire du Canada et voyages que les frères mineurs recollects y ont faicts pour la conversion des infidèles* (4 vols., Paris, 1866).

[Shirley] C. H. Lincoln (ed.). *The Correspondence of William Shirley* (2 vols., New York, 1912).

[Talon] "Correspondance entre la cour de France et l'intendant Talon pendant ses deux administrations dans la Nouvelle-France," *RAPQ*, 1930-1.

Tonti, Henri de. *Dernières découvertes dans l'Amérique Septentrionale de M. de La Sale* (Paris, 1697).

[Winslow] "The Journal of Colonel John Winslow," Nova Scotia Historical Society Colls., III and IV.

Secondary Works

Biggar, H. P. *The Early Trading Companies of New France* (Toronto, 1901).

Bishop, Morris. *Champlain: The Life of Fortitude* (Carleton Library, Toronto, 1963).

Brebner, J. B. *The Explorers of North America, 1492-1806* (Anchor Books, New York, 1955).

———— *New England's Outpost: Acadia before the Conquest of Canada* (New York, 1927).

Cahall, R. DuB. *The Sovereign Council of New France* (New York, 1915).

Campbell, G. G. *The History of Nova Scotia* (Toronto, 1948).

Caron, Abbé Ivanhoë. *La Colonisation du Canada sous la domination française* (Quebec, 1916).

Casgrain, Abbé H.-R. *Un pèlerinage au pays d'Evangéline* (Quebec, 1887).

Chapais, Thomas. *Jean Talon, intendant de la Nouvelle-France, 1665-1672* (Quebec, 1904).

———— *The Great Intendant* (Chronicles of Canada, Toronto, 1920).

Colby, C. W. *Canadian Types of the Old Régime, 1608-1698* (New York, 1910).

Colden, Cadwallader. *The History of the Five Indian Nations of Canada* (Ithaca, 1958).

Crane, V. W. *The Southern Frontier: 1670-1732* (Ann Arbor, 1929).

Doughty, A. G. *The Acadian Exiles* (Chronicles of Canada, Toronto, 1920).

Eccles, W. J. *Frontenac, the Courtier Governor* (Toronto, 1959).

———— *Canada under Louis XIV* (Toronto, 1964).

———— *The Government of New France* (Canadian Historical Association Booklet 18, Ottawa, 1965).

Faillon, Abbé E.-M. *Histoire de la colonie française en Canada* (3 vols., Paris, 1865-6).

Fauteux, J.-N. *Essai sur l'industrie au Canada sous le régime français* (2 vols., Quebec, 1927).

Filteau, Gérard. *La Naissance d'une nation: tableau du Canada en 1755* (2 vols., Montreal, 1937).

Frégault, G. *La Civilisation de la Nouvelle-France* (Montreal, 1944).

———— *Iberville le conquérant* (Montreal, 1944).

———— *François Bigot: administrateur français* (2 vols., Montreal, 1948).

———— *Le Grand Marquis: Pierre de Rigaud de Vaudreuil et la Louisiane* (Montreal, 1952).

———— *La Société canadienne sous le régime français* (Canadian Historical Association Booklet 3, Ottawa, 1954).

———— *La Guerre de la Conquête* (Montreal, 1955).

Garneau, F.-X. *Histoire du Canada depuis sa découverte jusqu'à nos jours* (2 vols., Paris, 1913-20).

Gipson, L. H. *The British Empire Before the American Revolution* (13 vols., rev. ed., 1958-61).

Giraud, Marcel. *Histoire de la Louisiane française* (2 vols., Paris, 1953-8).

Gosselin, Mgr. A.-H. *La Mission du Canada avant Mgr. de Laval, 1615-59* (Evreux, 1909).

Gosselin, Abbé Auguste. *Vie de Mgr. de Laval* (2 vols., Quebec, 1890).

—— *L'Eglise du Canada depuis Mgr. de Laval jusqu'à la conquête* (3 vols., Quebec, 1911-14).

Gowans, Alan. *Church Architecture of New France* (Toronto, 1955).

—— *Building Canada: An Architectural History of Canadian Life* (Toronto, 1966).

Graham, Gerald. *Empire of the North Atlantic: The Maritime Struggle for North America* (Toronto, 1950).

Groulx, Chanoine Lionel. *Histoire des Canadiens-Français,* I: *Le Régime français* (Montreal, 1950).

Hamelin, Jean. *Economie et société en Nouvelle-France* (Quebec, 1960).

Harris, R. C. *The Seigneurial System in Early Canada* (Quebec, 1966).

Hunt, G. T. *The Wars of the Iroquois* (Madison, 1940).

Innis, H. A. *The Cod Fisheries* (Toronto, 1940; rev. ed., Toronto, 1954).

—— *The Fur Trade in Canada* (New Haven and Toronto, 1930; rev. ed., Toronto, 1956).

Jaray, G.-L. *L'Empire français d'Amérique, 1534-1803* (Paris, 1908).

Jenness, Diamond. *The Indians of Canada* (Ottawa, 1955).

Jouvé, O.-M., O.F.M. *Les Français et le Canada . . . 1615-29* (Quebec, 1915).

Jury, W. and E. M. *Sainte-Marie Among the Hurons* (Toronto, 1965).

Kellogg, L. P. *The French Régime in Wisconsin and the Northwest* (Madison, 1925).

Kennedy, J. H. *Jesuit and Savage in New France* (New Haven, 1950).

Lanctot, Gustave. *L'Administration de la Nouvelle-France* (Paris, 1929).

—— *A History of Canada, 1600-1763* (3 vols., Cambridge, 1960-6).

Langlois, Georges. *Histoire de la population canadienne-française* (Montreal, 1934).

Leach, P. E. *The Northern Colonial Frontier, 1607-1763* (New York, 1966).

McLennan, J. S. *Louisbourg from its Foundation to its Fall* (Toronto, 1965).

Marion, Séraphin. *Relations des voyageurs français en Nouvelle-France au XVIIe siècle* (Paris, 1923).

Martin, F. X. *The History of Louisiana from the earliest period* (New Orleans, 1882).

Morisset, Gérard. *Coup d'oeil sur les arts de la Nouvelle-France* (Quebec, 1941).

—— *L'Architecture en Nouvelle-France* (Quebec, 1949).

Munro, W. B. *The Seigniorial System in Canada: A study in French colonial policy* (Cambridge, Mass., 1907).

Nute, Grace Lee. *Caesars of the Wilderness* (New York, 1943).

Pargellis, Stanley. *Lord Loudon in North America* (New Haven, 1933).

Parkman, Francis. *France and England in North America* (10 vols., Boston, 1851-92).

Penhallow, Samuel. *History of the Wars of New-England with the Eastern Indians* (Cincinnati, 1859).

Pouliot, Léon. *Etude sur les Relations des Jésuites de la Nouvelle-France, 1632-1672* (Paris, 1940).

Rameau de Saint-Père, E. *Une Colonie féodale en Amérique* (2 vols., Paris, 1889).

Riddell, W. A. *The Rise of Ecclesiastical Control in Quebec* (New York, 1916).

Rochemonteix, C. *Les Jésuites de la Nouvelle-France au XVIIe siècle* (3 vols., Paris, 1895-6).

—— *Les Jésuites de la Nouvelle-France au XVIIIe siècle* (2 vols., Paris, 1906).

Roy, J.-E. *Histoire de la seigneurie de Lauzon* (5 vols., Lévis, 1897-1904).

Roy, P.-G. *Old Manors, Old Houses* (Quebec, 1927).

———*The Old Churches of the Province of Quebec* (Quebec, 1925).

Rumilly, Robert. *Histoire des Acadiens* (2 vols., Montreal, 1955).

Salone, E. *La Colonisation de la Nouvelle-France* (Paris, 1906).

Stacey, C. P. *The Siege of Quebec, 1759* (Toronto, 1959).

Talbot, F. X. *Saint among the Hurons: the Life of Jean de Brébeuf* (New York, 1956).

Traquair, Ramsay. *The Old Architecture of Quebec* (Toronto, 1947).

Trudel, Marcel. *Histoire de la Nouvelle-France*, I: "Les vaines tentatives," 1524-1603 (Montreal, 1963); II: "Le comptoir," 1604-1627 (Montreal, 1966).

———*The Seigneurial Régime* (Canadian Historical Association Booklet 6, Ottawa, 1956).

———*Atlas historique du Canada français* (Quebec, 1961).

———*L'Esclavage au Canada français; histoire et conditions de l'esclavage* (Quebec, 1960).

Vattier, Georges. *Esquisse historique de la colonisation de la province de Québec, 1604-1925* (Paris, 1928).

Webster, J. C. *The Career of the Abbé Le Loutre in Nova Scotia* (Shediac, 1933).

———*The Forts of Chignecto* (Shediac, 1930).

Wintzerling, O. W. *Acadian Odyssey* (Baton Rouge, 1955).

[Wraxhall] C. H. McIlwain (ed.). *Peter Wraxhall's Abridgement of the New York Indian Affairs* (Cambridge, Mass., 1915).

Wrong, G. M. *The Rise and Fall of New France* (2 vols., Toronto, 1928).

Chapter II (1760-91)

[Allen, E.] *Ethan Allen's Narrative of the Capture of Ticonderoga and of His Captivity and Treatment by the British* (Burlington, 1849; Corinth Books, New York, 1961).

[Arnold, B.] Abbé Honorius Provost (ed.). "Papiers Arnold, 1775-6," *Revue de l'Université Laval* (November 1947-June 1948).

———Kenneth Roberts (ed.). *March to Quebec: Journals of the Members of Arnold's Expedition* (New York, 1938).

Aubert de Gaspé, Philippe. *Mémoires* (Ottawa, 1866).

[Baby, François] "Journal par Messrs François Baby, Gab. Taschereau et Jenkin Williams . . . 1776," *APQ* 1927-28, 430-98; 1929, 137-40.

Baby, Juge L.-G. *L'Exode des classes dirigéantes à la cession du Canada* (Montreal, 1899).

Bracq, Jean-Charlemagne. *The Evolution of French Canada* (New York, 1924).

Brooke, Frances. *The History of Emily Montague* (London, 1769; Ottawa, 1931).

Brouillette, Benoît. *La Pénétration du Continent américain par les Canadiens français, 1763-1846* (Montreal, 1939).

Brunet, Michel. *La Présence anglaise et les Canadiens* (Montreal, 1958).

Burt, A. L. *The Old Province of Quebec* (Minneapolis, 1933).

———*The United States, Great Britain, and British North America: the Revolution to the Establishment of Peace after the War of 1812* (New Haven and Toronto, 1940).

Buxton, G. *L'Influence de la révolution américaine sur le développement constitutionnel du Canada* (Paris, 1929).

Caron, Abbé Ivanhoë. *La Colonisation de la Province de Québec: Débuts du régime anglais, 1760-1791* (Quebec, 1923).

[Caroll, Charles] Mayer Brantz (ed.). *Journal of Charles Caroll of Carrolton during his visit to Canada in 1776, as one of the commissioners from Congress* (Baltimore, 1876).

Cavendish, Sir Henry (ed.). *Debates of the House of Commons in the year 1774, or the Bill for making more effectual provision for the Government of the Province of Quebec* (London, 1839).

Chapais, Thomas. *Cours d'histoire du Canada*, I, *1760-1791* (Quebec, 1919).

Charland, R. P. Thomas-Marie. "La Mission de John Carroll au Canada et l'interdit du P. Floquet," *Société canadienne de l'histoire de l'Eglise catholique* (1933-4), 45-6.

Clark, S. D. *Movements of Political Protest in Canada, 1640-1840* (Toronto, 1959).

Codman, John. *Arnold's Expedition to Quebec* (New York, 1930).

Coffin, V. *The Province of Quebec and the Early American Revolution* (Madison, 1896).

Coupland, R. *The Quebec Act* (Oxford, 1925).

Craig, G. M. *Upper Canada: The Formative Years, 1784-1841* (Toronto, 1963).

Creighton, D. G. *The Empire of the St. Lawrence* (Toronto, 1956).

Davidson, John. "The Growth of the French Canadian Race in North America," *Annals of the American Academy of Political and Social Science*, VIII (September 1896), 213-35.

Force, Peter (ed.). *American Archives*, Series IV and V, 1774-6 (9 vols., Washington, 1837-53).

Ford, W. C. (ed.). *Journals of the Continental Congress, 1774-1789* (31 vols., Washington, 1904).

Germain, Dom Aidan Henry. *Catholic Military and Naval Chaplains, 1776-1917* (Washington, 1929). Chapter I is devoted to the careers of Abbé Chartier de Lotbinière, Abbé de la Valinière, Père Floquet, S.J., and Abbé Gibault in the service of the Congress.

Gosselin, Abbé Auguste. *L'Eglise au Canada après la Conquête* (2 vols., Quebec, 1916-17).

Graham, Gerald S. *British Policy and Canada, 1774-91* (New York, 1930).

———*Empire of the North Atlantic* (Toronto, 1958).

Groulx, Abbé Lionel. *Lendemains de Conquête* (Montreal, 1919-20).

———*Histoire du Canada Français depuis la découverte*, II, *1760-1850* (Montreal, 1952).

———*L'Enseignement français au Canada, I: Au Québec* (Montreal, 1931).

Guilday, Peter. *The Life and Times of John Carroll, Archbishop of Baltimore, 1735-1815* (2 vols., New York, 1922).

Harlow, V. T. *The Founding of the Second British Empire, I, 1763-1793* (London, 1952).

Henry, Alexander. *Travels and Adventures in Canada and the Indian Territories between the Years 1760-1776* (New York, 1809).

Innis, H. A. *The Fur Trade in Canada* (rev. ed., Toronto, 1956).

Kennedy, W. P. M., and Lanctot, Gustave (eds.). *Reports on the Laws of Quebec, 1767-70* (Ottawa, 1931).

[Knox] A. G. Doughty (ed.). *Historical Journal of the Campaigns in North America* (3 vols., Champlain Society, Toronto, 1914-16).

Lanctot, G. (ed.). *Les Canadiens français et leurs voisins du sud* (Montreal, 1941).

Langlois, G. *Histoire de la population canadienne-française* (Montreal, 1935).

[Laterrière] *Mémoires de Pierre de Sales Laterrière et de ses traverses* (Quebec, 1873).

Laurent, Laval. *Québec et l'Eglise aux Etats-Unis sous Mgr Briand et Mgr Plessis* (Montreal, 1945).

Maheux, Abbé Arthur. *Ton Histoire est une épopée, I: Nos débuts sous le régime anglais* (Quebec, 1941).

————French Canada and Britain: A New Interpretation (Toronto, 1942).

Martin, Chester. Empire and Commonwealth: Studies in governance and self-government in Canada (Oxford, 1929).

Maseres, Francis. The Canadian Freeholder (London, 1777-9).

McIlwraith, J. N. Sir Frederick Haldimand (Toronto, 1906).

Metzger, Charles H. The Quebec Act: a Primary Cause of the American Revolution (New York, 1936).

Neatby, Hilda. The Administration of Justice under the Quebec Act (Minneapolis, 1937).

————Quebec: the Revolutionary Age, 1760-1791 (Toronto, 1966).

Ouellet, Fernand. Histoire économique et sociale du Québec, 1760-1850 (Montreal, 1966).

[Ray] Sister Mary Augustina. American Opinion of Roman Catholicism in the 18th Century (New York, 1936).

Shortt, A., and Doughty, A. G. (eds.). Documents Relating to the Constitutional History of Canada, 1758-1791 (2nd ed. rev., Ottawa, 1918).

Smith, J. H. Arnold's March from Cambridge to Quebec (New York, 1903).

————Our Struggle for the Fourteenth Colony (2 vols., New York, 1907).

[Smith, William] L. F. S. Upton (ed.). The Diary and Selected Papers of Chief Justice William Smith, 1784-1793 (2 vols., Champlain Society, Toronto, 1963-5).

Têtu, H., and Gagnon, C. O. (eds.). Mandements, lettres pastorales et circulaires des évêques de Québec, II (Quebec, 1888).

Trudel, Marcel. Louis XVI, le Congrès américain et le Canada, 1774-1789 (Quebec, 1949).

————L'Eglise canadienne sous le régime militaire, 1759-1764 (2 vols., Montreal, 1956-7).

————Le Régime militaire dans le Gouvernement des Trois-Rivières, 1760-1764 (Trois-Rivières, 1952).

————L'Influence de Voltaire au Canada (2 vols., Montreal, 1945).

Van Tyne, C. H. The Loyalists in the American Revolution (New York, 1929).

Verreau, Abbé H.-A. (ed.). L'Invasion du Canada (Montreal, 1873).

Wallace, W. S. The Maseres Letters, 1766-1768 (Toronto, 1919).

————Documents Relating to the North West Company (Champlain Society, Toronto, 1934).

————The United Empire Loyalists (Chronicles of Canada, Toronto, 1914).

[Washington, George] J. C. Fitzgerald (ed.). The Writings of George Washington (39 vols., Washington, 1931-44).

Wrong, G. M. A Canadian Manor and its Seigneurs, 1761-1861 (Toronto, 1908).

Chapter III (1791-1834)

An Apology for Great Britain (Quebec, 1809).

Aubert de Gaspé, P. Mémoires (Quebec, 1866).

Audet, F.-J. Les Députés de Montréal, 1792-1867 (Montreal, 1943).

Audet, L.-P. Le Système scolaire de la Province de Québec (6 vols., Quebec, 1950-6).

Bibaud, M. Histoire du Canada et des Canadiens sous la domination anglaise (Montreal, 1844).

Bouchette, J. A Topographical Description of the Province of Lower Canada, with Remarks upon Upper Canada, and on the Relative Connexion of Both Provinces with the United States of America (London, 1815).

———— The British Dominions in North America . . . (2 vols., London, 1832).

Burt, A. L. *The United States, Great Britain, and British North America* (New Haven and Toronto, 1940).

Caron, Abbé Ivanhoë. *La Colonisation de la Province de Québec: Les Cantons de l'Est, 1791-1815* (Quebec, 1927).

Chapais, Thomas. *Cours d'histoire du Canada, II: 1791-1814; III: 1815-1833* (Quebec, 1921).

Christie, Robert. *A History of the Late Province of Lower Canada* (6 vols., Quebec, 1848-55).

"Cockloft, Jeremy." *Cursory Observations, Made in Quebec, Province of Lower Canada, in the Year 1811* (Toronto, 1960).

Cowan, H. I. *British Emigration to British North America* (rev. ed., Toronto, 1961).

Craig, G. M. (ed.). *Early Travellers in the Canadas, 1791-1867* (Toronto, 1955).

———*Upper Canada: The Formative Years, 1784-1841* (Toronto, 1963).

Creighton, D. G. *The Commercial Empire of the St. Lawrence, 1760-1850* (Toronto, 1937).

Cruikshank, E. A. (ed.). *The Correspondence of Lieut. Governor John Graves Simcoe . . .* (5 vols., Toronto, 1923-31).

Dionne, N.-E. *Les Ecclésiastiques et les royalistes français réfugiés au Canada* (Quebec, 1905).

———*Les Trois comédies de Status Quo* (Quebec, 1909).

Garneau, F.-X. *Histoire du Canada, II: 1712-1840*, (Paris, 1920).

Groulx, Abbé L. *L'Enseignement français au Canada, I: Dans le Québec* (Montreal, 1930).

———*Histoire du Canada Français*, III (Montreal, 1952).

———*Nos luttes constitutionnelles* (Montreal, 1916).

———*Notre maître, le passé*, III (Montreal, 1944).

Innis, H. A., and Lower, A. R. M. (eds.). *Select Documents in Canadian Economic History, 1783-1885* (Toronto, 1933).

Kingsford, W. *History of Canada*, VIII (Toronto, 1897).

Knaplund, Paul. *James Stephens and the British Colonial System* (Madison, 1953).

Lanctot, G. (ed.). *Les Canadiens français et leurs voisins du sud* (Montreal, 1941).

Laterrière, Pierre de Sales. *A Political and Historical Account of Lower Canada* (London, 1830).

Lower, A. R. M. *Canadians in the Making* (Toronto, 1958).

Lucas, Sir Charles (ed.). *Lord Durham's Report on the Affairs of British North America* (3 vols., Oxford, 1912).

MacDonald, N. *Canada, 1763-1841: Immigration and Settlement* (London, 1939).

Manning, H. T. *The Revolt of French Canada, 1800-1835* (Toronto, 1962).

Millman, T. R. *Jacob Mountain, First Lord Bishop of Quebec* (Toronto, 1947).

Pierson, George. *Tocqueville and Beaumont in America* (New York, 1938).

[Papineau] "Correspondance de Joseph Papineau, 1793-1840," *RAPQ 1951-3*, 165-299.

———"Lettres de L.-J. Papineau à sa femme, 1820-39," *RAPQ 1953-5*, 187-442.

"Report of the Select Committee of Emigration from the United Kingdom," *Parliamentary Papers*, 1826-7, V.

"Report of the Select Committee on the Civil Government of Canada," *Parliamentary Papers*, 1828, VII.

"Report of the Select Committee to Inquire and Report how far the Grievances complained of in 1828 . . . have been redressed," *Parliamentary Papers*, 1834, XVIII.

"Reports" of the Gosford Commission, *Parliamentary Papers*, 1837, XXIV.

Tocqueville, Alexis de. *Journey to America* (New Haven, 1959).

Turner, F. J. (ed.). "Correspondence of French Ministers, 1791-1797," *American Historical Association Annual Report 1903*, II.

Williamson, Chilton. *Vermont in Quandary* (Montpelier, 1949).

Chapter IV (1834-9)

[Bourget] "Correspondance de Mgr. Ignace Bourget, 1837-40," *RAPQ 1945-6*, 137-224.

Brebner, J. B. "Patronage and Parliamentary Government," *CHAR 1938*, 22-30.

[Buller] "Buller's Sketch of Lord Durham's Mission to Canada in 1838," *CAR 1923*, 341-69.

"Carmellus" (A. Thorn). *Anti-Gallic Letters* (Montreal, 1836).

Caron, Abbé Ivanhoë. "Les Evénements de 1837 et 1838," *RAPQ 1925-6*, 146-329.

Chapais, Thomas. *Cours d'histoire du Canada*, IV.

Chauveau, P.-J.-O. *F.-X. Garneau et son oeuvre* (Montreal, 1883).

Christie, Robert. *A History of the Late Province of Lower Canada*, IV and V (Quebec, 1848-55).

Corey, A. B. *The Crisis of 1830-42 in Canadian-American Relations* (New Haven and Toronto, 1941).

Craig, G. M. *Upper Canada: The Formative Years, 1784-1841* (Toronto, 1963).

—— (ed.). *Lord Durham's Report* (Carleton Library, Toronto, 1963).

Creighton, D. G. *The Commercial Empire of the St. Lawrence, 1760-1850* (Toronto, 1937).

David, L.-O. *Les Patriotes de 1837-8* (Montreal, 1930).

DeCelles, A. *The "Patriotes" of 1837* (Chronicles of Canada, Toronto, 1916).

[Derbishire] N. Storey (ed.). "Stewart Derbishire's Report to Lord Durham on Lower Canada, 1838," *CHR XVIII*, I (January 1937), 51-62.

[Durham] *Report on the Affairs of British North America from the Earl of Durham* . . . (London, 1839). (Contains appendices not in Lucas edition).

Fairchild, G. M., jr. *Lower Canadian Affairs in 1837* (Quebec, 1910).

Fauteux, A. *Patriotes de 1837-8* (Montreal, 1950).

Filteau, G. *Histoire des patriotes* (3 vols., Montreal, 1938-42).

Garneau, F.-X. *Histoire du Canada*, II (Paris, 1920).

[Girod] "Journal of the late Amury Girod," *CAR 1923*, 370-80.

Groulx, Abbé Lionel. *Histoire du Canada Français*, III.

Kingsford, W. *Canada*, IX and X (London, 1898).

Lanctot, G. (ed.). *Les Canadiens français et leurs voisins du sud* (Montreal, 1941).

[Lartigue] Desrosiers, Abbé L.-A. (ed.). "Correspondance de Mgr J.-J. Lartigue," 1819-26, *RAPQ 1941-2*, 345-496; 1827-33, *RAPQ 1942-3*, 1-174; 1833-6, *RAPQ 1943-4*, 207-334; 1836-8, *RAPQ 1944-5*, 173-226; "Correspondance de Mgr Lartigue et son coadjuteur Mgr Bourget, 1837-40," *RAPQ 1945-6*, 39-224.

Lucas, Sir Charles. *Lord Durham's Report* (3 vols., Oxford, 1912).

[Mackenzie, W. L.] *Mackenzie's Own Narrative* (Toronto, 1838).

Mandements des évêques de Montréal, I (Montreal, 1867).

Mandements des évêques de Québec, III (Quebec, 1887).

Martin, C. "Lord Durham's Report and its Consequences," *CHR XX*, 2 (June 1939), 178-94.

New, C. *Lord Durham's Mission to Canada* (Carleton Library, Toronto, 1953).
——— "Lord Durham and the British Background of His Report," *CHR XX*, 2 (June 1939), 119-35.
Ouellet, Fernand. *Histoire économique et sociale du Québec, 1760-1850* (Montreal, 1966).
——— *Louis-Joseph Papineau: A Divided Soul* (Canadian Historical Association Historical Booklet 11, Ottawa, 1960).
Poutré, F. *Echappé de la potence: souvenirs d'un prisonnier d'Etat en 1838* (Montreal, 1869).
Report of the State Trials before a General Court-martial Held at Montreal in 1838-39; Exhibiting a Complete History of the Late Rebellion in Lower Canada (Montreal, 1839).

Chapter V (1840-9)

Chapais, Thomas. *Cours d'histoire du Canada*, IV, V, VI.
Cornell, P. G. *Alignment of Political Groups in Canada, 1841-67* (Toronto, 1962).
Creighton, D. G. *The Commercial Empire of the St. Lawrence* (Toronto, 1937).
DeCelles, A. *Lafontaine et Cartier* (Montreal, 1907).
Doughty, A. G. (ed.). *Elgin-Grey Papers, 1846-1852* (4 vols., Ottawa, 1937).
Gérin-Lajoie, A. *Dix ans au Canada de 1840 à 1850* (Quebec, 1888).
Groulx, Abbé Lionel. *Histoire du Canada français*, III.
——— *Notre maître, le passé, IIIe série* (Montreal, 1944).
Huston, J. (ed.). *Le Répertoire national* (Montreal, 1893).
Innis, H. A., and Lower, A. R. M. (eds.). *Select Economic Documents, 1793-1885* (Toronto, 1933).
Knaplund, P. (ed.). *Letters from Lord Sydenham to Lord John Russell* (London, 1931).
——— "The Buller-Peel Correspondence regarding Canada, 1841," *CHR VIII*, 1 (January 1927), 41-50.
Longley, R. S. *Sir Francis Hincks* (Toronto, 1943).
Ouellet, F. *Histoire économique et sociale du Québec, 1760-1850* (Montreal, 1966).
Tucker, G. *The Canadian Commercial Revolution, 1845-1851* (Carleton Library, Toronto, 1964).
Turcotte, L.-P. *Le Canada sous l'Union* (2 vols., Quebec, 1871-82).

Chapter VI (1849-67)

Audet, L.-P. *Le Système scolaire de la Province de Québec* (6 vols., Quebec, 1950-6).
Belvèze, Commandant de. *Lettres choisies, 1824-75* (Bourges, 1882).
Bibaud, M. *Histoire du Canada* (Montreal, 1843).
Boyd, J. *Sir George Etienne Cartier, Bart.* (Toronto, 1914).
[Cartier] J. Tassé (ed.). *Discours de Sir Georges Cartier, Bart.* (Montreal, 1893).
Cauchon, J. *L'Union des Provinces de l'Amérique Britannique du Nord* (Quebec, 1865).
Chapais, Thomas. *Cours d'histoire du Canada*, VI.
Chauveau, P.-J.-O. *L'Instruction publique au Canada* (Quebec, 1876).
Cooper, J. I. "G. E. Cartier in the Period of the 'Forties'," *CHAR 1938*, 71-8.
Creighton, D. G. *The Road to Confederation: the Emergence of Canada, 1863-1867* (Toronto, 1964).
[Crémazie] Abbé H.-R. Casgrain, (ed.). *Les Oeuvres complètes d'Octave Crémazie* (Montreal, 1882).

Doughty, A. G. (ed.). *Elgin-Grey Papers* (4 vols., Ottawa, 1937).

[Garneau] *Centenaire de l'histoire du Canada de F.-X. Garneau* (Montreal, 1945).

———"Voyage en Angleterre et en France," in *La Littérature canadienne*, I (Quebec, 1863).

Lanctot, G. *F.-X. Garneau* (Toronto, 1925).

Malchelosse, G. (ed.). *Sulte: Mélanges historiques* (Montreal, 1919).

Marion, S. *Les Lettres canadiennes d'autrefois*, IV (Ottawa, 1944).

Masters, D. C. *The Reciprocity Treaty of 1854* (Carleton Library, Toronto, 1963).

——— *Parliamentary Debates on Confederation of the British North American Provinces* (Ottawa, 1951).

——— *American Provinces* (Ottawa, 1951).

Mousseau, J.-O. *Contre-Poison* (Montreal, 1867).

[Parkman] M. Wade (ed.). *Journals of Francis Parkman* (2 vols., New York, 1947).

Roy, Mgr. Camille. *Nos origines littéraires* (Quebec, 1909).

Shippee, L. B. *Canadian-American Relations, 1849-1874* (New Haven and Toronto, 1938).

Waite, P. B. *The Life and Times of Confederation, 1864-1867* (Toronto, 1962).

——— (ed.). *Confederation Debates in the Province of Canada, 1865* (Carleton Library, Toronto, 1963).

Chapter VII (1867-96)

Barthe, U. (ed.). *Wilfrid Laurier on the Platform, 1871-1890* (Quebec, 1890).

Blanchard, R. *L'Est du Canada français* (2 vols., Montreal, 1935).

——— *Le Centre du Canada français* (Montreal, 1947).

——— *L'Ouest du Canada français* (2 vols., Montreal, 1953-4).

——— *Chroniques, Humeurs et Caprices* (Montreal, 1873).

Buies, A. *Petits chroniques pour 1877* (Quebec, 1878).

——— *La Lanterne, 1868-9* (Montreal, 1884).

Chiniquy, Charles. *Manuel des sociétés de tempérence* (Quebec, 1844).

——— *The Priest, the Woman and the Confessional* (Toronto, 1944).

Trudel, Marcel. *La véritable figure de Chiniquy* (Trois-Rivières, 1955).

Coats, R. H. and Maclean, M. C. *The American-born in Canada* (Toronto, 1943).

David, L. *Histoire du Canada depuis la Confédération* (Montreal, 1909).

Desilets, L. *Exposé sommaire* (Rome, 1884).

Desrosiers, A., and Fournet, L.-J. *La Race française en Amérique* (Montreal, 1911).

Hamon, R. P. E. *Les Canadiens-français de la Nouvelle Angleterre* (Quebec, 1891).

Hansen, M. L. and Brebner, J. B. *The Mingling of the Canadian and American Peoples* (New Haven and Toronto, 1940).

Hudson, T. *L'Institut Canadien de Montréal et l'Affaire Guibord* (Montreal, 1938).

Innis, H. A., and Lower, A. R. M. *Select Economic Documents, 1783-1885* (Toronto, 1933).

Innis, M. Q. *An Economic History of Canada* (Toronto, 1938).

Lamontagne, L. *Arthur Buies, homme des lettres* (Quebec, 1957).

Langlois, Georges. *Histoire de la population canadienne-française* (Montreal, 1934).

Maheux, Abbé A. "Le Nationalisme canadien-français à l'aurore du XXe siècle," *CHAR 1945*, 58-74.

Mandements de Montréal, III, VI, X.

Mandements de Québec, nouvelle série, I-IV.

Pouliot, Père L. *Mgr Bourget et son temps* (2 vols., Montreal, 1955).
Rumilly, R. *Histoire de la province de Québec*, I-VI (Montreal, 1942).
Skelton, O. D. *Life and Letters of Sir Wilfrid Laurier* (2 vols., Carleton Library, Toronto, 1965).
Sulte, B. *Histoire des Canadiens-français, 1608-1880* (Montreal, 1882-4).
Turcotte, L.-P. *Le Canada sous l'Union* (2 vols., Montreal, 1871-2).
Wade, M. "Sir Wilfrid Laurier," in C. T. Bissell (ed.), *Our Living Tradition*, I (Toronto, 1957).

Chapter VIII (1818-97)

Barthe, U. (ed.). *Wilfrid Laurier on the Platform* (Quebec, 1890).
Blegan, T. W. "James Wickes Taylor," *Minnesota Historical Bulletin*, I (November 1915).
The Canadian North-West (2 vols., Ottawa, 1915).
Creighton, D. G. *Sir John A. Macdonald* (2 vols., Toronto, 1952-5).
De Kiewiet, C., and Underhill, F. H. (eds.). *Dufferin-Carnarvon Correspondence* (Champlain Society, Toronto, 1955).
Denison, G. T. *Soldiering in Canada* (Toronto, 1900).
Department of Militia and Defence, *Report upon the Suppression of the Rebellion in the Northwest Territories, and Matters in Connection Therewith, 1885* (Ottawa, 1886).
Epitome of Parliamentary Documents in connection with the North-West Rebellion (Ottawa, 1886).
Giraud, M. *Le Métis Canadien: son rôle dans l'histoire des provinces de l'ouest* (Paris, 1945).
Gluek, A. C., Jr. *Minnesota and the Manifest Destiny of the Canadian Northwest.* (Toronto, 1965).
Hamon, Père E. *Les Canadiens-français de la Nouvelle Angleterre* (Quebec, 1891).
Howard, J. K. *Strange Empire: A Narrative of the North West* (New York, 1952).
[Macdonald] J. Pope (ed.). *Correspondence of Sir John A. Macdonald* (Toronto, n.d.).
—— *Memoirs of Sir John A. Macdonald* (Toronto, n.d.).
Morice, R. P. A. G., O.M.I. *Dictionnaire historique des Canadiens et des Métis français de l'Ouest* (Quebec, 1908).
—— *History of the Catholic Church in Western Canada* (2 vols., Toronto, 1910).
Morton, A. S. *A History of the Canadian West to 1870-1* (London, 1939).
Morton, W. L. *Manitoba: A History* (Toronto, 1957).
The Queen vs. *Louis Riel* (Ottawa, 1886).
Rumilly, R. *Histoire de la province de Québec*, V-IX.
—— *Mgr Laflèche et son temps* (Montreal, 1938).
[Selkirk] P. C. T. White (ed.). *Lord Selkirk's Diary* (Champlain Society, Toronto, 1958).
Skelton, O. D. *Life and Letters of Sir Wilfrid Laurier*, I (Carleton Library, Toronto, 1965).
Stacey, C. P. *Canada and the British Army, 1846-1871* (Toronto, 1937).
Stanley, G. F. G. *The Rise of Western Canada: A History of the Riel Rebellions* (Toronto, 1936).
—— *Louis Riel* (Toronto, 1963).
Taché, Mgr. A. *L'Amnestie* (Montreal, 1874).
—— *Encore l'amnestie* (Montreal, 1875).

Taylor, J. W. "Canadian Relations with British America, 12 June 1860," 39th Congress, 1st Session, House Executive Documents No. 128, Serial 1263.

———"Relations between the United States and Northwestern British North America," 37th Congress, 2nd Session, *House Executive Documents*, *X*, No. 146, Serial 1138.

Wade, Mason. "The French Parish and Survivance in Nineteenth Century New England," *Catholic Historical Review* (July 1950), 163-89.

Weinberg, A. *Manifest Destiny* (Baltimore, 1935).

Chapter IX (1867-1904)

[Aberdeen, Lady] J. T. Saywell (ed.). *The Canadian Journal of Lady Aberdeen* (Champlain Society, Toronto, 1960).

Acton, Lord. *History of Freedom and Other Essays* (London, 1907).

Asselin, Olivar. *Pensée française* (Montreal, 1937).

Bodelson, C. A. *Studies in Mid-Victorian Imperialism* (New York, 1925).

Bonenfant, J.-C., and Falardeau, J.-C. "Cultural and Political Implications of French-Canadian Nationalism," *CHAR*, *1945*, 56-73.

[Borden] H. Borden (ed.). *Robert Laird Borden: His Memoirs* (2 vols., Toronto, 1938).

Bourassa, H. *Great Britain and Canada* (Montreal, 1902).

——— *Grande-Bretagne et Canada* (Montreal, 1902).

——— "Les Canadiens-français et l'Empire britannique," *La Nouvelle France*, II, 1 (January 1903).

——— "The French Canadians in the British Empire," *Monthly Review*, (September 1902).

Brown, B. A. *The Tariff Reform Movement in Great Britain, 1881-95* (New York, 1943).

Buchan, John. *Lord Minto* (London, 1924).

Canada First: A Memoir of the Late William A. Foster, Q.C. (Toronto, 1880).

Caniff, W. *Canadian Nationality: Its Growth and Development* (Toronto, 1875).

Chamberlain, J. *Foreign and Colonial Speeches* (London, 1897).

Creighton, D. G. *Sir John A. Macdonald*, II (Toronto, 1955).

Denison, G. T. *The Struggle for Imperial Unity 1869-95* (London, 1909).

Dilke, C. W. *Greater Britain: Saxon Sketches* (New York, 1869).

——— *Le Drapeau national des Canadiens-français* (Quebec, 1904).

Evans, W. S. *The Canadian Contingent and Canadian Imperialism* (Toronto, 1901).

Gagnon, M. A. *Olivar Asselin* (2 vols., Montreal, 1962).

Garvin, J. L. *Life of Joseph Chamberlain* (4 vols., London, 1934).

Gauvreau, J. *Olivar Asselin: précurseur d'Action française* (Montreal, 1937).

Groulx, Abbé L. *Une croisade d'adolescents* (Quebec, 1912).

Hobson, J. A. *Imperialism* (New York, 1902).

Labat, G. P. *Le "Livre d'or" of the Canadian Contingents in South Africa* (Montreal, 1901).

Maheux, Abbé A. "Le Nationalisme canadien-français à l'aurore du XXe siècle," *CHAR 1945*, 58-74.

[Paquet, Mgr.] Chanoine E. Chartier (ed.). *Bréviaire du patriote canadien-français* (Montreal, 1925).

Pope, J. (ed.). *Confederation Documents* (Toronto, 1895).

Rumilly, R. *Histoire de la province de Québec*, VIII-XI.

Seeley, J. R. *The Expansion of England* (London, 1883).

Skelton, O. D. *Life and Letters of Sir Wilfrid Laurier* (2 vols., Carleton Library, Toronto, 1965).

—— *Life and Times of Sir Alexander Tilloch Galt* (Carleton Library, Toronto, 1965).

Smith, Goldwin. *Canada and the Canadian Problem* (London, 1891).

—— *Devant la tribune d'histoire* (Montreal, 1903).

Straus, W. L. *Joseph Chamberlain* (Washington, 1942).

Tupper, Sir Charles. *Recollections of Sixty Years in Canada* (London, 1914).

Tyler, J. E. *The Struggle for Imperial Unity, 1869-95* (London, 1938).

Wade, M. "Olivar Asselin," in R. L. McDougall (ed.), *Our Living Tradition*, V (Toronto, 1965).

Chapter X (1905-11)

[Borden] H. Borden (ed.). *Robert Laird Borden: His Memoirs* (2 vols., Toronto, 1938).

Bourassa, H. *Les Ecoles du Nord-Ouest* (Montreal, 1905).

—— *Le Projet de Loi navale: sa nature, ses conséquences* (Montreal, 1910).

—— *La Convention douanière entre le Canada et les Etats-Unis* (Montreal, 1911).

—— *The Reciprocity Agreement and its Consequences* (Montreal, 1911).

—— *La Conférence impériale et le rôle de M. Laurier* (Montreal, 1911).

—— *Le 5e Anniversaire du Devoir* (Montreal, 1915).

Dafoe, J. W. *Laurier: A Study in Canadian Politics* (Carleton Library, Toronto, 1963).

—— *Clifford Sifton in Relation to His Times* (Toronto, 1931).

Ewart, J. S. *The Kingdom Papers* (Ottawa, 1912).

Ferguson, G. V. *John W. Dafoe* (Toronto, 1948).

Groulx, Abbé L. *L'Enseignement français au Canada, II: Les écoles des minorités* (Montreal, 1932).

Laurendeau, André. "Henri Bourassa," in R. L. McDougall, (ed.), *Our Living Tradition*, IV (Toronto, 1962).

[Laurier] A. DeCelles (ed.). *Les Discours de Sir Wilfrid Laurier de 1889 à 1911* (Montreal, 1920).

—— *Les Discours de Sir Wilfrid Laurier de 1911 à 1919* (Montreal, 1920).

Lavergne, A. *Trente ans de vie nationale* (Montreal, 1935).

Neuendorf, G. *Studies in the Evolution of Dominion Status* (London, 1942).

Rumilly, R. *Histoire de la province de Québec*, XII-XVI.

Skelton, O. D. *Life and Letters of Sir Wilfrid Laurier*, II (Carleton Library, Toronto, 1964).

INDEX TO VOLUMES ONE AND TWO

Franchi, Cardinal, 367
Franciscans, 86
Francoeur, J.-N., 754, 755, 756, 760, 769, 909, 922
Francoeur, Louis, 946
Francq, Marcel, 982
Franquelin, Jean-Baptiste, 26
Fraser, G. K., 1054
Fréchette, Louis, 306, 371, 385, 386, 387, 388, 509, 516
Freeland, Dr. Anthony, 659
Freemasonry, 577, 643, 727, 840, 937, 1008
Frégault, Guy, 1077, 1114, 1115
French Revolution, 87, 94, 96, 98, 99, 100, 101, 158, 167, 331, 340, 342, 350, 610, 981
French Revolution (1830), 341
French Revolution (1848), 194, 256, 299, 341
Frigon, Augustin, 897
Frontenac, Louis de Buade, Comte de, 20, 21, 22, 23, 25, 26, 30, 39
Froude, J. A., 452

G

Gage, General Thomas, 49, 75
Gagnon, David, 176, 182
Gagnon, Ernest, 387
Gagnon, Ferdinand, 433
Gagnon, Jean-Louis, 904
Gagnon, Onésime, 832, 962, 1019, 1074, 1081
Gale, Samuel, 136, 153
Galipault, J.-P., 964
Galipeault, Antonin, 690
Gallèze, Englebert, 612
Galt, Sir Alexander Tilloch, 314, 316, 319, 320, 327, 361, 449, 458, 460, 462, 463, 465, 541, 884
Galt, G. F., 666
Gambetta, Léon, 352
Garceau, Napoléon, 508, 509, 517, 554, 556, 575, 587, 617, 665, 675, 680
Gariépy, Wilfrid, 660, 841, 856, 912
Garneau, Alfred, 306
Garneau, Madame Constance, 1005
Garneau, François-Xavier, 181, 212, 285–9 passim
Garneau, Sir Georges, 721, 729
Garneau, Major René, 989, 1082
Gaspé, I.-A. de, 131
Gaspé, Philippe Aubert de, elder, 288
Gaspé, Philippe Aubert de, younger, 291
Gaudet, Brig.-Gen. F. M., 669, 768
Gault, Charles Ernest, 663, 759
Gaulthier, Jean-François, 27
Gauthier, Archbishop Charles Hugues, 657, 680
Gauthier, Archbishop Georges, 650, 660, 694, 695, 736, 827, 909

Gauthier, Joseph, 182
Gauthier, L.-J., 742, 783
Gauthier, Dr. Pierre, 846, 851, 856, 912, 987
Gautier, Théophile, 302, 306
Gauvreau, Dr. Joseph, 635, 866
Gélinas, Gratien, 1077
Gendreau, J.-E., 879
Gendron, L.-H., 832
Genest, Père, 976
Genest, Samuel, 628, 634, 659, 690, 722
Geoffrion, Aimé, 617
Geoffrion, Victor, 508
George III, 47, 53, 68, 98, 127, 228, 243, 428
George V, 503, 555, 558, 678, 679, 731, 772, 776, 782, 834
George VI, 847, 856, 911, 922, 1012
Georgian Bay Canal, 593, 640
Gérin, Léon, 896
Gérin-Lajoie, Antoine, 293, 294, 295, 296, 306
Gérin-Lajoie, Paul, 1108
Germain, Lord George, 75
Gervais, Honoré, 528, 611, 896
Ghent, Treaty of (1815), 123
Giffard, Robert, 14, 26
Gilbert, Arthur, 587, 588, 589
Gilbert, Lt.-Col. L.-J., 685
Gill, Charles, 522, 612
Gillis, Clarence, 1061
Gipps, Sir George, 153
Girard, Marc-A., 404
Girod, Amury, 167, 177, 178, 214n.
Girouard, Joseph, 164, 177, 178, 192
Gisbourne, W., 456
Glackmeyer, Edouard, 286, 287
Gladstone, W. E., 157, 224, 250, 272, 451, 462, 469, 477, 493, 501, 513
Glenelg, Lord, 182
Glennie, Mrs., 659
Glennie, A. C., 659
Gobeil, Samuel, 832, 1042
Gobineau, Comte de, 867
Godbout, Adélard, 909, 938–46 passim, 958–67 passim, 980–8 passim, 1002–17 passim, 1054
Goderich, Viscount (later Earl of Ripon), 138, 139, 157
Godfrey, John Milton, 720
Gore, Col., 172, 173, 174, 175
Gosford, Lord, 153, 154, 155, 156, 163, 164, 165, 166, 167, 168, 171, 176, 225, 501
Gosselin, Mgr. Amédée, 613, 665
Gosselin, Abbé Auguste, 613
Gouin, Léon-Mercier, 964
Gouin, Sir Lomer, 515, 518, 553–61 passim, 583, 611, 620, 648, 662, 676, 718, 724, 729, 744, 782, 789, 796, 798, 895
Gouin, Oscar, 735

Tilley, Sir Leonard, 457
Tonnancour, Lt.-Col. L. J. G., Sieur de, 68
Tonty, Henri de, 21
Topp, Brigadier, 960
Tournefort, Joseph de, 27
Townshend, General, 49
Tracy, Marquis de, 17
Tremblay, Léonard-D., 813, 846, 851, 856, 984, 1055, 1056
Tremblay, Major-General Thomas-Louis, 643, 768, 965
Trent affair, 318
Trihey, Lt.-Col. H. J., 685
Trollope, Anthony, 449
Trudeau, Pierre-Elliot, 1109
Trudel, Senator F.-X.-A., 348, 354, 355, 371, 372, 373, 374, 376, 417, 418
Trudel, Marcel, 1115
Tryon, Governor, 69
Tucker, Walter Adam, 1049, 1050, 1057, 1066
Tupper, Sir Charles, 319, 397, 436, 456, 464, 466, 478, 482, 486, 505, 526, 565, 569, 789
Turcot, F.-M., 177
Turcotte, Edmond, 959, 989
Turcotte, Edouard, 1082
Turcotte, Louis-Philippe, 385
Turenne, Marshal, 25
Turgeon, Père, 423
Turgeon, Adélard, 553, 554, 556
Turner, General R. E. W., 667
Turriff, J. C., 743
Turton, Thomas, 183
Tweedsmuir, Lord, 838, 848, 849, 911

U

Union Bill, 130, 221, 224, 225, 226, 229, 231, 233, 240, 246, 249, 257, 262, 267, 268, 276, 286, 317
Union Démocratique, 963-4

V

Vachon, Archbishop Alexandre, 897, 946, 956
Vaillancourt, Cyrille, 968, 1002
Vaillancourt, Emile, 955
Vaillancourt, J. A., 560, 577, 611
Valade, Dr. F.-X., 414
Valinière, Abbé Huet de la, 77, 81
Vallée, Dr. Arthur, 413, 898
Vanfelson, George, 144, 154, 155
Van Horne, Sir William, 410, 591
Vanier, Anatole, 635, 866, 884, 889, 891, 895, 901, 903
Vanier, General Georges, 938, 946, 1116
Vanier, Guy, 661
Vanutelli, Cardinal Legate Vincenze, 579, 580, 582

Vanzetti, Bartolomeo, 414
Vaudreuil, Governor, 30, 35, 44
Vaughan, Cardinal, 439
Vegreville, Father, 406
Verrazano, Giovanni da, 6
Verreau, Abbé Hospice-Anselme, 385
Versailles, Joseph, 516, 525, 526
Versailles, Treaty of, 797, 798
Verville, Alphonse, 547, 548, 555, 631, 742
Verville, J.-A., 846
Vespucci, Amerigo, 6
Vetch, Samuel, 22
Veuillot, Louis, 303, 340, 341, 351, 354, 374, 872, 873
Vézon, Joseph Fournerie, Sieur de, 80
Victor-Emmanuel, King, 850
Vien, Thomas, 685, 796
Vienna, Congress of, 331
Viger, Bonaventure, 171, 174, 175, 176, 182
Viger, Denis-Benjamin, 104, 131, 132, 136, 137, 138, 143, 184, 185, 232, 245-50 passim
Viger, Jacques, 290
Viger, L.-M., 167
Villeneuve, Cardinal Archbishop, 641, 748, 827, 885, 906, 907, 909, 933, 934, 942, 943, 953, 956, 1003, 1014, 1015, 1081

W

Wakefield, Edward Gibbon, 183, 448
Walker, Thomas, 67, 71
Wallace, Dr. Clarke, 413, 425
Walsh, Vicomte, 306
Walsh, John C., 576, 637, 638, 639
Walsh, Bishop Louis, 634
War Measures Act (1914), 648
Ward, Sir Joseph, 593
Washington, Treaty of (1854), 591
Washington, Treaty of (1871), 464
Watkin, Sir Edward William, 314
Watson, Col. David, 669, 689
Watteville, Régiment de, 393
Wedderburn, Alexander, 62, 64
Weir, Lt., 173, 175, 182, 193
Wellington, Duke of, 122, 136, 225, 241, 242, 500, 501
Westgarth, W. E., 455
Westminster Conference (1871), 453
Westminster Palace Conference (1866), 327; (1884), 456
Westminster, Statute of, 732, 805, 818, 821, 822, 925, 958, 962
Wetherall, Lt.-Col., 172, 173, 174, 175
Whalen, Father M.-J., 669
White, G. S., 1055
White, R. S., 854
White, Stanley, 1076
White, T. M., 467
White, Sir Thomas, 727, 773, 775, 776